LIVIN(

MW01515422

Twentieth-Century Conflict in Canadian
and American History and Memory

Canada and the United States: we think of one as a peaceable kingdom, the other as a warrior nation. But do our expectations about each country's attitudes to war and peace match the realities?

In *Living with War*, Robert Teigrob examines how war is experienced and remembered on both sides of the 49th parallel. Surveying popular and scholarly histories, films and literature, public memorials, and museum exhibits in both countries, he comes to some startling conclusions. Americans may seem more patriotic, even jingoistic, but they are also more willing to debate the pros and cons of their military actions. Canadians, though more diffident in their public displays of patriotism, are more willing than their southern neighbors to accept the official narrative that depicts just wars fought in the service of a righteous cause. A provocative book that complements critiques of contemporary Canadian militarism such as *Warrior Nation*, *Living with War* offers an intriguing look at the relationship with the military past on both sides of the border.

ROBERT TEIGROB is an associate professor in the Department of History at Ryerson University.

ROBERT TEIGROB

Living with War

Twentieth-Century Conflict in Canadian and American History and Memory

UNIVERSITY OF TORONTO PRESS
Toronto Buffalo London

© University of Toronto Press 2016
Toronto Buffalo London
www.utppublishing.com
Printed in Canada

ISBN 978-1-4426-4408-3 (cloth)
ISBN 978-1-4426-1250-1 (paper)

∞

Printed on acid-free, 100% post-consumer recycled paper
with vegetable-based inks

Library and Archives Canada Cataloguing in Publication

Teigrob, Robert, 1966–, author
Living with war : twentieth-century conflict in Canadian and American
history and memory / Robert Teigrob.

Includes bibliographical references and index.
ISBN 978-1-4426-4408-3 (cloth)   ISBN 978-1-4426-1250-1 (paper)

1. War and society – Canada. 2. War and society – United States.
3. Militarism – Canada. 4. Militarism – United States. 5. Collective memory –
Canada. 6. Collective memory – United States. 7. Canada – History,
Military – 20th century. 8. United States – History, Military – 20th century.
I. Title.

HM554.T44 2016   303.6′60971   C2015-907841-5

This book has been published with the help of a grant from the Federation for the
Humanities and Social Sciences, through the Awards to Scholarly Publications
Program, using funds provided by the Social Sciences and Humanities Research
Council of Canada.

University of Toronto Press acknowledges the financial assistance to its publishing
program of the Canada Council for the Arts and the Ontario Arts Council, an
agency of the Government of Ontario.

Canada Council   Conseil des Arts
for the Arts   du Canada

ONTARIO ARTS COUNCIL
CONSEIL DES ARTS DE L'ONTARIO
an Ontario government agency
un organisme du gouvernement de l'Ontario

Funded by the   Financé par le
Government   gouvernement
of Canada   du Canada

Canadä

Contents

Illustrations

Acknowledgments

At the outset I didn't appreciate what an (irresponsibly) ambitious project I had taken on, and the fact that it actually made it to print is a testimony to the sustenance I received from a variety of sources. All of my colleagues in the Ryerson History Department, along with many friends in the Faculty of Arts and the wider university, provided unwavering support. Departmental colleagues Ross Fair, Carl Benn, and Tomaz Jardim took considerable time from their own work to talk through various aspects of the project; Art Blake read a draft of the book proposal and suggested a reorganization that I adopted; Jenny Carson did her best to keep me *compos mentis*.

I am grateful for the financial support provided by my department, faculty, and university that enabled me to hire several capable students to assist my research. Sarah Lambert, Daniel Dishaw, Catherine Melo, Mark Unwin, Jane Hoysack, and Colin McCullough all did fine work; the latter also reviewed an earlier draft of the manuscript and offered valuable commentary during his tenure as a postdoctoral fellow at McMaster University.

Beth Bailey and Fredrick Logevall furnished sound advice on conceptualizing this project, while the anonymous (and demonstrably wise) readers at UTP went above and beyond in providing recommendations that were both timely and indispensable. Stefan Fergus worked ably and efficiently in compiling the index, and Jon Weier helped me mull over ideas and alerted me to some relevant resources. For their guidance and inspiration, I also thank Ken Reddig, Henry Krahn, Lawrence Wittner, Barry Ferguson, and Lorraine and John Janzen-Kooistra.

Once again, the good people at UTP handled the project adeptly. In particular I would like to thank acquisitions editor Lennart Husband, who provided his typically-superb support and counsel, and managing editor Frances Mundy, whose guidance and professionalism were, as usual, first-rate. Copyeditor Anne Fullerton slayed some of the longer sentences, and it is my hope that she was paid by the word rather than the manuscript for wading through these rather expansive ponderings.

An earlier version of chapter three appeared as "Empire and Cultures of Militarism in Canada and the United States," (*American Review of Canadian Studies* 43. 1 [March 2013]). Portions of another article, "Glad Adventures, Tragedies, Silences: Remembering and Forgetting Wars for Empire in Canada and the United States," (*International Journal of Canadian Studies / Revue internationale d'études canadiennes* 45–6 [2012]), found their way into this volume at various points. Photographers John Goodwin and Rita Crane kindly granted permission to reprint photographs from their collections; filmmakers Rick Tejada-Flores and Judy Ehrlich of Paradigm Productions furnished a poster from one of their films; Ali Qadeer provided splendid cover-design and dog-sitting services; my friend and canoe bowman Rob Ridgen of the Yukon Archives lent a photograph and the story that went with it. For their capable assistance, I am grateful to the staffs at Library and Archives Canada, the Canadian War Museum, the Archives of Ontario, the Library of Congress, Guelph University's Archives and Special Collections, the New York Public Library, and the Toronto Reference Library.

Members of my family on both sides of the 49th parallel have been a constant source of encouragement in both my personal and professional endeavours; over the years and at a somewhat halting pace I came to acknowledge their wisdom regarding the value of hard work and a solid education. Special thanks to my brother Gerald, who has shown me time and again how to keep my chin up regardless of circumstance. I am also indebted to a host of Winnipeggers (past and present) for their lifelong and valued friendship. To them I say, be forewarned that I am planning another trip home to recharge the batteries (this time during the warmer months).

This book is dedicated to Suzanne, whose contributions cannot be adequately measured or expressed.

LIVING WITH WAR

Twentieth-Century Conflict in Canadian and American History and Memory

Introduction

Are Canadians fonder of their nation's military exploits, more protective of the memory of their wars and soldiers, than Americans are of their own? The question may, at first, seem profoundly naive. According to time-honoured self-perceptions, Canadians are an "unmilitary people" who inhabit a "peaceable kingdom" – descriptors crafted, to no small extent, with the expressed purpose of differentiating their experience from that of their "more warlike" southern neighbours. Nor are Canadians alone in drawing such distinctions. Particularly in its post-Second World War manifestation, international observers frequently cast US foreign policy as singularly belligerent, not to mention imperialistic, short-sighted, unilateralist, arrogant, and hyper-nationalistic, to enumerate a considerably condensed list of unflattering adjectives. Shortly after the 9/11 terrorist attacks, Canadian journalist Peter Scowen's book bearing the unambiguous title *Rogue Nation: The America the Rest of the World Knows*, summed up the delusions shared, in his view, by Americans as a whole: "They prefer to take it on faith that every covert and overt military operation undertaken by their armed forces and intelligence services overseas since the Second World War has been, and will be, carried out to further America's highest ideals and spread democracy across the globe, thus making them immune from criticism or justifiable counterattack. If only that were true."[1]

Yet the United States, which to its detractors suffers from a pathological addiction to both war and unquestioning patriotism, has also produced a powerful current of self-censure when it comes to assessing the conduct of international relations in general, and foreign war in particular. From the War of 1812 through the Mexican-American War, the War of 1898 (or "Spanish-American War"), the First and Second World

Wars, Korea, Vietnam, and the recent conflicts in the Middle East, US society has witnessed deep, immediate, and resilient divisions over the morality and value of entering a conflict, the conduct of its troops, the crafting and implementation of its military strategy, and its overall wartime objectives. As American historian Susan Brewer observed, fierce debates over "American national identity and purpose" have attended every US military venture from the dawn of the republic to the present.[2] Alongside an admitted enthusiasm for employing warfare as an instrument of foreign policy, then, there exists in American culture a profoundly ambivalent attitude towards the nation's wars and its fighting forces. Dissent, it would appear, is as fundamental to the American experience as the exercise of military might, and many of those who spoke passionately against the will to war – including Henry David Thoreau, Jane Addams, W.E.B. Du Bois, Mark Twain, Andrew Carnegie, William Jennings Bryan, and Martin Luther King Jr – remain familiar and revered figures in American popular consciousness.

The same cannot be said of Canada, or at least, of English Canada. Here, memory and public discourse offer fewer examples of thoroughgoing criticisms of Canadian military exploits. Instead, the legacy of the national wartime experience is best characterized by a blend of celebration (particularly where deeds of heroism can be mustered as evidence) and silence (particularly where experiences and actions do not ennoble the nation's image). In contrast to those in America, outspoken Canadian opponents of their nation's wars have been both fewer in number (including in relative terms) and frequently overlooked in the recounting of English Canada's history. Figures and events associated with military victory – General James Wolfe, Laura Secord, Juno Beach, *In Flanders Fields*, Sir Isaac Brock, Billy Bishop, Passchendaele, and of course, Vimy Ridge – are esteemed by many Canadians. Some citizens also carry the torch for individuals associated with lost martial causes, such as Wolfe's adversary Louis-Joseph de Montcalm; Gabriel Dumont, commander of the doomed Métis forces in the Northwest War of Resistance; and Jean-Olivier Chénier, martyred commander of the 1837 Lower Canada Rebellion. By contrast, the names Peter Brock, Muriel Duckworth, Margaret Rae Luckock, George Woodcock, Ernie Regehr, Charles Yale Harrison, and James Endicott – prolific and well-positioned Canadian critics of war all – would doubtless draw blank stares from a vast majority of their fellow citizens (though Farley Mowatt and perhaps J.S. Woodsworth would induce more than a few nods of recognition). Polls conducted over the past twenty years reveal that Canadians consistently rival Americans – and outdistance their NATO allies – in their levels of support for the use of force to resolve international dilemmas and in their "hypothetical casualty tolerance" in foreign military operations. Such circumstances suggest that Canadian society may be more militaristic than is generally recognized, if we take Andrew Bacevich's definition as a starting point: militarism, he wrote, involves "a romanticized view of soldiers, a tendency to see military power as the truest sense of national greatness, and outsized expectations regarding the efficacy of force."[3] Bacevich provided his definition in a discussion of American cultural perceptions of war after 9/11, but it is telling how well it can also reflect significant aspects of Canadian opinion.

Of course, public attitudes towards any issue ebb and flow over time, and since the early 1990s, and particularly after Prime Minister Stephen Harper's Conservative Party attained power in 2006, Canadians were exposed to a coordinated and well-financed campaign to view themselves first and foremost as "courageous warriors." The Harper government rewrote immigration manuals to accentuate Canada's role in international conflicts, inscribed the Vimy Ridge Memorial on the twenty dollar bill, required that members of the armed forces be present at citizenship ceremonies, and took pains to paper over the less bellicose and more multilateralist Liberal Party imprimatur on foreign policy. The government's accomplices in this task at the Canadian Defence and Foreign Affairs Institute and the University of Calgary's Centre for Military and Strategic Studies have engaged in two decades of relentless attacks on Canadians' regard for peacekeeping, insisting instead that citizens embrace their "true" heritage as warriors. Two recent examinations of this public relations offensive – Ian McKay and Jamie Swift's *Warrior Nation: Rebranding Canada in an Age of Anxiety* (2012), and Noah Richler's *What We Talk about When We Talk about War* (2012) – chronicled these efforts with some precision. American-born historian Michael Fellman, who relocated to Canada at the height of the Vietnam War, maintained that the campaign had made significant gains. "Militarism is seeping into Canadian ideological and institutional life," he warned in 2007, "with highly dangerous short-term and long-term implications. Yet we hear precious little outcry from the public or in the media, and this relative silence only encourages those controlling the levers of power to continue this development."[4]

Whether the majority of Canadians now truly value war-fighting over peacekeeping, or whether any recent alterations to citizens' self-image regarding their international role will endure, remain open questions. Less disputable is the fact that the success of these recent efforts to bolster the image of Canadian fighting forces owes much to the dearth of counter-narratives to the tales of military glory that have long populated English-Canadian history books, popular culture, and media. In other words, McKay, Swift, Richler, and Fellman are right in identifying a new emphasis on a war-fighting identity to the exclusion of all others, but if we take a long view of the relationship between English Canada and the nation's military engagements, we can gain insight into why these recent efforts have been met with what Fellman called "precious little outcry": veritably, outside Quebec, reservations about the rectitude of Canada's wars have been articulated rarely and cautiously, the grandeur of Canada's martial legacy infrequently questioned, the benefits of the wars seen to outweigh their detriments. Even the halcyon (or hellish, to some observers) days of Pearsonian internationalism and substantial commitments to peacekeeping – an era also shaped by the tragedy in Vietnam and the prospect of nuclear annihilation – did not give rise to a significant body of scholarly or popular cultural production that re-examined previous Canadian conflicts with anything approaching the censure visible in American reckonings of war (from that or any era). In surveying cultural output on the twenty-first-century War in Afghanistan, Richler argued that "the few decent film or television documentaries that have been produced about the fighting have mostly originated in the United Kingdom ... the United States ... and Europe ... Canadian documentaries have consistently focused, with the sort of patriotic obsequiousness that is the mark of civilian society's willing complicity with state-generated messages, on the tough work of Canadian troops and the emotional circumstances they and their families must tolerate."[5] And this is nothing new. Patriotism, complicity with state-generated messages, and a particular esteem for soldiering are the stuff of which English Canadian remembrance of war is made. Of course, Canadians can point to moments when their nation opted out of American-led wars that proved especially ill-advised – namely, Vietnam and Iraq – and congratulate themselves for their more pacific and reasonable character (and castigate the Americans for their folly). As Richler observed, however, even when Canada finds itself in what some consider similarly imprudent and unwinnable missions, the critical bearing significantly recedes.

That deviations from this norm – most pointedly, the 1992 CBC documentary *The Valour and the Horror* and the Canadian War Museum's exhibit on the Second World War's Allied Bomber Command – have spawned indignant backlash among English Canadians is a testament to how unusual and unwelcome challenges to English Canadian memory of war can be. As David Bercuson and S.F. Wise observed in their ruminations on *The Valour and the Horror* row, "Canadians are not usually disposed to debate their history, and especially not those aspects that are military in nature. Conscription, yes; the Normandy Campaign, no." Historian and journalist Gwynne Dyer reported that the original and sometimes unflattering look at Canada's wars presented in the 1986 documentary and accompanying book *The Defence of Canada* evoked "a concerted howl of rage from the Canadian military history establishment, who condemned it down to the last man. (They were all men at that time, of course)."[6] All of this is to say that while the Harper government's campaign to tout martial values is clearly the most intensive manifestation of Canada's valorization of warfare, it is possible to overstate the novelty of the nation's deference to an epic version of its military past. In truth, as this study will argue, the continuities in English Canada's attitudes towards war are profound and revealing.[7]

This apparent hallowedness with which Anglo-Canadians have viewed their nation's military history and armed forces calls for an analysis of a series of seeming paradoxes. The most immediate of these includes Canadians' conception that they are not inherently warlike, nor are they afflicted with the level of flag-waving patriotism and sense of national mission witnessed south of the border. Equally intriguing is the fact that since the early twentieth century, Canada's most significant military contributions involved partnerships with the United States. Canadians fought the same wars, on the same side, employed similar strategies, and possessed many of the same ultimate objectives as the United States in the First World War, the Second World War, and the Korean War.[8] To applaud and reiterate the abundant US-based criticisms of America's wars, as many Canadians do, while simultaneously underscoring the fundamental nobility of Canadian military ventures represents a seeming incongruity that begs further examination.

A comparative survey of scholarly and popular interpretations of Canadian and American involvement in the major wars of the twentieth century – as well as the rituals, monuments, and other public testimonials to the legacy of conflict – provides an opportunity to come to terms with some of these disparities and paradoxes. The turn of the twentieth century marked the beginning of a relative alignment of US and British (and therefore Canadian) interests in global affairs, and thus saw Canadians and Americans fighting with, rather than against, one another for the first time. Canada-US cooperation would go on to develop its own rationale, reinforced by the 1940 Ogdensburg Agreement establishing the Permanent Joint Board on Defence, and later NATO and NORAD, leading to a greater convergence of foreign policy interests and actions, and thus productive opportunities for parallel analysis. It is also the case that the variety of national responses to the First, Second, and Korean wars cannot be understood in isolation. These responses were built upon the legacies of previous conflicts, and later filtered through lessons gleaned from subsequent foreign entanglements (in particular, Vietnam, Iraq, and Afghanistan), an interdependence that necessarily brings other wars into this conversation from time to time. Two conflicts not shared by Canada and the United States nonetheless call for parallel examination: the War of 1898 and the South African War were virtually coterminous campaigns that were conducted under similar auspices; they devolved into analogous levels of brutality; and they were frequently conjoined in the minds of Canadians and Americans of the era. Both would drag on into the first years of the twentieth century, and serve as unnerving harbingers of the total wars that would soon convulse the globe; both served as significant steps on the path to a heightened international role for each nation.

The relationship between war and memory is particularly conducive to a trans-national, comparative approach, as international conflict amalgamates – to an unprecedented though provisional degree – the national destinies of various states, be they allies or adversaries. Under these circumstances, the differing and sometimes contradictory remembrance of similar events can reveal a great deal about perceptions of both self and other. As Jay Winter and Antoine Prost explained in their preface to the English-language edition of their survey of French, German, and British histories of the First World War, "it may be refreshing for English readers to recognize how unusual their own thinking is on the Great War, when placed alongside that of readers who bring to the subject entirely different assumptions." This type of juxtaposition, then, can serve to test often murky claims about national experiences and identities. How can one, for instance, identify nations as "warlike" or "peaceable" in isolation? Compared to whom or what? Likewise, if a people believes its soldiers are the world's finest – and the list of nominees for this garland is both lengthy and not infrequently weighted towards the nationality of the nominator – some relative supporting data should be expected.[9]

Absent comparators, however, we are often left with a host of untested and often competing claims. For instance, Desmond Morton argued that Canadians "have no affection for militarism or the military cast of mind," elsewhere going so far as to describe citizens' historical "disdain for military institutions." Donald Schurman corroborated this "lack of enthusiasm for military matters," and yet revealed that "it is indeed almost impossible to imagine Canadian writers protesting in print, either against World War One or its successor. Support for the military goals of the war was a hallmark of the colonial English Canadian." Donald Creighton called Canadians "a profoundly unmilitary people," while offering the seemingly contradictory insight that "the War of 1914–18 was the greatest experience that the Canadian people had ever known, or would ever know." Elsewhere we are informed that the supposedly "peaceable kingdom" inhabited by an "unmilitary people" was in fact forged in war, that Canada has always been a "warrior nation," that its soldiers "have consistently proven second to none," and that, according to Canadian General Rick Hillier, those same soldiers "are our credentials" to the wider world.[10]

A nation which exhibits no affection for militarism while begetting generation after generation of the world's finest soldiers, which disdains military institutions yet hesitates to voice opposition to military operations, which embraces an image of both a disinterested international mediator and a war-fighter, is a conflicted nation indeed. One possible explanation for these heterogeneous conclusions about the Canadian character is that we are not really dealing with a single nation at all, but a permanently disparate assemblage of regions, nations, ethnicities, and classes – in the time-honoured (and oversimplified) dichotomy, a mosaic rather than a melting pot. But if we do posit Canada as an integrated nation, at the very least the suppositions underlying the various testaments to militarism and peacefulness need to be measured according to a broader international context in order to make more reliable claims regarding the "national character." For this same reason, it is sometimes helpful to stray beyond the tight Canada-United States focus that otherwise underlies this study to include data from other nations – with those that round out the core members of the "Anglosphere" (Australia, New Zealand, and especially Great Britain) representing the most opportune sources of comparison. Such a move also recognizes the enduring insight underpinning J.B. Brebner's influential 1945 work *North Atlantic Triangle*, that "the *interplay* between the United States and Canada – the Siamese Twins of North

America," is an essential driver of both nations' development. Furthermore, understanding that interplay also requires bringing Britain into the conversation at key junctures, "whether in the realm of ideas, like democracy, or of institutions, or of economic or political processes."[11] This triangular interplay developed especial potency around the turn of the twentieth century, when Anglo-Saxons the world over developed a powerful sense of unity and shared destiny as agents of a Providential mission to civilize the globe. In this context, national discourses and identities, never purely "national" under any circumstances, reveal the deep inspiration of an international (and especially English-speaking) dialogue – even as each nation developed responses to issues like war and peace that were mediated by their own distinctive circumstances.

If Canadians' relationship to militarism is marked by some seemingly irreconcilable paradoxes, the contradictions inherent to the US martial experience are better known, and more widely maligned. The nation was born in hostility to standing armies, yet today equips more than two million soldiers with the most formidable military technologies on the planet – through an arrangement described ominously by their war-hero president Dwight Eisenhower as "the military-industrial complex." Early generations of Americans were instructed to avoid entangling alliances and any hint of partiality in their relations with fellow states, and to remain isolated from regions beyond their sphere of influence; yet today the United States operates more than 700 military bases outside its own borders, accounts for more than 40 per cent of all global military spending, and oversees the world's dominant military alliances.[12] These are no mean inconsistencies. However, as is the case with Canada, placing America's domestic deliberations over war and peace into comparative perspective also reveals unexpected discoveries – for instance, a nation more deeply committed to democratic ideals, reflection, renewal (and yes, peace) than is commonly conceded by many beyond its borders.

Positioning national experiences of warfare alongside one another should not be construed as an effort to issue blanket endorsements or condemnations of either country's attitudes towards armed conflict; indeed, these divergent national attitudes have produced outcomes deserving of both credit and censure. The opposition to war in the US experience, the willingness to confront and defy official policymaking surrounding international conflict, have certainly contributed to moments many Americans and non-Americans consider ennobling. Of these, the widespread condemnation over the seizure of territory and subject peoples following the War of 1898, the well-founded hesitation to send their sons into the bloodletting of the First World War, and the determined effort to end the American involvement in Vietnam are among the most celebrated. At the same time, the propensity for defiance and discord also led to blood in the streets and a domestic bombing campaign sparked by the same conflict in Vietnam; seemingly intractable political gridlock in the nation's capital over any number of contentious issues; and a tendency in some quarters to believe that vast and diabolical conspiracies underlie nearly every episode of consequence in American history (including, but not limited to, the decision to join the First World War, the assault on Pearl Harbor, and the 9/11 attacks). English-Canadians' more optimistic impression of both government power and governmental calls to arms, meanwhile, contributed to a jingoistic dash into wars of dubious morality that posed no threat to their territory (the South African War, and arguably, the First World War), but also to an immediate military challenge to fascist aggression in 1939. Canadian soldiers returning from battles their government required them to fight have not encountered widespread, collective opprobrium for the misconduct of a few from their ranks, a situation faced by many conscripted American veterans of the Vietnam War.[13]

Of course, the very idea of "national" attitudes is highly contentious, a point reiterated by social and cultural historians for many decades now (even those analysing countries possessing a more integrated and commonly accepted understanding of nationalism than Canada). No collectivity, no matter how cohesive, possesses a single "mind" in the ways that previous scholars like American historian Perry Miller sought to describe it. Rather, to paraphrase Walt Whitman, nations contain multitudes. They are made up of an array of peoples possessing various identities and points of view born of their culture, ethnicity, language, class, religion, gender, sexuality, region, generation, and so on. At the same time, nation is *also* an important source of personal identity, one often under-appreciated by analysts championing – or seeking to usher in – a new, borderless age of "post-nationalism." Especially in times of war or other perceived national crisis, this "outmoded" model of self-definition can experience a rather miraculous renaissance – not infrequently with the assistance of government-sponsored efforts to encourage and enforce fealty to the state and its mission. Moreover, while national identities are by nature fragmented and contested, they are not created equal: polities inevitably generate and sustain a dominant cultural viewpoint, one that can be approximated by taking stock of the frequency and visibility of particular messages about who we are, what we believe, where we came from, where we are going. Governments have distinct advantages in delivering such messages, as do journalists, corporations, writers, filmmakers, and academics, to cite a few of the more prominent cultural gatekeepers. When the stories these well-positioned sources tell about the nation are in relative alignment, we can begin to decipher an outlook that may be described as "national." The emergence of a backlash against those who challenge the authorized version of national identity and purpose also serves to provide a keener understanding of the dominant viewpoint (even as these challenges can reshape mainstream attitudes over time).[14]

Importantly for our purposes, the diversity of ethno-cultural identities – more precisely, the percentage of those outside the dominant rubrics of both Anglo-Saxondom and whiteness – has always been greater south of the border than in English Canada, providing one significant source of the divergent attitudes towards war cited above.[15] In times of interstate conflict, ethnic/national origin often takes centre stage in formulating individual and group responses, a process guided by concerns for kinfolk abroad, historic grievances or affections towards the various states involved (as well as towards their own government), and domestic anxieties about the loyalty of ethnic minorities. From the earliest days of European settlement onward, the inhabitants of what would become the United States constituted one of the more motley aggregations of the globe's peoples, and these ethno-cultural variations helped to cultivate spirited debates over national interests and trajectories. Here we run up against the limits of the mosaic-melting pot binary: Americans as a whole may possess a more cohesive and coherent understanding of their core myths and symbols than Canadians; in wartime, however, US officials have been forced to contend with a greater percentage of residents with blood ties to the enemy, and in the case of Americans of colour, residents who faced systematic legal marginalizations that blunted their enthusiasm for the great overseas cause. Other significant bases for distinctly English-Canadian and American views of war include sometimes vastly differing views of imperialism (a consistent source of global tensions throughout the modern era), as well as particular interpretations of the nature of government and of citizens' relationship to it – an important consideration when crafting attitudes to violence conducted at the state's bidding.

Foundation myths – the often epic tales of national origins that seek to bind a state's citizenry to a common purpose and inscribe collective values – play an exceptionally weighty role in shaping views of past wars, and obligations to present and future conflicts. From antiquity onward, these foundation myths display a near-universal emphasis on heroic struggles against hostile outsiders, which has rendered warfare something of a prerequisite for the emergence of an "authentic" polis. On this count, the American epic is relatively unambiguous (if the foundational Revolutionary War left certain political, economic, and social questions unresolved, these would be hammered out in the dreadful crucible of the nation's Civil War). The Canadian foundation myth is decidedly murkier and more contested, an alleged deficit that has led many of its citizens to dissect each past war for evidence of national advent (and upon locating it, to consider critiques of that conflict an implicit challenge to national honour).

Naturally, the question of who tells the story of war also matters a great deal. Here again we find a greater variety of identities, political leanings, and approaches among American chroniclers of foreign conflict (a substantial and growing ratio of women, to cite one example), and a corresponding constellation of verdicts on the nation's martial past. While Canadian analysts from various fields have applied a greater range of theories, methods, and themes to a range of issues over the past several decades, these new approaches have only recently begun to influence the understanding of Canada's wars. For most of the twentieth century, the keepers of the nation's wartime legacy remained a relatively small, frequently self-referential, and in terms of their approach to the field, fairly traditional lot. Those inclined towards new approaches to research tended to avoid military subjects, while the nation's military historians, as historian Laurel Halladay pointed out, were "skilled at patrolling the borders of the field." This is another way of saying that the apparent Anglo "consensus" on Canada's military legacy is less an organic reflection of the varieties of Canadian war opinion than the outcome of a specific project to naturalize and universalize a median Canadian view. As we will see, this is a process that has a habit of reducing "Canada" to "English Canada," and often winnowing the latter down further to "Ontario." Leading English Canadian historians, as historian Carl Berger explained, long envisaged a world moulded by their Ontario upbringing, graduate work at Oxford or the University of Toronto, and a professional career in their home province.[16] In a similar vein, the nature and workings of the Canadian media, Canadian law, and the nation's governing structure and culture have exhibited a greater capacity than their American equivalents to harmonize messages around centralized, statist, elite "norms," and to dampen potentially dissenting views. On an important level, then, the greater respect and cautiousness Canadians have afforded the handling of their martial past appears as a plain fact when seen through mainstream political and cultural artefacts of the nation at war; it becomes a somewhat shakier proposition when the lens is directed towards those at the margins of the frame and attempts are made to recover their wartime experiences. Such acts of recovery, as will be noted at several points in the following study, are not absent from the Canadian record, but they have been undertaken with greater frequency in American considerations of war.

Each of the above themes – imperialism, governance, demographic makeup, foundation myths, and authorship – provides a caster on which this study of various national attitudes to war rolls.[17] Surely, establishing and conveying the variety of national attitudes to any matter is a daunting task, and none more so than war, a most traumatic personal and collective experience that influences nearly all aspects of life and thought. Sources such as war memorials and commemorations, political speech, museum exhibits, opinion polls, journalism, film, literature, and music help to trace national attitudes to war, while printed works categorized as histories (including scholarly and popular works, as well as textbooks) constitute particularly enlightening source materials for this task. This is not to suggest that historians control public discourses related to armed conflict, or that they replicate unerringly wider cultural/national views. When it comes to popular perceptions of war, however, historians inhabit a particularly authoritative position – more so than in the construction of collective understandings of the political (where political scientists obviously hold considerable sway), social and cultural (which historians share with anthropology, sociology, and others), economic, intellectual, or any other subset of social inquiry. War is often considered the historians' special purview – and under Herodotus, a fifth-century B.C. Greek writer often referred to as the "Father of History" for his multi-volume record of the Greco-Persian wars, the font of the discipline itself. On significant war-related anniversaries, the media turns to historians, affording them space on television screens and in the nation's most prominent newspapers to tell us what happened and why it matters; when new wars threaten or break out, historians are summoned to place humanity's seeming addiction to mass violence into context. Moreover, historians synthesize a range of cultural artefacts that reflect and shape common responses to war, permitting an analysis that taps into broad cultural production. As such, the following survey tells a story of twentieth-century war, of comparative national identities and cultures, and to a lesser extent, of some of the major developments and trends within the discipline of history.

Of course, the sheer volume of output on this subject serves as an inherent challenge to such a project: given the synergies between war and cultural production in general, and historical writing specifically, both nations boast a surfeit of potential source material. The sources appraised here were selected with an eye to factors such as their influence among academics and the wider public, sales figures, controversy generated, and perceived representativeness. Any informed observer of the subject could take exception to some of the choices and exclusions that are inevitable in such a project. The objective of this study, however, is to provide as faithful a gauge as possible of the general outlook regarding past wars – their necessity, efficacy, accomplishments, morality, and importance to the national story – rather than a comprehensive inventory. The sample included here reveals clear themes and sometimes profound distinctions in national cultures of war, and while any expansion of source materials would doubtless add further colouration to the themes revealed in the following pages, it is hoped that the broader conclusions would be sustained.

The book's first two chapters present an overview of the various and frequently divergent ways Canadians and Americans have talked about their international conflicts, from the earliest journalistic accounts to the war-related ceremonies, histories, films, speeches, and exhibitions of the present era. The remainder of this study offers a series of propositions on the cultural, demographic, and legal bases for what are sometimes starkly dissimilar national representations of war. The earliest chapters are presented chronologically; for the sake of variety, and because certain topics are more diffuse and difficult to handle in a linear fashion, subsequent chapters alternate between a chronological and thematic presentation.

In 2008, British-born historian and public intellectual Tony Judt argued that "the United States today is the only advanced country that still glorifies and exalts the military, a sentiment familiar in Europe before 1945 but quite unknown today." Was Judt correct in his assumption of American exceptionalism in this matter, or in a move all-too-familiar to America's northern neighbours, had he simply ignored

Canada? Consider the inventory of factors he provides for this "singularly" American trait: Over the course of the twentieth century, and unlike much of Europe and Asia, the United States avoided civil war, occupation by foreign armies, territorial dismemberment, and mass civilian deaths through combat. The nation remembers most of their conflicts from this era as "good wars," and found itself "enriched rather than impoverished by its role in the two world wars and by their outcome." As any student of Canadian history understands, Canada, too, has passed through each of these way stations along the road to military glorification and exaltation. Historian Arthur Lower put it bluntly: "all of Canada has benefitted (economically) from every war, first and last, in which it has been caught up in."[18] What's more, Canada has been spared those chapters of the American story that cast the greatest aspersion on such thinking – namely, the wars in Vietnam and Iraq (not to mention the Civil War, by far the most devastating conflict in US history).

This overall synchronicity of twentieth-century military experiences contributes to national cultures which are given to celebrate rather than regret war. Nevertheless, while many Americans glorify war unreservedly, others push back forcefully against such thinking. English Canadian representations of their wars, by contrast, have displayed a narrower range of opinion, one that is weighted more heavily towards straightforward veneration. "Living with war" in the United States, then, is synonymous with intensive debates, even in the midst of a given conflict, while "Living with war" in English Canada is more closely associated with a reserved deference to the cause and to the dictates of government.[19] This is not to deny the presence of a critical posture towards war among Canadians, nor the fact that the nation has served as a considerably more peaceful international presence than the United States. The point, rather, is that challenges to nationalistic, orthodox understandings of war have moved more slowly and cautiously into the English Canadian academic and popular imagination. While this reticence has provided considerable leverage to recent efforts to align Canadian identity with the courageous warrior, it is one with deep, if often underappreciated, roots.

PART ONE

Reconnaissance: Martial Orientations

Chapter One

Conflict in the Age of High Imperialism

Tony Judt was certainly correct in his observation that the United States continues to glorify and exalt warfare, an attitude the majority of Europeans have learned, via terrible ordeal, to distrust. Few Americans would deny their nation's predisposition towards military veneration; rather, the debate has centred on whether this orientation has been profitable or damaging to national and global interests. In taking stock of US involvement in the War of 1898 and the Great War, journalist and future Republican senator Arthur Vandenberg lauded his nation's willingness to utilize American might to "serve human-kind ... with a purity of dedication unmatched in any other government on earth." Surveying this martial legacy in the wake of the Cold War and midst a "war on terror," some recent observers claimed for the United States the mantle of the world's first truly benevolent empire, one that fights for the universal good rather than self-interest. Other Americans found less to admire, as titles to their recent indictments of their nation's keenness for war attest: *The New American Militarism: How Americans Are Seduced by War; Imperial Delusions: American Militarism and the Endless War; National Insecurity: The Cost of American Militarism; The Hollywood War Machine: US Militarism and Popular Culture*, and the list goes on.[1]

For generations, America's northern neighbours have considered it nearly a precondition of loyal Canadian-ness to cleave to the more sinister views of US militarism, a posture that has found most resonance when the United States entered controversial wars of choice. In 1968, as dissent over American involvement in Vietnam deepened, writer Margaret Atwood's poem "Backdrop Addresses Cowboy" ridiculed a "Starspangled cowboy," a self-righteous anti-hero "innocent as a bathtub/full of bullets," who leaves only "a heroic trail of desolation."

During that same conflict, fellow Canadian literary icon Farley Mowat charged that the will to violence was a permanent American virus that preyed upon native and foreigner without prejudice, holding that the United States "engaged in almost every form of domestic and external brutality, aggrandizement, degradation of the individual, and destruction of freedom." A later generation of Canadians expressed similar opinions about the American character during that nation's debacle in Iraq – as did the older but un-mellowed Mowat and Atwood.[2]

Certainly the United States is a more militaristic society in the sense that the nation has, since its inception, used warfare as an instrument of foreign policy on more occasions and to greater cumulative effect (be it positive or negative) than Canada. Beginning with its war of independence from the British, Americans have participated in eleven major international conflicts (and one civil war), initiated seven of those, and used their military forces and covert personnel beyond US borders on hundreds of occasions in order to protect and expand their own, as well as multilateral, interests. Since Confederation, Canadian armies have fought in six international conflicts – always as a junior partner – never launched a war of aggression, and played a starring role in the founding of the UN peacekeeping tradition.[3]

Now if one accepts the premise that undergirds this study – that Canadians, and more pointedly English Canadians, display a greater inclination than Americans to esteem their wars, or at least a greater hesitation to criticize them – these differing national experiences provide a simple explanation: Canadians have been more selective in the use of force and participated in fewer conflicts, none of which were instigated by the nation or fought for aggression or territorial aggrandizement. In the popular imagination, Canadian wars are "good wars," those aimed at preserving liberal ideals, restoring international order, helping those in peril, and punishing belligerent and malevolent regimes. To J.L. Granatstein, the nation's most visible military historian, Canada's military legacy can be summed up in four words: "sacrifice, freedom, resisting aggression."[4]

This justification for Canadian pride in its military certainly has merit. Canadian history reveals no Vietnams, no forcible seizure of contiguous terrain – although the Métis and their indigenous allies defeated in the rebellions of 1871 and 1885 might hold a different view. While its citizens participated, sometimes with boundless enthusiasm, in British campaigns to secure the imperial hold on India and South Africa, Canada never warred to claim overseas territory for itself.

Its troops have been welcomed as liberators, most notably by the inhabitants of France, Belgium, and the Netherlands (though certainly not by the Boers of South Africa; the response from the Afghan people was decidedly mixed). In never initiating an international conflict, Canadians are freed from nagging questions about whether the violence could have been avoided through their own labours; instead, the nation joined confrontations already underway in order to defend their friends, uphold important principles, and restore international order.[5] Yet such an explanation for the esteem Canadians hold for their military accomplishments cannot account for the fact that even in wars that share striking parallels – and most pointedly, in wars fought side by side with the United States that neither nation had a hand in initiating – the premise holds: while America certainly glories in war, its citizens have also demonstrated a greater readiness than English Canadians to second guess, and often slander, their nation's military exploits. This chapter provides an overview of public attitudes towards early-twentieth-century conflicts in order to underline this divergence.

At the close of the nineteenth century, both Canada and the United States engaged in military campaigns that represented both profound historical departures and fateful precedents for each nation. Canada joined Britain in suppressing the Boers in the South African War; this confrontation marked the Dominion's first official dispatch of troops to a foreign military confrontation, and in the words of Canadian historian Carman Miller, "served as a dress-rehearsal for the First World War." The Americans challenged a deteriorating Spanish empire in Cuba, Puerto Rico, and the Philippines, and the resulting War of 1898 would lead to the acquisition of the nation's first overseas possessions and the beginnings of a truly global foreign policy. Writing with the perspective afforded by a century of subsequent developments, cultural historian Virginia Bouvier went so far as to assert that the years surrounding the conflict "were perhaps most critical to the shaping of American identities and U.S. foreign policies in the twentieth century."[6]

Clearly, important aspects of these conflicts differ. Though the United States teamed with local insurgents in their war with Spain, the Americans considered the matter a largely unilateral affair; Canada, along with Australia and New Zealand, fought in South Africa as a junior partner. The United States mustered more than 300,000 troops for their fight, while just over 7,000 Canadians volunteered for service in the Transvaal. Nevertheless, comparing these wars makes sense for a number of reasons. For one, these were wars of imperialism, among the last great battles in service of a project contested by growing numbers within and beyond the metropole during the era. In addition, the conflicts were virtually coterminous. The United States declared war against Spain in April 1898, and though hostilities between the primary combatants ended just four months later, the ensuing war between the Filipinos and their American occupiers continued – officially – until key rebel leaders surrendered in the summer of 1902 (and unofficially for decades thereafter). The clash between Britain and the Boers began in October of 1899, and this battle would also grind on (unexpectedly for imperialists anticipating an efficient rout) until approximately the same time the United States announced the end of official Filipino resistance. Combat deaths – just over 3,000 American and nearly 300 Canadian – represent roughly equal percentages of the total population.[7]

These parallels in time and ambience fed the perception that the two wars were, in essence, one. This view was buoyed by a widespread understanding among Anglo-Saxon elites that foreign policymaking must obey the self-evident laws of racial and linguistic hierarchy, a kind of nineteenth-century "clash of civilizations" that pitted English-speaking peoples against the world's "lesser breeds." As Edward Kohn's study of turn-of-the-century Canada-US relations demonstrated, challenges to the international status quo from Germany, Japan, and Russia, along with the increasing currency of social Darwinism, moved leaders of English-speaking nations to advance the notion that Anglo-Saxon peoples should unite to fulfil their global, and manifest, destiny. Under this reasoning, "the wars with the Spanish, Filipinos, and the Boers were not unconnected, but constituted parts of a larger, highly significant picture that drew the English-speaking peoples of the world inexorably closer together." Binding the Anglo-Saxon world, too, was a growing unease that historians Marilyn Lake and Henry Reynolds called "the apprehension of imminent loss," a realization that resistance to white rule was gaining ground the world over. This sense of siege intensified expressions of white identity, solidarity, and militancy, leading African American intellectual W.E.B. Du Bois to prophesy in 1900 that "the problem of the twentieth century is the problem of the color line." In subsequent writings, Du Bois was explicit about the root of "the problem": namely, the "new religion of whiteness" born in the nineteenth century, one predicated on that race's obsession with "ownership of the earth forever and ever, Amen."[8]

In this spirit of racial camaraderie and calling, many English Canadians "urged American involvement in Cuba and their annexation of the Philippines," with Toronto's *Globe and Mail* congratulating the United States for its willingness to keep "the ragged little beggars" in line. When the South African War began the following year, noted Kohn, "the United States supported Great Britain for the same reason the British had supported America a year earlier: both nations recognized their mutual interests in a world with shifting lines of power." In his Christmas message of 1899, J.A. Ewan of *Canadian Magazine* maintained that both battles must continue until "the Boer and Filipino have been made to realize that the Anglo-Saxon race never errs, that it makes war only for the benefits of humanity." Opponents of this purported Anglo-Saxon "destiny" also linked the conflicts: Mark Twain wrote of "Christendom's ... pirate raids" against the Filipinos and Boers in his ominous article "A Greeting from the Nineteenth to the Twentieth Century." Meanwhile, in a display of anti-imperialist solidarity, Filipinos in South Africa joined Boer forces to take up arms against Britain.[9]

Parallels also exist regarding the stated – and unstated – rationales for war. Supporters of both the American and British actions underscored the emancipatory nature of the operations, citing the oppression of colonized Cubans and the disenfranchisement of the mostly English "Uitlanders" in South Africa as primary motivations. Less altruistic and inspirational grounds, including access to markets and resources, and the need to shore up or establish "prestige" as international powers, received considerably less public airing. Finally, official assurances of a quick and convincing victory for the Americans and the British soon withered as a result of determined counterinsurgencies. This led to frustration, growing public discontent, and the deployment of increasingly pitiless offensives that relied upon torture, the internment of civilians, and scorched-earth campaigns against rebellious zones. For this reason, both conflicts are often viewed as antecedents to the "total wars" of the twentieth century that are characterized by large-scale atrocities and escalating percentages of civilian causalities.[10] For our purposes, it is also important to underline a fundamental incongruity in the ways the wars have been remembered: while the War of 1898 evinces a palpable sense of discomfort and indignation on the part of many Americans, the Canadian response to the South African War can be best characterized as an amalgam of facile commemoration and wilful neglect.

To be sure, neither conflict has maintained much purchase over the popular imagination in either the United States or Canada; the wars' bluntly imperial nature, racial overtones, and brutality have rendered them less valuable to the service of nation-building than other conflicts.

US officials and public institutions, rarely accused of introversion when it comes to commemorating victories in battle, remained silent at the centenary anniversary of the War of 1898. The Canadian government, meanwhile, sponsored what the CBC called a "solemn ceremony" to mark the centennial of the "Boer War," though the broadcaster conceded that this was a conflict "many Canadians know little about" before providing a markedly partisan and sanitized primer on the most rudimentary aspects of the conflict. Popular culture, too, has steered clear of these confrontations. Few works of fiction produced in Canada and the United States use the wars as their subjects, while Hollywood produced just two, little-remembered films on the confrontation with Spain. The *New York Times'* film critic of the day found the first of these, Paramount's 1927 silent film *The Rough Riders*, dry and uneven. "The comedy relief that reigns in the first chapters of this photoplay," wrote Mordaunt Hall, "is missing for quite some time in the latter episodes," a deficiency that participants from all sides who experienced firsthand the horrors of the war surely found entirely appropriate.[11]

However, for those whose ostensible goal is simply to comprehend and represent the past, rather than buttress any official national objectives, the wars would appear a productive site of inquiry, one that would at the very least provide criteria and caveats for potential involvement in future conflicts. On this, Canadians have appeared more than a little reticent, generating relatively little in the way of scholarly or public debate regarding the South African War – this from a country that has otherwise displayed an ongoing fascination with its participation in foreign conflicts. This comparative silence owes something to the relatively small Canadian contingent sent to bolster British claims to the region, and to a decidedly limited national influence over the course of the battle. However, this historic neglect is also rooted in the fact that the war does not accommodate itself neatly into the discourses of heroism, rectitude, nation-building, and uncomplicated notions of victory that characterize national understandings and commemorations of other Canadian conflicts.

US analysts, meanwhile, have taken up the task of interrogating their *fin-de-siècle* imperial war with some enthusiasm, producing a considerable breadth of literature that cross-examines official discourses regarding the origins and goals of the clash, and that measures the divide between their nation's stated ideals and the events of 1898. Indeed, one of the more striking features of US popular and academic accounts of the war is the sheer volume of the output. The passion and perceived

1.1 Despite its general enthusiasm for America's foreign conflicts, Hollywood has struggled to weave a tale of valour and righteousness out of the expansionist War of 1898. Paramount's 1927 silent film *The Rough Riders* was one of the few to take up the challenge, but few were moved. (Paramount Pictures, 1927.)

significance of the debates spawned by the conflict can be measured, in part, by the existence of more than a half a dozen essays and one monograph dedicated solely to the vast US historiography surrounding the war (to go along with numerous similar surveys of non-US scholarship). Unsurprisingly, many of the earliest accounts of the war, written in an era still awash in the jingoistic euphoria that marked US participation and victory, and one still beholden to social Darwinist theorizing which could invoke "the white man's burden" without irony or ignominy, lauded the US intervention and ensuing triumph. In 1900 for instance, Protestant clergyman Josiah Strong, whose previous book, *Our Country* (1885) had done much to convince Anglo-Saxon Americans that both heaven and humanity craved US global leadership, published *Expansion under New World Conditions*. Redeploying the racial theorizing which had animated his earlier justification for America's civilizing mission, Strong insisted that true freedom could only be achieved under the rule of law, a juridical condition alien to foreign races, inborn to Anglo-Saxons, and perfected under the US governmental system. This happy coincidence of American supply and foreign demand necessitated a protracted period of US guidance – rather than immediate independence – for areas delivered from Spanish rule in 1898. And for Strong, this extension of US hegemony was only the beginning; in fact, only two potential obstacles lay between Anglo-Saxons and their global destiny. "Is there any doubt that this race," he queried, "unless devitalized by alcohol and tobacco, is destined to dispossess many weaker races, assimilate others, and mold the remainder until, in a very true and important sense, it has Anglo-Saxonized mankind?"[12]

This avowal of the righteousness of US actions has been reprised repeatedly in the century since the conflict, endorsing US diplomat and future Secretary of State John Hay's declaration that this had been "a splendid little war." A biography of President McKinley published in 1901, the year of his assassination, referred to the US intervention as "a war for humanity, for America could no longer close her ears to the wails of starving people who lay perishing, as may be said, on her very doorsteps." According to H. Addington Bruce (an American journalist whose Canadian birth and education at Toronto's tony Upper Canada and Trinity colleges helped to nurture a fondness for imperial pursuits), the United States went to war "in the great cause of humanity" – no great bombshell in a volume titled *The Romance of American Expansion*. Paul L. Haworth, writing in 1920 on the heels of a later war which traumatized his nation and the globe, found solace in the earlier US action in

Josiah Strong.

1.2 Dawn of the Anglosphere? The Reverend Josiah Strong's popular gilded-age books on America's mission looked forward to the day when his clean-living brethren would, through a combination of dispossession and assimilation, "Anglo-Saxonize mankind." Accord with that social-Darwinist vision led influential figures throughout the English-speaking world to advocate "racial" unity in international affairs. (Edward Marshall, "'Back to the Farm a False Cry' – Josiah Strong," *New York Times*, 25 December 1910.)

Cuba, calling it "one of the most admirable chapters in human annals." Similarly, Randolph Greenfield Adams' 1933 history of the nation's international relations identified the deliverance of the Cubans as "one of the most creditable pages in American foreign policy." Such views faced increasingly potent challenges in the latter half of the twentieth century, but they have proved durable nonetheless. Writing in 1993, military historian James Bradford held that the United States did not enter the war to forward any goals besides restoring regional order and "maintain[ing] the principle of self determination," marking the first time the nation had taken up arms "out of a sense of moral obligation," and anticipating the core values embodied in President Woodrow Wilson's Fourteen Points. This line of thinking taps into a long tradition of American exceptionalism, chosen-ness, and destiny; such themes were made explicit in Arthur Vandenberg's contention that the war with Spain confirmed America's unparalleled capacity for selflessness.[13]

However, a great many US analysts of the war have – *from the beginning* – found roughly the opposite of "purity" in the motives for US intervention, or romance in the carnage that followed. Some emphasized the blundering and duplicity of the McKinley administration's prewar diplomacy with Spain; others depicted an effete federal government capitulating to public demands for a war of retribution after the explosion that sank the USS *Maine* in Havana Harbor, a public incited by the "yellow journalism" purveyed by the Hearst and Pulitzer newspaper empires.[14] Stephen Crane, one of the era's most celebrated writers, covered the war as a journalist and wrote damning poetry and a memoir that emphasized the savagery and pointlessness of it all. His 1899 poem "War is Kind" reproached those who upheld any notions of "the excellence of killing" on behalf of honour, the state, humanity, or any other pretext. In its fourth stanza, Crane wrote:

> Hoarse, booming drums of the regiment,
> Little souls who thirst for fight,
> These men were born to drill and die.
> The unexplained glory flies above them.
> Great is the battle-god, great, and his kingdom
> A field where a thousand corpses lie.[15]

Later American writers operating from "realist" theoretical paradigms did little to ennoble the sacrifice of the fallen. Counseling loyalty only to narrow national interests rather than ideals, mission, altruism, or any other moral abstraction, many realists viewed the decision to intervene as a spasm of illogic. George Kennan's *American Diplomacy*, for instance, handled the late-nineteenth-century dalliance with imperialism as "a momentary psychological lapse" that interrupted to the broader arc of US history. Others less bound to hardnosed realism sought to reclaim some measure of national honour by depicting a noble mission gone sour. Spurred to righteous action by Spanish depredations against the Cuban people, US officials then fell prey to the seductions of territorial gain, betraying Spain's erstwhile colonial subjects and the American people alike. It is important to point out that many of these interpretations share an underlying desire to cast the episode as unrepresentative of an "authentic" and more honourable – or at least more sensible – America. Still, aberrations, accidents, fits of madness, sudden shifts in policy, and other mechanisms summoned to salvage a broader and wiser national trajectory still serve to brand *this* war, which resulted in the deaths of thousands of Americans, a mistake.[16] In a strictly nationalist vein, then, this is tantamount to claiming that these soldiers died in error, and in futility. Whether such interpretations can withstand the weight of evidence is a rather different question than whether analysts of the war are willing to censure their nation's wartime conduct and, by extension, affix varying degrees of senselessness to the sacrifice of US service personnel (to say nothing of civilians or enemy combatants).

Moreover, a host of Americans have taken a much harsher line, emphasizing the immorality and futility of war as a diplomatic tool, and the centrality of premeditated territorial acquisition and self-interest in US intervention. This dystopian perspective found expression through the dozens of peace organizations that were founded during and immediately after the war, and which listed on their membership rolls some of the nation's more influential industrialists, lawyers, bankers, educators, and former diplomats. Recriminations continued in the analysis of the highly influential Progressive historians of the interwar period, who applied a materialistic interpretation of class conflict to both domestic and international history. Not surprisingly, Progressives like Charles Beard and Vernon Parrington underscored the commercial advantages of divesting the Spanish of territory from the Caribbean to Southeast Asia, along with the sizeable blow to claims of altruism entailed by these moves. Because their works served as the standard textbooks in high school and college history courses until the mid-twentieth century, many Americans would be forced to confront an unflattering portrait of their nation's internationalist turn.[17]

Nor did the savagery of the civilizing operations escape notice. At first, many Americans cheered the dashing exploits of Teddy Roosevelt's Rough Riders in Puerto Rico and the quick rout of the Spanish forces in all of the War of 1898's theatres. But as the Filipino insurrection against American occupation intensified, the Anti-Imperialist League – the largest peace organization spawned by the conflict – made the inhumane conduct of American troops a regular trope of their speeches and pamphlets. In 1899, the League published *Soldiers' Letters: Being Materials for the History of a War of Criminal Aggression,* a compilation of American troops' correspondence home that revealed episodes of torture, the bayoneting of the wounded, and the execution of prisoners by US personnel. In a speech to Congress, Senator George Frisbie Hoar condemned the shameful acts carried out in the name of America, including the slaughter of "uncounted thousands of peoples you have desired to benefit," the establishment of concentration camps, "the burning of human dwellings, and the horror of the water torture." Public outrage over these revelations led to Senate hearings on the conduct of US forces, and the court-martialing and imprisonment of numerous soldiers. *The Conquest of the Philippines by the United States,* a polemical work by NAACP president Moorfield Storey and Filipino national Marcial Lichauco published in 1926, featured an entire chapter on the brutality and treachery of US forces on the Philippine islands, with unflinching depictions of scorched-earth campaigns, concentration camps, torture, the killing of civilians, the mutilation of the dead, and the strict press censorship which concealed these atrocities from the American public.[18]

The war was likewise excoriated by Walter Millis, a New York journalist and best-selling military historian, in his 1931 volume *The Martial Spirit.* Millis applied irony, understatement, and black humour to deflate romantic notions of the glamour of war, revealing a military campaign marked by farce rather than heroism. Outlining a century-long history of US covetousness towards Cuba, Millis argued that while the American people wanted *Cuba libre,* US officials simply wanted Cuba. And once the decision to intervene was made, policymakers experienced conspicuous difficulties reigning in their appetites: "But if we were after all setting out to conquer the Philippines," wrote Millis, "what about Porto Rico, which was so much more easily available? And if the Filipino insurgents were to be gently steam-rolled, might not even the Cubans, in spite of all of our hopes, turn out to be unprepared for self-government?" Likewise, 1898 became a preferred target for the "New Left" historians who rose to prominence in the years surrounding the Vietnam War and focused – at times monolithically – on the commercial impulses orchestrating US foreign affairs. In subsequent decades, the conflict with Spain inspired a multitude of analyses informed by postmodernism, feminism, and internationalist economic frameworks – including dependency and world systems theories – that emphasize the unequal and exploitative character of international capitalism. Along the way (and repeatedly), the student of these works is instructed that the episode was driven by unvarnished covetousness, a blend of racial animus and cultural paternalism, and a yearning to reinvigorate regressive visions of American manhood; that US intervention violated international law and the nation's core principles; that government officials and journalists intentionally misinformed the public on the nature and objectives of the conflict; and that US soldiers engaged in unpardonable acts of criminality, particularly against Filipino insurgents.[19]

The sour mood so dominated appraisals of 1898 that some US commentators worried that the negativity would do lasting harm to patriotism and the nation's international image. In 1958, Harvard history professor Frank Freidel titled his account of the conflict *Splendid Little War*, a phrase he employed without irony in an attempt to reclaim it from war critics. In taking stock of collective attitudes towards the war, Freidel lamented the predominance of a decidedly pessimistic appraisal of the conflict that had begun with such idealism: "In the ensuing years, with the innocence destroyed, the war seemed less than a crusade and far from splendid," with Americans now "jeering at what had been spurious or ridiculous." Freidel's efforts, however, could not have anticipated or weathered the withering assault that Vietnam-era New Left historians launched against the war with Spain – and on American internationalism in general. In 1978, as the dust began to settle over these latest broadsides, naval historian James Field tried gamely to pick up where Freidel left off. Summaries of 1890s US expansion constituted "The Worst Chapter in Almost Any Book" of American history, as the title to Field's essay famously charged. To the author, analysis of the era's foreign policy was marred by overheated charges of racism, jingoism, and greed to explain what was in fact a haphazard and unintentional expansion. "The result," he wrote, "is an inverted Whig interpretation of history, differing from its predecessor primarily in that now the children of darkness triumph over the children of light."[20]

Those seeking to right the upturned house of Whig, to accent once again history's inexorable march towards enlightenment, may have found solace by turning to English Canadian representations of the South African War. Here, reproach and regret, even for one of the grimmer episodes in modern imperial history, remained scarce commodities through much of the twentieth century. Anglo newspapers and magazines strained to outdo their competitors in lavishing praise on the imperial forces and their cause. Like Josiah Strong's rendering of the War of 1898, the earliest Canadian books dedicated to the conflict in South Africa were marked by heavy doses of jingoism, as well as racial and religious justifications for empire that were grounded in

Anglo-Saxons' congenital "genius for self-government and organiza-tion" and their role as the earthly proxies of Divine will. Importantly, these volumes also emerged in the midst of the conflict itself – that is, before the war's unexpected duration and undeniable barbarity chal-lenged notions of the grandeur of the empire and the cause. A handful of soldiers' memoirs and regimental histories appeared in the ensuing decades, but those waiting for a book-length analysis of the entire war's military, social, and political implications for Canada would grow very old indeed. The first postwar monograph, and thus the first to chronicle the war to its distinctly bitter conclusion, would appear more than nine decades after the fighting ceased. *Painting the Map Red*, Carman Miller's 1993 lifeline to those holding their breath for the sequel, puzzled over the silence surrounding the war. "Most historians," Miller noted, "agree that the South African War had a profound impact upon Canadian life and politics … But despite its admitted importance, more than ninety years after Canadian troops first landed in Cape Town, there is still no compre-hensive study of Canada's participation in the war."[21]

Prior to the publication of Miller's work, those interested in broaden-ing their understanding of Canada's role in the episode were required to mine general historical surveys. The effort could hardly be consid-ered satiating, however, as these analyses of the conflict are marked by narrowness, insularity, and above all, remarkable brevity. In fact, in most of these volumes, the conflict barely registers, with historians from George Wrong to Donald Creighton to W.L. Morton dedicating only two or three paragraphs to Canada's first foreign war in otherwise exhaus-tive examinations of the nation's history. In his polemical (and emphati-cally grumpy) *Who Killed Canadian History?*, J.L. Granatstein included a chapter on Canadians' duty to understand their military past, recalling fondly the nation's participation in the world wars, less fondly its peace-keeping operations, and its inaugural international conflict not at all. Canadian authors who did mention the operation were united in evad-ing discussions of its causes, issues, and in many cases, even principal combatants – though they did little to hide their contempt for the Boers, who had the gall to defy both Britain and the inevitability of industrial progress. On the whole, the focus remained essentially national in scope, fixed on the war's impact on Canada's Dominion status and internal unity; the economic causation emphasized by American Progressives' studies of the War of 1898 found little purchase north of the border.[22]

In addition to appearing ahistorical, this overall disavowal of context is notable for at least two reasons. First, failure to exhume the myriad sources of the conflict and the broader stakes and implications involved does not permit an informed and comprehensive discussion of whether Canada was justified in participating in the South African War. Liberal Prime Minister Wilfrid Laurier may have found it politically expedient, both domestically and with respect to imperial relations, to send troops, and participation may (or may not, depending on the writer) have spurred Canadian sovereignty and an emergent nationalism. Regardless, these factors alone do not appear sufficient as *casus belli* or *casus foederis*, as the case may be.

Second, beyond Canadian borders, the South African War has generated more scholarly and popular writing than any other aspect of that region's history, while the war's origins have proven the most controversial issue in South African historiography. Before the 1993 publication of Miller's volume, however, readers confined to Canadian renderings of the war would have little idea that the hostilities emerged after nearly a century of tension between Britain and the Boers; that the British were generally understood to have provoked the war; that British society itself was deeply divided over the propriety of the conflict; that British mining interests had a decided interest in pressing the issue and manipulated the news coverage presented to empire readers; that beyond the empire there existed a "near-universal public sympathy" for the Boers; that Cape Colony prime minister and mining magnate Cecil Rhodes' catastrophic and unauthorized Jameson Raid of 1895–6, intended to spark a broad revolt against the Boer government, received worldwide condemnation; or that the importation of cheap Chinese labour to work the mines in the immediate aftermath of the British victory in 1902 undermined the already-tenuous claim that Britain fought for ideals rather than profit. In all, wrote the eminent British historian A.P. Thornton, the empire experienced "a loss of moral content" in the Transvaal, "from which it never completely recovered."[23]

Canadian suffragette and politician Nellie McClung shared these misgivings. In her 1945 memoir *The Stream Runs Fast*, McClung recalled that she and her Manitou, Manitoba neighbours wondered whether gold and diamonds "had kindled all the flame of conquest" in 1899, as "there seemed to be no good reason for fighting the Boers." Robert Page provided a rare international perspective of Canadian representations of the conflict in two slender volumes, *Imperialism and Canada* (1972), and a Canadian Historical Association "Historical Booklet," *The Boer War and Canadian Imperialism* (1987). Canadian writer June Callwood likewise furnished more context on the war in two short (and

1.3 Nellie McClung, posing circa 1910 with her son Mark and dog Philip outside their Winnipeg home, suspected less philanthropic motives for the British clash with the Boers than those put forward by the empire's supporters. While McClung maintained that her neighbours in the small farming community of Manitou shared these misgivings in 1899, English-Canadian newspapers and politicians expressed near-universal support for the imperial forces. (Castor Studio, Library and Archives Canada, C-008482.)

unarguable) revelations than most of the surveys that predated her 1981 popular history combined, reporting that the decision to go to war "divided Britain itself" into pro-imperial and pro-Boer factions, and that Cecil Rhodes' appetite for diamonds had served to inflame the region.[24] Outside these accounts, such themes rarely found their way into English Canadian assessments for much of the twentieth century.

If the lead-in to the South African War is generally underdeveloped in Canadian renderings, the summary of the conflict itself and its eventual resolution is doubly so. Indeed, in volume after volume, the discussion of the episode ends once the decision is made to send troops – an extraordinarily curious posture for any story of war (wherein "Who won?" is generally a leading query). A few general surveys mentioned the number of volunteers sent to South Africa, while almost none counted the dead or wounded. George Wrong stated simply that the troops "did good service," without revealing who prevailed or under what circumstances. Desmond Morton likewise noted only that the men "performed well," while Stephen Leacock claimed that the soldiers found "a glad adventure" in the Transvaal. The *Canadian Military Gazette*, surveying a post-bellum South Africa that had sickened many British observers, went so far as to proclaim that the conflict with the Boers proved that warfare was "becoming more humane, more restrained, more Christian." Once again, Robert Page supplied a rare rejoinder to the widespread applause, acknowledging in a brief paragraph that imperial forces came to adopt a scorched-earth policy and herded women and children into "poorly run" refugee camps, tactics which "led to extensive criticism of the war by 1902."[25]

By the early 1990s, then, Carman Miller confronted a considerable lacuna in the historical record. His exhaustive description of the soldiers' experience, something virtually ignored outside the regimental histories of the conflict, revealed that the troops were plagued by "weak and ineffectual leadership," ordered into ill-advised offensives with often-disastrous results, and appalled by the brutality and mayhem that surrounded them (and in which they took part). In non-Canadian accounts, this aspect of the war received scrutiny from the beginning; for instance, British journalist and future Liberal Member of Parliament J.M. Robertson's muckraking reports from the field, collected in a 1901 publication bearing the unambiguous title *Wrecking the Empire*, made it plain that imperial forces employed shockingly cruel methods in their efforts to bring the Boers to heel. British women like Emily Hobhouse who travelled to the war zone were instrumental in exposing the dreadful conditions in the camps, where poor nutrition and disease killed nearly 30,000, most of whom were women and children (more than double the number of those killed in battle on both sides). David Nash would later argue that revulsion over such tactics initiated a tradition of peace politics that flourished in the United Kingdom throughout the twentieth century. It is unclear from Canadian accounts whether the

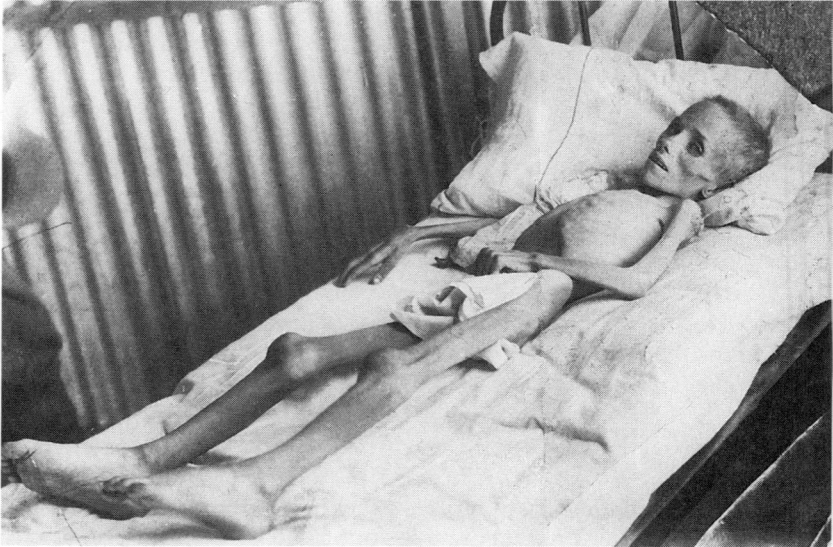

1.4 Activist Emily Hobhouse sought to appeal to the conscience of her fellow Britons with her disturbing reports and images from South African concentration camps, like this 1901 photograph of dying inmate Lizzie van Zyl (aged 6 or 7). Hobhouse's critics contended that the girl arrived at the camp in an emaciated state, while war opponents believed Hobhouse's claim that pitiful camp rations were to blame, and flooded the mailboxes of British politicians with copies of the image. Within a year, a number of British serials had reproduced the photograph, but no Canadian publisher followed suit. (http://public.fotki.com/SAgenealogie/abo/konsentrasiekampe/page2. html, accessed 2 January 2014.)

war haunted Canadians in similar ways; Carl Berger went so far as to hold that the "experience in South Africa did *nothing* to change" Canadians' perception "that war was more a manly triumph over the obstacles of nature than massive and indiscriminate slaughter" (emphasis added). [26]

What is clear is the fact that the story of the South African War, as rendered by English Canadians, served to encourage something of a false binary that continues to be upheld by many in that nation – one that separates countries that go to war for noble reasons and that always conduct themselves with bravery and honour from those who do not. While the atrocities that scandalized wartime Britain eventually found a small place in Canadian reckonings of the event, this component of the affair (which outside of Canadian accounts remains one of the war's primary lessons), continues to receive light treatment. In his extensive 2008 survey of Canada's regimental history, prominent Canadian military historian David Bercuson left out the scorched-earth tactics, well poisonings, and concentration camps, writing only this of the battlefield experiences of Strathcona's Horse, a Canadian unit that arrived to find the war moving into its most vicious stage: "It gained a reputation for fierceness in combat, and rumours circulated that the Strathconas took no prisoners."[27] "Fierceness" certainly sounds finer than "brutality," the former being an attribute to which all effective soldiers should aspire. "Reputations" and "rumours" may or may not be deserved (although it is also the historian's duty to follow up on them and render judgment as to their reliability); regardless, the use of such terms gives the Strathconas' story the aura of legend while granting them plausible deniability over any allegations of wrongdoing.

Granatstein was only partially more forthcoming, conceding that Canadian forces took part in "brutally effective" policies of incarceration, looting, and burning. The author also reiterated the Strathconas' "reputation for fierceness," reported they earned the nickname "The Headhunters," and made cryptic reference to the fact that "the guerilla war had inevitably turned into a brutal struggle, but later investigation cleared the Strathconas and their colonel of all [unspecified] charges." Chris Madsen's more thorough and less jaunty depiction of events fills in some of these gaping cavities in the plotline. "Canadian troops became intimately involved in the nastier aspects of the South African war," he revealed. In addition to their contributions to the scorched-earth policy, the Strathconas systematically executed Boer prisoners, an act Madsen called "malicious" and "murder" (under military law, a synonym for "taking no prisoners"). On another occasion, according to a Canadian eyewitness, drunken non-commissioned officers from the regiment shouted and sang as they fired revolvers at Boer prisoners. As Madsen observed, Australians who a year later "committed remarkably similar crimes" were tried and executed; the Canadians were spared only because Lord Kitchener, who for a variety of reasons took such incidents quite seriously, had not yet assumed command from the more indifferent Lord Roberts. In all, one need not rely on the idioms of "rumour" and "reputation" when the facts lay the sometimes-unflattering realities bare. Evasion of those realities continues to be a hallmark of Canadian remembering, a truth reflected and reinforced by a 2013 account of the war intended for a juvenile audience titled *Doing Canada Proud: The Second Boer War and the Battle of Paardeberg*.[28]

Little more than a decade after these wars' pointedly astringent conclusions, another, more extensive international conflict beckoned. Unlike their southern counterparts, Canadians were enthusiastic first-responders to the call to arms for what would soon be called the Great War. As Berger suggested, this keenness owed some measure to the absence, in the intervening years, of anything approaching a compre-hensive, much less disapproving, consideration of the nation's previous war for empire. As is commonplace in the midst of war, contempora-neous chroniclers frequently err on the side of heroism and embel-lishment in recounting the exploits of their countrymen in the field, and Canadian newspaper baron Max Aitken (later Lord Beaverbrook) was not one to defy tradition. After his appointment as head of the Canadian War Records Office in London, Aitken produced journalistic accounts of the Canadian Expeditionary Force's First Division, penned the bestselling *Canada in Flanders* (1916), and established the Canadian War Records Office, all of which sought to fulfil the objective he had disclosed to prime minister Robert Borden: "to enshrine in a contempo-rary history those exploits which will make the First Division immortal." By 1918, Aitken's CWRO had churned out more than a dozen works whose partisan ardour led some irritated Britons to ask whether "it was only the Canadian Corps and a few British units" that had confronted and overcome the Germans.[29]

After this, and in an echo of the South African War, the historical record of the Canadian experience in the First World War grew strangely cold – a surprise and offence to many in a nation of 8 million that had suffered 67,000 dead and more than twice that wounded, and who wished to see their stories told. While the historians' evasion of the previous South African campaign may be attributed to fear of controversy only by infer-ence, in the case of the First World War the charge can be made explic-itly. Archer F. Duguid, official historian of the Department of National Defence, refused access to official archival records of the war to all but regimental historians. His motivation, as he explained it, was twofold: First, he himself would produce the story of the CEF in a seven-volume series (a pledge that by 1947, and after twenty-five years of effort, had fallen six volumes short of the mark, resulting in the unceremonious cancellation of the project's funding). Second, under Duguid's watch, no writer would "embarrass" the soldiers or the nation through criticism of the war effort. As Tim Cook noted, "for Duguid, making these war records available would only result in 'dreadful things' happening in the 'hands of those who do not understand.'" Historians of the 1920s and 30s, both popular and professional, looked elsewhere for their topics, and the regimental histories – works produced largely by amateur historians hired by the regiments, and intended to memorialize the actions of their members rather than deliver a broad and dispassionate account of the war – became the *de facto* national historical record until the 1962 publication of George Nicholson's official history of the CEF.[30]

In the meantime, historians from other Great War nations produced a scholarship on the conflict noted for its magnitude and range of opinion, including highly critical assessments of their own countries' conduct and culpability. Britons in particular engaged in intensive second-guessing about the (in)capacities of their Great War military leadership, with former Prime Minister David Lloyd George's *War Memoirs* referring to British generals as a group "regarding thinking as a form of mutiny." Commenting on the frank and often savage treatment of British commanders (a.k.a. "the donkeys," after Alan Clark's immensely popular revisionist account by that same name), Canadian historian Andrew Godefroy wondered why Canadian commanders have been spared such recriminations: "One would think," reasoned Godefroy, "that Canadian Great War generals, in turn, would have received at least some similar negative popular attention from our own public, not silence."[31] While other nations wrestled publicly and bluntly with the legacy of the war to end all wars, another global conflict loomed. Once again, Canadians were expected to craft an appropriate response equipped with a decidedly gaunt body of serious analysis of their nation's previous conflict.

With experienced historians largely absent from the crafting of Canada's First World War record in the interwar years, citizens relied on such cultural commodities as journalism, memoirs, plays, works of poetry and fiction, sermons, war monuments, films, and fine art in order to make sense of the affair. Despite this broad range of source materials, explains Jonathan Vance, the messages they conveyed were remarkably similar: the terrible toll the war had exacted had been, without question, worthwhile; the loss was both necessary and transformative for Canada and the world. To buttress this conclusion, these sources cast the war as an uncomplicated morality play between good and evil, as a defence of righteousness, humanity, civilization, truth, even Canadian soil, and as a bloodletting unleashed solely through German aggression. In 1919, newspaper editor J.W. Dafoe summed up an attitude towards the Great War that has proven extremely durable to the English Canadian imagination. "Generation after generation for centuries to come," he eulogised, "will follow the Canadian way of glory over the battlefields of France and Flanders, with reverent hearts and shining eyes, learning anew the story that will doubtless always remain the most romantic page in our national history."[32]

On this, Dafoe proved prescient. In sermon, song, editorial, painting, and stained glass, the Canadian soldiers' sacrifice was habitually equated with that of Christ himself, who had likewise laid down his life to vanquish wickedness. Religious allegory also suffused the two most significant monuments to the war, Ottawa's National War Memorial and the Canadian National Vimy Memorial. The former depicts soldiers passing from west to east through an arch, and thus from death to resurrection; the latter is an obvious homage to a cathedral. And while the designers of these federally commissioned memorials aimed to avoid triumphalism and the glorification of war (in Canadian philosopher Randal Marlin's words, the Vimy Memorial conveys "grief, pain, and suffering rather than false pride and triumphalism," while the original name for the stoic National War Memorial was to be the "War and Peace Memorial") such was not the case at the local level. Here, communities across the land commissioned monuments through the interwar years that exemplified victory – "the single most important theme in war memorials erected by Canadians," noted Vance – rather than tragedy or lament.[33]

The most enduring testament to the Canadian experience, John McRae's 1915 poem "In Flanders Fields" imagines the dead exhorting the living, using romantic Victorian-era idioms, to continue the carnage in order to validate the previous sacrifice (a logic that, if applied by all belligerents, could only breed perpetual war). "Take up our quarrel with the foe," insist the dead; otherwise "We shall not sleep." In American historian Paul Fussell's words, here is "recruiting-poster rhetoric apparently applicable to any war ... a propaganda argument ... against a negotiated peace." (The Canadian government agreed, employing lines from the instantly famous poem on posters advertising First World War victory bonds.) McRae's themes stand in pointed contrast to the stark, modernist war poetry accentuating horror and futility, penned by the likes of Siegfried Sassoon, Edmund Blunden, and Wilfred Owen, that is most remembered in Britain. As Donna Coates, a scholar of Commonwealth war literature observed, Canadian Great War poetry as a whole exhibits "a remarkably uniform naïveté ... a surfeit of patriotic slogans

1.5 Long before American cultural historian Paul Fussell called it "recruiting poster rhetoric," the Canadian state recognized the practical value of "In Flanders Fields," using lines from John McRae's celebrated poem to promote victory bonds. ("Be yours to hold it high!," Archives of Ontario, C 233–2–1–0-7; "If ye break faith," CWM 19710080-004 © Canadian War Museum)

and an excess of praise – for Canadian soldiers' great deeds" and "for the growing self-reliance and maturity of Canada as a nation." Fussell's influential work *The Great War and Modern Memory* revealed that after the horror of the trenches, British war chroniclers traded their Victorian romanticism – what Fussell called "high diction" – for a spare, ironic, and gritty realism; in Canada, by contrast, "high diction" remained a dominant mode throughout the conflict and beyond. This persistence of war romanticism scarred some of the very men it sought to immortalize. As historian Jeffrey Keshen observed, the epic version of the war, conveyed to Canadians through a steady diet of buoyant and heroic accounts of battle, created an "intellectual chasm" between those on the home front and the returning, and often jaded and mentally broken, members of the CEF. Keshen argued that reintegration under such circumstances was doubly stressful, rendering soldiers' adjustment to peacetime more difficult in Canada than in other Allied countries.[34]

Outside Quebec, challenges to this largely affirmative Canadian Great War myth – from women's groups, some professors and clergy, and soldiers with negative views of the conflict – were relatively infrequent and muted when placed alongside the conversations occurring beyond the nation's borders. The European and American fervour for antiwar memoirs and novels that emerged after the war, including Eric Maria Remarque's *All Quiet on the Western Front,* Robert Graves's *Goodbye to All That* and a multitude of others, was decidedly less pronounced in Canada. A rare Canadian addition to the antiwar genre, American-born Charles Yale Harrison's *Generals Die in Bed* so roused veterans that they called on the federal government to ban the book. The sensitivity to Harrison's contribution owed much to its incongruity with previous and overwhelmingly affirming Canadian war literature, wherein, noted Peter Webb, "politicians are rarely corrupt, soldiers are seldom bewildered, the enemy never deserves sympathy as a partner in misery and generals never saunter safely home to die in bed."[35]

Of course, Canadians were not limited to the perspectives generated within their own country, and some diligently followed the more raucous Great War post-mortems turned out elsewhere. Canadian social democrats had long trained a good degree of their attention on the activities of British socialists, including the Fabian Society and its closest political expression, the British Labour Party. The Canadian variants of these – the League for Social Reconstruction and the Co-operative Commonwealth Federation, both founded in 1932 – included academics like Frank Underhill, Eugene Forsey, Frank Scott, and Harry Cassidy.

When Cassidy was appointed head of the United Nations Relief and Rehabilitation Administration training program in 1944, he made plain to his trainees the influence that interwar British condemnations of the First World War and the Versailles Treaty, like J.A. Hobson's *The Morals of Economic Nationalism* and John Maynard Keynes' *The Economic Consequences of the Peace*, had exerted on Canadian leftists. The latter text in particular, which described the Versailles Treaty as a vindictive, unjust, and dangerous "Carthaginian peace," caused a sensation on both sides of the Atlantic. Translated into eleven languages (including German) within a year of its December 1919 publication, it became an international best-seller and played a significant role in turning British and American public opinion against the Treaty of Versailles – just as the US Senate began deliberations on whether to ratify the agreement and join the League of Nations.[36]

Keynes' views also found devotees among some Canadian conservatives. Physician, author, and McGill University professor of medicine Andrew Macphail's sense of duty to country and empire ran so deep that in 1914, at age 50, he took leave of the civilian duties that had made him one of Canada's most prominent public intellectuals to serve in a field ambulance corps on the Western Front. This gesture, along with his literary contributions, led to his knighthood in 1918. Following an experience at the front that dissipated some of his enthusiasm for the glories of warfare, Sir Andrew anticipated, and then championed, the basic contours of Keynes' thesis in a series of lectures and articles, and came to a conclusion "even more pessimistic than Keynes" on the prospects for peace in the new world order forged out of the Great War sacrifice.[37]

Prolific Nova Scotian author, Great War veteran, and steadfast conservative Will R. Bird likewise experienced a disillusioning through the crucible of war, as his 1930 war memoir *And We Go On* revealed. Bird's work displayed the deepest respect for courage and sacrifice of his fellow soldiers, less empathy for the simplistic dichotomies between the warring factions – the German soldiers weren't "horned devils" any more than the British were "haloed champions of Christianity," noted one of Bird's fellow soldiers – and no patience for the inept, haughty, and often sadistic officers under whom the rank-and-file members of the CEF toiled. This was no antiwar novel in the tradition of those that claimed modern, industrialized killing turned all those it touched into dehumanized brutes; many of Bird's soldiers demonstrate an astounding capacity to retain their essential goodness in the face of indescribable horror. Nevertheless, the memoir raised troubling questions about the poisonous elitism and the inequality of suffering that plagued a fighting force that was, paradoxically, touted as a guardian of democracy and a template for national unity. In Bird's account, the officers who had exhibited so much manly bluster when berating the troops during drilling activities remained safely out of harm's way midst the worst of the battles; afterward, medals were doled out to a few soldiers who deserved them, and to a few whose elite social backgrounds had endeared them to the higher-ups (this from an author decorated for bravery himself).[38]

As Ian McKay and Robin Bates argued, a case like Bird's muddies the binary in postwar English-Canadian opinion suggested by Vance – namely, that the public was split between a small group of "neutralists, non-interventionists, and isolationists" on the one hand, and the vast majority who wholeheartedly endorsed the purpose and conduct of the war on the other. Bird is an apparent outlier in such a schema, a war supporter who nonetheless disparaged the way it was fought and what it revealed about his country. But Bird may not be such an unreliable barometer for public attitudes when one considers that following the war, he was one of the more visible and respected spokesmen for veterans, publishing articles in national magazines and delivering public speeches on veterans' concerns, penning more stories about the war, and by his own count giving slide presentations to at least 106 branches of the Canadian legion.[39] Bird's version of the war, then, bore at least some consonance with those who had, like him, lived it firsthand. As an aggregate, English Canada may have cleaved to an optimistic and conservative vision of the war, as Vance suggests. However, influential figures like Macphail and Bird, who defended the war's purpose while simultaneously stressing the harm it did to individuals, the nation, and the world, disrupt aspects of the myth and the degree of its hold over English Canadians, along with any notion that the myth's challengers arose only from the political left. Nevertheless, as we will see, doubts about the war raised by a range of Canadians were no match – either in their vigour or popularity – for those submitted by their southern neighbours.

The most public contest over Canada's Great War myth occurred in 1927 when an Ontario journalist charged that, in a bid for personal glory, Canadian Commander Arthur Currie had needlessly wasted soldiers' lives in the last hours of the war; Currie sued the paper for $50,000 and received $500 in damages. However, these challenges generated a backlash that, according to Vance, only strengthened the dominant view of the conflict and bolstered attention to, and reverence for, November 11 commemorations. Purveyors of the epic version of the war believed it would unite a nation separated by language, race, and region, and just as importantly, ensure that Canadians would not hesitate to heed future calls by national leaders to take up arms.[40]

On the second count, at least, promoters of the myth were correct. (Indeed, Noah Richler's 2012 survey of modern Canadian discourses regarding war reveals the persistence of high diction in discussions of the First World War all the way through Afghanistan, language that Fussell called a prerequisite for seducing young men into battle.) On the first count – that the war would provide the bond even the founding myth for an emerging nation – war defenders faced a quandary. While mid-century historians such as C.P. Stacey and W.L. Morton correctly identified a war-related upsurge in patriotism among large segments of the population, the conflict had also served to fracture the citizenry along ethnic, regional, class, and religious lines. Upholding the nation-building myth would require a disregard or understating of these fissures. The most obvious wartime cleavage, between anglophones and francophones over the issue of conscription, was so visible that it could not be ignored in creditable retellings of Canada's Great War contribution (although Ontario school history textbooks published between the wars managed to duck the issue). However, other stories languished in the mainstream accounts of the episode: from the war front, those of the maimed, the psychologically ruined, and the deserters; at home, those of the pacifists, draft resisters, non-francophone conscription opponents, conscientious objectors, and ethnic minorities associated with the enemy, who faced *de jure* and *de facto* proscriptions.[41]

In fairness, outlining the particularisms of the national community was not a priority in most early- and mid-century English Canadian histories regardless of topic; on the whole, historians sought to map a common national narrative, one that would foster a sense of loyalty to an ethnically and culturally Britannic Canada. Writing in 1974, Robert Craig Brown and Ramsay Cook took a new and hard look at the myth of English-Canadian wartime unity, providing extensive evidence that the conflict degraded relations not just between English and French, but also "between new and old Canadians, between classes, and between city and country." As a result, Canadians faced the next decade not with a new spirit of concord and self-assurance, but with profound discord and anxiety. Great War studies that followed began to demonstrate a greater acknowledgment of these fissures.[42]

While in subsequent decades the field would be marked by a significant broadening of vision, core elements of Canada's First World

War story that emerged between the world wars proved extremely durable. Germany was disproportionately, if not solely, to blame; morality, international law, and even national survival demanded a forceful Canadian military response. The paradoxical equation of a ruinous war fuelled by nationalism and the very creation of the Canadian nation began to face sustained challenges in the latter half of the twentieth century. Pierre Berton's immensely popular 1986 work *Vimy* questioned whether that "coming of age" battle was simply "used as a convenient symbol ... to stand for a more complicated historical process that, in the end, was probably inevitable." It concluded that whatever the answer, no real or imagined gains for the nation could justify "the loss of thousands of limbs and eyes and the deaths of five thousand young Canadians." Even so, the birth-of-a-nation myth remains powerful among Canadian historians, journalists, and officials, as does the emphasis on the singular heroism, pluck, and hardiness exemplified by Canadian troops.[43]

Indeed, if Canadians soldiers had, in Desmond Morton's words, "performed well" in South Africa, this relatively reserved language had no place in the nation's First World War record. Canadians have long been told that their Great War army was the preeminent fighting force in that global conflict, a motif that emerged during the war itself. As Jeffrey Keshen observed, jingoistic reporting, geographic distance from the horrors of the Western front, and governmental "news management" combined to forge an image of Canadian troops "who, through their extraordinary bravery, won the hardest and most important battles ... and thus emerged as a singular and heroic force in transforming Canada from colony to nation." The passage of time did little to temper these themes, or the swashbuckling language in which they were rendered. In George Stanley's 1960 account, the members of the CEF upheld a military legacy that finds no parallel in the history of warfare. "No men have fought better," he stated categorically. John Swettenham concurred in his 1965 First War survey, calling the CEF "a balanced fighting unit that could not be matched by the Central powers, nor – if performance was a criterion – by the Allied armies" (claims pitch-perfect to the ears of Australian Alastair Thompson, although he grew up listening to similar declarations about Anzac forces). Desmond Morton applauded the CEF in slightly more measured tones in 1993: "Between 1914 and 1918 Canadians helped create one of the best little armies in the world."[44] A corollary to these claims is that the Canadians almost singlehandedly turned the tide at various critical junctures in the war, variations on a theme disparaged by British readers of Max Aitken's hagiographies to the CEF that seemed to suggest that Canadians alone subdued the Germans.

Canadian media organizations followed a similar script. To mark the 50th anniversary of the beginning of the Great War, CBC radio aired the multi-part series *Flanders' Fields* based primarily on interviews with veterans. Although inspired by the tremendously successful BBC television series *The Great War* from that same year – a series whose bleak rendering of the conflict reflected and fed an increasingly anti-war atmosphere among British historians and the general public – Tim Cook noted that "the sense of futility from recent British war historians was not evident" in the CBC version. While many of the Canadian veterans shared stories of horror and anguish, the overall message of the series, according to the broadcaster's promotional advertisement, was one of "sacrifice and endurance and an indomitable cheerfulness; of hardship and of victory; of trust in their comrades and pride in their Corps and their country." The National Film Board's four-part *Battle of Vimy Ridge* (1997) showed audiences "how innovative tactics combined with iron courage and heroic self-sacrifice" enabled "Canadian soldiers to transform a field of slaughter into a field of glory," according to its promotional advertisement. (The series also revealed how far the NFB had moved from potentially unsettling depictions of Canada at war since the uproar over the 1992 production *The Valour and the Horror*.) The heroic version likewise found cinematic expression in Paul Gross's 2008 film *Passchendaele*. "Who we are was actually forged in those battlefields," explained Gross, who wrote, directed, and starred in this homage to Canadian martial prowess and valour at the Third Battle of Ypres. Here, Canadians helped to gain territory in Belgium at incredible cost, territory that was lost five months later and subsequently described as strategically inconsequential. The basic thrust of Gross's message – that the war did great things for the nation – differs little from that conveyed to Canadians from the war's immediate aftermath onwards. Gross told a reporter that he made the film to remind Canadians that "we were ferocious fighters, the most feared of the Allied troops."[45]

Sometimes too ferocious. British writer Robert Graves noted that in the First World War, "the troops with the worst reputation for acts of violence against prisoners were the Canadians (and later the Australians)." Graves recounts Canadians' testimonies of prisoner-of-war executions and other atrocities, and although he conceded that troops tended to treat such stories as "a boast, not a confession," recent research by Tim Cook confirmed the routine execution of surrendering

Germans by Canadians – the "false" charge that had so rankled critics of *Generals Die in Bed*. In this 2006 article, Cook accused Canadian military historians of "burying this harsh reality," a reality that historians from the United States, Britain, and Australia had demonstrated a greater inclination to confront.[46]

Such strategic evasions are in keeping with Canada's dominant Great War storyline. Victory, rather than regret for the mutual losses brought on by four years of slaughter, remains a cornerstone of Canadian representations. By extension, works written from an internationalist perspective, or that stress the universality of all soldiers' suffering and the ultimate futility of the conflict (common in the reckonings of Canada's allies and foes alike) remain rare. The names Passchendaele, Ypres, Flanders, and in particular Vimy Ridge, have retained a sanctity with few rivals in English Canadian popular consciousness, while pilgrimages to battle sites, begun shortly after the war itself, remain popular among Canadians. "The First World War remains by all odds the greatest event in Canada's history," wrote C.P. Stacey, the mid-century *doyen* of Canadian military history, a view that carries a great deal of sway to the present. In all, as Canadian historian Terry Copp noted, while English-speaking Canadians generally concede that the war took a terrible toll on innocent lives, these bleak sentiments have been tempered by "an imaginative version of a war in which their soldiers won great victories and forged a new national identity."[47]

Yet another aspect of the Great War and Canadian memory has remained relatively constant: challenges to the war myth that was formulated in the interwar period still invoke a vigorous and emotional backlash. In 1982, the National Film Board of Canada released *The Kid Who Couldn't Miss*, a documentary on Canadian First World War ace Billy Bishop that questioned whether some of Bishop's air victories were fabricated, including the attack on a German airfield that led to his receipt of the Victoria Cross. While the evidence for many of Bishop's claims is indeed lacking (and some fellow pilots considered him a devious self-promoter), the cross-examination of a Canadian war hero generated something of a national crisis. The Senate held hearings into the film's veracity, and War Amps CEO and serial defender of Canadian martial honour Cliff Chatterton produced a counter-documentary and book (the latter bearing the rather lurid title *Hanging a Legend: The NFB's Shameful Attempt to Discredit Billy Bishop, VC*). The battle to restore Bishop's name continues in print and on film. Less conspicuous and somewhat less feverish disputes have centred around the performance of Canadian commanders in the Second Battle of Ypres and the so-called learning curve Canadian troops underwent – or didn't, as the case may be – as they gained battle experience over the course of the war.[48] Although these questions have produced animated quarrels among professional and popular historians, they remain matters about how, rather than why, Canadians fought. More fundamental questions – Was the war necessary? Just? Worthwhile? Was the enormous scale of the Canadian contribution warranted? – appear to be largely settled among English Canadians.

In his February 2000 review of Niall Ferguson's *The Pity of War*, a volume that called Britain's decision to enter the Great War "the greatest error of modern history," *National Post* journalist Robert Fulford identified a disparity between the willingness of Britons to challenge their national mythologies and a Canada "content to stick with the clichés of the past." "All my life," Fulford sighed, "I have been reading that Canada became a nation on the battlefields of France." In truth, Fulford argued, the massive death toll and internal division that accompanied Canadian participation rendered the war "the unmaking of Canada as much as it was the making."[49]

It is rare that such claims are permitted to stand unopposed. Within days, history-profession heavyweights David Bercuson and Jonathan Vance provided op-ed responses in the *Post* that reprimanded Fulford for undervaluing the war's contribution to Canadian autonomy and identity. Jeffrey Keshen later presented a succinct summary of the dispute, and concurred with Bercuson and Vance on at least one count: that Canadian historians "have not glossed over the divisiveness caused by the Great War." To support this claim, Keshen provided a footnote listing five works written between 1938 and 1980 that foreground the war's contribution to national discord. The list itself raises several issues. For one, it is not very long. Granted, Keshen provided a sample rather than an exhaustive inventory, but it is telling that in the context of Canadian historiography he felt moved to remind readers that potentially unflattering accounts of the nation's wartime experience do indeed exist, and to call out a few by name (although one was authored by American Elizabeth Armstrong). As we will see, American historians might find it equally challenging to name five works that are generally laudatory about their nation's involvement in that same conflict. Second, the bulk of the reproach in the listed books is aimed at the divisiveness wrought by conscription, with the remainder trained largely on the antidemocratic measures taken by the Borden government to smother potential dissent. These studies are not, then, broad renunciations of the war in general, or of Canada's participation or martial conduct in it. And to repeat, the divisiveness they chronicle is simply inescapable: the conscription debate precipitated deadly riots, a national election, and a major realignment of the federal parties, while the War Measures Act enabled shameful abuses. Any general account of the war's impact on Canada must accommodate these rather dramatic facts. Nor does a frank airing of the national rift over the war necessarily amount to regret for Canadian participation or sympathy for French Canadian opposition – anglophone writers can just as easily point to opposition from Quebec as evidence of the province's intrinsic menace to both nation-building and sensible and effective policymaking. As such, the works offered as evidence of a willingness to cross-examine Canada's Great War mythologies take up this challenge rather meekly. The larger question stalking Fulford's lament – where is a Canadian equivalent to the fresh, iconoclastic, and potentially unsettling analysis found in *The Pity of War*? – remained unanswered. More recently, Canadian military historian Major John Grodzinski made a similar point with the simple observation that "Britain enjoys a lively scholarship on the Great War that is perhaps more honest and soul-searching than that being conducted in Canada."[50]

Major Grodzinski might well have added the United States to his list of candid soul-searchers. This despite the common conception that Americans display a weakness for heroes and a healthy, if sometimes myopic, self-esteem about their past, qualities which should lend themselves to a triumphalist rendering of their First World War encounter. Indeed, Americans might be expected to recall the sacrifice of the Great War in nobler terms than even Canadians, if one accepts the basic contours of a storyline that goes something like this: The United States, alone among the Great Powers, exhibited commendable restraint in avoiding the headlong rush into the catastrophe of August 1914, and was drawn into war in April 1917 by a series of submarine attacks on its merchant ships and citizens. Thus spurred to righteous indignation by an actual physical attack, Americans poured into Europe and helped transform a nearly four-year stalemate into an Allied victory. President Woodrow Wilson, lionized the world over for his vision and leadership, crafted the Fourteen Points which helped to encourage a German armistice, then travelled to Europe to head up peace negotiations. Though Wilson could convince neither European leaders nor American members of Congress to embrace the more idealistic components of his plan for global governance and reconciliation (with the victorious Allies balking at "peace without victory" and self-determination, and Congress at the League of Nations), the next global war would largely vindicate his overall vision. Accordingly, that later confrontation would lead Europe's statesmen to become the globe's foremost Wilsonians, and previously isolationist US politicians to endorse, and agree to host, the new version of the League. In short, Americans bore no responsibility for the war's outbreak, joined for good reason, helped to turn the tide, and attempted to dictate peace in terms that could well have averted the Second World War.

The account is, by and large, affirming, and better still, fortified by (mostly) solid evidence. Yet Americans do not commemorate specific battles, commit patriotic Great War poetry to memory as schoolchildren, or mark November 11 (known in the United States as "Veterans Day") with the reverence seen in Canada. In 2000, historian Gary Mead observed that the American campaigns of the Second World War, Vietnam, and even the "forgotten" Korean War have been "microscopically scrutinized. But who remembers," he wondered, "the two million Americans shipped to France in 1917–18, never mind the two million more who joined but never even crossed the Atlantic?" Historian John Milton Cooper concurred, relegating America's second experience (following the Civil War) with total warfare to the category of "America's 'forgotten wars.'" While veterans' groups continue to press federal lawmakers, there is still no national memorial to the Great War in Washington DC.[51]

This neglect owes in part to the fact that of all the major powers involved, the US experience was the shortest, as most American troops did not see action until 1918. But there is much more to the widespread forgetting than that. Remembrance of the US contribution has been impaired by the ambivalence and regret that have marked America's First World War legacies to far greater degrees than that of Canada. Intensive debates over the desirability and morality of entering the conflict gripped the United States for nearly three years prior to April 1917, providing future war opponents with a ready list of objections to participation: that this was a battle for empire; that historically, Americans had recused themselves from the violence seemingly endemic to Europe for good reason. As the conflict evolved, further objections emerged: that British and Germans alike violated international laws meant to safeguard the transport of neutral peoples and goods; that the United States demonstrated favouritism in protesting German violations and ignoring Britain's; that the horror of the trenches and industrial-age butchery should be avoided at all cost; that the interests of Wall Street, rather than average Americans, would be served.[52]

After the 1917 resumption of indiscriminate German U-boat attacks on American shipping, however, popular opinion moved towards an endorsement of participation on the grounds that "the Hun" menaced both broad principle (the rights of neutrals) as well as American security – and possibly, the nation's very existence. Almost as soon as the conflict ended, however, Americans came to heed and contribute to an emerging body of international analysis that complicated the conclusion that Germany bore sole responsibility for the war. If war guilt could not be so easily affixed, was US intervention necessary, desirable, or defensible, from either a strategic or moral standpoint? Was Article 231 of the Treaty of Versailles – the so-called war-guilt clause – therefore a travesty? Further, did the wartime behaviour of Germany's adversaries – including the United States – blur the notion that the Germans alone were aggressors and villains? And where was the new world order that Wilson had promised as a repayment for American sacrifices?[53]

Convoluted and often unsettling answers to these questions resulted in a collective sense of ambiguity and self-doubt regarding America's wartime experience. "The sense of a wasted war and a failed peace," observed historian Jerald Combs, "permeated the historical atmosphere of the 1920s and 1930s." In short order, Americans from all points on the political spectrum came to consider Great War participation an error – and with roughly 126,000 of their fellow citizens dead and 234,000 wounded, an error of dreadful magnitude. The 1920 presidential election, to a large measure a referendum on Wilson's handling of the war and the peace, saw the Democratic ticket lose the popular vote by more than 26 per cent, the widest margin of any major party in the nation's history. The Democrats lost, moreover, to a little-known Republican "compromise candidate" Warren Harding, who promised little more than a return to pre-war "normalcy" and was so deficient in political talents and personal integrity that he continues to round out the bottom of most presidential rankings. Revealingly, as John Milton Cooper observed, of all American wars from Independence through Vietnam, this "would be the only war besides Korea and Vietnam not to propel a military commander or hero into the White House."[54]

In this general turning against the Great War, historians led the charge. Sidney Fay's three-part article, "New Light on the Origins of the World War" (1920–21), was one of the first of the American "revisionist" accounts on the conflict – a label embraced by many of the craft's practitioners who challenged narrowly nationalistic interpretations of the war's origins. By 1928, Fay had expanded his ideas into a massive, two-volume study on Great War origins. He dedicated himself to the long view of the European conflict, beginning his story with

1.6 Warren G. Harding, 29th US president, in 1920. American participation
in the Great War was on trial in that year's presidential campaign, and the
Democrats suffered a drubbing of historic proportions at the hands of a
supremely unqualified and unscrupulous candidate, one who promised little
more than a return to pre-war "normalcy" in foreign and domestic matters.
Although Providence afforded him just two years to muck things up, and in
spite of some stiff competition, Harding continues to land at the bottom of
most presidential rankings. (PRES FILE - Harding, Warren – Informal Photos,
Library of Congress, Washington DC.)

the 1870–1 Franco-Prussian War and churning out more than 500 pages
of Great Power hermeneutics before even mentioning Archduke Ferdinand, whose assassination sparked the international inferno. Along the
way, the reader is informed that secret alliances, nationalism, imperial
rivalry, and popular-press jingoism underlay the calamity of August
1914, sins from which no major European power could gain absolution.
Notably, Fay believed that Britain may have forestalled the conflict

by being forthright of its intentions to provide a military response to German aggression.[55]

Fay's text is noted for its measured and painstaking claims, and the relative humility with which they are offered. Not so his contemporary Harry Elmer Barnes, University of Columbia historian and serial revisionist (at times reversing even his own truculent claims, using still more truculent prose). In *The Genesis of the World War* (1926) Barnes corroborated much of Fay's explanation for the roots of the conflict, but also highlighted broader cultural pathologies that plagued Western Civilization as a whole: the social Darwinist thinking which justified power politics, an educational system which promoted uncritical nationalism, and above all, the "cult of war" which accorded foremost social prestige to the military profession. Barnes fulminated against such views: "War, instead of promoting the noblest of emotions," he declared, "brings forth, for the most part, the most base and brutal elements and processes of human behavior." And in the long and tawdry history of human conflict, the most recent manifestation had been, without dispute, the worst. "Never was any previous war so widely proclaimed to have been necessary in its origins, holy in its nature, and just, moderate and constructive in its aims," wrote Barnes. "Never was a conflict further removed in the actualities of the case from such pretentions" (despite the offence taken, he noted, towards Great War revisionism by unnamed "Canadian and English writers"). Just two pages later, Barnes reprised the charge, holding that "the World War was unquestionably the greatest crime against humanity and decency since the missing link accomplished the feat of launching *homo sapiens* upon his career."[56]

It is doubtful that such appeals to evolutionary biology won Barnes adherents among the growing ranks of American religious fundamentalists – nor would his proposal that "advocates of pacific international relations ... link hands with the proponents of birth control" in order to reduce the demand for resources, and by inference, armed battles for those resources. In an era marked by bitter legal and cultural clashes over evolution (the Scopes trial riveted the nation in 1925) and birth control (Margaret Sanger served jail time the previous decade for operating a birth control clinic in Brooklyn), these were provocative moves indeed. Yet despite this apparent willingness to cause offence and a rhetorical approach given to rant rather than nuance, Barnes was no fringe figure. His disparaging views on the war found wide readership in academic journals, in a series of twelve articles he wrote for the popular weekly *Christian Century*, and just two years after the bestselling *Genesis*, in another book he penned on the First World War with similar conclusions, *In Quest of Truth and Justice*. In the interwar years, Barnes proved an extraordinarily popular and respected historian and journalist, an individual "acclaimed, by scholars and laymen, as one of the foremost intellectual leaders of his time." In other words, in the American context, these caustic observations belonged to the mainstream, and were echoed widely in the popular press; "revisionism" had become orthodoxy. When the US government joined France in crafting the 1928 Kellogg-Briand Pact outlawing war, the revisionist impulse had also come to shape international law.[57]

Throughout the interwar years, a host of US analysts (many on the left) would continue to denounce the economic motivations for US intervention and the wider imperial covetousness that drove the conflict, arguments which enjoyed special appeal in the anti-business atmosphere of the Great Depression. *Merchants of Death*, a 1934 Book-of-the-Month Club selection, exposed the vast profits made by American arms manufacturers. The American chapter of the Women's International League for Peace and Freedom played a leading role lobbying for the creation of the Senate Munitions Committee, a body charged with investigating whether business interests conspired to bring America into the conflict. Led by Republican Senator Gerald Nye, the committee's 93 hearings, followed carefully in the popular press, found no smoking gun (as it were). The hearings did, however, demonstrate that munitions manufacturers flaunted neutrality policies in providing arms to belligerents and enjoyed enormous profits and governmental favouritism, fueling suspicions that corporate interests had subverted the popular will. Walter Millis's best-selling *Road to War: America 1914–1917* (1935) deepened the disillusionment. This exposé, which in 1939 *Life* magazine called "among the top books of the past quarter-century" in terms of its influence on American policy and opinion, attributed US intervention to diplomatic blundering, pressure from American financial interests, and the influence of British propaganda.[58]

Many Americans on the right, for their part, lamented the naiveté of Wilson's crusading spirit and the disavowal of traditional American isolation from European matters (a sentiment harboured by some liberals as well). And citizens of all political persuasions condemned the seemingly vindictive peace hammered out at Versailles. Even members of Wilson's inner circle, like former Secretary of War Newton Baker, conceded that the Kaiser posed little danger to US security, much less the nation's very survival. The first public opinion polls on US participation in the Great War, conducted in 1937, found that

70 per cent of respondents considered US entry into the conflict a mistake. For a political culture known for its factiousness, the relative unanimity of America's Great War renunciation is striking; nearly as remarkable to the modern reader is the role of historians in driving such reconsiderations. Taking into account the passage of the Neutrality Acts of the 1930s, which prohibited US economic interactions with belligerent powers, Jerald Combs observed: "Perhaps at no other time has American historiography had so direct an impact on American politics."[59] For a large percentage of Americans, then, the war was viewed as a tragic waste visited upon the nation by special interests and foreign manipulation.

American popular culture echoed and enhanced the sense of gloom. The antiwar novel, what historian John Bodnar called "an entirely new genre of fiction," found expression and wide readership through such works as John Dos Passos's *Three Soldiers*, Ernest Hemingway's *A Farewell to Arms*, Ford Maddox Ford's *No More Parades*, William Faulkner's *Soldiers' Pay*, and Dalton Trumbo's *Johnny Got his Gun*; the latter was inspired by a Canadian soldier who had lost his limbs and all senses in the war. While Hollywood studios at first produced a number of exultant Great War films (with particular fondness for aviation), in the most popular silent film of the decade, *The Big Parade* (1925), the lead character is subjected to the horror of the trenches and is forced to undergo the amputation of a leg as the result of his wounds. The film became a template for a series of subsequent American productions that took a hard look at the war, including *The Dawn Patrol* (1930) and *Men Must Fight* (1933). As Bodnar observed, "it was not until nearly 1940 that Hollywood and others began to reinvigorate the more reverential look at the 'Great War' in order to push public opinion towards supporting another American intervention into a European struggle."[60]

Not all Americans turned on the war. Many veterans' remembrances were "warmly nostalgic," observed historian Steven Trout, and some of their fellow citizens continued to hold glamorous, romantic notions of warfare following the conflict. In the twenties and thirties, the American Legion promoted a positive remembrance of the US contribution and the role it played in unifying the nation and assimilating citizens of disparate identities during the twenty months of their nation's involvement. The organization's efforts, however, were undercut by the racial segregation it upheld in Legion Halls, and its promotion of an aggressive nationalism and war "preparedness" that, according to Trout, struck many Americans as "war mongering" and "all but synonymous with fascism."[61]

For the remainder of the twentieth century, American collective appraisals of the war would undergo sometimes radical oscillations, but the constant here was ambiguity, doubt, and wrangling over the conflict's place in the American narrative. The Second World War served to discredit the US tradition of isolationism, and as a result, many historians (if not the general public) began to ameliorate their criticisms of Great War participation. In the latter half of the century, renewed and sometimes catastrophic US interventionism – most notably in Vietnam – cooled opinion once again to the war that built momentum for American globalism. Even those who cut Wilson some slack for bringing the nation into the war continued to hammer away at particulars. Cold War-era realists belittled the president's utopianism, which held that international relations could be built around moral and legal ideals rather than the threat and use of force, and which contributed to the illusion that principle, rather than national security, was at stake. In other words, by leading the United States into war, Wilson had done the right thing for the wrong reasons. New Left scholars were less charitable, recasting Wilson's supposed utopianism as base self-interest. His goal, they maintained, was to re-mould the international political economy along American lines by replacing formal colonialism with open-door liberalism, thereby unlocking previously closed mercantilist empires for US investors while proscribing true self-determination. In all, as Gary Mead wrote, over the course of the century "American popular consciousness increasingly concluded that participation was from the outset an error, that the practicalities of it were badly handled, and that ultimately all that sacrifice did nothing for U.S. domestic interests."[62]

Who, then, were the heroes of First World War America? In the years following the conflict, many Americans found bravery, honour, and prescience in the words and deeds of those who had opposed US participation from the beginning. In 1937, Congress marked the twentieth anniversary of the American entry into the conflict with a special commemoration for their 56 colleagues who had voted *against* Wilson's declaration of war. Wisconsin Senator Robert La Follette, reviled in the press and threatened with expulsion from office for voting against US intervention, was named one of the top five senators in history by a senate committee in 1959, one of the top seven in 2000, and tied with Henry Clay for the greatest senator in US history in a 1982 poll of US historians. William Jennings Bryan, who resigned as Secretary of State in 1915 to protest Wilson's increasingly belligerent attitude towards Germany, was the subject of a number of admiring biographies in the 1920s and 30s. Jane Addams, a well-known and highly respected reformer prior to the war, sank to pariah status after 1917 – "the most dangerous woman in America" according to war enthusiast Theodore Roosevelt – for her opposition to the conflict and support for conscientious objectors. During the 1920s, her reputation once again ascendant, she was shortlisted for the Nobel Prize six times. Dozens of prominent individuals from both the United States and Britain, including Woodrow Wilson and his wartime nemesis La Follette, nominated Addams for the award, which she finally won in 1931. Similarly, while aspects of their radicalism limit the possibility of universal admiration among Americans, Great War opponents like labour leader Eugene Debs, anarchist Emma Goldman, black intellectual W.E.B. Du Bois, and pacifists Norman Thomas and A.J. Muste remain significant and esteemed figures in historical works on the era.[63]

In 1980, Howard Zinn, author of the immensely successful *A People's History of the United States*, summed up the conflict thusly: "no one since that day has been able to show that the war brought any gain for humanity that would be worth one human life. The rhetoric of the socialists, that it was an 'imperialist war,' now seems moderate and hardly arguable. The advanced capitalist countries of Europe were fighting over boundaries, colonies, spheres of influence … " Zinn remains a polarizing figure for his radical politics, but on this count, at least, his views appear blandly nonpartisan when situated within the broader trajectory of American thought. Similarly, in introducing their edited volume on the history of American war resistance, both leftist Murray Polner and conservative Thomas Woods Jr concede that while the Second World War "may have been a necessary war … that war was but a continuation of the unnecessary World War I." In English Canada, such views continue to invite bitter recrimination from some quarters – particularly under a federal regime committed to equating Canadian identity with military heroism. Quebec activist and future New Democratic member of parliament Alexandre Boulerice's hardly disputable reference to the war as "butchery" in 2007 was dredged up six years later by conservative media outlets and the prime minister himself, who called the remark "outrageous, inflammatory, unacceptable." The Veterans Affairs minister demanded a formal apology, while a spokesman for a Canadian veterans lobby equated the comment with "spitting" on the legacy of the First World War – and recommended that Boulerice leave Canada for "whatever country he wants to go to."[64] If Boulerice ever considers taking sanctuary in a country where his opinions would provoke little umbrage, he does not have far to go.

Chapter Two

Wars Good, Cold, and Forgotten

If the collective memory surrounding the necessity of the First World War is marked, for Americans at least, by a persistent ambiguity and turmoil, that of the Second is considerably less so. Here, the world confronted a singular evil in Nazism, and an unprecedented challenge to the international order in the militant expansionism of the Axis powers. Accordingly, the Second World War also goes by the moniker the "good war," wherein liberal democracies (and their communist ally), provoked by indisputable desecrations of international law, state sovereignty, and human decency, banded together to eradicate these appalling regimes. Questions have been raised about the Allies' complicity in building the preconditions for the rise of extremism – for instance, in the continent-wide stumble into the First World War; the treatment of Germany, Italy, and Japan at Versailles; the US abnegation of internationalism after 1919; the supposed unfairness, in the view of the Japanese, of the Washington Naval Treaty; the American demand for full repayment of First World War loans; and the wilting of other European states before Hitler's demands in the 1930s. However, almost no post-Second World War observer could legitimately contest that, once the blitzkrieg had been launched, a military response was compulsory in order to stop the murder, pillage, rape, enslavement, and genocide orchestrated by Germany, Italy, and Japan. Following the First World War, some analysts from nations on both sides of the conflict surmised that a German victory would have been benign, or at least not catastrophic, for the future of Europe and the globe; no sane person could offer similar conjectures after the Second.[1]

Little wonder, then, that the defeat of the Axis powers occupies a place of unrivalled prestige in the national memory of Allied nations, and Canada and the United States are no exception. For these two nations, war memory is also mediated by the fact that, Pearl Harbor aside, no fighting took place on home soil, thus sparing the domestic population from the widespread suffering visited on the civilians of nearly every other war participant. The economic privations wrought by the Great Depression had been banished by the demands of wartime production, and in consequence, the economic and military power of each nation grew relative to other states between 1939 and 1945. By war's end, the United States had supplanted Britain as the indisputable leader of the globe, while Canada revelled in its brief standing as the world's fourth-ranked military power. No two war participants, it could be argued, experienced the war in such positive ways.

Accordingly, official war commemorations place the veterans of the conflict front and centre in the pantheon of national heroes. For the United States, the "good war" gains additional cachet by being surrounded by the dubious (the First World War), the overlooked (Korea), and the disastrous (Vietnam). The fighting in pivotal theatres – most notably the Netherlands, Anzio, Sicily, and Juno Beach for Canadians, and for Americans, Pearl Harbor, Omaha Beach, Iwo Jima, and Okinawa – is commemorated in state-sponsored ceremonies, iconic photographs, and documentary and feature films, not to mention an ongoing outpouring of books. For their ability to mobilize and eventually prevail against totalitarian adversaries, NBC news anchor Tom Brokaw called the Americans who came of age during the war the "greatest generation," and the label stuck. The war became a touchstone for moral conviction, excellence, self-sacrifice, and national unity, qualities to which subsequent generations have, so the argument often goes, generally failed to measure up.[2]

The war's myriad "lessons" have cast a long shadow over public debates. To this day, officials need only invoke the memory of Hitler, the Munich Conference, or "appeasement" in order to legitimize military action against an international adversary. Indeed, effective leadership in times of crisis, along with a preference for toughness over compromise in response to a seemingly-intractable foe, now goes by the label "Churchillian" (one affixed to George W. Bush, to cite one example, in the days following the September 11, 2001 attacks.) When in 2011 American-born Canadian academic Michael Fellman decried the militarization of Canadian citizenship ceremonies, J.L. Granatstein shot back with a predictable line about Fellman's freedom to speak being guaranteed by the war against Hitler, and with the sophomoric canard that without the service of veterans in that war, "Fellman would have grown up speaking German."[3] (As Fellman grew up in Wisconsin, Granatstein's jibe implied that a Nazi victory in Europe would have brought about the fall of the United States.)

All of this is to say that, in comparison to other potential reserves of patriotism and nation-building, the Second World War is the mother lode. "In the search for a usable past," noted Michael Adams, "Americans increasingly return to this best war ever." The same could be said for Canada. As Margaret MacMillan observed, "behind much of the current fascination with World War II lies the feeling, certainly on the Allied side, that it was the last morally unambiguous good war." Not surprisingly, challenges to the nobility and heroism of the Allied effort – in the United States, over the Smithsonian's proposed *Enola Gay* exhibit, and in Canada over the CBC documentary *The Valour and Horror* and the Canadian War Museum's exhibit on Bomber Command – have generated some of the most ferocious debates over war and memory in either country's history.[4]

And yet. Once again, surveying the national treatments of the Second World War, the assessments of the war's origins, motives, prosecution, and outcomes, we find that while Americans can be as sanguine, not to mention jingoistic, triumphalist, self-assured, and protective about their wartime past as any national community, they can also be unexpectedly harsh on that same past. Clearly, US popular and scholarly opinion endorses, by wide margins, the propriety of the nation's involvement and conduct in the Second World War. After all, the nation had been attacked, civilians and military personnel killed, its navy, air force, and infrastructure battered in the air raid of December 7, 1941. Moreover, that attack had been perpetrated by a regime in league with Hitler and one that shared many of Nazism's most repugnant traits, including an utter disdain for the sanctity of the individual that forms a core of Americans' self-concept. Accordingly, the rectitude of US intervention and the cause for which the nation fought has been confirmed repeatedly by mainstream historians, the press, Hollywood films, and bestselling memoirs. The themes presented were frequently positive and self-congratulatory: the war had been fought for democracy, our way of life, and international law. Americans, by many accounts, had single-handedly won the war, and thus deserved to dictate the peace and assume their role as global leader. Cold War fears of communist expansion, and America's new-found role as a global security force aimed at checking that expansion, proved advantageous to the recollection of a conflict that cemented the nation's internationalist bearing.[5]

Still, even among those who applauded participation, the penchant for often intensive self-censure persisted. Following Pearl Harbor, a widespread feeling emerged that America itself was at least partly to blame for the calamity – for disengaging from European matters, for embracing the illusion that oceans rendered them invulnerable, for failing to comprehend and prepare adequately for the vicissitudes of twentieth-century international affairs. In the popular press, a nation had been roused to manhood, despite its best prewar efforts to cling to adolescence; had the maturation come sooner, some offered, perhaps the wars in Europe and Asia would never have materialized. In short, there was little running from "root causes" here. In 1943, prominent liberal columnist Walter Lippmann published what he termed a "severe criticism of American policy" since 1900, one which castigated the naivety of the American people and their leaders for believing that neutrality and isolationism would bring peace. Lippmann himself had held similar beliefs in the interwar years, and his *U.S. Diplomacy: Shield of the Republic* served as a forthright *mea culpa* for these miscalculations. Political affairs columnist Dorothy Thompson, called the second most influential woman in America after Eleanor Roosevelt in a 1939 *Time* magazine piece, likewise blamed herself (as well as US officials and the general public) for abetting the prewar naivety regarding the emerging international crisis. This despite the fact that as a correspondent in Germany, Thompson had roundly condemned the ruthlessness of the Nazi regime, and had been expelled by Hitler personally for her views. In the four years that Americans battled totalitarian war machines in Asia and Europe, they also expended considerable energy battling themselves, conducting seven highly partisan investigations aimed at uncovering the truth about (and affixing blame for) Pearl Harbor. After the war, some went so far as to blame Franklin Roosevelt himself for orchestrating the attack as a means of drawing the nation into an unwanted and unnecessary war.[6]

While enthusiasm for the conspiratorial interpretation of US involvement faded, highly unflattering representations of the nation's wartime experience remained common. A series of best-selling Second War novels – notably, written by American veterans of the conflict – interrupted the postwar triumphalism, suggesting that a fight against evil did not automatically render the Allies noble or the story of the war heroic or inspiring. Norman Mailer's *The Naked and the Dead* (1948) represented the violence, masochism, and will to subjugate that marked the campaign against the Japanese as extensions of America's longstanding maladies, and as proof that the capacity for evil was not bred by fascism alone. The "hero" in James Jones's *From Here to Eternity* (1951) is decorated posthumously for his bravery during the Pearl Harbor attack, when in truth he was AWOL and inebriated during the raid and shot and killed for resisting arrest. In the following decade, Jones published *The Thin Red Line* (1962), an account of soldiers fighting not for humanity, national honour, or any other grand moral or strategic objectives, but simply to maintain a semblance of their own sanity. Other anti-heroic war novels included Joseph Heller's *Catch-22* (1961), and Kurt Vonnegut's *Slaughterhouse Five* (1969), which depict an Allied effort characterized by atrocity, farce, bungling, and recklessness. In John Bodnar's words, books like Vonnegut's disrupted the national atmosphere of self-congratulation "by refusing to see World War II as inspirational and by attaching the memory of the war to a narrative of loss rather than one of victory." These accounts share not only a bleak view of the war and what it did to individuals and the nation, but also a bleak view of an imagined future sullied by militarism, open-ended global contests for power, and an attendant erosion of individual autonomy and worth. These works are also united by their standing as some of the most highly regarded American novels of the twentieth century, and by the fact that all became Hollywood films (with *From Here to Eternity* also adapted twice for television and once for an upcoming, and presumably fairly joyless, musical.[7])

New Left historians would also challenge the facile commemoration of the good war. While denying the conspiratorial aspect of the earlier Roosevelt critics, they nonetheless agreed that the president's Japan policy had been needlessly belligerent and dangerous. For William Appleman Williams (another Second War vet) and many of his followers, the policy was a component of the larger American open door objective, one which saw the closed economic empires being constructed by Germany and Japan as a threat to national prosperity. While Franklin Roosevelt spoke of "four freedoms" and employed the exalted language of the Atlantic Charter, his administration's underlying motivation for participation, argued Williams in 1959, was materialistic rather than idealistic. Williams did not deny the necessity of stopping fascism; rather, he held that without the economic imperative, the American administration simply would not have acted. Gabriel Kolko went further, contending in his 1968 study *The Politics of War: The World and United States Foreign Policy, 1943–1945* that US officials viewed Japan and Germany, *as well as* America's wartime allies, as economic rivals to be overcome. For Kolko, the war was as much about securing markets and resources at the expense of Britain, the Soviets, and the Third World, as it was about defeating fascism.[8] As the Vietnam War raged, these were no fringe opinions.

If American objectives have proven contentious, so too have the methods employed to defeat the Axis powers. *War without Mercy*, John Dower's seminal study on cultural attitudes during the Pacific war, demonstrated that both the Japanese and American campaigns were "fueled by racial pride, arrogance, and rage," with the dehumanization of the Japanese so absolute that Americans came to believe that their enemy "deserved no mercy and virtually demanded extermination." Extermination of two cities via atomic bombings, meanwhile, became an issue of particularly intensive debate. Beginning in the mid-1960s, the traditional justifications for the bombings – that they saved hundreds of thousands of Allied and Japanese lives, destroyed important military targets, and were essential to the Japanese surrender – began to face increasing scrutiny. Revisionist accounts provided additional and considerably less noble motivations to the discussion: a desire to intimidate the Soviets in the emerging bipolar order, revenge for Pearl Harbor, racism, curiosity over what the bomb could do to a "real" target, the need to justify the two billion dollars spent on research and development. Revisionists also advanced the notions that the Japanese were on the verge of surrendering, and that the Truman administration's casualty estimates for a land invasion were wildly and purposely inflated. Entire sections of academic libraries were soon populated with works wrestling with the morality and necessity of the bombings. The debate went mainstream in 1995 when the Smithsonian Institute proposed an exhibit on the *Enola Gay*, the B-29 aircraft that had dropped the bomb on Hiroshima, an exhibit intended to present the historiographical controversy candidly. After a ferocious public squabble which saw veterans, Congress, and journalists pulling in one direction and most of the professional historians involved pulling in the other, the Smithsonian cancelled the interpretive component of the exhibit and simply displayed the remains of the bomber – although the wider debate continues unabated. Even so, as defenders of the exhibit noted, "the preponderance" of American historians who wrote on the bombings "held that the war could have been brought to an end without an Allied invasion or the atomic bombing of Japan."[9]

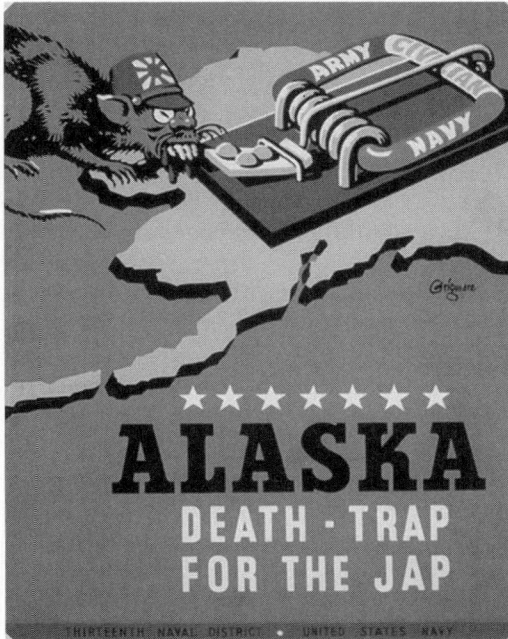

2.1 In 1986, historian John Dower published the first specialized study of the race hatred that amplified the gruesome fighting in Pacific theatre. To Dower, the public tolerance, even acclamation, for the atomic bombing of Japanese civilians had been abetted by a steady propaganda campaign focused on reducing the enemy to the level of vermin. (Edward T. Grigware, Washington: WPA Art Project, [between 1941 and 1943], LC-USZC2-985, Library of Congress Prints and Photographs Division.)

The intensity of the contest over *Enola Gay* was not merely rooted in the fact that the sometimes-unsettling conclusions of historians had now reached the public. Rather, the timing itself was critical, as the debates emerged alongside a growing public reverence for military history in general, and that of the Second World War in particular. The reasons for this upsurge are manifold. Following the lead of President Ronald Reagan, many influential Americans encouraged their fellow citizens to reinvigorate their pride in American military achievements, a message that resonated with a generation eager to overcome disappointments of Vietnam. Indeed, the term "good war" itself was a product of the post-Vietnam era, and a conscious effort to harken back to better military legacies; the atmosphere of optimism would gain further oxygen from the triumphalism that followed the collapse of the Soviet Union. Other reasons for the trend find many correlates in Canada. The passing of the generation that lived through the world wars led to a desire to retrieve their stories before it was too late, and various milestones – the 50th anniversaries of Pearl Harbor, D-Day, VE- and VJ-Day, and the like – brought increased public, governmental, and media attention to the conflict. The emergence of the internet abetted genealogical research, dissemination of personal stories, and the traffic in memorabilia, and cultural industries fed the boom by producing exhibits, books, films, and television programs dedicated to history and war. As was the case with *Enola Gay*, these cultural products themselves generated highly publicized battles over their fairness and accuracy, which only brought additional attention to the events they depicted.[10]

Cultural historians have also pointed to broader social forces which underwrote a generalized "memory boom" and "heritage phenomenon": vast changes wrought by modernization, globalization, and immigration led some to seek solace in a "simpler" time, to "a space of stable relationships, known boundaries, and a sense of place." Hollywood director Steven Spielberg hit on a common theme: speaking to an audience at the June 2000 opening of the National D-Day Museum in New Orleans (itself a testament to the war's public renaissance), he revealed that he made the 1998 film *Saving Private Ryan* to honour his "dad's generation" and to tutor younger Americans about the moral clarity and selflessness that characterized Second World War Americans – ethics that, by implication, later generations had lost. To film historian Robert Niemi, Spielberg presented viewers with an image of "the near-saintly dedication and manly heroism of the American GI" that was as propagandistic as it was fanciful. That image also proved extraordinarily popular. The 2001 Hollywood production *Pearl Harbor* (in which roughly equal portent is afforded the air assault and a love triangle) and bestselling books like Stephen Ambrose's dashing *Band of Brothers* and Brokaw's *Greatest Generation* reflected and enhanced the positive attention afforded the war-era Americans and their triumph.[11]

For many Americans in the academy and culture industries, however, the "memory boom" provided an opportunity not to piggyback on the warm nostalgia by publishing genial supplements to the feel-good aura, but to write directly against what they considered the growing mythmaking that accompanied the trend. Beginning in the mid-1980s, the Second World War was subjected to a slew of what David Farber called "tough-minded accounts of a nation riven by conflict, jaded by the distance between home front and battleground, mired in horrors, and often blinded by ignorance." Second World War veteran Paul Fussell, whose ground-breaking study *The Great War in Modern Memory* (1975) depicted the cultural transformations experienced by Europeans forever traumatized by trench warfare and mechanized killing, revealed that his revulsion for armed conflict was born in his own experiences in the "good war." In *Wartime: Understanding and Behavior in the Second World War* (1989), Fussell made his demythologizing agenda plain. "For the past fifty years," he explained, "the Allied war has been sanitized and romanticized almost beyond recognition by the sentimental, the loony patriot, the ignorant, and the bloodthirsty. I have tried to balance the scales." A memoir of similar intent, *Doing Battle – The Making of a Skeptic* (1996), followed, wherein Fussell revealed the revulsion he felt over fellow GI's bloodlust (murdering German POWs while engaging in "good-ole boy yelling" and laughter, or finding "deep satisfaction" in shooting a prone enemy who was already "twitching"). The author goes so far as to call America's Second World War's ground campaign an "unintended form of eugenics, clearing the population of the dumbest, the least skilled, and the least promising of all young American males."[12]

Many of these new works used the tools of social history and cultural theory to excavate the voices of marginalized social actors whose war had not been so "good." Farber himself was a willing accessory to the "tough-minded" revisionism he observed in the field as a whole, co-authoring with Beth Bailey an account of the tumult that war brought to Hawaii – via the Japanese attack *and* the subsequent influx of American servicemen destined for the Asian theatre. Here troops encountered "the first strange place" of their wartime experience, a land where the majority of civilians were non-white and where, after the arrival of troops, men outnumbered women by as much as 100 to one. Violence frequently accompanied attempts to maintain and renegotiate the boundaries between race, sex, and gender. Similarly, a reader of Michael C.C. Adams's *The Best War Ever* (1994) quickly becomes aware that the title is bitterly ironic. That this was undeniably "a necessary war" did not, for Adams, make it "good." The home and battle fronts teemed with atrocities, psychoses, class conflict, censorship, propaganda, and racial and sexual violence (much of the latter perpetrated by enlisted men). In other words, in its effect on individuals and society this was a war like any other – the "inherently destructive" outcome of the ultimate failure in human interactions, "wasteful

of human and natural resources, disruptive of normal social development." Adams was moved to write his polemic after observing officials and journalists utilize a "folkloric" version of the Second World
War to rally public support for the 1991 Gulf War, with the author
fearing that the "good war" could inspire future "human catastrophes
in the questionable belief that history shows wars will cure our social
problems and make us feel strong again." Fussell expressed similar
worries, writing that "there has been so much talk about 'The Good
War,' the Justified War, the Necessary War, and the like, that the young
and innocent could get the impression that it was really not such a
bad thing after all. It's thus necessary to observe that it was a war and
nothing else, and thus stupid and sadistic ..." A number of subsequent
reassessments of Second World War America made similar claims,
and like Adams's work, became staples on college history syllabi
(although none could bump *The Best War Ever* from its standing as the
military history book undergraduates were most likely to plagiarize).
In 2000, filmmakers Rick Tejada-Flores and Judith Ehrlich provided
a response to the jingoistic Hollywood representations of America at
war, releasing *The Good War and Those Who Refused to Fight It*, a documentary narrated by popular actor Ed Asner that "pay[ed] tribute to
the extraordinary courage and idealism" of Second World War American conscientious objectors.[13]

The quotation marks John Bodnar employed in the title to his book
The "Good War" in American Memory made it clear that by 2010, it was
difficult to employ the descriptor without serious qualifications, a truth
made plain in the author's handling of the multiple and often contradictory understandings of the war's purpose, impact on, and lessons
for, America. Bodnar's account reveals that despite the decades of "sanitized and romanticized" imaginings of the war derided by Fussell, the
war's meaning has always been in flux and fiercely contested, from
the first days of US involvement to the present. In other words, recent
historians producing "tough accounts" are not inventing wartime fissures or imposing today's standards of morality or identity politics on
past events (frequent accusations hurled at "revisionists"), but merely
recovering and conveying the myriad wartime experiences of those
who may not have enjoyed access to the public ear.[14] In many of these
more critical and complicated accountings, wartime Americans are not
always as laudable as advertised, nor, by implication, are subsequent
generations synonymous with a precipitous slide towards selfishness,
greed, decadence, or any of the other vices ostensibly alien to the "greatest
generation."

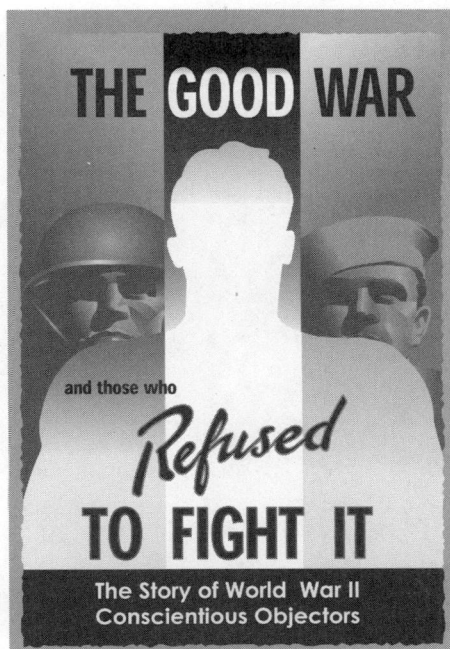

THE GOOD WAR

and those who

Refused

TO FIGHT IT

The Story of World War II
Conscientious Objectors

2.2 Allied soldiers surely displayed courage and idealism in the fight against fascism; so, too, did those who took a principled stand against participation in the killing despite immense public pressure to enlist, according to the makers of this 2000 US documentary. (Poster design by John Mattos, © Paradigm Productions, www.paradigmproductions.org).

Most of the above understandings of the Second World War – positive and negative – find expression in English Canadian representations of the conflict, but the censorious accounts have been fewer in number, milder, more apologetic for raising what may be construed as inconvenient truths. Following the war, a few veterans produced novels depicting soldiers as flawed and often un-heroic figures, but sales were modest, and unlike those produced by their American counterparts, the books did not become part of the nation's literary canon. The most audacious of these, Earl Birney's satirical novel *Turvey: A Military Picaresque* (1949), told the story of a simple-minded private (as Birney wrote, one "with the intellectual and soldierly capacities of a farmyard duck") who craves sex, booze, and battlefield action but spends most of his time in the company of inefficient and farcical military bureaucrats.

2.3 After Europe descended once again into war, Canadians re-invoked the CEF's consummate reputation for soldiering in Flanders, with those safely on Canadian soil demanding spectacular victories against Hitler in order to burnish the legend. These inexperienced infantrymen of the Queen's Own Cameron Highlanders, finally given the opportunity to engage the enemy in August 1942, are wading into a bloodbath. (Library and Archives Canada, PA-113245.)

Though a modest success, the book was banned by many Canadian libraries for its realistic depiction of soldiers' often earthy dialect. More solemn and influential assessments of the war generally concluded that, as with the First World War, the Second did great things for Canada: despite some rough moments in English-French relations, the conflict enhanced Canadian unity, patriotism, the nation's international standing, and its sterling reputation for soldiering. As C.P. Stacey and Richard Foot wrote, "despite the bloodshed, the war against Germany and the Axis powers transformed Canada's industrial base, elevated the role of women in the economy, paved the way for Canada's membership in NATO, and left Canadians with a legacy of proud service and sacrifice embodied in names such as Dieppe, Ortona and Juno Beach."[15]

As some historians conceded, however, the reputation for unrivalled heroism and prowess gained by Canada's Great War soldiers (through, as Keshen explained, a carefully managed and not entirely forthright public-relations campaign), would give later troops much to live up to. Historian Edgar McInnis observed that during the Second World War, a Canadian public eager once again for accounts of valour demanded "an even more shining role than the Canadian forces had played during the last war." As the war against Hitler moved into its third year without any significant Canadian engagements, a senior military officer noted with some unease that "the people in Canada are calling for blood." Tragically, their demands would be answered at Dieppe, where Canadian Lieutenant General Harry Crerar insisted that untried Canadian troops form the core of the raiding force. This suicidal mission produced a casualty rate of nearly 70 per cent of the roughly 6,000 (mostly Canadian) infantrymen. A similarly impossible and catastrophic encounter in Hong Kong confirmed that Canadian soldiers were not in fact unassailable. To W.L. Morton, "troops who had been raised on a legend of invincibility" had been given "a stern lesson in the trials of war." Yet Morton could not give up entirely on the notion of Canada's intrinsic soldiering capacity, maintaining that despite the utter failure at Dieppe, "one thing only came to Canada from the operation, namely, assurance that the Canadian Army was still of the quality of the old army of 1914–1918, which had made the reputation of Canadian troops."[16]

Some historians questioned whether any men could match the reputation established in the Great War, and suggested a mixed record for the Canadian forces. John English noted that Canadian troops could have done better in the battles that followed the Normandy landings, but placed the blame squarely on the commanders, not the troops. Others anointed the Second World War Canadians as the fitting heirs to those of the First: "Canada's soldiers," wrote J.M.S. Careless, "who had distinguished themselves in rapid advances in the First War, had won no less credit in the Second for their record in bitter, sustained fighting." Edgar McInnis conceded that the earlier campaigns were uneven, but that fighting in Italy finally "bore out the reputation of Canadians as shock troops." The Canadians quickly became, in C.P. Stacey's estimation, "battle hardened soldiers who had mastered every aspect of their task."[17]

As with the earlier wars, circumstances that challenged the upbeat take on the nation's efforts in the Second World War languished in Canadian representations from the beginning. American historian John

2.4 The remains of a young boy who had sought refuge in the arms of a firefighter during "Operation Gomorrah," a week-long bombardment of Hamburg that killed more than 40,000 and injured nearly as many in July 1943. For many years, area bombing was handled more gingerly in Canadian war accounts than in those of their allies. When the Canadian War Museum's 2005 exhibit on Bomber Command included photographs like this depicting the consequences of area bombing, critics declared the images unduly inflammatory. (Image reprinted from Sheldon Richmond, "Killing Noncombatants," *The Journal of Historical Review* 18. 1 [January/February 1999], 38.)

Dijoseph's work on the area bombing of German cities revealed that the practice proved controversial among the British public even as their nation faced the prospect of a Nazi takeover, with a "sizable minority" of wartime Britons, including residents of cities turned to rubble by the Luftwaffe, voicing opposition to any targeting of urban areas. According to Granatstein and Morton, during the war "none raised a voice against it in Canada." Canadian historians, observed Donald Schurman, were likewise slower than their allies to acknowledge the controversial nature of the bombing campaign – a campaign, it bears noting, that Canadian officials and pilots had no part in authorizing or directing. In one important respect, however, the analysis of Canada's

Second World War differed from that of both the South African and Great Wars: professional and amateur historians alike began to fill library shelves with volumes chronicling the Canadian effort almost as soon as the troops returned home.[18]

By the 1970s, however, interest in these accounts, and in those of Canada's First World War, began to wane. Official multiculturalism, an influx of immigrants from non-traditional geographies, and the emergence of Canada as a leading practitioner of UN peacekeeping led some to wonder about the relevance and utility of Canada's martial and imperial past. Among historians, the rise of social and cultural history contributed to a de-emphasis on nation-building narratives and a new interest in the distinctive stories of women, ethnic groups, and the working class, along with the local and regional varieties of experience endemic to the vast and disparate nation. The study of Canada's past wars, formerly undertaken by historical generalists and military specialists alike, became in Tim Cook's words, "a sub-discipline, isolated from the mainstream of historical studies as a separate activity to which other historians – and most students of history – seemingly needed to pay little attention." "Seen as didactic and narrative," Cook explained, "military history was dismissed as being uncritical and untheoretical, and therefore even more out of step with the march of academic historians." Add to these trends a very unpopular contemporaneous US mission in Vietnam and an ongoing threat of thermonuclear war – both of which served to sour attitudes towards militarism in Canada and around the globe – and the dearth of military history in the seventies makes a great deal of sense. As Colin McCullough's study made clear, Canadians of the era came to embrace the image of peacekeeping enthusiastically, and high school history textbooks frequently devoted entire chapters to Canada's UN peace operations. After the Cuban Missile Crisis, citizens who balked at the prospect of being vapourized over a quarrel between the White House and the Kremlin were somewhat less likely to be labelled communist dupes. By the 1980s, the collapse of détente and the intensification of the arms race under Ronald Reagan had brought unprecedented numbers of anxious Canadian citizens (like their American counterparts) to peace organizations.[19]

War-related cultural production that emerged from the period reflected some of these changes. Canadian analysts did not demonstrate the kind of wholesale condemnation of their nation's wartime motives, conduct, and character offered by some of their American counterparts; however, histories such as C.P. Stacey's *Arms, Men and Governments*, J.L. Granatstein and J.M. Hitsman's *Broken Promises:*

A History of Conscription in Canada, and Daphne Read's *The Great War and Canadian Society,* demonstrated a new willingness to criticize military failings, and to depict the often damaging effects of war on Canadian unity, specific ethnic groups, and the soldiers themselves. These works also reflected the broadening of the field beyond the traditional focus on high politics and battlefield strategy. In 1977, Timothy Findley published *The Wars,* one of the more successful and celebrated Canadian antiwar novels. In this work, Robert, a Great War Canadian soldier and the novel's protagonist, endures the terror of trench warfare and a sexual assault perpetrated by fellow soldiers, but cannot endure the wanton disregard for the life of men and animals at the front permitted by a senior officer. Robert kills the officer, is captured and court-martialed, and dies blind and insane a few years after the war at age twenty-five. In his introduction to the 2005 Penguin's Modern Classic edition, fellow Canadian writer Guy Vanderhaeghe called the book "both a marvelous work of art and a passionate indictment of the first cruel idiocy of the twentieth century." Second War veteran Farley Mowatt followed with the bestselling *And No Birds Sang,* a memoir of the author's involvement in the Italian campaign that traces his metamorphosis from naive and enthusiastic enlistee to sardonic (and misanthropic) antiwar activist.[20]

W.A.B. Douglas and Brereton Greenhous's *Out of the Shadows: Canada in the Second World War* exemplified the new candour towards Canada's wartime past. The authors, moonlighting from their regular tasks at the Department of Defence Directorate of History, furnished forthright and often extended criticisms of Canadians at war: of battlefield inexperience and ineffectiveness, area bombing – "a malevolent, technological, impersonal battle waged primarily against women and children" – anti-French prejudice in the Canadian forces, the despotic War Measures Act and policy of Japanese internment, and the fatuous inflation of Canada's contribution. "It has to be admitted," the authors confided in the Epilogue, "that in the final analysis Canada's effort was not essential to winning the war." A reviewer conceded that this was probably true, but worried about Canadians' capacity to stomach the news, as "such a statement is bound to anger, and to hurt, many people in this country."[21] While many of the book's conclusions are unflinching, the authors' preface reads rather like an extended episode of flinching, as they brace for an anticipated backlash against these heterodoxies. In its efforts to prepare Canadians accustomed to affirming war stories for a new and potentially vexing challenge, the preface provides a measure of how unusual such challenges have been. They authors warned:

The reader should bear in mind that any honest book about Canada at war is not going to be limited to a list of gallant deeds and glorious achievements ... Many Canadian mistakes are recounted, not because Canadians necessarily made more mistakes than others but simply because this is a book about Canadians at war. The Americans, British, French, Germans, Japanese, and Russians also made mistakes, but the recitation and study of their blunders is a matter primarily for their own historians.[22]

A few works that followed took aim at the stock heroic rendering of Canada's war effort and its contribution to national unity and progress. Ruth Roach Pierson for example, found that women involved in nontraditional, war-related work faced overwhelming levels of hostility, along with considerable pressure to reassume traditional roles after 1945; while liberation was the watchword overseas, Canadian women would have to wait. The tolerance for the recital of mistakes, missed opportunities, and transgressions had clear limits, however. This the CBC would learn after airing the 1992 series *The Valour and the Horror*, a revisionist look at Canada's wartime contribution by Terrance and Brian McKenna that questioned, among other matters, the probity of the Allied bombing of German civilians. Media historian Jeanette Sloniowski argued that the depth of public furor over the production was unprecedented in the history of Canadian broadcasting. "The fate of [*The Valour and the Horror*] proved," noted Jeffrey Keshen, "that Canadians wanted to remember the Second World War as a good war, for the CBC took so much flak from military historians, veterans, and politicians that it never gave the sordid mess another airing." Not all observers dismissed the production as a "sordid mess" – the Department of National Defence (DND) itself produced an official three-volume history of the Royal Canadian Air Force in 1994 which validated the claims of bombing ineffectiveness that so riled war defenders. But as Keshen observed, military historians did indeed lead the flaying of the CBC and the McKennas. David Bercuson and S.F. Wise counterattacked with *The Valour and the Horror Revisited*, while Granatstein dismissed the massive, painstakingly documented, four-author DND study as implausible.[23]

A decade later, when the Canadian War Museum included a panel on Allied bombing that referenced the fact that the tactic remains controversial, the response was equally vitriolic. Although revisionist interpretations of Canadian military history had never been popular, the broader cultural climate helped elevate the level of outrage aimed at bombing critics to new heights. At the end of the century, Canada, too, was caught up in a "memory boom" – one built upon some of the same cultural, demographic, and technological transformations witnessed in the United States (although a boom that in Canada was as passionate about the First World War as it was the Second). And as was the case south of the border – where elites from the president on down helped to bolster the sentiment – the burgeoning interest in past wars was not entirely a spontaneous grassroots expression. In Canada it was assisted by the expanding nationwide network of Security and Defence Forum research centres established at Canadian universities and funded by the Department of National Defence, and later by the Canadian Defence and Foreign Affairs Institute (2001), along with Stephen Harper's Conservative Party.[24]

As we have seen, many American historians seized upon the memory boom to counter what they considered the rising influence of naive "folklore" surrounding the war; on this front, their Canadian counterparts have been considerably more restrained. As late as 2004, Keshen noted that despite the proliferation of works dedicated to the war's negative aspects and impact published in Britain and the United States from the 1970s onward (and particularly after 1990), "Canadian historians have not reminded us that even a good war can have lots of bad people, or at least people who could be perceived as bad when seen through the prism of wartime anxiety or prudery." Were wartime Canadians simply more upstanding, loyal, orderly, polite, and courteous than citizens of other Allied nations, or than later generations of Canadians? Or have Canadian analysts of the war disregarded, unintentionally or otherwise, its more sordid aspects? Keshen's own study pointed to a generalized disregard, finding that evidence for a much more nuanced and less gallant image of Canadian soldiers and civilians "looms very large" in governmental records, in the wartime mass and local media, and in the memories of the many Canadians the author interviewed to assemble his book.[25]

Some subsequent Canadian works further challenged the "sanitized and simplified" picture of the war decried by Keshen. Fourteen years after a ground-breaking American study of the experiences of gay US servicemen in the Second World War, Paul Jackson's *One of the Boys* chronicled the Canadian side of that often bitter struggle for equality. Margaret MacMillan's *The Uses and Abuses of History* employed the Canadian War Museum controversy as a starting point for an examination of the ways Canadians and others construct and often burnish the past for present ends; political scientist Randall Hansen's *Fire and Fury* roundly condemned the morality and value of area bombing – and provided extensive evidence that the Americans who participated in it took greater pains to avoid civilian deaths than the British and those under their command.[26]

On the whole, however, Canadian histories emphasizing these less glamorous themes remain a rare commodity compared to those produced by their wartime allies; the notion that the good war's image should be moderated or complicated has not gained as much ground among Canadian historians. As their contents soon make clear, book titles like *The Good Fight* and *The Last Good War* are to be taken at face value. In fact, some of the same authors who extolled the First War as a vital chapter in the preservation of human freedom tamed some of their enthusiasm for that conflict in order to bolster the Second. "Whereas the First World War was a battle of rival imperialisms," wrote J.L. Granatstein with a frankness not seen in his earlier work on the Great War, "the following world war was *genuinely* a struggle for survival against a monstrous evil, a just war, the last good war" (emphasis added). Terry Copp produced two bestselling volumes of Canada's Second World War valour that shared a basic thesis: that Canada's contribution to victory had been greatly underrated, that "the Canadian citizen army that fought in the Battle of Normandy played a role all out of proportion to its relative strength among the Allied Armies." Such works routinely include a lengthy meditation on the war's primary lesson: that despite the dreamy idealism that clouds many individuals and that can, from time to time, capture (dangerously) the public as a whole, *this* conflict serves as irrefutable evidence that war is a permanent and necessary mode of human interaction, that war solves problems, is a force for justice, and is fought by heroic men against evil foes.[27]

In this sense, Michael C.C. Adams was right: the war is eminently *usable* because its (atypical) necessity slides easily into goodness, and goodness into proof that wars provide a reliable mechanism for elevating individuals and civilizations alike – in all, that "it is usually better to fight than talk."[28] In other words, the war's lessons as rendered in these Canadian accounts are not unlike those employed by politicians who evoke appeasement whenever they face an intractable international foe – regardless of that foe's consonance with Hitler's views, methods, or objectives. Terms like "the last good war" also imply that (some? most? all?) wars prior to the Second were similarly worthwhile and honourably fought, that the more proximate and thus more glaring shortcomings of subsequent conflicts are aberrations. But given the widely understood uniqueness of fascism's threat and malevolence, one could also argue that in the history of Canadian and American foreign engagements, the Second World War was "the first and last

good war" (if we use the term "good" in the more circumscribed sense
of "absolutely necessary"). To do so, however, would draw attention
to the war's exceptionality, not its universal justification for military
spending and war-fighting and against, for instance, conciliation and
peacekeeping.

Whether or not the Second World War can truly be considered unreservedly good, in calling it the "last" of such conflicts, even exponents
of the "good" thesis seem to have given up on its successor, the Korean
War. The move is not new. The conflict is so marginal in public consciousness that there would be some justification for simply omitting
that episode from a work on twentieth-century war and memory –
although this would only perpetuate an injustice suffered by the war's
victims and participants from the outset. Canadian and American historians have paid far less attention to the conflict than that afforded
the world wars, and in the case of American scholars, to Vietnam and
even the 110-day War of 1898. A 1998 survey of US secondary school
textbooks found that, on average, they dedicated less than 50 lines to
the Korean War, while only 73 per cent stated that the fighting ended
with a cease-fire as opposed to a peace settlement. Comparatively few
films or works of literature take the war as their principle subject, and
veterans have often felt excluded from the rituals of official commemoration. American veterans waited until 1996 for the unveiling of the
Korean War Veterans Memorial in Washington, DC, while a privately-
funded "Korean War Wall of Remembrance" listing the names of the
Canadian dead was dedicated in Brampton, Ontario in the following
year.[29] Some Americans may be familiar with at least one of the war's
battles, the dramatic landing at Inchon; it is likely that fewer percentages
of Canadians have heard of Kapyong, where outnumbered Canadian
and Australian forces halted the advance of a Chinese division head-
ing for the South Korean capital of Seoul. Yet even this incident, in a
metaphor for the conflict as a whole, was about defence, about holding the line. There would be no Vimys or Iwo Jimas around which to
rally public sentiment, no Korean War memorials inscribed on national
currency, no mass pilgrimages to battle sites, no poetry committed to
memory by school children.

Explanations for the relative neglect and ambivalence abound.
Neither Canada nor the United States was attacked, nor were any of
their long-time allies. Korea was in a distant, little-known, and often
disparaged corner of the globe. Citizens who in the recent past had
watched their governments enact anti-Asian immigration and domestic policies were now being urged to put their lives on the line for Asian

peoples, as well as a South Korean government many saw as autocratic. The war was prosecuted under the flag of the United Nations, a neophyte international body that could not inspire the same type of allegiance as nation or empire. To one of its principle architects, a war which involved more than twenty nations, killed as many as four million people, and bull-dozed much of the peninsula was not a war at all: Haunted by the perennial ghosts of Munich, President Harry Truman ordered troops to the fight immediately and without the congressional approval mandated by the Constitution, and thereafter called the war a "police action" in order to deflect accusations of illegality. So great was the official denial that for more than a year after the hostilities began, Americans killed in action and returned for burial in national cemeteries were provided grave markers listing only their name, rank, and date of birth. The army finally relented to pressure from the families of causalities, but still could not bring itself to call the cause for which these men died a war, marking their graves simply "Korea." The conflict's obscurity was reinforced by the fact that, facing no shortages, rationing, or conscription, those on the home front were largely unaffected.[30] Moreover, the war's objectives were unclear from the outset, and fluctuated dramatically as it progressed – most significantly and stupidly when UN forces shifted focus from preserving South Korea to gaining the entire peninsula, a move which brought in the Chinese and multiplied the carnage. Most importantly, the war itself became a deadly stalemate, and the fighting ceased not with the vanquishing of the enemy, but through a cease-fire and a still-patrolled and volatile demilitarized zone. Totalitarian North Korea, a lunatic regime that UN forces sought to eradicate, remains a problem vexing South Korea, the global community, and American international relations to the present.

On the matter of forgetting, much is also made of the war's proximity to the far more substantial Second World War. Here, the sometimes overzealous applause for the good war and greatest generation does few favours to those caught up in the Korean War. The implied corollary is that the Korean affair was not noble, and that those who fought it failed where their more capable forbearers succeeded (even as many of the same members of the generation that prevailed in the Second could not do so in Korea). In the United States, such aspersions emerged during the conflict itself, as it became clear that American forces would not dispatch their foes with the expected ease. Their troops, many US observers concluded, simply did not possess the physical and moral strength or the "gumption" exhibited by those that had routed the Axis. Following the conflict, even the American Legion turned on Korean

War veterans, accusing them of tarnishing the Second War victory, of disloyalty, of being "soft on communism." In an evidently durable trope, blame for this alleged attenuation in loyalty, honour, and military valour was placed at the feet of the "liberal education" imposed on American youth that sapped the "American people's spirit of devotion to a common cause" (although it is hard to imagine that schooling had devolved so drastically in five years). Some Canadian veterans of the war reported similar condescension from Second World War veterans.[31]

Later historians would reprise the charge that the troops lacked patriotism. Even Paul Edwards wrote in his otherwise sympathetic lament for the war's neglect that the American "soldiers were not equal to the standards established in World War II," that they were "soft, spoiled, and often poorly led." The Canadian Army's official history of the conflict offered similar judgments about the first contingent of Canadians sent to Korea, a charge repeated in subsequent assessments by Canadian, British, and Australian analysts.[32] If war provided the ultimate gauge of citizens' individual and collective mettle, it would follow that those who did not prevail would face ambivalence, neglect, even resentment. Other variables that shape the outcome of all wars – geography and climate, familiarity with the terrain, the degree of cooperation from civilians, the proximity and strength of the enemy's allies, blind luck, and, especially in modern, mechanized conflict, technology – cannot be marshaled to excuse the disappointing outcome in this case without also devaluing the role of individual capacity and courage in previous triumphs.

In this sense, Korea would have to be forgotten. This despite its significance as a forerunner of the type of conflict both Canada and the United States would face on more than a few occasions: a limited war aimed (during one phase at least) at "regime change," though one in which the Western-backed alternative was no model of democracy or human rights. Here, too, was a conflict of both a civil and international nature, and one that would therefore require winning "hearts and minds" along with traditional battlefield engagements, even as indiscriminate civilian deaths at the hands of both factions mounted. Efforts to gain favour were further confounded by Koreans' long encounter with colonialism and the false promises of benevolent uplift offered by earlier self-appointed mentors. For each of these particular circumstances, "Korea" could be interchanged with "Vietnam," "Iraq," "Afghanistan," "Libya." There are lessons to be learned from the Korean War – for instance, that such conflicts are unfathomably complex, resistant to measurable successes, and often catalysts for future bloodletting – but these are not the types of morals on which proponents of a "warrior culture" prefer to dwell.[33] Thus the unrelenting focus on the lessons furnished by the good war.

Given this neglect, clashes in the United States and Canada over the meaning of Korea have been less publicized than those played out over other wars, and more confined to specialists; likewise, the conflict's less-than-satisfying "conclusion" has given works on the war a more critical and reserved tone. In view of the patterns established above, however, it should not surprise that the most stinging critiques of the UN mission emerged from Americans. Many positive accounts of America's role in the conflict did emerge in the years immediately following the war, works which, as Paul Edwards observed, "heralded the American effort in Korea as having some of the qualities of a 'good war,' one fought for precise and understandable reasons." In this view, the war was a simple product of international communist aggression funneled through a Soviet puppet (North Korea) against a liberal democracy (South Korea), and the United States was merely doing its bit as a loyal member of the UN to protect the sovereignty of member nations. "Yet even in the most committed of these accounts," Edwards continued, "the moral affirmations and patriotic justifications that had dominated early World War II histories often appeared out of place."[34]

More caustic interpretations are manifold. American historians, who in the case of previous wars delivered plenty of self-censure even in examining their nation's martial victories, veritably revelled in the opportunities provided by an ill-starred foreign engagement. In 1952, while the war still on and its outcome uncertain, leftist journalist and historian I.F. Stone published *The Hidden History of the Korean War*. This incriminatory account could be called revisionist – except that the orthodox, nationalistic representation hardly had time to take root in the literature. After decades of influential (and often best-selling) dystopian offerings on US wars, some American analysts no longer waited for the official version of events, but struck pre-emptively at the anticipated, one-dimensional depictions of a good and necessary fight against a demonstrable evil. Stone blamed much of the instability in the two Koreas on President Truman's unwavering and unwarranted support for South Korean strongman Syngmann Rhee, a phony democrat whom Truman "ought to have despised." Stone also wrote frankly of American atrocities, revealing the use of napalm against North Korean towns and cities and confessing that the tactic smacked of "an indifference to human suffering … which makes me as an American deeply ashamed." Lt. Col. Melvin Voorhees, Public Information Officer and Chief Censor for the US military, published *Korean Tales* in the same year. The book offered up equal portions of tragedy and travesty, much of the latter supplied by Commander-in-Chief of the UN forces, General Douglas MacArthur. The general, Voorhees revealed, made a habit of dashing off to the front in his private, four-engine luxury aircraft (which always reserved seats for the Tokyo bureau chiefs of leading American and British news services) to take credit for a recent or upcoming operation. MacArthur's fondness for the camera and himself not only robbed his frontline generals of much of the credit; on more than one occasion, it also served to give communist forces advance notice of UN offensives.[35]

As with the assessment of all America's previous wars, the Vietnam conflict brought renewed attention to Korea, although the "lessons" of Vietnam seemed especially apposite to a previous (unwinnable) war in Asia. Stone's "hidden history" remained so after its initial publication, too hazardous for a society enduring the McCarthyite witch-hunt; the book found a new publisher and a wide audience in 1970, by which time "credibility gap," a term not employed by Stone but germane to his thesis, had become a household term. New Left historians incorporated and expanded Stone's findings. American bungling, overconfidence, cultural ignorance and insensitivity, misinterpretation of the intentions of the Soviets and the Chinese, war crimes, and preoccupation with the extension of the open door were regular themes. In light of the catastrophic conflict in Indochina, scholars identified the Korean War as the cognitive stepping stone between "the highly romanticized memory of World War II" and "the structurally critical response unleashed during the war in Vietnam." Cultural histories of the Korean era found that wartime American writers, filmmakers, and journalists turned increasingly to unromantic, realist imagery to represented "the damaging rather than the edifying consequences of battle," "cynical and critical depictions of the armed forces," and "implicit and explicit critiques of the nation's military commitments overseas."[36]

Vietnam, then, served as the culmination rather than origin of a cultural shift towards a more pessimistic appraisal of soldiering and militarism. In Lisle Rose's *Roots of Tragedy: The United States and the Struggle for Asia, 1945–1953* (1976), the "tragedy" is Vietnam, with the underappreciated failures in Korea setting the stage for the more widely known catastrophe that would follow. Likewise, in calling his indictment of the conflict *Korea: The First War We Lost* (1986), war veteran Bevin Alexander defied the notion that Vietnam was the nation's first truly calamitous foreign engagement. Other Korean veterans critical of the war's justifications and prosecution produced similar, dissenting accounts.[37]

In the early 1980s, Historian Bruce Cumings began building a career and a considerable reputation by highlighting the civil (rather than Stalinist or Maoist) foundations of the conflict. Complicating the international dimension of the conflict also deflated one of the war's primary rationales: that monolithic communism was "on the march" and demanded an immediate Western military response. Marilyn Young concurred, arguing that Rhee's unpopularity among South Koreans rendered the conflict "not only a civil war between the two halves of an artificially divided country, but a civil war *within* the South" (emphasis in original). Cumings also drew attention to the reprehensible nature of both the North and South Korean regimes (the latter a haven for Koreans who had collaborated with the ruthless Japanese colonial administration), and to the "world economy logic" underlying the US decision to protect and extend their alliances and markets in the region. Atrocities, he informed readers, were common on both sides, racism was rampant among American troops and commanders alike, and the "liberal" regime the UN sought to defend was so loathed by many South Koreans that they welcomed their Northern assailants as liberators (and joined guerilla insurrections in support of Kim's army).[38] This passage from his 2010 account of the war captured the desolate themes Cumings had been working for three decades:

> Here was the Vietnam War we came to know before Vietnam – gooks, napalm, rapes, whores, an unreliable ally, a cunning enemy, fundamentally untrained GIs fighting a war their top generals barely understood, fragging of officers, contempt for the know-nothing civilians back home, devilish battles indescribable even to loved ones, press handouts from Gen. Douglas MacArthur's headquarters apparently scripted by comedians or lunatics, an ostensible vision of bringing freedom and liberty to a sordid dictatorship run by servants of Japanese imperialism.[39]

Cumings, along with the many Korean War detractors from the United States who followed, laid much of the blame for the two-year deliberations over a cease-fire on American diplomatic miscalculations and deception; his work also made much of allegations that US forces engaged in bacteriological warfare. This charge was first leveled by Canadian missionary and activist James Endicott after his 1952 visit to China, and it made him a pariah in his home country. (An incensed *Winnipeg Tribune* revealed that Endicott himself was the source of the WMDs: "The germs and maggots and crawling things are products of your warped mind," the paper's editors charged. "You carry pestilence with you and breathe it on clean things.") Endicott's claims were repeated in a 1998 book co-authored by his son Stephen and American historian Edward Hagerman. When a 1999 Associated Press report claimed that American soldiers had, under orders, massacred civilians at No Gun Ri, the incident became standard fare in the accounts of American revisionists. No matter where one comes down on these still-contested claims, it is difficult to argue with American historian William Stueck, one of the more widely-published American defenders of the war. In their focus on "developing the dark side of the US relationship with Korea," Stueck observed, many of his colleagues were determined "to lambaste the United States for virtually every crime imaginable."[40] But such is the nature of American contests over war remembrance.

The dynamic confrontations over the origins, conduct, and meaning of the Korean War have contributed to a steady flow of book-length American reconsiderations and responses; among historians, at least, the war is no longer underrepresented in the overall national story, and the ongoing battles over the meaning of Korea have frequently reached the mass media. By contrast, the complete oeuvre of Canadian specialized studies on the conflict can still be carried from the library by a solitary – and not particularly brawny – researcher in one trip. Lt. Col. Herbert Fairlie Wood called his 1966 official history of Canadian Army participation *Strange Battleground*, a title whose accent on peculiarity served as a kind of apology for the frustrations, failures, and confusion that this most atypical of wars would bring. Although arguments for American, UN, and South Korean culpability in the onset of hostilities – and arguments against US bombing of cities and deployment of napalm – had been in circulation since the conflict itself, Wood made no reference to these controversies. The author discussed the use of napalm only on Chinese soldiers and only in terms of its strategic and psychological value (conclusion: effective). Such a treatment of the issue went hand-in-hand with Wood's claim that this conflict, which in the history of wars involving Canadian and American forces killed unprecedented percentages of civilians, was "a business-like war" conducted not so much by soldiers defending a threat to their homeland, but by cool, detached "technicians." This job description also accounted for the "less than total commitment" he claims the troops put forward.[41]

Written in the waning years of American involvement in Vietnam, Denis Stairs' *Diplomacy of Constraint* focused on the diplomatic relationship between Canada and the United States during the Korean conflict, and argued that in participating, Canada did the Americans and the

world a considerable service in attempting to reign in their neighbour's
more belligerent and impulsive tendencies. The thesis reinforced the
view, prized by many Canadians, that they were an eminently reasonable and moderate people; it was also affirmed in several subsequent
Canadian and American handlings of the war. Some of the efforts at
"containing America," as Stairs phrased it, succeeded ("do not use the
atomic bomb"), while others ("do not provoke China") went unheeded.
Stairs framed these Canadian mediation efforts, along with the nation's
somewhat disenchanting encounter with American leadership and
"limited war," as important precursors to the Canadian peacekeeping
tradition.[42] For Canadians of the day, at least, Korea could indeed provide
valuable lessons.

In the trickle of subsequent Canadian re-evaluations of Korea, many
of the vibrant, provocative, sometimes uncorroborated, and seemingly
unavoidable commotions convulsing US understandings on the war
hardly registered. John Melady's *Korea: Canada's Forgotten War* presented
Syngman Rhee in wholly flattering tones, and provided no qualification to the notions that the war began simply because "Russia was
pulling the strings," or that "Canadians died for the cause of peace in
Korea." Several authors correctly pointed out that Canadian officials of
the day believed that Stalin had ordered the invasion, but fail to inform
readers that declassified Soviet documents have since undermined this
simplistic understanding of war origins. David Bercuson's *Blood on the
Hills*, Brent Byron Watson's *Far Eastern Tour*, and William Johnston's *A
War of Patrols* wrestle with the effectiveness of the Canadian ground
forces, but not the righteousness of the cause in Korea. In Bercuson's
view, Canadian troops sent to prop up an authoritarian regime paradoxically "helped hold the line of freedom"; further, in facilitating the
transformation of a local conflict into a wider, protracted, and devastating regional war, Canadian forces served "the cause of international
peace and security." Melady's new Preface to the second edition of *Canada's Forgotten War* provided a further clarification of the stakes: "Had
Canada and its United Nations partners not intervened when they did,
all of Korea might now resemble the wretched police state that lies
north of the 38th parallel." In his Introduction to the second edition of
Ted Barris's *Deadlock in Korea* – like Melady's account, a book reissued
to capitalize on the sixtieth anniversary of the war's outbreak – Bercuson
echoed this simplistic storyline. With the 1953 ceasefire agreement,
he wrote, "South Korea was saved; today it is a prosperous, free, and
democratic state." Omitted, and seemingly purposely obfuscated by Bercuson's hasty transition from 1953 to "today," was an acknowledgment

that from the appointment of Rhee until 1992, South Koreans suffered under a series of military dictatorships disposed to executing political opponents and opening fire on peaceful demonstrators, regimes that enjoyed the considerable support of the United States, Canada, and other Western trading partners. In this sense, South Koreans loosed the shackles of their own "wretched police state" *despite* the actions of the West. [43]

Regardless of whether the American-led UN response to the conflict was prudent, or whether the war as a whole can be considered a victory, at least the most celebrated battle involving Canadians was – although the title of a book on the incident, *Triumph at Kapyong*, still seems jarring and a little disingenuous in the context of the larger ambiguities, failures, and tragedies that marked the war. The story of Kapyong, wrote the author, "sparkles" with the peerless qualities exhibited by the Canadian troops: "courage, initiative, modesty, and an uncomplicated, rock-solid belief in themselves ... On one April night six decades ago, they were wonderful." And despite the fact that US soldiers made up over 96 per cent of UN ground forces, the book suggests Canadians might have been the linchpins of South Korea's deliverance: because of Kapyong, "the Korean War did not end abruptly in April 1951 in a communist victory."[44]

This is not to say that these accounts were unrelentingly or, in some cases, even generally positive. For a conflict as unsettled and frustrating as Korea, a degree of censure is inevitable. Some had harsh words for the poor training, discipline, and morale that marked the Canadian effort, and especially for the public and governmental indifference to the plight of the troops. Watson's *Far Eastern Tour* delivered a most dyspeptic analysis of "governmental neglect and high command imprudence" that meant "the wartime experiences of Canadian infantrymen in Korea were far more difficult and unpleasant than they need have been." For the author, these failures at the top were instrumental in encouraging the decidedly less-than-wonderful conduct of many Canadian soldiers, including rampant alcohol abuse, acts of racism and violence towards non-combatants, and the highest rates of venereal disease among UN forces.[45] Yet for Watson, Bercuson, and others who underscored the darker side of the conflict, Canada's Korean War served as a caveat about what befalls an underfunded, underappreciated, and unprepared military – an outlook rather different, in other words, from a generalized critique of warfare's morality or its efficacy as a diplomatic tool. The wider indictments of the war's justification, overall purpose, conduct, and aftermath that have so animated its American chroniclers, and the more universal warnings they have raised about the application of military solutions to international relations dilemmas or about the over-reliance on the lessons of Munich, have not found a place in Canadian specialized studies on the war.

A recent cultural analysis of Canada's relationship with the peoples of Asia in the first half of the twentieth century provided a considerably darker image of the nation's involvement in Korea. While acknowledging that "many Canadian soldiers conducted themselves with discipline and integrity" and that some "displayed a strong sense of humanity towards the Korean people," historian John Price made it plain that Canadians also committed uncounted acts of shocking cruelty against soldiers and civilians alike. In addition to presenting graphic descriptions of widespread torture, rape, and murder, what made Price's handling of the matter unique was the author's connection between these acts and the long and bitter legacy of anti-Asian bias that afflicted Canadian society as a whole. These atrocities could not, in other words, be solely attributed to the isolated incidents, bad apples, the savagery of war, inadequate training, the adversity of the mission, or any other palliative rationalizations: these acts were, rather, a reflection of an undeniable aspect of the nation itself. That truth is underscored by the fact that, while roughly sixty of the Canadian troops involved were found guilty of rape, murder, and other violent crimes and sent to Canada to serve hard time, most were released immediately upon their return home. In Brent Byron Watson's incontestable conclusion, this was merely "another example of the institutional racism that seems to have permeated the upper echelons of the Department of Defence." Yet despite court records and media reports that authenticate the depth of the problem, the inclination to excuse or raise doubts about such incidents endures. "Stories continue to persist," wrote Granatstein in 2011, "some possibly true, of how Canadians pitched grenades into roadside huts indiscriminately or killed prostitutes rather than pay them. In a war of great cruelty, such atrocities seemed almost incidental."[46]

Placed into the context of their other major wars of the twentieth century, discernible patterns in Canadian and American war analysis and remembrance are reconfirmed by Korea. While Americans surely glory in war, condemnation is also a fundamental and unavoidable theme, one that generally commands a vocal minority and has on occasion emerged as the prevailing perspective on a given conflict. The sometimes bitter repudiation of the nation's wars, moreover, has not been confined to academics, elites, leftists, or any other subgroup variously accused of an ingrained patriotic deficit. And while Vietnam certainly amplified the penchant for demythologizing America's wars and the nation's wider sense of international mission, the tragedy in Indochina simply reinforced opinions expressed regularly and bluntly in earlier eras by citizens of various identities, ideological perspectives, and influence. Alongside an undeniable tradition of uncritical war triumphalism, American discourse has gestated a vibrant "reverse heroic" mode, wherein the crude delineations of good (us) and evil (them) are – sometimes just as crudely – reversed.[47] While most US opinion falls between these polar extremes, the range of options presented to and by Americans contemplating their military legacy is considerable.

English Canadians have handled their wartime legacy with greater reverence, caution, and respect – a generalized trait recognized, as indicated in the foregoing, by observers such as Andrew Godefroy, Donald Schurman, John Grodzinski, Tim Cook, and Jeffrey Keshen when they placed Canadian estimations of war into a broader bilateral or international perspective. While condemnation is surely present in assessments of Canada's military past, it has never exhibited the depth and profile witnessed south of the border. Accordingly, when Canadians surveying the writing of their nation's wars describe a given work as a "critical" history, the reader will generally find an author willing to highlight such phenomena as flawed strategies, battlefield errors, inadequate equipment and military funding, bureaucratic bungling, and the challenges to national unity; something short, in other words, of the kind of fundamental repudiation of war principles, purposes, methods, and consequences that gain a "critical" rating in the US context.[48] In Canada, wars that brought victory, national unity, international recognition, and the preservation of the international liberal order, remain cornerstones of national memory – even as the triumph, harmony, respect, and freedom achieved through conflict are sometimes more limited and complicated than touted. Those conflicts that cannot support the equation of warfare with positive national development, meanwhile, are largely absent from public remembrance – as they are, though to a lesser extent, in the United States – *and* vastly underrepresented in Canada's historical literature. Thus far we have focused primarily on the "how" of war representation and remembrance. The more complicated and compelling question is "why."

PART TWO

Excavation: Inquiries into the Development of War Habits

Chapter Three

Wars for and against Empire

Modern imperialism – the quest for international hegemony inaugurated by sixteenth-century Western European expansion and competition – has exerted an impact on the globe that can scarcely be overstated. It inspired exploration, technological innovation, scientific discovery, and environmental plunder, and led to a worldwide remapping of flora, fauna, and disease. It simultaneously enriched and impoverished millions, depriving untold numbers of imperial subjects not only of their traditional livelihoods, but also of their lives. The pursuit of empire transformed and eradicated ethnic groups and cultures, integrated economic markets, and revolutionized concepts of governance, religion, human rights, and racial identity. It was undertaken by a host of peoples in the name of ideologies ranging from monarchism to liberalism to communism to fascism, and left no human society untouched. It is the DNA of the current, globalized world.[1]

Modern imperialism also fed wars – of conquest, colonial competition, and resistance – that have been among the most destructive in history; in contemporary Africa, Eastern Europe, South Asia, and the Middle East, vestiges of the "great game" of European imperial rivalry continue to animate clashes within and between states. Furthermore, as war has served as one of the more consistent means of preserving and extending imperial control, international conflicts face regular scrutiny for evidence of imperial motivations. More often than not, such evidence can be marshalled, as the threshold of proof can be pegged at a rather low level: any belligerent – and particularly those from the wealthier strata of nations – that is thought to prosecute a conflict out of self-interest rather than self-defence, altruism, or principle is susceptible to charges of imperialism. And history provides few examples of nations willing to sacrifice their wealth and citizens solely in the interests of ideals or foreign peoples.

That imperialism exhibits a profound impact on the arc of both US and Canadian history, then, comes as no surprise, nor should the fact that important aspects of that impact are analogous. The environs that would become Canada and the United States served as a magnet for British settlers, and thus developed into outposts of history's most extensive formal empire. Although relations between aboriginal peoples and those of European descent were generally more turbulent in the United States, both settler societies countered indigenous resistance with asymmetric violence as they expanded westward, and both eventually achieved autonomy from the British metropole. But when we triangulate the matters of nation, empire, and war, difference, rather than similitude, emerges as the dominant theme. Over the course of the first half of the twentieth century, Canadians fought for the British Empire vigorously and – in the case of many English Canadians – candidly and without apology. As Canadian military historian Donald Schurman observed, "it is indeed almost impossible to imagine Canadian writers protesting in print, either against World War One or its successor. Support for the military goals of the war was a hallmark of the colonial English Canadian." As the twentieth century progressed and imperialism's reputation entered an irreversible decline, more and more English Canadians muted their imperial justifications for Canada's wars, leading some to question their nation's participation, and others to accentuate other motivations. Americans, by contrast, have resisted joining conflicts they considered imperial in nature, entered wars with the expressed purpose of reigning in the practice of imperialism, instigated military operations to expand their territory and install or shore up US-friendly regimes (while denying any imperial motivation), and along the way become the most dominant power – or empire – in world history.[2] In other words, profound complication, contradiction, and mutability converge at the nexus of these national encounters with war and empire.

Indeed, it was war itself that helped furnish these two societies with dichotomous attitudes to empire. The US War of Independence, a middle- and upper-class tax revolt that, in the interest of gaining mass appeal and moral authority, metamorphosed into a lucid challenge to colonialism and inherited rule, provided important intellectual foundations for the distinct societies that would inhabit British-controlled North America. For Americans, the conflict with Britain stirred a disdain for imperialism, a sentiment the United States has promoted tirelessly in word, and often in deed, from its inception to the present. Anti-imperialism provided much of the ideological basis for Thomas Jefferson's Declaration of Independence, as well as the Monroe Doctrine of 1823 warning European powers about further colonization of the Western Hemisphere. Contempt for empire coloured America's initial opposition to the Great War and Woodrow Wilson's agenda at Versailles, as well as later US officials' broadsides against fascism and Communism. The refrain has not fallen out of fashion. Shortly after the 2003 US invasion of Iraq, Defence Secretary Donald Rumsfeld defended adamantly the emancipatory impetus for the campaign, insisting, "We're not imperialistic. We never have been."[3]

To be sure, the idealism embedded in such libertarian pronouncements was generally married to practical considerations: the early leaders of the new and relatively weak republic feared that a continued European presence in the Western Hemisphere would threaten American security and limit territorial and economic expansion; Wilson's call for freedom of the seas, the removal of economic barriers, and an adjustment of colonial claims provided succour to both anti-imperialists and US investors, and so on. Further, the nation has on numerous occasions throughout its existence behaved in a candidly imperialistic fashion, with Latin America frequently serving as the site of encroachment. Yet, neither these generally unstated supplementary motives behind anti-imperialist discourse nor the outright breaches of the principle diminish the fact that vigorous anti-imperialism is a staple of American rhetoric. This credo forms a core component of national identity – one that places the nation both outside and at the vanguard of history – and to trammel upon this notion is to undercut much of the basis of American exceptionalism. In this way, anti-imperialism unites Americans from across the political spectrum as few issues can: from those on the left who may reject the notion of exceptionalism yet oppose imperialism on universal moral and legal grounds; to those on the right who employ anti-imperialism to bear out the unique; and to some, divine mission of their nation. As Bill Kaufman pointed out, over the course of American history, conservatives have generated some of the most forceful condemnations of empire, fearing that US expansion would enlarge executive power at the expense of the demos, increase military expenditures, and bind the nation to "entangling alliances."[4]

The American Revolution provided vastly different lessons for Canadians, serving as confirmation that the Crown safeguarded the general welfare and promoted carefully managed, organic reform, thus

serving as a bulwark against the excesses of both rampant individualism and mob rule. The battle between American Patriots and British
forces led to assaults by the former against fellow colonists who refused
to take up arms against the King, or who enlisted in British regiments
against the revolutionaries. The British defeat led more than 40,000 of
these loyalists to relocate to British North America, where their fidelity
was reinforced through a series of rewards: grants of farmland, the protection offered by British laws and institutions, and eternal recognition
by the Crown, in the form of having the letters "U.E." (for "Unity of the
Empire") affixed to their names, and to those of their descendants. As
such, the loyalists' allegiance to empire was confirmed by an esteemed
and unshakable public mark. As Norman Knowles wrote, the loyalist
experience contributed to a series of ideas generally associated with the
group in Canada: "unfailing devotion to the British Crown and Empire, a
strong and pervasive anti-Americanism, suffering and sacrifice endured
for the sake of principle, elite social origins, and a conservative social
vision." In truth, as Knowles and others have demonstrated, these characteristics simplified differences among what was in fact a fairly diverse
assemblage, and have been modified and reconstructed over time in
order to suit a range of shifting political requirements.[5] Yet in the same
way that the US anti-imperial ideal retains its power despite its sometimes erratic relation to fact, the issue here is not whether the loyalist
myth aligns with reality, but that it is widely believed to be authentic;
gives loyalism its cultural potency. And the most enduring element of
the loyalist tradition is its devotion to the empire.

Of course, the loyalists did not find an unpeopled land when they
immigrated to British-held Quebec. More than 70,000 inhabitants, the
majority of French origin and the remaining consisting of members
of various indigenous tribes, already resided in the region. Over the
course of the nineteenth century, however, increased migration from
Britain led to the numerical and political dominance of Canadians of
British origin; by 1901, they comprised 60 per cent of the population,
while those of French origin made up 30 per cent. Political and cultural
influence increased accordingly, and by the time of Confederation, the
loyalists had assumed the mantle of Canada's founding fathers; heroic
nation-builders around whom nascent patriotic sentiment might crys-
tallize. Naturally, Quebec's francophones could never reconcile themselves to equating loyalism with the truest form of Canadianism or the
nation's "founding," nor could the remnants of Nova Scotia's French-
speaking Acadian population. Britain's mid-eighteenth-century efforts

to deport the latter group *en masse* contributed to Acadians' lingering bitterness towards the empire, and the embrace of their own distinct creation myth in the 1847 epic poem *Evangéline*, by American Henry Wadsworth Longfellow. Here, a recently betrothed couple forcibly separated by the British deportation reunite decades later through sheer coincidence and with the husband near death. *Evangéline* sold well, both in the United States and especially among Acadians, stimulating an incipient Acadian nationalism, and after 1887, serving as the masthead for the leading Acadian newspaper. Loyalism, then, served as a patently incomplete and provocative claim to national identity; demographic facts, however, provided anglophiles with a distinct advantage in their attempts to codify "Canadianness" and its interdependence with the British Empire. Further, as historian Jerry Bannister argued, Canadians need not possess a loyalist or even a British lineage to embrace key components of the loyalist outlook. Chief among these are the mutually-reinforcing ideas of a fondness for the monarchy, British political institutions, and a powerful central state, and an affiliated distaste for both the United States and "the belief in revolution as an acceptable political choice."[6]

Significantly, the achievement of Dominion status and a growing sense of Canadian nationalism throughout the late nineteenth century did not mean attenuation of fealties towards anglophones' ethnic homeland. As Carl Berger argued, the era's English Canadians viewed a commitment to empire as a form of Canadian nationalism, a dual loyalty that emphasized Canada's role as a partner in empire, as well as the pre-eminence of British political institutions, values, and traditions. The fact that they shared a border with a more powerful neighbour that sought to deliver a rather different set of political and cultural values to the entire continent – on some occasions, most notably in 1812, through force of arms – only enhanced English Canadians' bonds to Britain. For Canadians, casting off the yoke of empire under such circumstances would be roughly equivalent to unilateral disarmament in the face of a clear and present danger.[7]

When at the close of the nineteenth century each nation became involved in separate imperial wars – in the case of the United States, a war that added colonial possessions to the republic, and for Canada, a war to defend British imperial possessions – these national responses to empire would be sharpened, contested, and redefined. For Americans, the War of 1898's association with imperialism rendered the conflict one of the more controversial episodes in the history of US foreign relations, although it was considerably less contentious at the war's outset. By and large, Americans supported their nation's declaration of war in April 1898, convinced that their government sought simply to deliver aggrieved Cubans from their Spanish overlords. Ensuing events would present a sizeable challenge to this straightforward appraisal, as US forces engaged their Spanish counterparts not only in Cuba, but widened the war to include attacks on the Spanish-held Philippines, Guam, and Puerto Rico. Moreover, while observers have long wrestled with the question of whether the McKinley administration embarked on its challenge to Spain in order to acquire territory, overseas territorial acquisition was an undeniable outcome of the battle, with the Treaty of Paris (1898) ceding control of the Philippines, Puerto Rico, and Guam to the United States.[8]

The president himself protested perhaps too much against charges that the United States was now following in the footsteps of the much-maligned Europeans. At a speech in Boston given while the Filipino insurrection raged, McKinley stood before portraits of three American presidents identified as "Liberators" – Washington, Lincoln, and in no great fit of modesty, himself – and declared: "No imperial designs lurk in the American mind." In his subsequent assessment of the Filipino situation, McKinley revealed a talent for softening bad news via obfuscation that twenty-first-century audiences might describe as positively Rumsfeldian: the president "reasoned" that it was "not a good time for the liberator to submit important questions concerning liberty and government to the liberated while they are engaged in shooting down their rescuers." To many Americans, however, the "rescuers" were in fact engaged in an unambiguous betrayal of the ideal essential to their very existence as a nation: that a people held an inalienable right to govern themselves. In June 1898, indignation over the proposed annexation of the Philippines inspired the formation of the Anti-Imperialist League, an organization which by 1899 amassed over 50,000 members – "the largest antiwar organization per capita in American history" – and included such noted and disparate figures as Grover Cleveland, Jane Addams, Mark Twain, Andrew Carnegie, W.E.B. Du Bois, Booker T. Washington, Samuel Gompers, John Dewey, and Henry James. Although expansion was carried out under a Republican administration, the League's opprobrium over the deviation from cherished US ideals found broad bipartisan support; as Mark Twain wrote to League organizers after reviewing the group's membership roll, "I am gratified to find that there's a multitude of sane people in the Republican party yet, and in the rest of the nation."[9]

Prominent federal politicians also took a leading role in challenging America's imperial turn. William Jennings Bryan, McKinley's Democratic opponent in both the 1896 and 1900 presidential elections, and Republican Massachusetts Senator George Frisbie Hoar were among the war's most consistent and acerbic critics. Likewise, anti-imperialism served as the basis of denunciations of the terms of the Treaty of Paris from prominent American clergymen, presidents, and professors at many of the nation's leading universities, the editorial boards at the *North American Review, Nation, Harper's*, most African American newspapers, and though he was in the employ of war advocate Hearst, renowned journalist Ambrose Bierce. "Republic or empire?" was the oft-voiced query, implying that colonial holdings invalidated the very basis of governmental authority as outlined in the US Constitution. Denunciations of expansion could also arise from less noble impulses, including anxieties over the "dilution" of American racial stock through the incorporation of non-white peoples. Varina Howell Davis, widow of Confederate President Jefferson Davis, wrote in an 1898 newspaper column that annexation would bring "fresh millions of foreign negroes, more ignorant and more degraded" than even those in the United States. In the American context at least, notions of Anglo-Saxon supremacy could both rouse and deflate enthusiasm for expansion.[10]

The first years of the twentieth century witnessed the publication of a number of American novels which echoed these progressive, and sometimes odious, anti-imperial themes. Academics critical of overseas expansion also entered the fray. Economists pointed to the inequities and exploitation inherent in imperial financial arrangements, while legal scholars stressed the constitutional inadmissibility of holding foreign peoples. In 1906, Johns Hopkins political scientist Horace Flack published an 88-page journal article assessing the legality of the US intervention in Cuba, weighing the justifications provided by the McKinley administration against international and US law, the Constitution, and the evidence. In careful, dispassionate prose, Flack concluded that Americans had flouted neutrality laws prior to the declaration of war, that the *Maine* explosion should have been investigated by an impartial tribunal, that the Cuban situation threatened neither US national security nor American lives or property, and that the Spanish government took considerable pains to diffuse the approaching conflict and meet US demands. He then turned to the humanitarian justifications that had proven so effective in gaining public assent for intervention. Writing in an era that held only embryonic notions of international responsibility towards a state's abuse of its own citizenry, and that possessed no independent international organizations with which to adjudicate such matters, Flack found that interventions by individual states on purportedly moral grounds are rife for exploitation. In fact, the very case he assessed provided a handy example. "It could be claimed that [US intervention] was moral," he conceded, "*were* there no questions of self-interest involved" (emphasis in original). He concluded that the war could not be justified under any criteria, and that the objective of *Cuba libre* could very well have been obtained through diplomatic means rather than arms. Altruistic sentiment – the liberal internationalists' justification and the realists' blight – took a back seat in this account; rather, Flack found that economic and strategic aspirations guided America's Cuba policy before, during, and after the conflict. Shortly after the publication of this article, historian Elbert Benton came to nearly identical conclusions in a book-length enquiry, though he found that the Cubans' lack of governmental experience meant that the Platt Amendment, at least, was "not unjust."[11]

Initially, American supporters of a war for expansion abounded as well; in fact, dissenters remained in the minority, as measured by postwar congressional approval of territorial acquisitions, the overall tenor of newspaper coverage, and McKinley's victory in the 1900 federal election, where the imperial question loomed large. However, war proponents faced the burden of squaring their nation's anti-imperial ideal with its postwar acquisition of overseas property, and to do so they adopted a number of interpretive strategies. "Saving the appearances" in this instance could involve simply denying or downplaying the imperial nature of US involvement, and stressing instead that altruistic motives provided the prevailing inspiration for intervention, a tack that carried additional complications. For one, such a defence was based mainly on assessments of US actions towards Cuba, certainly the fuse of the conflict, but just one of the theatres of engagement once the war was underway. Cuba did indeed undergo a transformation from colony to nation as a result of the war, while the citizens of Puerto Rico, Guam, and the Philippines simply witnessed a changing of the imperial guard. Second, Cuba's "independence" was restricted profoundly by the rights of US intervention guaranteed by the Platt Amendment, presented to the Cubans in 1902 as a condition of US withdrawal from the island. War supporters attempted to reconcile Cuba's undeniable protectorate status by ignoring Platt outright, underselling its impact on Cuban autonomy, or presenting the measure as a prudent and beneficent curative for the irrationality and political immaturity of the Cuban people. "There was no 'public,' in the Anglo-Saxon sense, educated and fit for self-government," argued John Truslow Adams (writing, paradoxically, in the midst of a war against Nazism and its racial essentialisms), "but there were plenty of the unfortunate type of South Americans who take naturally to political agitation and insurrection." Other war supporters simply conflated the attitudes of the American people towards the conflict with those of their nation's leaders. The former did indeed view the war in highly idealist hues, as a blow against foreign tyranny in keeping with the dearest values of the nation. The latter had long considered Cuba, less than 150 kilometers from American shores, a "natural" extension of US territory, and according to war critics, employed the discourses of self-determination, "*Cuba libre!*," and altruism in service of less magnanimous objectives.[12]

Still other war defenders contended that overseas empire was simply "accidental," that American leaders stumbled into war, then stumbled upon territory whose inhabitants, once again, were unfit for self-rule. McKinley himself maintained that he had no desire to take the Philippines, and "when they came to us, as a gift from the gods, I did not know what to do with them." Felix Adler, founder of the secular-humanist Society for Ethical Culture, initially declined a request to join the Anti-Imperialist League by arguing that while he was "strenuously and unalterably opposed" to imperialism, the fact that the United States now found itself with foreign charges instilled a feeling "that the civilized races have certain duties toward the backward races ..." As we have seen, a long line of observers depicted the conflict as an irrational, unintended, and/or uncharacteristic episode in US history, one that was thrust upon an unwitting nation. "This escape hatch is familiar," countered war critic Walter LaFeber. "In Samuel Flagg Bemis's seminal text on American diplomatic history [published in 1938] ... the grand story of American expansion rolls along until the narrative encounters 1898. Bemis could handle the next thirteen years only by calling them an 'aberration.'"[13] (Nor does the "accidental" thesis sit well with McKinley's decision to press for annexation of the Hawaiian Islands shortly after his inauguration in 1897. Overseas expansion, it would appear, was neither anathema nor *terra incognita* to the president.)

Other war defenders, led by Theodore Roosevelt, naval historian Alfred Thayer Mahan, and economic historian Brooks Adams, counselled a less puritanical observation of America's traditional anti-imperial creed, arguing that the nation would never achieve its destiny as a global leader unless it adopted the tactics of other Great Powers (what came to be known as America's "large policy"). Moreover, in assuming leadership over the peoples of their newly acquired territories, defenders of the large policy held that the United States would implement a singularly enlightened and benevolent – that is, an "exceptional" – colonial regime. American administrators would dedicate themselves, to degrees unmatched in imperial history, to the betterment of subject peoples through the establishment of "universal" liberal institutions and the grooming of their wards for self-government. In this view, imperial acquisition was not a deviation from US ideals, but a logical extension of the nation's Providential mandate to lead and uplift. US Army General and large policy supporter James Harrison Wilson offered one of the more comprehensive justifications for seizing foreign lands, counselling, "let us take this course because it is noble and just and right, and besides because it will pay."[14]

On the whole, however, the War of 1898's imperial aura proved contentious and vexing. It served as the primary basis of war opposition, while war supporters were required to close their eyes to imperial realities, emphasize the haphazard nature of territorial expansion, point to the exceptional qualities of American governance, or propose important modifications to national values. And by 1902, noted David Hendrickson in his recent and exhaustive account of the debates over US foreign policy, popular opinion soured on the war and the wider imperial project. "In the disappointments of the Philippines and the rousing popular opposition to England's fight against the Boers in South Africa," he observed, "imperialism was discredited."[15]

Anglo-Canadians' accommodations of "England's fight" were less varied, with few voices offering disparaging words for their nation's participation. In fact, the closing years of the nineteenth century found the Dominion swept up in an empire-wide surge of Britannic jingoism, a sentiment encouraged by the "new" imperialism's competition for colonies, the scientific racism that measured national and racial progress according to the extent of one's colonial holdings, and the diamond jubilee of Queen Victoria's reign. "They were proud," notes Phillip Buckner of the era's English Canadians, "to see large parts of the map of the world painted red" – an attitude that, at the very least, pardoned the wars of conquest that had reddened the globe. Some in Canada pushed for formal imperial federation or even envisioned their nation taking over as the centre of empire, a goal that meaningful contribution to imperial defence would only enhance. Local and regional

" EXPANSION."

The water-cure method of extorting from Uncle Sam the confession that an Empire is better than a Republic.

3.1 In this 1902 cartoon from the Progressive Chicago newspaper *The Public*, President Theodore Roosevelt and other "imp-ish" members of his administration force Uncle Sam to expand via the "water cure," a gruesome method of torture deployed by American forces against Filipino insurgents. Such tactics provoked public outrage, Senate hearings, and numerous courts-martial, along with a widespread feeling that America's "large policy" was undermining the nation's special calling. (*The Public*, 31 January 1902.)

historical societies proliferated throughout *fin-de-siècle* Ontario, with their members paying particular attention to preserving – and often embroidering – the story of the War of 1812 and the heroism of such figures as Sir Isaac Brock and Laura Secord. Such commemorative efforts fed Canada's so-called militia myth, the post-1812 idea that untrained but sturdy Canadian farmers and frontiersmen made for superior soldiers. Accordingly, Canadian entry into the conflict was endorsed heartily in the press and pulpit on grounds that stressed the nation's duty to empire, along with the liberal principles that allegedly motivated British intervention. To the editors of the *Canadian Military*

Gazette, the rationale for Canadian participation was plain: "insult the mother ... [and] you must settle with the sons." (Many Canadians trusted that such resolve would also ensure the corollary: that insults to the sons would rouse the mother.) And like Theodore Roosevelt and other pro-imperialist Americans, Canadian imperialists maintained that war would also reinvigorate "martial values" in a citizenry softened by wealth and leisure.[16]

Journalist and historian Goldwin Smith brought a British tradition of anti-imperial liberalism when he immigrated to Canada in 1871 at the age of 48, but when the South African War broke out, he found maddeningly few English Canadian sympathizers. Smith considered the imperial connection the primary motivation not only for anglophiles' support, but for that of the Liberal government as well. "The Canadian government under Sir Wilfrid Laurier," he explained to an American friend (in an analysis that undervalued considerably the challenge of governing the "two solitudes") "is a mere sycophant of the Tory and Imperialist government of England." On Canada's west coast, meanwhile, distance from, and disdain for, the national government compelled citizens to focus almost solely on the imperial connection, using war support to corroborate the claim that they were Britons rather than Canadians. Editorial support for the war from British Columbia publications was so impassioned that the *Nelson Reader* was led to comment, "one would think it was B. C. that was at war with the Boers, and not the British Empire."[17]

Like later historians summarizing Canada's role in the war, contemporary observers avoided impartial evaluations of its causes, conduct, and aims. Canada's first self-described "history" of the South African War, T.G. Marquis's *Canada's Sons on Kopje and Veldt*, was in fact a contemporaneous account written before the conflict was a year old. Marquis employed official military and governmental reports, as well as correspondence from Canadian soldiers, in an unabashed hagiography to his nation's contribution. The soldiers were "heroically fighting the Empire's battles," while the letters they wrote demonstrated a virility, singleness of purpose, and courage that characterized romantic, Victorian notions of honour. "Manly letters these!" Marquis exclaimed. "No boasting; all showing that the soldiers realized the awfulness of war but with no thought of leaving the field till the work they had volunteered to do was accomplished." Presbyterian minister and Queen's University principal George Munro Grant provided an introduction to the work, one that made plain the reverend's commitment to empire, race, and "muscular Christianity" – the Victorian-age belief. that male athletic endeavour fostered Christian morality, and furnished young men with the vigour required to defend and extend "civilization" (read: "the empire"). Though Grant conceded that the war did not imperil Canada any more than if it "had broken out in Saturn," nonetheless, "an electric current flashed across the Continent, from Halifax to Victoria, thrilling all English-speaking hearts at any rate, and a cry went up that the war was Canada's as well as England's." And while the response demonstrated Canada's unequivocal commitment to "the Empire ... freedom, [and] equality for all white men," it proved also that "we are henceforth a nation ... one that will require military build-up in order to defend itself."[18]

Grant's reference to the rapture experienced by "English-speaking hearts" hints at the linguistic divisions exposed and broadened by the Laurier government's decision to commit troops to the conflict, a theme underdeveloped in Marquis's subsequent handling of the story. The omission of domestic politics was rectified to a degree in W. Sanford Evans's *The Canadian Contingents and Canadian Imperialism: A Story and a Study* (1901). Evans was an educator and journalist who in 1893 founded the Canadian Club, a non-partisan, non-sectarian organization dedicated to promoting Canadian nationalism, and the largest of many clubs dedicated to the same goal around the turn of the century. Evans lauded Canada's participation in the South African War as an act of a maturing nation, though a nation that remained British in character and allegiance. For this reason, and like Grant, Evans saw no contradiction between loyalty to Canada and the empire; the British traditions, wrote the latter, "are the only common national traditions."[19]

From the outset, then, the war could be employed to advance decidedly partisan ends: that Britishness constituted Canada's sole and rightful identity, that loyal Canadians supported involvement in South Africa, and that francophones lay on the losing side of both the participation debate and history itself. Just as important, and in stark contrast to American debates over the War of 1898, these accounts made it clear that Canadians need not fret over the imperial character of the campaign. For these authors, "empire" was a concept that invoked honour rather than discomfort. The tales of valour in the Transvaal conveyed by Marquis and Evans thus spoke to and enhanced a renewed commitment to militarism and empire among the era's English Canadians. Indeed, the war would launch a *pro*-imperialist league: the Federation of the Daughters of the Empire (later the Imperial Order Daughters of

Empire), founded in 1900 midst the patriotic zeal that seized much of English Canada during the conflict. As Katie Pickles explained, to this organization, "Canada was to become a nation through conformity to a grand narrative, the contents of which were to be based upon British democracy and constitutional monarchy [and] the Christian myths and saintly symbols of the British Isles."[20]

French Canadians were as estranged from such an organization as they were from the South African conflict itself. While leading Quebec clerics pledged support for the war in hopes of forestalling charges of disloyalty and maintaining a productive relationship with Ottawa, many francophones considered the Canadian contribution an act of colonial servility and a dangerous precedent. Quebec MP Henri Bourassa emerged as the spokesperson for the latter, condemning the war in parliamentary debates and his 1902 book *Great Britain and Canada*. Holding that Confederation was intended as a French-English alliance of equals, Bourassa pointed out that francophones "do not ask that our English-speaking fellow countrymen should help us to draw closer to France; but on the other hand, they have no right to take advantage of their overwhelming majority to infringe on the treaty of alliance, and induce us to assume, however freely and spontaneously, additional burdens in defence of Great Britain." Such musings, along with later opposition to conscription in the Great War, led anglophiles to label Bourassa a traitor and lunatic. A mid-twentieth-century study of his thinking summed up the response from the English language press: Here was "Bourassa the Dirty, fomenter of strife, breeder of rebellion, hater of all things British, cowardly misrepresenter of facts, journalistic snake in the grass." Anti-French sentiment was so intense in English Canada during the South African War that even Governor General (and Briton) Lord Minto expressed unease. In a letter to his brother in England, he observed: "French Canada does not wish to be mixed up in Imperial Wars and is lukewarm, but at home apparently you do not call a man disloyal if he disapproves of the war – here if he is only lukewarm and is French Canadian he must be a rebel."[21]

As the war descended into a horrendous stalemate and atrocities by both sides entered the public record, the grandeur of the "civilizing" mission became harder to endorse. While observers from Britain assailed their nation's conduct with vehemence, their English Canadian counterparts, prey to what Desmond Morton called "a naive military enthusiasm," generally did not. This despite the fact that accounts of the bitter realities of the battle found their way across the Atlantic; as

Goldwin Smith wrote in November 1901 to New Yorker Edward W. Ordway of the Anti-Imperialist League, "the atrocities of the South African War are, I think, beginning to toll on Imperialist sentiment here." In a parliamentary speech from the same year, Bourassa catalogued some of the more repellent aspects of British campaign and its effects on the region's women and children, and called for a negotiated settlement to the conflict. But rather than spark a movement against the war and a broader public re-examination of Canada's obligation to imperial defence, English-Canadians responded to the revelations with relative silence. Smith's slim 1902 publication on Canada and the war entitled *In the Court of History: An Apology of Canadians Opposed to the Boer War*, puzzled over the disparities between the British and Canadian responses. In Britain, he correctly noted, opposition to war was widespread and influential, shaping election debates, parliamentary inquiries, and press coverage, with outrage over the war's conduct helping to restrain the British military's "sanguinary excesses" and push officials towards a diplomatic solution. "But Canada, on the other hand," he continued, "has been simply swept in the train of the dominant part in the Imperial country. In our Parliament free speech has been drowned in clamour. Our public press almost universally has been a transcript of the jingo press of England. Thus the main facts of the case have never been allowed to come before the Canadian people."[22] Anglo-Canadians, it seemed, were more unrepentant imperialists than Britons.

What was true in Smith's day remained the case for much of the twentieth century. A war that did little to bolster the reputation of imperial forces was, it appears, best left to languish in the historical record and the public imagination. The jingoistic Canadian poems and songs that proliferated in the early days of the war were soon forgotten. Canada's role in the victory at the Battle of Paardeberg – the Vimy Ridge of its day for early century Canadians – had little lasting impact on public school curricula, war commemorations, or (until 2009) citizenship manuals. War memorials proliferated in communities across the country in the years immediately following the conflict, but unlike those commemorating subsequent wars, the unveiling of monuments dried up rapidly within a decade. South African War memorials do not form the backdrop of Remembrance Day ceremonies, where the conflict is rarely invoked by name. Historians could not avoid the war altogether, but focused almost exclusively on constitutional questions raised by Britain's request that Canada provide troops, to wider questions of Canadian sovereignty and identity, and to the parliamentary debates which served to fracture the government and the citizenry, along regional and linguistic lines. Left unaddressed were questions about the war's causes and conduct, matters that could cast aspersions on both nation and empire.[23]

Canadians' support for the war simply reinforced Goldwin Smith's conviction that his fellow citizens would overcome their puerile attachments to the empire, and thereby attain political adulthood through political union with their republican – and more authentically liberal – neighbour. Smith missed the mark, however, in several important respects. First, English Canada was not as unified in its backing of the war as he, and many later observers, presumed. A variety of individuals and organizations opposed the conflict on anti-imperial and/or pacifist grounds, including farm and labour groups, traditional peace churches, dissenting clergy and congregants from mainline Protestant congregations, citizens of German and Irish descent, and the Woman's Christian Temperance Union. Moreover, wrote Carman Miller, a "large amorphous body of English-Canada opinion, almost entirely ignored by historians of the war ... adopted a more tentative position" than either war supporters or foes.[24] Yet Smith could be forgiven for failing to appreciate the full volume of this combination of dissent and apathy, as organizations dominated by ethnic minorities, women, and labour generally experienced difficulty in making their voices heard. When contrasted with the industrialists, ex-presidents, senators, and lawyers who led the anti-imperial charge in the United States, Canadian opponents of empire suffered a glaring scarcity of political capital, not to mention sheer numbers. Smith also erred in suggesting that a North American union would rid Canada of the curse of empire. By this point, the Americans were wrestling with the imperial question to degrees unprecedented in their history – and sometimes arriving at very illiberal answers.

The advent of the First World War only added fuel to an already combustible American debate on the matter of empire. The initial US decision to opt out of the conflict rested on a number of factors, including the tradition of isolationism from European affairs, the multiethnic makeup of the American population, the commercial advantages of neutrality, and in the war's early stages, indignation over violations of that neutrality committed by *both* sides in the conflict. The US commitment to anti-imperialism also played a decisive role. To war critics like labour leader Eugene Debs and Republican senators Robert La Follette and George Norris, the battle in Europe was fundamentally a

3.2 British-born historian and journalist Goldwin Smith, pictured here some time before his permanent relocation to North America in 1868, believed Canadians would transcend their fatuous zeal for empire through formal union with their republican neighbours. To later critics of Canada's subservience to US foreign policy like James Minifie and John Warnock, NATO and NORAD served to fulfil a portion of that vision, although certainly not the anti-imperialist bit. (LC-BH82–4719B, Library of Congress Prints and Photographs Division, Washington, DC.)

clash of morally equivalent, predatory empires, an interpretation in keeping with traditional American perceptions of European societies as decadent, rapacious, and addicted to violence. Great Britain, La Follette pointed out in the debate over US entry, was "a hereditary monarchy, with a hereditary ruler, with a hereditary House of Lords, with a hereditary landed system, with a limited and restricted suffrage for one class and a multiple suffrage power for another ..." The Women's Peace Party, created in 1915 under the direction of Jane Addams and fellow women's rights activist Cary Chapman Catt, argued that a world free of warfare rested on the termination of colonial regimes, along with disarmament and the establishment of a global peacekeeping organization.[25]

Even those Americans who discerned moral discrepancies between the belligerents, including the pro-British Woodrow Wilson himself, held colonial rivalries responsible for much of the tension that had produced war. Prior to US entry, Wilson spoke sardonically of "England's having the Earth and Germany's wanting it." After joining, Wilson made the attenuation of colonial rule and the wider principle of self-government central to his war aims – an ode to domestic opinion, his own convictions, and less publically, the commercial advantages of open door trading networks. The sense of moral superiority begat by the nation's republican heritage precluded an official alliance with Imperial Britain and France; instead, the United States would participate as an "Auxiliary Power," a mostly semantic distinction that presented a nation somehow embroiled in and simultaneously above the fray, positioned to arbitrate the war's conclusion in accordance with American values. The Wilson administration's commitment to anti-imperialism involved serious contradictions, including the contemporaneous US military engagements in a half-dozen Latin American countries (another reason Wilson was at first reluctant to commit an already-busy US Army to Europe), and the president's own and particularly keen racism, which led him to doubt the capacity for self-government among non-white peoples.[26] Nonetheless, Wilson's Fourteen Points included a commitment to the "absolutely impartial adjustment of all colonial claims"; of all the points, this one most clearly aligned with US ideals, and provided Americans with a *casus belli* that reaffirmed their nation's essential rectitude and fitness for global leadership.

Wilson's idealistic call for widespread decolonization fell well short of its goal. While the map of Europe was redrawn in an effort to align national boundaries with ethnic makeup, the former colonies of defeated powers were transferred to the victors under the auspices of League of Nations "mandates," and the vast colonial holdings of victorious powers left intact. This bending to old-world status quo served as a fundamental, though often underappreciated, source of the US refusal to join the League of Nations. League opponents are generally, and often rightly, presented as devotees of American exceptionalism and isolationism who chafed at the prospects of placing US troops under foreign command and relinquishing the congressional prerogative to declare war; however, Wilson's domestic foes also expressed a principled commitment to republican ethics. La Follette, who voted against US participation in the League, held that the "peacemakers" at Versailles had "locked the chains on the subject peoples of Ireland, Egypt, and India." Fellow progressive Republican William Borah argued that the League's commitment to safeguarding its members' territory meant the United States would be committed to the tawdry task of defending Britain's global empire, a charge echoed with especial resentment by Irish-Americans. The mulish persistence of imperialism following a war the nation had entered in order to enshrine US-style liberalism on a global scale only augmented the sense (bolstered by revelations of British propaganda and stateside profiteering, as well as the seeming vindictiveness of the peace) that American blood had been shed in vain. "Of all the great disillusionments in American history," David Hendrickson wrote, "the crushed hopes of a liberal peace may take first prize in depth and suddenness." Thus viewing their most significant contribution to matters of international war and peace in a decidedly negative light, the militaristic impulse lost considerable ground among Americans.[27]

In Canada, the imperial question provided clarity, rather than ambiguity, to the issue of Canadian Great War participation. Lacking its own foreign policymaking apparatus, and obliged to defend the British Empire by virtue of its Dominion status, the Canadian government's only decision involved the extent to which the country would participate. Even the boundaries between the British and Canadian militaries were blurred: a 1907 Imperial Conference determined that Britain and the dominions "would adopt the same organization, tactics, and training so that, in time of war, the armies could be easily integrated"; as a result, Canadian soldiers trained in Britain, and British officers took positions in the Canadian military. When war came, the Canadian Expeditionary Force was classified as an "Imperial" contingent operating under the auspicious of Britain's Army Act, and until 1917, commanded by a British officer.[28]

While the legal status of Canada vis-à-vis the European conflict was beyond doubt, this did not in itself guarantee public assent for the cause. On this, the Conservative government of Robert Borden may have harboured concern, as in the decade that followed the conclusion of the South African War, some Canadians began to question whether the price of empire was commensurate with its rewards. The settlement of the Alaska Boundary Dispute, which saw Britain sacrifice Canadian interests in the name of concord with the United States, proved a rallying point for critics of empire. Toronto lawyer John S. Ewart argued in a series of books that the settlement, coming just a year after Canadian forces returned from their service to the metropole in South Africa, demonstrated that an independent Canada could fare no worse in the international arena than it had under the "shelter" of a scandalously indifferent Britain. Yet when war came in 1914, these hesitations were largely jettisoned; Donald Creighton hardly exaggerated in claiming that "Canada entered the war with almost unbelievable unanimity." For a conflict that posed no direct threat to Canadian soil, the vigorous pro-war sentiment – what Tim Cook called "an orgy of military pageantry" – owed largely to the nation's connection to, and abiding affection for, Britain. Canadian First War veteran D.E. Macintyre recalled that "nobody stopped to debate the causes of the war, or who was responsible for it; all we cared about was that Britain was at war with the most powerful and efficient army in the world and needed help." Indeed, 64 per cent of those who volunteered for the First Canadian contingent were British-born, a testament to the influx of British immigrants in preceding decades, and to their continuing allegiance to the land of their birth.[29]

Prime Minister Robert Borden made clear Canada's war aims and the synchronicity between nation and empire in his 18 August address to a hastily summoned Parliament, promising that Canadians "will be united in a common resolve to put forward every effort and make every sacrifice necessary to ensure the integrity and maintain the honour of our Empire." On the eve of war, the editors at Montreal's English-language *Daily Star* likewise made no distinction between the identities of Britons and Canadians, writing that if England loses, "*we* will pass finally from the roster of great nations, and our Empire will become one of the defaced mileposts which mark the tragic road by which the human race has journeyed" (emphasis added). Later defenders of the righteousness of the cause would emphasize the violation of Belgian neutrality, the rapaciousness of German militarism, and the wider threat that nation posed to the international liberal order, but to Canadians of the day, the majority of whom were born in Britain or of British ancestry, the fact that the empire was imperilled provided the overarching justification for participation. As historian O.D. Skelton reported in his survey of Canadian history published shortly after the war, the nation's initial enthusiasm for the war arose out of "deep and abiding sympathy with the mother country," a sympathy even a liberal nationalist like Skelton clearly shared. Only later, as a result of (sometimes embellished) revelations of Germany's "callous and ruthless policies," continued Skelton, "Canada comprehended the magnitude of the danger threatening all the world."[30]

Given this widespread public endorsement of the empire, it is not surprising that the role of European imperialism in general, and of British policy in particular, in the spurring the conflict has received far less attention in Canada than the United States. Canadian historians like Skelton, and later J.M.S Careless, simply blamed Germany's expansionism, militarism, depravity, and tyranny; other writers began with Franz Ferdinand's assassination and provided a mechanistic description of the immediate steps to war; some provided broader contextual background while depicting a Britain removed from the quarrels of the continent and struggling alone and in vain to prevent the catastrophe; still others began with the Canadian reaction to a conflict already underway. In recent decades, a few Canadian First War accounts began to take a longer, and less partisan, view of war origins. Britain, too, bore some blame for the war, having contributed to "the intrigues of European diplomacy," wrote Granatstein et al. in 1983. Tim Cook's *At the Sharp End* (2007) placed British expansionism, as well as its arms build-up, front and centre in contextualizing August 1914. Recently, Andrew Iarocci also pointed to the "expensive maritime arms race" conducted by Britain and Germany in their quest for dominance. Such nods to a more generalized European will to duplicity, violence, and expansionism remained a staple of US war accounts throughout the twentieth century, a fact not lost on tory Donald Creighton: in reviewing US objections to the Peace of Versailles and the mandate system which brought additional overseas holdings under British control, Creighton sighed over Americans' "ingrained suspicion of the sinister power of British imperialism."[31]

In the interwar years, few Americans would have taken offence to Creighton's characterization. In fact, anger over British embellishments and outright inventions of German atrocities in Belgium, and over the British blockade of Germany which led to German attacks on American merchant ships, contributed to a 1920s campaign to purge the alleged pro-British bias plaguing US schoolbooks. The general anti-imperial aura bolstered the postwar standing of proponents of Progressive or "New" History. Richard Hofstadter, a mid-century historian whose education in the 1930s coincided with the high point of Progressive influence on the field, wrote that these scholars "gave us the pivotal ideas of the first half of the twentieth century. It was they who seemed to be able to make American history relevant to the political and intellectual issues of the moment." Although the Progressive school's seminal text, Frederick Jackson Turner's "frontier thesis," famously viewed expansion as the source of American distinctiveness and success, later practitioners conditioned by the perceived excesses of American expansion and their revulsion towards the Great War generated strong disavowals of empire. What unified all of the interpretations, Hofstadter explained, was the belief that "economic and political conflict" formed history's central trope, an approach that served as a radical departure from more conservative, consensual, and statist models of history.[32] Here, for instance, is Parrington's laconic encapsulation of the American story:

> From the first we have been divided into two main parties ... On one side has been the party of the current aristocracy – of church, of gentry, of merchant, of slave holder, or manufacturer – and on the other the party of the commonality – of farmer, villager, small tradesman, mechanic, proletariat. The one has persistently sought to check and limit the popular power, to keep control of the government in the hands of the few in order to serve special interests, whereas the other has sought to augment the popular power, to make government more responsible to the will of the majority, to further the democratic rather than the republican ideal – let one discover this and new light is shed on our cultural tendencies.[33]

Beard's *The Rise of American Civilization*, the highly regarded, best-selling survey co-authored with his wife Mary Ritter Beard, is representative of this outlook. Unlike many of their pre-First World War colleagues, the Beards depicted the War of 1898 not as a deviation in the American plotline, but a continuation of an imperial arc begun by the nation's economic elites prior to the Civil War (and made explicit in the Monroe Doctrine and the idea of Manifest Destiny). Culpability for the Great War, meanwhile, was here shared by the Great Powers; those asserting only German malfeasance told a "story for babes." US participation, initially defended by Charles Beard in 1917, was now cast as a folly driven to a significant extent by advocates of the open door policy, a policy which would also guarantee future conflicts with other imperial powers. And though the authors clearly disapproved, the fact that this imperial course had marked American foreign policy for nearly a century at the time of writing, and that the public had endorsed pro-expansionist presidential candidates at the polls from McKinley onwards, gave their chapter on imperialism an air of resignation. The 1898 imperial turn in US foreign policy, they wrote, "evoked some discontent among old-fashioned Americans."[34] However, these principled "old-fashioned Americans" were confronting a powerful cultural tide: "As a matter of record," the Beards argued,

> Anglo-Saxons seldom looked upon imperial conquests so simply and so harshly as Roman and German philosophers; according to their cosmic view, there were always ethical elements to be taken into account ... the poet Kipling voiced the same spirit in his lines celebrating the imperial call as a solemn command to take up the White Man's burden, to seek another's profit and work another's gain, a flame communicated to the American branch of the race.[35]

As he confided to fellow historian Arthur Schlesinger, Charles Beard's own contempt for "the burden" went back at least to his days as a graduate student. "I left the G.O.P. on imperialism in 1900," he recalled, "and have found no home anywhere since that year." While America's imperialist inclinations provided the focus of just one chapter in the Beards' sweeping chronicle of their nation's history, other historians of the interwar period attacked European militarism and colonialism with renewed vigour, while also demonstrating unprecedented negativity towards past and ongoing US imperialism in Latin America and Asia, and towards the violence rooted in the nation's nineteenth-century westward expansion. The reinvigoration of US anti-imperial ideals had tangible effect: the Neutrality Acts of the mid-1930s signalled both a general reprimand of American participation in the First World War and a rejection of future sacrifice in support of European empires; in Latin America, Franklin Roosevelt's "Good Neighbor Policy" led, by 1940, to the removal of every US marine and the annulment of treaties sanctioning American intervention.[36]

In Canada, too, the interwar years witnessed something of a reexamination of the nation's relationship with empire, as questions raised somewhat timidly after the affair in South Africa now received a more candid ventilation. On the one hand, these conflicts required Canadians to confront the price of empire; on the other, the immense sacrifices made in defence of Great War Allies led to a widespread feeling that

Canadians had earned a greater measure of sovereignty. Petitioning along these lines emerged in the midst of the Great War itself, and led to the 1917 transfer of command of the CEF from a British to a Canadian officer and Britain's acquiescence to the Dominions' demands for greater input into Allied decision making. Following the war, all serious talk among Canadians of imperial federation ceased, and the desire for greater autonomy led Canada and the other Dominions to petition successfully for independent status in the newly formed League of Nations (a move that rankled Americans, who feared imperial affections would produce a monolithic pro-British voting bloc).[37] In 1931, the Statue of Westminster granted Canada its own voice in international affairs. A war entered in defence of empire was now widely touted as Canada's war of independence.

Greater autonomy from Britain also permitted (and necessitated) closer ties to the old loyalist bogey, the United States. Fighting alongside that nation for the first time softened anti-Americanism that had nourished a good deal of English-Canada's unwavering loyalty to Britain. After the American entry, Canadian Minister of Finance Thomas White, whose fidelity to empire stimulated his opposition to a reciprocity treaty with the United States in 1911, reflected the changing mood in a letter to US Treasury Secretary W.G. McAdoo. While acknowledging some past traumas in the bilateral relationship, White contended that "in our attitude towards constitutional liberty and all social problems our people are very much alike and understand each other better I think than any other two peoples in the world today. The struggle in a common cause will I am sure greatly cement our friendship and respect for one another." Following the war, frustrations with the violence seemingly endemic to European society led both nations to adopt a more isolationist, and continentalist, bearing. Continentalism touched the academy as well, with greater percentages of Canadian scholars looking to the United States, rather than Britain alone, to pursue graduate degrees, and organizations like the Carnegie Foundation providing funding to scholarship endorsing the idea "that North American history was the story of partnership emerging from confrontation."[38]

However, care should be taken not to drive the autonomy thesis too far. The treatment of those who questioned the practice of following Britain into past and potentially future conflicts reveals the limits of Canadians' sense of independence from Britain in the years between the wars. University of Toronto professor Frank Underhill, a historian inclined to see the history of Canada in North American rather than

3.3 English Canadians expressed some qualms about the British tie in the wake of the Great War; French Canadians were considerably more forthright. When Union government solicitor general and conscription advocate Arthur Meighen ran for prime minister in 1925, the Quebec daily *Le Soleil* reminded readers of his (apparently breezy) willingness to sacrifice his countrymen to the imperialist brute. ("The Trafficker in Human Flesh," *Le Soleil*, 29 October 1925. Source: "The Prime Ministers of Canada," http://www.prime-ministers. ca/meighen/bio_1.php, accessed 1 February 2014.)

merely British terms, held a particularly low view of the imperialism and
Canada's obligation to defend the British variant. Underhill called the
League of Nations "a society of retired burglars defending the principle
of property," and in the mid-1930s, went so far as to suggest to his students that both Britain and Germany bore responsibility for the advent
of the First World War. Modern Canada must, Underhill insisted, make
it clear "to the world, and especially to Great Britain, that the poppies
blooming in Flanders fields have no further interest for us." For utter-
ing such heresies, Ontario's Liberal Premier Mitchell Hepburn threatened to introduce legislation in 1939 to fire Underhill, a move endorsed
lustily in the Ontario press and by Conservative opposition leader
George Drew.[39]

Underhill may well have known what he was in for. As he observed
in a 1933 article on Goldwin Smith, Smith's adopted city of Toronto –
the North American nirvana for members of the Protestant, royalist
Orange Order – was not the happiest place for a friend of republicanism or the United States. Nor did the University of Toronto provide
refuge for a liberal nationalist like Underhill, as evidenced by vigorous attempts by the board of governors to convince Underhill to quietly resign, and by the university library's cancelled subscription to
the US-based *New Republic* following an article critical of the British
royals. On observing Underhill's rough treatment, fellow Canadian
historian Arthur Lower offered a succinct observation from Winnipeg,
writing to Underhill, "you would be much happier in another city."
Yet by the mid-1930s, as Europe appeared to be girding for another
war, Lower conceded privately to Underhill that the "Imperialistic
wolf-hounds" were also "baying to high heaven out here." Indeed, in
1938, the editor of a University of Saskatchewan student newspaper
was sacked for printing an article which stressed the futility of the
First World War slaughter; meanwhile, a media frenzy greeted Carlyle
King, an English professor at the same institution (and former under-
graduate student of Underhill's at Saskatchewan), after his admonition against Canada's participation in another war to defend British
possessions. Such challenges to imperialism, Britain, and the First
World War – exceedingly mild when placed alongside American estimations of the same issues – generated accusations of sedition from
purportedly "autonomous" Canadians. In the end, the imperialists
carried the day, as both Underhill and King pledged to cease all public
statements about international affairs in exchange for retaining their
university appointments.[40]

Carlyle King's concerns over Canada's fate in the next war were no mere abstractions. Like many observers of global affairs in the thirties, he perceived imminent danger in Europe. (In Asia, meanwhile, a conflict simmering between Japan and China since 1931 had escalated dramatically in 1937.) The September 1939 outbreak of war in Europe would raise further questions about the nature and extent of the autonomy supposedly gained by Canadians at Vimy, as Parliament offered little resistance to once again following Britain into war. Wrote Philip Buckner, "the decision – taken virtually automatically and without substantial opposition in English Canada – to enter the Second World War, revealed how deeply English-speaking Canadians felt about their British heritage and their commitment to the mother country." This is not to deny that humanitarian ideals were at stake in more visible ways in 1939 than in 1914, or that the nature of the regimes that launched a war of aggression was reprehensible – facts presented forcefully by war supporters. In addition to reprising the claim that a victorious Germany would ultimately seize Canada, Parliamentarians endorsing intervention pointed to the dire and undeniable threat to democracy and international law posed by Nazism, and maintained that both Britain *and* France sustained values and institutions dear to Canadians.[41]

Still, the arguments presented before Parliament endorsing a full commitment to the Second World War effort echoed many of the imperial themes that inspired a Canadian commitment to the First, and indeed, to the South African War. Whether by design or circumstance – and though there were more pressing matters to discuss – the emergency war session of Parliament commenced with the recitation of a letter from King George VI to the Canadian people following his trip to the Dominion that summer, wherein he thanked his subjects for their hospitality and praised the abundant virtues of the nation. To deny aid to a now-imperilled sovereign following such flattery would strike some members as the epitome of gracelessness. H.S. Hamilton, Liberal Member of Parliament for Algoma, spoke passionately and at some length about the need to defend both France and England (though not Poland, the nation at that moment in direst need), but ended with a paean solely to Britain, to "the things England stands for ... [and] the forms of life she has largely been responsible for bringing into the world." Social Credit leader J.H. Blackmore raised only the threat to Britain and to "the existence of all British peoples," stating, "I believe in the British people, I look with astonishment on their miraculous history ... I cannot escape the conviction, sir, that there is for this people and those associated with them a great mission to perform, a great goal to achieve." Blackmore closed with a statement as true as it was infuriating to the handful of Quebec and CCF representatives who deemed Canadian participation the act of a colonial subordinate: "The King and Queen of Great Britain are Canada's king and queen," he implored. "How can Canadians contemplate with calmness the leaving of those two inadequately protected?"[42]

In the United States, the outbreak of war stirred what historian Arthur M. Schlesinger Jr called "the most savage national debate in my lifetime," one whose venom eclipsed even the abundantly vituperative, subsequent rows over McCarthyism and Vietnam. Opponents of US participation appealed to the tradition of isolationism, the perceived folly of the First World War, and, once again, the alleged moral equivalence of European powers locked in a never-ending contest for continental and global dominance. Even after Hitler's takeover of most of Western Europe, the largest-selling religious serial in the nation, *The Christian Century*, continued to call for neutrality and a negotiated settlement. "Our citizens with virtual unanimity contemplate a Hitler victory with profound apprehension," its editors wrote, "but it does not follow that they contemplate a British victory without grave misgivings as to its effect upon Europe, upon the rest of the world, and upon America's future."[43]

Those who counselled US entry gained increasing public favour after the startling German victories of 1940 and the greater scrutiny of Nazism that accompanied the regime's expansion; here was an abhorrent ideology antithetical to the very foundations of US ideals, one that sought aggressively and openly to repudiate international law and thwart America's economic interests and global mandate to lead. The late Woodrow Wilson, ridiculed since the League debates for his idealism, internationalism, faith in collective security, and general hauteur, underwent a miraculous rehabilitation, at least on the first three counts. US analysts now moved to embrace the necessity of a new world order built on American values and leadership, though they continued to condemn Wilson's failure to sell that vision, a tragic character flaw that helped consign the globe to another episode of unfathomable violence. Though these shifts in opinion were visible before Pearl Harbor, the Japanese attack served to cement them among policymakers and the general public, along with the affiliated truth that vast oceans no longer sheltered the United States from foreign aggression.[44]

Even so, while the idea of moral equivalence of European governments collapsed, the notion that imperialism in general was both

indefensible and an inveterate source of global tensions remained relatively constant among Americans of all political stripes throughout
the war. Before US entry, Roosevelt and Churchill's Atlantic Charter
outlined their blueprint for a world purged of totalitarianism and war,
including a pledge to "respect the right of all peoples to choose the form
of government under which they will live." While Churchill denied that
the clause applied to the British Empire, Roosevelt and the American
people considered it a universal guarantee. *Life* magazine provided
an apt summation of the national mood in an October 1942 editorial,
maintaining that "one thing we are *not* fighting for is to hold the British
Empire together" (emphasis in original). "As the American public saw
things," observed Mary Ann Heiss, "the war was being fought for the
ideas set for in the Atlantic Charter – freedom, self-determination, anti-
colonialism, global cooperation ... On the surface, at least, it seemed
the nation's policy goals were in sync with its anticolonial heritage and
messianic mission to remake the world in its own image." As Roosevelt
proclaimed, "We of this hemisphere have no need to seek a new international order; we have already found it."[45]

Below the surface, however, lay factors which guided US leaders
away from their firm anticolonial stance. Pressing their European
Allies on the issue could harm wartime relations and the economies of nations engaged in a life and death struggle against fascism;
later, as the Axis powers wore down, fears of postwar Soviet expansion encouraged similar hesitance regarding a rapid decolonization
that would both weaken West European powers and create newly-
independent nations vulnerable to Soviet influence. The global fight
against communism, coupled with the fears of another postwar economic depression, also motivated the United States itself to project
its power internationally to degrees unprecedented in its history –
through the wartime seizure of strategically important territory in the
Pacific, and the establishment of the US-led International Monetary
Fund and World Bank; through foreign assistance initiatives like the
Marshall Plan and the Point Four Program of technological assistance to "developing" countries, which required recipients to realign
aspects of their economies in accordance with US demands; through
peacetime military alliances, which contributed to the establishment
of hundreds of US bases in foreign nations; through the continued
pursuit of an "open door" international trading regime, which abetted the global dominance of American products, capital, and culture;
and through military interventions and covert operations aimed at

installing or shoring up US-friendly regimes and undermining leftist governments.[46]

Should this expansion of American influence be called an empire? In the first decades of the Cold War, most Americans were inclined to answer in the negative. In these years, noted cultural historian John Fousek, the US media "generally suggested that the United States stood apart from, and above, the traditions of European imperialism and colonialism." "Even in the African American press," he continued, "European colonialism received scorn and vilification that US foreign policy was largely spared." Similarly, the consensus-school historians and political scientists who came to dominate postwar scholarship – and who chafed at Progressive history's focus on conflict as the "natural" state of American society – tended to view the rapid expansion of US power as a necessary and essentially defensive step to contain a debased and truly imperialistic adversary. Consensus scholars argued that the United States was uniquely suited to guide global affairs because the nation had broken the destructive, Old-World mould of nation-building: America's history, geography, and political institutions, the argument went, yielded a people of singular affluence, equality, social mobility, harmony, and pragmatism, and who therefore had much to offer a world wracked by ideological extremism and endless war. In pointed divergence from Europe, America had no feudal hierarchies to overcome, no record of imperial plunder for which to apologize. (This was particularly true if the image of a certain and potentially unsettling previous conflict could be titivated; thus the timing of Frank Freidel's *Splendid Little War* [1958], which sought to rehabilitate the altruistic interpretation of the turn-of-the-century conflict with Spain.) Above all, these writers stressed the essential unanimity and resilience of Americans' core beliefs across time and space. In his seminal 1948 consensus history *The American Political Tradition*, Richard Hofstadter reviewed a broad range of seemingly dissimilar American political leaders and found a common "ideology of self-help, free enterprise, competition, and beneficent cupidity upon which Americans have been nourished since the foundation of the Republic."[47]

Consensus advocates exhibited less – well – *consensus* on the practicalities of exporting American-style liberalism wholesale. In *The Genius of American Politics*, Daniel Boorstin argued that since that genius had been gestated under "a peculiar and unrepeatable combination of historical circumstances," the United States had "nothing in the line of a theory that can be exported to other peoples of the world." For this reason, he warned, "nothing could be more un-American than to urge other countries to imitate America." The exceptional nation would forever remain so. Daniel Bell's *The End of Ideology: On the Exhaustion of Political Ideas in the Fifties*, on the other hand, suggested that American-style liberal pragmatism formed the terminus of all sincere quests for the good life, a conclusion whose implications for the rest of the globe were rather obvious. Such reasoning helped propel "modernization theory" to the centre of mid-century American foreign assistance programs – with "modern" used interchangeably with "American." As Nils Gilman wrote in his history of the theory, "the language and practice of modernization expressed a confidence that the United States should be a universal model for the world and a sense that the United States had a duty to promote this model." To postcolonial societies retarded by dysfunctional governance, agrarian economies, and an unscientific world view, US academics and officials offered a series of prescriptions to accelerate the "inevitable" but sometimes halting pace of development towards urbanization, industrialism, and free-market liberalism (and away from the ersatz remedies offered by their Cold War adversary).[48]

Democracy sat much lower on this list of priorities, at least in the short term. In their efforts to shepherd the needy into modernity, American officials often demonstrated what Gilman called a "ruthless willingness to apply unrestrained state force," preferring dictatorships that endorsed or tolerated the modernization model over democracies that might choose another path. Intervention in Vietnam was but one of the many unsavory outcomes of the project to remake the globe. The notion of exceptionalism itself was battered by these efforts, as the distinctions between European empire-building and American modernizing became difficult to discern in practice. For Americans associated with the emerging New Left, their nation's traditional proscriptions against imperialism as an invitation to incessant warfare had never been so apt.[49]

By the late 1960s, then, the consensus view had lost much of its sheen. Not only did foreign audiences express hostility to the imposition of "universal" US institutions and values, but postwar Americans also began to challenge the idea that harmony best described their nation's story. The Civil Rights struggle, protests over the Vietnam War, and the politics of identity chipped away at notions of national homogeneity and reinvigorated the importance of conflicts over wealth and power to US history. A new generation of scholars with such leanings began to emerge in the 1960s, reprising many of the themes of Parrington, Beard, et al. However, this was not simply the Progressive school warmed over.

While reasserting the centrality of economics to the understanding of social conflict and change, the so-called New Left historians and their progeny paid increasing attention to the roles of such factors as race, culture, and ideology in contests over power. The evident contradictions between the nation's professed commitment to anti-imperialism and its actions abroad made US foreign policy a particularly fertile field of inquiry.[50]

None of this generation of historians was as influential as William Appleman Williams. Trained at the University of Wisconsin under Progressives Merle Curti and Fred Harvey Harrington, Williams' early work took a second look at Frederick Jackson Turner's frontier thesis. While disagreeing with Turner's proposition that America's economic and democratic vitality required an ever-expanding frontier, Williams argued that *belief* in this fallacy assumed canonical status by the end of the nineteenth century. Thus transformed from "an idea into an ideology," the thesis impelled the territorial acquisitions of 1898 and a wider "open door" policy in areas outside America's traditional sphere of influence. Williams' landmark 1959 study *The Tragedy of American Diplomacy* extended these themes, depicting a nation that, since the 1890s, had pursued a conscious and aggressive imperialistic foreign policy in an effort to ward off domestic conflict and economic disaster. That the policy was unnecessary for economic and social well-being, harmful to both the American character and the outside world, and a repudiation of the ideal of self-determination rendered the history of US foreign affairs "tragic." Williams feared that the story could well take a far more disastrous turn, as he held the open door policy primarily responsible for the Cold War standoff with the Soviet Union, a clash that could precipitate nuclear annihilation.[51]

It is difficult to find a more unflattering interpretation of American foreign policy and *casus belli*, for Williams represented aggressive expansion as a deep-seated national pathology. Not only did he trace the roots of the imperialist desire back to the Founding Fathers themselves, but Williams impugned the citizenry as a whole, rather than merely the nation's elites: The open door policy, he argued "integrated and formalized the frontier thesis, the specific demands of businessmen, workers, and farmers, and the theory which asserted that the American economic system would stagnate if it did not expand overseas."[52] To Williams, the fulcrum on which this project turned, the episode which fully embedded the imperial course in the nation's *weltanschauung*, was the War of 1898. US participation in subsequent wars advanced this

ultimately destructive course, and the 1947 Truman Doctrine institutionalized aggressive expansion of US markets as America's "grand
strategy" throughout the Cold War.

It is difficult, as well, to identify a more influential single work on
US international affairs. *Tragedy* became a bestseller, resulting in two
reprints (1962 and 1972) in which the author refined his views and
responded to critics. He quickly attracted a multitude of disciples, some
emerging from his graduate seminars at Wisconsin and others simply
converted after encountering the book; more than any other figure,
Williams established the legitimacy and vigour of New Left history in
the United States. John Lewis Gaddis, himself an eminent international
relations scholar (though one who disputed *Tragedy's* overall thrust),
called Williams "the most influential diplomatic historian of his generation." In the mid-1970s, following a war in Vietnam that seemed to confirm the centrality of imperialism to US foreign policymaking, Howard
Schonberger commented on the "increasing domination of the historiography of American foreign policy" by acolytes of Williams. Even
twenty-five years after its publication, a *Reviews in American History*
retrospective on the book's impact argued that "few but the narrowest studies of episodes in American foreign relations will be written,
if they are to shine, without an awareness of and an accommodation
to [*Tragedy*]." The post-9/11 reinvigoration of American militarism and
unilateral interventionism generated renewed interest in Williams and
his ideas.[53]

In subsequent decades, scholars inspired by postmodernism, social
constructivism, feminism, and the so-called cultural turn – all of which
interrogate the ways meaning is made, reinforced, and resisted –
further broadened the source of the imperialist drive from the narrow
focus on politics, economics, and interests towards cultural and ideological factors. The significance of race to growing American hegemony
was one of the more consistent themes. Thomas Paterson outlined some
of the effects of racialized thinking on US foreign policy: "First, those
who presume to be superior do not negotiate with those they deem
inferior; diplomacy is thus downgraded, whereas war is elevated as an
instrument of policy. Second, superiors expect to win wars against infe-
riors; so war becomes an attractive method to gain foreign policy objectives and to civilize a retrograde world." Walter Williams stressed the
role of race in the legacy of expansionism by considering US interactions
with Native Americans as a component of international relations; in his
view, the desire to annex the Philippines was simply a continuation of

the relentless expansion of US territory that had marked the nation's nineteenth-century Indian policy. Thus, in the same way that Euro-American continental expansion could not be fully comprehended without the rationalizing discourses of "civilization" versus "savagery," so too the seizure of foreign territory could not be undertaken without some assurances that Anglo-Saxon Americans were confronting beings who were by some important measure "lesser." This long view of US encounters with non-Europeans also dealt a particularly lethal blow to the "imperialism-as-aberration" school, and would be incorporated into subsequent works by a multitude of analysts. Though few writers suggested that ideas of Anglo-Saxon supremacy served as the primary motivation for US empire-building, many agreed that notions of racial and cultural superiority both justified and shaped American relations with foreign peoples. Racialized thinking and the rationalization it provided for America's hegemonic aspirations would undergird analysis of US policymaking in the War of 1898, Wilson's intrusions into Latin America, the decision to drop atomic bombs, the aversion to a negotiated settlement in Korea, and the Vietnam War.[54]

Apprehensions and outright anger over the incremental dismantling of the anti-imperial creed go far in explaining the profound ambivalence some Americans have expressed towards the Second World War. On the one hand, that conflict eliminated the scourge of fascism, and this fact more than anything else put the "good" in the good war; on the other, the devastation of dominant European and Asian powers and the crumbling of their empires allowed the United States to emerge as the globe's dominant actor, a position that postwar policymakers would seek to guard and enhance with considerable fervour. Observers need not share the opinion of William Appleman Williams and Gabriel Kolko that a single-minded drive for markets and resources served as a premeditated and fundamental motive for US participation in the Second World War to grant that the nation emerged from the conflict on an imperial trajectory. The opportunities and "lessons" furnished by the war led directly to renewed interventionism in Latin America, the ousting of uncooperative governments in the Middle East and Africa, a global network of military alliances and bases, and the devastating campaigns in Southeast Asia.

For those predisposed to frowning on manifestations of empire, the Second World War thus became synonymous with the death of a worthy American ideal. Prior to this, argued Andrew Bacevich, most Americans viewed any pretentions towards US global leadership as inherently symbolic, as providing an example to foreign peoples who might wish to emulate those aspects of the American experiment that struck them as both laudable and apposite to their local situation. "With the advent of World War II," Bacevich explained, "the tradition of America as exemplar – now widely and erroneously characterized as isolationism – stood almost completely discredited. In Washington after 1945, it carried no weight at all. In official circles, fixing the world now took precedence over remedying whatever ailments afflicted the United States." Fellow historian and critic of empire Chalmers Johnson also decried the impulse to "fix the world," crediting "the continuous military buildup" and the expansion of US military bases overseas that began after 1941 with the ruination of the nation's special genius. And like Bacevich, he railed against his fellow citizens' confounding gift for denial, for their capacity to maintain, in Bacevich's words, "the cherished American tradition according to which the United States is not and cannot be an empire." "We do not think of these overseas deployments as a form of empire," Johnson wrote; "in fact, most Americans do not give them any thought at all until something truly shocking, such as the treatment of prisoners at Guantanamo Bay, brings them to our attention. But the people living next door to these bases and dealing with the swaggering soldiers who brawl and sometimes rape their women certainly think of them as imperial enclaves, just as the people of ancient Iberia or nineteenth-century India knew that they were victims of foreign colonization."[55]

Meanwhile, the 1980s "cultural turn" in humanities scholarship helped to popularize broader definitions of what an empire is and what it does. Armies, bases, and considerable control over international financial and political institutions were some of empire's more obvious expressions; however, the ability to export and "naturalize" ideas that served particular agendas came to be understood as a fundamental building-block of American empire (or any other hegemonic project). Emily Rosenberg traced the rise of "liberal developmentalism" to highlight the idea that culture serves not only to inspire imperial ambitions (i.e., justifying the act of seizing foreign territories from those deemed "inferior"), but also forms a core constituent of ensuing imperial rule. That is, the effective exportation of "soft power," of values and ideologies, can be as important to the establishment and maintenance of empire as economic, military, and political control. The unprecedented globalization of American mass culture following the Second World War, a product of both market demand and extensive and often covert

US-sponsored efforts to attract "hearts and minds" to American-style liberalism, was frequently cast by those within and outside the United States as imperialism's latest mode (in Richard Wagnleitner's memorable phrase, the mode of "coca-colonization"). Feminist scholarship drew attention to the gendered nature of the imperial project, and to the masculinist impulses that helped motivate territorial expansion and shape US hegemony. These new lines of inquiry brought increasing numbers of women and ethnic minorities to scholarship on war and empire, and broadened considerably that scholarship beyond the traditional precincts of military history.[56] Just as importantly for our purposes, they solidified the imaginative link between the Second World War and the final eclipse of what many Americans considered one of their great gifts to the world: the natural right to self-determination. As Bacevich and Johnson observed, not all Americans viewed the postwar projection of US influence as imperial in nature, but those who did were forced to reckon anew with a global conflict that had vanquished whatever remained of the anti-imperial creed. Indeed, a measure of the "toughness" exhibited by many American analysts towards the Second World War has its roots in a lament for the lasting damage the conflict did to their national experiment.

Only in recent years has it been possible to find a supporter of US global expansion who uses the term "empire" in a non-pejorative sense. "If an empire," Maier noted in 2003, "post World War II was the empire that dared not speak its name. But these days, on the part of friends and critics alike, the bashfulness has ended." Neoconservative historian and columnist Robert Kagan was one of the first to reclaim the term from critics of US foreign policy, calling the United States a "benevolent empire" in a noted 1998 *Foreign Policy* essay; four years later, likeminded columnist Charles Krauthammer lauded the fact that "people are coming out of the closet on the word 'empire.'" "Nowadays," concurred Christopher Hitchens in that same year, "if you consult the writings of the conservative and neoconservative *penseurs*, you will see that they are beginning to relish that very word." The relishing was not confined to analysts of American foreign policy, but was also on full view among the crafters of that policy. The aphorism on Vice-President Dick Cheney's 2003 Christmas card tied US global hegemony to providential destiny, enquiring, in a phrase taken from Benjamin Franklin, "And if a sparrow cannot fall to the ground without His notice, is it probable that an empire can rise without His aid?"[57] Embrace of the term, however, may belong to a particular, and waning, historical moment, one that had much to do with the atmosphere of Cold War triumphalism and the aggressive unilateralism and moral certainty ushered in by the 9/11 attacks. In the wake of US troubles in Iraq and Afghanistan, as well as an economic downturn that attenuated America's global influence, simplistic praise for the salvific power of Pax Americana may appear less sustainable to contemporary observers. And in the end, the merits of that debate – whether the United States is a good, bad, neutral, or non-empire – are less germane to the purposes of this study than the fact that for vast the majority of the nation's history, empire remained a profane word in the US lexicon, and the extent to which imperialism was seen to motivate past conflicts has shaped citizens' attitudes to those conflicts in profound ways.

In Canada, the Second World War and its aftermath reinvigorated the related phenomenon of greater independence from Britain and growing interdependence with the United States. The 1940 Ogdensburg Agreement established a coordinated bilateral defence of North America, essentially rendering Canada a protectorate of the United States, and when the latter joined the war in 1941, the two nations tightened considerably their economic, political, and military relationship. The Bretton Woods system placed Canada under a global economic order ultimately administered by the Americans, and the war's contribution to economic infirmity in Britain and vigour in the United States meant that, by the end of the conflict, the Americans had replaced Britain as Canada's largest foreign investor and trading partner. In 1946, the passing of the Canadian Citizenship Act legally defined citizens as primarily Canadian, rather than British subjects. By 1949, Cold War fears impelled Canada to co-found, with little domestic dissent, the US-led North Atlantic Treaty Organization (NATO) – an organization that would transfer a good deal of the nation's foreign policymaking initiative to the United States – and to join the US-led Korean War the following year. J.B. Brebner's *The North Atlantic Triangle*, which posited that Canada could not be understood solely through its British pedigree, captured and enhanced the growing atmosphere of cooperation. In the realm of culture, the Second World War brought into disrepute the racialized thinking that had undergirded talk of Anglo-Saxon supremacy and the importance of blood ties between Canadians and Britons.[58]

Yet once again, the idea that postwar Canada quickly sloughed off its imperial bonds overlooks important evidence to the contrary. In fact, a key building block in rallying English Canadian support for the Korean War centred on the idea that the United States had at last set aside its anti-imperial prudery and joined Britain in its global, civilizing mission. While American officials, conscious of the poisonous legacy of imperialism among Koreans and potential coalition partners, took pains to downplay any connections between past colonial intrusions and their current efforts to repel the North Korean invasion, influential Canadians applauded what they viewed as America's acquiescence to the British model of world ordering. The *Globe and Mail* wrote that "the United States, by its leadership in Korea is only catching up with Britain," a sentiment echoed in editorials from across Canada. The move softened the potential opposition to entering a war under US, rather than British, direction, and allowed for sometimes smug digs at previous American admonitions of British colonial pursuits.[59] While fascism had undermined long-held notions of Anglo-Saxon supremacy, one need not ascribe to objectionable racial hierarchies to express a preference for British institutions, traditions, and values.

Such partialities and affections for cultural Britishness were expressed most pointedly by leading postwar Canadian intellectuals like J.M.S Careless, Harold Innis, Donald Creighton, W.L. Morton, and George Grant, by many of the nation's most prominent newspapers and magazines, and by the Massey Commission and the Progressive Conservative Party. Evidence for the continued emotional ties to Britain can be measured by the vigorous backlash that accompanied Canada's growing cultural, military, and economic integration with the United States. "Canada had become an autonomous nation during the First World War," wrote Creighton; "she reverted to the position of a dependent colony during the second." Innis agreed, arguing that the country had mutated "from colony to nation to colony." Grant's celebrated 1965 polemic *Lament for a Nation* bemoaned the selling-out of Canadian interests and values in the name of continentalism, and glorified a bygone Canada typified by cultural Britishness, political and religious conservatism, and an aversion to modernity (in other words, Grant's was not a plea for sovereignty, but for Canada's subservience to the "right" empire). That a book with such seemingly archaic leanings became a rallying point for a new generation of Canadian nationalists from across the political spectrum points to the continued importance of British identity to English Canadian nationalism; here, British traditions served as the surest bulwark against Americanization. The fact that most English Canadians of the era descended from immigrants from the British Isles, and Britain remained the largest source of Canadian immigrants until the 1960s, only reinforced these loyalties.

Magnus Eisengrim, the protagonist in Robertson Davies's 1975 novel *World of Wonders*, explained Canadians' enduring fondness for Britain thusly: "The notion that everybody wants the latest is a delusion of intellectuals; a lot of people want a warm, safe place where Time hardly moves at all, and to a lot of those Canadian that place was England."[60]

At what point, then, did English Canada outgrow the imperial mindset? For Philip Buckner, the period from 1957 to 1967 witnessed the emergence of a truly independent Canada, a decade that featured the Canadian-British fractures over the Suez Crisis, as well as a raucous flag debate and the nation's heady centenary celebrations. The mid-century liberalization of immigration laws broadened considerably the nation's ethnic makeup, and along with the rise of Quebec separatism, led Canadian officials to promote multiculturalism, rather than British-ness, as the true marker of national identity. An emerging leftist critique of Canada's increasing deference to the militant foreign policy of the United States – a nation CBC Washington correspondent James Minifie called the "star-spangled Devil" in his polemic for a non-aligned Canadian – joined the conservative reprimand of continentalism. Like Minifie, many of these "new nationalists" would draw inspiration from a growing worldwide rejection, in word and deed, of the legitimacy of empire. These processes reflected what José Eduardo Igartua called the "de-ethnicization" of English Canada, a "quiet revolution" that paralleled, both in time and impact, the more generally recognized Quiet Revolution transforming Quebec at the same time.[61]

In foreign policy, the nation's formative contribution to the UN peace-keeping tradition provided Canada with a foreign presence independent of both Britain and the United States, one that finally reconciled the historic breach between French- and English-Canadian concepts of international responsibility. Historian W.A.B. Douglas noted that "it would be an unwarranted presumption to claim that there was a 'Canadian way of war,'" as Canadian military doctrines have generally reflected those of Britain, and later, America; Pearsonian internationalism, while not a conventional "way of war," could provide Canada's military with a distinctive international brand.[62] In an effort to broadcast the increased autonomy of Canadian forces to the wider world (of particular importance for a nation engaged in peacekeeping operations in postcolonial settings), the anachronous term "Royal" was removed from both the navy and air force in 1968. In the academy, the growth of social and cultural history diverted attention away from single, grand narratives of national development and towards an appreciation for the

THE RIGHT ROAD IS STRAIGHT AHEAD

3.4 In the wake of the Suez Crisis, Toronto cartoonist Les Callan submitted
that the appropriate route for Canada was unambiguous. (*Canadian Liberal
Monthly*, 28 November 1956.)

variety of the Canadian experience; those who stood outside – whether
by choice or compulsion – traditional notions of (Britannic) Canadian-
ness, were now given voice.

Curiously, while American scholars from the New Left-era forward
trained a range of fresh analytical tools on the re-examination of their
nation's wars, their Canadian contemporaries generally demurred.
With few exceptions, social and cultural approaches were harnessed
to bring new insights to Canada's *domestic* sphere. Works on Canada's
wars maintained their traditional connections to narrative history and
biography, and resisted the kind of theorizing on race, culture, gender,

and hegemony that led American analysts to new understandings – and often piercing critiques – of war's contribution to empire-building and a racially ordered international system. Perhaps this is not so curious after all, if we take into account the relative aversion to controversy in Canadian war writing. Approaches inherently critical of the operations of power would hold little allure to those accustomed to affirmative accounts of military engagements and the wider legacies of Britannic civilization.[63]

The enigma of this latent conservatism in Canadian war-related studies was compounded by another: that the emergence of a more fully autonomous and unified Canada, one increasingly certain of its distinctive domestic and international identity and very prospects for survival, turned out to be something of an anathema to the nation's war chroniclers. Rather than taking pride in a nation that seemed at last to be finding its own place and voice (and emerging from the shadow of empires), many of the more well-positioned military historians condemned what they saw as the quixotic idealism of peacekeeping, along with the peril to national unity and resolve posed by the "multicultural mania" blighting government and academy alike. Instead, Canadians should envision themselves as war-fighters and, not incidentally, recognize their duty to answer the call whenever their largest trading partner appeals for military assistance. In other words, Canadians should feel no shame over their evolution, in Harold Innis's sardonic maxim, "from colony to nation to colony."[64]

At a certain level, these anxieties over the rise of a more confident and independent Canadian identity and policy make sense. On the one hand, peacekeeping lacks much of the glamour, moral certitude, and triumphalism associated with conventional military narratives. As Thomas Hardy observed in a statement both true and potentially worrying to those who recount the feats of Canada's men and women in uniform: "War makes rattling good history; but Peace is poor reading." On a more fundamental level, this more diverse and independently-minded Canada might come to reappraise the sense of grandeur associated with wars fought at the behest of others. In the words of McKay and Swift, in the imagination of some of the nation's more prominent military historians (or "new warriors"), "the great events in Canadian history were those in which the British and American empires were built and defended. It is in the rush of Canadian soldiers to defend those empires that Canadians should find their national identity."[65] Giving Canadians free reign to find that identity where they saw fit, especially in an era marked by increasing immigration and ethno-cultural diversity, might lead to fragmentation, disunity, and a failure to assign warfare a central role in the national story and character.

A central conundrum surrounding the new warriors' approach is that the national story is by nature fragmented and often discordant (or rich and multilayered, to put it another way); shooting the messenger will not obviate this fact. Wars entered primarily because of colonial bonds provide some of the clearest examples of this truth; that the imperial trappings of the South African War and the two world wars rendered the conflicts profoundly divisive among Canadians is simply beyond question. In the past, the primary fissure ran between English- and French-Canada, but as the nation's population diversified, the numbers of citizens who harboured antipathies to imperialism in general, or to its British variant in particular, multiplied. One way to surmount this fractiousness is to focus on ideals and values, to assert that Canadians fought not merely or primarily because they were British subjects obliged to safeguard imperial territory, prestige, and economic might, but because the values embodied by Britain were both exemplary and universal (at least in the case of the world wars; evidence for the benevolence motivating British operations against the Boers has proven more difficult to locate, a circumstance that provides further incentive to forget that conflict). As Vance observed, praise for the merits of the British way of life was customary in the days when English Canadian nationalism sat comfortably with imperialism; as affections for empire waned, the emphasis on values helped combat the notion that Canada fought simply out of imperial duty. Thus, a recent Canadian study called the world wars a straightforward "defence of liberty, justice, and ... the British Empire," conflicts fought "for the same liberal ideals." Another volume closes reverently with the words of First World War Prime Minister Robert Borden, who praised "the valour of those Canadians, who, in the Great War, fought for the liberties of Canada, of the Empire, and of humanity."[66]

This simple conflation of the British Empire with liberty poses additional challenges, however. Andrew Smith argued that Canadians should give "2½ cheers" for the British Empire, and provided much evidence to support his claim that "British imperialism brought significant benefits to Canada" in the realms of law, governance, and economics.[67] But such praise for empire obscures the fact that there existed many forms of British imperial governance. The British connection did indeed benefit English Canadians greatly, and provided both profits and losses to the historical ledgers of francophones and indigenous peoples. But clearly there exists a divide between the colonial experiences of Canada, New Zealand, and Australia on the one hand, and those of Ireland, South and East Asia, the Caribbean, and Africa on the other. The vast numbers of Canadians who trace their roots to this latter assortment of geographies – those who did find a privileged place in the empire, who fought in Britain's wars based on false promises of increased sovereignty and better treatment, and who had to attain their independence through revolt rather than genial negotiation – may well chafe at the ironies of celebrating the essentially liberating character of British imperialism. Wars fought to "preserve" or "defend" the empire, words used without complication in many Canadian accounts, also granted Britain a continued capacity to rule, sometimes ruthlessly, over tens of millions of subjugated peoples who did not eulogize their imperial ties.

A second strategy for bolstering both Canadian nationalism and the prestige of wars entered, first and foremost, because of the Dominon's ties to Britain, involves simply remarrying nationalism with imperialism. This approach harkens back to the anglophilic aura of the late nineteenth century, when the mutually reinforcing notions of militarism and imperialism were at their zenith, when George Parkin's map of the British Empire – with Canada positioned proudly at its hub – adorned the walls of every English Canadian schoolroom, when Goldwin Smith bristled at his fellow countrymen's antiquated affections for the Crown, and when 60 per cent of Canadians traced their ancestry to Britain. In the twenty-first century, the move would seem a debilitating anachronism in a nation that has, since the Great War, moved consistently away from the monarchical connection and sought to establish an independent identity. Yet this is precisely the tack taken by the Conservative government under Stephen Harper. The recently revamped citizenship manual (2009) placed increased emphasis on both the monarchy and Canada's military history, pictures of the Queen replaced Canadian paintings at government buildings, and in August of 2011, the Conservatives restored the title "Royal" to the Canadian navy and air force. The latter move proved especially surprising: there was little ongoing debate over the 1968 renaming of the armed forces, no groundswell calling for the restoration of imperial idioms.

In retrospect, the timing of the announcement was no accident: Prince William and wife Catherine, the "good royals," had just completed a popular tour of Canada, during which the prince extolled the

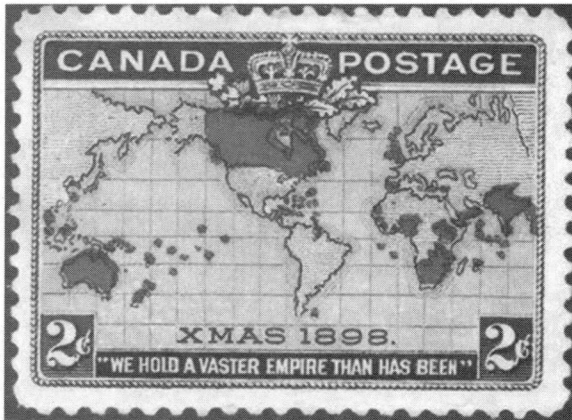

3.5 Next in line for reintroduction? The Canadian Postmaster General featured the ubiquitous Parkin map on the Christmas 1898 stamp, along with a humble nod to the empire's reach. (Bertram W.H. Poole, *The Postage Stamps of Canada*, n.d. National Archives of Canada.)

"vital contribution made by Canadians who fought for freedom in the wars of the twentieth century," and donned khakis to pilot a Sea King helicopter in military training exercises. Official justifications for the change remained cryptic: a desire to enhance "pride" in the military, to renew patriotism, and to restore an allegedly "lost" national identity. Granatstein himself, not one lacking in pride for Canadian military accomplishments, called the move "abject colonialism."[68] Once again, Canadians were presented with the disheartening (and divisive) paradox that without their British pedigree, they lack a distinct national heritage.

Of course, the chairman of the Monarchist League of Canada applauded the move as a reminder of who ultimately commands the nation's armed forces: "they're not the Prime Minister's or the Defence Minister's," he noted, "they are the Queen's."[69] This is both technically correct and farcical in practical terms, as any unilateral attempt by Elizabeth II to muster Canadian troops would quickly reveal. The politics behind the rebranding initiative are transparent enough: the change was part of a larger program of undermining the Liberal Party's imprint on Canadian foreign policy, which included armed forces amalgamation, peacekeeping, and the broader strategy of replacing British symbols in an effort to make them more representative of modern, multi-ethnic Canada. Reinvigorating the monarchical connection also isolates the New Democratic Party, whose time-honoured aversion to the empire was only reinforced by the federal party's 2011 electoral coup in Quebec, where support for the monarchy is virtually non-existent. Harper's victory in that same election proved that a federal majority could be attained without catering to the interests of Quebec. Just as importantly, reconnecting the military and the monarchy permits a more enthusiastic celebration of Canada's martial past: the seeming contradiction inherent in conflicts that demonstrated both Canada's imperial subservience and its sovereignty is thus nullified. Whether modern Canada as a whole will buy into a nationalism built on imperial legacies – whether this will rally or disunite Canadians of various ethnicities, remains an open question.

In all, Americans have displayed a decided antipathy to the concept of imperialism – an antipathy that is near-universal when they consider the expansionist projects of foreign states. Many have also scrutinized their own nation for evidence of imperial taint, and particularly in the case of war, found much to condemn. Those seeking to return the nation to its anti-colonial ideals face a stiff challenge, however, both from the "facts on the ground" associated with America's unprecedented and undeniable global reach, and from a recent movement to acknowledge and embrace the idea of an imperialistic United States. Canada, too, is at something of a crossroads as it wrestles with the often-contradictory legacies of loyalism and multiculturalism, of militarism and peacekeeping, and of nationalism and imperial ties. Here, and in pointed contrast to the United States, the imperial bond has inspired a sometimes-reflexive defence of past military endeavours. And although concerted attempts to sustain a usable, nationalistic martial past would appear to be complicated by the colonialist hue of Canada's wars, this dilemma may be reconciled if recent, state-sponsored attempts succeed in reconstituting empire as both a self-evident good and an enduring pillar of Canadian nationalism.

Chapter Four

Political Cultures: The Architecture of Governance

An American tourist who stumbled across the summer 2011 debates over restoring the "royal" designation to Canada's navy and air force may well have enjoyed a supercilious chuckle on learning that Canada's armed forces still "belong to the Queen" (our apocryphal sightseer having excised that complication some 235 years prior). Subsequent clarifications of who actually controls the fate of the men and women in uniform – not the House of Windsor after all, nor Canada's Parliament, but the Canadian cabinet, a few dozen souls who are themselves beholden to a significant degree to the will of the prime minister – may have induced bewilderment, or concerns over the democratic deficit seemingly afflicting the process. Recent generations of Canadians, observing (also with a measure of nationalistic conceit) the seemingly relentless dispatching of American forces to foreign locales *and* a federal legislative system paralysed by partisanship, might be equally surprised to learn that only Congress can declare war. Had federal legislators truly toned down the bitterness and posturing to reach consensus on the use of force on so many occasions? The further revelation that Congress has issued such declarations only five times and provided sometimes-vague consent for military action in roughly a dozen other instances would, once again, bring little closure to the matter. Were the countless other military engagements unlawful? Is the American president any less constrained on the matter than Canada's prime minister? Why do members of Congress and the American people tolerate this state of affairs? Or do they? Clearly, these distinctive protocols and practices regarding the use of force are confusing, contradictory, and – as they provide opportunities for a select few to deploy lethal force in the name of the nation – open to charges of despotism. These protocols also underline clear differences in governmental regimes, differences that can have profound effects on why wars are entered, how they are prosecuted, and how they are ultimately remembered.[1]

The influence of governmental regimes on attitudes to war can be approximated through two approaches. The first focuses on the structure of government as represented in its foundational ideological principles, the laws and traditions that animate it, and the institutions through which it finds expression; we might call this the "hardware" of governance. As this chapter illustrates, although both nations are liberal democracies sharing important characteristics and values, subtle and sometimes profound differences in the nature and evolution of governance have generated regimes that seek and resist consensus in differing ways, a fact readily observable in deliberations over war. A subsequent chapter will address the second – and thoroughly interrelated – matter of citizens' attitudes towards government and their relationship and obligations to it, and to wider questions of authority in general; these cultural habits and assumptions make up the "software" of governance. Both of these aspects of governance converge to form what can be designated a "political culture," or "the way of life of a political community or polity," in Nelson Wiseman's elegant definition.[2] Charting the development of ideas about the role of government, how it gains legitimacy, and the rights and responsibilities of citizenship provides a frame through which historic attitudes towards state-sponsored violence may be comprehended.

Here again, the US War of Independence looms large. Not only did it discredit imperialism, it also reflected and enhanced a profound distrust for governmental authority. The Revolution did not fashion these views *ex nihilo*; it merely built upon the sense of autonomy generated by those fleeing, among other things, religious and ethnic conflict, debt, and the law, and establishing relatively autonomous communities in the "wilderness." It took the break from Britain, however, to make distrust of government a pillar of Americanism. Thomas Paine's January 1776 pamphlet *Common Sense*, with its vilification not only of the abuses of George III but of the very idea of monarchy, helped to transform a protest against England's maltreatment into a quest for complete autonomy under a republican government. "Of more worth," offered Paine in his pamphlet, "is one honest man to society and in the sight of God, than all the crowned ruffians that ever lived."[3] The Declaration of Independence that followed elevated citizen surveillance of government to a near sacrament, holding that when a given regime fails to reflect the consent of the governed, "it is [the citizens'] right, it is their duty, to throw off such Government, and to provide new Guards for their future security." Following the revolution, the "new Guards" established by the framers of the Constitution were hamstrung intentionally in an effort to prevent the aggregation of power in any single individual or institution. The Bill of Rights, meanwhile, codified the principle that federal power could not undermine citizens' liberties, thus enhancing the aura of individual prerogative and governmental constraint. Government's role, in other words, was simply to defend the "natural rights" of citizens and then get out of the way.

This is not to deny that the Constitution is a rather conflicted document, at once inimical to the rise of despotism *and* to the power of the people. By the time it had been hammered out and ratified in 1789, the new nation had already witnessed popular uprisings that threatened not only governmental authority, but, in their calls for the redistribution of wealth, the security of private property. Would Jefferson's call to "throw off" governments that lost public favour result in perpetual revolution? Alarmed political elites were thus moved to insulate government from the immediate reach of the populace through such measures as the electoral college (which provided for the indirect election of the president), executive nomination of the lordly Supreme Court Justices (whose terms are limited only by the length of their mortal coil), and the six-year appointment of senators by state legislators (a practice that survived until 1913). Only members of the House of Representatives, junior partners to senators who serve just two-year terms, would be elected directly by the people. In its attenuation of direct democracy, and in its preservation of the pre-war economic status-quo, the period from 1776 to 1789 witnessed, in constitutional historian Russell Kirk's view, "a revolution not made but prevented."[4]

Still, checks against the aggregation of power, of the will to despotism, survived the anti-democratic tendencies of the framers; fears of the tyranny of the masses were leavened by the potential tyranny of any single individual or branch of government. Checks and balances designed to constrain executive and legislative prerogative render consensus-building a prerequisite for action on foreign policy or any other matter of state, and overlapping jurisdiction between government branches means that conflict and gridlock are built deliberately into the system. The latter tendency is exacerbated by the fact that representatives and senators are elected on mostly local issues, and may place local concerns ahead of national interests in their deliberations over foreign policy. The selection of candidates through the primary system (which replaced selection by state and district conventions in the early twentieth century) enhanced the ability of the local population to shape the issues.[5]

This obligation to consensus, and the difficulty in obtaining it, is only intensified by the relative weakness of American political parties, when compared to those in parliamentary systems. Since the emergence of the two-party system in the 1790s, politicians elected to Congress have demonstrated a considerable measure of independence from "official" party positions, and party whips have not been afforded the clout witnessed in parliamentary systems.[6] Thus, while Republicans, for instance, generally served as the standard-bearers for US isolationism in the first half of the twentieth century and their Democratic counterparts proved more consistent internationalists, the inability of parties to regulate their members' votes on such matters has blurred the lines between these camps. In part, this volatility exists simply because nonconformity in voting carries less political hazard in the United States than it does in its parliamentary counterpart: majority parties do not "fall" when they lose a vote in Congress, as they can in a framework where the executive is determined by the makeup of the House of Commons rather than the outcome of a separate, stand-alone public plebiscite.

American politicians' autonomy can also be traced to the independence of mind fostered by a culture that places a premium on the dictates of individual conscience, and a national experiment built on intensive and freewheeling public debate – attitudes reflected and enhanced by the First Amendment's guarantee of freedom of speech and belief. On this outlook Tocqueville expressed some hesitations, observing in 1840 that Americans "owe nothing to any man, they expect nothing from any man; they acquire the habit of always considering themselves as standing alone ..." His contemporary Ralph Waldo Emerson exalted that same outlook, counselling, "a man is to carry himself in the presence of all opposition as if every thing were titular and ephemeral but he."[7] Regardless of their estimations of the value of such an orientation, few observers of the United States deny that the will to individualism represents an important strain of American self-perception.

The nature of political fundraising also plays a role in weakening party loyalties and buoying individual autonomy. Since the earliest days of the republic, candidates themselves, not the party, have borne responsibility for the bulk of campaign fundraising, and candidates may spend any amount of money they raise; until the early 1970s, contributions were largely unregulated and undisclosed. Such a system bred pervasive and widely-acknowledged abuses; as Mark Twain observed, "I think I can say, and say with pride, that we have legis-latures that bring higher prices than any in the world." Nineteenth-century Pennsylvania Senator Simon Cameron outlined the ethical horizon of elected officials rather liberally when he declared, "an hon-est politician is one who, when he is bought, stays bought." The emer-gence of so-called political action committees in the 1940s ensured that previously enacted laws prohibiting direct contributions from labour and business groups could be easily circumvented through the crea-tion of organizations that fronted for unions and corporations. A series of campaign finance reforms introduced over the course of the twenti-eth century aimed to regulate and disclose political funding, but none guaranteed that successful candidates would not reward their donors with political benefits and favourable votes.[8]

Once again, this state of affairs has contributed to a high degree of volatility in voting patterns: candidates must triangulate the wishes of their party, constituents, and donors, and the latter two groups gener-ally represent a wide variety of interests that do not align precisely with centralized party platforms. The suspicion that moneyed interests asso-ciated with the defence industry could manoeuvre politicians towards military "preparedness," ever-expanding arms budgets, and (in order to validate the outlay and perpetuate the cycle), war, has been a fixture in popular consciousness at least since Senator Gerald Nye's commit-tee on the First World War munitions industry began hearings in 1934. The Cold War emergence of what President Dwight Eisenhower called the "military-industrial-complex" only increased the stakes, cash, and defence-industry lobbying. Less common, though also in play, is the practice of endowing politicians with financial incentives to oppose militarism. In the early 1960s, atomic scientist Leo Szilard established the Council for a Livable World, arguing that "the combination of the sweet voice of reason and substantial campaign contributions" might convince legislators to scale back the arms race and work for concili-ation with the Soviet Union. From the 1960s until his death in 2008, philanthropist Stewart Mott poured millions of dollars into the cam-paigns of those who pledged to work for peace, arms control, and other liberal causes, leading Charles Colson, White House chief counsel to Richard Nixon, to include Mott on the president's infamous "enemies list"; Mott, Colson declared, offered "nothing but big money for radic-lib candidates."[9] Given the profitability of war-related industries, the contest is decidedly lopsided. The point, however, is that this is a system in which such individual pliability on matters of war and peace, along with a range of other issues, is both possible and often handsomely rewarded.

The multicultural composition of the United States, born of a comparatively liberal approach to immigration that has permitted newcomers from a wide variety of origins, further inhibited party cohesion on matters of foreign policy. Especially from the mid-nineteenth century onward, the United States developed a uniquely heterogeneous population, leading to a concentration of minority groups in various electoral districts and the emergence of powerful ethnic lobby groups. By the beginning of the twentieth century, New York City held the second largest concentration of Germans in the world after Berlin, and major northern and eastern American cities as a whole became home to waves of newcomers from southern and eastern Europe In the first decade of the twentieth century, south- and east-European *émigrés* made up 70 per cent of all European immigrants to the United States. These new arrivals were soon joined by African Americans fleeing the segregation, lynching, poverty, and – notably for our purposes – virtual exclusion from the political process that marked the American South, in a major demographic realignment known as the Great Migration. The lands west of the Mississippi, meanwhile, served as a destination for millions of Germans, Scandinavians, and southern- and eastern-Europeans.[10]

Although the population density of the American west was dwarfed by that of the eastern seaboard, the "Great Compromise" hammered out during the 1787 constitutional deliberations provided each state two senators regardless of population. Given the large percentages of non-Anglo-Saxons in many western states, by the beginning of the twentieth century the compromise had the effect of affording minority opinion considerable influence in the upper house. Add to this the fact that the Senate is the more influential congressional body in general – and even more so in the area of foreign affairs – and senators like Idaho Republican William Borah's apparently outsized impact on his nation's foreign relations begins to make sense. First elected in 1907 to represent a scant 300,000 residents in a nation of nearly 100 million, Borah's rigorous isolationism and anti-imperialism resonated with the many Idahoans of German, Irish, and Scandinavian descent. He would serve the state until his death in 1940, and along the way become the Republican's foreign affairs expert and a pivotal figure in the US rejection of the League of Nations in 1919. To howls of protest from groups like the American Legion, the Daughters of the American Revolution, the American Federation of Labour, and chambers of commerce, Borah was also the Senate's most committed exponent of official recognition of the Soviet Union, a measure finally adopted by Democrat Franklin Roosevelt in 1933. Borah's particular constellation of views would have made for difficult campaigning in many states and often put him at odds with members his own party, who christened him "The Great Opposer," but he never faced a serious challenge to his seat from the distinctive collection of Idahoans. The story is similar for the likes of Robert La Follette (Wisconsin), George Norris (Nebraska), and Asle Gronna (North Dakota), senators representing populations small in numbers but big on anglophobia, and men not coincidentally at the forefront of opposition to America's entry into the First World War and Wilson's League of Nations.[11] The notion of "states' rights," then, is no abstraction, but is written into the framework of US governance. By extension, so too are the peculiar viewpoints that distinguish the disparate inhabitants of American states and regions.

As a whole, the demographic transformations that marked the nation around the turn of the twentieth century provided a challenge to the relatively close bonds forged in the previous decades between US international interests and those of the broader Anglo-Saxon world. This led politicians to craft positions that spoke to the particular interests of voters of a variety of (sometimes overlapping) ethnic and religious minorities: Irish, German, Roman Catholic, Eastern Orthodox, Jewish, Black, Hispanic, and so on. To influential Canadian observers of the day, this remarkable profusion of ethnic variation served as evidence that Americans could not be considered suitable partners in any scheme for continental unity, for the United States had ceased to be an Anglo-Saxon nation. "Once it was," lamented Colonel George Taylor Denison, a founder of the Canada First movement that advocated for imperial federation, "but since the revolution it has been the dumping ground of Europe, and they are forming a community there entirely different in characteristics from ours." Other Canadians were quick to point out that the presence of millions of black Americans sullied further that nations' genius and any claims to authentic Anglo-Saxondom. In matters of foreign affairs, the various ethnic minority groups that rendered the United States "entirely different" have on many occasions exerted pressure on government to address the concerns of their kinfolk abroad, and have often advocated positions at odds with the population as a whole: sometimes more pacifistic and at other times more belligerent, and in general more anti-imperialist and anti-British than the median American view. As diplomatic historian Alexander DeConde observed, the outbreak of the First World War "quickened the ethnic consciousness of minority groups." In consequence, Washington became "a lobbying battleground between rival interest groups emotionally entangled in the war," a battleground so volatile that leaders feared US entry could precipitate civil war.[12]

In 1915, Woodrow Wilson bared his frustrations over the domestic discord wrought by war in Europe in a speech to recent immigrants at a naturalization ceremony. "You cannot become thorough Americans if you think of yourselves in groups," he lectured. "America does not consist of groups." As it turned out, Wilson was right to be concerned – and somewhat overconfident about the conformist influences of the American polity. Two years after his tutorial on citizenship, fifty-six federal legislators (more than one-third of these from his own Democratic party), voted against his request for a declaration of war against Germany; the bulk of these naysayers were clustered in middle and western states. As historian Melvin Small observed, "all the other major powers over the past two centuries have had to contend with ethnic minorities. But the democratic United States has been the only one among them that lacks the ability to suppress the cacophony of voices from electorally powerful ethnic groups."[13] In foreign affairs at least, the "melting pot" was anything but.

Harry Truman understood this well. In defending his strong support for the creation of Israel to state department officials in 1945, Truman put it bluntly: "I have to answer to hundreds of thousands who are anxious for the success of Zionism. I do not have hundreds of thousands of Arabs in my constituents." In 1972, foreign policy mandarin George Kennan chafed at the policymaking dilemmas faced by a government accountable to a pluralistic citizenry, lamenting, "our actions in the field of foreign affairs are the convulsive reactions of politicians to an internal political life dominated by vocal minorities."[14]

All of these factors – individualism, party weakness, "debts" to donors, demographic pluralism – are intensified by the sheer scale, in both geographic and demographic terms, of US society. In a vast and diverse nation dominated by just two federal parties, a myriad of local and regional, cultural, and class concerns cannot but pull those parties in multiple directions, and render any precise definition of "Republican" and "Democrat" impossible. For instance, the so-called New Deal coalition that dominated US politics from the Great Depression to the late sixties sought to balance the interests of recent immigrants, northern urbanites, blacks, intellectuals, and labour unions with those of white southerners – the latter a constituency marked by pronounced hostility to each of the former. A Democrat from New York City was a vastly different creature than one from Little Rock, a truth that obviated attempts at internal consistency, produced epic congressional battles *between* Democrats, spawned third-party presidential candidates backed by disaffected southerners, and under Republican Richard Nixon's successful "southern strategy" to woo white southerners to the party of the reviled Lincoln, saw the coalition crumble under the weight of its internal contradictions. It was only with the increasing polarity inspired by the "culture wars" of the late twentieth century that America's two traditional parties became more internally consistent, and less willing and able to build bipartisan consensus.[15]

As the above circumstances suggest, altering the course of the American ship of state is intrinsically demanding. In order to pass any initiative, even presidents from parties holding a majority in both houses have been forced to generate broad bipartisan support for their positions – within a political culture that, paradoxically, extolls and rewards independence of mind. Note, for instance, that while the United States was hardly a docile presence on the international stage after 1900, since that date Congress has consented to formal declarations of war only in the case of the world wars – and just five times in all since independence. On four of those occasions, Congress assented to the president's request only after hostilities had already begun. Constitutional scholars generally agree that, except in the case of "a sudden attack on the United States," the power to initiate war belongs solely to Congress. In practice, however, the executive branch has applied a much more elastic understanding to its war powers in an effort to circumnavigate a potentially fractious Congress.[16] Accordingly, presidents have used a range of quasi-constitutional means to engage enemies abroad, from open-ended and nebulous congressional authorizations (Vietnam and Iraq) to semantic smokescreens (the Korean "police action") to covert actions (abundant). Both world wars, meanwhile, provided tangible threats to American interests, security, and values well before US entry, but presidents were required to wait for repeated and increasingly audacious attacks on American merchant ships in the case of the first, and a direct strike on US soil in the case of the second, before they felt they possessed the political capital to obtain a declaration of war from Congress. Even Franklin Roosevelt, who oversaw a strong

Democratic majority in both houses and governed during a high tide of executive authority over the other branches of government, could do little to move congressional opinion towards war before Pearl Harbor – despite his protracted and spirited efforts to do so.

Those same spirited efforts point to a further outcome of the inherent intractability of US policymaking: presidents who wish to sell a course of action to Congress have frequently resorted to embroideries and outright falsifications in order to gain assent. Roosevelt himself engaged in a series of deceptions designed to entangle his nation in the conflict prior to Congress's 8 December 1941 declaration of war – despite assuring in his 1940 re-election campaign that "your boys are not going to be sent to any foreign wars." He presented the "cash and carry" provision of the 1937 Neutrality Act as well as the March 1941 Lend-Lease bill as measures that would maintain American security *and* neutrality, rather than patent efforts to align with anti-fascist European governments and draw his nation into the Allied war effort. After ordering the US navy into what amounted to an undeclared war to shepherd supply ships across the Atlantic that same year, Roosevelt resorted to his most flagrant deception. When the USS *Greer* – a destroyer issued secret orders to help Britain's Royal Air Force stalk enemy U-boats – came under German fire, Roosevelt framed the attack as an unprovoked act of piracy.[17]

Indeed, pliability with the truth is something of a constant among US presidents seeking congressional consent for foreign aggression, a theme that runs from James Polk's spurious claim that Mexican soldiers attacked their American counterparts on US soil (thus instigating the 1846–48 Mexican-American War), to Woodrow Wilson's fierce condemnations of German violations of freedom of the seas and utter silence on the British variant, to Lyndon Johnson's nearly pitch-perfect reprise of the *Greer* incident in describing attacks on US vessels in the Tonkin Gulf (paving the way for the massive escalation of US forces in Vietnam). "FDR's deviousness in a good cause made it much easier for [Johnson] to practice the same kind of deviousness in a bad cause," noted Arkansas Senator J. William Fulbright in 1971; here again, it is worthwhile to note that the censure arose from a member of the president's own Democratic Party. George W. Bush's avowal that Saddam Hussein possessed weapons of mass destruction and helped mastermind the 9/11 attacks was merely the latest in a rather ignoble line of presidential prevarication – although the Bush regime may have set the standard in this regard. Indeed, the US non-profit and non-partisan Center for Public Integrity found the administration made a total of 935 false statements between 2001 and 2003 regarding Iraq's alleged threat to the United States.[18]

Even when presidents do not rely on blatant fabrication, successful pitches of foreign policy initiatives frequently rely on moralism, exaggeration, fear-mongering, and fervent appeals to patriotism. Diplomatic historian Fredrik Logevall found all four at work in the crafting of the Truman Doctrine, first outlined by the Democratic president in a 1947 speech seeking support from a Republican-controlled Congress for the Cold War policy of containment. To Logevall, the policy was promoted under a series of trumped-up claims: "cooperation with the Soviet Union was impossible for the foreseeable future, for its leaders possessed an omnivorous and insatiable appetite for power. The only language they understood was deterrence and preponderant military force. Soviet-American friction therefore did not result from clashing national interests, but from the moral shortcomings of Kremlin leaders." Truman's address painted global affairs in bleak, apocalyptic terms, a battle between two ways of life that only America could wage and, for the sake of all humanity, must win. In framing the issues thusly, Truman had clearly heeded the advice of Republican Senator Arthur Vandenberg, who recommended that the president "scare the hell out of the American people" in order to move traditionally isolationist Republicans towards the unprecedented global role entailed by containment. Truman was frank about his motives in his reply to a letter from Secretary of State George Marshall, wherein Marshall wondered whether the president's speech "was overstating the case a bit." Truman responded that based on his "contacts with the Senate, it was clear that this was the only way in which the measure could have passed." On Korea, Truman again used simplistic and unsubstantiated claims to build domestic support for participation: the North Korean invaders were simply "bandits and thugs" motivated by their hatred of freedom, and ordered into the attack by their Soviet overlords. In this case, however, Truman circumvented the dilemmas inherent in congressional cross-examination by simply ordering an immediate dispatch of US troops to the peninsula in what he called a "police action." A recent study of the pre-war rhetoric of five presidents since Truman found that they had taken his lesson to heart. Presidents Kennedy, Johnson, Nixon, Reagan, and George H.W. Bush all "presented in detail a terrible, shocking and shameful story … [and] a pattern of unprovoked and intentional evil. Total innocence and virtue was on our side; total guilt and wickedness on the other."[19]

The moralistic flavour of US foreign policymaking was further enhanced by what historian C. Vann Woodward called "free security," or the luxury, unparalleled in the modern era, of developing a nation without attendant fears of foreign invasion. Between 1815 and 1941, American foreign policy could assume virtually any shape its architects chose, and engage with the other great powers almost entirely on American terms – or not at all. In such a context, Americans found it easy to heed George Washington's injunction against entangling alliances and to conceive of themselves as apart from, and above, Old World intrigues and violence. In Woodward's summation, "the national myth that America is an innocent nation in a wicked world is associated to some degree in its origins and perpetuation with the experience of free security." Absent tangible security threats, factors such as civic and religious ideology came "to play an inordinate role in shaping America's response to the world," as Andrew Preston wrote. Accordingly, President McKinley framed the seizure of the Philippines as a humanitarian mission rather than a stepping stone to Asian markets. Woodrow Wilson brought his nation into war not merely because German submarine attacks threatened American commerce and security, but because those attacks constituted "a warfare against mankind," against wrongs "that cut to the very root of human life." Wilson articulated America's wartime goals in equally expansive and momentous terms. US participation, he averred, would "vindicate the principles of peace and justice in the life of the world," and make the world "safe for democracy." The United States would "fight without rancor and without selfish object, seeking nothing for ourselves"; rather, their aim would be to "bring peace and safety to all nations and make the world at last free." Here, the desire to avert a potential impasse in Congress coalesced with long-standing American notions of perfectionism, chosen-ness, and destiny to fashion a series of war aims as high-minded as they were unattainable. In an effort to cement these themes in the public imagination, Wilson created by executive order the blatantly propagandistic Committee on Public Information, mandating that it depict the "absolute justice of America's cause" and the "absolute selflessness of America's aims."[20]

While the political culture outlined above has often bred discourse marked by oversimplification, falsehoods, self-righteousness, and hyper-nationalism, it can also provide decided advantages for those challenging the national will to war. The relative weakness of the executive and political parties, coupled with the congressional prerogative to declare war, renders Congress a highly visible forum for airing

4.1 The "benevolent assimilation" of the Filipinos included shipping more than a thousand of the newly conquered wards to the 1904 St Louis World's Fair as a "live exhibit." For seven months they were required to perform their "primitive" rituals for fair patrons, including a daily butchering, grilling, and eating of a dog, a rare and ceremonial event back home. (US Library of Congress Prints and Photographs Division.)

what are often widely divergent and pungently-expressed views on matters of war and peace. While fractiousness is hardly rare among members of Congress, debates over the rectitude of military actions are responsible for some of the most volatile and memorable debates in congressional history. After casting a vote to censure President Polk on the grounds that the Mexican-American War had been "unnecessarily and unconstitutionally begun by the President of the United States," Illinois Congressman Abraham Lincoln compared Polk's sundry and often-contradictory pronouncements on the war to "the half-insane mumbling of a fever dream." "His mind," Lincoln rhapsodized, "tasked beyond its power, is running hither and thither, like some tortured creature on a burning surface, finding no position on which it can settle down and be at ease." Many of Lincoln's colleagues agreed, as the vote to censure the president passed 85 to 81. In his 1902 commentary on President Theodore Roosevelt's handling of the Philippine insurrection, Senator George Frisbie Hoar, a member of the president's own Republican Party, offered a mock tribute: "Your practical statesmanship has succeeded in converting a people who three years ago were ready to kiss the hem of the garment of the American and to welcome him as a liberator, who thronged after your men when they landed on those islands with benediction and gratitude, into sullen and irreconcilable enemies, possessed of a hatred which centuries can not eradicate."[21]

The Democrats' 1900 election platform had foreshadowed Hoar's attacks, blasting an ongoing war to degrees unheard of, as we will see, in war debates among Canada's federal parties. Marrying soaring idealism with baser racial hypothesizing, the Democrats judged the war in the Philippines an utter miscarriage:

> We condemn and denounce the Philippine policy of the present administration. It has involved the Republic in an unnecessary war, sacrificed the lives of many of our noblest sons, and placed the United States, previously known and applauded throughout the world as the champion of freedom, in the false and un-American position of crushing with military force the efforts of our former allies to achieve liberty and self-government. The Filipinos cannot be citizens without endangering our civilization; they cannot be subjects without imperiling our form of government; and as we are not willing to surrender our civilization nor to convert the Republic into an empire, we favor an immediate declaration of the nation's purpose to give the Filipinos, first, a stable form of government; second, independence; and third, protection from outside interference, such as has been given for nearly a century to the republics of Central and South America.[22]

Similar examples abound. After Woodrow Wilson implored Congress to declare war on Germany, Progressive Republican Senator George Norris denounced the unsavory influence of Wall Street lenders and munitions manufacturers on the call for US entry, which "has brought us to the present moment, when Congress urged by the President and backed by the artificial sentiment, is about to declare war and engulf our country in the greatest holocaust that the world has ever known … I feel that we are about to put the dollar sign upon the American flag." In 1970, George McGovern, a Democratic senator from South Dakota who would run for president in 1972, rose to address his colleagues in support of a bill calling for an end to the Vietnam War. That war, argued McGovern, stood as "the cruelest, most barbaric, and the most stupid war in our national history." McGovern then laid the blame for the conflict squarely on the shoulders of his colleagues, who had given President Johnson *carte blanche* for his escalation. "Every senator in this chamber is partly responsible for sending 50,000 young Americans to an early grave," he charged. "This chamber reeks of blood. Every senator here is partly responsible for that human wreckage at [military hospitals] Walter Reed and Bethesda Naval and all across our land – young men without legs, or arms, or genitals, or faces, or hopes." While these arguments did not always win the day, their venom, visibility, and often cogency, meant that principled stances against war penetrated popular consciousness, and were often vindicated by subsequent events and shifts in opinion. Indeed, such statements appear regularly in anthologies of great American speeches, and serve as required readings in courses on US history.[23]

Nor have the debaters always limited themselves to verbal sallies. In 1856, South Carolina Democratic congressman Preston Brooks was so incensed over Massachusetts Republican senator Charles Sumner's denunciations of pro-slavery violence in Kansas that he caned Sumner nearly to death in the Senate chamber, while fellow Democrat Laurence Keitt held horrified onlookers at bay with a pistol. Such immoderations, doubtless acts of political suicide in nations beholden to more staid political traditions, did little harm to professional careers in this case: in the next election, both Democrats involved were returned handily to Congress (whereupon Keitt incited a 50-member brawl after a Republican wandered too closely to the Democratic zone of the House floor.) Historian Williamjames Hoffer counted eight such corporeal altercations between 1798 and 1856; four featured canes, three involved pistols, and one led to an out-of-chamber duel that left a congressman dead. The rancour expressed in Congress, in other words, can be extraordinarily tangible; this combined with the notion that compromise reveals weakness and moral laxity, and one is left with a potentially explosive scenario. Of course, the most palpable expression of this combustibility is the American Civil War, which claimed 750,000 lives and ended only when the South had spent its men and resources. The war came, observed Brenda Wineapple, because by 1860 there remained no "incentive to budge, to question one's own righteousness, to create the grounds on which a compromise might occur."[24] In all, the broad freedom to speak enjoyed by American legislators includes the liberty to chastise other politicians, frequently from one's own party, on

SOUTHERN CHIVALRY — ARGUMENTversus CLUB'S.

4.2 Debating by other means: Brooks' caning of Sumner is the most notorious of several instances when words proved inadequate for the men of Congress. The original caption for this widely-reproduced lithograph, "Southern chivalry – argument versus club's" [sic], suggests an artist more sympathetic to Sumner and his cause than the tittering senators observing the assault. (John L. Magee, 1856.)

matters of war and peace. These fierce clashes in both word and deed have enjoyed a considerable impact beyond the walls of the Capitol building.

War opponents have also gained advantage from the fact that while US leaders are prone to exaggerations and an overreliance on moral rather than self-interested justifications for war, such excesses and obfuscations provide highly visible targets for administration opponents, and offer the possibility of acute domestic blowback as war supporters' own words are turned against them. Rookie congressman Lincoln first entered the national consciousness in 1846 by challenging President Polk's false charge that Mexican soldiers precipitated war by entering American territory, demanding to know the precise spot on which hostilities began. William McKinley's declaration that God himself had ordered the seizure of the Philippines so that Americans could uplift and Christianize the islands' "little brown brothers" generated extensive and inventive ridicule from those who witnessed the ensuing carnage, and suspected baser and more temporal motivations. McKinley's claim moved William Lloyd Garrison Jr, son and namesake of the famed abolitionist, to rework the lyrics to "Onward Christian Soldiers" thusly: "Then onward, Christian soldier! Through fields of crimson gore/ Behold the trade advantages beyond the open door." After Wilson's war message in 1917, Senator George Norris reminded his colleagues that Wilson's call rested on the fact that Germany had unlawfully declared certain international waters war zones, then noted dispassionately: "The first war zone was declared by Great Britain. She gave us and the world notice of it on the 4th day of November, 1914." Robert La Follette concurred, and added that the president also misled in characterizing the conflict as a straightforward war for democracy, citing British imperial holdings as evidence of the autocratic practices of America's proposed allies. For his part, President Truman initially painted Korea as a life-and-death struggle against an enemy bent on global domination. As the war descended into a bloody and protracted draw, his administration began to downplay the conflict's significance, arguing that "the United States must concentrate on the global threat and not over-commit to one of the many fronts in the fight against communism." The about-face contributed to disillusionment over the war from citizens and lawmakers alike.[25]

Subsequent war presidents likewise found that the prodigality they employed to bring Congress onside would serve to tarnish their foreign policymaking legacies beyond repair. The Pentagon Papers, leaked in 1971 to the *New York Times* and *Washington Post* by former Pentagon analyst Daniel Ellsberg, revealed that President Johnson had lied repeatedly and often outlandishly about American motivations, goals, tactics, and progress in Vietnam in order to gain congressional and public support. The leaked information revealed "a humiliation of Congress," charged Michigan Democrat Lucien Nedzi, a veteran of both the Second World War and Korean War, who like every Democratic *and* Republican member of the House, had trusted the Democratic president's avowals about the nature of the Tonkin Gulf incident and therefore voted to give him free reign in Vietnam.[26] (Here, unrestrained Cold War paranoia and the false assumption that Johnson – the "peace candidate" in the 1964 presidential race – would undertake a measured response to the North Vietnamese "attack" overrode the fractiousness more typical of war-related deliberations.) As political theorist Hannah Arendt observed shortly after Ellsberg's disclosures:

> The crucial point here is not merely that the policy of lying was hardly ever aimed at the enemy (this is one of the reasons why the papers do not reveal any military secrets that could fall under the Espionage Act), but was destined chiefly, if not exclusively, for domestic consumption, for propaganda at home, and especially for the purpose of deceiving Congress. The Tonkin incident, where the enemy knew all the facts and the Senate Foreign Relations Committee none, is a case in point.[27]

Nearly four decades after the Tonkin vote, George W. Bush built congressional and international backing for the invasion of Iraq on dubious and politicized intelligence about Saddam Hussein's weapons programs; when these claims withered under the weight (or absence) of evidence, so too did much of the president's support in Congress.[28] Lacking these calculated embroideries, presidents would have faced the prospect of failing to gain congressional assent, or undertaking (perhaps more limited) actions under more realistic rationales. Neither of these alternatives would provide war opponents with the depth and richness of manure that has fertilized American bitterness towards such conflicts as the First World War, Vietnam, and Iraq. The painstaking justifications for war crafted by the executive meant that some of the more controversial conflicts would forever, and sardonically, bear the names of their foremost salesman: the War of 1812 became "Mr. Madison's War," the Mexican-American War "Mr. Polk's War," and – although he had inherited it from his three predecessors – Johnson's deceptions and catastrophic escalation made the Vietnam War his very own.

Canada's political regime provides distinctive counterpoints to the structure and practice of American governance. The configuration of Canada's governmental system was adopted from that of Britain (and under that nation's consent and oversight) rather than overhauled to prevent the aggregation of executive power, confirming Canadian elites' faith in benevolent, centralized authority. This attitude demonstrated an affirmation of the British link; in fact, many of the era's English Canadians viewed Confederation as a step towards "a general imperial consolidation" that would eventually result in a formal "Federation of Great Britain and her Dependencies." This general orientation to governance also served as a rebuke of the perceived excesses of the "mobocracy" and sectionalism seen in the United States (a nation still smoldering from civil war when the Canadian fathers gathered in Charlottetown). That universal male suffrage came to Canada only in 1918, almost a century after it was adopted in the United States (and decades after New Zealand and Australia), confirmed and fortified the more elitist bent of Canada's political culture.[29]

Tellingly, when Canada's founding fathers expressed fears of tyranny, it was a tyranny not of the Crown or the executive, but of the majority. As a corollary to the faith in "benign" centralized control, then, Canadian governance became equated with the successful mediation of group rights – primarily those of English- and French-speaking constituencies, and to a lesser but still important respect to those of indigenous and religious communities. A strong state, so the argument goes, is essential to protecting French Canadians from English, and all citizens from both American influence and the nation's unique climatic and geographic challenges. These attitudes help to explain why even conservative Canadian politicians have traditionally endorsed a relatively high degree of state activism compared to their American counterparts. If government was a (barely) necessary evil to many Americans, traditional Canadian thinking was more likely to frame it in more affirmative terms, as a partner, rather than an enemy, to human freedom.[30]

The differences between Canada and the United States on these matters can certainly be overstated. After all, both nations possessed a common inheritance in British liberalism; both represented, at a fundamental level, projects to enshrine a liberal order dedicated to the primacy of the individual (a designation limited for many years to affluent, Caucasian males) and *his* right to property, equality before the law, and certain civil liberties. Similarly, in dedicating their efforts to creating "a climate favourable to money-making," nineteenth-century Canadian elites' overarching allegiance was to the preservation and enhancement of their rank, not to any altruistic notion of *noblesse oblige* or the common good, held political theorists Janet Ajzenstat and Peter Smith. In other words, Canadian state-building's debt to liberalism (not to mention the political ideals of the United States) was long undervalued. Instead, Canadians habitually inflated the impact of "toryism's supposedly 'organic' view of society," a view that was believed to instil "a sense of the common good that is superlatively absent in liberalism" – and most superlatively absent in the American strain of liberalism.[31]

.W. Jefferys   C-96362 Public Archives of Canad

Loyalists Drawing Lots for Their Lands, 1784

4.3 In this illustration by early-twentieth-century artist C.W. Jefferys, well-groomed loyalists draw lots for land, displaying the orderliness and gentility that would reach mythological proportions in subsequent assessments of Canadian political development. (C.W. Jefferys, National Archives of Canada, C96362.)

This is not to suggest that liberalism meant precisely the same thing on both sides of the border. Against any such conflation, two caveats can be raised. First, recognition of liberalism's centrality to the project of Canada does not require a complete dispatch of the influence of loyalism and its "tory touch," an influence most clearly distinguished when the United States is used as a frame of reference. Traits attributed to loyalism that encouraged the embrace of "a beneficently powerful

central state" – order, lawfulness, rank and hierarchy, a preference
for communal over individual rights, and elite-managed reform over
revolution – may not form the *sine qua non* of Canadian political culture, but they are certainly more salient to the Canadian record than
the American. The second caveat concerns the idea that while earlier
analysts habitually oversold the tory impact on Canadian state formation, this faithful reiteration served to provide the loyalist founding
myth a disproportionate stature in the public imagination. In these
continual reverberations, the political values and behaviours associated with loyalism were frequently equated with the most authentic
expressions of Canadianism, regardless of their relative sway over the
nation's founding and subsequent development.[32]

Canadians' penchant for viewing the forty-ninth parallel as a *cordon
sanitaire* inoculating an enlightened, cooperative altruism against a feral,
Darwinian free-for-all had much to do with the overzealous embrace of
the tory edition of Canadian development. Thanks to political institutions unrivalled in their capacity to foster social harmony, opined the
Canadian Methodist Magazine in 1880, "we are free from many of the
social cancers which are empoisoning the national life of our neighbours. We have no polygamous Mormondom; no Ku-Klux terrorism;
no Oneida communism; no Illinois divorce system; no cruel Indian
massacres." The *Methodist's* paean to the essential concord enjoyed by
Canadians (thanks to a beneficently powerful central state) was rich
even by late-nineteenth-century standards, and would become more
untenable with the subsequent expansion of market liberalism, industrialism, urbanization, and immigration; at the same time, the magazine's presumptions continue to resonate in various incarnations to
the present. Of course, Canadians often denounced, sometimes with
impressive vehemence, political parties, individual politicians, partisanship, political corruption, the influence of special interests, and so
on.[33] Until recently, however, few Canadian parallels could be found
for the deep-seated fears of "big government" or the "imperial presidency" that have animated so much American discourse, war-related
and otherwise.

Canada's parliamentary system also offers reasons why the nation
has not witnessed the degree of fractiousness and intra-party squab-
bling embedded in American foreign policymaking. Since a government can fall when it loses the confidence of the House of Commons,
federal political parties generally enforce strict discipline over their
members by "whipping the vote," and can threaten with expulsion

from caucus those who deviate from the script. Because of this requisite unanimity, power is highly centralized in the party leadership; as William Cross and John Chrysler observed, "in virtually all aspects of party life, including control of the party's purse strings, recruitment of staff, and organization of electoral strategies, the party leader is supreme." In contrast to the US system of checks and balances, majority federal governments in Canada face virtually no limits on centralized power, save for those prescribed by the division of jurisdictions between federal and provincial governments. The system is best characterized as a fusion, rather than separation, of powers, with Canadian cabinet ministers charged with both executive and legislative tasks.[34]

In the first half of the twentieth century, centralized control was particularly acute, with the dominant political organizations operating as cadre, rather than mass, parties. As Dan Azoulay observed, the era's Liberal and Conservative parties were "organized by the top party leadership, financed by a small number of well-connected party supporters in central Canada and characterized by minimal input from a relatively small membership."[35] And although Canada, too, adopted a bicameral legislature, its un-elected Senate served largely as a reviewing body for the work conducted in Parliament, and over time came to "function" as a sedentary paddock for aging patronage appointees, thus limiting the forums for consequential and spirited debate on matters of national significance. Not that the consent of the Senate or even of the House of Commons is needed before Canada commits to a foreign conflict: as mentioned above, and in further testament to the extraordinary powers of the executive, the decision rests entirely with the prime minister and his or her cabinet.

Canada's ethnic makeup provides further clues to the inclination towards foreign-policy consensus in Parliament. Immigration laws operant until the 1960s limited the entry of what were deemed "inassimilable races," leaving north- and west-European, and especially British, peoples to top census rolls well into the twentieth century. This is not to say that ethnic enclaves did not exist or that their members remained silent on international matters. After the turn of the twentieth century many members of Parliament came to represent ridings comprised of large percentages of "non-canonical" Canadians: for example, Jews in Montreal; Germans in Kitchener and Vancouver; Métis, Icelanders, Ukrainians, and Mennonites in the West; First Nations peoples clustered in various ridings throughout the North and West (rendering the 49th parallel in the west more like a borderland region, with populations on both sides exhibiting similar ethno-cultural characteristics). However, in addition to the fact that many of these groups were concentrated in rural areas far from centres of power, their political impact was limited by structural components of the nation's political system. Here again, centralized party discipline served to moderate the particular interests of any riding, and none more so than constituencies marked by potentially nonconformist views. Furthermore, representation in Parliament is assigned primarily according to population; aside from an ode to regional parity built into the mostly toothless Senate, there is no mechanism for also giving each region or province (which may, as in the case of Manitoba, feature a small population and a high percentage of non-canonical groups) equivalent and tangible influence on policy formation through a second chamber like the US Senate, where both Idaho and New York State possess identical clout. In this sense, the ostensible commitment to group rights clashes with the realities of political parties that are conditioned by the configuration of the parliamentary system to speak with one voice.

Of course, there is no analogy in the United States for an ethnic group like Canadian francophones, who throughout the twentieth century comprised roughly a third of the national populace and expressed a fairly cohesive and often oppositional outlook on their country's foreign policy. However, it can be argued that a state required to mediate the interests of two principal ethnicities – one possessing a clear numerical advantage – faces a more predictable, if not always more manageable, foreign policy dilemma than a state forced to contend with a number of divergent and politically powerful minority groups. Aside from a potential backlash from francophones (hardly an insignificant concern, as discussed below), Canadian leaders were able to manoeuvre the state into both world wars without the same degree of uncertainty facing their American counterparts, who confronted a myriad of potential fissures mapped out along ethno-cultural fault lines. The German, Irish, and East European presence in Canada, for instance, was small, dispersed, and politically neutralized by the nature of the country's political regime. Note, for example, that many Canadians of German, Ukrainian, and Irish descent expressed enmity to both the South African and First World Wars, and these groups voted heavily against conscription in 1942. Yet they enjoyed no independent and well-positioned advocates like Senators Borah or La Follette to register their concerns at the federal level (thus encouraging the myth that Quebecers stood largely alone in contravening the will of the rest of

Canada). As Desmond Morton noted, antiwar opinion certainly existed in early- to mid-century English Canada, but those possessing such leanings "found few outlets for their views." While many French Canadians certainly questioned the logic of following Britain into conflicts that posed no immediate threat to Canadian soil, potential francophone opposition was tempered by the fact that their country was not taking up arms against their European kin – to the extent that francophones even retained strong kinship ties to France. While the editors at Montreal's *La Presse* urged readers to form a regiment and "join France's heroic army" in 1914, such appeals did not prompt a stampede to Quebec recruiting stations. Many in that province bore a lasting grudge over France's willingness to dump its North American colony in the settlement to the Seven Years' War, and were dismayed by the secularism initiated by the French Revolution.[36]

An important qualification is required at this juncture. While American leaders fretted that their multiethnic composition meant joining conflicts in Europe could incite political stalemate, public revolt, or even civil war, there is no US parallel for the disharmony and bitterness provoked by the Canadian government's introduction of conscription in both world wars. The discord was so intense that it fractured the party unity that is normally the hallmark of parliamentary systems, provoked riots, and in the case of the Second World War, created a crisis that at points virtually paralysed the federal government. Upon entering that war, MP Ernest Lapointe, the Quebec lieutenant in Prime Minister Mackenzie King's cabinet, helped convince King to promise not to invoke conscription on the grounds that "it would wreck the Canadian war effort, destroy the national unity, and might even mean civil conflict." When King abandoned the pledge in 1944, he wrote in his diary that he believed "a situation of civil war in Canada would be more likely to arise" if his government *did not* introduce the measure.[37]

Anxieties over Canadian unity afflicted all federal governments to varying extents, and none more than that of the ultra-cautious Mackenzie King. In the interwar period, this scenario provided Quebec with a strong – and to many resentful Canadian anglophiles, disproportionate – voice in foreign affairs, prodding federal policymaking towards more isolationist, peaceable, and continentalist positions. But again, lacking a politically potent constituency of citizens with ethnic ties to the belligerents, Canadian leaders could commit the nation to European wars and British imperial ventures with the confidence that the move would not, in and of itself, inspire overwhelming waves of rebellion (either

"The National Maple in Danger"   Citizens' Union Committee.

Quebec Must Not Rule All Canada

4.4 While Quebecers believed themselves to be perennial losers of the debates over Canadian foreign policy, this Unionist campaign advertisement, like some later English-Canadian historians, took the opposite view. (*Toronto Telegram*, 14 December 1917.)

within party ranks or in the country at large). That state was achieved only by obliging citizens to fight oversees, a measure that laid bare French- and English-Canadian fissures over concepts of national identity, loyalty, and security, and over the scale of Canada's responsibilities to the crises abroad. While francophones were not alone in dissenting from the majority English Canadian view on these matters, the voices of others whose ethno-cultural affiliations led them to similar conclusions found, to reprise Morton, "few outlets." Accordingly, the conscription rows and the wider disputes over Canada's international duties were presented habitually in the French-English binary; this was at once an oversimplification of the variety of ethnic responses to the wars, and an accurate rendering of the ways in which the conflicts played out at the federal level.[38]

In all, the high degree of centralization and discipline that marks mainstream parties has precluded the type of regional and ideological elasticity (and in-fighting) seen in American political parties. One effect of the inflexibility and similitude is that Canadians whose interests did

4.5 Alberta Premier William Aberhart was the father of the social credit movement, but on matters of foreign policy, this "protest" party fell into line. ("100 Outstanding Albertans," Calgary Stampede website, http://corporate.calgarystampede.com/getting-involved/western-legacy-awards/100-years, accessed 12 January 2015.)

not align with the political bases of the Conservatives or Liberals were moved to form their own federal and provincial parties. But outside Quebec-based parties and the CCF, non-traditional "protest" parties focused primarily on domestic issues – monetary reform, social security, farmers' and workers' grievances, fair taxation – and the most successful, the Socreds, were positively anglophilic. The founder and spiritual leader of the Canadian social credit movement, Alberta Premier Reverend William Aberhart, was convinced that Anglo-Saxons constituted one of the lost tribes of Israel, and that the triumph of the British Empire would usher in the second coming of Christ, or vice versa. Their regional focus, meanwhile, consigned all of these upstarts to permanent third party status. They lacked the funding, organization, and broad appeal to seriously challenge the two dominant parties, and by extension, the nation's general orientation in foreign affairs.[39]

All of this points to the fact that, for Canada's majority governments at least, foreign policymaking has been a far more straightforward and less combative process than it has in the United States. If a ruling party, and more specifically, the cabinet, wishes to pursue a course of action, the outcome is preordained by the seat distribution of Parliament. Legislative congestion, authentic deliberation, and vote bartering of the likes witnessed in the United States can occur only during minority governments; otherwise, even the most controversial motions can gain parliamentary assent. When impassioned dissent from the majority

position is articulated, it serves primarily to appease the particular outlook of an opposition party, the dictates of a member's own conscience,
and/or the sentiments of his or her constituents; on the big issues, the
outcome of the vote is rarely in doubt (if the opportunity to vote is even
tendered).

These characteristics of Canadian governance present obvious advantages to officials contemplating matters of peace and war: lacking the
prerequisite to convince potential sceptics of the necessity of a course
of action, Canadian political leaders have been less reliant on the exaggeration or invention of national security threats. The moralism that
characterizes policymaking in the United States is not absent from the
Canadian context; as we have seen, a belief in the superiority of British
civilization meant that initiatives in defence of Britain were presented
habitually in language that extolled the pre-eminence of empire. And
on the question of war, Canadian leaders have heightened the stakes
to degrees that strained credulity, as in the sombre declaration that an
enemy victory in either of the two world wars would lead to the German seizure of Canada. Yet the requirement to manufacture consensus through any available means is largely absent in a parliamentary
system. Canadian executive and legislative discourse provides no USS
Greers, Tonkin Gulfs, or phantom WMDs to stain the image of past military actions and provide traction for war critics. Instead, war aims have
been presented in ways that, when compared to the American context,
are clearer, more limited and achievable, and generally agreed-upon
by a plurality of English-speaking Canadians of the era: defence of the
empire and the values for which it stands (with "empire" tantamount
to "civilization"), the upholding of international law and the rights
of neutral nations, and increased standing within the empire and on
the international stage. Canadians did not enter conflicts buoyed by
promises from their leaders that participation would bring an end to
the very institutions of warfare and imperialism, or "make the world
at last free." Rather, they hoped to preserve British civilization, pun-
ish aggression, assert their own claims to nationhood, and in the case
of Korea, contain communism and lend credibility to the incipient
United Nations and its collective security mandate. To the extent that
these goals were considered met, they helped to vindicate the sacrifices
made. What is more, Canadian leaders have been spared – or spared
themselves – the more nagging dilemma of justifying or obscuring their
instigation of an international conflict. As evidenced by the examples of
the Mexican-American, Vietnam, and Iraq wars, efforts to make a case

for deliberate breaches of international peace have led to some of the more spectacular presidential distortions.[40]

The above circumstances help to account for the lack of intra-party discord and a majority government's relative ease in enacting policy. But they should not obscure a basic truth about the Canadian system: namely, Parliament is by design an adversarial arena. Unlike the US Congress, where seats are arranged in a semi-circle facing the speaker, Canada's governing and opposition parties confront one another dauntingly across the aisle. Certain odes to civility are built into parliamentary proceedings – comments are addressed through the Speaker, and opponents are addressed not by name but as "the Honourable Member." However, Parliamentarians routinely train their rhetoric, gaze, and gestures directly at their foes, and in distinct contrast to the US Congress, the opposition is afforded the regular opportunity to question (read: assail) the ruling party, and most pointedly, the prime minister and his or her cabinet (who in this instance might long for the juridical *and* physical separation of powers enjoyed by their American counterparts). Intensive media coverage of Question Period renders what is the most combative component of Parliament the primary avenue through which citizens learn of the workings of government – a truth not lost on MPs, who have always played to the scribes, and later the cameras, in an effort to sway the (increasingly cynical) public.[41]

Do such arrangements lend themselves to more combative legislative discourse than that witnessed in the US Congress? Or has a national outlook that lays claim to orderliness and respect for authority, and that recognizes at least some obligation to respecting differentiated group interests in the name of national harmony, produced comparatively less histrionics and grandstanding – or to put it another way, less assertiveness, gravity, and memorability – in legislative discourse? Any disparities here are difficult to measure. At times the House has abided by the example of long-serving Liberal leader Wilfrid Laurier, who stated, "I have before me as a pillar of fire by night and as a pillar of cloud by day a policy of true Canadianism, of moderation, of conciliation." At other times – over issues of trade reciprocity with the United States, Anglo-Canadian naval relations prior to the First World War, conscription, the adoption of a distinctly Canadian flag (rendered especially testy by the ruling Liberal's minority status) – the oratory could become passionate, and sometimes malicious, personal, and puerile. At the very least, however, the Canadian parliamentary record reveals a greater disinclination to resort to physical assault. The sole example

4.6 "On guard" indeed: political adversaries in Canada's House of Commons are separated only by a few metres and a pair of Hansard reporters adept at transcription – but not necessarily physical intermediation. (18th Canadian Parliament, 1938, CGMPB / Library and Archives Canada / C-024358.)

occurred in 1878 after Guillaume Cheval, M.P. Rouville, played a Jew's harp while Vancouver Island member Arthur Bunster, un-affectionately dubbed the "ass of the House," attempted to speak. More recent House of Commons deliberations suggest that MPs have abandoned much of the pretense towards decorum, respect, and issues-based debating they maintained in the past, and that ruling parties have grown fonder of scripted, empty responses and the use of closure to suppress debate, a measure previously considered extraordinary and thus rarely invoked. For these reasons, wrote Frances Ryan rather unarguably in a 2009 article in *Canadian Parliamentary Review*, "Canadians have been steadily losing faith in Parliament and Parliamentarians" (and presumably could offer up a lavish list of contenders for the modern House's most noteworthy ass.) [42] But the generally unreserved bitterness that marks more recent governing- and opposition-party relations should not be grafted unmodified onto understandings of past Parliaments, when greater measures of courtesy and accord were expected, if not always extended.

At issue here is the fact that House of Commons deliberations over Canada's decision to go to wars from South Africa to Korea generated fewer sparks than might be anticipated, given that taking up arms is the gravest course any nation can choose. On the matter of war, major-party discipline merged with the ideological consonance between parties – and perhaps, with a fuller commitment to courtesy – to produce "debates" that scarcely qualify as such when contrasted to equivalent American deliberations. As Conservatives fashioned themselves the party of Protestant English Canada and British imperialism, they were hardly a brake on majority Liberal governments contemplating war in 1899 and 1939. In fact, Prime Minister Laurier's Liberals faced no opposition from Anglo MPs from either party over the dispatch of troops to South Africa; rather, the bulk of the condemnation from English Canada – expressed most pungently by Ontario Conservatives – centred on the conviction that the volunteer force of 1,000 was wholly insufficient.[43]

In a pattern that would re-emerge in later conflicts, South African war opponents confronted the quandary of obeying their conscience and constituents, or the bidding of their party. Quebec Liberal MP, cabinet member, and war opponent Henri Bourassa chose the former, resigning his seat rather than bowing to the will of his Liberal colleagues on South Africa. In his letter of resignation, he asked "whether Canada is ready to give up its prerogatives as a self-governing colony, its Parliamentary freedom ... and revert to its former status as a Crown colony." Re-elected by acclamation and sitting now as an independent, he moved a resolution requiring that Parliament decide the nature and extent of any future military engagements. This relatively modest proposal, one that would do little to impede majority governments favouring participation in foreign conflicts, marshalled only ten supporting votes in the 213-seat House. In a measure of the power of the executive over Canadian foreign affairs, Laurier committed 1,000 troops to the conflict in October 1899 by order-in-council without consulting Parliament, and another 1,000 less than three months later using the same procedure.[44] The absence of democratic consultation over foreign military engagements is remarkable enough, made more so because this was Canada's first official dispatch of troops abroad, a then-unprecedented step that would indeed establish a precedent and fundamentally alter the course of the nation's history.

Fifteen years later, Prime Minister Borden's Conservatives received the full endorsement of the Liberals – and even the backing of Bourassa – over Canada's commitment to the war against Germany. In fact it was Laurier, now in opposition, who provided the most impassioned and memorable rallying cry, promising that when Britain was imperilled, Canada would not equivocate. "When the call comes," Laurier assured Parliament, "our answer goes out at once, and it goes in the classical language of the British answer to the call of duty: 'Ready, aye, ready.'" Canadians following House of Commons deliberations on the matter would be treated to a litany of similar endorsements. Only Borden's 1917 call for conscription broke the solidarity over Canada's commitments to the First War, spurring passionate debates not over the wider rectitude of the conflict and Canada's participation in it, but over the limits of the nation's wartime obligations. A majority of English-Canadian Liberals so disagreed with Laurier's opposition to conscription that they broke party ranks to join a Unionist party under Borden, one that decimated the so-called Laurier Liberals in the 1917 election. In further testament to the extraordinary powers of a majority government, that electoral victory had been virtually guaranteed by the 1917 Wartime Elections Act, which for the first time afforded the franchise to women – but only those with sons, husbands, and brothers serving in the CEF; the same despotic legislation disenfranchised COs and "citizens of enemy origin naturalized since 1902." Following the war, Parliament acclaimed – without a recorded vote – Canada's endorsement of the Treaty of Versailles and membership in the League of Nations.[45] The anti-imperialism and isolationism that drove successful opposition to these measures in the United States (and provided some separation between Republicans and Democrats on America's foreign policy obligations) enjoyed considerably less support in Canada; by virtue of their willingness to defend the British Empire, anglophone members of Canada's principal parties were, in a sense, *de facto* internationalists.

While America's responsibilities towards the Second World War generated incendiary clashes in Congress between and among Republicans and Democrats, Canada entered the fray in the war's first days, and with near unanimity. At the outbreak of the conflict, the ever-cautious Mackenzie King maintained that he would "let Parliament decide" whether Canada would go to war. However, with his party holding more than 70 per cent of the seats in the House of Commons, and King and his cabinet bent on participation, the ode to parliamentary agency on the matter was more than a little disingenuous. As Granatstein and Morton wrote, the prime minister, "a sentimental anglophile, an Imperialist and a monarchist," never entertained the possibility of Canadian non-participation. Add to this the fact that the opposition Conservatives and third-party Socreds harboured some of the nation's most fervent monarchists, and the outcome of the discussion that followed was never in doubt. King and the ruling Liberals voiced enthusiastic endorsements for Canadian participation on the familiar grounds of the nation's links to Britain and Canada's duty to humanity and international law, endorsements whose passion – at least on Canada's duty to safeguard the king and queen – was eclipsed by that of Conservative and Socred leaders Robert J. Manion and J.H. Blackmore.[46]

Although a majority of Quebec MPs endorsed Prime Minister King's call for Canadian participation in the Second World War, the province also furnished three parliamentary dissenters. One need not agree with their claim that this was a battle solely over interests rather than principles to grant other aspects of their critique merit. One justification for Canadian participation struck Independent Liberal Maxime Raymond as profoundly ironic in light of the sovereignty otherwise touted by his parliamentary colleagues. "We are being asked to fight for the defence of liberty, when, in this very Canada of ours, it is being proclaimed that when England is at war, Canada is at war – in other words, we have not even the liberty of living in peace, when no one is doing anything to disturb it." Fellow Liberals Liguori Lacombe and Wilfrid Lacroix concurred, and provided prophetic warnings that the war would once again invite conscription and enduring domestic discord.[47]

Prior to the debate, King may have entertained apprehensions about the response of the CCF. Founded in 1932 on a manifesto that included an avowal to "refuse to be entangled in any more wars fought to make the world safe for capitalism," the party had captured seven seats in their first-ever federal campaign in 1935. After intensive internal deliberation, however, the CCF resolved to support the dispatch of Canadian troops to Europe in the fall of 1939, Hitler's expansionism having dampened their belief that all war was, at its root, an outgrowth of class conflict. The party's co-founder and conscience, J.S. Woodsworth, stood alone in breaking ranks, an act that led to his ouster as CCF leader. "While we are urged to fight for freedom and democracy," Woodsworth argued in his speech opposing participation, "it should be remembered that war is the very negation of both." In a statement that drew jeers,

Woodsworth testified that if one of his own children should refuse to
join the impending Canadian war effort on the basis of personal conviction rather than "cowardice" and faced imprisonment or execution
for their stand, "I shall be more proud of that boy than if he enlisted for
the war." It was through such unwillingness to compromise that historian Frank Underhill, a deep admirer of Woodsworth, called him an
"untypical Canadian." In the sense that "true Canadianism," to quote
Wilfrid Laurier, meant "moderation" and "conciliation," Underhill
was correct. Indeed, Woodsworth's willingness to defy even his own
party on matters of principle is something more common to American legislative practice – and for differing reasons, to that of Quebecers
battling the centralizing prerogatives of federal political parties. In the
end, Woodsworth stood alone, as even Quebec opponents of Canadian
participation muted their defiance. In the voice vote over the Canadian
declaration of war taken among the 245 members of the House, Woodsworth alone expressed opposition. In a step that surprised only those
who forgot it was required, the Canadian Senate then approved the
decision of the House unanimously.[48]

A little more than a decade later, the circumstances surrounding the
conflict in Korea conspired to render parliamentary deliberations over
the matter even more harmonious. First, the Liberal government of
Prime Minister Louis St. Laurent held one of the most commanding
majorities in Canadian history. Second, the war featured an array of
justifications that could please almost everyone: internationalists (with
CCF-ers and Liberals among the most committed) cheered the war's
UN authorization; continentalists (the preferred orientation of some
Liberals) counseled strong support for the United States; and Empire
Loyalists (a designation still worn proudly by Progressive Conservatives and Socreds) found comfort in the participation of the British.
Nearly all members, and even most Quebecers, could agree that a war
that curbed godless, international communist expansion was in the
national and/or celestial interest. Finally, with Parliament scheduled
to recess on 30 June, just days after the North Korean attack, some
analysts suspected that tough and seemingly crucial questions about
the war's origins, the influence of the United States on UN policy, and
Canada's responsibilities in the matter were "ignored in the inexorable
processes of prorogation and railway schedules to Canada's far-flung
constituencies."[49]

Whatever the origins, all three opposition parties supported the
Liberal's immediate offer of support and military observers, seeming,

in the words of Denis Stairs, "actually to compete for opportunities to support the government position" and contending "that Canada should be doing more ... The fact that the government," Stairs continued, "was being urged by democratically elected legislators to take a more active part in an ominously expanding conflict was intriguing."[50] *Ottawa Journal* reporter Norman Smith concurred:

> There was the Canadian Parliament begging its executive members to send ships or troops or planes to fight in a far-off mountainous land where no Canadians are and whose economic interest to Canada is less than that of Smiths Falls. And the begging was being done though nobody had declared war on anybody. It was being done, too, without any speeches of appeal or pressure having been made by the executive.[51]

When Quebec Liberal MP Jean-François Pouliot expressed hesitations about the American influence over the UN action and Canada's obligations to a distant, unknown land, fellow Quebec Liberal Maurice Boisvert shot back that it was "the duty of members of this Parliament to endeavour to get everyone in the country to back the policy of the government." An enraged Pouliot stormed from the House, "thus removing from the chamber its only serious malcontent," noted Stairs. Two months later, a reconvened and presumably tanned and refreshed parliamentary body revisited the issue of Canada's obligations to Korea. This time, only four MPs (two Quebec Progressive Conservatives and two Independents from the same province) condemned the Liberals' Korea policy in a special parliamentary session, accusing the government of downplaying the civil nature of the conflict, endorsing a US-led imperial agenda, and shifting Canada's colonial subservience from Britain to the United States. Badly outnumbered, their criticisms went nowhere. "In retrospect," conceded Stairs, "some of their observations appear surprisingly perceptive."[52]

As the above examples demonstrate, opposition in the House to Canadian participation in war has been submitted by the few Parliamentarians from French Canada willing to break the otherwise durable and rigorously policed bonds of party loyalty, or in the case of J.S. Woodsworth, from members of marginalized third parties (members further marginalized within their party for their stance). While, in the main, federal governments sought to craft a foreign policy that would not unduly antagonize Quebec, the ability of francophone opinion to shape that of the broader English-speaking public was limited at the best of times; midst the patriotic frenzy that often accompanies calls to arms, such opposition can generate rancorous backlash (not to mention accusations of disloyalty and sedition). Likewise, isolated "untypical Canadians" from third parties can be dismissed with relative ease. Accordingly, their words of hesitation and dissent remain occluded, belittled, forgotten. The titanic congressional debates over the proper resolution of the War of 1898, American intervention in both world wars, and the Treaty of Versailles – debates which at various stages could have tipped in either direction – have correlates in Canadian parliamentary discourse only over the matter of conscription (and even here, the outcome was predetermined by the support for the measure outside Quebec). Through the consensus that has otherwise typified House deliberations over foreign conflict, the notion that Canada's participation in wars was appropriate, natural, inevitable, beyond question, is written into the national tradition.

However, this "certitude" also involves something of a sleight of hand. Because of the homogenizing nature of parliamentary discourse, the near-unanimity of war support exhibited in the House has always outstripped the degree of consensus evident in the population as a whole. As a consequence, the majority of constituents who harboured doubts about Canadian participation in the major wars of the twentieth century – whose ancestral ties, pacifism, anti-imperialism, quest for greater Canadian autonomy, or any other "eccentricity" placed them outside the pro-war consensus – would not possess a representative on Parliament Hill willing or able to express sympathy for their stance.

America's military legacy also features its own democratic deficits on the matter of war: an executive that has fabricated, withheld, or massaged licentiously the evidence required by elected representatives to make informed decisions about international affairs; presidents who have used force without congressional assent (or even knowledge); leaders who have promised outcomes that they were in no position to deliver. When combined with a political system predicated on conflict, intractability, freewheeling debate, and individual prerogative, and one that provides greater voice to constituents from the margins, the upshot is fairly predictable: an exceptionally messy, volatile, and wide-ranging dialogue on war.

Chapter Five

Political Cultures: The Citizen
and the State

Randolph Bourne took seriously the founders' commandment to hold governmental and military authority to account; to this Progressive-era American journalist, war only deepened these burdens of citizenship. Writing in the aftermath of his country's 1917 metamorphosis from neutrality to belligerence, Bourne railed at the ease with which democratic and autocratic governments alike could "slide" their nation into war, maintaining that even in "representative" systems beholden to checks and balances, foreign policymaking had a tendency to revert to "the private property of the Executive part of the Government." Even in traditionally anti-statist America, he argued, warfare instigated instantaneous and alarming transformations: "The citizen throws off his contempt and indifference to Government, identifies himself with its purposes, revives all his military memories and symbols, and the State once more walks, in august presence, through the imaginations of men." Senator Robert La Follette shared these concerns about war's transformative faculties, insisting that once the nation becomes embroiled in war, a citizen "must be most watchful of the encroachment of the military upon the civil power. He must beware of those precedents in support of arbitrary action by administration officials which, excused on the pleas of necessity in war time, become the fixed rule when the necessity has passed and normal conditions have been restored."[1]

For his part, Bourne was more than a little apprehensive about a state's willingness to cede its power. In fact, he argued, "State is essentially a concept of power" – that is, an institution reflecting the will of its most aggressive citizens, and one that craves unrestricted centralized authority. Since warfare furnishes unparalleled levels of citizen subservience, he argued that "war is essentially the health of the State." "Only when the State is at war," he continued, "does the modern society function with that unity of sentiment, simple uncritical patriotic devotion, cooperation of services, which have always been the ideal of the State lover." But Bourne's libertarianism and idealism would not permit him to accept the past as prologue; war, he held, could be banished, but only by curbing the power of the state. "We cannot crusade against war without crusading implicitly against the State. And we cannot expect ... to end war, unless at the same time we take measures to end the State in its traditional form." Bourne's foil to state power was the nation, an essentially cultural understanding of a people inhabiting the same territory and supporting just enough bureaucracy for "internal administration" – "a federation of free communities," as he called it. "The State is not the nation," he explained, "and the State can be modified and even abolished in its present form, without harming the nation. On the contrary, with the passing of the dominance of the State, the genuine life-enhancing forces of the nation will be liberated."[2]

Bourne is one of those fascinating American paradoxes: an influential public intellectual, like Mark Twain, Mary Harris "Mother" Jones, Jane Addams, Robert La Follette, I.F. Stone, and Martin Luther King, who is at once quintessentially American in outlook and method *and* subjected to accusations of disloyalty. All of these figures spoke reverently about the Declaration of Independence and the Constitution, and drew many of their core messages from close and faithful readings of the fundamental components of those documents and wider American values, and all spoke passionately about the right to free speech and the value of dissent enshrined by the much-vaunted First Amendment. "Radical journalism," wrote Bourne, "seems to be the most direct means of bringing one's ideal to the people, to be a real fighter on the firing line."[3] Yet all paid dearly in their day for challenging authority and popular opinion, with the accusation "un-American" a common, and profoundly incongruous, charge.

Sanctions against Bourne included his firing from *The New Republic* for his antiwar writings, and the shuttering of the office at his new magazine, *The Seven Arts,* by a publisher who feared that Bourne's work would invite charges under the 1918 Sedition Act. In a letter to a friend, Bourne mourned, "the magazines I write for die violent deaths, and all my thoughts are unprintable." In a pattern that lends credence to Tocqueville's concerns over the "tyranny of the majority," a society adamant about upholding the sanctity of individual conscience also has the habit of pummelling those who take the notion most seriously. As American historian Max Paul Friedman observed, there exists "a tendency among those most outraged over anti-Americanism to eliminate from their idea of America so much of what is characteristic about the place," including "its extraordinary diversity," and "its polity founded on a tradition of dissent."

Twain wrote: "It is by the goodness of God that in our country we have those three unspeakably precious things: freedom of speech, freedom of conscience, and the prudence never to practice either of them." The famously caustic utterances of Twain himself, along with those of his fellow "anti-Americans" cited above, underline the hyperbole of the quip. Still, the backlash visited on those who disrupted comfortable conventions explains why some Americans might chose "prudence" over outspokenness.[4]

At the same time, while Americans have often been unkind to their more forthright contemporaries, they also have a custom of rejuvenating the names of the dissidents in the longer term. Indeed, immediately following the war, the theme of a government running amok over individual freedoms became standard fare in law journals, the popular press, and general histories of America's Great War experience, while in subsequent decades, a multitude of specialized studies appeared that lambasted the Wilson administration's anti-German propaganda campaign, assault on civil liberties and war resisters, and implementation of the draft.[5]

Bourne, an avowed leftist, also serves as a reminder that not all Americans who railed against "big government" were clustered on the right of the political spectrum, just as US conservatives' emphasis on low taxation and small government led many, despite the common assumption of their bellicosity, to take an active antiwar stance. While the previous chapter focused primarily on what has transpired within the formal mechanisms of the federal governance, the story is incomplete without the other half of the equation – that is, citizens' understandings of their role in the political process. Here again we can identify general traits that, at least in their degree of emphasis, are particular to Canada and the United States, and bear directly on the ways each society grapples with war. If the rationale behind democratic governments is to generate policy reflective of both the general will of the populace and the greater good of the polity, American leaders wishing to "slide" their nation into foreign conflicts would have to, by turns, placate and muzzle an exceptionally diverse and obstinate collection of sceptics.

In deploying the term "State lover" to enervate supporters of Woodrow Wilson's wartime repressions, Bourne aimed for a nerve. As with individualism, Americans have tended to embrace its ideological kin, anti-statism, to degrees unmatched in Western societies; while the British departed the American colonies in 1781, the generalized suspicion of governmental authority did not leave with them. Despite the implementation of a political system that reflected the will of the governed to an extent then-unmatched among nation-states, and despite the establishment of constitutional checks against authoritarian tendencies, wariness and often outright hostility towards government became an enduring component of the national fabric. Notwithstanding their desire to craft a system of governance by and for "we the people," Americans acquired a peculiar capacity to imagine their representatives as alien, as "Other." As political scientist Samuel Huntington observed, "opposition to power, and suspicion of government as the most dangerous embodiment of power [constitute] the central themes of American political thought," elsewhere noting that "the idea that people *should* trust their government is a radical departure from that tradition" (emphasis in original).[6]

One response to this suspicion of government involves seeking to render it as small as practically possible – and then, in the idyllic world of neoconservative libertarian and anti-tax crusader Grover Norquist, condensing it further. "I don't want to abolish government," assured Norquist in 2001, "I simply want to reduce it to the size where I can drag it into the bathroom and drown it in the bathtub." Deep distrust of government can be affirmed even by those who champion the role of a powerful, activist state in the redress of social ills. Radical journalist I.F. Stone, a keen supporter of the most interventionist government in American history, Franklin Roosevelt's New Deal regime, summed up his approach to reporting succinctly: "Now in the job of covering a capital, there's really certain basic assumptions you have to operate on. The first is that every government is run by liars, and nothing they say should be believed."[7] Declarations of affection for the nation are expected; the term "state-lover" carries roughly the same gist as "dupe," "swindler," or "sycophant."

In testimony to the power of anti-statism and individualism, many Americans have advocated and practiced civil disobedience, or the deliberate violation of laws in order to achieve political objectives coupled with a willingness to suffer the consequences, as a means of establishing and reinvigorating American ideals. This strain of activism runs from Boston's tea-chucking "Sons of Liberty" to the Patriots in the American Revolution, and on through the Abolitionists, Henry David Thoreau (who refused to pay taxes to protest the Mexican-American War), the Suffragettes, Martin Luther King and the Civil Rights activists of the 1950s and 60s, Vietnam War resistors, anti-nuclear activists, and a range of smaller, and sometimes disturbing, groups and figures (including the original Tea Partiers' self-appointed twenty-first-century heirs). The lessons Americans have gleaned through these efforts include the idea that civil disobedience can be effective, that citizen-activists have the right and capacity to change laws and attitudes through defiant public engagement. In 1970, looking back on a decade rife with strategic, collective law-breaking in the name of racial, gender, and sexual equality, nuclear disarmament, peace in Vietnam, the reorientation of the Democratic Party, and a range of related and unrelated causes, American legal scholar Edward Levi found the practice embedded in the very legal praxis of his nation. It is, he wrote, "one of the most serious oddities of our law": the fact that a citizen "is encouraged or in some sense compelled to establish a significant legal right through a personal act of civil disobedience."[8]

Levi's contemporary, political scientist Wilson Carey McWilliams agreed that tactical law-breaking is foundational to the effective workings of American jurisprudence. The court's "tasks," he argued, "depend, in part, on public action," concluding that "the court acts, in fact, to authorize disobedience to otherwise legitimate authority, and it depends on citizens who will take advantage of its authorizations." The esteem for individual conscience combines with distrust of the state, and for some, a sense of national mission, to foster a climate where "criminality" aimed at purifying the law and society becomes a most American act – one "primarily American in origin and substance," in the words of political theorist Hannah Arendt.[9] And as suggested by the above list of episodes in civil disobedience, military ventures have been high on the list of the insubordinates' targets. These experiences, together with the strains of chosen-ness and perfectionism that have captivated various Americans throughout their history, help explain the presence of a broader base of idealism among some Americans – one that seeks to expose and purge perceived deficiencies, including the resort to warfare, from the national experience (and in the singular optimism of the Wilsonian moment, from the globe itself).

Certainly, the degree of anti-statism has waxed and waned, often in accordance with perceptions of national security threats. Until the

Second World War, the protection provided by the combination of vast oceans and weak neighbours (i.e., "free security") allowed the republic to flourish without the degree of centralization required in states facing more immediate threats, permitting the small-state ideology to gain increasing purchase over the American imagination. An extreme variant of this view – anarchism – enjoyed its heyday in the decades surrounding the turn of the twentieth century, stimulated by extreme disparities in wealth, the palpable influence of moneyed interests on government policy, and the violence employed by state and corporation alike in order to restrain aggrieved groups. That immigrants brought traditions of labour radicalism with them, and suffered some of the worst exclusions, made them overrepresented in the movement (further marginalizing it). Even so, as David Goodway argued, the anarchist ideal had deep roots in the American experience, "growing out of the values of the American Revolution and Jeffersonian democracy," and exhibiting a considerable influence on the outlook of such thinkers as Emerson and Thoreau. Conversely, in times when crises threatened the nation as a whole and not merely its most vulnerable citizens, Americans have often turned to the otherwise-reviled state for deliverance. The governmental activism of the New Deal gained wide acclaim in the midst of the Depression; in the early, anxiety-ridden years of the Cold War, Americans rallied around Truman's call to contain communism, muting much of the anti-governmental rhetoric that otherwise formed a staple of US political discourse.[10] Similar trends were observable during "hot" wars and following the 9/11 attacks.

Adherence to anti-governmental sentiment has also varied according to region, cultural group, class, and gender. Since the earliest days of the nation, white southerners have appealed to "states' rights" as a means of reigning in the excesses of centralized authority (and protecting the institutions of slavery, and later, segregation), going so far as to take up arms against the federal government over the issue. By contrast, women, blacks, and other marginalized groups have often called for the expansion of federal power to tackle social and economic inequalities. Brenda Gayle Plummer's study of mid-twentieth-century African American internationalism revealed that, to the mortification of American officials, blacks embraced a higher power still – that of the United Nations – when their own government failed to uphold UN Declaration of Human Rights' clauses guaranteeing equality. Still, as Gary Wills has shown, distrust of government, social superiors, and authority in general has claimed, and continues to claim, committed

5.1 A branch of the American tradition: British artist and socialist Walter
Crane pays tribute to the American anarchists executed after the 1886
Haymarket riots in Chicago. (*Liberty Magazine*, London, 1894.)

and sometimes fanatical adherents from across the American political spectrum.[11]

Wills and others have argued vigorously and convincingly against the commonly held US beliefs that federal power has been antithetical to American progress, and that the sweep of their nation's history is marked by the devolution from a laissez-faire Eden to a coercive and authoritarian centralized bureaucracy. Such "myths," as American legal historian William Novak called them, overstate "the so-called natural development of individualism, private rights, civil society, free labour, and a free economy in American history ... [and obscure] the more historical and 'artificial' role of collective decision-making, public law, government, and regulation in American political-economic development." In reality, as Wilson Carey McWilliams, and more recently E.J. Dionne Jr have argued, American political discourse reveals a constant struggle to balance the virtues of individualism and community obligation (or liberalism and republicanism, as the founders called them). Yet many Americans have held firm to the conviction that the ideal government is something approaching no government, that the centralization of power represents the corrupting influences of European tradition (leading agitated American conservatives to rail against "the Swedenization of America"), that the American model is, or should be, exceptional in its minimalism. "That government is best which governs not at all," counselled Thoreau, an abolitionist and pacifist whose view on this matter at least has enjoyed broad support from slaveholders, American militia groups, and the National Rifle Association, among others.[12]

In no small irony, many of the previously discussed factors contributing to the volatility and individual prerogative inherent to the American legislative process also make significant contributions to citizens' cynicism regarding their government. The Constitution's framers introduced checks and balances to make policymaking ponderous and reflective rather than effortless and impulsive, but this deliberate awkwardness led to persistent doubts about the government's ability to "get things done." The immoderations associated with limitless fundraising tainted politicians as craven and pliable, while blurring the lines between the platforms of Republicans and Democrats. The weakness of political parties, along with candidates' courting of special interests (business, labour, ethnic groups, and the like) further muddied party distinctions, leading many potential voters to question whether either party truly stood for principle or the greater good. Perhaps most significantly for our purposes, the rhetorical excesses required to override congressional gridlock on matters of foreign policy – an overreliance on fear, embellishment, half-truths, and moralism, along with an associated disinclination to acknowledge self-interest – provided a rather predictable recipe for subsequent citizen discontent and cynicism once a fuller measure of the facts and costs associated with the policies was revealed.[13]

On the question of war, then, a nation born in distrust for authority has been provided much on which to nourish its original suspicions. A great deal of this generalized, public disenchantment echoes the disillusionment and disgust voiced by elected representatives over the unreliable claims made by the executive to win votes for military action. McKinley's assurance that the United States engaged in "benevolent assimilation" predicated on "the temperate administration of affairs for the greatest good of the governed" rang hollow when Americans learned that "uplift" involved concentration camps, widespread torture, and the indiscriminate liquidation of hundreds of thousands of America's new wards. "It is a matter of congratulation that you seem to have about finished your work of civilizing the Filipinos," Andrew Carnegie wrote to a member of McKinley's cabinet in the early stages of the insurrection. "It is thought that about 8000 of them have been completely civilized and sent to Heaven. I hope you like it." Woodrow Wilson's overselling of the selflessness, nobility, and global transformation that would mark US intervention in the Great War was bound to produce widespread bitterness once the dust had settled and the ledger calculated. In truth, revenues generated for American defence-related industries were at once handsome and, to many Americans, vulgar; *pace* the embellished and simplistic claims of German malfeasance purveyed by Wilson and the Committee on Public Information, culpability for the war's origins and excesses lay, to varying degrees, on all sides, and the world was scarcely closer to an American-led millennium of peace and justice following the conflict than it had been prior to 1914. As Randolph Bourne observed after US intervention, "the penalty the realist pays for accepting war is to see disappear one by one the justifications for accepting it."[14]

The widespread abjuration of the Great War in American popular consciousness achieves a good deal of logic when read in the light of the unbridled idealism and misinformation that surrounded US intervention, and in the ensuing appraisals of who had won and lost in the process. Polls from the late 1930s revealed that fully 82 per cent of Americans supported the markedly anti-capitalist notion that "the manufacture and sale of war munitions for private profit should be prohibited," and that 70 per cent believed US participation in the war was a mistake – a figure that dropped just two percentage points in a survey conducted after the September 1939 German invasion of Poland. Americans were also inclined to believe that the system itself was to blame, that reforms were needed to constrain the ability of the state, and especially the executive, to manoeuvre an unsuspecting or reluctant nation into war. Pollsters found strong majorities in favour of the proposal that declarations of war and the imposition of the draft should require authorization in a national referendum, and that Congress "was more to be trusted than the president to keep the United States out of war." As the statement implies, war was a malady manufactured elsewhere and one that the nation should "keep out of" on principle, but one for which the executive branch seemed to exhibit a fatal attraction. Trust in the assurances of their leaders – according to Samuel Huntington, never a commodious resource at the best of times – had been further sullied by the illusions spun by the president and by the mendacity of the CPI. In this case, the deception proved particularly tragic: subjected to the overheated demonization of "the Hun" during the First World War, Americans were slower to believe, and act upon, reports of the Nazis' "final solution."[15]

The zenith of anti-governmental sentiment likely occurred in the wake of Vietnam and Watergate – episodes that stained foreign and domestic affairs, as well as Republican and Democrat alike. Surveys revealed that the percentage of citizens who felt they could "trust the federal government" stood at a remarkable 75 per cent in the first year of the Johnson administration. The figure was buoyed by the certainties of the Cold War, the memory of the recently martyred President Kennedy, Johnson's promotion of benevolent government intervention through his "Great Society" programs, and the legislative progress made on race relations confirmed by the 1964 passage of the Civil Rights Act. By the late 1970s, with the Great Society programs eviscerated in order to prosecute a disastrous war, progress on civil rights stagnant, and a president driven from office for his Mafioso-like machinations, the figure had bottomed out at 25 per cent. When a later administration's assurances that Americans invading Iraq would find weapons of mass destruction and a populace that welcomed them as liberators proved baseless, support for the operation plummeted.[16]

Deep-seated fears of centralized authority have also led many Americans to be apprehensive about any war, regardless of the pretexts under which it may have been instigated. The basic reasons are twofold: First, enlightenment-era republican philosophy (which owed a good deal to British liberalism) depicted warfare as an ailment incubated exclusively by monarchies – and paid for, in blood and taxation, by the people. Government "of the people" would therefore eliminate wars of aggression, and wars of defence would be necessary for republics only so long as covetous kings ruled foreign lands. (The same belief moved Canadian liberals like Goldwin Smith, also nurtured by the British liberal tradition, to press for a termination of the imperial yoke.) President George Washington's warning to avoid permanent alliances and maintain a "defensive posture" demonstrated the logic of a people convinced that monarchy and warfare were synonymous.[17] Second, warfare itself was such a pernicious force that it had the capacity to return a free people to the chains of tyranny. As James Madison, author of the Bill of Rights and fourth president of the United States, argued:

> Of all the enemies to public liberty war is, perhaps, the most to be dreaded, because it comprises and develops the germ of every other. War is the parent of armies; from these proceed debts and taxes; and armies, and debts, and taxes are the known instruments for bringing the many under the domination of the few. In war, too, the discretionary power of the Executive is extended; its influence in dealing out offices, honors, and emoluments is multiplied; and all the means of seducing the minds, are added to those of subduing the force, of the people ... No nation could preserve its freedom in the midst of continual warfare.[18]

Anxieties over the power of wartime governments to "subdue" the people led Madison and other architects of the Constitution to consider including the option to refuse military service in the Bill of Rights. The provision was featured in an early draft of the Second Amendment concerning citizen militias, as the framers believed – wrongly, according to subsequent Supreme Court rulings – that the Constitution limited citizens' military obligations solely to the militia, not the federal army or navy.[19]

A portion of this fear of professional soldiers was inherited from Britain, where Oliver Cromwell's New Model Army had ably demonstrated the harm such a force could do to liberty and the rule of law. The American colonists' own encounter with Madison's devilish vortex – war, debts, taxation, and tyranny – exacerbated the angst. The Seven Years' War led the English Parliament to impose higher taxation imposed on the thirteen colonies – famously, without allowing the colonists representation in the legislative process. A series of new and newly enforced levies were to be a means of paying down the Crown's war debts and funding the colonists' continued defence, in the form of a British standing army. Tensions soon emerged over the presence of British regulars. Writing in the *Boston Gazette* in 1768, Boston politician and future revolutionary leader Samuel Adams advised that "even when there is a necessity of the military power, within a land, which by the way rarely happens, a wise and prudent people will always have a watchful and jealous eye over it; for the maxims and rules of the army, are essentially different from the genius of a free people, and the laws of a free government."[20]

Adams was right to be concerned, for trouble was brewing. The British army would soon be deployed not for the colonists' protection, but to subdue the latter's burgeoning and fairly predictable mutiny against taxation, despotism, and in turn, military repression. Rather than giving in to rebel demands, the British government's response involved heaping on additional servings of military force and direct rule over the colonies, both of which would require additional sources of revenue. Wound into this ever-constricting spiral of cause and effect, insult and injury, reaction and overreaction, both the Revolutionary War and the new nation's antimilitaristic creed represent consummate examples of determinism (with a more recent variant, to continue the force-engenders-submission doctrine, being the assurance that extra-judiciary executions of alleged terrorists in predatory drone attacks – attacks that have also produced extensive "collateral damage" – will *reduce* the number of America's international enemies.) No surprise, then, that the Declaration of Independence's laundry list of George III's abuses included the presence of standing armies "among us, in Times of Peace," and the Crown's efforts "to render the Military independent of and superior to the Civil Power." The panacea, to the framers of the Constitution, would be to discourage the establishment of permanent armies and, as we have seen, to place the decision to make war in the hands of Congress. These measures had resonance. As historian Richard Rubenstein wrote, when Tocqueville toured America a half century after its divorce from Britain, he marvelled at Americans' disinclination "to engage in foreign wars, and the absence among them, except for a handful of professional soldiers, of any cult of military power and glory."[21]

On this matter – that permanent, standing armies were unnecessary and unwelcome – Americans and Canadians were in relative accord.

This attitude was transplanted to Canada via British traditions and, more surprisingly, from the loyalists who quit American territory but not all the ideals upheld by their Revolutionary War tormentors. Thus the esteem of the citizen militia in both national traditions, an esteem built upon aggrandized tales of martial accomplishments. (Rough plotline: individual civilians hear the bugle call and drop fishing net, field hoe, and rucksack filled with pelts, and fuse into a cohesive and deadly battalion that draws upon the same skill sets, brawn, and resolve that brought success in gentler times.) Canadians did not need a standing army, wrote editors of the *Toronto Globe* in 1870, "because they possess the best possible constituents for a defensive force in themselves. The finest soldiers are men whose own stake and interest in the conflict impel them to respond to the call to arms."[22] But lurking behind this paean to self-reliance was the belief, or at least the hope, that the British navy and army would defend Canada should the need arise – and until the early twentieth century, few Canadians held illusions about who, specifically, might pose a threat to their nation. Canada was not, in other words, blessed with free security.

Opposition to a professional Canadian army, then, was only partially due to its latent threat to liberty. In truth, when Canadians spoke pejoratively of "standing armies," they also reflected a set of mutually-supporting, pragmatic assumptions: the presence of British regulars (to most English Canadians, not repressive occupiers but guardians against American territorial avarice) made a Canadian contingent redundant; armies were costly, and in the context of British protection, wrote Granatstein, "a drain on the nation's resources, nothing more"; if the Americans ever turned on Canada and Britain decided not to intervene, a Canadian army would be overrun. "Any attempt at resistance would be useless," wrote a militia officer. "We should be as a child in the hands of a giant, and immediate submission would be our inevitable lot." Accordingly, Canada's first Militia Act, drafted a year after Confederation, created "no more than a modest auxiliary for the British regular garrison which really defended Canada," observed Desmond Morton.[23] Significantly, the Dominion's founders issued no generalized warnings about dangers of armies and warfare to liberty, and included no checks on the growth or exercise of military power in the Constitutional Act of 1867, instead simply reiterating that the British sovereign remained the commander-in-chief of Canada's forces.

Over the next few decades, the hostility Canadians maintained towards permanent, home-grown and -funded standing armies began to abate. As the threat from the United States moderated, Britain determined that its troops would best serve imperial interests elsewhere, and in 1871 removed the garrison defending Canada. While some Canadians of the era may have relaxed their suspicions that the United States sought continental domination, internal threats from indigenous groups, the Métis, and radical labour could and did disturb the peaceable kingdom, confirming the usefulness of full-time, professional soldiers to the maintenance of order (even if in these years the professionals were referred to as a "Permanent Active Militia" rather than an official Canadian army). Meanwhile, the escalating competition between European colonizers for territory and wards in Africa and Asia led to a role reversal in metropole-colony expectations: Britain now appealed to Canada and the other Dominions for military assistance in the great civilizing crusade for empire, first in the Sudan in 1884 and fifteen years later in South Africa (with more urgent requests pending). These appeals for a "common defence" of empire generated an enthusiastic response among a cadre of Canadian advocates for compulsory military training and the expansion of the Dominion's armed services, men mostly of British heritage and elite status residing in Ontario who considered militarism an antidote to the emasculating influences of urban, bureaucratic drudgery. A powerful, homegrown force ready to defend the far reaches of the empire would also alleviate the shame of appealing to the British – of forever remaining a dependant – should a threat to Canadian soil materialize. Stephen Leacock epitomized this view when in 1907 he explained his support for a Canadian-British military partnership: "I that write these lines," Leacock declared, "am an Imperialist because I will not be a Colonial."[24]

Leacock was by no means alone. By the early twentieth century, older hesitations about militarism were becoming increasingly unpopular, even hazardous. In a context where British holdings were at once unprecedented in scale, confronting mounting challenges from colonial subjects and European rivals, and central to many Canadians' pride and self-concept, warnings against militarism and standing armies could be construed as deliberately anti-British, anti-imperialist, and ultimately disloyal. At least one of these charges – that of anti-imperialism – Goldwin Smith would not deny. In order to further his longstanding campaign against empire, Smith also became a leading opponent of the compulsory cadet training that was spreading to Canadian schools in years between the South African and First World Wars. Such training, Smith argued, "is a desperate attempt to lead into the wrong path those not yet capable of choosing for themselves, and to infect the whole rising generation with the military microbe now so actively at work in the brains of a few." But Smith's view was losing ground, and a surge of militant imperialism eroded much of the previous hesitations to the professional armies that, as those on both sides of the debate understood, formed the vanguard of the march of empire.[25]

To the south, too, opposition to standing armies was under assault. Despite the anti-militaristic ideals of American republicanism, the new nation would grow to become synonymous with warfare. In the nineteenth century, major conflicts with Britain, Mexico, and Spain were interspersed with, and sometimes components of, the myriad campaigns against indigenous groups that began in the earliest days of settlement and persisted into the twentieth century. Burgeoning economic ties with Latin America were accompanied and often stimulated by US naval and marine incursions in the region. Even though they remained small by European standards, standing armies became a permanent feature of government expenditures and the executive-branch toolkit, and as the framers warned, centralized power grew apace. As a member of congress, Abraham Lincoln had voted to censure President James Polk for "the most oppressive of all Kingly oppressions": the ability of one man "to make war at pleasure." Once in the White House himself, Lincoln mustered the state militia, extracted funds from the treasury to fund the military, suspended habeas corpus, and blockaded southern states deemed to be in rebellion against the federal government – all without congressional consultation, much less approval. Although Lincoln's actions were taken to prevent the dissolution of the country rather than initiate a foreign war, the president himself conceded that they might be illegal in his subsequent request that Congress approve them retroactively. Predictably, rebellious southerners cried tyranny, but Congress and the Supreme Court endorsed Lincoln's maneuverings. However, as was the case with FDR and the USS *Greer* incident, controversial actions taken for what many considered noble ends raised fears that a model had been established – in Lincoln's case, a precedent "for transcendent executive power during emergencies that exist only in the hallucinations of the Oval Office," in Arthur Schlesinger's notable phrase.[26]

Despite these transformations, citizens who opposed the state's growing fondness for militarism possessed a clearly defined and commonly recognized reservoir of political thinking on which to draw. The threat to constitutional principle and individual freedom posed even by

THE VAMPIRE.

Abe.—"COLUMBIA, THOU ART MINE, WITH THY BLOOD I WILL RENEW MY LEASE OF LIFE—AH! AH!"

5.2 Blood-sucking tyrant Abraham Lincoln menaces Columbia, goddess of
liberty. (Matthew Somerville Morgan, "The Vampire," *Comic News*,
26 November 1864, The Western Reserve Historical Society, Cleveland, Ohio.)

"good wars" moved a range of Americans to maintain the "watchful and jealous eye" over military power counselled by Samuel Adams. The Anti-Imperialist League predicated its resistance to the War of 1898 on disapproval over the growing militarism of, and executive control over, US foreign policy – not merely over the nation's "imperial turn." Like many of the academics who bore that label and came to dominate the field in the interwar years, progressive historian Vernon Parrington added the issue of class to the traditional concerns about war's impact on liberty and national creed. Warfare, he argued, constituted the greatest threat to democracy because it furnished governmental *and* business interests with the optimal conditions under which to magnify their authority at the expense of the commons. For Parrington, the war with Spain was one of the worst offenders, as it provided a two-pronged assault on American liberal ideals: it strengthened what he called "the aristocracy" at home while denying self-government abroad.[27] To Americans accustomed to viewing any aggregation of power with distrust, these were worrisome trends indeed.

The differences between Americans and Canadians on attitudes towards the state can be quite stark. The disparities have also been embellished by a tendency to undervalue and underreport the dissent, anti-authoritarianism, and resistance that have also been components of the Canadian story; once again, this erasure functions to separate (and hierarchicalize) the two national communities and provide Canadians a means of self-definition. As Ian McKay pointed out in *Reasoning Otherwise*, despite a veritable explosion in the numbers and influence of Canadian leftists between 1900 and 1920, the nation's libraries contain significantly fewer works on early century radicalism than the repositories of other comparable nations, observing that "Canada is unusual in this respect." Similarly, labour historian Kenneth Tunnell argued that the underreporting of labour violence in Canada by his colleagues in the field served as means of setting the nation apart and above the "violence, bloodshed, and near-anarchy" to which they consigned American labour history. To emphasize dissent and repression in Canadian history, then, would counter the claims to the "peaceable kingdom" that English and French Canadian elites have upheld as an antidote to the corruption, immorality, lawlessness, and hedonism incubated by American republicanism. It would, in other words, corroborate Canadian historian Frank Underhill's assertion that his nation was not as distinctive as his fellow citizens believed or hoped, that in fact, "the United States is simply Canada writ large."[28]

Underhill's conflation of the cultural sensibilities of the neighbouring countries has never been terribly popular. In the words of historian Jeffrey Brison, "in the mythology that pervades discussions of the political cultures and of the 'essential' national characteristics of Canada and the United States, simplistic juxtapositions have tended to reign supreme." Some of these juxtapositions would include statist versus anti-statist, deferential versus disorderly, communal versus individualistic, consensual versus conflicting. Especially following the Second World War, wrote Michael Gauvreau, Canadian elites cultivated and embellished these distinctions though a conscious and coherent "rhetorical strategy and a set of cultural institutions and policies dedicated to manufacturing national consciousness." Failure to underscore and preserve these distinctions, these intellectuals believed, would result in nothing less than the Americanization, and therefore eradication, of the Canadian national character. These views undergirded the conclusions of Massey Commission (1949) and a host of other governmental initiatives that sought to shield Canadians from American mass culture through state promotion of an anglophilic nationalism in broadcasting and the arts. In other words, as is the case with Americans who oversell the so-called natural development of individualism in their history, it is also possible to overstate the grassroots and organic development of these "essential" Canadian affinities for the state, deference, and consensus. These characteristics were, in part, outcomes of an elite-driven project to preserve a particular kind of Canadianism – and not incidentally, to tutor the mid-century waves of newcomers in the proper approach to citizenship in their new land.[29] All states and social elites wish, of course, to be obeyed and revered, but here we have a particularly opportune synergy between that desire and the definition of what it meant to be authentically Canadian: namely, one who is deferential to authority.

While the disparities can and have been overstated and overdetermined, it is not particularly courageous to claim that, when compared to the tumult often witnessed in the United States, civil society in Canada has often appeared more civil. Writing in 1970, Carl Berger observed that "the greater obedience to the law by Canadians compared to Americans was not some imaginative invention but a feature which nearly everyone who has contrasted the two countries has remarked upon." Indigenous peoples, long vital to the economic viability of European colonists and fur-trading companies alike, and often inhabiting zones far from white settlement, were not subjected to the kind of continuous, and often shockingly sadistic, armed assaults perpetrated by land- and resource-hungry Euro-Americans. Anarchism, the most profound testament to anti-statism, "has never generated much support" in Canada according to the *Canadian Encyclopedia*, "although small groups of activists have existed sporadically in larger cities and anarchist ideas have lightly influenced a number of writers." Attempts to locate anarchism in the Canadian record generally result in the revelation that Russian-born US citizen Emma Goldman, deported to the Soviet Union in 1919 for her activities, spent her last days in Toronto, and that writer George Woodcock (born in Canada but raised in Britain) supported the cause. As a recent study by Travis Tomchuk makes plain, such an assessment underrates the significance of early twentieth-century anarchists to the Canadian left (and the substantial interplay between Canadian and American anarchists); even so, the movement never approached the popularity witnessed in the United States. The socialist movement in general took longer to coalesce in Canada than in much of the Western, industrialized world, providing supporters of Canadian liberalism assurances that theirs was indeed a more peaceful and consensual order (and leaving them entirely unprepared for the shock of the widespread leftist revolt that began in the last years of the Great War and produced considerable success at the ballot box between the wars).[30]

There was, then, some basis for the national clichés. Canadian Sociologist S.D. Clark believed that the natural environment played a leading role in fashioning them, arguing that America's geography "favoured individual enterprise and limited political interference," while the challenges posed by the Canadian landscape called for "large-scale bureaucratic organizations and widespread intervention by the state." Here, then, was a people that needed the state, and a nation less defined by the warrior than the bureaucrat; in this view, its citizens were thus bound to exemplify the classic organizational virtues of order, deference, hierarchy, and collective limitations upon individual autonomy.[31] And to reiterate, English Canadians did not consider themselves "occupied" by a hostile foreign army, but rather protected by British troops from an expansionist neighbour, and the Fathers of Confederation did not compose the rules for their society immediately following an encounter with military oppression.

Frank Underhill did not dispute that some of these differences existed, nor did he celebrate them, considering Canada's more submissive and conservative variety of liberalism the unfortunate result of the fact "that the first great liberal democratic upheaval in nineteenth-century

Canada, the movement of Papineau in Lower Canada and of Mackenzie in Upper Canada, the movement which was our Canadian version of Jacksonian democracy, was a failure." Canadian quiescence, to
Underhill, was simply the product of a people who had yet to fully
dispense with a feudal mentality. As Charles Taylor observed, "increasingly, Underhill came to view Canadian politics as an insipid and
immature variant of the stirring activities which occurred within the
great republic."[32]

If Underhill considered the anti-authoritarian commotion south of
the border "stirring," Canadian Tories had long been "gratifyingly
appalled," in the words of historian S.F. Wise, by the same performance,
considering it an object lesson in how *not* to go about organizing a society. Political theorist Katherine Fierlbeck ascribed some of these tory
sensibilities to Edmund Burke, who valued "a civility born out of the
medieval codes of chivalry ... a sense of moderation and measure in
action and behaviour, and an acceptance of duty and one's place in
the social landscape." "Respect for authority, for example," Fierlbeck
continued, "is quite evident in the Canadian political tradition, and
evidence of this deference has ranged from the peaceful opening up
of the Canadian West, in comparison to the violence of American frontier settlement, to modern gun laws." Note again the rhetorical strategy: the "opening" of the Canadian West was not, in fact, particularly
"peaceful." While armed clashes were considerably rarer north of the
border, in the years following Confederation the federal government
did most of its killing by stealth rather than armies and massacres,
deliberately promoting starvation and disease to clear western regions
for the advance of "civilization." But *in comparison to the violence of the
American frontier*, the Canadian version of settlement was more pacific.
Thus, Canadians respect authority.[33]

As Fierlbeck was quick to point out, Canadians' attitudes towards
government were far from monolithic, and could include strains of
anti-statism. Some of the clearest expressions of the mien emerged
from francophones committed to ultramontanism in the late nineteenth
and early twentieth centuries. "This [anti-statist] characteristic is not
remarkable," observed Fierlbeck of Quebec's affiliations for the idea,
"as the Church itself had taken on many of the dominant functions of
the state (including education, health care, and social assistance) and
would find any expansion of state activity quite threatening." Francophone anti-statism, then, was not a repudiation of authority in general, but a product of a contest between two rival masters. Indeed,

the French-Canadian variant of ultramontanism ran so deep, noted Fierlbeck, that some observers designated it "more orthodox than the Pope." Here, then, is an additional basis for the anti-conscription sentiment so prevalent among francophones. By contrast, concerns over state power or "big government" failed to rally significant numbers of English Canadians until the 1970s, when conservative organizations like the National Citizens' Coalition and the Canadian Federation of Independent Business formed to protest the taxation policies of Pierre Trudeau's Liberal government. And despite this adaptation of American political discourse by those on the right, Canadians from across the political spectrum have embraced a government program, Medicare, as a core feature of Canadian identity; a national plebiscite conducted through a CBC television series anointed Medicare's "father," Saskatchewan politician Tommy Douglas, the "Greatest Canadian."[34]

It should thus not surprise that while many Americans fretted that the expansion of wartime governmental powers served as a profanation of a coveted national ideal, English Canadians responded with considerably less alarm. Historian Donald Creighton, for instance, applauded the expansion of centralized power during the First World War, holding that "the federal government was rapidly regaining the paramount position which the Fathers of Confederation had intended it to have and which it had gradually lost during the long years of laissez faire and peace." The "paramount position" Creighton lauded found its basis in the War Measures Act of 1914, which provided the Borden government extraordinary powers to censor, arrest, detain, deport, and regulate all aspects of production and distribution, transportation, and communication. Minister of Justice C.J. Doherty explained that the war made it "necessary for the people of Canada to place their confidence in us for the time being," and Parliament concurred, passing the act unanimously after little debate.[35]

Measures taken under the act included the internment of more than 8,500 "enemy aliens," the majority of whom were Ukrainians whose homeland had been divided by Austria-Hungary and Russia and whose overseas kin fought on both sides of the conflict (but in greater numbers for the Allies). Until Ukrainian-Canadian historians began to intervene in the matter in the mid-1970s, most English Canadian historians who reflected upon the episode joined Creighton in declaring the internment an act of state benevolence, one that housed and fed impoverished immigrants and sheltered them from nativist persecution. Borden's Conservatives incarcerated foreign nationals because

5.3 First World War "enemy aliens" interned at Spirit Lake, Quebec circa 1915.
(Library and Archives Canada, PA-170620)

they sought "to safeguard the rights of aliens," wrote Robert Craig
Brown and Ramsay Cook (in logic that bears faint echoes of the "we-
destroyed-the-village-to-save-it" justifications expressed by American
commanders in Vietnam). Other measures associated with the state's
"paramount position" included a press censorship harsher than that
undertaken in the United States and Britain, one that included the outright prohibition, in print and at public meetings, of the use of nearly a
dozen central and eastern European languages.[36]

In recent decades, Canadian historians and legal scholars have
expressed far less sanguinity regarding the extension of federal authority than Creighton and his contemporaries. Creighton's views, however,
reflected a commonly held faith that state power would, on balance, be

used wisely and for the greater good; they were also directly at odds with the attitudes voiced by many Americans towards government that helped to stimulate intensive criticism of warfare and its propensity to spur and condone governmental expansion and abuses. Over the years, Canadian war opponents have built their stance on a range of foundations – J.S. Woodsworth, James Endicott, and Muriel Duckworth on the Social Gospel, Charles Yale Harrison on his experiences in the trenches, George Woodcock on anarchism, radical labour leaders on international working-class solidarity. But none of these bases of war opposition enjoyed the kind of enduring and widespread appeal that inspired the main current of American antimilitarism. While citizens of both countries found arguments in British liberal theory to constrain the prerogatives of the state, Canadian antiwar activists could not rouse large numbers of their fellow citizens simply by drawing upon a latent pool of hostility to governmental authority. "The lack of a revolutionary mythology in Canada," Jerry Bannister maintained, "meant that there was no foundational principle of natural justice – no *liberté, égalité, fraternité, ou la mort!* – to legitimize opposition to the laws of a sovereign state."[37]

If the framers of the US Constitution considered war the most dreaded enemy to public liberty, they considered free speech – and more pointedly, an unfettered press – one of the surest guardians of that liberty. In the constitutional debates, observed John Byrne Cooke, "no right was more often proclaimed inviolable" than press freedom, "the most essential safeguard of the liberties the Revolution had been fought to secure." Here the framers built upon a venerable British tradition of freedom of the press that was also inherited by English Canadians, and then added the unparalleled measures of American suspicion of authority and faith in the common sense of an informed public. As Thomas Jefferson stated in 1787, he would prefer "newspapers without a government" to "government without newspapers." The corrective to despotic tendencies, as historian of journalism Jeffrey A. Smith wrote, would be "limited government and unlimited citizen debate."[38] As such, the relationship between the press and government would be essentially and necessarily adversarial.

At times, journalists willing to expose the repression and corruption of powerful individuals and institutions became influential and revered figures, known in the Progressive era as "muckrakers," and later in the century as investigative reporters. In wartime, however, the commitment to this journalistic duty, and the wider adherence to the principle of free speech, has waxed and waned. Unbridled press jingoism did much to construct overwhelming public support for the War of 1898; despite the apparent guarantees of the First Amendment, government repression and censorship along with war-enhanced patriotism worked to constrain critical reporting during the world wars.[39]

To some Americans, however, war was precisely the moment when unfettered speech was most needed. Indeed, we can see some of the clearest examples of Madison's embedded tension between war and republican liberty in the public reaction to measures employed to prosecute "total war" in the first half of the twentieth century. In addition to establishing the propagandistic Committee on Public Information upon US entry into the First World War, the Wilson administration issued the Alien Act, Alien Enemies Act, Espionage Act, and Sedition Act, officially in order to safeguard national security, and unofficially, to silence dissent. These laws forbade such acts as criticizing war conduct or aims, discouraging men to register for the draft, or questioning the government or the Constitution – such breadth suggests an administration far less optimistic about the benefits of the First Amendment than many of its citizens, as well as a regime bracing for American-style candour. Robert La Follette suspected as much, noting that the "forcible measures which we understand are being ground out of the war machine in this country is the complete proof that those responsible for this war fear that it has no popular support." In truth, despite La Follette's claims and Wilson's fears, many American politicians and citizens of the time expressed support for these measures out of war-bred and CPI-enhanced patriotism, fears of having these expanded war powers used against them, or some combination of both. However, while the fact that more than 2,000 Americans were arrested under these acts and roughly 1,000 convicted bespeaks a demonstrably overzealous inclination to police speech, these figures also signal a widespread refusal to self-censure.[40]

The "overzealous policing" thesis clearly trumps inferences of calculated civil disobedience in many cases – for instance, in the postmaster's clampdown on a magazine that called for higher taxation and less borrowing to finance the war, or in the sedition conviction for the maker of a 1917 film about the US War of Independence (wherein American colonists bayoneted British troops, an ill-timed history lesson for the British Tommies and American Doughboys striving to maintain a constructive relationship). Other Americans seemed intent on openly flouting the new laws in order to bring attention to the soiling of the revered

First Amendment. Socialist Charles Schenck, taking special note of the proscription against interference in military recruitment, mailed out roughly 1,500 leaflets urging men to resist the draft. In the Supreme Court challenge to his subsequent arrest, Schenck cited the constitutional guarantees of free speech; nevertheless, the court upheld the new wartime legislation, as it did in every other challenge brought before it prior to the Second World War. In a speech given in North Dakota, fellow socialist Kate Richards O'Hare took direct aim at prohibitions against hindering the draft, calling "the women of the United States ... nothing more nor less than brood sows, to raise children to get into the army and be made into fertilizer." She was convicted under the espionage act and sentenced to five years in prison. Many prominent Americans expressed indignation over the government's shredding of civil liberties. Charles Beard called for the release of "political prisoners whose offense was to retain Mr. Wilson's pacifist views after he abandoned them." After one of his colleagues was fired by Columbia University for opposing the war, Beard resigned from the university faculty in protest. Alarmed clergy, conservative lawyers, and Progressive reformers formed the National Civil Liberties Bureau in 1917, an organization dedicated to preserving First Amendment rights and the rights of conscientious objectors. Following the war it continued its mission as the renamed American Civil Liberties Union.[41]

The intensive public hostility towards citizen repression and government deceit in the Great War would bear at least some fruit the next time the nation became involved in war. Wartime abuses certainly did not disappear during the Second World War – the internment of more than 100,000 residents of Japanese descent represents one of the gravest violations of civil liberties in the nation's military past (and an act that would generate a multitude of mostly incriminatory scholarly and popular considerations from the late 1940s onward). For those who feared the war would once again bend both constitutional principle and the truth beyond recognition, however, the news was not all bleak. Understanding that Americans were appalled by the excessive idealism and baseless propaganda produced by the Committee on Public Information, the Roosevelt administration's Office of War Information (OWI) sought to regain public confidence by toning down the rhetoric over the war's course and aims; terms like "realistic," "hard headed," and "practical" were common in agency communications. Though still on the books, the Espionage Act was rarely used (and one of the few wartime convictions under the measure was overturned by the Supreme Court in 1944).[42]

Hollywood, too, became somewhat more nuanced, producing propaganda films under the guidance of the OWI that exhibited greater
sophistication than the crude "hiss and boo" features – "To Hell with
the Kaiser," or "The Kaiser, the Beast of Berlin" – produced in the First
World War. In testimony to American's individualistic bent, many of
these Second World War films endorsed both individualism *and* the
collectivism rarely celebrated in peacetime but required to prevail in
armed combat. Cultural historian Lary May outlined a typical plot: a
go-it-alone American maverick is steadily made to realize that, for the
good of the nation, he must learn to become an effective team player
in an army platoon/bomber crew/battleship. (It is probably superflu-
ous to add, this being Hollywood, that both victory *and* romance follow.) The storyline could also apply to a nation heretofore unwilling
to temper its sovereignty for the sake of an international wartime alliance or collective security organization. Here again, the OWI proved
discerning, maintaining that internationalism meant a world ordered
according to American values and institutions, and under the nation's
ultimate leadership.[43] Of course, this new approach to international
affairs would also require a repudiation of not only isolationism, but
also of limited government and the anti-militaristic creed promoted by
many influential Americans from the nation's founding onward.

Clearly, the Madisons, Parringtons, Bournes, and La Follettes lost this
argument rather convincingly. Permanent, vast, and expensive standing armies, entangling alliances, "the encroachment of the military
upon civil power," and the amplification of executive authority in military matters became permanent fixtures in American life following the
Second World War. These transformations served as the preconditions
for a rise to global dominance that *Time* publisher Henry Luce would
celebrate as "The American Century." But the Cold War entrenchment
of the so-called national security state should not obscure the fact that,
until the mid-twentieth century, such matters were under intensive
negotiation; this led to significant citizen resistance against the related
phenomena of military ventures, expanding government, and threats to
individual liberties. Even those like Arthur Schlesinger who acknowledged the need for a strong state in the face of the communist threat
fretted about the potential for despotism, as he argued in his influential 1949 book *The Vital Center*. And despite (or because of) the ascendance of the military-industrial complex and a nation on a permanent
war footing, war opposition based on anti-statism remains a powerful
stream of wider antiwar thinking, one that continues to find support

on both the right and left. The sentiment helped to invigorate Vietnam-era protestors, draft resisters, and organizations like Vietnam Veterans for Peace, which emerged in 1967 – before opposition to the war had reached the mainstream – and swelled into a mass movement boasting tens of thousands of veterans from chapters in all fifty states and Vietnam itself. The organization claimed the authority to confront their government based on clearly stated and widely understood notions of citizen duty: the veterans, noted historian Andrew Hunt, "sought to narrow the gap between the ideals and the reality of American society," and "came to see themselves as inheritors of a legacy of radical resistance in the United States dating back to the American Revolution." Hunt himself contended that, owing to their status as current and ex-soldiers, Vietnam Veterans for Peace "challenged the Nixon administration more than any other antiwar or New Left organization."[44]

Vietnam was a uniquely divisive affair, and the notion that firsthand witness to the horror and futility would work actively against their own government – even while the nation was at war – is perhaps not as striking in this situation as it would be in others. More notable is the idea that thousands of American veterans of all conflicts from the Second World War (the "good war") forward would come together to form Veterans for Peace (VFP), an organization born in the mid-1980s that has grown to include more than 120 local chapters. VFP's goals are not modest: its members pledge to work "to restrain our government from intervening, overtly and covertly, in the internal affairs of other nations," and more ambitious still, "to abolish war as an instrument of national policy." The group's approach to "restraining" their government can be particularly robust: in 2005 it called for the impeachment of George W. Bush for "war crimes and crimes against humanity" conducted in Iraq, and in 2011 asked Congress to impeach Barack Obama for "illegal wars in Iraq, Afghanistan, Pakistan, Yemen, Somalia, and Libya," among other actions the group deemed contraventions of US and international law. To an extent, such nerve can be viewed as an extension, rather than a repudiation, of soldierly and citizen responsibility within a culture that gives license to call out social superiors and to warn against the growth of tyranny at home and abroad.[45]

This adversarial relationship between citizen and government has also inspired innumerable polemics from historians, journalists, political scientists, cultural theorists, and a range of other professionals and laypersons left and right that rail against the growing militarization and centralization of the state in an effort to call their nation back to its original credo. Once again, some of the most pointed have emerged from the pens and keyboards of former soldiers and state security personnel. Korean War veteran, former consultant to the CIA, and one-time loyal cold warrior Chalmers Johnson wrote a series of bestselling books that excoriated his nation for trading republicanism for empire, and democracy for a "domestic dictatorship." Johnson's arguments gained power from their ability to draw on the revered "founding fathers." "The founders of our nation," he wrote in 2006, "understood [the relationship between empire and dictatorship] well and tried to create a form of government – a republic – that would prevent this from occurring. But the combination of huge standing armies, almost continuous wars, military Keynesianism, and ruinous military expenses have destroyed our republican structure in favor of an imperial presidency. We are on the cusp of losing our democracy for the sake of keeping our empire."[46] Madison's dire warnings, in other words, had gone unheeded.

In a series of books and articles, historian and former US Army officer Andrew Bacevich echoed Johnson's general critique, as well as the latter's panacea for the dangerous sprawl of American militarism and empire: namely, a return to "an earlier credo, nurtured across many generations until swept aside by the conceits of the American Century." Despite the passage of centuries and the increasing complexities and interconnectivities of the current age, for Bacevich, the blueprint for America's relationship with the globe was set down, unerringly, many years ago. America was to be a world leader, "a city upon a hill," but one that led by suasion rather than force. "For the Founders, and for the generations that followed them, here was the basis of a distinctively American approach to leadership, informed by a conviction that self-mastery should take precedence over mastering others. This Founders' credo … transcended partisanship, blending both idealism and realism, emphasizing patience rather than immediacy, preferring influence to coercion."[47] In other words, the United States truly is – or was – an exceptional nation with a mandate of uplift, though in its pure form the mandate was to be realized through soft power – by attracting others to a demonstrably superior way of life. Here exceptionalism, antimilitarism, and isolationism (a term Bacevich rejects in favour of a not dissimilar emphasis on America as stay-at-home "exemplar") are restored to the centre of national identity. Questions could be raised regarding the near-beatification afforded eighteenth-century political theorists and their ability to divine a faultless *weltanschauung* applicable to any age, or regarding the simple partition between the laudable pre-Second

World War America and the fallen internationalist variety. Indigenous communities, Latin Americans, and many foreign policy analysts have been more apt to find continuities rather than ruptures in the arc of American expansion and the preference for leading via coercion rather than example. Still, opinions like those of Johnson and Bacevich resonate because they appeal to the core and unique aspects of the nation – and as Nixon discovered when confronted by Veterans for Peace – because of these authors' credentials as soldiers, as eyewitnesses to the implementation and effects of modern US internationalism. They have taken seriously the citizen's duty to remain vigilant for abuses of power, and to speak forcefully when they perceive deviations from the nation's authentic republican and libertarian tradition as set down in its founding documents.

Journalists and news organizations who consciously framed themselves as keepers of the constitutional flame reacted with similar alarm to the postwar growth and projection of US military power. I.F. Stone, who according to his biographer D.D. Guttenplan shared "Thomas Jefferson's view of a free press as the keystone of American liberty," had the nerve to pick apart the US government and Army version of the Korean War in the midst of the conflict (and while Senator McCarthy cowed journalist and politician alike through his Senate witch-hunts). Investigative journalist Seymour Hersh gained international renown in 1969 for exposing the My Lai Massacre and the military's attempt to cover it up, and subsequently built an award-winning career out of excavating and disseminating allegations of military malfeasance – including the Abu Ghraib prison scandal – as a means of exposing corruption in, and restoring the constitutional balance to, foreign policymaking.[48]

Two years after My Lai, the *New York Times* and *Washington Post* published scandalizing excerpts from the Pentagon Papers in defiance of the US Attorney General, claiming privileges guaranteed by the First Amendment's protection of free speech. In upholding this right, the Supreme Court credited the newspapers that revealed state secrets for providing an indispensable service to the nation. Writing for the majority, Justice Hugo Black commended the *Times* and the *Post* for their "courageous reporting" and for "nobly" doing "precisely that which the Founders hoped and trusted they would do." "Only a free and unrestrained press," Black argued, "can effectively expose deception in government. And paramount among the responsibilities of a free press is the duty to prevent any part of the government from deceiving the people and sending them off to distant lands to die of foreign fevers and foreign shot and shell." In his homage to the purpose and power of free speech, frank avowal of a government that deceives, and acidic condemnation of the deadly consequences of unchecked power, Black reflected values that were so embedded in the American self-concept that "every citizen – liberal and conservative alike – could comprehend and champion" them.[49]

Days before the Supreme Court handed down its ruling, Daniel Ellsberg, a senior military analyst working at the Pentagon, confessed to leaking the top secret Pentagon Papers to the press. He explained that he did so as a patriot compelled by an urgent desire to reign in an imperial presidency and an immoral war, and as a citizen inspired by a tradition of principled civil disobedience. Forced underground by a massive FBI manhunt, Ellsberg was nonetheless – and to the deep embarrassment of the bureau – located and interviewed by Walter Cronkite of CBS News. Here, Ellsberg outlined what he considered the primary lesson of the Pentagon Papers' release: that "this is a self-governing country. We are the government. And in terms of institutions, the Constitution provides for separation of powers, for Congress, for the courts, informally for the press, protected by the First Amendment ... I think we cannot let the officials of the Executive Branch determine for us what it is that the public needs to know about how well and how they are discharging their functions."[50]

Many Americans agreed. For revealing state secrets that humiliated the US government and armed forces and impaired their ability to successfully prosecute an ongoing war, Ellsberg became "an instant celebrity," receiving a prolonged ovation when he appeared before a live audience on the *Dick Cavett Show* while awaiting trial on espionage charges. The charges dismissed after revelations of gross government misconduct, Ellsberg was maligned as a traitor *and* widely celebrated as an American hero by voices from across the political spectrum – a fact not lost on President Nixon. As Ellsberg's trial wound down, Nixon fulminated to his chief of staff (a rant, like many others, that the president kindly recorded for posterity) that "we have the rocky situation where the sonofabitching thief is made a national hero and is going to get off on a mistrial. And the *New York Times* gets a Pulitzer Prize for stealing documents ... *What in the name of God have we come to?*" (emphasis in original).[51]

In subsequent decades, Ellsberg became an *éminence grise* for the American free-speech and antiwar movements, receiving numerous awards and honours, contributing to publications celebrating other whistle-blowers, and being called upon to weigh in whenever a new leak of classified government documents appeared. He would refer to both Bradley Manning and Edward Snowden, US government operatives who divulged massive amounts of sensitive and explosive material relating to national security during the "war on terror," as heroes of American liberty and guardians of the Bill of Rights. And again, it is not simply that a handful of individuals thought it proper to expose abuses of power, but that so many fellow citizens applauded actions aimed at weakening the hand of the executive and the military. Polls showed Americans evenly split on the "hero v. traitor" question in both the Manning and Snowden cases, with campaigns launched to offer Manning, sentenced to 35 years for espionage and theft, a presidential pardon; both Manning and Snowden received nominations for the 2013 Nobel Peace Prize. The "Bradley Manning Support Network" put up billboards in the nation's capital urging his release and featuring the slogan "Blowing the whistle on war crimes is not a crime." Between June 2010 and September 2013, Courage to Resist, an American organization founded at the outset of the Iraq war to support GIs who opposed the conflict, raised more than $1.4 million from over 23,000 online donors for Manning's defence.[52]

Some of these challenges to American military activities from the likes of Bacevich, Chalmers Johnson, and Pentagon whistleblowers would undoubtedly have arisen even without the trappings provided by the American political tradition. Especially following the Second World War, the numerous foreign engagements initiated by successive US administrations and the thoroughly related mushrooming of the "defence" industry's economic and political influence have no equivalent among modern nations, and would raise concerns in any polity. Nor have all Americans bemoaned the magnification and militarization of the state – especially when presented with the alternative of passing off global leadership to another nation, foreign alliance, or worst of all for some conspiracy-minded citizens, the United Nations. But it is the relatively common understanding of their nation's origins, founding ideologies, and special role as an exemplar for a better and more peaceable world that undergirds the volume, outrage, and relative popularity of publications, organizations, and individuals that have challenged their government and its wars. As the founders counselled and subsequent events seemed to confirm, authority (whether governmental, military, or otherwise) covets growth, and warfare provides one of the pretexts for, and instruments of, that expansion. To those upholding

this view, authentic citizenship is synonymous with a continuous interrogation and checking of power, and all wars are brought under suspicion for their potential contribution to the advance of "tyranny."

Clearly, the adherence to this model of citizen and journalistic
responsibility has a tendency to go in and out of fashion. Following
the 9/11 attacks, for example, major news organizations repeated the
Bush administration's justifications for an attack on Iraq so uncritically
that the *New York Times*, hardly the worst offender, was moved to print
a public apology for its servility. Still, a tradition of anti-statism and
an accompanying contempt for the "standing armies" and the drain
they place on democracy and public monies have time and again provided a credible and commonly understood mechanism for intervening
forcefully, if not always successfully, in public policy debates. In a 2013
interview with a Chinese reporter, Edward Snowden rejected the labels
supporters and opponents tried to affix to him. "I'm neither traitor nor
hero," he offered. "I'm an American."[53] Regardless of one's opinions of
his actions, in the sense that they aligned with a resilient tradition of
American thought, Snowden spoke truth.

It is difficult to imagine a member of the Canadian security establishment who trafficked in state secrets defending their actions through a
similar appeal to patriotism and national tradition. Indeed, if Canadians
have demonstrated greater trust in authority, they have also exhibited
less enthusiasm for that other pillar of American anti-statism – the right
and the duty of citizens to call out perceived abuses of power. Once
again, a component of this reticence was structural. The British North
America Act of 1867 creating the Dominion of Canada was never democratically approved, and in some aspects, like the un-elected Senate,
decidedly antidemocratic. Most importantly, while the act included
provisions for language and denominational education rights, it featured nothing analogous to the American Bill of Rights. "The fathers
of Confederation," noted legal historian Dominique Clément, "had
little stomach for the constitutional rights favoured by their southern neighbours, and the decision to avoid entrenching a bill of rights
was perfectly consistent with the British tradition of Parliamentary
supremacy." The power of Parliament, in other words, was supreme
and unconstrained, while rights of individual citizens remained vague
– preserved in a British tradition of an "implied bill of rights" that was
itself subject to the discretion of Parliament.[54]

To an extent, then, the greater deference to authority exhibited by
Canadians in comparison to their American neighbours was an outcome

of legal restraint rather than a straightforward reflection of individual or community choice or an aspect of "national character." The republican-versus-Westminster governmental structure cannot fully account for these disparities, however. As Andrew Parnaby and Gregory Kealey wrote of the period between Confederation and the Great War, "the profound suspicion so prevalent in Victorian England of spies, spying, and secrecy found few reflections in Canada. The suspension of habeas corpus, political arrests without charges, mail seizure, secret agents, perhaps even agents provocateurs – all were present in these formatives years of the new nation-state and all went unopposed but for the victims." To Jerry Bannister, the loyalist tradition is an important part of this story. "Whereas liberalism fuelled the development of modern individualism," he wrote, "loyalism offered expedient means to restrict civil liberties in the interests of the state. Loyalism offers a key to understanding the seemingly illiberal nature of [Canada's] liberal order."[55]

Over the latter half of the twentieth century, a good deal of these national differences ebbed, and several recent works have charted an interrelated "decline of deference" and rise of a more American-style rights culture in Canada over that span (while coming to differing conclusions about the desirability of this trend). Although wartime repression proved instrumental in accelerating appeals for citizen liberties and governmental restraint, the changes occurred incrementally over many decades. In the first years of the Great War, Canadian officials were so confident in public support for, or at least quiescence regarding, the conflict that they felt no need to create the kind of pro-war propaganda agencies established in the United States and Britain to maintain popular support. Only in 1917 did the Borden administration change course, creating the Union Government Publicity Bureau to encourage public compliance with the increasing obligations entailed by conscription, conservation of consumer goods, and the issuance of war bonds. Prior to this, civil society willingly provided much of the propaganda that an official agency might otherwise coordinate: English Canadians heard powerful affirmations of the rectitude of the Allied effort and Canada's indispensable contribution to it from such sources as advertisers, school teachers, authors, clergy, and the mainstream press.[56]

In fact, the press proved to be so jingoistic that the stifling levels of press censorship permitted under the War Measures Act, and enforced by Chief Censor Lieutenant-Colonel Ernest J. Chambers, would appear unnecessary – that is, until one discovers that Chambers leveled much of his opprobrium at foreign-language newspapers produced in

Canada, and especially at publications produced outside the country. As Keshen revealed, roughly 90 per cent of the 253 publications banned originated in the United States. Even the fourteen newspapers of the mainstream William Randolph Hearst newspaper chain made the list, and remained there after US entry into the war moved Hearst from war opponent to enthusiastic supporter. Doubtless the Wilson administration would have relished the powers afforded Ernest Chambers, but the First Amendment denied the US government the kind of latitude that allowed Canada to simply ban the use of the languages of their wartime adversaries in print or public meetings, or to shutter the offices of an "unpatriotic" English-language serial without fear of a court challenge. The US government's creative solution to the meddlesome manacles of the First Amendment involved denying offending publications access to the federal mail system, a practice that bankrupted some papers and saw others delivered privately or sold on street corners.[57]

This is not to suggest that, outside Quebec, intensive resistance to both the war and the governmental measures undertaken to prosecute it did not exist. While English Canada, with its large measures of British makeup and emotional connection to the empire, exhibited less outspoken opposition to the conflict than the United States, not all displayed unqualified loyalty to the cause. Kealey noted that organized labour "blithely ignored" a law banning wartime strikes, as well as the "Anti-Loafing Law" requiring that all Canadian men from sixteen and sixty years of age secure gainful employment. The introduction of conscription likewise inspired "a storm of protest" from unions (to go along with deadly riots in Quebec). Five thousand farmers assembled in Ottawa in 1918 to condemn the Borden government's broken promise that their field-hand sons would be exempt from the draft. Some wartime citizens challenged the provisions of the War Measures Act in court, and one Alberta judge lamented that his country's wartime legislation gave the government more authority than war measures enacted in Britain, "where bombs are dropping from zeppelins and the guns of war can be heard."[58]

As was the case in the United States, in the numerous arrests, prosecutions, convictions, and internments of Canadian residents conducted under the aegis of wartime powers, it is often difficult to determine whether a given target was actively resisting the war or simply rendered guilty by association (with a union, socialist organization, ethnic group, etc.). More apparent is the fact that large percentages of real or perceived war opponents were relatively poor and clustered on the political left. Many of these were recent immigrants who brought with them traditions of radicalism and socialism, traditions that helped them make sense of the maltreatment they received from the Canadian state. In other words, they had not been conditioned in the art of deference, and were willing to make this known. As Ian McKay observed, "in the context of a hierarchical and conservative liberal order ... the word democracy was associated with American mob rule." Thus, when Canadian leftist serials "hoisted the flag of 'Democracy' into the mastheads of their publications of the 1890s, they were being deliberately provocative [...] demanding a 'capacity to judge' that the Canadian liberal order was not predisposed to recognize."[59] To a considerable extent, conformity was a virtue handed down from above, and resisted by those whose interests it did not serve; in Canada, social rank (more pointedly, the lack thereof) played a more pivotal role in inciting anti-state sentiment than it did in the United States, where mainstream journalists, lawyers, judges, clergy, and the Founders themselves could be as wary of power as the powerless.

It is of little surprise that for decades, historians who chronicled Canada's First World War reflected the deference often assigned to the nation as a whole, ignoring or downplaying many of the less consensual aspects of the Great War story, and as we have seen, offering some extravagant apologias for state suppression. Writing in 1993, Kealey noted that US historians had paid "far more attention" to their state's war on leftists during the conflict, that "class tensions have been largely ignored" in conventional Canadian accounts. While there certainly has been much catching up on this front since Kealey's piece, for most of the twentieth century there was nothing approaching the public and academic outcry against governmental abuse that became a permanent feature of American remembrance of the conflict, and little effort to excavate the stories of those who did not conform neatly to the nationalistic mythology of the war. Amy Shaw's 2009 account of Canadian conscientious objectors to the conflict, for instance, marked the first systematic study of this group, despite the fact that these dissenters' stories provide one of the surer means of addressing foundational questions about the war and Canada's responsibilities: Under what circumstances is state-sanctioned violence justifiable? Did this war meet the criteria of a just war for the European powers involved? For Canada? Should a liberal democracy compel citizens, through conscription, to fight and kill in its name, even when its territory is not directly threatened? Can individuals opt out of a decision that was arrived at through due process?

To what extent did answers to these queries differ between Canada and other warring states, including their autocratic adversaries? The magnitude of such questions has drawn many more American (and as Shaw notes, British) analysts to the story of war resisters in their nation, and this collective consideration of war opposition has served to place resistance firmly within the story of the war itself.[60]

While a range of influential postwar Americans turned on the governmental repression surrounding the war as quickly as they turned on the war itself, in the 1920s the recoil against wartime proscriptions in Canada was limited mostly to the leftists who had borne the brunt of the state's authoritarian measures. Organizations like the Workers' Political Defence League and the Canadian Labor Defence League emerged in the early twenties to oppose the harassment of the left, with the latter claiming a membership of 20,000 within a few years of its founding. Owing to the radical makeup of these organizations, along with a continuing faith in the righteousness of the war and the seeming exoticism (and Americanism) of the discourses of rights, few other Canadians came on board. The first true national civil liberties organization – that is, one dedicated to defending rights on principle, not just the freedoms of those who shared the organization's political leanings – was formed in 1937 when "a few left-liberals and social democrats," alarmed by the profligate authoritarianism of Quebec Premier Maurice Duplessis and his government, formed the Canadian Civil Liberties Union (CCLU).[61]

In that same year, volunteers from both the United States and Canada began arriving in Spain to join the Republican cause in their civil conflict against the fascist Franco regime. On the surface, the outsized Canadian contribution – nearly 1,700 volunteers, compared to roughly 3,000 from the far more populous United States – appears to undermine the assumption of greater Canadian deference, as both governments had declared participation illegal. Many of the Canadian recruits, moreover, viewed the opportunity in distinctly anti-statist hues, as a chance to hit back against their own government and its violent response to Depression-era labour activism. One recruit noted a widespread desire among the volunteers "to actually fight against the people, against the same kind of people, whom they thought were responsible for their condition, and who were oppressing them here in Canada." However, a closer look at precisely who was signing up for that fight suggests that this spirit of defiance was, to a notable extent, a recent graft onto the Canadian body politic. More than three-quarters of the Canadian volunteers were immigrants, the highest percentage of any foreign contingent; only one

5.4 "Very, very working class": Canadian volunteers in the Spanish Civil War, 1937. The photograph is attributed to Canadian architect Hazen Sise, one of a handful of university-educated Canadians to join the Spanish Republicans. (City of Vancouver Archives, AM54-S4-: Mil P330.)

third of the Americans belonged to the same category. Historian Michael Petrou noted that the British contingent included a number of "middle- and upper-class volunteers, often writers and intellectuals," while roughly five hundred of the Americans were college students or recent graduates. In contrast, Petrou could find only 32 Canadians who had experienced any form of higher education. Most foreign fighters who joined the Spanish Republicans were united by leftist politics, but the Canadian contingent stood out for its marginality, for its dearth of older-stock and better-off volunteers willing to flout their government's ban and confront the growing scourge of European fascism. "I considered them to be far more proletarian," noted an American commissar who fought alongside the Canadians. "They were very, very working class. The overwhelming majority – it was stamped on them."[62]

Many of these Canadian volunteers had been recruited through labour unions, ethnic organizations, and the civil liberties groups

that emerged following the First World War. After the outbreak of the
Second, the most prominent of these rights organizations, the CCLU,
diverted much of its attention away from Quebec Premier Duplessis
and towards the federal government led by Mackenzie King, which
had again passed a far-reaching War Measures Act. King himself operated with great trepidation on the matter of conscription, as it had
proved deadly to unity and to some protestors in the last conflict. But
unlike the US administration, which had been stung by intensive interwar criticisms of its repression of civil liberties in the previous war and
thus attempted to pursue a kinder and gentler application of its Espionage and Sedition acts, the Canadian government again provided itself
a more draconian blueprint for civilian control than that of either the
United States or Britain.[63]

King's Liberals would find many opportunities to utilize the War
Measures Act to the fullest. The internment of 20,000 residents of
Japanese descent was patterned on the American model, and federal
authorities detained a number of Germans and Italians. Parliament
had banned the Communist Party in the spring of 1940 and maintained
the sanction even after the Soviets joined the Allied cause – making
Canada unique among Western nations of the era. A long list of other
groups faced similar proscriptions once the war began. The Jehovah's
Witnesses, who as self-styled members of God's Army considered
secular military service a conflict of interest, had their literature cen-
sored in the First World War; during this conflict, the sect itself was
simply outlawed. When members continued to practice their beliefs,
state prosecutors, police, and violent mobs responded aggressively. The
Technocracy Association, an obscure utopian group dedicated to bet-
tering the world through scientific innovation (and whose leadership
initially questioned the war), also menaced the state enough to make
the blacklist.[64]

The War Measures Act would be extended following the Second
World War to give the federal government a free hand in dealing with
the Canadians who had been accused of spying by defecting Russian
embassy employee Igor Gouzenko in September 1945. Following on
the heels of the widespread violations of citizen freedoms during the
war, the rough treatment of alleged Canadian spies proved something
of a tipping point for the Canadian rights movement. Membership in
the CCLU increased and new rights groups were founded; they were
joined in their calls for a codified bill of rights by federal politicians to
the left and right of the ruling Liberals who had witnessed firsthand the

immoderations of parliamentary supremacy (and who, confined con-
tinuously to the opposition benches, did not enjoy the opportunity to
manipulate the levers of these considerable powers).

International events were also influencing Canadian rights' discourses. The horrors of the Second World War, and most pointedly, the
Holocaust, inspired a global "rights revolution" and moved the newly-
created United Nations to enshrine a Universal Declaration of Human
Rights; as the name implied, all member states were expected to champion it. Still clinging to the principle of parliamentary supremacy, and
having experienced through the War Measures Act the full extent of
its prerogatives, King's Liberal government considered opposing the
Declaration. If maintained, this stance would have put Canada in
league with Saudi Arabia, the Soviet Union and its puppet states, and
apartheid South Africa. Sobered by the company they were keeping
and pressured by the United States, the Canadian delegation voted
for the measure when it was brought before the General Assembly in
December 1948.[65]

Those petitioning for a Canadian Bill of Rights would wait until the
election of John Diefenbaker's Conservatives; the legislation finally
appeared as a federal statute, and one therefore still subject to parliamentary supremacy, in 1960. A bill of rights would not be constitution-
ally guaranteed until 1982, when Pierre Trudeau's Liberal government
repatriated the constitution and made a "Charter of Rights and Freedoms" its opening section. Canadian accounts of war written in this era
began to reflect the increased attention to domestic rights and government wrongs, while Canadian opinion polls conducted between 1960
and 2000 revealed "dramatic declines in public confidence and respect"
for governmental institutions. As a result, observed Bradley Watson,
"with respect to the theory and practice of civil rights, the drummers
that Canada and the United States march to are no longer so different
from one another." While certainly not the only factor, this "decline in
deference" may help to explain why the Afghanistan War registered
lower levels of support among English Canadians than any other conflict in the nation's history. It should nevertheless be noted that the
"decline" can be overstated: while Americans responded with considerable outrage after Snowden's leaks revealed the shocking extent of
their government's domestic surveillance program, analogous practices in Canada outlined in the same set of documents "drew crickets
in Ottawa," noted *Globe and Mail* reporter Josh Wingrove. University
of Ottawa law professor Michael Geist bristled over the disparities

between the forceful reaction of the American public and "the shameful Canadian silence on surveillance."[66]

While certain historic disparities have attenuated, for much of Canada's history the will and ability to speak freely and challenge ruling authorities found fewer advocates and outlets in that nation than the United States. As a consequence, specific absences stand out: civil disobedience, long a staple of American resistance to a host of perceived ills, war among them, was less conspicuous in Canada's first century. Prior to the emergence of the *Front de libération du Québec* (FLQ) in the 1960s and the growing first nations' activism in recent decades, one of the more prominent examples of civil disobedience in Canada involved nude marches and property destruction by British Columbia Doukhobors protesting compulsory school attendance in the early- to mid-twentieth century. Founded by a handful of Second World War veterans, the anti-war group Canadian Veterans Against Nuclear Arms emerged in 1982, but it closed shop in 2011 (at a time when recent and ongoing wars were adding substantial numbers to American antiwar veterans groups). The early-twentieth-century American mania for muckraking journalism never enjoyed the same sway in Canada – except vicariously, as Canadians devoured American magazines like *Collier's* and *McClure's* to sate their hunger for scandal and evidence of greater Canadian reasonableness. Mid-twentieth-century journalists like Blair Fraser and Frank Underhill were certainly not afraid to call out the actions of their government in times of peace or war: during the Korean War, Fraser's articles in *Maclean's* and Underhill's editorials in the *Canadian Forum* spoke frankly and disparagingly about racism in the Canadian forces, Canadian support for the repressive regime in South Korea, and the acquiescence of their nation to the dogmatic and belligerent foreign policy of the United States. Since the 1980s, journalist and war historian Gwynne Dyer's doubts about the necessity of Canada's twentieth-century wars and alliances have tied both the Department of National Defence and the country's dominant military historians into knots (or rather into a collective knot, as their critics insist the two groups have been joined at the hip for some time). But it is impossible to find a widely read Canadian journalist in the mould of I.F. Stone or Seymour Hersh, who to borrow a phrase from William Stueck's estimation of his fellow Korean War historians, seemed determined "to lambaste the United States for virtually every crime imaginable."[67] That brand of seemingly-infinite antagonism towards the state was bred under a particular set of circumstances not replicated in Canada.

This infinite antagonism has a variety of outcomes. As the forgoing suggests, Americans' suspicions regarding the powerful have on many occasions served them well, helping citizens to restrain executive imperiousness, sift through the misinformation particularly endemic in wartime, and challenge violations of national ideals. However, the anti-authoritarian posture can be taken to considerable extremes, towards an inclination to view virtually every official utterance as a deception in service of a malignant conspiracy. The post-9/11 era, which combined the memory of an appalling national trauma with the proliferation of information technology capable of broadcasting un-vetted personal opinions around the globe, has been particularly amenable to such wanton theorizing. Yet as several authors point out, it is really nothing new in American history. Historian Richard Hofstadter, writing in the wake of the McCarthyite witch-hunt of the 1950s, called it the "paranoid style in American politics." Hofstadter found its roots in the populist revolt against "the system" in the late-nineteenth century, a system that seemed stacked deliberately and cunningly against agrarian interests. Emily Rosenberg traced the foundations of conspiratorial thinking back to the distrust of rulers fostered by George III. More recent excavations identified its origins in the Puritans and their struggle against Satan (embodied in Indian peoples, and at Salem, in fellow Puritans), who was in no mood to see their holy experiment succeed. The conspiratorial bearing has been fueled at times by notions of utopianism and exceptionalism, by the conviction that the nation was meant to be spared the struggles and vicissitudes that befell unexceptional states, and that problems arising in the United States were therefore the work of a cadre of saboteurs. Beginning in the mid-nineteenth century, the nation's growing ethnic diversity "deepened suspicions of unfamiliar identities and gnawed at the sense of internal security." Whatever its bases, the American penchant for theorizing along these lines is undeniable. What other country features so many of these intrigues that it boasts its own 925-page encyclopedia of conspiracies? [68]

Not surprisingly, the trauma of war has proven fertile for wild and uncorroborated conjectures about the forces supposedly seeking to ground the American ship of state. In Real Enemies: Conspiracy Theories and American Democracy, World War I to 9/11, Kathryn Olmsted cited the First World War as a watershed moment in the growth of conspiratorial thinking, fueled by the expansion of the federal bureaucracy, the military, intelligence gathering, and executive power. In his bitter condemnation of the First World War, for example, Harry Elmer Barnes charged that

Woodrow Wilson had deliberately invited German U-boat attacks to incite the public. As Jerald Combs wrote, Barnes mapped out the tangled web of deceit in meticulous detail, considering "Wilson a willing conspirator with the bankers, munitions makers, Allied propagandists, and pro-Allied advisers Ambassador Walter Hines Page, Secretary of State Robert Lansing, and Colonel Edward House to drag the United States into the war."[69]

Following the Second World War, accusations emerged that President Franklin Roosevelt, a supposed closet warmonger frustrated by the passive and neutral bearing of the citizenry, either knew of the impending Pearl Harbor attack or deliberately provoked it. To diplomatic historian Charles Tansill and other isolationists on the right who had always seen in New Deal liberalism the work of a proto-dictatorship, the loss of 20 warships, nearly 200 planes, and 2,402 American lives was a small price to a tyrant hell-bent on manufacturing an anti-democratic "back door to war." The president's provocative trade embargo and the freezing of Japanese assets in the United States, along with the transfer of the Pacific Fleet from the relative safety of San Diego to a US base within reach of enemy aircraft, furnished all the proof of malice the FDR-haters required. Even some progressive supporters of Roosevelt's New Deal, including the (until then) respected historians Charles Beard and Harry Barnes joined the conspiracy camp, hurling an admixture of allegations about the president's motives for inviting the attack: a desire to preserve the British Empire, shut down the New Deal, expand US access to foreign markets, ensure re-election, and the Manichean list goes on. It is little surprise that a scheme requiring a vast, coordinated, and entirely undetected collusion, not to mention the desired reaction from a foreign power and a president of amaranthine callousness, proved entirely groundless. But the conspiracy train kept rolling. The Korean War, critics maintained, was Harry Truman's Trojan horse for establishing the supremacy of the United Nations over all sovereign countries, including America. In 2011, career dissenter Seymour Hersh told the *Guardian* that the official version of the death of Osama bin Laden was "one big lie, not one word of it is true."[70]

It is not difficult to understand why Hersh might have doubts, as he has personally uncovered sensational governmental deceptions in the past. This points once again to a conundrum not unique to the United States, but one particularly intensive in the context of its political culture. Official fabrications, silences, and misrepresentations have been commonplace in the manufacturing of a climate conducive to policy implementation – including and often most pointedly, that surrounding warfare. A people disposed to conspiratorial thinking – according to some analysts since the arrival of the Puritans – sometimes has a hard time creating mythological explanations more creative than those grounded in the facts. For our purposes, there is a larger point to be made about the demonstrated will to dismantle orthodoxies, to cross-examine, to lay blame, to cast aspersions on matters for which American blood was shed – whether or not there exists good (or any) evidence on which to base such claims. To the extent that these theories gain adherents, they add further doubts, ambiguities, and pessimism to public perceptions of conflict. To be sure, some Canadians have dabbled in conspiracy when assigning blame for disastrous military engagements like the 1942 raid on Dieppe, but comparatively speaking, the Canadian record on this is quite sparse.[71]

In sum, and to put it most simply, since states prosecute wars, attitudes towards the state will shape attitudes to war. The steps taken to execute wars – including expanded governmental authority, the implementation of strategies designed to build and maintain domestic support, and the growth in military and executive power – will also influence the public legacies of conflicts. Members of a society holding civil liberties at the centre of their self-concept who see those liberties trammelled in the name of a given war may align their views of armed conflict accordingly. They may also, as we have seen, choose to realign their stated veneration for civil liberties, weak states, and small armies. Plainly, an unwavering commitment to individual rights has not been universal among Americans, and those who spoke against wartime proscriptions sometimes found themselves in dangerous and lonely places. Still, as a result of the nation's political, legal, and cultural inheritance, dissenters possessed a greater license and vocabulary to table their opposition than their counterparts in Canada. Nonetheless, some Canadians have also voiced similar regard for individual freedoms and concerns over their abandonment during wartime. Moreover, Canadians can be grateful that in the realm of controversial foreign engagements, their leaders have provided them less examples to wrestle with, and that in recent years, individual liberties have received greater measures of protection. Canadians and Americans may have arrived at a similar place on issues surrounding the state and the individual, but differences in levels of trust and acquiescence afforded their governments, and the relative ability of those governments to dampen dissent, has left an indelible mark on the reckoning of each nation's wars.

Chapter Six

Matters of Faith

The European idea of the nation-state that grew out of the 1648 Treaty of Westphalia held that, in the name of domestic harmony, political boundaries should be drawn around groups of people who shared a common identity. Blood, history, language, and religion thus became touchstones of belonging, and the "imagined community" that emerged from such a rubric became a powerful tool for motivating citizen fidelity and sacrifice. The outcomes of this configuration could be most impressive: witness the global empires constructed by Western European nations, a project that tied individual and corporate initiative to the interests of both church and state, creating a global community that by 1900 had been remarkably Europeanized; likewise, the rapid industrialization that followed Germany's 1871 unification and brought that nation to great-power status within a generation. The effects of this radical disjuncture between "us" and "them" could also be lethal, as evidenced by the systematic violence that accompanied imperial expansion, competition between European states, ethnic pogroms within states, and efforts by the colonized to regain territories and identities consumed by the great nationalist spectacle of expansion. To Lloyd Kramer, "[n]ationalist movements and ideologies have arguably contributed to more violent conflicts than any other political or ideological force in the contemporary world."[1]

Despite the best attempts of many Canadian and American elites, the European model did not – *could not* – take root in the same way in these nations. A variety of groups already occupied these regions prior to the arrival of European settlers, groups who, despite the longings of many of the new arrivals, had no interest in simply vanishing from the scene. What's more, through a combination of design and happenstance, these fledgling settler societies would be peopled by a disparate variety of immigrants who did not conform to the definitions of "us" posited by the earliest European settlers, and who were therefore constantly challenging and reshaping the delineation of who "we" were. To a greater degree than their European precursors, the United States and Canada would develop polities characterized by their hybridity. Instead of a national fidelity developed around the ethnos, civic virtues would be marshalled – although not without a fight from those who favoured the ethnic archetype – to serve as the symbolic bond for these unusually diverse societies.[2]

Of course, "diversity" itself is a heterogeneous and slippery concept, one that can be measured in a number of ways. From the 1960s onward, American and Canadian historians paid increasing attention to the influence of race, class, and gender on the multifarious attitudes and experiences of their nation's constituents. The effects of the social and cultural turn in the writing of history have been considerable, broadening and complicating understandings of "national" outlooks that were heretofore measured by trolling through the archival leavings of male elites. Until recently, scholars gave comparatively less attention to the role of religion in shaping public attitudes, despite the fact that, as Samuel Huntington observed, religion is often the most cherished of personal identity markers, one that often inspires little appetite for compromise. Perhaps betraying their own subjectivities on matters of faith, social and cultural historians often puzzled over the incongruities between the "true" interests of women, ethnic minorities, and workers, and their actual beliefs, affiliations, and voting patterns – many of which have been shaped by religion. As historian Phillips argued in *American Theocracy*, "we can begin by describing the role of religion in American politics and war with two words: *widely underestimated*" (emphasis in original). Tocqueville would have agreed, marvelling at both the assortment of American sects and their influence on public policy in the 1830s. "Next to each religion," he reported, "is a political opinion that is joined to it by affinity. Allow the human mind to follow its tendency and it will regulate political society and the divine city in a uniform manner; it will seek, if I dare say it, to *harmonize* the earth with Heaven" (emphasis in original).[3] Whether such harmony verifies Marx's famous equation of religion with opium has, of course, much to do with one's opinion of the former.

Lest we think that the Americans have always had the upper hand when it comes to the impact of religion on the *civitas*, we should consider the claims of Mark Noll, who has published extensively on the religious history of both nations. Noll maintained that the influence of faith was so ubiquitous in early-twentieth-century Canadian public life that, in this era, Canada could make a stronger claim for being a "Christian nation" than the United States. Gordon Heath's study of this same era rightly called the Christian church Canada's most influential public institution, one fundamental to "the formation of public morals, religious beliefs, and political sentiments."[4] Significantly for our purposes, on discourses surrounding life-and-death issues like war, religion has been granted a prominent place; further, as revealed below, religious leaders have served variously as some of the more zealous supporters *and* opponents of war. Although their views do not always align precisely with those of their congregants, in times of national crisis, religious sentiments hold considerable sway over those in and beyond the pews, including the makers of national policy. And core aspects of the fusion of religion and politics have shown remarkable durability and consistency over time.

Indeed, religious conviction – along with commercial ambition – provided the most powerful motivations for the earliest European settlements in the "new world," with these impulses often operating in concert. Jamestown, whose establishment by the Virginia Company of London in 1607 made it the first permanent settlement in what would become the United States, was primarily a business venture. The Pilgrims who founded Plymouth Colony thirteen years later, on the other hand, were born in dissent from the established Church of England, and crossed the Atlantic to escape religious discrimination and to found a religious utopia. Other dissenters soon joined them in New England, including Congregationalist and Presbyterian Puritans driven by similar sensibilities, interdictions, and ambitions. However, it is possible to make too much of these discrepancies between Virginians and New Englanders. The mostly Anglican Virginia settlers were, like most Europeans of the era, a deeply religious people who wished to bring salvation to indigenous peoples (the Virginia Charter of 1609, for instance, mandated church attendance and twice-daily public prayers for all settlers, and death to those absent). Meanwhile, the Pilgrims and Puritans received funding from enterprising London financiers, and being good Calvinists, equated hard work with holiness, and profitmaking with their status as "the elect."[5]

None of these groups exhibited particular aversions to employing armed conflict to further their ends, as evidenced by their theological sanction of "just warfare," as well as ample demonstration in both the British and colonial settings that these believers took to heart Clausewitz's definition of war as "politics by other means." While religious doctrine did provide certain proscriptions against the resort to arms, none of these groups could be described as anything approaching pacifistic. In fact, the inveterate competition between Catholics and Protestants for souls and terrain in the Americas, along with sometimes-fierce resistance from indigenous populations, moved American colonists to liberalize previous definitions of a "just war." The Puritans in particular, whose especially acute sense of exceptionalism led them to consider themselves demonstrably superior not merely to Indians and Catholics, but to all other Protestants, came to rationalise any measures used to defeat the enemies of their "holy endeavour." Accordingly, the previous prohibitions against inhumane conduct and the killing of civilians that formed a pillar of just war theory were, in practice, jettisoned. The only criterion of the theory that remained – *is the cause just?* – was, for the Puritans, moot: any action undertaken to protect and expand the realm of God's elect was by definition virtuous.[6]

Thus freed from any ceiling on the use of force, New England colonists battled indigenous communities like the Pequot and the Wampanoag in military campaigns whose savagery and indiscriminate killing horrified other Indian tribes who had allied with the colonists. "Obliteration – total and final annihilation – of the Satanic enemy was the ultimate if unobtainable object," wrote American historian Bernard Bailyn in *The Barbarous Years*, elsewhere marveling at "the scarcely believable ferocity of the English troops, their frenzied butchery, which can only be explained, as they later explained it, by the dreaded fear of the Antichrist." Bloody religious battles in England between Puritans and the Crown in the mid-seventeenth century only furthered the Calvinist-inspired distrust of both monarchy and secular authority in general, and elevated warfare to near-sacramental status in the minds of colonists. Puritan minister Thomas Sutton made the ecclesiastical mandate of warfare explicit, telling his New England parishioners, "above all creatures, God loves souldiers; above all exercises, commends fighting; above all actions, he honors warlike and martiall designes." And despite the asymmetry that characterized nearly every European-Indian battle (when King Philip's War ended in 1676, for instance, nearly half of the prewar indigenous population of 11,600 lay dead, while 800 colonists, representing just 1.6 per cent of their original number, suffered the same fate), the Puritans considered themselves the true victims

6.1 English colonists vanquish the infidels with shocking barbarity in this
nineteenth-century engraving showing the attack on the Pequot fort in Mystic,
an assault which killed virtually all of the fort's roughly 700 inhabitants. Most
of the dead were women, children, and the elderly, and were either burned
alive when the colonists set fire to the fort, or shot while trying to escape.
(United States Library of Congress Prints and Photographs Division.)

of these confrontations. Deploying an interpretation that would mark
future American and Canadian assessments of their soldiers' experiences, the colonists viewed the hardship wrought by their Indian
enemies as both a punishment for sin and an analogue to Jesus' own suffering and redemption. These themes – that an exceptional people were
required to take up arms to extend freedom and rid the world of evil,
and that the righteousness of their cause justified the means required to
prevail in battle – have proven resilient in the American imagination.[7]

As immigration to the American colonies grew, so too did the diversity of faiths practised by the colonists. Most adhered to some variant of

Protestantism – even in Catholic-friendly Maryland, the "papists" constituted a minority of the population. Nevertheless, growing numbers
of Baptists, Lutherans, and Dutch-Reformed, to cite some of the more
prominent, eroded the early dominance of Anglicans and Puritans.[8]
A couple of dynamics associated with this increasing diversity are of
particular significance: first, the further development of individualistic
concepts of faith, and second, the emergence and flourishing of pacifist
sects.

Regarding individualism, and as with the Pilgrims and Puritans, it
is important to note that several of these groups emphasized the pre-
eminence of personal conscience, or came to the position as a result
of the powerful influence of Puritan thought in the colonies and the
distance from old-world regulatory bodies. These dissenting believers
were keen to expose real or imagined governmental violations of personal liberty, and held that authority ultimately rested not in the state
or any overarching religious organization, but in the local church and
in the mind of the believer. These sentiments would be enhanced by the
religious persecution some groups faced as minorities in certain American colonies, such as Anglican-dominated Virginia, and in the case of
the Baptists and Presbyterians, in Congregationalist-dominated New
England. Similarly, a number of Anglican congregations, influenced by
liberal views emanating from some of their fellow congregants in England, became less devoted to the Crown, ritual, and hierarchy, bringing
England's fissure between "High-" and "Low-Church" Anglicanism
to America as well. This reverence for individual conscience and local
authority also bolstered the conviction that clergy had a right and a
duty to weigh in on matters of public policy, a calling many American
churchmen would come to pursue with decided fervour.[9]

Here, then, we have another font of the independence of mind and
anti-statism (not to mention anti-Catholicism) that characterizes much
of American identity, a radical disavowal of the primacy of secular
authority, and a faith-based source of American libertarian ideals that
Preston called "Christian republicanism." The so-called Great Awakening of the early- to mid-eighteenth century furthered this regard for
individual conscience, as evangelical preachers instructed the faithful
to place ultimate trust in their "inner light," rather than secular or even
religious authorities. Not surprisingly, Congregationalists, Baptists, and
Presbyterians – some of the more committed exponents of individual
conscience prior to the Great Awakening, and the denominations that
showed greatest enthusiasm for this "evangelical turn" – formed the

core support for the patriot cause in the American Revolution. These allied religious and political developments led adherents of dissenting congregations to connect the purest forms of human freedom to the particular world view encouraged by their faith. The genius of American liberty, they argued, was made possible by the individual freedom that could only be fully realized by a believer answerable solely to God.[10]

This exaltation of the "inner light" also helps account for the remarkable multiplication of American Protestant sects, as individuals and groups split off from traditional churches in a perpetual quest to pursue the true spiritual path revealed to them through divine guidance. As Hudson observed, this circumstance "was to give a perfectionist cast to much of American religious life and to foster the uninhibited experimentation by smaller fringe groups that was to be the dismay of European churchmen." By the end of the nineteenth century, even American Catholics, a group allegedly afflicted by slavish obedience to papal authority, began to demonstrate an autonomy that prompted a series of encyclicals from Rome aimed at reining in increasingly irrepressible American bishops.[11]

The second notable dynamic related to the increasing fragmentation of American religious life concerns the fact that seventeenth- and eighteenth-century immigration to the colonies included growing numbers of believers from pacifist sects. These newcomers found like-minded neighbours in the war-wary Baptists, whose opposition to state-sponsored violence led the Massachusetts General Court to pass a 1640 statute making it illegal to question "the lawfulness of making war." Fleeing Europe, in large measure because of their radical refusal to take up arms, Mennonites, Moravians, Dunkers, and the Society of Friends (or "Quakers") found refuge in societies noted for their greater measures of tolerance than those of the Old World. The Quakers in particular featured members of considerable influence like William Penn, founder of Pennsylvania, and John Woolman, an early champion of abolitionism. As a group, they would take considerable pains to imbricate themselves into the most significant issues of the day, including debates over religious tolerance, slavery, Indian policy, and war. By the time of the American Revolution, Quakers stood as the fifth largest denomination in the colonies. Each of these pacifist sects sought to distance themselves, on principle, from the rebellion against Britain, and the American revolutionaries encouraged the sense of disassociation with some gusto, subjecting members of peace churches to fines, verbal and physical abuse, and public humiliations. High-Church Anglican clergy, meanwhile, generally opposed that same conflict on the grounds that it was "an unjustified rebellion against constituted authority," an authority particularly dear to those whose head of church and state were one and the same.[12] For these reasons, many High Anglicans and members of pacifist sects decamped the newly independent republic for Britain, Canada, or other British-held terrain.

Religion and commerce also motivated the earliest successful European settlements in what would become Canada, with the early-seventeenth-century French monarchy and priesthood seeking to procure profits from farming, fishing, lumber, and furs, as well as souls from the conversion efforts of the Franciscans and Jesuits. And, like their colonial neighbours to the south, the early colonists at New France wished to create a religious utopia in the wilderness, one administered through their earliest permanent settlement at Quebec. After this, some of the similarities begin to erode. Unlike the American colonists, most of the French settlers were members of an established Roman Catholic Church, a fact that dissuaded religious independence, experimentation, and fragmentation. Further, while many of the earliest Europeans found the New World acutely inhospitable, the settlers of New France confronted a particularly forbidding array of environmental challenges. Unforgiving weather and disease resulted in slow population growth and a heavy reliance on the French homeland for support long after the American colonies achieved self-sufficiency. The existence of the powerful and hostile Iroquois (made more hostile by Samuel de Champlain's military campaign against the group, launched within a year of Quebec's founding) also proved a consistent threat to French settlement for much of the seventeenth century, again requiring the continual intervention of the French crown.[13]

Owing to these circumstances, New France existed in a thoroughly dependent relationship with old France. Serious dissension directed at the home country would threaten the colonists' very survival, and the French crown and church could exercise a degree of authority over the settlement – what historian Terry Crowley termed "a sometimes stifling control" – that would have been impossible in the American colonies. Two decades after Quebec's founding, King Louis XIII's advisor Cardinal Richelieu provided a measure of the Crown's sway over New France, banning non-Catholics from moving to the colony and implementing the semi-feudal seigniorial system along the St. Lawrence valley, with all lands owned by the king. Prospective French emigrants who craved greater levels of religious, political, and economic freedom, like the

Huguenots who had heretofore found refuge in New France, looked for more amenable environs; many would find these in the English colonies to the south.[14]

Quebec, on the other hand, would function as a theocracy, with its established church noted (and in the case of Protestant observers, frequently scorned) for its emphasis on hierarchy and submission to authority. However, while Quebec's religious authorities sometimes sanctioned violence against indigenous communities using a rationale akin to that of the Puritans – that any threat to the work of God deserved to be vanquished – the prevailing tenor of the aboriginal-settler relationship proved more pacific than that found in the English colonies. Rather than seeking to eradicate "heretical" beliefs and practices, and the heretics themselves if they resisted, Quebec's Jesuits quickly "gave up the idea of Frenchifying the Indians," wrote historian James Axtell. Instead, the priests practiced what Axtell called "a brand of cultural relativism," adopting aspects of the indigenous lifestyle and identifying components of aboriginal cosmology that could be channeled towards an appreciation for Christianity. These English-French disparities became a source of embarrassment for English missionaries and a source of contention for the indigenous peoples they proselytized. When an English minister offered to establish a school for the children of New York's Onondaga tribe in 1772, the tribe's rejection came with a pointed admonition: "Brother, you must learn of the French ministers if you would understand, & know how to treat Indians. They don't speak roughly; nor do they for every little mistake take up a club & flog them."[15]

While the British conquest of Canada in 1760 raised francophones' fears of a state-sponsored de-Catholicization campaign, the Quebec Act of 1774 served to safeguard the survival of the church by allowing it to collect tithes. Protestantism would come to Canada not through British attempts to reengineer the world view of French Catholics, but through missionary efforts targeting indigenous groups like the Mohawks (who as late as 1812 comprised the largest single group of Anglicans in Upper Canada); through Protestant migration to the Atlantic coast in the aftermath of the Acadian expulsion; and with the arrival of the loyalists. Those fleeing the American Revolution were far from a homogenous lot; the refugees were made up of a range of individuals and groups who felt threatened by the prospect of the "tyranny of the majority," including religious and ethnic minorities, recent arrivals to the thirteen colonies, indigenous peoples, and blacks. At the same time, many from this motley assemblage were united by their high regard for the protection offered by the English Crown. American colonists belonging to religious congregations known for individualism and anti-monarchical leanings obviously felt less compunction to abandon the beginnings of an experiment founded on republican ideals, and as a result, the high degrees of individualism and anti-statism visible in mainstream American Protestantism were not reproduced to the same degree through emigration to British North America. Along with Anglicans, whose desire to relocate to areas maintained by Britain is readily understood, came some of the more conservative elements of the Presbyterian and Methodist churches – and comparatively few of the unruly Baptists.[16]

In Canada these refugees found kindred souls in clerics like Scottish-born, nineteenth-century Anglican Bishop John Strachan, who considered the American Revolution the inevitable consequence of a people ruined by a "mania for undefined liberty and licentiousness." Such a "mania" constituted the antithesis of the precept so central to the Anglican world view: the need for order. Order served as the fundamental prerequisite for creating a stable society, which was in turn the prerequisite for liberty; the Americans, with childlike impatience, had subverted the very foundation of freedom in a doomed effort to achieve it. For Anglican leaders in both Britain and Upper Canada, the antidote to the "American mania" was clear: a state-sponsored or established Anglican Church. Without this, they reasoned, Canada too would be plagued by disunity, rebelliousness, and a lack of respect for the divinely inspired Crown and social order – the very pestilences that hatched the American Revolutionary War.[17] Thus, while the conflict with British "tyranny" helped to inspire the architects of America's Constitution to protect individual conscience by proscribing the state establishment of religion, Canadian and British Anglicans derived precisely the opposite lesson from the same body of evidence.

US attacks on Strachan's adopted city of York during the War of 1812 did little to moderate the Bishop's disdain for the dissipations of American republicanism. In fact, York was spared potential American plundering only through Strachan's own negotiations of surrender in 1813. After this, Strachan became even firmer in his conviction that Upper Canada should serve as a sanctuary for those faithful to state and church – and more pointedly, to the Church of England. The war had also disrupted connections between American and Canadian chapters of the same denominations, compelled Canadian congregations with ties to the United States to demonstrate their loyalty to the empire, and

6.2 A grim-faced Bishop Strachan in an undated photo, perhaps pondering the spectre of American liberalism. (John Connon/Thomas Connon, Photographer, Connon Collection, XR1 MS A267022, University of Guelph Library Digital Collections.)

reoriented the focus of Canadian immigration from the United States to Great Britain. In short, Canadian Protestantism as a whole became more statist, conservative, Britannic, and anti-American, augmenting characteristics already apparent before 1812. The Roman Catholic Church, too, remained loyal to Britain during the war, leading British officials to give up whatever illusions they maintained about turning the Church of England into Quebec's established church; thereafter, Catholic dioceses expanded rapidly throughout Canada.[18]

Clearly, none of these groups could eclipse the Anglican Church in the contest for Britishness, and the post-1812 political, cultural, and demographic shifts outlined above go far in explaining why the period

between the war with the United States and Canadian Confederation marks the high tide of Anglican influence in Canada. By virtue of
their commitment to England, Anglican clergy of the era were inex-
tricably bound to both the colonial and imperial government, viewing their church as a public institution and "guardian of the imperial
tie," and themselves as representatives of the Crown. As historian William Westfall noted, "the state supported and to a considerable degree
controlled the church in the colony, while the church accepted, indeed
glorified, the close relationship that these ties created." The newspaper
The Church, the official organ of Canadian Anglicanism (and one bearing a fitting title, given that the sect longed for the day when it would
represent all English Canada), made little distinction between "secular" and "sacred" in an 1845 editorial, averring that "a certain form of
Christianity has been interwoven with the framework of the British
Constitution." As Robert Choquette observed, between the Proclama-
tion of 1791 (which set aside Crown-owned "clergy reserves" to fund
the Anglican Church) and the mid-nineteenth century, the Church of
England acted as "a department of the state," deriving both income
and a good deal of regulation from secular authorities in both Canada
and England. The blurring of the church-state divide occurred even
on an individual level: Anglican clergy like Strachan were core members of Upper Canada's Family Compact, an ultra-conservative cadre
of British loyalists that dominated the government and judiciary; Jacob
Mountain, bishop of the Anglican diocese in Quebec, served on the legislative councils and executive committees of both Upper and Lower
Canada. Owing to their strong connections to the empire and a social
order that relied heavily on patronage, Anglicans were disproportionately represented among Canada's governmental, military, and business elites, and thus held considerable sway over public discourse in
pre-Confederation Canada.[19]

Not surprisingly, the church inherited certain obligations in return
for state support and protection, not the least of which being the duty to
defend the state against internal and external threats, along with restrictions on the right of clerics to comment on public policy. Although
successful challenges from other sects and the ascendance of political
liberalism ended the Anglican monopoly over the clergy reserve system
and thwarted Bishop Strachan's dream of a thoroughly Anglicanized
Upper Canada, continued immigration from Britain meant that by mid-
century, the Anglican Church stood as the largest single denomination in
Upper Canada. While scholars continue to debate whether the Anglican

Church was truly the established state church of Upper Canada, it certainly believed itself to be so, a stance that was reinforced by demands from other congregations to *disestablish* the church. The Presbyterian Church, for its part, considered itself the Scottish associate of Anglicanism, with the same claims to establishment status. Rather than rescind the special status these sects enjoyed as a means of recognizing the increasing plurality of the populace, the government of Upper Canada under John A. Macdonald simply added to their number by providing similar privileges to Roman Catholics and Methodists.[20]

The 1854 cessation of financial support from the government severed the direct link between Anglicanism and state, with clerics now maintaining that the church, rather than society at large, served as the primary conduit through which God communicated to the world. Though moderated, Canadian Anglicanism's strong connections to state and empire remained powerful well after Confederation, helping to foster a climate where support for metropole and King were frequently equated with the true Canadian outlook, particularly in Canada's most populous province. As Westfall observed dryly, this nineteenth-century religious culture "survived for a long time, and the shadow it cast covered much of the province into the twentieth century, giving Ontario a moral reputation that unnerved those who might be unmindful of its social benefits." And with the formal ties to the state cut, Anglicans became more ecumenical, forging links to other mainstream Protestants and thereby generating new avenues through which non-Anglicans' fealty to empire could be channeled. "In the process there had been movement from both sides toward the centre," wrote Grant. "There would be no established church, but neither would the churches be private organizations catering merely to the spiritual needs of their individual members."[21] In other words, the disestablishment of Anglicanism allowed other churches to express a greater measure of support for the state, since the state no longer appeared to favour a single, rival congregation. In this sense, each took on something of a semi-established status; each saw the others as collaborators in a vital national and global endeavour.

In all, argued Westfall, by the end of the nineteenth century "the distinction between church and dissent had been overwhelmed by the Protestant consensus" an ecumenical outlook that persisted into the twentieth century. Indeed, in contrast to the multiplication of church bodies characteristic of American Protestantism, turn-of-the-century Canadian Protestants expressed a good deal of "hospitality to proposals for church union," a mindset that "pointed to a bad conscience about the divisions that already existed." Fittingly, the preamble to the 1925 Basis of Union of the United Church of Canada – the era's most profound testament to the desire for unity – pledged that the new church would "foster the spirit of unity in the hope that this sentiment of unity may in due time, so far as Canada is concerned, take shape in a Church which may fittingly be described as national." American historian William Katerberg observed that while the existence and influence of "civil religion" at the national level is more often associated with the United States, "*within particular regions*, relations between religious, social, and political establishments may have been tighter in Canada. Most obvious in this vein was Roman Catholicism in Quebec; close behind were the culturally powerful mainline Protestant denominations of Ontario" (emphasis in original).[22]

Not all Canadian sects or individual churchgoers pledged similar levels of obedience to state and empire. Links between US and Canadian churches that had been severed during the War of 1812 were restored over the course of the century, providing an avenue through which the American evangelical movement influenced believers in Canada as well. However, the differing cultural climate to the north smoothed some of the more "disorderly" qualities of the evangelical mindset, including its superabundant enthusiasm, emotionalism, and lack of deference to church and state. Similarly, the utopianism and millennialism that exerted a strong influence among American believers never had the same influence to the more stoic and reserved Canadians. But the relative absence of Canadian millennialism and perfectionism also removed another potential avenue for challenging the rectitude of war, since many American end-times evangelicals laboured tirelessly to purge their society of all ills in order to speed the second coming of Christ. Their list of evils was sweeping, and included individual iniquities like swearing, drunkenness, dueling, and card-playing, as well as institutional wrongs like slavery, poverty, and warfare. Voluntary associations dedicated to these goals proliferated, furnishing US believers with abilities in organization, fundraising, and publicity that would serve them well from the antebellum era to the present.[23]

Immigrants to Canada from Christian pacifist congregations hardly shared the enthusiasm for the prerogatives of the state displayed by the Protestant consensus. However, Quakers, the group that had been most outspoken on the issue of war in the American (and British) context, made up at their peak only 0.05 per cent of the Ontario population (a scant 7,300 of the 1,396,091 residents recorded in the 1861 census), and declined to roughly 1,000 in the entire nation by the beginning of the twentieth century. In terms of sheer numbers, Christian pacifism in Canada would largely be represented by Mennonites, a group that, through various waves of immigration, claimed nearly 50,000 adherents at the outset of the Great War and continued to grow steadily throughout the century. But in contrast to the Quakers, many adherents of the Mennonite faith were rural, inward-looking, committed to the German language, and distrustful of both higher education and involvement with the state, factors which moderated their influence on broader Canadian culture. As peace historian Peter Brock pointed out, Quaker pacifism was "integrational" while the Mennonite variety was "separational." The sect was also highly decentralized and hesitant to liaise with other denominations, not to mention secular organizations.[24]

Mennonites had also learned from their Anabaptist forbearers that open challenges to state authority led to harsh persecution, and thus came to embrace relocation over protestation when official policy contradicted their core beliefs. Their early experiences in Canada would give Mennonites little assurance that they had finally found a haven of tolerance for their dissenting views. As Ross Fair's study revealed, Mennonites and other religious pacifists fleeing the newly established American republic received a far less charitable welcome in Upper Canada than is generally acknowledged. For decades, they were denied British citizenship, and adult males were required to pay an annual fine in lieu of military service (and had their goods and chattels seized if they failed to do so). Following the War of 1812, Bishop Strachan was so frustrated by the lack of wartime cooperation from pacifist congregations like the Mennonites that he sought to close the border to these groups, arguing that they had been "a clog" in the war effort and that "our population is too small to allow a large portion to be non Combatants."[25]

Although Mennonites became more active in the wider peace movement following the Second World War, their experiences and outlook constrained the influence of their antiwar views prior to that conflict, and rendered the later spirit of activism a divisive issue within the church. In fact, the numerically challenged Quakers often took the lead in defending the nation's pacifists, lobbying the First World War Union government, for instance, on behalf of all Canadian conscientious objectors. Owing to these factors, it is not surprising that, as Amy Shaw has noted, both Britain and the United States possess a good deal more primary and secondary materials on conscientious objection than Canada. This dearth owes a great deal to the demographic and ideological characteristics of Canada's religious dissenters, along with, as Shaw observes, "the eager insecurity of a colony anxious to prove its maturity and imperial goodwill." In other words, the attitudes of Canada's pacifists, imperialists, and nationalists conspired to tamp down the story of wartime dissent: Mennonites were not prone to trumpet their nonconformity, and members of the mainstream – keen on depicting a unified, rising international power – were likewise disinclined to emphasize the presence of dissention in their midst. The disinclination could assume alarming proportions. Following the Great War, judges who had presided over tribunals of men appealing their conscription burned the court records associated with their cases because, explained one, the documents "were full of hatred and bitterness and would have been a living menace to national unity."[26]

English-Canadian Protestantism's near-universal support for a war in South Africa fought at the behest of the British Empire, then, was largely foreordained – and as the era's most influential public institution, ecclesiastical support mattered a great deal. In sermons, press interviews, and editorials in church publications, clerics from Canada's four largest Protestant denominations endorsed the justness of the cause on the grounds that a British victory would result in the extension of suffrage, the cessation of slavery, and the rehabilitation of the backward and debased Boers (who, though nominally Christian, exhibited a stunted or blatantly false understanding of the Word). Even the internment of women and children could be defended: on the one hand, in a battle where good and evil were so clearly demarcated, ends justified means; on the other, reports of rampant disease and death in the camps could be attributed to Boer slovenliness rather than British maltreatment. In fact, argued some, internment would provide an ideal opportunity to introduce the incarcerated (whose deaths in squalid conditions, it bears repeating, numbered nearly 30,000) to the benefits of modernity.[27]

Mainline Protestant understandings of the war's relationship to empire, meanwhile, demonstrated how far non-Anglicans had moved towards establishment-type thinking on these matters. As Gordon Heath's study revealed, the Protestant consensus as a whole, and not just the Church of England, understood the role of empire within a "providential framework," holding that "Britain had a divine mandate to wage war in defence of justice and liberty for the oppressed." The Christmas editorial of the official magazine of Baptist-funded McMaster

University wrote that because of this mandate, "Britain is to-day dying red the African veldt with the life blood of her sons," a sacrificial act that "is in truth the essence of the teaching the Master taught some nineteen hundred years ago among the olive groves above Jerusalem, and upon the sunny vine-clad slopes of Judea." Underpinning these assumptions lay the mutually-supportive beliefs in social Darwinism, which held that Britain's status as the world's most powerful empire proved the racial superiority of Anglo-Saxons, and the Social Gospel, which urged believers to carry the benefits of their higher civilization to the backward and downtrodden. In a context where distinctions between the Kingdom of God and the Kingdom of Britain were frequently undetectable, criticism of the actions of imperial forces could invite accusations of both sedition and sacrilege.[28]

At the same time, like so many committed Canadian imperialists of the era, Protestant clerics were also dedicated nation-builders, and viewed the war as a means of advancing Canada's position within the empire. Churches helped to define soldiering as a solemn national duty, providing Communion to troops at special "send-off services" and encouraging donations to the "Patriotic Fund" supporting the war effort, even though this reduced parishioners' contributions to the church itself. And like the Puritans besieged by Indian resistance, some English-Canadian churchmen viewed the trials and tribulations in South Africa as punishment for collective sins, and extolled war as an opportunity to purify the nation. As Heath reported, church editorials referred to the dead as martyrs who "had given their lives in the 'sacred' task of nation building" – sentiments that would be reprised in subsequent Canadian encounters with war.[29]

Of course, Canadian Mennonites frowned upon the empire's aggression (even more so because they found kindred spirits in the Boers, who had also emigrated from the Netherlands in search of religious freedom). Having been spared the dilemma of conscription, however, Mennonites and other pacifist sects could vent their opposition quietly among themselves, rather than being required to defend their unwillingness to fight in public. Thus, in contrast to the condemnations of Britain's alleged greed and cruelty emanating from some American and British churches, English Canadians heard few hesitations about the righteousness of the clash in the Transvaal from the pulpit. Even Methodists, who in 1884 had issued a declaration calling for arbitration as a substitute for warfare, refused to condemn the conflict in its initial stages, and in 1902 formally declared their support for the British cause (paradoxically, around the same time that the war's atrocities had disillusioned many British clergy). The Woman's Christian Temperance Union's early and consistent opposition was thus both bold and a striking anomaly among Protestant Canadians. In fact, noted Carman Miller, the WCTU was "the only organized Protestant body to oppose the war." Francophone Catholics, for their part, expressed some grave and understandable misgivings about a war against an agrarian, unassimilated, linguistic, and religious minority within the British Empire. Such reservations led to charges of disloyalty from the Anglican's *Canadian Churchmen* and helped to lay the groundwork for the tradition of French-English division over Canada's foreign conflicts. It should nonetheless be noted that French Canadian opinion was in fact less homogenous than English Canadians believed, as the protection offered by the imperial connection, along with ultramontanist support for efforts to spread Christian civilization, led some francophones of the era to endorse British imperial pursuits.[30]

As was the case for Canada's *fin-de-siècle* war, the vast majority of American Christians supported US intervention in Cuba. However, a good deal of this support was conditional, predicated on the belief that the military operation was essentially a mission of mercy aimed at relieving the suffering of the Cuban people and eliminating the scourge of tyranny from Latin America. Spanish depredations against the Cubans were undeniable and appalling – nearly 100,000 civilians died in Spanish *reconcentrados* – and American newspapers made the most of the dreadfulness in a bid to increase circulation. Accordingly, American Protestants, who like their northern neighbours were infused with the crusading spirit of the Social Gospel and the righteous manliness of muscular Christianity, demanded action. And like their Canadian counterparts, mainline American Protestants of the era embraced the twin assumptions that God favoured both Anglo-Saxons and *their* nation above all – and had therefore marked them as His special agents of global transformation. After the American victory at Manila in May 1898, Congregationalist minister and popular author Lyman Abbot told the readers of his weekly *Outlook*, "the Nation is simply the hand of Providence; its task was made for it by its history, and they who fall in the doing of the task fall in a noble cause."[31]

At the same time, waves of late-century immigration meant that the conflict with Spain coincided with an era, noted Preston, "when American religion became more pluralistic, more complicated, and more diffuse." Despite this increasing fragmentation, the belief in the nobility – indeed, necessity – of intervention was so universal among Americans that even believers from churches who did not share the same fervor for militarism, racial destiny, and nationism expressed few misgivings. Pacifist sects like the Quakers and Mennonites remained opposed to all use of violence, but the depth of the humanitarian crisis in Cuba, alongside the fact that President McKinley was one of their own, subdued some of Methodism's traditional concerns over war (although Southern Methodists, who had witnessed firsthand the consequences of armed conflict during the Civil War, remained hesitant). Catholics, by this point nine million strong and thus a significant political force, by-and-large supported a war even against a Catholic adversary: the conflict, they reasoned, would deliver their co-religionists in Cuba and the Philippines from Spanish tyranny, while their public endorsement of intervention would speed the acceptance of the Catholic church in Protestant-dominated America (although Catholics bristled when pro-interventionist Protestants spoke of Filipinos as a people yearning for conversion to the true faith). Leaders of Mormon and Jewish groups, whose numbers had also increased substantially in the previous decades, likewise offered their support as a means of gaining greater public favour. American Jews also found solace in the fact that the United States was willing to resort to arms in order to support principles of freedom and justice; for a community closely monitoring the ongoing maltreatment of French officer Alfred Dreyfuss, that willingness seemed in direct contradistinction to the reactionary nature of European regimes.[32]

This virtual unanimity among non-pacifist religious groups would be fractured by both the imperial question and the severe measures undertaken to subdue the Filipino uprising against US occupation, a turn of events that shocked American and Filipino alike. Presbyterian minister Henry Van Dyke spoke for the latter in his 1898 Thanksgiving Day sermon when he lamented, "never has fate sprung a more trying surprise upon an unsuspecting and ingenuous people." Religious pacifism, largely silenced when the American Civil War demonstrated that state violence could be employed for emancipatory ends, regained its voice as the conflict with Spain evolved. Groups that had endorsed the action as a rare example of military power deployed in the service of humanity were "appalled" by the transformation of the mission and began to peel away from the pro-war camp: church leaders led an unsuccessful campaign to exclude provisions for annexation of the Philippines from the Treaty of Paris; the Federal Council of Churches organized a department of peace; twenty-nine of the country's most prominent Protestant, Catholic, and Jewish leaders gathered to establish the Church Peace Union. The American chapter of the WCTU reversed its initial support and became an outspoken critic, a course followed by prominent African Methodist Episcopal and Catholic bishops, who attacked the racial and religious chauvinism that fed American atrocities against Filipinos. These critics were joined by a number of Protestant clergy, like Unitarian Reverend H.M. Simmons of Minneapolis, who connected the racial violence of the American south with the tactics of US forces abroad. President McKinley, Simmons charged, was "sending great armies around the world ... to lynch a people for merely wanting to practice the principles which we have taught." Support for the war among Protestant missionaries remained strong, but the heterogeneity and individual prerogative that characterized much of the American religious milieu joined with the nation's republican creed to give rise to stern rebukes of a government and army that were, at that moment, entangled in a gruelling foreign conflict. Plainly, the oft-stated tenet that it is a citizen's solemn duty to cast aside all doubts and rally around the flag once a nation is at war holds less purchase among Americans than is sometimes maintained. As Reverend Van Dyke declared in his aforementioned Thanksgiving Day homily, "if the test of loyalty is to join in every thoughtless cry of the multitude, I decline it. I profess a higher loyalty – *allegiance to the flag, not for what it covers, but for what it means*" (emphasis in original).[33]

Similar patterns – near-unanimous support for the duration of the war from English Canadian mainstream church leaders, and among their American counterparts, a range of responses shaped by ideological diversity and shifting circumstances on the battlefield – would mark religious-based responses to the Great War. Although the ideology of progressivism had contributed to an upsurge in pacifism among church groups, when the conflict in Europe broke out, Canadian Protestant leaders promptly shed their more irenic inflections. Once again they framed the war, at its root, as a contest over religion, holding that this was less a battle between men and nations for territory or freedom than a struggle for the preservation of Christianity itself. "War is never wrong," the *Presbyterian Record* instructed, "when it is a war against wrong." Like the conflict with the Boers, this was a holy war between the elect and the damned, though one that again saw Christian fighting Christian. As even the more guarded Methodists concluded, "German religion had become the exact antithesis of Christianity," and Germany and its Kaiser could well be agents, or the very embodiments, of the anti-Christ. Once again, imperialism, nationalism, and Providential destiny were conflated, with preachers championing conscription and urging Canadians to vote for the wartime Union government "in the name of God and Country." In fact, few groups were as unwavering in their support of the war effort as Canada's Protestant clergy; of these, Anglicans, not surprisingly, were in the forefront. In all, observed Carl Berger, the "Christian approbation of war" so dominant during the South African conflict would be "re-echoed a thousandfold during the First World War."[34]

Francophone Catholics again expressed greater ambivalence, with many considering the struggle in Europe to be outside Canada's national interests. English-speaking Ontario Catholics, however, a group that numbered roughly 280,000, generally endorsed the war for reasons that mirrored those of Protestant Canada (an opportunity to sacrifice for the cause of Christ), and that echoed American Catholics' desire to gain acceptance from a Protestant-dominated polity. As Mark McGowan's study of Toronto's Catholics found, participation in and support for the war "marked the culmination of their community's decades-long process of integration into Canadian society." The Catholics of New Brunswick, Prince Edward Island, and especially Nova Scotia also demonstrated strong support for the conflict and volunteered for the Canadian Expeditionary Force in numbers disproportionate to their percentage of the total population.[35]

The few English Canadian church leaders who opposed the conflict walked a lonely road. J.S. Woodsworth and William Ivens, Methodist clergymen and committed social gospellers, left the ministry for their staunch antiwar stance – Woodsworth by choice, and Ivens via compulsion. Members of historic peace churches, excluded from compulsory service by the Military Service Act, faced public harassment, mockery in the press, condemnation from pro-war clerics, and occasional incarceration; individuals from mainstream congregations who claimed conscientious objector status received, in Wright's words, "virtually no support from their local clergymen."[36] On the whole, English Canadian churches would serve as a bastion of loyalty to the war effort.

However, this was a new kind of confrontation – a "total war" of unprecedented scale, a machine-age slaughter of unimaginable horror. Canadians began to develop grave doubts that a righteous and all-powerful God would call on so many of the nation's young men to die such gruesome deaths on His behalf. Redeploying time-honoured approaches that aimed to link warfare with the ultimate sense of purpose, Protestant clergy sought to make sense of the suffering by presenting the soldiers' experience as a mirror of the redemptive suffering of Christ himself. In Jonathon Vance's words, "each death was an atonement, each wound a demonstration of God's love, and each soldier a fellow sufferer of Christ."[37]

Not all men of the cloth toed the official line. Following the war, some Canadian Great War chaplains resigned their orders as a result of their experiences at the front, and many Protestant clerics came to adopt a penitent spirit over their Great War endorsement and a more pacifistic tone in general. "I want to escape that utter depression of the soul that overwhelms me when I think of Ypres and Passchendaele, the hell of Lens, the mad ruin that stretches from Vimy and Arras to Cambrai and Valenciennes," confessed Presbyterian chaplain (and future moderator of the United Church) E.H. Oliver. Even so, many Church leaders' straightforward equation of Jesus and the Canadian infantryman endured into the postwar era even as the clerics of other participating nations turned forcefully on the notion of war and their role in consecrating it. "Years after the armistice," observed Wright, "church publications continued to feature stories of battlefield heroism, soldiers' memoirs, wartime poetry, and victory hymns ... Sermons written for bereaved local congregations, perhaps more than any other media, perpetuated this heroic interpretation of the war through the early 1920s."[38]

The continuing equation of Flanders' fields and the highest ideals of Christ can be seen in the postwar elevation of the Western Front into "a new Holy Land," one which inspired reverent pilgrimages to battlefields and cemeteries from Canadians, and in the 1936 unveiling of the Vimy memorial, a cathedral-like edifice suffused with Christian symbolism. For those at home, the religion-war nexus found its most obvious expression in the many monuments, tablets, plaques, and stained glass memorials to the war that proliferated in churches after 1918, and which reiterated the motif of soldiers' Christ-like sacrifices. Such aesthetic representations were also common in British churches, but apart from military chapels and veterans' buildings, virtually unknown in the United States, where positive views of the war did not survive long enough to be implemented in ecclesiastical architects' plans.[39] As discussed below, Canada's mainstream Protestant churches developed more nuanced, ambivalent, and sometimes hostile attitudes towards warfare in the ensuing decades; however, their earlier fervour for

6.3 Canadian chaplain E.H. Oliver was forever traumatized by the horrors he witnessed in places like Passchendaele, here pictured following the 1917 battle that left hundreds of thousands dead. (George Metcalf Archival Collection, Canadian War Museum, 19930013–512.)

empire and militarism became a permanent feature of Canada's houses of worship.

It may be difficult for some modern observers to account for the stability of the triumphalist and Godly renderings of the Great War among Canadian church leaders. In part, it stemmed from the main-line churches' history of fealty to nation and empire, and the accompanying desire to separate the Canadian experiment from – and elevate it above – the American. With this came a reluctance to condemn the actions of a state whose very existence always appeared more tenuous than that of their older, more prosperous, and more assertive neighbour (not to mention the more established civilizations of Europe). Intensive self-criticism, in other words, could undermine a people who were not yet fully aware of themselves as such. In a similar vein, in its immediate aftermath, the war was already being touted as Canada's coming of age, its war of independence. Second-guesses about the necessity of the carnage would call into question the purported basis of the nation itself (among clergy who, as we have seen, underscored the basic unity of nation, church, and empire). In part, the unyielding appeal to the sacredness of the endeavour was based on the sheer scale of Canadian casualties, which, to even begin to accept, had to carry with them the profoundest meaning. Post facto questions of the sacrifice would, for many congregants facing indescribable loss, simply be too much to bear. When a few of the pious did indeed question the righteousness of warfare, the state could be counted on to rein them in, as members of the Canadian Fellowship of Reconciliation discovered in 1931 when Toronto police descended upon an organizational meeting in an effort to disperse the seditious assembly.[40]

At least prior to the spring of 1917, Canadians who opposed the Great War on religious grounds would have found many friends (not just of the Quaker variety) south of the border. American religious leaders remained highly unsettled on the righteousness of the Great War in its early stages; prior to US entry, they could express candidly their reservations without the prospect of undermining their government or dividing their congregants, who might otherwise have sons, brothers, and husbands in the trenches. This liberty merged with longstanding American traditions of exceptionalism, isolationism from European "decadence," and religious fragmentation and autonomy, to produce a wide array of often harsh denunciations of the overseas crisis. After an autumn 1914 trip to Britain, France, and Germany, renowned American missionary John Mott excoriated the "holy war" mentality that had seized clerics and laypeople on both sides of the conflict; the experience led him to found the American Fellowship of Reconciliation upon his return to the United States.[41]

Uncomfortable memories of American churches' initial enthusiasm for the War of 1898 undergirded these recriminations. That conflict had discredited the concept of "progressive war" and spurred an unprecedented rise in American pacifism, even among mainline congregations. In an expression of both the depth of antiwar sentiment and the American penchant for diffusion and splintering, at least forty-five groups dedicated to peace in general, to keeping the United States out of the war, or both, emerged before 1917. Among the more prominent

were the Anti-Preparedness Committee, the American Union Against
Militarism, the Christian Socialist League, the Church Peace Union, the
American Fellowship of Reconciliation, the Women's Peace Party, the
American Peace Society, the League to Enforce Peace, and the American
Neutral Conference Committee. Representatives from all major peace
groups met in 1916 in New York City for a "Conference of Peacemakers." Although diverse, these organizations were united by the fact that
they were either specifically religious in origin and nature, or counted
prominent religious leaders among their founders and core membership. Pentecostals, advocates of both pacifism and a particularly
uncompromising anti-statism, voiced ringing denunciations of possible US intervention and conscription. American Catholics, dominated
as they were by clerics and congregants from Ireland, expressed little
enthusiasm for fighting alongside Britain.[42]

Not all American sects were similarly inclined. Particularly from
Protestant denominations with historic ties to the British Isles there
emerged, from August 1914 on, calls for intervention on behalf of
the Allies and bitter denunciations of German militarism and autoc-
racy. As the conflict continued and the British blockade spurred
increasingly audacious German attacks on merchant ships and the
deaths of Americans at sea, the isolationism, pacifism, and neutrality that had previously marked the less-anglophilic church
officials' attitudes to the conflict dwindled. President Wilson, the
thinking went, had done all he could to avoid war. Now, with the
true depravity of Germany laid bare, both Protestant and Catholic
ministers began to present congregants with a stark choice: America could continue to endure German humiliations and face the
prospect of a Europe dominated by what was increasingly viewed
as an evil regime, or it could willingly subject itself to suffering –
just as Christ had – in order to redeem humanity. Wilson's presentation of war aims was particularly well-aligned with this type of
reasoning, as a war fought for no personal gain, for the restoration
of justice, and for a new millennium of American-led international
harmony held considerable appeal to believers who trusted in the
divine mission of their nation. As the ecumenical Federal Council of
Churches maintained in a cable to Wilson, the president's proposed
League of Nations was nothing less than "the political expression
of the Kingdom of God on earth." Even Christian fundamentalists –
a new term for conservative Protestant evangelicals who clung to
biblical inerrancy, and who expressed great devotion for their country

6.4 The Reverend Billy Sunday strikes a commanding pose in this 1908 studio portrait. (C.U. Williams, Bloomington, Indiana.)

and great suspicion towards their government – now came on board. After US intervention, popular fundamentalist evangelist Billy Sunday was invited to offer a prayer in the House of Representatives, and presented a particularly stark outline of what was at stake in the battle against Germany. "Thou knowest, O Lord," prayed Sunday, "that no nation so infamous, vile, greedy, sensuous, bloodthirsty ever disgraced the pages of history," concluding that "if you turn hell upside down, you will find 'Made in Germany' stamped on the bottom."[43]

Sunday never revealed precisely *how* he had gained such a revelation, but his views, if not their flamboyant allocution, were shared by many clerics from more staid religious traditions. And in a fashion not atypical to the US setting, once these Americans signed on to the campaign, they did so with rather remarkable and single-minded zeal. After Congress approved Wilson's war message, the pacifism that had characterized many mainstream religious bodies in the first years of the conflict all but vanished, leaving socialists virtually alone in their opposition to US participation. Even the traditionally antiwar Unitarians lent their support, as did ecumenical organizations – like the now paradoxically named Church Peace Union – that had been created for the expressed purpose of keeping the nation out of war. American Roman Catholic leaders, displaying roughly the opposite of the ultramontane sentiment so popular in Quebec, backed Wilson's peace proposal over a rival plan put forward by Pope Benedict XV; their allegiance to the state, always a concern for those who feared American Catholics placed papal decree above that of the president, had been endorsed by US Cardinal James Gibbons on the eve of American intervention. "The primary duty of a citizen is loyalty to country," he counseled his flock and assured non-Catholics. "This loyalty is exhibited by absolute and unreserved obedience to his country." The Cardinal's words would be heeded. "Without backing from church hierarchy," wrote historian Christopher Capozzola, "... only nine Catholics in the entire United States are known to have claimed conscientious objector [CO] status" out of a total of 65,000 COs nationwide. A broad range of church leaders formed the National Catholic War Council to back the war effort. American Jews, many of whom had embraced both socialism and pacifism at the beginning of the conflict, rallied around the flag to demonstrate loyalty, back a Democratic president, and relieve the suffering of European Jews caught up in the conflict. German aggression against the United States, the hyperpatriotism that attended American entry, and the coercions orchestrated and inspired by the Committee on Public Information rendered opposition to war not only unpopular but dangerous. As was the case in Canada, even members of traditional peace churches, whose principled refusal to fight was both longstanding and officially recognized by the Selective Services Act, faced verbal and physical assault.[44]

In the interwar period, many American churchmen issued very public expressions of shame over their role in promoting hatred and militarism during a conflict that had in fact done little to bring about the kingdom of God on earth, and that had instead so enriched the war-related industrialists whom many Americans were now calling the "merchants of death." A 1931 poll of nearly 20,000 US clergy found that fully 80 per cent endorsed *unilateral* disarmament, while hundreds of the nation's most prominent ministers made a public pledge to never again endorse warfare. The Federal Council of Churches did the same, in language that underscored the anti-statist currents of American religious thought, acknowledging that "we look back with shame upon the blind servility with which the Christian church gave itself to the government of the United States in 1917 and 1918." In all, Christian groups passed hundreds of antiwar resolutions between the wars: the Evangelical Synod of North America testified that "to support war is to deny the Gospel we profess to believe"; the General Conference of the Methodist Church called warfare "the greatest social sin of modern times; a denial of the ideals of Christ"; the Presbyterian General Assembly issued the simple declaration that "the Church should never again bless a war"; the Congregational General Council was even more straightforward, proclaiming that "the Church is through with war!" Ray Abrams's *Preachers Present Arms*, a caustic indictment of the Protestant clergy's role in building support for the conflict, became the standard inter-war interpretation of American church-state relations during the Great War. Once again, the idea that the teachings of Christ were irreconcilable with individual and collective violence moved to the mainstream among US Protestants – at the same time that pacifism was limited to what Vance called a "small minority" in Canada. Disciples of Christ minister Kirby Page outlined the kind of uncompromising commitment to nonviolence ascendant among American Christians, maintaining that "the following of Jesus Christ is infinitely more important than the maintenance of political liberty at the expense of his principles." While not all religious groups went this far (some antiwar resolutions left openings for wars of defence) the general mood was undeniable.[45]

The churches did more than issue *mea culpas* and vow to withhold their support for future war; they also became leading advocates for the instruments meant to prevent it. "Virtually every major denomination," noted Gerald Sittser, supported the League of Nations and "urged the Senate to ratify it." Denominations and ecumenical organizations expressed similar levels of enthusiasm for international disarmament and US participation in the Permanent Court of International Justice (the latter which, as with the League, the Senate rejected). When in the late 1920s most of the world's nations endorsed the Kellogg-Briand Pact renouncing war, the churches were euphoric: the General Conference of Southern Methodism rhapsodized that the treaty "is shot through with the light that shone in Bethlehem. The inspiration is the man from Galilee." Charles Clayton Morrison, editor of the nation's most widely-read religious periodical, the ecumenical *Christian Century*, declared, "today international war was banished from civilization." While the celebration proved premature, Morrison expressed support for uncompromising pacifism even after Europe and Asia descended into chaos, arguing as late as October 1941 for peace talks with Hitler rather than a US military response to Nazism.[46]

Such views distressed influential Christian realist theologian Reinhold Niebuhr, whose belief in the essential sinfulness of humanity led him to conclude that a commitment to absolute pacifism would only speed the triumph of evil over good. "Pacifism is usually the creed of only a small minority in any nation," he lamented in a 1940 article for *The Nation*. "It has achieved more than minority proportions in contemporary America largely because our churches are almost unanimous in their espousal of it." As Niebuhr's broad censure of "our churches" suggested, Catholic misgivings about US participation in the new European war were also widespread, rooted in the general climate of anti-militarism and the anti-British attitude among the many congregants of Irish, Italian, and German descent. Catholic opposition was also nurtured by a lamentable forbearance for European fascism, a by-product of the anti-Semitism prominent among some church leaders (including Ontario-born and -educated radio commentator Father Charles Coughlin, whose nationally circulated newspaper *Social Justice* serialized the full text of *The Protocols of the Elders of Zion* in 1938). Protestants also embraced anti-Semitism with unprecedented vigour in the interwar years as the nation grappled with increased immigration, urbanization, and economic crisis. Many religious individuals and organizations opposed US entry into war because they saw no need to assist European Jews, or considered the Jews the font of the socialist/capitalist/whatever-ideology-you-revile conspiracy to control global finance and consign the globe to perpetual violence. The targets of the bigots' vitriol were alone among major US religious groups in expressing consistent and passionate calls for intervention. The generalized atmosphere of anti-Semitism contributed to the indifference towards European Jews desperate to escape Nazism. Only 140,000 Jews were admitted to the United States between 1933 and the outbreak of war in 1939, and just 21,000 were admitted during the Holocaust.[47]

Hitler's shocking advances in the spring of 1940 begin to erode the antiwar unanimity Niebuhr disparaged, and Pearl Harbor shattered it convincingly, leading the majority of religious leaders and organizations to support US entry. Yet, scarred by their experiences in the First War, significant numbers of American church leaders remained ambivalent, and not just those from traditional peace churches. *New Republic* editors were aghast at the "notably lame, halting and sometimes shameful" levels of support for the war effort from mainstream clerics, while the *Catholic Worker* provided no succour to the *New Republic*, vowing even in the aftermath of Pearl Harbor to "continue our pacifist stand." After the Japanese attack, Charles Clayton Morrison grudgingly accepted what he called the "unnecessary necessity" of this war, but sought to rein in pulpit jingoism by reprinting selections from *Preachers Present Arms* in his *Christian Century* magazine.

6.5 Father Charles Coughlin delivered a message not unlike that of European fascists to Depression-era Americans. (Boston Public Library [Creative Commons].)

While many churchmen came to the conclusion that the United States had a responsibility to halt totalitarian aggression, they also moved quickly to help shape a new international order in hopes that this war would truly be the last. The results of a 1942 Federal Council of Churches' conference on a "Just and Durable Peace" were praised in the pages of *The Christian Century*, which also published an 80-page handbook summarizing the conference's conclusions. So motivated were the conference delegates to eliminate the scourge of war that they called for measures that would have been as unpalatable in pre-war America as they are in its modern incarnation, including "world-wide freedom of immigration" and "strong immediate limitations on national sovereignty." The report also singled out "the shortsighted selfishness of [US] policies after World War I" as a primary cause of the calamity then confronting the globe. American officials would later credit the report for creating "the climate of American opinion that was indispensable to the establishment of the United Nations."[48]

American church leaders did not simply set their sights on the post-bellum world, nor did they reserve their criticisms for the failures of previous US policy. Throughout the war, faith-based condemnations of the aerial bombardment of cities, the draft, and Japanese internment hounded the Roosevelt administration. Greatest indignation would be reserved for Harry Truman following the atomic bombings of Hiroshima and Nagasaki. Denunciation from American Catholic leaders was nearly universal ("the most powerful blow ever delivered against Christian civilization and the moral law" charged the *Catholic World*). Fundamentalists and conservative evangelicals appeared less troubled, but thirty-four prominent mainline Protestant leaders denounced the decision in a letter to Truman, while their official church publications condemned the bombings. The Federal Council of Churches commissioned a 1946 study of the ethics of nuclear warfare that concluded "we have sinned grievously against the laws of God and the people of Japan." As historian Paul Boyer observed, "the greatest concentration of critical comment on the Hiroshima and Nagasaki bombings came from the churches"; over the next decades, religion would provide the glue to the increasingly strident movement to eliminate nuclear weapons. Here again Catholics, with their particularly strong emphasis on the sanctity of life, were in the forefront.[49]

While Canada's mainline Protestant clergy were less likely than those in the United States to openly question the necessity of the First World War in the interwar years, some Canadians blamed the church leaders' often-overheated patriotism for helping to fracture national unity and fuel the slaughter in Europe. Stung by such criticisms, and in a tacit acknowledgment that they may have some merit, representatives of the Protestant consensus demonstrated greater hesitancies as tensions between European states once again mounted. Outright pacifism never gripped Canadian mainline churches to the degree witnessed in the United States; as historian Robert Wright found, "in spite of their profound disgust with the carnage of mechanized war, most Canadian clergymen refused to take the position that there was no evil greater than war itself." Still, Canadian church leaders of the 1930s expressed an increased commitment to various strains of internationalism, isolationism, neutrality, and mediation than they had in the lead-in to the Great War. All of the largest Protestant denominations expressed strong support for the League of Nations, disarmament, and the Kellogg-Briand Pact.[50]

As was the case in the United States, the Canadian churches' hesitation to immerse themselves into the troubles of Europe, along with more longstanding racial and religious chauvinisms, slowed their endorsement of a campaign to open the nation's borders to German Jews. The churches finally came around in February 1939, long after Nazi interdictions against the Jews were widely known, and too late to make a meaningful impact on Canada's shameful prewar policy of all-but-banning Jewish *émigrés*. By that time, noted Wright, even the secular press supported liberalizing immigration – "a sign, some churchmen admitted, that perhaps the Christian church in Canada had failed to take its rightful place on the cutting edge of Canadian opinion on the matter." The relatively lacklustre effort did little to move Ottawa bureaucrats. During the war, noted legal scholar Dominique Clément, Canada remained "among the least hospitable destinations for Jewish refugees," with only about 5,000 permitted entry by 1945. Taking their cues from a Vatican that enjoyed a rather alarmingly close relationship with Italian fascism, Canadian Roman Catholics within and outside Quebec were likewise slow to raise concerns over the character of the emerging European regimes. In fact, a degree of Quebec opposition to both the Second World War and the second instalment of conscription was predicated on an undisguised antisemitism among some of that province's inhabitants, and after 1940, widespread support for the collaborationist Vichy regime.[51]

After Canada's official declaration of war against Germany, Canada's mainline Protestant churches worked to build public consensus for participation; this time, however, their efforts displayed considerably less fervour than they had in 1914. Anglican clergy could hardly turn their backs on a conflict that provided an unparalleled threat to their ancestral homeland and their "Defender of the Faith" (i.e., King George VI), but their endorsements lacked the fever and certitude that marked their Great War rallying. In October 1939, sixty-eight United Church ministers signed a "A Witness Against War," a statement that "sought not to turn the United Church against the war effort but rather to temper the church's patriotism and remind it of its responsibility to those within its fold for whom war was unconscionable." Like their American counterparts, wartime ministers revived their prewar enthusiasm for internationalism in both church and state affairs as a means of encouraging a more cooperative postwar order, participating in the planning for the World Council of Churches (est. 1948), and endorsing the United Nations enthusiastically. Outside the Jehovah's Witnesses, pacifist sects faced less scorn for their stance from the government and the public, including mainline churches. In part, this owed to the fact that COs were now granted the option of undertaking alternative service, an option that Mennonites embraced with some enthusiasm.[52]

Canadian church leaders demonstrated a greater willingness to raise objections to aspects of the Allied prosecution of the war, although they generally exhibited greater restraint than their American colleagues. While US church leaders issued strong public condemnations of Allied area bombing, and their British counterparts joined the US Bombing Restriction Committee, the handful of Canadian clergy who expressed reservations did so more quietly, adding their names to a cable sent to congratulate Anglican leaders in Britain who had protested the policy in the House of Lords. The relative silence on the issue dumbfounded one of the few to break it, United Church minister Lavell Smith. "Our bombers are described as cutting swaths of utter destruction across a city," he wrote in the *United Church Observer* in early 1944. "Our political leaders promise the enemy worse things to follow. Yet I listen in vain for the voice of the Canadian Church to condemn such indiscriminate bombing." Historian Stephanie Bangarth's comparative study of Japanese-Canadian and -American internment revealed that, unlike those in America, Canadian churches "chose not to raise public alarm" over the issue because they maintained greater confidence in their government and its commitment to "British precepts of justice and fair play." When Mackenzie King's Liberals proved more illiberal than the Roosevelt administration and began to prepare the ground for deportation, the churches moved to the forefront of the effort to block the measure, and joined the broader campaign for the protection of human rights in Canada. The experience did much to reorient clergy away from the establishment-type thinking that had exerted such a powerful influence on their mission, and towards acting in "a prophetic role, often against the state, in order to inhibit state repression and to advocate for oppressed peoples."[53]

Denunciations of the atomic bombings emerged from some Protestant organizations, and most vehemently from the Canadian branch of the pacifist Fellowship of Reconciliation. The FOR branded the act an "atrocity" whose perpetrators "stand condemned before the bar of justice and mercy." In the Anglican magazine *Canadian Churchman*, Vancouver clergyman Cecil Swanson counseled, "if we never thought war evil before, surely we must do so now, and bend all our energies towards developing world peace." On the whole, however, even religious pacifists in Canada "were slow and almost reluctant" to confront the atomic issue, according to peace historian Thomas Socknat.

As in the United States, the most consistent and vigorous admonitions emerged from the Catholic Church, with Montreal's *Le Devoir* basing its own denunciations on the fact that the *Osservatore Romano*, the voice of the Holy See, condemned the action. However, unlike their American counterparts, Canadians were not calling out the actions of their own government, which had no say over the decision to drop the bombs. And although Canadian Catholics were as appalled by the bombings as their co-religionists in the United States, the majority of the former were French-speaking, once again curbing the influence of these views in English Canada.[54]

Following the war, the "just and durable peace" churches on both sides of the border yearned and toiled for would be pre-empted by the burgeoning East-West rivalry for geostrategic dominance. This "cold" war would in fact provoke and sustain hot conflicts around the globe, along with counter-insurgency, political assassinations, a complex web of military alliances, and an arms race of unprecedented scale and risk. Despite the blatant contradictions between the shape of the new world order and the high ideals clergy had articulated during the Second World War, the churches' opposition to their own governments' readiness to confront ("contain") this new enemy was tempered by a number of factors. For one, Communism was officially atheistic, and its proponents spoke openly (and rather too assuredly) of the coming worldwide revolution that would sweep away the old order – religion included. Other factors for religious support for containment provide clues as to why the fiercest anticommunism could generally be found south of the border: If communism is understood as the ultimate expression of state power over the individual, it was bound to be particularly upsetting to congregants who glorified the authority of the individual believer before God. Among those with decided and religiously sanctioned suspicions about the state, collectivism, group rights, and governmental schemes for economic redistribution, the Soviet Union represented the ultimate foil, and ultimate evil.

Such fears moved Canadian believers as well, particularly Catholics and conservative Protestants. But the striking incongruity between the ideals of communism and those of the American fundamentalists and conservative evangelicals in particular helps to explain why the Christian right – which had been marginalized and widely ridiculed since the 1925 Scopes Trial over its contempt for modernity and science – came to occupy an increasingly prominent position in American life following the Second World War. Victory in that war and the enhanced international standing that followed only strengthened the belief that the United States had a God-given mission to redeem the world, rendering these ideas "as active and powerful as they had been at any moment in the nation's history," according to historian Alan Brinkley. Stirred by its battle with international socialism, the American state took on a shape more pleasing to conservative Christians, moving away from the centralized planning and pragmatic coalition-building of the New Deal and the war years, and towards an agenda that championed individual responsibility, extreme moralism in the framing of international affairs, and a greater role for religion in the public square. God was added to the pledge of allegiance in 1954, and two years later, "In God We Trust" replaced the now unnervingly communalist *E Pluribus Unum* as the nation's official motto.[55]

These transformations in political culture, along with the spectre of an international foe viewed as a direct threat to their dearest principles (and that could bring on the Apocalypse by unleashing its nuclear arsenal), led Christian conservatives to set aside some of their concerns about their own government. Always fiercely patriotic and simultaneously suspicious of both the state and other sects, a new breed of more ecumenical evangelicals like Billy Graham became fixtures in the White House, and presidential candidates jockeyed for their endorsement. In a calculated effort to raise the profile of religion in the political arena, Graham held revivals on the steps of the Capitol building in Washington DC and prayer sessions at the Pentagon. Anticommunism would provide a dependable and overarching component of Evangelical leaders' calls for personal and national renewal. As Graham told a 1949 revival audience two days after the revelation that the Soviets had detonated their first atomic bomb, "communism is a religion that is inspired, directed, and motivated by the Devil himself who has declared war against Almighty God."[56]

While the Christian right should not be credited as the sole source of transformations in American policymaking during the Cold War and its aftermath, it cannot be denied that some of the nation's more recent foreign endeavours reflect the priorities of religious conservatives: a crusading mentality; the sense that America's Providential role as a redeemer nation and a chosen people can override the call to be peacemakers, justifying the use of overwhelming force even torture against their enemies; a preference for an unyielding America-first foreign policy over multilateralism and an associated disdain for restrictive international laws and governing bodies. The United Nations and

6.6 Previously a movement deeply suspicious of the state, conservative evangelicalism began migrating towards the mainstream in the crusading atmosphere of the Cold War. Here Billy Graham and wife Ruth arrive at the White House to conduct an ecumenical service on Richard Nixon's first Sunday in the White House, January 1969. (Courtesy of Nixonfoundation.org.)

its peacekeeping efforts, central to Canadian identity in the Cold War years, do not fare well on such a menu of priorities. As Andrew Preston remarked, "the very bases of evangelicalism and fundamentalism are ideological, theological, and cultural purity grounded in a refusal to compromise with the irreligious and the immoral." Ed Dobson, past board member of Jerry Falwell's Moral Majority, put it succinctly: "politics is essentially the art of compromise and negotiation, and fundamentalists don't place a high value on compromise and negotiation." Graham concurred, arguing in the dying days of the Korean War that the United Nations had failed "to stand up to Russia," because the international body lacked the moral certitude born of faith in God. "There can be no bargaining," he admonished, "no parlaying or compromising with evil." Contempt for the United Nations could also arise out of the belief that the world body is inimical to Israel, a nation whose preservation fundamentalists view as key to the unfolding of the end times. Historian Paul Edwards suggested that the much of the confusion and controversy over both the Korean and Vietnam wars had to do with their contradiction of the "authentic" American story, wherein the nation fights to fulfil God's divine plan. "Such a belief," Edwards observed, "makes limited peace [or defeat] appear a violation of God's will, thus likely to invoke divine displeasure."[57]

But to suggest that Christian conservatism accounts for the totality of US Cold War religious thinking is to read present American public discourses into the past. Before conservative evangelicals and fundamentalists moved to the political mainstream – a process that accelerated in the last decades of the century – postwar religious thinking could moderate the nation's belligerent, crusading, and unilateralist impulses as well as amplify them. Liberal Protestants, Catholics, and Jews spoke out against both containment and NATO, calling them simplistic military panaceas to what were in fact multifaceted and delicate international dilemmas born of poverty, inequity, and colonialism. Although both conservatives and liberal clergy supported the Korean War (the former because it sought to frustrate communism's global march, the latter because it was endorsed by the United Nations and seemed to breathe new life into the idea of global governance) this support was not unconditional, and Christian progressives castigated the US government for its unilateralist attitude to the conflict. "Make this truly a U.N. venture," *Christian Century* editors implored in the war's early stages. "It has hardly been so far. The impression so far has been that decisions have been made in Washington and communicated to Lake Success." As the war dragged on, the same magazine slammed the United States and its allies for its scorched earth policy, a strategy that was annihilating "the whole apparatus of a society." By the mid-1950s, the National Council of Churches (formerly the FCC) voiced deep unease over the hawkish foreign policy of the Eisenhower administration – a policy shepherded, ironically, by former chairman of the organization's Committee on a Just and Durable Peace, and now secretary of state, John Foster Dulles. Harshest condemnations for US Cold War policy emerged in response to Vietnam, and from nearly all points on the religious spectrum. A powerful (and now mostly forgotten) evangelical *left*, forged in the struggles over war in Indochina, civil rights, and second-wave feminism, emphasized the correlation between war and global inequality and campaigned vigorously to end both.[58] In all, the depiction of a stable, uncomplicated, anti-communist consensus does not square with the complex responses of a range of Americans; what is more, despite the anti-religious agenda of their international foe, church leaders were often in the forefront of gainsaying Cold War dogma, national self-righteousness, and bellicosity in foreign affairs.

In postwar Canada, the ebbing of British power and the empire's hold over the Canadian imagination came together with fears over nuclear weapons and a longstanding dis-ease regarding the United States; in response, Protestant clerics articulated increasingly pointed critiques of the state, nationalism, warfare, the arms race, and global inequality. These attitudes provided added momentum to a more general critique of injustice and inequality that had been developing since the beginning of the century under the rubrics of Progressivism and the Social Gospel, with clerics demonstrating a growing willingness to interpose themselves – "American-style" – into the realm of politics. The Church of England, formerly a haven for militant imperialists, spawned the Anglican Pacifist Fellowship in 1937 as war threatened Europe, and the magazine *Anglican Peacemaker* in 1947 as tensions between the superpowers mounted. The Canadian arm of the movement denounced the formation of NATO, arguing that Canadians were being "conditioned" for future wars against communism. The United Church became a haven for "peace-lovers," including Canada's most noted – and notorious – pacifist, the Reverend James Endicott, whose invectives against Cold War militarism earned him legions of devotees and enemies. Throughout the long standoff with the Soviets, the United Church frequently took the lead in calls for peace, international mediation, and greater attention to the plight of the global south.[59]

Catholic leaders, too, encouraged a greater commitment to social activism and peacemaking, particularly after the liberal tone of the Second Vatican Council of the mid-1960s. International lay organizations like Catholic Action ("the most important social action movement of the Catholic Church in Canada," according to Robert Choquette) took these appeals seriously, often taking progressive stands and using assertive tactics that exasperated the church hierarchy. By the end of the 1960s, a wide chasm had developed between church and state over such issues as the federal government's complicity in the Vietnam War and its economic relations with the apartheid regime in South Africa. In short, most of the trappings of the old establishment culture had withered. "Whereas it was relatively easy a century ago to find churchmen and churches who clearly sided with the economic establishment and exploiters," observed Choquette, "by the beginning of the twenty-first century it has become more and more difficult to do so."[60] In their independence and challenges to secular – and sometimes church – authority, Canadian congregations were coming into greater alignment with ideas and approaches that had characterized American religious life for generations.

However, postwar liberal congregations expressing these newfound or more longstanding commitments to peace, arbitration, and multilateralism confronted a mounting demographic challenge. Between 1960 and 2000, the percentage of Canadians belonging to the United Church fell from 20 to 9.6, while the Anglicans experienced a drop from 13 to 6.9, and the Presbyterians from 4 to 1.4. Official figures for Catholicism remained around 40 per cent, but from the 1960s onward, active participation in that church dropped significantly among Quebecers, and almost as sharply in English Canada. (Beginning in the 1980s, liberal Catholics faced additional challenges from a papacy committed to undercutting the progressive activism of priests and the laity inspired by Vatican II.) In the United States, membership in progressive Protestant churches likewise fell markedly, while the fundamentalist Southern Baptist Convention grew to eclipse all other Protestant denominations by the end of the twentieth century.[61]

Several developments common to both countries contributed to the demographic contraction of more liberal variants of Christianity. For one, in the toxic anti-communist atmosphere that accompanied the Cold War, Christian progressives who opposed war and the arms race found themselves red-baited. Based on suspicions that his peace activism was conducted at the behest of Moscow, James Endicott was booted from the CCF party in 1948, branded an opponent of God by *Maclean's* editor Blair Fraser and "public enemy number one" by numerous Canadian dailies, and pressured to leave the United Church. The shunning was more widespread in the United States. For instance, Joseph Matthews, a Methodist missionary appointed as Joseph McCarthy's research director, contributed a 1953 article to the influential monthly *The American Mercury* entitled "Reds and Our Churches." Here, Matthews disclosed that, as evidenced by their support for peace and disarmament, "the largest single group supporting the Communist apparatus in the United States today is composed of Protestant clergymen," who faithfully restock the Communist Party with "agents, stooges, dupes, front men, and fellow travellers" (and who, perhaps most shockingly, "outnumber professors two to one" in fulfilling these functions for the Kremlin).[62]

Mainline churches also faced other, more prosaic challenges. Religious experimentation, atheism, the growth of the welfare state, and immigration eroded both the dominance and the social role of the traditional churches. Postwar refugees expanded Jewish and Eastern

Orthodox congregations in both countries. Beginning in the 1960s, both societies liberalized their immigration policies, leading to increasing percentages of newcomers from Muslim, Hindu, Buddhist, Sikh, and Confucian traditions. By the end of the century, there were more Muslims in the United States than either Presbyterians or Episcopalians, and Los Angeles boasted the largest variety of Buddhist sects in the world. In Canada, the Muslim population grew by 129 per cent between 1991 and 2001, while the numbers of Hindus, Sikhs, and Buddhists each increased by nearly 90 per cent. While these recent immigrants held a range of views on issues of war, peace, and foreign obligations, their influence on the ways past wars were remembered faced some considerable constraints. On the one hand, as more recent arrivals, it was difficult to gain the public ear on debates over these nations' more distant past; on the other, the desire to adapt themselves to their new homelands may have served to dissipate the desire to confront orthodox versions of the national story.[63]

The decline in old-line congregations also has roots in the social upheavals wrought by immigration, civil rights, feminism, the sexual revolution, abortion rights, and Vietnam. These phenomena encouraged an ecclesiastical forked road: both a weakening of religiosity and a migration to more conservative forms of traditional faiths (and away from congregations that sought to accommodate themselves to these cultural transformations). These social clashes were fiercest in the United States, where the accompanying retreat to religious conservatism was also more profound. With the growth and increasing politicization of the American religious right from the Reagan years onward, any discussion of the "religious" impact on US politics became shorthand for the influence of the Christian *right*. But Canadian fundamentalism and conservative evangelicalism, at first a largely Baptist phenomenon that had little influence over mainline churches, has also experienced rapid growth in recent years at the expense of old-line Protestantism. Although politically engaged, in its early incarnation the Canadian version of the movement tended to press the government on domestic issues like abortion, euthanasia, homosexuality, and educational curricula. As Marci McDonald's recent study on the rise of Christian nationalism in Canada points out, however, some of the nation's conservative evangelicals – like their American counterparts – are increasingly committed to the aggressive protection and extension of Judeo-Christian civilization and inimical to extending olive branches to the perceived enemies of their world view.[64] In both postwar Canada and the United

States, then, the resistance to war espoused by the mainline Protestant churches increased as their total numbers decreased, primarily at the expense of non-belief and conservative evangelicalism; the former has no intrinsic position on state-sponsored violence, while the latter has demonstrated less enthusiasm for peacemaking, reconciliation, and multilateralism than more liberal variants of Christianity.

Plainly, the influence of religion on Canadian and American perspectives on war is far from homogenous. As these societies developed and perceptions of national mission and national security changed, the church proved a versatile wellspring of ideas for citizens seeking to make sense of these transformations. Doctrinal creed could be used to champion pacifism and belligerence, nationalism and internationalism, imperialism and independence, chauvinism and ecumenicalism, and all points in between – even within a single denomination, a single cleric, and a single believer. The plurality of faiths in both nations only added to the complexity and diversity of religious interpretations of conflict, setting Canada and the United States apart from the more homogenous religious traditions of many European states. Historically, the plurality has been strongest in the United States, a function of that country's more varied population and the continual multiplication of sects inspired by such factors as individualism, perfectionism, and anti-authoritarianism. These factors also undergird the sometimes wild oscillations between outright pacifism and intensive bellicosity that have characterized wide swathes of American religious thought and practice. And church leaders have not kept their opinions to themselves, alternately exhorting their nation to assume a more aggressive or pacific posture than that deemed appropriate by their government. Such attitudes are not absent from the Canadian religious experience, but the symbioses between the church and state has always been stronger in that nation. Accordingly, the Canadian churches' position on warfare has proven less subject to volatile reorientations, and until the mid-twentieth century at least, more consonant with the injunctions of state and empire.

Chapter Seven

Race

Visitors to the US National World War II Museum in New Orleans bask in a profoundly reverent psalm to the country's contribution to the toppling of fascism. The exhibits are designed, notes the official website, to convey "the epic and global scale of *the war that changed the world*" (emphasis in original). Viewers could be forgiven for leaving with the impression that those epic changes were effected primarily by the Americans themselves, who, although they countenanced a handful of foreign allies, seemed to tally all of the key goals unassisted. *Beyond All Boundaries*, the 4-D movie narrated by Tom Hanks, delivers the war's origins, battles, and outcomes in motifs that the most flamboyant Broadway producer might well find wantonly bathetic. Patrons young and old swoon over the gleaming machines of industrialized killing in the "U.S. Freedom Pavilion" sponsored by Boeing, a firm that, despite its standing as the world's second largest weapons manufacturer, did not see fit to recuse itself from such a naked conflict of interest.[1]

The "greatest generation" refrain fades, however, when the exhibits turn to issues of race. Over thirty panels in the permanent collection reference the racism that pervaded every facet of American society, from the segregated military to the discrimination in wartime industries, from the internment of racial minorities to the profound chauvinism with which white Americans regarded their darker-skinned foreign foes. Photos of black soldiers returning home to facilities with segregated entrances, and wartime posters depicting the Japanese as repugnant vermin abound. Even the panel describing the 2.5-ton CCKW Hard Top transport truck displayed in the Freedom Pavilion points out that many of the drivers "were African American, reflecting a segregated military in which blacks were often relegated to

7.1 Wartime dehumanization of the Japanese led mass-circulation magazines like *Life* to depict American atrocities with stunning nonchalance. This "picture of the week" from the magazine's 22 May 1944 edition came with the caption "Arizona war worker writes her Navy boyfriend a thank-you-note for the Jap skull he sent her." The National World War II Museum in New Orleans features an enlarged reproduction of the image as part of its extensive treatment of the bitter racism that marked the War in the Pacific. (Copyright Ralph Crane, used with permission of Rita Crane.)

non-combat but essential roles." As presented here, an inanimate tool of war, one that formed the backbone of the supply lines established to sustain the Allied rollback of the Nazi empire, carries the permanent odour of the nation's racism and hypocrisy.

The Canadian War Museum reveals the considerable variation that exists between these neighbouring countries when it comes to matters of race. Visitors to the Ottawa institution are told that Canadians of all backgrounds clamoured to enlist in the nation's foreign conflicts, that Great War volunteers from First Nations were "accepted because of their warrior reputation," and that many aboriginal peoples, like decorated Ojibwa soldier Frances Pegahmagabow, excelled in their roles. Discussions of who recruiters turned away focus on restrictions related to age and physical capabilities (are *your* teeth, modern visitor and ersatz recruit, good enough "to chew the sometimes rock-hard military food"?). A single panel alludes to the fact that Japanese Canadians hoping to join the battle against fascism faced unspecified "official barriers," while another board mentions that following the Second World War "aboriginal veterans had difficulty getting some benefits." The museum allows that the internment of "enemy aliens" in the world wars was the product of "deep prejudice," but as rendered here, that prejudice exerted only a trifling influence over the make-up of the Canadian military and its conduct abroad. What follows are some second thoughts on the comprehensiveness of that portrait.

While the previous chapter pointed out that the Christian church constituted one of the most influential public institutions in both the United States and Canada, it no longer maintains the stature it once held. In the face of the growing diversity of belief and the ascent of non-belief, overt religious influence on public policy, at least in Canada, became less discernible, while the more durable impact of religion in the American public square faced increased scrutiny and opposition.[2] But when we parse other components of identity, we again find that historically (and despite the widespread currency of its melting pot myth), American society possessed a greater range of potential responses to war in the form of its greater ethno-cultural or "racial" variation.

The latter categorization is particularly problematic from a biological perspective, as its scientific basis has long been discredited. But it remains useful as a category of social analysis, since race has served as the most durable means of social ordering and exclusion in modern, Western societies.[3] Little wonder, then, that those excluded on this basis – those that have been "racialized" – have undertaken a careful reconsideration of the full spectrum of "truths" established and reproduced by a dominant culture that for generations took as its starting point the inferiority of non-white peoples. Racialized thought and behaviour, in other words, *ipso facto* yields a systematic interrogation of prevailing wisdom – not the least of which the wisdom of participating in armed conflicts that are justified by the obligation to export liberal ideals denied to some at home. Under these circumstances, racialized groups excluded from the full benefits of citizenship have seized the opportunity provided by war to call out their nation's double standard, demand redress, and raise doubts about the idealistic rationales furnished by supporters of the war. Taking into account the uneven commitment of their nations to concepts like freedom and equality on their own soil, could their governments be trusted to implement them abroad? Were other, more salient motivations in play in the decision to go to war? Could the same racial ordering and mechanisms for race-based dominance operating at home be introduced or reinforced, unwittingly or by design, through victory overseas? A previous passage outlined some of the influences of marginalized groups on the way political representatives craft foreign policy; here, the focus is on the voices of minorities themselves, and the degrees to which those voices can make themselves heard in the wider national conversation.

From one angle, Canada has always exhibited a greater measure of ethnic diversity: in addition to its comparatively larger percentage of indigenous peoples, it includes a francophone community that, throughout the twentieth century, comprised nearly one-third of the Canadian populace. Canadians frequently referred to the two solitudes as distinct races well into that century, believing the English and French embodied profoundly divergent and immutable characteristics. On this, many English-speaking writers did not go out of their way to flatter Canada's francophones. In a tradition that built upon both the Durham Report of 1838 and the pioneering and reductionist analysis of nineteenth-century American Francis Parkman, English Canadians frequently cast the relationship between the two "founding peoples" as a struggle between the agrarian, backward, and submissive French and the dynamic, politically progressive, and entrepreneurial English. To the latter, it was clear which "race" would and should prevail, and that francophones who failed to assimilate or bow to Anglo dominance were simply impeding the nation's – and indeed civilization's – foreordained advance. In Durham's words, the French "must be given" the national character of the British, "of the great race which must, in the lapse of no long period of time, be predominant over the whole North American Continent." The Durham-Parkman thesis enjoyed a long and distinguished run. "For many decades," wrote D.R. Owram, these views "were echoed in popular histories and even by those who claimed to be revising him."[4]

The second-class treatment was not confined to the analysis of historians. In fact, Canadian writers of the era were accurate in referring to the French and English as separate races, for in practice, the imagined biological distinctions did indeed serve as a pretext for differential and unequal treatment. In other words, race operated here as it always does, as pseudo-science with very real social outcomes. In addition to the alienation born of English conquest, francophones found themselves on the losing end of the liberal economic order even within their own province, as anglophones clustered in Quebec's largest cities came to dominate industry, banking, and much of the province's wealth. Discrimination in hiring, along with the fact that much of the province's business was conducted in English, helped to consign francophones to the least-skilled sectors of the labour market; the resulting economic inequalities persisted into the 1980s. Moreover, following Confederation, many French Canadians came to the opinion that their ability to influence public policy did not correspond to their status as one of Canada's founding peoples. Rather, Quebecers discovered that on key issues of national debate they were simply one province among many, and thus a province perpetually subordinate to the will (or "tyranny") of the English majority. Regardless of the party in power, the federal cabinet rarely included more than a single token minister from Quebec, and francophones remained underrepresented in the civil service until the latter half of the twentieth century. Francophones in and beyond Quebec feared – and many English Canadians hoped and actively worked for – the day when the French would be fully assimilated into a Britannic, and thus fully integrated, Canada. Between the late 1880s and the First World War in particular, wrote Meisel, Rocher, and Silver, French Canadians were subjected to a "bullying and anglicizing wave" that swept the nation and revealed profound fissures over the very idea of Canada.[5]

The campaign during those years to eliminate French-language rights outside Quebec boosted the dreams of the assimilationists and the sense of isolation of French Canadians; warfare would cement the sense of betrayal within the francophone imagination. The salient point is that French Canadian resistance to the nation's wars was not merely an outcome of distinctive aspects of their ideology – i.e., Roman Catholicism's emphasis on the sanctity of life, or francophones' vision of a fully sovereign Canada, a vision stirred by their past and adverse encounter with imperialism. Rather, ongoing grievances and differential treatment were fundamental to the shaping of dissenting francophone opinions on war.

A people increasingly convinced of their subordinate status was naturally conflicted about offering their sons to a nation that had demonstrated a fluctuating commitment to the interests, or even the existence, of francophones. To be *conscripted* to do so via the will of the English majority was an affront of another order of magnitude, and simply confirmed many French Canadians' worst fears about their fate within Confederation. To make matters worse, the Canadian military that fought in wars from South Africa to Korea was a mostly unilingual organization plagued by anti-French bias. In fact, encouraging francophones to fight – and when that failed, requiring that they do so – was viewed as a component of the campaign to anglicise the French, to speed the elimination of the French language and the province's allegedly regressive, inward-looking world view.[6] The opposition to war and the outrage over conscription expressed by leading francophones finds explanation in this complex array of sensibilities, complaints, and slights.

Francophones themselves made these connections plain. As the British and Boers girded for war in the summer of 1899, the Laurier government passed a resolution in the House of Commons calling for the extension of voting rights to all British subjects in the region, a change that would be modelled on the example of Canada, where "men of different races, but races of equal rank" received equal treatment. Forwarded to the Senate for "sober second thought," three French-Canadian representatives suggested the addition of "a paragraph to sustain the rights of British subjects in Manitoba," where over the previous decade the French-speaking Métis population had been divested of lands, French eliminated as an official language, and the rights to Roman Catholic education (guaranteed by Parliament at the province's founding) had been abridged.[7]

During the First World War, Henri Bourassa likewise made the links between domestic inequities and foreign obligations clear, juxtaposing the call for more French Canadian soldiers with the government of Ontario's 1912 legislation – subsequently upheld in the courts – requiring the province's schools to teach in English only. Writing in 1915, Bourassa maintained that Ontario shared with Germany an insistence on "one emperor, one empire, one flag, one language," and was thus precisely the kind of regime Canadians were being sent abroad to dismantle. "French Canadians," he wrote in his own Montreal daily *Le Devoir*, "are enjoined to fight the Prussians of Europe. Shall we let the Prussians of Ontario impose their domination like masters ...?" Armand Lavergne, the Liberal MP for Montmagny, echoed the ironies of marching off to relieve oppression abroad while countenancing it at home. "Until they have been completely freed of this persecution," he stated of Franco-Ontarians, "I cannot consider for an instant the idea of deserting their cause for a somewhat interesting adventure in a foreign country." When the pro-conscription Union government was swept to power while winning just three seats in Quebec (in urban, Anglo-dominated ridings), French Canadians witnessed the nadir of their influence over public discourse and policymaking; the ensuing talk of secession from Canada that seized the province was hardly unpredictable. Mackenzie King's promise at the outset of the Second World War to refrain from conscription rendered the reversal of that pledge – again, driven by fervent English-Canadian appeals for a policy anathema in Quebec – doubly offensive. Being compelled to fight for a nation that consistently subsumed the will of francophones to that of the English majority became a defining issue of Quebec nationalism and separatism. Meeting in Quebec in the early 1960s to organize the modern sovereignty movement, delegates cited the fact that the federal government had "imposed" conscription on French Canadians and forced them "to serve our country in a unilingual English army" as proof that Confederation could not preserve the interests and cultural identity of francophones.[8]

In all, distinctive aspects of their ideology, along with systematic discrimination based on their ethnicity, meant that French Canadians were destined to serve as a persistent source of opposition to war. However, unlike many dissenters in the United States, linguistic differences placed at least some limits on the ability of francophones to influence the cultural atmosphere of English Canada (although Anglo-Canadians sometimes took pains to advertise francophone war opposition in order to invalidate the latter's true "Canadianness," as discussed below). And while their grievances were well-founded, francophones were not asked to sacrifice on behalf of a country that denied them the right to vote, restricted their movements, and conducted or condoned systematic physical violence against them. Such circumstances did indeed affect some Canadians and Americans, but these were residents set apart by the particularly obstinate divide of skin colour. Lacking the status of "visible minority" and the harsher proscriptions that went along with it, the basis of francophones' complaints were likewise less visible to many Anglo-Canadian observers.

Consider, for example, English Canadian historians' explanations of the sources of francophone opposition to the South African War. Arguably the least justifiable and certainly the least popular conflict in post-Confederation Canadian history (a judgment reinforced by the general disregard for the war in the overall record), Quebec's qualms about participation have nonetheless spawned a series of one-dimensional and belittling assessments of the francophone "character" and "mind" – and often little sympathy for francophone disenchantment with the war or the nation as a whole. Indeed, the dispute between the British and the Boers contained elements easily recognizable to English writers: in South Africa, so the narrative went, the British confronted a simple, pastoral people of alien speech who were seemingly unwilling or unable to surrender to the inevitability of industrial progress. The *Toronto Evening News* set the tone early in a wartime editorial denouncing francophone opposition, calling French Canadians the "Canadian Boers." The innumerable English-Canadian condemnations of the Boers' alleged backwardness thus carried supplementary and rather undisguised implications about the drag francophones placed on the national trajectory. J. Castell Hopkins attributed francophone opposition solely to ignorance: "The people of Quebec," he averred in 1901, "had not yet been educated up to the point of participation in British wars and Imperial defence." Others depicted a people plagued by a contemptible naiveté and narcissism. As Britain faced its hour of need in the Transvaal, wrote W.G. Hardy in 1960, "French Canada shrugged its shoulders and turned back to its farms and its church bells." More than one English-Canadian historian framed francophone war opponents, and their spokesperson Henri Bourassa, as irrational extremists for suggesting that Canada's interests were not served by shoring up distant imperial possessions. Castell Hopkins himself could not bring himself to name the "rash young Member of Parliament who resigned his seat as a protest," and lauded both federal parties for supposedly treating "the matter as of no importance." To George Wrong, Bourassa was "a man of fiery eloquence and extreme views," while war opponents were still cast as "extremists" in Granatstein et al.'s 1983 publication, *Twentieth Century Canada*.[9]

Arthur Lower seemed poised to bring empathy to his explication of Francophone hesitations, beginning his 1946 discussion of the troop debate with a sardonic (and rather Freudian) discussion of Canadian imperialists' "pent-up urges" for foreign imperial adventures, and the "jingoistic rejoicing" that followed the sating of said urges. Yet Lower, writing at the conclusion of a global war that once again had threatened the unity of his nation, saved his harshest words for francophones, contrasting English Canada's supposed internationalism and cosmopolitan world view with that of French Canadians. The latter, he maintained, "had little memory of anything but a parochial existence on the banks of the St. Lawrence which was its entire world, possessed almost no interests outside of its own parishes and was possessed by the complete absorption in itself that characterizes the French race." Thusly (and perplexingly) upbraiding war supporters and opponents alike, Lower moved directly to a meditation on the difficulties faced by Laurier in "bringing harmony between the two races" (a mission that may well have been advanced by banning the translation of Lower's own volume into French).[10]

Extremist, ignorant, naive, parochial, self-absorbed, anachronistic, anti-modern – the assumptions regarding French Canada set down by Durham and Parkman cast a long shadow indeed. Absent is any sense that Canadian liberalism may have let Quebec down at any level; that francophones might have reason to demur over participating in wars on behalf of a nation engaged in a "bullying" campaign of assimilation; or that wars to enshrine justice and equality abroad might strike some Quebecers as at least faintly hypocritical. To the extent that these English writers were able to convince their audience that francophones' antiwar position was founded primarily on irrational, adolescent sensibilities, they also helped to preserve the affirming image of a nation that fought as an uncomplicated champion of liberal values – along with the disaffirming and paradoxical image of *Quebec* as the betrayer of those values. Donald Creighton's monograph summarizing the first one hundred years of the Canadian experiment made this abundantly clear. "French Canadians," he explained, "were colonials and isolationists who saw no reason why Canada should try to play a major part in world affairs … Their dominating purpose was the defence of their own provincial culture, not the establishment of world peace and security."[11] Such reductionist conclusions about the source and nature of francophone sentiments not only purges English Canadian chauvinism from the historical record; it also fails to account for the fact that, when placed in a larger North American context, French Canadians' disinclination to become embroiled in the vagaries of European power politics was hardly unusual.

If the economic and political marginalizations faced by francophones were often underappreciated by English Canadians, the inability among whites as a whole to detect the more systematic exclusions faced by people of colour would require considerably more effort. In both Canada and the United States, that effort would entail an ability *not* to

7.2 No pretext for opposing conscription other than a contemptible indifference to the fate of humanity: Sir Wilfrid Laurier plays politics in this 1917 Unionist campaign poster. (Library and Archives Canada, ANC-C93223.)

see the "whites only" signs affixed to the doors of businesses until the mid-twentieth century, to *not* be aware of the neighbourhood covenants that prohibited a range of groups from certain districts of the community on account of their skin colour, to *not* be alarmed at the presence of various non-white citizens at polling stations before certain points of time (e.g., Native Americans prior to 1924, Asians in both countries before the late 1940s, Canadian First Nations before 1960, blacks in the American South prior to 1965). Given the especially grave contradictions between wars for freedom and their own rank in the social order, it should not surprise that people of colour would provide some of the more venomous and persuasive denunciations of each nation's martial contributions to the salvation of foreign peoples. Here the words of Edward Cooper, editor of the *Colored American*, come to mind. Upon hearing President McKinley's call for the "benevolent assimilation" of the Filipinos, Cooper wrote, "our white friends have a habit of expending their sympathy upon the black man who is farthest off."[12]

While racial minorities faced similar restrictions in both nations, the disparity in the presence of racial minorities as defined (and delimited) by the colour of their skin is significant. Throughout the twentieth century, blacks made up approximately 10–12 per cent of the US population. In fact, the number of American blacks alone eclipsed the total population of Canada in every twentieth-century census, growing from nearly 9 million in 1900 to nearly 30 million in 1990. By the beginning of the twenty-first century, blacks were surpassed as America's largest minority by Hispanics, a group that had grown rapidly since the Second World War, while the percentage of Americans identified themselves as non-white rose steadily from just over 12 per cent in 1900 to nearly 30 per cent by the end of the century.[13]

Canadians of colour, on the other hand, made up just 3.5 per cent of the population according to the 1901 census, a figure bolstered by the relatively high numbers of indigenous peoples residing in the recently acquired, and not yet "developed," Canadian north and west. The paucity of non-Europeans in Canada was not accidental. The nation was to be, as Sir John A. Macdonald told the House of Commons in 1869, "a White man's country," a designation that would be ensured through immigration regulations welcoming newcomers from the United States and western and northern Europe, countenancing limited numbers of south- and east-Europeans, and barring, taxing, or severely restricting "inassimilable" peoples. As a result, the percentage of people of colour reported in 1901 was not eclipsed until the 1971 census, after the liberalized immigration policies of the 1960s led to an influx of new-comers from non-traditional sources, and an increase in the total percentage of those of non-European origin to 4.4. By 2001, as a result of the continuation of these trends and a census questionnaire that allowed individuals to cite more than one ethnicity, the proportion of Canadians who declared at least a portion of non-European parentage had risen to roughly 17 per cent.[14]

While people of colour on both sides of the border faced marginalizations that generated adversarial attitudes towards mainstream society, the wide national disparity in overall percentages matters. In the United States, citizens of colour provided a vital pillar of the Democratic Party coalition from the New Deal onward, and the importance of their labour to industry and agriculture could exert a significant impact on federal policy. The tens of millions of racial minorities provided a critical mass that sustained a wide variety of newspapers and journals, radio stations, voluntary organizations, political lobbies, independent religious denominations, advocacy groups, and in the case of blacks, their own colleges and universities. The leading civil rights organization in the United States, the National Association for the Advancement of Colored People (NAACP), counted 90,000 (predominantly black) members and 300 local branches in 1919, a membership figure nearly equivalent to the total number of Canada's indigenous peoples, that nation's largest ethnic minority group (though a "group" comprised of a range of disparate cultural and linguistic communities). By the end of the Second World War, the NAACP boasted nearly half a million members. Historian Robin Winks outlined some of the disparities in publishing: in 1915, J.R.B. Whitney of Toronto established the weekly *Canadian Observer*, hoping to establish it as the official voice of black Canadians. By 1921, the *Observer* was gone, leaving no serials printed for African Canadians at a time when there were 492 such publications produced by and for African Americans. A few papers for Canadian blacks appeared in the interwar years, but as of 1939, the London, Ontario-based *Dawn of Tomorrow* was the last one standing, and by then the erstwhile weekly was appearing only a few times a year. The ethnic publications that flourished in Canada over the course of the twentieth century tended to be those that served linguistic minorities in their native tongue – rendering their views less accessible to most Canadians of the day, and not incidentally, to future historians conducting their work in English.[15] Racialized Americans possessed, in other words, a greater capacity to make their voices heard.

7.3 Boards cover broken windows at Chinese businesses following the 1907 anti-Asian riots in Vancouver. (Library and Archives Canada, C023555.)

But there is more to the relative visibility of aggrieved groups than mere numbers: the conspicuousness of the adversity they face certainly contributes to the intensity of their resistance, and it can be argued that one finds more abundant, and prominent, expressions of acute racism in the American narrative than the Canadian. This is partly a function of scale: on the one hand, more frequent encounters with racialized individuals provide more opportunities for expressions of racism; on the other, higher percentages of racialized minorities provide a greater level of perceived threat to those that seek to maintain hierarchies that work in their favour. It should not be surprising, then, that some of the more flagrant episodes of racial animus in modern Canadian history were set in British Columbia, a province with significant percentage of residents of Asian descent, and in Nova Scotia, home to large numbers of African Canadians (some of whom took to referring to their province as "the Mississippi of the North"). In the main, as Robin Winks wrote in an observation that could be applied to racialized Canadians as a whole, Canada's black community was not "sufficiently numerous, organized, or politically oriented to make up a voting bloc, gain power, or to attract hatred because of their political potential."[16]

Canadian blacks and other minorities certainly attracted hatred, discrimination, and violence, but as Winks' quote implied, anxieties over their ability to gain influence in the public sphere never approached levels witnessed in the United States. Persistent fears over the potential power of American blacks, in particular, provoked a consistent and brutal backlash. Lynching, an act of white terrorism aimed largely at policing racial boundaries in the American South, claimed approximately 5,000 (mostly black male) victims in the century following the Civil War, and just one in Canada over that same span. While such acts of terror could have a chilling effect on levels of resistance among Southern blacks, the millions of blacks and their allies beyond the region could not be cowed into silence by the threats of white Southerners. Outrage over the persistence of lynching and over the federal government's unresponsiveness to it allied and unified the African American community and their supporters, inspiring a coordinated and prominent anti-lynching campaign among progressive reformers and anti-racist groups. (The lone Canadian lynching victim, meanwhile, an aboriginal youth named Louie Sam, was murdered by an American mob that crossed the Washington-British Columbia border to avenge a murder that Sam, as was later revealed, did not commit.[17])

Significant episodes of racial violence did erupt in Canadian communities – for instance, in 1784 in Shelbourne and Birchtown, Nova Scotia over labour competition between blacks and whites; in Vancouver in 1887 and again in 1907 over the rising numbers of Asians; in Depression-era Toronto by nativist groups against Jews; in Halifax in 1919 when returning Canadian troops and local whites destroyed Chinese restaurants; and in that same city in 1991 after several black men were denied access to a nightclub. The American record of race riots is considerably more extensive – such incidents have been chronicled, by way of comparison, in a two-volume, 930-page, 300-entry *Encyclopedia of American Race Riots*. The World Wars proved particularly conducive to creating the conditions for racial violence, as millions of blacks relocated to urban centres to work in war industries; others served overseas and returned home expecting compensation for their sacrifice in the form of the same freedoms they had helped deliver to Europeans. Whites wedded to the status quo in the workplace, neighbourhood, and the broader social hierarchy were instrumental in fomenting more than twenty-five riots in the bloody "Red Summer" of 1919 alone; a similar wave of major racial violence swept the nation in 1943. If numerical strength, subjugation, and resistance exist in a triangular relationship, the greater visibility of activism and militancy among American minorities finds additional explanation in these conditions. In 1951, William L. Patterson of the leftist Civil Rights Congress went so far as to claim that the "institutionalized oppression and persistent slaughter of Negro people in the United States on the basis of 'race'" met the UN definition of genocide.[18] The charge, leveled in the midst of rigorous McCarthyite proscriptions against "anti-American" discourse and the hyper-patriotism of a nation at war, provides a measure of both the intensity of American racial repression and the disinclination of those repressed to temper their resistance.

Canada's proximity to, and preoccupation with, the United States has also worked to amplify perceptions of national differences regarding race. America, the thinking goes, is the nation confounded by a "race problem"; an "ideology of racelessness" thus emerges as one means of establishing Canada's status as un- (or anti-)American. In the nineteenth century, as the American battle over slavery propelled the nation towards civil war, a powerful myth emerged that the institution had never existed in Canada (approximately 3,000 people of African descent toiled as slaves in what would become Canada before 1834). Through much of the twentieth century, historical studies of the African Canadian experience portrayed Canada as a blameless "haven of refuge" offering social and legal equality to blacks fleeing American repression – assumptions that dissolved under the weight of later scholarly analysis, but still retain power in contemporary discourse.[19] As discussed in the previous chapter, Canada's interactions with its First Nations peoples have also been held up as evidence of a more tolerant society, although scholars continue to debate the merits of those claims. Regardless, these dynamics have given struggles over racial matters a lower profile in the recounting of the Canadian story.

The visibility of America's "race problem" has also been enhanced by the attention paid to all things American by supporters and detractors alike the world over. The international influence of US culture, politics, and finance rendered the American story an international concern, and the ability of American liberalism to remedy the plight of blacks – what Swedish economist Gunnar Myrdal famously called "an American dilemma" in his 1944 book of the same title – provided something of an acid test for US claims of global leadership, particularly among people of colour within and beyond US borders. Accordingly, by the mid-twentieth century, the US State Department's file included an international cultural exchange program whose mandate included reversing negative perceptions of American racial politics among foreign governments and peoples. Racial activists, understanding the power they wielded under such worldwide scrutiny, simply redoubled efforts to publicize their predicament in hopes of compelling concrete measures, rather than mere public-relations campaigns, from Washington. Prominent black newspapers and journals circulated widely within and beyond the nation's borders, broadcasting the gains and limits of the American freedom struggle to a worldwide audience, and leading dailies like the *Pittsburgh Courier* actively cultivated a transnational audience by running columns by correspondents from Africa and Asia.[20] The dissent born of state-sanctioned inequalities, a relationship as old as the American republic itself, would grow more conspicuous with the rise of American hegemony.

For a number of reasons, African Americans have often taken the lead on public debates over race, war, and peace. As a significant demographic force with a long history of anti-slavery and anti-racist agitation, the community developed strong, interconnected, and highly politicized institutions and organizations. Moreover, as a people living in a society that countenanced voting restrictions, discrimination in housing, and "Jim Crow" segregation, and that ignored consistent acts of terror against the black community, African Americans could readily sympathize with colonized peoples beyond their borders who faced similar affronts (some of whom were their ethnic kin). In fact, since the beginning of the twentieth century, African American spokespersons have articulated a vision of their community as a "nation-within-a-nation," an internally colonized people who linked their experiences with colonized and racialized peoples abroad. In consequence, US conflicts that appeared to support an imperial agenda – on the part of America or its allies – faced highly publicized and sometimes-withering critiques from American blacks. While many African Americans joined the Anti-Imperialist League during the War of 1898, a group of Illinois blacks who wished to make the links between foreign and domestic tyranny considerably more explicit formed the National Negro Anti-Expansion, Anti-Imperialist, Anti-Trust, Anti-Lynching League (or NNAEAIATALL for "short"). In 1907, leading black intellectual W.E.B. Du Bois, a firm supporter of the Anti-Imperialist League, wrote to its president Moorfield Storey asking for a copy of a photograph published

7.4 The aftermath of the Bud Dajo massacre. W.E.B. Du Bois hoped the image would find a wide audience. ("Trench at Bud Dajo," 1907. Library of Congress, LC-DIG-ds-04272.)

in one of the organization's pamphlets. Du Bois hoped that the image, *After the Battle of Bud Dajo* – which depicted US Marines posing triumphantly over a pile of mangled corpses following the butchery of roughly 1,000 Filipino Muslim men, women, and children – could be enlarged, framed, and distributed throughout the United States in order to impress upon Americans "what wars and especially what Wars of Conquest really mean."[21]

Throughout the First World War, US officials fretted about the wartime loyalty of the Black community, whose leaders routinely disparaged the imperial character of the European regimes and the war itself. In these years, African Americans were also carefully monitoring their nation's actions towards the Philippines, along with as a series of ongoing military occupations in Latin America. The most distressing was in Haiti, whose overwhelmingly black population made it "the only independent Negro government in the New World," as Du Bois noted in a letter to Wilson weeks after the 1915 US invasion. As a result, many

African Americans were no more trusting of their country's foreign agenda than they were of European imperialism. Desperately needing their labour (especially in agriculture) and compliance with the draft, and witnessing rising violence between blacks and white civilians and soldiers, inveterate racist Woodrow Wilson was moved to appoint conservative black leader Emmett Scott as special assistant to the secretary of war. Working in coordination with the Committee on Public Information, Scott strove to convince African Americans that this was not "a white man's war" or a battle for empire, but "a war of all the people under the Stars and Stripes for the preservation of human liberty throughout the world."[22]

American officials were mostly underwhelmed by the results. In June 1918, the Wilson administration instructed Scott to moderate a secret and what would prove to be contentious meeting between administration officials and black newspaper editors and leaders, who were urged to tone down their persistent criticisms of the war effort. While many complied, federal agents continued to expend considerable resources monitoring and suppressing outspoken journals like *The Crisis*, the official organ of the NAACP edited by Du Bois, and *The Messenger*, a black socialist newspaper edited by A. Philip Randolph and Chandler Owen that called on African Americans to resist the draft. Undercover operatives infiltrated meetings of advocacy groups like the NAACP, along with black unions and army units, and jailed black leaders like Randolph and Owen who failed to demonstrate satisfactory support for the conflict.[23] Reigning in black volatility was proving an onerous task.

If the First World War was, to many black critics, the predictable upshot of imperial rivalries run amok, the Second seemed a prime opportunity to finally eradicate the institution of colonialism itself. Fascist expansion and pogroms justified by racial supremacy demonstrated the logical and dreadful outcome of race-based theories of rule. Allied talk of the importance of self-government to international stability and prosperity – ideas fundamental to the Atlantic Charter and FDR's Four Freedoms – inspired enthusiastic endorsements of the war effort in the black press and from a broad range of Americans of colour. NAACP leader Walter White, sensing momentum on the colonial issue and drawing on the growing power of black voters in northern electoral districts, corresponded with Roosevelt frequently and was able to secure several meetings with the president in order to press the matter.[24]

It soon became clear that the administration did not share the black community's level of enthusiasm for the dismantling of empires; for

Roosevelt, the desire to maintain the goodwill of European allies necessarily restrained America's anti-imperial efforts. Voices like White's,
however, could not simply be dismissed, and throughout the war,
American officials were forced to play the demanding, zero-sum game
of appeasing their most important international allies and their non-
white constituents over the postwar fate of colonized peoples. Concerns about the wartime loyalty of British-held India, for instance, led
to widespread appeals that Indians be granted independence following the war in exchange for their contributions to the conflict. Walter
White again led the way, proposing jointly to the president and British
Ambassador Lord Halifax that the United States send a high-level commission to the subcontinent to devise a formula for India's role in the
war and its postwar fate. Including African Americans in the proposed
commission would, White argued, demonstrate "to the colored peoples
of the Far East and of the world, that discrimination based on race is not
the sole manifestation of the attitude of the United Nations."[25]

As historian Daniel Aldridge observed, after the president and the
ambassador "feigned great interest in White's suggestions and gradually let the matter drop," and the British instead incarcerated Gandhi
and other Indian nationalist leaders, White became more outspoken
and uncooperative. In August 1942, he cancelled his promised Office of
War Information radio broadcast intended for Japan that would have
confirmed African American support for the Allied war effort. In a letter to White, Roosevelt expressed sympathy with White's frustrations
and urged the NAACP "to be realistic" about the timeline for decolonization, but much of the "bonhomie and good will" that had marked
their earlier relationship had been eroded. NAACP officials would later
vent that the 1944 Dumbarton Oaks Agreement laying the groundwork
for the United Nations demonstrated a "total lack of consideration" of
the colonial question and threatened to withhold support for the proposal as a result. Fearful of repeating Woodrow Wilson's failure to rally
a cross-section of Americans behind the idea of international governance, the US Secretary of State invited the NAACP to serve as a consultant to the US delegation at the spring, 1945 United Nations Conference
on International Organization held in San Francisco.[26]

Regrettably, the death of Roosevelt, who for all of his hesitations
remained one of the more committed anti-imperialists in his administration, along with the growing anxieties over Soviet global influence
and the obstinacy of European colonial powers, helped to frustrate the
high hopes many people of colour held for a thoroughly anti-colonial

UN Charter. Although fears of international communism and of being tarred as a communist sympathizer subdued some critics of imperialism as the Cold War became entrenched, the issue was not entirely abandoned. Prominent black Americans spoke out against the 1949 establishment of NATO on the grounds that the organization would shore up the military capacity of the European colonial powers and undercut the authority of the United Nations, an organization that many blacks hoped could still be marshalled to advance the twin agendas of civil rights and decolonization. When US forces intervened in Korea, mainstream African American publications and organizations initially lent their support. Black singer, actor, and left-activist Paul Robeson, on the other hand, charged that the policy of containment had simply become a justification for American imperialism, and warned that other regions of the global South were likely to face similar US incursions.[27] Robeson proved prescient. As discussed below, the projection of US power in the name of thwarting international communism saw American forces fighting primarily in postcolonial settings, leading African American spokespersons to draw unflattering parallels between the subjugation of people of colour under European colonialism, and their own nation's grand strategy in the Cold War.

The imperial trappings of US wars were not the only source of African American war resistance. American blacks had long bristled at the irony of being asked to lay down their own lives in order to spread liberty, equality, and democracy – ideals at the heart of every public appeal to arms since independence. The truth all too visible to African Americans was that a nation claiming a divine calling to extend liberal ideals did so with an army that for decades rejected black conscripts. Only when the attrition of the Civil War rendered African American fighters indispensable to the Union cause did the army relent, although African Americans served in segregated units with segregated blood supplies, and generally under white commanders, long after Hispanics and Native Americans had been accepted into regular combat units. Blacks were also consigned in disproportionate numbers to non-combat duties, limiting their ability to gain military honours and to thereby confirm their standing as the physical and intellectual equals of whites. (Du Bois acknowledged the potential for racial advancement inherent to military service even as he denounced it, writing, "how extraordinary and what a tribute to religious hypocrisy, is the fact that in the minds of most people, even those of liberals, only murder makes men.") And despite President Truman's 1948 executive order desegregating the military, blacks continued to fight

7.5 Delivering the fruits of liberty to the Cuban people in segregated units: the US Army's "Buffalo Soldiers" in 1898. (Library of Congress Prints and Photographs Division.)

in separate units for the first year of the Korean War, as military officials, backed by southern Democrats who controlled important congressional committees, simply ignored the new law. Outrage over this intransigence from the black press, the NAACP (which sent lawyer Thurgood Marshall to Korea to investigate), and liberal senators led senior officers to begin integrating units in the summer of 1951, but all-black regiments were not completely phased out until late in 1954.[28]

These restrictions were merely the military variation of the denial of basic rights experienced in society at large, yielding a range of responses to war from black leaders. As the above comments by Du Bois indicate, some argued that demonstrations of loyalty and conspicuous contributions to victory would advance the cause of racial equality. In a 1917 editorial in *The Crisis*, Du Bois urged fellow blacks to "forget our special grievances and close our ranks shoulder to shoulder with our white citizens" during the First World War. Such a strategy went hand-in-hand with campaigns to give blacks the opportunity to serve in the military on equal terms with whites, and thereby prove patriotism, aptitude, and manhood. A desegregated and meritocratic army, so the thinking went, would provide a microcosm for similar transformations in civilian life. While desegregation would have to wait, protests at black colleges and pressure from a range of organizations including the NAACP led the army to allow blacks to serve in combat units and to train as officers. By the time of the armistice, hundreds of blacks had served as officers, while Privates Henry Johnson and Needham Roberts, members of an African American regiment reassigned to the French, became the first Americans to receive France's highest decoration for valour, the *Croix de Guerre*. At least within the military, slow progress was being made. Another Du Bois editorial at war's end made the *quid pro quo* of his earlier call for "closing ranks" explicit. "We return. We return from fighting. We return fighting. Make way for Democracy! We saved it in France, and by the Great Jehovah, we will save it in the United States of America, or know the reason why."[29]

Similar efforts marked American entry into the Second World War. After Congress's declaration of war, the *Pittsburgh Courier*, the nation's most popular black newspaper with a circulation of 350,000 (a figure several thousand higher than the *Toronto Star*, Canada's best-selling newspaper), initiated a nationwide "Double-V" campaign. The *Courier* held that black contributions to victory over racist regimes abroad should be used as leverage to achieve victory over racism and segregation at home. The *Chicago Defender*, the *Amsterdam Star-News*, and other leading black newspapers signed on. In their widespread denunciation of the campaign as untimely and provocative, white newspapers helped to usher "Double-V" into the wider public consciousness; white citizens need not have expressed sympathy with the campaign to recognize that some Americans found an element of hypocrisy in their nation's war for freedom. For NAACP leaders, the conflict provided the opportunity "to persuade, embarrass, compel and shame our government and

7.6 African American intellectual and activist W.E.B. Du Bois, pictured here in 1918, expressed mixed feelings about black Americans' military obligations. (Photograph by Cornelius M. Battey, Library of Congress Prints and Photographs Division, LC-USZ62-16767.)

our nation" into concrete action on racial injustice. Recognizing the need to maintain African American support and subjected to persistent pressure from black leaders, newspapers, and organizations, the Marines and the Coast Guard admitted blacks for the first time, and blacks served as tank operators and pilots – also firsts. The exploits of the so-called Tuskegee Airman, an all-black fighter squadron trained at the black university in Tuskegee, Alabama, consistently made the front pages of black newspapers and won them grudging support in the mainstream media. Greater opportunities within the military did not necessarily translate into broader societal acceptance, however. When Tuskegee squadron member Charles Dryden passed through New York's Penn Station while on leave, an elderly white woman took him for a porter and ordered, "here, boy, carry my bag." Dryden replied that he was "an officer of the United States Army Air Forces," but the message was clear. For all of their advances within the military, black men like Dryden remained stereotyped and emasculated.[30]

Given the glacial rate of progress on race, other prominent black voices withheld support for foreign wars until the freedoms fought for abroad were enshrined at home. "Let us have a real democracy for the United States and then we can advise a house cleaning over on the

7.7 African Americans cited the exploits of the Tuskegee Airmen, like those pictured here in 1943, as evidence of a long-denied black capability. (United States Air Force photo courtesy of The Black Archives of Mid-America Collection, BA19.TUS2, 1943.)

other side of the water," wrote the editors of the *Baltimore Afro-American* in 1917. Other African Americans capitalized on the national emergency instigated by wars to demand better treatment as a precondition of support. In 1941, for instance, black union leader A. Philip Randolph threatened to hold a 100,000-person march in the nation's capital to protest racial discrimination in government agencies and the defence industries. Alarmed by the prospect of such a public exposé of the hypocrisy of the Four Freedoms in his own nation and unable to placate Randolph with vague promises, Franklin Roosevelt issued an executive order that banned discrimination in these sectors and established the Fair Employment Practices Committee to ensure compliance. "For the first time," wrote historian John Jeffries, "FDR had taken major public action on behalf of civil rights; indeed, for the first time since Reconstruction the federal government had created an agency committed to action toward equal rights for African Americans."[31]

Victories like this were significant but sporadic. As historian James Westheider observed, despite Du Bois' hope that black contributions to saving democracy in France would help salvage the American variant, racial conditions deteriorated categorically in the immediate aftermath of the First World War. Two decades later, when blacks returned from a war against fascism to an America unwilling to dismantle segregation, "a certain hope died, a certain respect for white Americans faded," wrote black author James Baldwin. Their wartime service did, on the other hand, politicize many black veterans who believed their sacrifice should count for something. Consequently, black veterans of the Second World War and Korean War formed a core of the burgeoning Civil Rights movement of the 1950s and 1960s.[32]

The black veterans' move from military service to grassroots agitation signalled a wider shift in strategy among black activists. The long-held conviction that fighting abroad could be parlayed into the expansion of democratic rights and greater recognition at home had born little fruit, and talk of using military service as a weapon against racism began to fade. In the midst of an unfolding disaster in Vietnam, and in the context of a draft system that provided exemptions weighted towards privileged Americans, Martin Luther King Jr made the continued chasm between US ideals and the lived experience of African Americans explicit. "We were," charged King in a 1967 sermon at Manhattan's Riverside Church, "taking the young black men who had been crippled by our own society and sending them 8000 miles away to guarantee liberties in Southeast Asia which they had not found in Southwest Georgia and East Harlem. So we have been repeatedly faced with the cruel irony of watching Negro and white boys on TV screens as they kill and die together for a nation that has been unable to seat them together in the same schools." King's speech made headlines; it was, observed historian Joe Allen, a "bombshell" that infuriated the Johnson administration and led to venomous denunciations in the mainstream press. *The Washington Post* proclaimed that King had "diminished his usefulness to his cause, to his country, and to his people." Time has been kinder to the assessment of King's sermon, as it is now regarded, wrote Allen, as "one of the best antiwar speeches in American history."[33]

Adding to the African American disenchantment with military service was the fact that armed forces integration took place in an era when the United States became increasingly committed to the defence

7.8 Exactly one year before his assassination, Dr. Martin Luther King Jr delivers his historic speech linking the civil rights and antiwar campaigns at New York City's Riverside Church. Seated behind King (left to right) are Rabbi Abraham Joshua Heschel, historian Henry Steele Commager, and Dr. John Bennett, President of Union Theological Seminary in NY. (File: JG 1967-938-7, 04/04/1967, © John C. Goodwin.)

and extension of pro-Western regimes in postcolonial settings. As the percentage of racial minorities in the US armed forces multiplied – through conscription to support wars in Korea and Vietnam, and more generally as a result of woeful employment prospects for minorities in the regular workforce – more and more Americans of colour denied freedom by the United States were required to turn their guns on foreign peoples sharing a similar complexion and predicament. Black writer Clyde Taylor summarized African American thinking on Vietnam: "One attitude ... toward the Vietnamese revolutionaries among resistant Black people is 'No Vietnamese ever called me nigger!' A more radical reaction is 'We are all in the same boat.' The most radical response has been 'We are allies.'" Black activists also considered the financial costs associated with continual military campaigns particularly unseemly when so many African Americans confronted inadequate housing, education, employment opportunities, and health care. War, in other words, simply intensified black marginality. "By the 1960s," wrote historian Kimberely Phillips, "the idea of combat as a 'right' and a declaration of black citizenship and the military as 'equal opportunity' no longer retained its rhetorical and organizing power for civil rights struggles." Black activists committed to the principle of non-violence at home began to call on their government to uphold the same standard abroad. Depicting a state addicted to the use of violence against foreign foes *and* domestic dissenters, leading civil rights organizations became *de facto* antiwar organizations, and calls for racial justice were joined by equally strident appeals for international peace. The African American community, always wary about the use of force abroad, had been transformed into a pillar of American war opposition. Enlisted blacks became key figures in an antiwar movement emerging from within the military itself, and like their white counterparts, some African American deserters and draft resisters travelled north to seek refuge in Canada.[34]

Black antiwar exiles were tapping into a long tradition. Since the American Revolution, waves of African Americans quit their country for Canada, and found a land generally free of the more extreme acts of white terrorism that their own nation was unwilling to confront. They did not, however, discover an Eden of racial harmony and equality. Some black loyalists anticipating an improved racial climate under the leavening influence of the Crown found more bigotry in Canada than in the United States, and returned to the republic as a result. Upper Canada's Abolition Act of 1793 guaranteed fugitive American slaves freedom, and the prohibition of slavery by the British Parliament in

1834 removed whatever fears remained that blacks might be returned
to a condition of servitude; still, *de jure* and *de facto* discrimination obviated any claims to "racelessness" that Canadians harboured over the
course of the nineteenth and twentieth centuries. A hodgepodge of federal, provincial, and local laws and practices (many adopted directly
from the United States) sought to prevent or discourage non-white
immigration, citizenship, integration, business and labour competition,
and social mobility. In the nineteenth century, Ontario banned African
Canadians from running for office or serving on juries, and individual
counties prohibited blacks from buying land or obtaining a business
license. Segregation in public transportation, public spaces, and housing
was commonplace throughout the country until the mid-twentieth century, and non-whites encountered signs barring them from entrances to
hotels, restaurants, beaches, pools, public parks, and skating rinks. The
city of Edmonton eliminated the need for signage altogether, simply
banning all blacks from the city in 1911. While blacks had been granted
the franchise in 1834, Canadian residents of Chinese and South Asian
descent were denied the right to vote until 1947.[35]

Lacking the kind of numbers, resources, and organizational infrastructure enjoyed by their American counterparts, far fewer racialized minorities sought redress through the courts; when they did,
the absence of a bill of rights hampered successful legal challenges
to race-based statutes and practices. Indeed, no laws explicitly forbidding discrimination existed in Canada until after the Second
World War. While the law did not "impose segregation," observed
legal historian James Walker, a series of high court rulings "upheld
the right of Canadian individuals, organizations, and institutions to
discriminate on the grounds of 'race.'" Thus, some African Canadian
children in Ontario and Nova Scotia continued to attend segregated,
and markedly inferior, public schools well into the 1960s. An 1849
Ontario statue authorizing segregation in public education was not
overturned until 1964, ten years after the landmark Brown v. Board
of Education ruling in the United States. Likewise, non-whites were
denied access to some institutions of higher learning and professional
training programs until the 1960s.[36] Not surprisingly, this constellation of regulations and practices consigned many Canadians of colour
to the lowest rungs of the economic order.

Through it all, the original inhabitants of the land and the nation's
largest ethnic minority remained the poorest Canadians. Canada's
indigenous peoples were, like their American counterparts, internally

colonized, forced onto generally unproductive reserve lands, and presented with a set of alien political, economic, and legal arrangements
by a state whose authority they rejected. In addition to being subjected
to many of the day-to-day slights and indignities shared by other
non-European peoples residing in Canada, indigenous groups were
forced to hand over their children to a system of residential schooling
designed to rid them of their language, religion, and other aspects of
the "backwardness" that rendered them incompatible with the liberal
order. Exposés of the systematic abuse suffered by children in these
settings continue to make headlines today. The federal government
banned many traditional cultural practices with the same goal of assimilation in mind. Reserve territory "guaranteed" by treaty was frequently
appropriated at a later date, or squatted on or seized by whites. The
franchise was not extended to aboriginal peoples until 1960.[37]

Many of the supposed differences between the experiences of American and Canadian racial minorities were, therefore, simply imagined.
As Phillip Buckner wrote of the era before official multiculturalism:
"In reality – a reality that many Canadians still wish to deny – Canada
was not more tolerant of diversity than the United States." Given their
corresponding standing in the social order, racialized Canadians exhibited similar reactions to those in the United States when their respective federal governments took their nations into war. Some questioned
their obligations to a state and society unwilling to countenance them
as equals. Frequently overlooked in the Quebec-v.-Rest-of-Canada
depictions of the conscription crises, for instance, is the fact that thousands of Canadians of colour organized against the policy in a direct
protest of their disenfranchisement. Concerns over whether racial
minorities would serve were one thing; fears that their ill-treatment
might inspire active support for the enemy were quite another. At the
beginning of the South African War, rumours circulated that certain
aboriginal peoples, still incensed by their losses during the Northwest
Rebellion, intended sail to South Africa and train their rifles on British imperial forces. In fact, anxieties over arming racial minorities and
tutoring them in the art of modern warfare proved a persistent concern
among Canadian officials contemplating the makeup of their nation's
forces; similar apprehensions led to widespread opposition to black
enlistment in the US services prior to the Civil War.[38]

Other members of Canadian racialized groups chose to support various wars out of patriotism and the idealistic goals of fighting for democracy and self-determination. Many expressed the conviction that military

service would provide indisputable evidence of the qualities racist discourse insisted they lacked – loyalty, competence, and manhood – and
trusted that their contribution would spur more favourable treatment for themselves and their kin. Indigenous peoples also believed
participation would strengthen their desire for permanent inclusion
and autonomy (as opposed to their assimilation) within Canada –
sentiments not unlike those expressed by mainstream Canadians who
saw participation in the empire's battles as a means of enhancing their
nation's sovereignty. After Laurier dispatched the first contingent of
Canadian troops to South Africa in the fall of 1899, for example, a number of First Nations leaders delivered appeals to local Indian agents,
federal officials in Ottawa, and Britain offering military service. "The
Indians of the Saugeen Reserve," noted one letter, "are anxious to go
to the Transvaal in case another contingent be sent ... They are anxious
to show their loyalty." During the First World War, the Grand Indian
Council of Ontario sent a letter to individual tribes that recognized
the incongruities of sending their young men to fight for "liberty, freedom and other privileges dear to all nations, for we have none." Yet
the council encouraged enlistment and accepted conscription in order
to show other Canadians that indigenous peoples shared "the same
instincts" and the "same capabilities." That same conflict inspired a
deep desire to serve among some African Canadians, who wished to
show their gratitude for the refuge the nation provided "in the dark
days of American slavery," as Hamilton journalist George Morton
wrote in a letter to Minister of Militia Sam Hughes. J.R.B. Whitney, editor of the short-lived black weekly *Canadian Observer*, saw the conflict
as a way to demonstrate to Canadians the fighting prowess already
recognized, he maintained, by the enemy. "Germans Dread Colored
Soldiers in the Battlefield" read one *Canadian Observer* headline. As
little had been done to improve racial conditions in Canada between
the wars, the nation's entry into the Second World War was accompanied by a similar array of patriotic and practical arguments for full
participation.[39]

Like their American counterparts, however, Canadian racial minorities willing to die for their country, liberal ideals, and the advancement of their race were forced to contend with a military establishment
largely unmoved by the gesture. Unlike the situation in the US Army,
however, which established separate, mostly non-combat regiments for
black troops, many Canadian racial minorities attempting to volunteer
for military service were simply turned away. This was essentially an

issue of prejudice meeting scale, as the percentage of racialized Canadians was too low to provide a serious political dilemma for officials over the issue; too low for commanders to risk challenging the chauvinism of their white soldiers for the sake of a handful of potential additions; too low for the government to assume the considerable cost and effort of creating a segregated army. Accordingly, colonial secretary Joseph Chamberlain wrote directly to leaders of the Iroquois Confederacy who had offered troops for South Africa, thanking them for their loyalty and expressing regret at having to decline "their patriotic offer." Canada's Department of Indian Affairs dutifully followed the British line and informed local agents that indigenous peoples would not be permitted to defend the empire. Prospective black and Asian volunteers faced a similar response.[40]

Except for an outright ban on First Nations' enlistment, there was no official policy regarding Canadians of colour in the early stages of the First World War; the matter was placed in the hands of individual commanders and recruiters, who were generally unified in the practice of accepting only white applicants. When the oft-repeated assurance (from combatants on both sides) that the war would be "over by Christmas" proved a cruel hoax, Canadian officials prosecuting a total war came to see the illogic of rejecting willing applicants for overseas service. By the end of 1915, army recruiters were ordered to accept all able-bodied men. A handful of non-whites made their way into regular units, but most applicants continued to face rejection from military officials who simply ignored the directive from Ottawa. In a survey by Military Council of unit commanders, one officer explained that he refused black volunteers because it would be unfair to expect his "fine class of recruits" to be forced "to mingle with negroes." Another stated that neither he nor his men "would care to sleep alongside them, or to eat with them, especially in warm weather." The pervasive mingling-phobia could be mitigated, reasoned *Canadian Observer* editor Whitney, by organizing an all-black platoon. When Acting Minister of Militia and Defence A. Edward Kemp informed parliament that no efforts were underway to organize such a unit, Whitney, who had been advertising for recruits in his newspaper, wrote to the minister to inform him that he had one ready to go. He need not have bothered: a subsequent survey of Toronto-area commanding officers found none willing to accept the group. "At a time when Prime Minister Borden had committed Canada to the daunting task of keeping 500,000 men in the battlefields," wrote James Walker, "not a single battalion would take a Black platoon."

Vancouver-area Japanese Canadians who also raised their own unit were met with the same response.[41]

At the end of April 1916, facing critical manpower shortages and on the recommendation of an internal report which reiterated some of the more demeaning stereotypes regarding black capacity, Canada's military council authorized the creation of a single black construction battalion. A year later the black soldiers left for Liverpool in their own troop ship to avoid "offending the susceptibility of other troops" also making the crossing. Military officials discussed, and eventually rejected, sending this mobile ghetto across the Atlantic alone and unprotected rather than in a regular convoy during what was described as "one of the worst weeks of unrestricted submarine warfare."[42]

In their attempts to maintain and police imprecise and mutable notions of racial hierarchy and classifications of citizenship, Canada's military policies regarding ethno-cultural groups blended equal parts tragedy and farce. Some of the members of the all-black construction battalion had been pressed into service through conscription, a law considered applicable to all British subjects. In other words, Canadian minorities who were initially informed they were unwanted in the forces were now told they *must* serve. By January 1918, Borden's government revised the Military Service Act to exempt First Nations and Japanese on the grounds that they did not possess full citizenship rights (and that the government had no interest in extending them). Three months later, another order exempted all British subjects prohibited from voting at the federal level from military service; three months after that, East Indians were granted an exemption even though, deprived of the franchise, they had been covered by the previous order. Having long possessed the right to vote, African Canadians were given no such latitude despite their undeniable status as second-class citizens. Unsurprisingly, several years of humiliating rejection, news of the horrors of trench warfare, and reports from the handful of visible minorities in the CEF about the bitter racism they encountered from fellow soldiers dissipated much of the earlier enthusiasm for enlistment. Officers hitherto panicked by the prospect of abiding African Canadians in their units now complained to military headquarters that a number of blacks had slipped across the border to avoid performing their solemn duty. One Ontario commanding officer wrote to another recommending that "to obtain these men that rightfully belong to us," the military would need to actively hunt down uncooperative blacks. It is unlikely that the reason for black draft resistance advanced in the letter – that "the average

COLORED MEN!

Your KING and COUNTRY Need YOU!

NOW is the time to show your Patriotism ; Loyalty

Your Brothers of the Colonies have rallied to the Flag and are distinguishing themselves at the Front. ℂ Here also is your opportunity to be identified in the Greatest

LT. COL. D. H. SUTHERLAND
C. O. No. 2 Construction Battalion

Will you heed the call and do your share? ✄ ✄ ✄

War of History, where the Fate of Nations who stand for Liberty is at stake. Your fortunes are equally at stake as those of your white brethren

NO. 2 CONSTRUCTION BATTALION

Now being Organized All Over the Dominion Summons You. WILL YOU SERVE?

The British and their Allies are now engaged in a great forward movement. Roads, Bridges and Railways must be made to carry the Victors forward. The need of the day is Pioneers, Construction Companies and Railway Construction Companies. No. 1 Construction Company has been recruited. No. 2 Construction Company is now called for.

Lt. Col. D. H. Sutherland is in charge of the Company's Headquarters at Pictou; at Halifax applications may be made at the Parade Recruiting Station; elsewhere to any Recruiting Officer, or by letter to—

MAJOR C. B. CUTTEN, Chief Recruiting Officer, Halifax, N. S.

Royal Print & Litho Limited, Halifax N. S.

7.9 Although initially rejected for service despite their impassioned appeals, African Canadians were advised that their loyalty was on trial in this 1917 advertisement for the all-black No. 2 Construction Battalion. (*The Atlantic Advocate*, January 1917, Esther Clark Wright Archives, Acadia University.)

negro is rather 'afraid of the Army'" – would be moderated by such an approach.[43]

Perhaps most distressingly, little moral or administrative enlightenment was gleaned from the Great War experience of rejecting certain classifications of willing applicants in times of personnel shortages; when Canada joined the Second World War, many willing volunteers again found that they were unwelcome. As with the First War, Ottawa left the matter of recruitment up to the discretion of individual commanders, who once again responded to a survey on the enlistment of African Canadians with claims that "regular" troops would refuse to fight in, or even sign up for, an army that admitted blacks. The jarring dissonance between these sentiments and the rationale for a war against fascism did not appear to strike those queried. Moreover, while official recruiting policy stated that the army welcomed anyone demonstrating suitable levels of fitness and education, these variables could serve as stand-ins for race when commanders wished to discourage non-white recruits (in addition to the fact that poverty and segregation correlate strongly with poorer health and lower levels of education). While official statistics on the matter are unavailable, the Halifax district commander reassured Ottawa that many local blacks would be turned away for lacking educational qualifications, while historian Scott Sheffield suggested that rejection rates for First Nations were "significantly higher than the national average." Still, the army constituted the branch *most* welcoming to men of colour. Until 1943, the Royal Canadian Air Force simply prohibited the enlistment of men who were "not both of pure European descent and the sons of natural born or naturalized subjects"; the navy's proscription against enlistees not "of the white race" remained until after the D-Day invasion of June 1944.[44] And once again, groups willing to enlist in the army but discouraged or banned on the basis of skin colour would be ordered to do so when conscription was reintroduced in 1944.

The confusion, inconsistency, abrupt revision, and most of all, hypocrisy of the Canadian military's racial policies inspired abundant, vigorous, and compelling counterarguments from those most affected. During the First World War, letters from prominent African Canadians objecting to the near-universal rejection of black volunteers at a time of scarce recruits reached Prime Minister Borden and Minister of Militia Sam Hughes. When Borden's government introduced conscription, First Nations' peoples and Japanese Canadians delivered a wave of petitions to Ottawa and London protesting the imposition of citizenship duties on those who did not possess citizenship rights. Indigenous "anti-recruiters" hounded government recruiters sent to reserves, "reminding Indians of their grievances and the many government promises made to them which had been broken throughout history."[45]

The reprisal of prejudicial recruiting in the Second World War incensed a group of black Halifax veterans, who were left to conclude that their Great War sacrifice had gone unrecognized, and wrote the minister of national defence to say as much. When First Nations were once again conscripted in 1944, a sympathetic Department of Indian Affairs Agent from British Columbia explained to his superiors that the low enlistment figures from his region were due to the Navy's blanket rejection of aboriginal applicants. "It is this discrimination against the B.C. Indian that has made them oppose being called up and put in the army," he wrote. Percy Ross, Chief of Victoria's Songhees Reserve, requested logic the government was unable to furnish, wondering "why Chinamen are exempt from compulsory military service and the Indians who originally owned the country" are not. Other letters, band resolutions, and petitions pointed to First Nations' exclusions from schools, hotels, government jobs, and the legislative process as fundamentally incompatible with their inclusion under the Selective Service Act. The fact that the wars were fought under the banner of bringing liberty to others only deepened the sense of betrayal.[46] Canada's visible minorities, in other words, articulated responses to their nation's wars that were frequently indistinguishable from those voiced by their American counterparts. The similarity of their plight, along with the links between Canadian and American racialized groups forged through transnational alliances – and in Canada, via the popularity of American-based minority newspapers and journals – provoked strikingly similar protestations against government policy and the wars themselves.

Distinct differences existed, however, in the ability of minority groups to make their grievances known to the wider public, and by extension, to find a prominent place in the national memory of the war. As indicated above, in Canada the preponderance of objections to exclusionary and prejudicial policies took place out of public view: in letters and petitions to politicians, Bureau of Indian Affairs agents, and military officers; in correspondence between First Nations' bands; in meetings where military recruiters sparred with draft resistors. Publications by and for racial minority groups being hard to come by, however, most public information on the activities and mood of racialized Canadians in wartime was set down in the mainstream media. Never a mainstay of sensitivity to the particular concerns of non-canonical Canadians, wartime patriotism and censorship intensified media organizations' emphasis on consensus, unity, and state boosterism. Accordingly, stories on the responses of racialized communities to war, when they appeared at all, were heavily invested in depicting a pan-Canadian support for the war effort. Thus, for instance, Second World War–era Canadians read in the *Winnipeg Free Press* that a Cree band from northern Manitoba decided to forgo its annual treaty payment from the BIA in 1940 in order to support the war. The *Brantford Expositor, Vancouver Sun, Cardston News*, and "numberless" other papers celebrated First Nations' donations to Victory Bonds. The *Toronto Star* presented a quote from a single British Columbia Native leader expressing loyalty to the war effort as verification, according to the headline, that "Indians to Assist as Canada at War." Other publications reported that residential schoolchildren made clothing to support the war effort and that women, children, and elders pulled together gamely to keep their reserves functioning in the absence of enlisted men. In all, wrote Sheffield, positive indigenous responses to the war effort were "eagerly reported in the nation's media."[47]

There were occasional exceptions to this pattern. In both world wars, indigenous opposition to conscription based on nineteenth-century guarantees that they would be exempt from such measures generated significant, and sometimes sympathetic, coverage in the press. But the widespread objections to military service based on the indignities of being refused service, denied access to high school, the workforce, and the voting booth, and treated as "children" and "wards," are generally confined to letters, memoranda, and petitions found in the files of the Department of Indian Affairs and other federal agencies. These were not the types of stories likely to be run by a wartime media committed to inspiring loyalty and unity, and to proclaiming the merits of a crusade for liberty conducted abroad. This despite Sheffield's finding that "the marginalized place of Status Indians in the social and legal landscape of Canada" –rather than treaty rights, worries over labour shortages on reserves, or any other concerns – served as "the most prevalent issue raised by First Nations opponents of conscription."[48]

Although the obstacles to full inclusion confronting Canadian and American racialized groups bore striking similarities, and wars fought to extend liberal ideals placed domestic racial exclusions under a particularly unflattering glare, the spotlight directed on American action and inaction on these injustices was always brighter. African

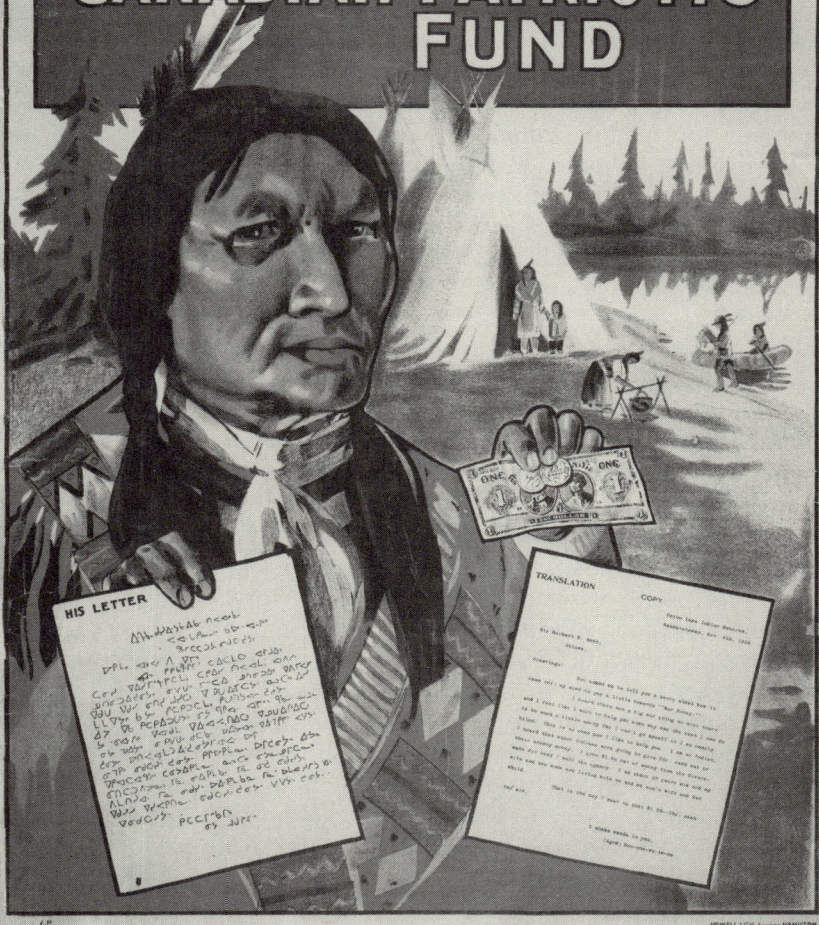

7.10 Canadian newspapers applauded First Nations' contributions to war finances, but it is unlikely that Native groups returned any salutations for this particular governmental "tribute" to their aid. (Toronto Reference Library, 1914–18. Patriotic fund. Item 1. L.)

Americans in particular used their numbers, organization, and the lessons of their long struggle for freedom and equality to prod their concerns into the national conversation about war. Presidents were compelled to appoint black officials to win African Americans to the cause and mediate the tensions between racial groups. Influential African American leaders enjoyed personal meetings and frequent correspondence with the president and his administration, permitting an airing of grievances and appeals for redress. By vowing to bring 100,000 disgruntled blacks to the streets of the nation's capital, A. Philip Randolph could force FDR's hand on an issue that alienated the Democratic president's southern wing. By threatening to withhold their support for the United Nations, the NAACP was granted a seat at the negotiating table when the time came to craft the organization's charter. Through the hundreds of newspapers and magazines published by the black press, African Americans could gain information on the ordeals, accomplishments, and campaigns of their kin without the gatekeeping conducted by dominant media organizations. The international stature of black leaders meant that a Sunday morning sermon condemning the Vietnam War made headlines in, and inspired a rancorous riposte from, the mainstream press.

Visibility did not always, or even often, translate into progress on the "American dilemma." In consequence, much of the fervour for viewing their nation's involvement in foreign conflict as a distinctive opportunity for racial gains ebbed over the course of the twentieth century. This disillusionment, coupled with an increasingly multiracial American military that was tasked with policing non-white peoples abroad, helped to fuse American racial activism with peace activism, adding vigour to the longstanding currents of anti-militarism and vigilance towards the state. Significantly for our purposes, the conspicuous clamour over race in wartime America made the issue an important component of the story of war itself. It is difficult to find a book-length survey of US involvement in the Second World War written since the 1960s that does not include some treatment of matters like the proposed march on Washington and the resultant desegregation of war industries, the Double-V campaign, the ironies of fighting Hitler with segregated forces, the barriers overcome by the Tuskegee airmen, the irreconcilable persistence of Jim Crow in the years following a war against fascism, and the momentum the Four Freedoms provided to modern civil rights activism. Indeed, in the spate of volumes produced since the 1980s that took aim at more romantic and pious representations of America at war, racial animus in the civilian and military realms was often *the* story. The innumerable specialized studies of the wartime experiences of non-white Americans at home and abroad have reinforced the stature of racial conflict in all its guises in the representation of the war.[49]

Even Tom Brokaw's hagiography to the "greatest generation" included an entire section entitled "Shame," comprised of five chapters dedicated to racial minorities' Second World War experience. "Any celebration of America's strengths and qualities during those years of courage and sacrifice," wrote Brokaw in his introduction to the section, "... will be tempered by the stains of racism that were pervasive in practice and in policy. As it was an era of great glory for America and its people, it was also, indisputably, a time of shame." Testimonials from racial minorities who suffered discrimination and violence in the military and the wider society followed (although in each case, Brokaw's volume emphasized the individual's ability to overcome prejudice and make a meaningful contribution to the war). One effect of this type of remembrance, as John Bodnar noted, is that it "resist[s] efforts to sentimentalize completely what had taken place in the early 1940s."[50] An acknowledgment of wartime racial struggles, even when soft pedaled, moderates the more simplistic and triumphal narratives of a righteous nation summoned to replace a foreign evil with a liberal democratic order it had perfected at home. The more that racialized voices are brought into the conversation, the more difficult it is to maintain unmitigated praise for what turns out to be a convoluted, paradoxical, and at times disgraceful and hypocritical wartime record.

That race plays a less prominent role in the recounting of Canada's military history should not surprise. This particular theme has never received the kind of attention directed at America's difficulties over the issue, a consequence of Canada's smaller percentage of people of colour and its proximity to the more conspicuous, headline-grabbing racial traumas of the United States. However, in many parts of the country, Canada's edition of Jim Crow proved just as comprehensive and long-lasting as its southern progenitor, and the nation's general racial attitudes and policies consciously echoed the practices deployed to maintain white dominance in the United States. The impact of racialized thinking was particularly striking in the Canadian military, where opportunities for those of colour tended to lag behind even those of the rigidly segregated American forces. Rather than being given an opportunity to prove themselves and gain social acceptance in their own, separate units, racialized Canadians who sought to enlist were simply rebuffed during the South

African War and in the first years of both world wars. When the opportunity to serve finally came, either through dogged campaigning for the right or via the obligation of conscription, the work was generally not the type that would win the recognition and gratitude these groups considered so vital to their broader social advance. At a time when African American squadrons flew over North Africa and Sicily, and blacks serving on US naval vessels battled German and Japanese warships on the high seas, the Canadian branches of these services clung to a strict, whites-only policy. Discrimination in war-related industries, meanwhile, was not banned until November 1942, more than a year after the practice was outlawed in the United States.[51]

While the fact that fewer Canadians were affected by racial ordering in civilian and military life helps to explain the lower profile afforded the issue in that country, it is another thing to suggest that such themes are unimportant to the larger story of war. For nations fighting under the banners of freedom, democracy, justice, and equality, the systematic denial of these principles and ideals at home has a place in the record, regardless of the numbers involved. As in the American context, mindfulness of the bitter racial animus faced by many Canadians can moderate some of the self-congratulation surrounding the deliverance of national virtues to a needy world, serving as a sign that a full remembrance of war includes an acknowledgment of societal failings and the pain they brought to some citizens. At the same time they were subjected to a wartime deluge of radiant proclamations about the virtues of their liberal democracies, visible minorities seeking to contribute to this great cause found that its promises were contingent on skin colour. As Winks observed of Canada's Great War ambiance, "the moment when the nation as a whole at last felt itself to be emerging as an identifiable culture on the world scene" also marked "the nadir for the Negro in Canada," whose social rejection was never more "painfully obvious."[52] Remembering in this way, then, affirms that while Canada may have important lessons to share with the world, there is also room for humility about the nation's own efforts to realize the ideals it claims.

Greater attention to the matter of race also serves as a reminder that while Canada fought wars, as Creighton wrote, to establish "world peace and security," some of those conflicts also sought to sustain, rather than dismantle, a racially ordered world system ("a world-girdling British imperial federation controlled by His Majesty's white subjects," in Desmond Morton's apt phrase). It was a theme that racialized Americans injected into their national conversation early and often, but one with a far lower profile in the Canadian record. When one learns, moreover, that white Canadians preparing to take on fascism expressed repugnance at the thought of conducting this task alongside blacks, and that many sent to Korea broadcasted in word and deed their deep contempt for Asians, we need to look to motivations for Canadian intervention that go beyond facile affirmations of the desire to rid the world of malevolent theories and regimes – to simply, as one volume on the Canada's Second World War effort concluded, "preserve the basic human right to be free."[53] That was certainly part of the story, though not the whole story, and for some civilians and soldiers alike, not the story at all.

The routine elision of such matters can also diminish the public's ability to contextualize more recent examples of individual or institutional racism: the hate crimes committed by the Canadian Airborne Regiment against blacks in their ranks and the citizens of Somalia whom the force was sent in 1992 to protect, conduct which included the torture and murder of a Somali teen (with soldiers posing proudly for the camera over their dying, blood-drenched victim); the delivery, in direct contravention of international law, of real and perceived enemies to the notorious torture chambers of the Afghan judicial system (an act sociologist Sherene Razack placed in a long line of the indifference and double-standards that governed Canadians' conduct towards "uncivilized" foreigners in peacekeeping and war). Such acts provoked justified outrage among Canadians, as well as a not entirely warranted claim that these indignities represented unique betrayals of a mostly-unblemished military legacy, one that had not previously known "racial sneers and killings." Where the incidents at My Lai and Abu Ghraib align with certain notions of US soldierly conduct harbored by a wide range of domestic and foreign critics (e.g. Mailer, Vonnegut, Fussell, Hersh, Atwood, and Mowat, to cite a few), Canadian reckonings of their own recent scandals frequently distinguished the "aberrant" conduct of the "bad apples" from the courageous shock troops, principled peacekeepers, and benevolent leaders of previous generations.[54] Those earlier Canadians certainly represented their country with distinction, but the biases they inherited from a culture that devalued racial minorities, along with the dehumanizing crucible of battle, could also inspire the types of ugly attitudes and deeds Canadians more commonly ascribed to other states and their armies.

In all, a discussion of the racial animosity that plagued Canada's military and wider culture has moved rather haltingly into the record of war. From the "first draft of history" furnished by journalists to the retrospections produced through much of the twentieth century, the perpetual quarrel between French and English Canada garnered most of the attention paid to ethno-cultural divisions in wartime Canada. Among English writers, this attention was often synonymous, as we have seen, with considerable confusion over why francophones dissented, and frequent dismissals of the idea that the French had legitimate grounds for complaint. Japanese internment gained greater notice beginning in the mid-1970s, providing a challenge to notions of national innocence and righteousness, and studies of the episode began to raise the complicated story of Asian Canadians' attempts to contribute to the World Wars. Around that same time, First Nations and Métis groups grew increasingly vocal about their omission from the national story of war and their difficulty in accessing veterans' benefits; as a result, historians were alerted to the experience of Canada's "forgotten soldiers," as historian Fred Gaffen called them in the title to his seminal work on the subject from 1985. Little was said of the role and plight of black soldiers in the World Wars until American historian Robin Winks gave the subject some attention in his 1971 monograph on African Canadian history. Little more was added until Calvin Ruck's 1987 study, aptly titled *The Black Battalion, 1916–1920: Canada's Best Kept Military Secret.*[55]

Still, if the paradox embedded in America's racial dilemma and its stated wartime goals provides a consistent leitmotif for US analysts, similar analysis is mostly consigned to specialized studies in Canada, and is absent or lightly handled in many general Canadian war accounts. A recent and encyclopedic study of the three-hundred year history of Canada's army, for example, mentioned the exclusions faced by black soldiers once, admitting that while they initially experienced difficulties enlisting in the First World War on account of prejudice, "pressures for men destroyed most such barriers."[56] With no subsequent discussion of matters like segregated units or the rejection of non-white volunteers in later wars, the reader is left to believe that any racial discrimination in the Canadian Army had been overcome, in that war and for all time. The short shrift given to the extensive and often bitter chronicle of racial minorities' struggle for respect and equal opportunity in the Canadian military is not atypical. While such an approach does little to illuminate an unflattering and often overlooked corner of the nation's past, it undoubtedly heartens those who view Canada and its armed forces as straightforward agents of freedom, as well as those who consider race a uniquely "American dilemma."

Chapter Eight

Making and Breaking Nations

Americans, even the more historically challenged among them, have little trouble identifying their country's birthdate. The fourth of July, 1776, is the most celebrated secular event on the nation's calendar, the date when representatives of the Second Continental Congress declared their official break from Britain and their resolve to continue the military insurrection against the metropole until the British absorbed the new reality. Those on the other side of the Atlantic may beg to differ on the exact timing, marking American independence on 3 September 1783, the day Great Britain grudgingly accepted their loss by signing the Treaty of Paris. Regardless, the larger event that precipitated the annulment of the British and American colonial union – namely, a military struggle that left tens of thousands dead on both sides – cannot be disputed. The nation was born in war.[1]

Despite the certitude surrounding the nation's founding, since independence many Americans of various eras have called for the re-birth or re-invigoration of a nation that had allegedly lost some of its original focus, purity, and determination. Frequently that regeneration, to the Jeremiahs promoting it, required additional bloodletting. The Republican "War Hawks," who pressed for a military response in order to restore American honour in the face of Britain's indignities in 1812, were the first of many to cite the ensuing conflict as the "Second American Revolution" – the final break from colonial subservience. In the 1860s, Southern secessionists used the same term for their battle with the North, again deploying the language of honour to rally fellow citizens to the cause of states' rights (and less publicly, to the right to own and traffic in human beings). Nineteenth-century campaigns against such foes as Mexico and the Plains Indians found their logic in similar claims about the cathartic and productive power of violent revenge – in these cases, following the humiliations at the Alamo and Little Big Horn. Likewise, as historian Kristin Hoganson made clear, American officials stressed the centrality of chivalric ideas of manhood and honour in American debates surrounding the decision to declare war on Spain in 1898. War advocates appealed to American manhood after the sinking of the *Maine* "not only because of their desire to redeem American honor vis-à-vis Spain, but also because they believed that American men *needed* a war – that their manly fiber was in doubt" (emphasis in original). Prior to that conflict, Assistant Secretary of the Navy Theodore Roosevelt went so far as to call President McKinley (who, it should be noted, had appointed Roosevelt to the post) a "chocolate éclair" for seeking a diplomatic solution to the crisis. And for Roosevelt, an advocate of "the strenuous life" for both men and nations, the specific enemy hardly mattered. As he confided in a letter to a friend as tensions with Spain mounted, "in strict confidence … I should welcome almost any war, for I think this country needs one."[2]

Although chivalric sensibilities are more frequently associated with the Victorian era, such discourses did not go out of fashion in representations of the next century's conflicts. After Pearl Harbor, war supporters depicted a nation that had been lulled into naive and childlike sleep by the false promises of isolationism, now roused to an avenging, national manhood. The Cold War era, to a range of recent analysts, instigated a "crisis" of American masculinity as economic transformations led more and more of the nation's men to exchange their overalls for the grey flannel suits of the urban (and "effete") office worker. American men had devolved alarmingly from the archetype proposed by Roosevelt: namely, the cowboy, who in the president's words, "will not submit tamely to an insult, and is ever ready to avenge his own wrongs; nor has he an overwrought fear of shedding blood. He possesses, in fact, few of the emasculated, milk-and-water moralities admired by the pseudo-philanthropists; but he does possess, to a very high degree, the stern, manly qualities that are invaluable to a nation." As cultural historian Suzanne Clark wrote, "manliness itself, and the old warrior ethic it invoked, was on trial" in the new, bureaucratized Cold War order.[3]

To Clark's colleague in the field Robert Dean, this perceived crisis in masculinity impelled the Kennedy administration to emphasize a warrior philosophy and "a rhetoric of polarized opposites against political opponents: manly strength and feminized weakness, youth and age, stoic austerity and debilitating luxury." While the Bay of Pigs served as a rather direct riposte to the administration's carefully fashioned self-image, the unyielding toughness Kennedy demonstrated (at least publically) during the Cuban Missile Crisis restored the president's manly lustre, serving as a "rephallusization of the Kennedy administration and the United States," in the words of one particularly lyrical observer. Following the 9/11 attacks, US military analyst William Deresiewicz equated an inflated reverence for the military uniform with an attempt to restore the nation's virility after the humiliation at the hands of Al Qaeda, with official pronouncements like President George W. Bush's "bring it on" betraying "a kind of desperate machismo." The pattern is clear: when honour is violated, a failure to answer the humiliation with bloodshed amounts to a communal emasculation. Violence, manhood, and nationhood each find their apogee in concert with the others. And in the case of JFK, the restoration of personal and national masculinity is worth even the risk of Armageddon. Indeed, the very willingness to usher in nuclear annihilation could in itself be considered the highest form of a kind of reckless, unbending manliness. In all, observed Emily Rosenberg, there exists a strong faith that progress in American history depends on episodes of "regenerative, violent warfare" conducted by "men of heroic, masculine qualities."[4] The forging of the nation becomes a never-ending and gender-specific project, one that requires periodic sacrifices that echo those made in the Revolutionary War. But to reiterate: despite the continual reprisal of the martial necessity, no one disputes that the nation does indeed exist, nor the event that precipitated its birth.

It is a truism – and a fundamental element of national identity – that Canadians lack such clarity regarding their founding myths. British General James Wolfe's victory over French General Louis-Joseph, Marquis de Montcalm on the Plains of Abraham in 1759 was surely a pivotal moment in Canadian annals, but its inadequacies as a reservoir of national unity are obvious. (In spite of this, Ontario schoolchildren were still obliged to sing *The Maple Leaf Forever*, an anthem exalting Britain, the Crown, and the rout of the French, well into the 1970s.) Canadians can point to no revolution that marks a clean break from empire, only a gradual, painstaking, and to some, eminently tedious march towards "responsible government" (even the term intimates a certain dowdiness). Indeed, the resilient connections between Canadian nationalism and British imperialism rendered the prospective taking-up of arms against the metropole a kind of injury to the self, as opposed to the more straightforward patricide committed by

8.1 Not a gun in sight: Canadian delegates talk their way to self-government at the London Conference of 1866. (John David Kelly, artist, 1889, Library and Archives Canada/C-006799.)

the Americans. In the Fathers of Confederation, Canadians, too, possess a patriarchal cadre of nation-builders, but while these men made fine speeches about the wisdom of domestic autonomy and French-English cooperation, none had cause to shout such pulse-quickening slogans as "Give me liberty or give me death!" (Patrick Henry urging the Virginia Convention to commit troops to the Revolutionary War), or "I only regret that I have but one life to lose for my country," (Continental Army soldier Nathan Hale from the gallows before being executed by the British for espionage).[5] Nor did Sir John A. Macdonald or any other Fathers of Confederation muster colonists to stirring battlefield victories in order to secure independence, as had America's first president.

Violent acts of repression and removal perpetrated against the impoverished and out-gunned native and Métis peoples may have exhilarated some nineteenth-century Euro-Canadians, but as potential examples of valour and nation-building, these incidents have not worn well. While the British North America Act of 1867 provided Canada a measure of legal autonomy, Confederation did not "forge a nation," if one accepts Benedict Anderson's oft-repeated equation of nation-hood with "an imagined community" of citizens bound by a common past and purpose: Quebecer's hesitations regarding their bonds to the Canadian community are well-rehearsed; for years, white British Columbians took their province's name literally, remaining emphatic anglophiles ill-disposed towards the government in central Canada decades after they joined Confederation in 1871; in the West as a whole, wrote historian Amy Knight, Canadian patriotism was "so weak that successive prime ministers up to the time of Mackenzie King had worried that the region might try to secede and join the United States"; a majority of Newfoundlanders and Labradorians have always considered their Canadian identity secondary to that of their region, and many continue to deem the 1949 decision to join Confederation a dreadful error; many First Nations peoples never recognized Ottawa's authority and continue to consider themselves sovereign entities within Canada. In Carl Berger's words, the authors of Confederation well understood that "the union of 1867 ... opened up, but did not guarantee, the prospect that the various regions and communities would one day form in fact what everyone called a 'new nationality.'" A century after Confederation, historian Ramsay Cook concluded that the project of national assimilation was far from complete and perhaps even unnecessary, that "Canadianism" was best defined by an amalgam of the "limited identities" – regional, ethnic, and class – that citizens continued to embrace. Little has transpired in the intervening years to suggest that Cook needs to radically alter his proposition.[6]

This relative absence of both national drama surrounding Canada's founding and national unity thereafter rendered Canada something of an outlier among modern nations. As British military historian Christopher Dandeker observed, "that the creation of the modern nation-state has, so far, been intimately connected with violence is attested by many examples," including those of the United States and Latin America in the late-eighteenth and early nineteenth centuries, Eastern Europe and the Middle East between the world wars, and the anticolonial struggles of the mid-twentieth century. The attainment of sovereignty thus provided these new states with a storehouse of valiant (and always malleable, and often embellished) episodes to bring together and inspire future generations. Not surprisingly, then, as historian Alan Gordon observed, the nineteenth century "saw both the entrenchment of nationalism and the rise of the hero cult across Europe and the Americas." Writing in 1882, French political theorist Ernest Renan made the connection between gallant deeds and nation-building explicit: "A heroic past, great men, glory (I mean the true kind)," he instructed, "this is the social capital upon which one founds the idea of a nation."[7]

Renan's insistence that a national polity needn't share a common ancestry, that it could be fashioned from any group of people who had simply "done great things together" and "wish[ed] to do more," served multi-ethnic nations like the United States and Canada well. The dilemma for the latter involved settling on those events common to both English and French (those of indigenous and non-canonical identities being of considerably less concern) and that were considered certifiably heroic. Many Canadian achievements have been called upon to serve as the "social capital" Renan claimed would construct a nation: simply surviving and learning to adapt in an alien and demanding environment; fashioning a functioning and increasingly representative polity out of disparate ethno-cultural groups; constructing a transportation and communication infrastructure across the world's second largest country; attaining sovereignty *without* resorting to bloodshed and maintaining that sovereignty while sharing a border with a powerful nation possessing designs on the entire continent; and later, crafting a Charter of Rights and a multicultural society that have become the envy of the world. All would qualify under Renan's definition of nationhood, rephrased only slightly in Frank Underhill's 1964 Massey lectures as "a body of people who have done great things together in the past and who hope to do great things together in the future." The military's role in many of these achievements was relatively minor; in fact, in the long struggle for equality and democracy in Canada, noted John Conway, "the military was used, often with protests from its own ranks, as an instrument of control and repression" – as a brake on the very freedom so often ascribed to the efforts of the armed forces themselves.[8] But none of the non-military episodes in nation-building offered above possessed the panache of a battle to the death fought against "tyranny" and for a new experiment in governance. Was Canada's past as heroic as that of other countries, or heroic at all? Was Canada even a bona fide nation? Arthur Lower's meditation on the divergent memories generated by the American Revolution is surely a mite dystopian, but just as surely he captured a sense of

Canadians' envy over the comparative stories of national origins. English Canada, he wrote,

> inherited, not the benefits, but the bitterness of the Revolution. It got no shining scriptures out of it. It got little release of energy and no new horizons of the spirit were opened up. It had been a calamity, pure and simple. And to take the place of the internal fire that was urging Americans westward across the continent there was only melancholy contemplation of things as they might have been and dingy reflection of that ineffably glorious world across the stormy Atlantic. English Canada started its life with as powerful a nostalgic shove backward into the past as the Conquest had given to French Canada: two little peoples officially devoted to counter-revolution, to lost causes, to the tawdry ideals of a society of men and masters, not to the self-reliant freedom alongside of them.[9]

If the American Revolutionary War served to equate Americans with heroism and Canadians with loss, then it followed that the latter would need to draw on other episodes of violent struggle to establish the building blocks of nationhood. Military endeavours, one might infer from Lower's lament, serve as the ultimate arbiter of winners and losers, of heroes, cowards, and goats. Indeed, in their demonization of others, the commitment of the individual to a larger, collective task, and the insistence on the justness of their cause, wars seem to fulfil the model for binding a national community outlined by a variety of Enlightenment-era European and American nationalists. As American historian Lloyd Kramer observed, these writers "stressed the danger of enemies, the need for sacrifice, and the national ideal as an essential component of human identity." "Nationhood happens," proposed Scottish political theorist Neil Davidson in 2000, "when some people, as a result of common experience (inherited or shared), feel and articulate the identity of interests as between themselves, and against other nations whose interests are different from (and usually opposed to) theirs."[10] Building a railway or a just society satisfies the "fellowship" criteria ably, but warfare – with its unambiguous provision of enemies, threat, and opposition – appears a surer route to marking all the boxes on the nationhood checklist.

Such faith in the productive, transformative power of communal violence is evident in the manifold efforts to identify the war, even the specific battle, which *made* Canada – for in what other manner, the logic goes, can a nation be truly born? Here, the First World War, and more narrowly, the Battle of Vimy Ridge reigns supreme. "The special appeal of Vimy Ridge," observed Jonathan Vance, "rested in its ability to bring together the religious and the nationalist." Begun on Easter Monday, the offensive combined a powerful amalgamation of symbols in the Canadian imagination – the rising of both Christ and the nation – an amalgamation reiterated by Canadian poets of great reverence and variable talent from the immediate aftermath of the battle onward.[11]

Historians, public officials, and cultural institutions, too, came to anoint Vimy as the moment Canada attained national manhood; there, the four Canadian divisions of the Canadian Expeditionary Force, comprised of soldiers from across the Dominion, fought together for the first time and achieved a stunning victory. Writing of the period leading up to the victory at Vimy, Donald Creighton rhapsodized that "in these months of tremendous accomplishment, the rise towards the maturity of nationhood was swift and confident, both at home and abroad," and that in a long string of gruesome battles of attrition fought by the CEF, "the victory at the ridge of Vimy was perhaps the most perfect of them all." Vimy, wrote H.F. Wood in 1967, was "Canada's Agincourt, no more, and no less." In 1996, the National Film Board released a documentary with the unambiguous title *Vimy: The Birth of a Nation*. The Historica Canada website reported that "Canadian bravery and valour led to the tremendous victory for the entire Allied Force and was considered the turning point of WWI." Historica's "Heritage Minute" video featured a voice-over recitation of a soldiers' letter home reporting what he felt at battle's end: "And mother, I thought, we *are* a nation. This is us." "Vimy Ridge had an extraordinary effect on the national psyche," Rene Chartrand declared in 2007, as it engendered "a consciousness of being proud citizens of a fully independent nation." It not only made Canada, but "made Canada into a country of heroes," enthused *National Post* columnist Joe O'Connor, who as a high school student envied all the glamour and violence in American history until he stumbled across "a founding national identity myth slathered in blood and guts and First World War glory."[12]

On this, the Harper government was unequivocal, with the prime minister calling Vimy Canada's sacred "creation story" and conveying this message from the dead at the 90th anniversary commemoration of the battle: "We may hear them say softly: I love my family, I love my comrades, I love my country, and I will defend their freedom to the end." Like fellow historian Margaret MacMillan, Michael Fellman sensed a presentist agenda in apocryphal testimony of the fallen.

Fellman observed that "national birth in blood sacrifice is important to emphasize when one wants to make the pitch for a current war and the re-militarization of a society." Five years later, the project continued apace: Vimy was the indisputable "birth of the nation" affirmed Governor General David Johnston at the 95th anniversary commemoration of the attack.[13]

British historians Gary Sheffield and Alexander Turner have argued that the desire to find the nation's birth at Vimy has given the battle a sanctity that has inured it to harder, more empirical truths: that Canadians did not fight alone at Vimy, but as part of a British imperial force, and that the battle was but a component of the wider Battle of Arras and not, as many Canadians have been told, anything approaching a turning point in the Great War. Canadian historian Paul Dickson pointed out that men born in the British Isles outnumbered the Canadian-born in the CEF divisions that fought at Vimy ("at a time," noted Dickson, "when seventy-seven per cent of Canadians were born in Canada"), deflating some of the enthusiasm for the "homegrown" character of the triumph. Nor had the participants, according to historian Wesley Gustavson, simply "jettisoned their British identity atop Vimy Ridge in favour of a Canadian one." In fact, notwithstanding the fictional letter writer's sentiments in Historica's Heritage Minute, the idea that Vimy marked the ur-moment of Canadian nationhood did not take hold in the public consciousness until the 1960s – stimulated in large measure by the confluence of Canada's centenary and the fiftieth anniversary of the battle. Other Vimy-deflators questioned whether a bloodbath producing more than 10,000 Canadian casualties should be consecrated as the national cornerstone, and pointed out that the heavy losses at Vimy helped usher in conscription, a move that permanently splintered the nation. Desmond Morton's more limited claims for Vimy's hold on the Canadian imagination reflected these misgivings. "For Canadians," he wrote in 1999, "Vimy Ridge was a nation building experience. *For some*, then and later, it symbolized the fact that the Great War was also Canada's war of independence" (emphasis added).[14]

Given these persuasive challenges to the Vimy myth, those who claim the war as a whole made the nation might appear to be on surer ground. After all, it was Canada's contribution to the entire war, not Vimy alone, that gave the country the eminence to sit as an independent nation at the peace table in Versailles, and that provided momentum for the 1931 Statute of Westminster. Frank Underhill's 1923 essay on the CEF argued that the war "made" Canada, a view reiterated so consistently it has become a cliché. C.P. Stacey, Pierre Berton, and W.L. Morton echoed Underhill's claim, as did Morton and Granatstein, who wrote assuredly that "for Canada the Great War was a war of independence." "Rich, prosperous, still struggling for unity," Granatstein stated in *Who Killed Canadian History?*, "present-day Canada was made in Flanders fields." But as discussed in Chapter Three of this volume, more recent analysts have disputed the belief that the First War challenged English Canadians' self-conception as loyal citizens of the British Empire. "Neither central argument of this 'death of Canadian imperialism' interpretation – that war bred nationalism and that post-war disillusionment was widespread in Canada – stands recent close examination," wrote John Herd Thompson, who pointed to the continued and intense post-war loyalty of Canadian officers to Britain's empire and culture, and a decided lack of post-war disillusionment among the general populace. Phillip Buckner argued that "participation in war *strengthened* the emotional ties between Canada and Britain and ensured the survival of the British connection even after the formal bonds were weakened" (emphasis added).[15]

Assigning the birthdate of Canada to the First World War also overlooks the fact that French-speaking Canadians existed for 300 years prior to the Great War, and considered themselves a nation (indeed, the term "Canadian" referred exclusively to French colonists until the 1791 establishment of Upper and Lower Canada). "From the earliest days of those settlements," explained Jean Martin, "the French colonists who settled along the St. Lawrence valley felt that they were living in a country called Canada or Kanata." James Wood, meanwhile, argued that at the end of the supposedly unifying international campaign, Canadians were "more deeply divided than ever before along lines of region, ethnicity, and class." Much of the division arose over the introduction of conscription and Borden's subsequent Order-in-Council removing exemptions and lowering the draft age. "Farmers, workers, French Canadians, the Prairie west, and Maritimers – groups whose disaffection from national life would become a defining characteristic of Canada in the 1920s and 1930s – all were united in their outrage" over the Union government's handling of the matter. The ironies of a nation gaining its identity and sovereignty through a global catastrophe ignited by fanatical nationalisms, through a war that created permanent fissures in the national fabric, has led to an amelioration of the earlier claims. Tim Cook acknowledged that Canadians may not necessarily have "gained their identity on the slopes of Vimy

Ridge" – although in the same paragraph he provided the more tempered claim that "the Great War signified Canada's coming of age."[16]

Challenges to the belief that Vimy, or the wider war, "made" Canada have inspired further sleuthing about national origins; the constant among many of the seekers is that the nation must have been "forged in war." The War of 1812, which journalist and historian Jeffrey Simpson called with certain justification "among the dumbest ever fought," has been summoned nevertheless as a formative and magnificent moment in national development. Mid-nineteenth-century politician and educator Egerton Ryerson held that the conflict unified the Upper Canadians and gave them a founding myth as glorious as any from antiquity: "The Spartan bands of Canadian Loyalist volunteers, aided by a few hundred English soldiers and civilized Indians, repelled the Persian thousands of democratic American invaders, and maintained the virgin soil of Canada unpolluted by the foot of the plundering invader." At the war's centenary, Ontario provincial archivist Alexander Fraser wrote that the conflict supplied "a saga of glowing tradition, an epic of patriotism, an historic pageant of men and women whose deeds will be our national inspiration and whose names will be our everlasting glory."[17]

Though the conflict languished in the public imagination following the world wars, the bicentenary of 1812 saw the Harper government reprise the motif that the British-American confrontation served as a shining moment in Canada's progress towards nationhood. According to the prime minister's official message on the war, the rediscovery of this "seminal event in the making of our great country" (a rediscovery shepherded along by the government's $28 million "information" campaign) would allow the nation to gain new appreciation for the "heroes who fought for Canada." In praising only the "Aboriginal peoples, local and volunteer militias, and English and French-speaking regiments" that participated in the conflict, the prime minister evaded any mention of the fact that British regulars formed the backbone of the imperial forces, or the fact that this was a war between the United States and Britain. That the episode featured blatantly treasonous acts by thousands on both sides of the border, and that Canada was merely a distant outpost of empire did not intrude on the government's glorious retelling of a battle that "laid the foundation for Confederation and established the cornerstones of many of our political institutions."[18]

American and Canadian historians continue to squabble about who truly prevailed in one of history's "dumbest" wars, but there is little room in the puffery from either side to call attention to the conflict's most conspicuous losers: namely, Aboriginal peoples. Whether they took up arms for Britain, the Americans, or sought to maintain neutrality, there was no winning. In American-held territory, indigenous groups were divested of lands and relocated to squalid reserves, while hopes for the creation of an independent First Nations state west of the Mississippi died when the British ceded those lands to the United States at the 1815 Treaty of Ghent. Mdewakanton Sioux chief Chetanwakanmani ("Little Crow") summed up the fruits of his people's alliance with King George III: in the final year of the conflict, half his tribe "died of hunger with shreds of skin in their mouths." Twenty-eight million dollars is surely enough to provide a relatively comprehensive accounting of the conflict and its outcomes, but including references to the betrayal and starvation that befell certain constituencies would be anathema to a PR campaign extolling the "heroes" who inaugurated the spirited march to nationhood. Instead, in a claim that begs for qualification, the federal government maintained that the conflict demonstrated and enhanced Canada's "respect for linguistic and ethnic diversity."[19] This being one of the war's chief lessons, any clarification on the ultimate fate of British-allied indigenous peoples – many of whose descendants continue to reside in Canada and were thus subjected to the same boastful campaign – was necessarily ignored.

Despite the considerable federal resources poured into informing the public about the myriad ways in which 1812 "[made] our great country," a 2013 survey revealed that the effort did little to elevate the image of the conflict in the minds of Canadians. In fact, pollsters found that Canadians would have preferred a campaign to mark the thirtieth anniversary of the 1982 Charter of Rights and Freedoms (a Liberal Party initiative on which the Harper government was virtually silent in 2012); those surveyed also expressed hope that significant attention would be paid to the 2019 centenary of women's suffrage. In short, respondents recognized factors other than participation in international conflict as significant, nation-building achievements worthy of public celebration. While the narrative of a nation "forged in fire" certainly roused some Canadians, others seemed equally moved by the idea of a nation forged in negotiation and incremental progress towards democracy and social justice.[20]

Nevertheless, establishing a nexus between warfare and national founding(s) remains a time-honoured and potent means of demonstrating the magnitude of any number of Canadian conflicts. And pinpointing the moment of national origin carries undeniable allure.

Like locating the source of a great river, it bequeaths the discoverer a certain degree of immortality (and the historian a certain bump in book sales); accordingly, a range of surveyors have endeavoured to fix or reposition the nation's date of birth in order to show why their war or battle truly mattered. English Canada's "electric" response to Britain's appeal for conscripts in South Africa proved one thing above all, according to George Munro Grant in his 1899 preface to the first book on Canada's role in the war: "We are henceforth a nation." A recent study of the 1866 Fenian raids on Canada pushed the national birthdate backward, claiming that this episode was not a relatively minor and amateurish military encounter, but rather, as its subtitle asserted, *The Battle that Made Canada*. The raids, so the argument goes, demonstrated the need for the unity and military preparedness that only Confederation could realize. Yet other observers did not espy a bona fide nation until Canada had put another eight decades and three international conflicts into the books; the Second World War, which marked the first instance of an independent Canada choosing war, became for many the culmination of Arthur Lower's "colony-to-nation" arc. As C.P. Stacey and Richard Foot wrote in the *Canadian Encyclopedia*, Canada's "status as an independent country, only shakily established in 1919, was beyond doubt after 1945." Authors who in other contexts had confidently cited the First World War as the nation's "war of independence" now recanted in order to canonize the Second. The Statute of Westminster, explained Granatstein and Morton in *A Nation Forged in Fire: Canadians and the Second World War*, "was only a paper statement of independence, and psychologically Canada remained the colony it had legally been in 1914" after the 1931 statute. It would take a second global conflict – fortuitously for Canadian development, just around the bend – to complete the national gestation. (Ironically, in a book that shared *A Nation Forged in Fire's* 1989 publication date, Granatstein suggested that the world wars were the *undoing* of Canadian independence. The economic burden of "Canada's herculean attempts to aid Britain" he wrote, "forced the country's sweet surrender to the United States," a neo-colonial subservience that the author, at that time at least, seemed to lament.[21])

The Korean War proved somewhat less yielding to this type of burgeoning-autonomy storyline: its prosecution was too American-dominated, its outcome too messy, and Canadians confirmed their continued association with the metropole by fighting in the Commonwealth Division. Historian John English made the seemingly obligatory attempt anyway, calling a chapter on the war "Becoming Adult." A recent edited collection of military history, *Forging a Nation: Perspectives on the Canadian Military Experience*, simply assigned the nation-building mantle to *all* wars fought in Canada from the colonial period to the present – and as the volume's title suggests, to no other factor. All Canadian wars having thus been claimed, one author selected an entirely foreign conflict as the moment of birth, titling his work *Blood and Daring: How Canada Fought the American Civil War and Forged a Nation* (the Canadian nation, that is).[22]

As the above efforts make clear, determining the moment of national origin is a considerably inexact science. Just as plainly, warfare is widely perceived as the ultimate maker of nations and a perennial source of auspicious outcomes for Canada. And to the query, "which war made Canada?" (the question "*what* made Canada?" demonstrating a naiveté about how these things work), the inevitable response in the wake of the above offerings is "all of them."

To Canadians who accept this premise, each conflict becomes, at its root, unimpeachable, an indispensable and hallowed step on the road to national autonomy and maturity. Unlike Americans, Canadians cannot call 1812 or the First World War foolish blunders, or the Second World War a direct and avoidable consequence of the "needless" First, without also destabilizing the alleged foundations of their nationhood. Such thinking also leads to the inevitable conclusion that soldiers represent the most important social actors ("the best citizens of our country" in the words of Canada's Defence Minister in 2011) since their contributions to national development eclipse those of all others. It was the sacrifice of soldiers, wrote Granatstein in a variation on this theme, that made Canada "this best of all nations." The Canadian-American variance over the perceived influence of war on national development can be acute, a testament to both Americans' comparative certitude regarding their international standing, and the luxury, born of that same certitude, of forgetting that the outside world may have influenced the evolution of the American state. As political scientist Robert Saldin made clear, American analysts of their nation's political development have grossly undervalued, and often simply ignored, the influence of warfare on the expansion and transformation of their state.[23]

It would be difficult for readers of Canadian war histories to make an analogous claim. Instead, many English Canadian analysts have accepted the logic laid down by the historian of the Canadian militia in 1902, even if later writers would generally be more circumspect – at least publicly – about those who refused to respond to the bugle call:

> The country realizes that its whole life has been stimulated, the standard of its manhood built up, the national character strengthened by the achievements of its sons in the Fenian Raids, the Red River Expedition, the Nile Campaign, the North-West Rebellion, and the South African War. True, the laurels have been moistened with the tears of Canadian mothers, but a price has to be paid for everything that is worth having. The mother of a coward does not often weep.[24]

The equation of past military exploits and soldiering with the very essence of Canadian-ness found its apogee under the Harper government (once again), and its decision to make military personnel a fixture at Canadian citizenship ceremonies, where new citizens are tutored on the most sacred ideals and symbols of the polity. An operational bulletin issued in early 2011 from Citizenship and Immigration Canada described military service "as one of the highest expressions of citizenship" and directed that members of the military should be seated next to the citizenship judge, present in the receiving line for new citizens, and permitted to give a short speech. The citizenship judge was instructed to state: "Thousands of brave Canadians have fought and died for [Canadian] rights and freedoms. The commitment to Canada of our men and women in uniform should never be forgotten or go unrecognized." Canada's core identity, to the crafters and defenders of the new policy, is that of a warrior, despite the nation's status as one of the globe's most pacific geographic zones over the nineteenth and twentieth centuries, and despite the relatively few inter- or intra-state military battles its soldiers participated in (again, compared to virtually every other nation on earth) over that same span. Here, then, is one of the more profound paradoxes of English Canadians' identity: they inhabit a space as faithful to the ideal of a "peaceable kingdom" as can be found in the modern era, and yet many emphasize martial contributions as a – or even *the* – fundamental signifier of belonging. A warrior posture stands in for a thoroughgoing warrior past.[25] British military historian Michael Howard posited something of an inverse relationship between citizens' experience with war and their fascination with it:

> There is no 'military history' as such of classical antiquity, or even of the Middle Ages. These were societies organised for war, constantly at war,

and their structure and their activity cannot be dissociated. 'Military history' as a speciality is a luxury which can be enjoyed only by atypically peaceful societies, and it is perhaps an indication of how peaceful our own society is today that military history in its narrowest operational sense should be enjoying so remarkable a boom.[26]

In an op-ed endorsing the new citizenship policy, David Bercuson presented a primer on the nation's history that ascribed the most significant twentieth-century advances in Canadian culture, communications, and international reputation to its participation in foreign wars (although in an article chronicling a century of military achievements, he simply ignored peacekeeping, Canada's most internationally-celebrated and distinctive contribution to the "modern multilateral world" he otherwise lauded).[27] To those might wonder why episodic troop deployments were more important in building the nation than the daily contributions of farmers, industrial workers, teachers, artists, politicians, journalists, entrepreneurs, poets, nurses, fishermen, or any other sector of the population – in other words, why representatives of these indisputable nation-builders are not also required at citizenship ceremonies – Bercuson simply noted that state existence is impossible without the security ensured by armed forces, that all other activities within a state have as their prerequisite a tranquil polis.

Such analysis overlooks the fact that from the outset of European settlement, a tranquil Canadian polis free from foreign (and sometimes internal) aggression has ultimately been underwritten by non-Canadians: until 1759 by the French government, then by the British and their unparalleled navy (including in the years *following* Confederation), and finally by the Americans and their nuclear arsenal (although they helped to assert Canadian sovereignty over Canada's far north, it was not the Canadian Rangers – Arctic residents deputized as reservists and equipped with First World War-issue Lee Enfield .303 rifles – who deterred a Soviet invasion during the Cold War). Few would suggest that representatives of these essential, non-Canadian guarantors of the nation's security should also be present when new Canadians take their oath. And once again, such endorsements are put forward without considering whether a mandatory military presence at citizenship ceremonies makes Canada an outlier among similar liberal democracies, as it in fact does. Britain, for instance, has no provision for military personnel at citizenship ceremonies (although when ceremonies are held in the Tower of London, Beefeaters may happen to be in the vicinity, noted a British official). In the United States, soldiers are invited to play a ceremonial role when naturalization proceedings are held at military bases or when all or most of the citizenship candidates are members of the armed forces; military participation in other cases is only optional. It would be specious to argue that the armed services have played a greater role in Canadian development than they have in Britain or the United States. The latter countries, however, demonstrate a more variegated attitude to their military legacy, and a similar equation of citizenship and militarism may have been deemed too controversial by government officials, if the notion struck them at all. By contrast, in a context where warfare in general is so closely affiliated with the existence and flourishing of Canada, the few critics of the new citizenship policy were called "silly," and cast as naïfs and "spouting" academics.[28]

Arthur Lower's previously cited anxieties over Canada's "two little peoples" and their "lost causes" and "tawdry ideals" points to another potential source of English Canada's celebration of its martial past: namely, an aura of insecurity. To its citizens, the nation may indeed exist – having been "born" or "made" or "forged" by an event or series of events. However, this act of naissance does not guarantee recognition or respect from others. As a junior partner in the wars of the twentieth century, as a "warrior nation" that only went into battle at the behest of more powerful international actors, the country seemed locked in a perpetual struggle to remain visible, to be taken seriously, to be treated as a mature and indispensable international player. While marching to war under the ultimate direction of other nations might simply confirm Canada's secondary rank, performing with distinction in those same wars could be parlayed into greater international recognition. Foreign conflict could, in other words, serve as both confirmation of, and cure for, subordinate status. "Canadians are almost always part of some larger enterprise," noted McKay and Swift, "whose supreme leadership resides with people from other countries. As if in compensation for their status ... Canadians have evinced an immense fascination in things military."[29]

We can see this sense of insecurity over the international standing of the nation – over prospects for its very survival – in various and often considerable efforts to downplay controversy or explicit challenges to the integrity of wartime Canada. As discussed previously, judges overseeing CO hearings destroyed court records because the documents "were full of hatred and bitterness and would have been a living menace to national unity." Official records from that same war's Canadian Expeditionary

Force were tightly controlled by the Department of National Defence historian Archer Duguid so that no writer would "embarrass" the soldiers or the nation through criticism of the war effort, an effort that for Duguid had finally furnished Canada with its own, and only, "national epic." While US historians such as Harry Elmer Barnes, Charles Beard, I.F. Stone, William Appleman Williams, and Walter LaFeber seemed to take a special delight in blasting away at America's contradictions, hypocrisies, and foibles, their Canadian counterparts were more likely to handle their nation's reputation with greater caution. For much of the twentieth century, the Canadian story rendered by historians was first and foremost a teleological and relatively benign account of the rise of self-government – from "colony to nation." University of Toronto historian Chester Martin's 1929 study *Empire and Commonwealth* called this meta-narrative the "transition from governance to self government in British North America." As such, "the iconoclastic temper," wrote Carl Berger of his nation's historiography, "expressed itself in Canada in a more tepid and limited fashion" than that witnessed in the United States or Europe.[30] Canadian historian Phillip Buckner concurred. "Until recently," he explained in 2004, "most Canadian historians were self-confessed nationalists and, though many present-day historians would deny the label, they continue to write from a nationalist perspective little different from that of their predecessors." Those whose primary goal is to acclaim and contribute to national progress, rather than impartially report on the nation, will shape their contributions accordingly. Here, Alan Gordon's observation comes to mind: "Historians have long been involved in the manufacture of national identity, as well as in its study" – some more candidly than others.[31]

The effects of such an orientation on the retelling of war stories are significant. Tough questions regarding Canada's military past could undermine the apparently precarious nation, while a more straightforward commemoration of war and the nation's unparalleled aptitude for soldiering could help to preserve and enhance the polity (and deflect potential slights from outsiders). As Margaret MacMillan wrote, "in countries that are, for whatever reason, lacking in self-confidence, the teaching of history can be an extremely sensitive matter." It is no surprise, then, that writers from the other Dominions – like Canada, relatively new nations overshadowed on the international stage by Britain and longing for greater notice – displayed similar traits. Their troops were, man-for-man, the most effective, their battles the most portentous, their considerable contributions perennially undervalued

in the histories of war penned by foreigners. It is this sensitivity that
also helps account for the relative dearth of humour, irony, farce, or
parody in Canadian war accounts, tropes which abound in the works of
US historians like Charles Beard and Walter Millis, or novelists Joseph
Heller and Kurt Vonnegut. "Only with the insecure," Richler offered,
"does humour becomes [sic] an assault on the fragile and ardently
defended construct of an ideology."[32]

Odes to the motif of insecurity, inferiority, invisibility, and the perceived ability of military sacrifice to vanquish them became recurrent
in English Canadian representations of the nation's wars. Participation in the South African War, claimed Canadian anglophiles of that
era, would speed the day when the underappreciated Dominion
would transcend Britain and become the centre of the empire. "We
have been children long enough," Colonel George T. Denison told a
meeting of the British Empire League at the war's outset, "let us show
the Empire that we have grown to manhood." While the lofty summit
as the empire's hub was never realized, a twenty-first-century writer
continued to hold that the unvarnished and brutish exercise in imperialism "bestowed on a recently independent Canada international
recognition, which is often only earned through military prowess and
sacrifice."[33]

But that recognition was seemingly incomplete, provisional, or illusory. Shortly after his country joined the First World War, Canadian
historian J. Castell Hopkins expressed relief that at long last, "Canada
was no longer an insignificant, dependent, unknown colony but a
nation with a nation's responsibilities." Others agreed that the twin
spectres of insecurity and invisibility had finally been vanquished
in Flanders. In a 1928 Queen's Quarterly article, political scientist and
Great War veteran (and alliteration enthusiast) Burton Hurd assured
readers that the conflict had at last "rid the public mind of the incubus
of an insidious inferiority complex. From 1914 dates a new tradition,"
he proclaimed, "a new sense of power, a new spirit of confidence."
In a Maclean's piece also published in 1928, war veteran, lawyer, and
future Progressive Conservative premier of Ontario George Drew produced a scalding indictment of the American pretense that the United
States had done most of the heavy lifting in the defeat of Germany. The
unpalatable corollary to the American version of events, noted Jonathan Vance, was that under this interpretation "the defence of Ypres
in 1915, the capture of Vimy Ridge, [and] the Hundred Days" became
minor events "that had little real impact on the outcome of the war."

Canada's substantial contribution to victory, so central to the project of recognition, was in danger of going unacknowledged. Drew's piece so resonated with slighted Canadians that *Maclean's* produced 100,000 offprints in order to meet demand.[34]

It was one thing for Canadians to assert that their army (and therefore their nation) had distinguished itself on the world stage; a respected foreigner making the same observation would strengthen the claim considerably. It was rare to find a popular Canadian high school text from the latter half of the twentieth century that did not include some portion of a quote from Lloyd George's *Memoirs* commending Canadian performance at the Battle of the Somme: *The Winds of Change* (1961) rendered it thusly: "Thenceforward they were marked out as storm troops; for the remainder of the war they were brought along to head the assault in one great battle after another." A textbook from the same era points out that it was an awestruck American war correspondent who reported that the Canadians' stand against the German gas attack at Ypres "was to be remembered as one of the heroic episodes of the war." Yet nearly a century after the Great War, Nathan Greenfield was still toiling to buttress the regard for Canada's contribution, penning an unequivocally heroic account of Canadian efforts at the Second Battle of Ypres. In addition to classifying *this* battle as the true "forging of Canada," Greenfield wrote *Baptism of Fire* to refute "those who believe that Canadian accomplishments are ipso facto second rate, or that there is something about Canadians that predisposes them, to borrow Jack Granatstein's phrase, to be 'the boy scouts of the world.'" "Second rate" heroics are not really heroics at all, and nations beholden to a boy scout mentality are nations that have yet to realize their full maturation and manhood. Seemingly – and despite Burton Hurd's 1928 guarantees that the nation had arrived – twenty-first-century Canadians were still battling the "incubus of an insidious inferiority complex." Pierre Berton recognized the power and stability of the complex in his 1986 account *Vimy*: "There is something a little desperate – a little wistful – in the commentaries of the twenties and thirties and even later, in which Canadians assured one another over and over again that at Vimy, Canada had at last found its maturity."[35]

The theme of Canada's international recognition – its perceived absence, and war's antidote to the ailment – would re-emerge with every deployment. Canadian General Rick Hillier bemoaned the fact that, despite the recognition bought by Vimy, by the Second World War Canada was again "much ignored by the rest of the world." Canada's contribution to the defeat of fascism allowed the nation to at last come "out of the shadows," as Brereton Greenhous and W.A.B. Douglas titled their record of Canada's role in the conflict. "Canada's effort was not essential to winning the war," they conceded, but added that the effort "was more than enough to win the respect of other nations and to earn for Canada a place in world affairs of a totally unprecedented kind." A textbook published in both languages at Canada's centenary, however, suggested the coming-out was ephemeral: "Canadians were disappointed both during the war and in later years that British and American news reporters and historians have concentrated upon the achievements of their own national forces and have found little space to deal with Canada's contributions." In 1950, Canadian journalists, politicians, and diplomats argued that participation in the Korean War would confirm Canada's new clout in a multinational world order and allow Americans to recognize their northern neighbours as "respected colleagues." However, these expectant Canadians soon "discovered that their voices were even less appreciated in *Pax Americana* than within *Pax Britannica*." General Hillier stressed recognition, rather than humanitarian or strategic goals, as the primary aim of the nation's military engagements – a kind of Canadian "grand strategy" that linked all conflicts from the South African War to the present. Hillier groused about the tendency to "fritter away Canadian impact through 'contributions' to larger missions" like the 1990s efforts in the Balkans, rather than taking on roles as distinct, and therefore conspicuous, Canadian units. When Canada was included on a *jihadist* hit list after 9/11, Captain Jon Hamilton of the Princess Patricia's Canadian Light Infantry told a Toronto reporter that "it was finally nice to be recognized by the enemy," to be "big enough to be recognized by guys who hate us, powerful enough to be recognized by those who hate Western society."[36]

In truth, and like Theodore Roosevelt's calls for regular military engagements in order to maintain America's national vigour, the use of warfare to confirm Canada's status as an authentic and internationally-respected nation is a never-ending project – despite the sovereignty and respect "won" at Paardeberg, or Vimy, or Juno, or Kapyong, as the case may be. Hence, as the Harper government announced that the Canadian mission in Afghanistan would end in 2014, *Globe and Mail* editors applauded the heightened international and domestic prestige they claimed the effort had purchased. "Canada earned respect within NATO," the *Globe* maintained. "The Canadian Forces gained in esteem among young people, who respected the military for doing battle against harsh odds ... And Canada at last shook off the myth of Canadian pacifism – of Canada almost solely as a peacekeeping nation, unable to shoot back – and reconnected with its past as a fighting force on the side of good, not shrinking from a challenge. Canada did its part with impressive resolve in an unwinnable counterinsurgency war."[37]

The passage groans under the weight of its internal contradictions, false assumptions, and uncorroborated claims. Simple appeals to right and wrong in this instance are muddled by the fact that "the side of good" included an Afghan government tainted by corruption, electoral fraud, entanglement in the drug trade, and the torture of prisoners handed over by Canadian forces. The notion of a "side of good" also had to accommodate an ISAF military legacy burdened by accidental and intentional civilian deaths, targeted, extra-judicial assassinations, and atrocities against soldier and civilian alike. The editors' claim that past peacekeeping efforts amounted to "shrinking from a challenge" would in fact face a vigorous challenge from the thousands of Canadian peacekeepers who had put themselves in harm's way since 1956, and witnessed more than one hundred of their countrymen die in an effort to forestall further violence in the globe's most hazardous zones. Finally, no explanation is provided as to why joining "an unwinnable counterinsurgency war" is a prudent expenditure of lives and resources – except, that is, by inference: Canada prevailed, according to the logic of the piece, by gaining respect. No evidence is provided to confirm that fellow NATO members or Canada's youth increased their affections for the nation and its military as a result of the mission, or that respect from these groups was lacking before this point. No matter: war, even when it cannot achieve its strategic or political aims, is ultimately and perpetually useful for a nation locked in a seemingly endless quest for esteem – the Hillier doctrine incarnate. The *Globe* editors themselves made the Sisyphusian nature of this project chillingly clear: "Enough is enough," they wrote of the admittedly unwinnable conflict that killed 158 Canadian soldiers and wounded more than 2000 others in body and untold numbers in spirit "– until the next one." As adventure novelist, stalwart imperialist, white supremacist, and fifteenth Governor General of Canada John Buchan wrote, "No great cause is ever lost or won, The battle must always be renewed, And the creed must always be restated."[38]

Faith in the ability of war-fighting to establish and burnish Canada's international reputation formed a central tenet of the Harper government's foreign policy, but it was a faith in the most literal sense – one sustained by longing and conviction, rather than empirical data.

We do, incidentally, possess data on why the global community has come to hold Canada in high regard – a standing confirmed by innumerable opinion surveys conducted since the mid-twentieth century. The nation's sterling reputation was achieved, if polls and foreign testimonials are to be believed, through its commitment to multilateralism, foreign aid, human rights, peacekeeping, mediation, North-South dialogue, bridge-building, disarmament, environmental protection, and the list of decidedly non-belligerent pursuits goes on. Evidence regarding the relationship between militarism and international standing could also be inferred by the 2010 failure of Canada to win a seat on the UN Security Council, a botched campaign overseen by a government that had cooled considerably to the attributes previously exalted in international polls, and warmed considerably to militarism and tough talk. Following that unprecedented snub, the Harper administration turned rejection into a virtue, replacing the earlier claim that greater bellicosity would earn international respect with the insistence that principle rather than any desire for approval drove the government's international agenda. Regardless of one's opinions on the suitability and efficacy of a more aggressive international posture, the evidence suggests Canadians should be wary of the oft-repeated platitude that global recognition "is often only earned through military prowess and sacrifice."[39] Nonetheless, the belief has exerted a strong influence over the ways the nation's wars have been justified and recalled.

Americans, too, have used the rationale of international recognition and prestige in calls to arms, though in that nation, the debate has taken on a different hue. Before the twentieth century, the discourses of prestige contained elements that would be recognizable to Canadians. At a time when the United States was still committed to isolationism, anti-imperialism, and small armies, some pro-war rhetoric found its basis in a desire to be recognized and play a more central role in world affairs. Supporters of the turn-of-the-twentieth-century "large policy" for American international relations argued that victory over Spain in 1898, along with a significant naval build-up, would force the Europeans to acknowledge and respect US power – sentiments in short supply in the capitals of Europe up to that point. In this, large policy advocates were quite successful. US diplomatic historian Norman Graebner told the story of a foreign diplomat in Washington who "observed that, although he had been at his post only a brief time, he had seen two different countries – the United States before the war with Spain, and the United States after the war." The latter incarnation was more self-assured, aggressive, outward-looking, and for European nations engaged in a bitter rivalry for foreign lands and peoples, now a potential ally or competitor. As a recent study of the US-European relationship pointed out, it was more than a case of simple well-wishing that led European heads of state to acknowledge Theodore Roosevelt's 1905 inauguration by showering the president with gifts; Kaiser Wilhelm II's present – a one-ton bronze bust of Kaiser Wilhelm II, towed to the White House by four overtaxed horses – was the most arresting, if not the most appreciated.[40] The two world wars would, of course, speed the rise of US economic, military, and political dominance, the Second providing the definitive confirmation that this would be "the American century." After 1945, going to battle in order to achieve international notice was no longer required. The nation could not fail to be discerned.

This did not mean, however, that wars would no longer be fought to enhance America's international image. As the world's undisputed hegemon, visibility was no longer at issue, but a new anxiety – credibility – seized the minds of American officials. US power would be fleeting, they reasoned, if the nation did not demonstrate a willingness to deploy it. According to this line of thinking, a disinclination to resort to war would only mean more war – and the nation would be forced to fight reactively, not at a time and place of its own choosing. "To sit by while Korea is overrun by unprovoked armed attack" argued State Department consultant and future Secretary of State John Foster Dulles "... would start [a] disastrous chain of events leading most probably to world war." The president corroborated the reasoning: "If aggression were allowed to succeed in Korea," Truman explained in a national radio address, "it would be an open invitation to new acts of aggression elsewhere." As the US involvement in Vietnam deepened, the doctrine of credibility helped to neutralise accusations that Americans were dying for a lost cause. Wrote Fredrik Logevall, "an early withdrawal from the war, so the argument went, would cause allies elsewhere in Asia and around the world to lose faith in the reliability of America's commitments and would embolden adversaries in Moscow and Beijing to pursue aggressive designs all over the globe." Credibility would later be trotted out as an underlying motivation for the Reagan administration's intercessions in Latin America, George H.W. Bush's call for a military response to Iraq's 1990 invasion of Kuwait, and interventions in Somalia and the Balkans under Bill Clinton. And once again, the Munich Conference – that most exceptional constellation of actors and circumstances – provided the cautionary tale, the iron law, and the ultimate rationale for the preference for shooting rather than talking.[41]

Case studies scrutinizing the creed suggest that the American pursuit of credibility through warfare could be just as quixotic as Canada's quest for recognition and influence via the same means. Logevall's analysis of the Vietnam War found that "neither friends nor foes around the world tended to see American credibility as being at stake in Vietnam." Indeed, the real threat to America's international standing concerned US support for the repressive South Vietnamese government, a point reiterated by diplomatic representatives from Britain, France, Japan, and Canada. By waging a ruthless and ultimately futile conflict to hold together an autocratic and incompetent state, America's image suffered permanent harm. The result, as the title to Logevall's study suggests, was "America Isolated." American political scientist Daryl Press took a macro approach to the credibility thesis, examining a range of twentieth-century crises to determine whether previous hesitations to use force by a given state had any influence on later perceptions of threat among that state's enemies. Press began his project convinced that he would finally confirm "that backing down reduced credibility," an article of faith among many governments and scholars that had never been confirmed by international relations theorists. Instead, he found that in case after case, the perceived power of a state actor at the moment of crisis, rather than any past hesitations to use that power, governed the behaviour of its adversaries. Chronic bluffer Nikita Khrushchev, for instance, issued an unending string of dire ultimatums in order to compel Western withdrawal from Berlin, withdrawal of foreign armies from Egypt during the Suez crisis, and American withdrawal of its naval blockade of Cuba. Press determined that Khrushchev's failure to act on his past threats had no effect on how seriously the West took the next one. The overarching question involved whether the Soviets possessed the means to follow through on the current warning. US adherence to the credibility doctrine, in Press's view, amounted to a "self-imposed rigidity created by excessive concern over its reputation." "Tragically," he wrote, "those countries that have fought wars to build a reputation for resolve have wasted vast sums of money and, much worse, thousands of lives."[42]

Citizens and officials of both Canada and the United States, then, have pointed war's salutary effects on their nation's international standing in order to justify participation in conflict and vindicate the losses incurred. The obvious national differences in the type of standing

already held, and the ways in which this rank could be altered or preserved through military action, raises a question. Are wars undertaken
by the world's preeminent power in order to maintain credibility less
vital to national identity, and thus less revered in collective remembrance, than wars said to galvanize national birth, maturation, and
global recognition? The prerogatives of credibility may serve to align
US policymakers behind calls for military action, and may prove inspirational to citizens confronting the international dilemma that their
leaders insist provides a test of America's standing. In the longer term,
however, these types of wars would not appear to carry the *gravitas*
and emotional appeal of contests synonymous with a nation's founding, coming-of-age, or arrival on the world stage. In other words, the
nature of the prestige sought, claimed, or attained bears come consideration. The fact that the two US conflicts most closely associated with
credibility – Korea and Vietnam – are also among the least popular in
American history may be instructive on this, although they also went
very badly. Swift triumph in both theatres would have seen these wars
commemorated in much different ways (although a certain percentage
of Americans would still consider them misadventures in imperialism).
It is nevertheless noteworthy that a similarly ambiguous and inconclusive campaign in Afghanistan has been called a Canadian success for its
ability to train the gaze of a range of actors – the nation's youth, NATO
allies, "those who hate Western society" – on the country and its martial
prowess. Lacking a similar battle with visibility, having attained the
unambiguous status of a hegemon, post-Second World War Americans
were presented a more difficult task in arguing that participation in a
foreign conflict in and of itself constituted any gain for the nation.

Certainly, one aspect of the war-as-nation-builder theme is indisputable: military campaigns routinely centralize and bureaucratize states,
swelling governmental authority and levels of taxation. However, other,
less mechanistic and more idealistic components of nation-building,
like unification of the citizenry and the protection and extension of their
highest principles, can easily be sabotaged by conflicts. This is perhaps
most evident in multiethnic countries organized, by necessity, around the
principle of civic nationalism. British historian Anthony Smith noted
that "every nationalism contains civic and ethnic elements in varying
degrees and different forms." Canadian political theorist Slobodan Drakulic concurred, pointing out that "nation-states have historically been
the states of some ethnies more than of others, in liberal or any other
polities, and that is because of their statism, which inevitably stratifies

ethnies as it does individuals and social groups." These processes have been especially evident in war, which by its nature stirs fears of disloyalty and sedition, of whether every individual and group is "doing their bit." While both Canadians and Americans can point to a proud legacy of civic nationalism based on adherence to liberal notions of equality and the rule of law, in times of international conflict, those positioned outside the dominant definition of citizenship have been harassed, silenced, and incarcerated. In this sense, the national ideal is at its most vulnerable in wartime, and thereafter must be painstakingly salvaged through the passage of time, through the recovery of the experiences of the ostracized, and sometimes, through formal apologies and monetary compensation.[43]

Here the story of francophone Paul Triquet is instructive. A Major in the Quebec-based Royal 22e Regiment (in the English press, the "Van Doos") during the Second World War, Triquet received the Victoria Cross for his bravery during the 1943 battle for Casa Berardi, Italy. Triquet's battlefield achievements heartened Canadians across the country, and perhaps none more so than the government officials who craved a genuine hero from Quebec in order to promote recruitment efforts, and later, the policy of conscription in that province (a policy that Triquet himself firmly opposed). Triquet, the only francophone and only Quebecer of the war's fourteen Canadian Victoria Cross recipients, returned to Canada before war's end and became an integral part of Ottawa's $30 million campaign to promote war bonds. From 1943 onward, as DND historian John MacFarlane explained in his biography of the Major, Triquet's story was deployed in service of a range of agendas: to demonstrate to English Canadians the loyalty and bravery of francophones; to remind Quebecers that their sons did indeed fight in wars that built the nation; to provide all Canadians with stories of anglophone-francophone cooperation and mutual sacrifice; to show that "good" francophones – those that supported and contributed to the pan-Canadian ideal in peace and war – would be rewarded and revered.[44]

The effects of these campaigns on the general public are harder to measure than the effects borne by Triquet himself. Uncomfortable with both public speaking and his designation as a hero, vilified by many in Quebec as a symbol of militarism and deference to English Canada and empire, and forced to maintain the sheen of role model by pretending that his failed marriage was intact, Triquet fell prey to anxiety, alcoholism, and violent outbursts. By 1947, he had become more of a burden than

8.2 A sculpture of Major Paul Triquet, one of the fourteen military figures in the Valiants Memorial that borders the National War Memorial in Ottawa. As biographer John MacFarlane noted, Triquet is largely forgotten in his home province. (Author photograph.)

an asset to the army's PR efforts, and was forcibly retired; he would spend much of his remaining years rebuilding his life and reputation.[45] The title of MacFarlane's biography – *Triquet's Cross* – provides an apt measure of the strain placed on individuals who are called upon to reconcile the divides hewn and aggravated by Canada's wars; in this sense, Triquet's own disintegration served as something of a metaphor for that of national harmony under the duress of war.

The Democratic Party well understood this notion of war as a potential nation-destroyer when it unveiled its official platform for the 1900 federal election midst the ongoing battle in the Philippines. "We oppose militarism," it stated. "It means conquest abroad and intimidation and oppression at home. It means the strong arm which has ever been fatal to free institutions. It is what millions of our citizens have fled from Europe ... We denounce it as un-American, un-Democratic, and un-Republican, and as a subversion of the ancient and fixed principles of a free people." More recently, Noah Richler made the rather indisputable claim that the greatest threats to the integrity of Canada lie within rather than without – chief among them the persistent challenge to reconcile the identities and aspirations of French- and English-Canadians.[46] Given the rifts along these lines generated and exacerbated by the nation's participation in international conflict, the hazards surrounding attempts to consecrate the nation's wars as the ultimate marker of Canadian-ness and arbiter of belonging are rather obvious. If war, to extend Randolph Bourne's aphorism, is the health of the state, it can also be a virus to the nation.

All of this is not to deny that deploying military history in the project of nation-building holds obvious advantages in both Canada and the United States: it draws on events whose magnitude renders them unforgettable, providing a common script for citizens of various ethno-cultural backgrounds; it tells a story of moral certitude and victory (with Korea, Vietnam, Iraq, and Afghanistan providing more complex storylines), buttressing the sense of special national mission; it brings purpose to the tragedy of death and physical and mental injury; it reminds citizens of their nobility and selflessness in rescuing foreign peoples from aggression and tyranny; it recalls a time when the disparate identities, loyalties, interests, and the petty grievances and disharmony that accompanied them were set aside, and the nation worked as one to overcome an existential threat. All of these claims are both warranted and somewhat more complicated than often advertised; the last in particular – the mythology of unity – has served as something of a perennial agitator, with those extolling the myth susceptible to undermining the very unity they pursue.[47]

In spite of these perils, many Americans and Canadians have looked to war as mechanism for building, reinvigorating, and defining their respective nations. In the United States, the belief that American progress depends on "violent, regenerative warfare" is both the source and outcome of a more violent approach to foreign affairs. Such a conviction has helped to propel the nation into war, and served to defend the war's legacy thereafter. These beliefs have not, however, inured particular wars from an iconoclastic gaze: only one conflict, the Revolutionary War, wears the sanctity of fashioning the nation, and it follows that this clash would be the least controversial, and most admired, in the nation's annals. Canadians, many of them determined to locate a gripping founding epic but unsettled on where each war ranks on the nation-building register – and unsettled, too, about their status as a bona fide nation and respected (or just plain visible) international presence – have handled their wartime past with greater measures of cautiousness and reverence. It is a general bearing that the government of Prime Minister Harper sought, with some success, to make the most of.

Conclusion

Warrior Nation? Few would deny the United States a claim to this title. From the earliest days of European settlement, relations between indigenous peoples and European colonizers served as a consistent source of violent, and sometimes apocalyptic, confrontations in the lands that would become the United States. The years that followed the founding of the nation – here again, through armed conflict – would see this trend continue, as Euro-American expansion and battles over resources fomented a series of genocidal clashes with indigenous groups that ground on until the turn of the twentieth century. In the meantime, Americans inaugurated conflicts with Britain, Mexico, Spain, and each other, and deployed force on dozens of occasions, along with the perpetual threat of force, in order to establish and maintain dominance over Latin America after formal European empires departed the hemisphere. And, as those who long for the return of a more irenic and circumspect America point out, these were the quiet years. Two world wars, most pointedly the second, along with the postwar challenge from a reviled ideological foe helped to inspire an American internationalism whose scope knows no rival in history, and one constructed and sustained through a variety of means: political, economic, cultural, and ultimately, martial. The predictable result has included the construction of a global network of interests, military bases, and alliances, along with military encounters large and small. War, in other words, has been a constant in American history, a tool employed recurrently to address a range of problems. As historian Kenneth Rose lamented in *Myth and the Greatest Generation: A Social History of Americans in World War II*, "virtually every American generation since the early 17th century [... has] had its own war." Harry Elmer Barnes, employing a phrase taken from his 1947 conversation with Charles Beard, decried the trend as "perpetual war for perpetual peace," an axiom that later served as the title to historian Robert Divine's damning analysis of the US appetite for war.[1]

The despair expressed by Rose, Barnes, Beard, and Divine over the persistence of warfare in American history points to another verity about this nation of warriors: the deeply held conviction among significant numbers of Americans that it was not supposed to turn out this way. *Europe* was the site of perpetual conflict, a fact that motivated a good deal of the migration from the old world to the new, as well as George Washington's admonitions against international alliances. Sharing a widespread and honestly earned fear of standing armies and of the anti-democratic pressures that warfare exerted on the polity, the Constitution's framers sought to make participation in war difficult and rare, and Americans expressed disapproval though not surprise when European monarchies marched off to war at regular intervals in their seemingly endless contest for imperial aggrandizement. The United States, by contrast, was surrounded by great oceans and weak states, providing an unprecedented (one might say "exceptional") opportunity for a peaceful foreign policy, one freed from the impulse to dominate others. The wisdom of such an outlook was reinforced by the increasing variety of immigrants from Europe and around the world, creating a society whose harmony would be riven by instigating or joining foreign fights.

An amalgam of analysts, interests, domestic pressures, and foreign events moved US administrations towards an increasingly militant international posture (remembering that militancy was the default setting towards indigenous groups from the beginning) and eventually, a quest for global hegemony. In manoeuvring the nation thusly, however, "large policy" champions – if that Gilded Age moniker may be extended more generally to advocates of robust and primarily unilateralist internationalism – were required to surmount the various and intersecting legal, cultural, and demographic constraints on war-making. Foreign military engagements thus became synonymous with simplistic, sanctimonious, and often outlandish justifications, the repression of minorities who opposed the mission or were seen as a threat to its execution, and a clampdown on dissent from those alarmed by these government dissipations. These unsavory by-products of warfare also help to explain the government's fondness for taking action covertly so as to preserve the administration's domestic and international reputation and circumvent the deterrents to warfare imposed by American ideals, popular opinion, and the Constitution.

There are many responses to this tension between American self-concept, values, and law, on the one hand, and the emergence of a warrior nation on the other. Many Americans, Robert Divine noted, simply continued to "think of themselves as a peace-loving people and the United States as a peaceful nation." Others embraced a warrior ethos as a necessary posture for a nation granted a special mission to transform the world in its own image. A third response involves an appeal to the ideals that promised a more pacific national experiment – anti-imperialism, anti-militarism, a constrained executive, popular sovereignty, government transparency, the rule of law – and emphasizes war's threat to these, the very notions that were supposed to set the nation apart. The popularity of this more defiant and idealistic response to war has fluctuated, sometimes with alarming speed and intensity, over the course of American history. Indeed, this variability in American public opinion serves as one of the leitmotifs of this study. Randolph Bourne observed the phenomenon firsthand after Congress gave assent to Woodrow Wilson's request for war. "The Middle West," Bourne wrote, "which had been soddenly pacifistic in our days of neutrality, became in a few months just as soddenly bellicose, and in its zeal for witch-burning and its scent for enemies within gave precedence to no section of the country." Following the war, Walter Lippmann generalized about the influence of US public opinion over foreign policy, arguing that the people had "compelled the government ... to be ... too pacifist in peace and too bellicose in war, too neutralist or appeasing in negotiation or too intransigent."[2]

Now any group of people confronted with the paradox outlined above – that believed they were meant to break the mould of the European penchant for armies, warfare, and foreign adventurism, but found themselves passing through the same wide gate on the broad way to militarism and empire – would offer some resistance to these developments. The fact that, at critical junctures, the American public was prodded along on this course via deceit and cant only intensified the opposition to these developments. However, what gave war opponents their special authority – and what also helps to account for some of the pointed oscillations in public opinion cited above – was that a good deal of their resistance relied on tools and traditions that their fellow citizens would recognize as intrinsically American. The sanctity of individual conscience – referred to by eighteenth-century evangelicals as

the "inner light," endorsed in the Bill of Rights, and extolled by governments as that quality which separated them from their enemies (even as
those same governments hounded those who took the principle most
seriously) – served as a durable building-block of war opposition. So
too did the notions that government is by nature a threat to liberty
and that true citizen loyalty was synonymous with the surveillance of
the state, a task that a free and inherently adversarial press was also
expected to carry out.

These purportedly core American ideals and traditions did not prevent authorities from running roughshod over them, especially in the
national crises precipitated by war; in this task, officials were often
joined enthusiastically by the press and the general population, whose
fear, self-interest, xenophobia, and racism frequently trumped allegiance to principle. In this respect, hypocrisy looms especially large in
the American story, as time and again the nation fell well short of its
often loudly professed creed. But in another respect, the undeniable
(and bountiful) violations of national dogma simply rendered some
citizens *more* hostile towards official policy, and made revered martyrs
of those who kept the faith in the midst of overwhelming coercion to do
otherwise; as such, historians and others have anointed many of these
stubbornly idealistic citizens as the nation's truest patriots. Minority
groups with the critical mass to influence national discourse have also
served as firsthand and voluble witnesses to the fact that America's
fitness for global leadership has been impaired by the unsatisfactory
implementation of liberty and equality at home, and to the fact that
the nation fought for a host of reasons beyond the perennial mantra of
delivering freedom to the downtrodden.

Plainly, none of these critical appraisals of American militarism prevented the triumph of a fundamentally bellicose foreign posture, and
in general these views have been in the minority. At the same time, the
presence and intensity of a critical posture towards American militarism is the consequence of a specific set of historical ideas and developments that have provided war opponents with a relatively consistent
and potent catalogue of objections. And at times, this critical bearing
has exerted substantial impact over the direction of US foreign policy:
in the first years of the twentieth century prior to American entry into
the Great War, when antiwar organizations and discourses proliferated; in the interwar efforts to curb the buildup of arms and the profits
of munitions manufacturers; in the movement to end the US presence
in Vietnam; and in the 1980s protests against the arms race that helped

move the Reagan administration towards reconciliation with the Soviets, to cite some of the more notable examples. At other times, intensive public efforts to prevent war simply fell on deaf ears. Responding in February 2003 to the largest antiwar protests in the United States since the Vietnam War (mass demonstrations against a merely *hypothetical* conflict, for the invasion was only a proposition at the time), President George W. Bush granted "that people are allowed to express their opinion," but added, "you know, size of protests – it's like deciding, 'Well, I'm going to decide policy based upon a focus group.' The role of a leader is to decide policy based upon, in this case, the security of the people."[3] At times, too, American critics of their nation's military legacy from across the political spectrum overreached in their attempts "to lambaste the United States for every crime imaginable," to reprise William Stueck's charge, fabricating accusations and theorizations that inhabited the realm of the grotesque and the loony, and that proved fundamentally counterproductive to their cause. US public debates over war, in other words, have proven exceptionally lively, freewheeling, messy, and sometimes hysterical. The "paranoid style in American politics," as Richard Hofstadter labelled it, has remained a durable trope in considerations of the rise of this warrior nation.

Canada's claim to warrior status is less straightforward. Its legal independence emerged in stages, and did not rely on the gun. It has avoided civil war. Armed conflict between indigenous groups and Euro-Canadians has been sporadic and brief when compared to the United States. Canada has never initiated an international conflict or invaded another country for territorial gain. As with (and to a great extent because of) the United States, Canada has not lived with any imminent threat of invasion for much of its history, at least not since its southern neighbour put aside any talk of sending its armies across the 49th parallel. Indeed, Canada has been blessed with what Margaret MacMillan rightly called "an extraordinary period, unusual in much of the world's history, of peace."[4] Canada did join the two world wars at their inception, though at the behest and under the ultimate direction of others, a scenario that also describes the nation's participation in the South African and Korean wars. At the end of the Second World War, Canada took a leading role in creating the United Nations and the idea of UN peacekeeping, instruments designed to discourage the use of force as a tool of foreign policy and to restore order in areas where conflict did emerge. On the other hand, while the Canadian government may have opted out of the Vietnam War, 30,000 Canadians volunteered

9.1 Ottawa native Mike Touchette (left) at a base in South Vietnam, summer 1968. Although often overlooked in the chronicle of the Vietnam War, roughly 30,000 Canadians fought to preserve the government of South Vietnam. Mike is wearing a Canadian beret with a Governor General's Foot Guards cap badge, signifying the unit in which he served prior to joining the US Army. (From the 1991 video *Canadian Images of Vietnam - 1965–1970*, photographer unknown, ©RRProductions, used with permission of Rob Ridgen, Province of Yukon archivist.)

in the US military's campaign aimed at preserving South Vietnam. Moreover, while Canada was an enthusiastic supporter of peacekeeping, it was hardly a neutral party in the superpower standoff, often using peacekeepers to protect and advance national interests. In sum, Canada's legacy in matters of war and peace is considerably variegated and defies any single label.

The insistence from some quarters that soldiering makes up Canada's primary identity is therefore complicated. As suggested above, when compared to much of the rest of the world, the nation has been a haven of peace for generations. On several occasions its soldiers have been summoned to foreign wars and played important roles in those conflicts, but there is nothing approaching the war-per-generation ratio that has marked four centuries of America's past, or the levels of collective violence faced by Europeans, or indeed most of the globe, over that same span. Moreover, the embrace of a warrior posture among modern Canadians would appear most apt in an unchanging world where, as political realists maintain, interstate warfare is both a constant and a prerequisite for survival. Such thinking overlooks a number of important considerations that have led to a marked deflation in the warrior image in other parts of the world. For one, the globe is more peaceful at present than at any time in history, and aside from Vladimir Putin's disgraceful but limited incursions into the territory of his weaker neighbours, interstate military conflicts have been all-but banished from previously war-prone Europe and are nearly as inconceivable elsewhere (in part because of the commitment to collective security, international law, mediation, and peacekeeping that Canada helped to nurture). By the end of the twentieth century, a growing number of political and military analysts had arrived at the conclusion that "people no longer believed that war was an effective instrument of policy, that 'victory' would ever be worth the price." Again, Margaret MacMillan: "Ways of thinking change, and what seemed perfectly normal two centuries ago is now quite literally unthinkable. War and conquest used to be quite standard ways of shifting boundaries about." In a similar vein, confronting terrorism and civil conflict with brute force has proven less effective than many of its advocates advertised, with even "victories" often effecting only short term gains that spawn unintended consequences and more violence in the longer run. To many, "warriors" are no longer the most suitable emblems of the national character. James Sheehan's book *Where Have All the Soldiers Gone?: The Transformation of Modern Europe* demonstrates how deeply much of that continent has repudiated the celebration of warriors, and the old notion that armed conflict was a "source of heroism, discipline, and comradeship from which a new political order could be built."[5]

Canadian defenders of the warrior ethos are apt to point out peacekeeping is a spurious template for the nation's image because, prior to the "aberration" of peacekeeping, Canadians took sides and fired at the enemy. It is certainly true that Canada's role as a peacekeeper is not as longstanding as its record of military engagements, nor can it be, international peacekeeping having been conceived only after the Second World War. Perhaps it is the case that nations, like international governance in general, can change, evolve, and adapt. English Canadians were

once proud to call themselves imperialists, too, but this undeniable historic fact is not perceived as an indelible marker of identity. Some ideas
simply outlive their usefulness, and come to be seen as the detritus of
an earlier, less-enlightened age. Tony Judt put it this way:

> Europe experienced the twentieth century – invasion, occupation, civil
> war, anarchy, massacres, genocide, and the descent into barbarism – to a
> degree unmatched anywhere else. The risks inherent in a 'war of choice'
> (Iraq), or the abandonment of international agencies in favor of unilateral
> initiative, or an excessive reliance on military power, are thus clearer to
> Europeans than most peoples ... The United States, by contrast, had no
> direct experience of the worst of the twentieth century – and is thus regret-
> tably immune to its lessons.[6]

If Canada's status as a warrior nation is a complicated matter in an
objective sense (i.e., in the measurable impact its soldiers have had
on national – and relative to fighters from other states – international
development), that status is arguably more verifiable in an imaginative sense (i.e., in the widespread esteem English Canada has afforded
the nation's wars, along with esteem's more reserved collaborator, the
hesitation to disrupt the broad national regard for Canada's military
record). Once again, Tony Judt's characterization of Americans' faith
in warfare and their immunity to its lessons bears some resemblance
to the attitude among many in Canada, who were likewise spared
firsthand experience with "the worst of the twentieth century." As this
study has argued, where Americans have been subjected to a dominant
account of military glory *as well as* a less-common but still powerful
challenge to the epic view of their nation at war, fewer and generally
more guarded examples of the latter have been available to English
Canadians. Instead, the ideas that war has served as a positive force in
Canadian development; that the nation fought on the side of good and
for all the right reasons; and that its soldiers perennially punched above
their weight, turned the tide of previously intractable conflicts, and
habitually conducted themselves with honour and bravery, have been
disrupted more rarely and more cautiously in Canadian reckonings.

This is not to deny the presence of antiwar attitudes and activism
among Canadians of various identities and eras. As discussed, peace
and disarmament movements enjoyed relatively strong support at various junctures, and often in the years when these causes also gained
favour in the United States: most notably, between the world wars,

during the American phase of the Vietnam conflict, and in response to the Reagan military buildup. What is more, in the latter half of the twentieth century, Canadians developed a genuine fondness for UN peacekeeping and relished their identity as one of the globe's foremost practitioners of the craft (a bearing that also carried an implicit critique of their more pugnacious neighbour). But in the case of wars in which Canada played a combat role, reverence, respect, glorification, and a desire to guard and enhance the reputation of the nation and its soldiers have prevailed in English-Canadian popular and scholarly histories and cultural production in general. Again, all of these tendencies are alive and well in American remembrance, but so too is a censorious "reverse-heroic" mode whose scope and depth is unmatched in Canada.

Recent efforts to equate soldiering with the highest form of citizenship, in McKay and Swift's words, to "rebrand" Canada as a nation of war-fighters, represent the most exaggerated and coordinated example of these phenomena. While it is difficult to ascertain the degree to which average Canadians warmed to these efforts, the rebranding campaign was not created *ex nihilo*, as it drew on (and amplified considerably) themes and idioms already in circulation. The campaign was able to make use of a favourable calculation of Canada's wars that has roots in the nation's emotional and blood ties to the British Empire, as well as a political culture that, in comparison to that of the United States, has placed greater faith in authority and greater power in the hands of governing elites. The historic symbiosis between church and state is also part of the story (most germane to the first half of the twentieth century), along with a desire to confirm that Canada is a bona fide nation and international power deserving respect (an ongoing project). To a significant degree, the rebranding initiative can be seen as merely the latest deployment of warfare as a means of fixing a single image of Canadian-ness, to at last vanquish the notion that the nation lacks unity, an identity, and an international eminence. In so doing, as suggested in Chapter 8, advocates for Canada as a "warrior nation" are doing battle with an extant and substantially affirmative image of the country held by many in the global community, an image built upon values, traditions, and initiatives rather different than those championed by Canada's "new warriors."

While the above factors did much to create a consensus of favourable opinion towards Canada's wars, this study has suggested that a measure of that consensus is illusory, that the construction of positive opinions has relied upon a longstanding underestimation or erasure of contrapuntal views and potentially disruptive facets to the affirming story of war. Those for whom the wars were not "good" have received considerably more attention from American chroniclers; likewise, ineffective or dishonourable troop performance – to varying degrees, an unavoidable characteristic of any nation engaged in conflict – has played a smaller role in Canadian accounts. The accent on consensus, orderliness, fair play, and respect has long been employed by Canadians as a means of differentiating themselves from Americans, and from certain angles, the stance has merit. These traits can also be overstated, and at times have been imposed from above – both by governmental regimes of the day and subsequent histories of Canada's conflicts – rather than emerging as an organic expression of the Canadian "character." This is another way of saying that Canada's endorsement of its wars, while widespread, is not as profound as the existing historical literature and cultural record implies. The damage done to English-French relations has certainly not gone unnoticed, but as we have seen, many anglophone writers have not been kind to francophone war opponents, or sympathetic to their grievances. Undue English-Canadian criticism of wars opposed by many French Canadians, by extension, could be read as a tacit admission that francophone hesitations proved prescient. "Our history books describe that controversy," Robert Fulford wrote of the 1917 Conscription Crisis, "but they don't mention the quite lively possibility that on this issue Quebec was absolutely right and the rest of Canada totally wrong."[7] Deploying a comparative approach to these matters reveals that French Canadians, routinely cast in English-language war accounts as backward, parochial agrarian relics, expressed attitudes to imperialism, militarism, and their country's responsibilities to Europe that would have resonated with significant numbers of Americans – many of whom claimed the label "progressive."

The relative dearth of critical assessments of Canada's military activities can also be traced back to specific characteristics of the writing of the country's military history. At times, government records on military operations were carefully guarded by official historians so that unsympathetic writers would not embarrass the nation or the armed forces through disclosures of failure, misconduct, or controversy. The "iconoclastic temper" did not seize Canadian practitioners the way it did in the United States and Britain, as Carl Berger observed, and for much of the twentieth century the ideological variation witnessed among the writers of American history was not as discernible in Canada. The "new" or Progressive history, revisionism, and the New Left scholarship, all of which stimulated lively critiques of the military impulse in the US, found few supporters among Canadian war chroniclers. Throughout this era, many leading Canadian historians were self-confessed nationalists, noted Philip Buckner, eager to promote the survival and flourishing of a nation whose prospects were sometimes doubted. Each of these dynamics portends an analysis of Canada's wars that is mostly affirming, and each echoes the more general response to war among the wider anglophone population. There is nothing peculiar about this symbiosis, as historians both reflect and shape popular opinion. Something less explicable happened in the last decades of the century: the field of Canadian history broadened markedly, but the writing of military history proved resistant to these innovations. "The non-porous nature of the parapets around military history," offered Canadian historian Laurel Halladay, "goes a long way toward explaining the animosity most new left or post-modern historians exhibit when faced with the work the field generates."[8]

American historians of the same generation, meanwhile, continued to broaden the study of American wars by applying approaches that were by turns innovative, disputatious, faddish, provocative, and often critical of the ways in which unequal power relations are sustained and challenged. In other words, many of these approaches carried with them intrinsic suspicions of state-sponsored violence, recognizing its capacity for building and maintaining elite control over foreign and domestic audiences alike. A range of scholars of various – and especially for the field of history, non-traditional – identities were drawn to the field, analysing the ways in which the tumult of war created the conditions to both reinforce and confront the subordinate status of women, minorities, and other aggrieved groups. The variety and volatility of US war discourses, longstanding characteristics of that population's ruminations on the subject, were thus further enhanced.

Halladay contended that similar developments in Canadian war historiography would more fully represent the interests and identities of an increasingly diverse population, and "thus do more for unity, patriotism and the military field than virtually anything that has already been written."[9] Canadian writer Randy Boyagoda made a similar point in a 2011 op-ed to the *Globe and Mail*, arguing for the greater internationalization of Canadians' understandings of war. Such a broadening of vision, Boyagoda held, would lead to a fuller comprehension of both the effects of conflict and the historical experiences of newer arrivals to the country. In his words,

> Fostering a more complex sense of the past is important for a pluralist
> country like contemporary Canada, in terms of maintaining its connec-
> tion to historic world events like the Second World War while also trying
> to engage and reflect the current concerns and historical experiences of
> its newer immigrant groups, from regions like North Africa and South
> Asia. Discerning unities between Canada's long-established peoples and
> its more recent immigrant communities would foster a shared sense of
> historical experience ... To that end, we should increasingly recognize
> more than European-origin Canadians and their descendants in the sto-
> rylines of war commemorations. Doing so would preserve, reflect, and
> enhance appreciation of our unexpectedly shared experiences, both heroic
> and tragic.[10]

Here, the obligations and opportunities of citizenship become dialecti-
cal. It is not only immigrants who must acknowledge the heroism and
sacrifice of Canadian soldiers (i.e., the Canadian Citizenship Guide
mandate); longer-term citizens may also gain a fuller understanding
of momentous events (and of their new neighbours) by learning how
episodes like the world wars affected populations beyond Canada's
borders. For nations like Canada and the United States that have been
spared direct experience of "the worst of the twentieth century," the
potential for enhanced understanding is considerable.

For those who share Halladay and Boyagoda's desire for new directions in Canadian understandings of war, there is significant reason for
optimism. As pointed out on several occasions in previous chapters,
more recent histories of Canada at war have begun to contest long-held
assumptions and approaches, and many of the critiques offered in this
volume of the straightforward, and often epic, nation-building framework of war representation have been drawn from these newer efforts.
Works from the likes of Margaret MacMillan, Jonathan Vance, Tim
Cook, Jeffrey Keshen, Amy Shaw, Ian McKay and Jamie Swift, Noah
Richler, Andrew Iacocca, and Laurel Halladay, to name but a few, demonstrate new ways to understand, complexify, and more fully colour in
Canada's military past. A few of the older generation of war writers –
Desmond Morton in particular – have also demonstrated an openness
to challenge the authorized version and dismantle orthodoxies.

The novelty of these approaches – in the sense of both their inno-
vativeness and their recent emergence – means that it will take time
and effort to introduce new angles of vision into the established, public narratives on war. And embarking on these new journeys is not

without its personal perils. As US historian Emily Rosenberg noted in her discussion of her nation's "history wars" of the 1990s, historians who confronted cherished national mythologies surrounding the Second World War, who drew attention to the myriad experiences and sometimes-contradictory understandings of the conflict among Americans and foreigners alike, were hounded for their "lack of patriotism" and their predisposition to "tamper with sacred national memories." Historians Tom Englehardt and Edward Linenthal, writing of the same era's titanic public battles over the meaning of war, remarked that they and their colleagues were placed "in the uncomfortable position of being blamed for creating the very problems whose complexities they set out to explore."[11]

The stakes are much higher, however, for those compelled to conduct military operations in the name of the population as a whole, for the foreign peoples caught up in those same operations, and for domestic minority groups brought under suspicion for their ethnic ties to potential enemies abroad. To them we owe an unencumbered, honest, and comprehensive conversation about war's efficacy, costs, and consequences, one that places abstract notions such as national pride, glory, and recognition on a lower plane than candid evaluations of war's impact on soldiers, civilians, domestic commitments to tolerance and the rule of law, and the cause of international stability and justice. Over the course of the twentieth century, Americans demonstrated a greater readiness to wrestle with this broad range of their wars' consequences than Canadians. And while these efforts did not forestall the rise of a militant empire, one can only speculate about the nature and number of foreign adventures and imbroglios the world's dominant power would have involved itself in (either through its own initiatives or via the appeals of others) without the leavening influence of America's war detractors. Canadians can be grateful that they do not face the same demands and incentives for the continual deployment of their military forces. A more "honest and soul-searching" approach to Canada's past wars, to echo the plea made by Major John R. Grodzinski, would provide Canadians a greater capacity to adjudicate the potential costs and benefits the next time such an appeal arises, as it always does.

Notes

Introduction

1 Morton, *Canada and War,* 1; Scowen, *Rogue Nation,* 28.

2 Brewer, *Why America Fights,* 9.

3 Miller, "Endgame for the West in Afghanistan?"; Bacevich, *The New American Militarism,* 2.

4 "Courageous warriors" cited in Lawrence Martin, "Harper Has Reached the Pinnacle – Now What?," *Globe and Mail,* 12 July 2011; Richler, *What We Talk About,* 65; McKay and Swift, *Warrior Nation;* Fellman, "Let's Talk about Creeping Canadian Militarism," *The Tyee,* 23 May 2007. http://thetyee.ca/Views/2007/05/23/CanMilitarism/, accessed 17 January 2012.

5 Richler, *What We Talk About,* 73–4. The author concludes that the effort could not eradicate affections for peacekeeping, which he claims are resurgent in the aftermath of an inconclusive and unpopular contribution to the War in Afghanistan (ibid., 323).

6 Dyer, *Canada in the Great Power Game,* 2.

7 Bercuson and Wise, *The Valour and the Horror Revisited,* 3; Andrew Bacevich made a similar point about the relative inability to effect radical changes in national trajectories over the course of one administration. He argued that the post-9/11 bellicosity of the Bush administration was no substantial realignment of American foreign affairs, but the elaboration of policies, sentiments, and trends deeply seated in that nation's history and culture (*The New American Militarism,* 4–5).

8 As discussed in Chapter 3, Canadian and American objectives surrounding the Great War could demonstrate considerable variance. Both nations, of course, sought the defeat of the Central Powers; however, Canada fought candidly for the preservation of the British Empire, while

President Woodrow Wilson made self-determination and the dismantling of empires central pillars of his nation's war aims.

9 Winter and Prost, *The Great War in History*, vii. Recognition of the value of comparative war studies led to the 1938 establishment of the International Commission of Comparative Military History, an organization still in existence (Douglas, "Marching to Different Drums," 249n22).

10 Morton, *A Military History of Canada*, x; Morton, *Canada and War*, 1; Schurman, "Writing About War," 231, 241; Creighton, *Dominion of the North*, 439; Creighton, *Canada's First Century*, 132; Stanley, *Canada's Soldiers*; Jack Granatstein, "Canada Always Was a Warrior Nation," *Ottawa Citizen*, 2 September 2012; Horn, *The Canadian Way of War*, 15; Hillier cited in ibid.

11 "Canada has never been a true 'nation-state,'" argued political scientist Shauna Wilton, who pointed to the failure of a succession of state-sponsored efforts to define a single and accepted concept of nationhood. "Today," Wilton offered, "Canada may be 'post-national' according to a more traditional definition of the nation on the basis of common or shared language, ethnicity and history" (Wilton, "Immigration Policy and Literature," 26); Brebner, *The North Atlantic Triangle*, xxv. For an unflattering discussion of the origins of the concept of the "Anglosphere" and its implications, see John Lloyd, "The Anglosphere Project," *New Statesman*, 13 March 2000. Lloyd writes, "This idea, or rather cluster of ideas, has similar origins – in the Anglo-American intellectual right, a milieu at once self-confident, vengeful, well funded and very sharp. It is based on the belief that the transatlantic right needs some kind of coherent internationalist vision to set against the corporatist European Union."

12 Chalmers Johnson, "America's Unwelcome Advances," *Mother Jones*, 21 August 2008, http://www.motherjones.com/politics/2008/08/americas -unwelcome-advances; Laicie Heeley, "U.S. Defense Spending vs. Global Defense Spending," *The Center for Arms Control and Non-proliferation*, April 24, 2013, http://armscontrolcenter.org/issues/securityspending/articles/ 2012_topline_global_defense_spending/, (accessed 7 February 2014).

13 While not denying that some returning veterans faced a hostile reaction, sociologist and Vietnam veteran Jerry Lembcke argued that stories of soldiers being spat upon or called "baby killers" represented urban myths crafted by those who sought to discredit antiwar activists. See Lembcke, *The Spitting Image*.

14 In his study of the seventeenth-century American Puritanism, for example, Miller took the "liberty of treating the whole literature as though it were the product of a single intelligence." (Miller, *The New England Mind*, vii). On the preliminary obituaries for the nation-state, see, for instance, Guéhenno, *The End of the Nation-State*. The collapse of communism,

the author argued, "marks the close of an era ... It brings an end to the age of nation-states" (x). Antonio Gramsci remains the most influential commentator on the ways power operates to create "hegemonic discourse" and notions of "common sense" among societies, and the ways hegemony can both absorb oppositional ideas and be transformed by them. For a good recent introduction to Gramscian thought and its influence, see Schwarzmantel, "Introduction," 1–16.

15 I use the term "English Canada" here and throughout broadly, to represent regions that feature an anglophone majority.

16 Halladay, "Renegotiating National Boundaries," 7; Berger, *The Writing of Canadian History*, 10. On the ways that tangible antiwar sentiment has been systematically downplayed in Canadian historiography, see Lara Campbell, Michael Dawson, and Catherine Gidney, "Introduction: War Resistance in Canadian History," in Campbell, Dawson, and Gidney, *Worth Fighting For*.

17 Here I have pinched a phrase from Davies, *The Deptford Trilogy*, 775.

18 Judt, *Reappraisals*, 6; Lower cited in McKay and Swift, *Warrior Nation*, 6.

19 On this point and in innumerable other instances throughout the text, I am indebted to the anonymous readers at the University of Toronto Press for helping to clarify my ideas and suggesting language that would assist me in doing so.

1 Conflict in the Age of High Imperialism

1 For an analysis of post 9/11 exaltation of the US military, see William Deresiewicz, "An Empty Regard," *New York Times*, 21 August 2011; Vandenberg cited in Perez, *The War of 1898*, 42. For a post-Cold War example of the embrace of the idea of empire, see Kagan, "The Benevolent Empire"; for a survey of the growth of this outlook after 9/11, see Hitchens, "Imperialism"; Bacevich, *The New American Militarism*; Boggs, *Imperial Delusions*; Goodman, *National Insecurity*; Boggs and Pollard, *The Hollywood War Machine*.

2 Atwood, *Selected Poems*, 70; Mowat cited in Azzi, "The Nationalist Moment in English Canada," 214. On recent Canadian opinion, see Scowen, *Rogue Nation*; Christopher Marquis, "World's View of U.S. Sours After Iraq War, Poll Finds," *New York Times*, 4 June 2003; Margaret Atwood, "Letter to America," *Globe and Mail*, 28 March 2003. Wrote Atwood: "When the Jolly Green Giant goes on the rampage, many lesser plants and animals get trampled underfoot."

3 The list of major US conflicts includes the War of Independence, the War of 1812, the Mexican-American War, the American Civil War, the War of 1898, the First World War, the Second World War, the Korean War, the

Vietnam War, the Gulf War, the Iraq War, and the Afghanistan War. It does not include the numerous campaigns against indigenous peoples, which American policymakers considered domestic or civil conflicts, conclusions at variance with the many indigenous groups who considered themselves autonomous nations. See Rubenstein, *Reasons to Kill*, 2. Canada's wars include the South African War, the First World War, the Second World War, the Korean War, the Gulf War, and the Afghanistan War. Once again, this does not account for Indian wars, which were, from the perspective of indigenous groups, wars against sovereign peoples for territorial gain. Nor does it include conflicts fought on Canadian soil before the creation of a partial or fully autonomous Canada, wars that nonetheless undergirded much of the imperial nationalism of the nineteenth and early twentieth centuries: the 1759 Battle of Quebec and the War of 1812 (discussed in greater detail in Chapter 8). Imperial loyalties were also verified and enhanced by the presence of Canadians in British contingents sent to fight the 1854 Crimean War, the Indian Rebellion of 1857, and the 1884–5 uprising against British occupation in the Egyptian province of Sudan.

4 J.L. Granatstein, "In Peacetime, Soldiers are Scorned," *Ottawa Citizen*, 5 July 2011.

5 I am speaking strictly of wars fought since Confederation – that is, by an autonomous, or semi-autonomous nation.

6 Miller, *Painting the Map Red*, xi; Bouvier, "Introduction," in Bouvier, ed., *Whose America?*, 1. While several hundred Canadians served in a British military expedition in the Sudan in 1884–5, these men were recruited, funded, and commanded by Great Britain (Benn, *Mohawks on the Nile*, 24). Thomas Schoonover goes so far as to claim that the war with Spain marked the beginnings of globalization as we know it (Schoonover, *Uncle Sam's War of 1898*).

7 I am not implying that imperialism no longer exists or that wars are no longer fought to advance the interests of empires; only that official appellations along these lines fell out of favour as the century progressed. The figure for American dead does not include those killed in the Filipino insurrection that followed the peace treaty with Spain.

8 Kohn, *This Kindred People*, 150; Lake and Reynolds, *Drawing the Global Colour Line*, 2; Du Bois cited in ibid., 1–2. The term "clash of civilizations," applied anachronistically here, comes from the influential and controversial essay on the post-Cold War international order by American political scientist Huntington, "The Clash of Civilizations?"

9 Kohn, *This Kindred People*, 9, 143; *Globe* cited in ibid., 43; Ewan, cited in Berger, *The Sense of Power*, 249; Twain cited in Donal A. Lowry, "'The World's no Bigger than a Kraal': The South African War and

International Opinion in the First Age of 'Globalization,'" in Osmissi and
Thompson, *The Impact of the South African War*, 278; Lowry, "The Boers
were the Beginning of the End?," in Lowry, ed., *The South African War
Reappraised*, 203.

10 See Nasson, "The War One Hundred Years On," in Cuthbertson,
    Grundlingh, and Suttie, *Writing a Wider War*, 3–17.

11 Bouvier, *Whose America?* 2–3; "Canada Marks Boer War Anniversary,"
    CBC News, November 10, 2000, http://www.cbc.ca/canada/
    story/1999/10/17/boer991017.html (accessed 7 July 2013); Mordaunt
    Hall, "Movie Review: *The Rough Riders*," *New York Times*, 16 March 1927
    (Twentieth Century Pictures' *A Message to Garcia* [1936] also depicted
    the war). The CBC report on the Boer War correctly noted that the Boers
    condoned slavery and – less credibly – that they provoked the war.
    Canada's dead (270 in total) were cited, as was the fact that the war ended
    in victory and provided Canadians with confidence they would draw
    upon in the world wars. No mention was made of the vast numbers of
    civilian dead or the savagery employed by imperial troops, tactics that
    provoked widespread international condemnation.

12 Strong cited in Pratt, *The Expansionists of 1898*, 6. For a discussion of
    Strong's ideas and their influence in American thought, see LaFeber, *The
    New Empire* 72–80. For examples of likeminded early accounts of the war,
    see Berger, *Under Northern Eyes*. On the historiography of the war, see
    Crapol, "Coming to Terms with Empire"; Field, "American Imperialism";
    Fry, "From Open Door to World Systems"; Fry, "William McKinley and
    the Coming of the Spanish-American War"; Healy, "One War from Two
    Sides"; Paterson, "United States Intervention in Cuba"; Smith, "William
    McKinley's Enduring Legacy" in Bradford, *Crucible of Empire*, 205–49; and
    Perez, *The War of 1898*.

13 Alexander McClure and Charles Morris, *The Authentic Life of William
    McKinley*, cited in Perez, *The War of 1898*, 41; Bruce, Haworth,
    Adams, and Vandenberg cited in ibid., 42, 38, 37, 42; James Bradford,
    "Introduction," in Bradford, *Crucible of Empire*, xiii–xiv. On Bruce's
    education, see "H. Addington Bruce," in Gilman, Peck, and Colby, *New
    International Encyclopedia*. For an excellent discussion of the American
    notions of exceptionalism, chosen-ness and destiny, see Fousek, *To Lead
    the Free World*, esp. 5–11.

14 The "blundering and duplicity" charge was first leveled by *The Nation*
    magazine in 1901. For other critiques, see Combs, *American Diplomatic
    History*, 79; Benton, *International Law and Diplomacy*, 32; Wilkinson, *Public
    Opinion and the Spanish-American War*; Wisan, *The Cuban Crisis*; and Trask
    The War with Spain, 56.

15 Stephen Crane, "War is Kind," in Polner and Woods Jr, *We Who Dared*, 92–3.
16 Kennan's position is summarized in Amy Kaplan, "Left Alone with America: The Absence of Empire in the Study of American Culture," in Kaplan and Pease, *The Cultures of United States Imperialism*, 14; for a similar interpretation, see Morgenthau, *In Defense of the National Interest*. For an example of the "accidental" thesis, see Offner, *An Unwanted War*. When figures from the Philippine-American War are included, roughly 7,000 U.S. soldiers died as a result of these conflicts (Dyal, *Historical Dictionary of the Spanish-American War*, 67).
17 Lutzker, "Themes and Contradictions in the American Peace Movement," 320–1; Jim Zwick, "The Anti-Imperialist Movement, 1898–1921," in Bouvier, *Whose America?* 171–92. On the Progressives' relationship with war, see Howlet, "Parrington's Opposition to War." For a discussion of the Progressives' orientation and considerable impact, see Hofstadter, *The Progressive Historians*, and Tyrrell, *Historians in Public*, 61.
18 Barnett, *Atrocity and American Military Justice*, 23; Welch, "American Atrocities in the Philippines," 239–40; George Frisbie Hoar, "Against Imperialism," in Ravitch, *The American Reader*, 339; Story and Lichauco, *The Conquest of the Philippines*, 126–54.
19 Millis, *The Martial Spirit*, 226. For surveys of the New Left historians and those that followed, see Fry, "From Open Door to World Systems"; Paterson, "United States Intervention in Cuba"; Schonberger, "William H. Becker"; and Perkins, "The Tragedy of American Diplomacy." For early views on the legality of the conflict, see Flack, "Spanish-American Diplomatic Relations"; and Benton, *International Law and Diplomacy*. On masculinity, see Kristin Hoganson, "'Honor Comes First': The Imperatives of Manhood in the Congressional Debate over War," in Bouvier, *Whose America?*, and Hoganson, *Fighting for American Manhood*. Issues of misinformation and press censorship, as well as atrocities committed by US soldiers, were raised in Storey and Lichauco, *The Conquest of the Philippines*, and by many subsequent authors included in the works listed above. Edited collections featuring many of the themes cited here include Bouvier, *Whose America?* and McCoy and Scarano, *Colonial Crucible*.
20 Freidel, *Splendid Little War*, 3, x; Field, "American Imperialism," 645. On Freidel's motivations, see Golay, *Spanish American War*.
21 On press coverage, see Page, *Imperialism and Canada*; and Berger, *The Sense of Power*, 236. Ibid., 117 (first quote); Miller, *Painting the Map Red*, xi (second quote). Early books on the war included Marquis, *Canada's Sons on Kopje and Veldt*; and Evans, *The Canadian Contingents*. As discussed in the following chapter, Canadian anti-imperialist Goldwin Smith produced

In the Court of History, a short book not primarily on the war itself but on what he considered Canadians' unwarranted support for it.

22 Wrong, *The Canadians*, 391; Creighton, *Dominion of the North*, 399; Morton, *The Kingdom of Canada*, 398–9; Granatstein, *Who Killed Canadian History?* For a summary of this body of work, see Teigrob, "Glad Adventures, Tragedies, Silences."

23 Iain Smith, "A Century of Controversy over Origins," in Lowry, *The South African War Reappraised*, 23; Lowry, "Introduction," in ibid., 4, 38; Alan Jeeves, "Hobson's *The War in South Africa*: A Reassessment" in Cuthbertson et al, *Writing a Wider War*, 235; Lowry, "Conclusion," in Lowry, *The South African War Reappraised*, 204–5; Thornton, *The Imperial Idea*, 109. On British war opponents, see David Nash, "Taming the God of Battles: Secular and Moral Critiques of the South African War" in Cuthbertson et al, *Writing a Wider War*, 266–86.

24 McClung, *The Complete Autobiography*, 350–1; Page, *The Boer War and Canadian Imperialism*, 10–13; Callwood, *Portrait of Canada*, 229.

25 Wrong, *The Canadians*, 391; Morton, *A Short History of Canada*, 125; Leacock, *Canada*, 198; *Canadian Military Gazette* cited in Keshen, *Propaganda and Censorship*, xii; Page, *The Boer War*, 15.

26 Miller, *Painting the Map Red*, 151; Nash, "The Boer War"; Berger, *The Sense of Power*, 236. On Robertson and other British war opponents, see Lowry, "Introduction," in Lowry, *The South African War Reappraised*, 10; and Lowry, "Conclusion," in Lowry, *The South African War Reappraised*, 211. On Hobhouse, see Albert Grundlingh "The National Women's Monument: The Making and Mutation of Meaning in Afrikaner Memory of the South African War," in Cuthbertson et al *Writing a Wider War*, 19; and Godby, "Confronting Horror," Methuen, 1902.

27 Bercuson, *The Fighting Canadians*, 123.

28 Granatstein, *Canada's Army*, 44; Madsen, *Another Kind of Justice*, 33; Horn, *Doing Canada Proud*.

29 Cook, "Quill and Canon," 504–5.

30 Cook, *Clio's Warriors*, 63–7, 147; Duguid cited in Cook, "Quill and Canon," 507; Vance, *Death So Noble*, 169; Nicholson, *Official History of the Canadian Army*. The lone volume to emerge from Duguid's ambitious project was his 1938 *Official History of the Canadian Forces in the Great War*.

31 Andrew Godefroy, "Introduction," in Godefory, *Great War Commands*, xii; George cited in ibid. For an excellent international summary of the evolution of First World War interpretations, see Winter and Prost, *The Great War in History*.

32 Vance, *Death So Noble*; Dafoe cited in McKay and Swift, *Warrior Nation*, 65.

33 Vance, *Death So Noble*, 35–72, 17 (last quote); Marlin, *Propaganda,* 340.
    On the National War Memorial, see Ferguson, "Canada's Response."
34 Fussell, *The Great War and Modern Memory*, 249; Vance, *Death So Noble*, 200;
    Coates cited in Richler, *What We Talk About*, 77; Keshen, *Propaganda and
    Censorship*, xvii. For a summary of British Great War poetry, see Sillars,
    Fields of Agony. As Sillars notes, British writers also produced poems that
    praised the war effort, but these were largely forgotten following the
    conflict as the sense of waste became increasingly dominant among the
    British public (7–8); Vance points out that Fussell focuses on the literary
    output of elites, whose attitudes experienced a more profound shift away
    from "high diction" than those of average citizens (*Death So Noble*, 5–6).
    There is doubtless merit in this argument, but my focus is on the war-
    related literature that has stood the test of time in each national context,
    regardless of the social position of the author. Using this criterion, the
    disparity holds: Britons have canonized a decidedly bleaker literature on
    the Great War than Canadians. For more on McRae's poem, see Holmes,
    "In Flanders Fields."
35 Vance, *Death So Noble*, 29–30; Schurman, "Writing about War," 241;
    Sillars, *Fields of Agony*, 8; McKay and Swift, *Warrior Nation*, 83; Webb, "A
    Righteous Cause," 46–7. As Richler notes, Harrison's work represented a
    rare example of an English-Canadian novel that emphasized the horror
    and futility of the Great War until Timothy Findley's *The Wars* (1977).
    More recently, novelists such as Jack Hodgins (*Broken Ground*, 1999), Allan
    Donaldson (*Maclean*, 2005), and Joseph Boyden (*Three Day Road*, 2005) have
    conveyed similar themes (Richler, *What We Talk About*, 25; 80–1).
36 Armstrong-Reid and Murray, *Armies of Peace,* 135; Hobson, *The Morals of
    Economic Nationalism*; Keynes, *The Economic Consequences*; MacMillan, *Paris
    1919,* 479.
37 Robertson, *Sir Andrew Macphail*, 182–4, 188–9, 192, 196 (quote). As Vance
    demonstrates, Macphail could be a staunch defender of the Great War
    myth, particularly in his public pronouncements (Vance, *Death So Noble*,
    33, 54, 75, 190). Robertson's biography paints a more enigmatic portrait of
    Macphail's response to the First World War: "To the observer attempting
    to make sense as a whole of Macphail and his attitude to the war and
    his experiences in it, one of the most striking impressions is that of
    contradictions. His views on a number of matters oscillated from one pole
    to another" (*Sir Andrew Macphail*, 189).
38 Bird, *And We Go On;* McKay and Bates, *In the Province*, 137–42; soldier cited
    in ibid., 141.
39 Vance, *Death So Noble*, 29; McKay and Bates, *In the Province*, 133.

40 Sharpe, *The Last Day*; Vance, *Death So Noble*, 212, 227–56.
41 Richler, *What We Talk About*, 197; Fussell, *The Great War*, 11. Stacey,
"Nationality," 10–19; Morton, *The Kingdom of Canada*; Nicholson, *The Canadian
Expeditionary Force*. Canadian disunity is outlined in Wood, *Militia Myths*,
242. For the earliest specialized study on linguistic divisions and the war,
see Armstrong, *The Crisis in Quebec*. On Ontario textbooks, see Theobald,
"Divided Once More," 4–5. Tremblay," Du suicide," provides a rare study
of soldier suicide in the CEF. For a recent study of Canadian soldiers found
guilty of cowardice or desertion, see Iacobelli, *Death or Deliverance*.
42 Cook and Brown, *Canada 1896–1921*, 320 (quote); 338. For studies that
expanded these themes, see Kealey, "State Repression of Labour"; and
Keshen, *Propaganda and Censorship*.
43 Berton, *Vimy*, 295, 307. Laurel Halladay outlines the continuities in Canada's
war histories in "Renegotiating National Boundaries"; Nathan Greenfield's
Baptism of Fire offers a contemporary example of the national survival
argument, citing an alleged battlefield taunt from a German soldier as
proof that the Kaiser had designs on Canada itself (7). Canadian analysis
of German culpability is addressed more extensively in Chapter 3. For
examples of recent efforts to complicate previous understandings of the
war's impact on Canada, see Hayes, Iarocci, and Bechthold, *Vimy Ridge*; and
Martin, "Vimy, April 1917." This matter is taken up in detail in Chapter 8.
44 Keshen, *Propaganda and Censorship*, ix; xvii; Stanley, *Canada's Soldiers*, 417;
Swettenham, *To Seize the Victory*, 26; Thompson, *Anzac Memories*; Morton,
When Your Number's Up, vii. For a discussion of the persistence of these
views to the present, see Keshen, "The Great War Soldier," 15.
45 Cook, *Clio's Warriors*, 208–9 (CBC quote); NFB cited in Keshen, "The Great
War Soldier," 15; Gross cited in Richler, *What We Talk About*, 83–5. On the
impact of *The Great War* series in Britain, see Black, *The Great War*, 219.
46 McKay and Swift, *Warrior Nation*, 74–5; Graves cited in ibid, 74; Cook,
"The Politics of Surrender," 664. Cook provides the following examples of
non-Canadian studies examining the killing of prisoners in battle: Noble,
"Raising the White Flag"; Ferguson, "Prisoner Taking"; Bourke, *An Intimate
History of Killing*; Grossman, *On Killing*; Dower, *War Without Mercy*.
47 Stacey cited in Cook, *Clio's Warriors*, 10; Terry Copp, "The Military
Effort, 1914–1918," in MacKenzie, *Canada and the First World War*,
35. For rare examples of internationalist war accounts by Canadian
authors, see Eksteins, *The Rites of Spring*; and MacMillan, *Paris 1919*. As
MacMillan observed, "in the early years after World War I, the dead were
commemorated in France and Britain as fallen heroes who had fought to
defend their civilization. It was only later as disillusionment about the

war grew that the British and French publics came to remember them as victims of a futile struggle" (MacMillan, *The Uses and Abuses*, 49). On the growing divide between the more jaded British representations and the more optimistic Canadian accountings in the latter half of the century, see Cook, *Clio's Warriors*, 208–9; Vance, *Death So Noble*, 57–60; Iarocci, *Shoestring Soldiers*, 268.

48 H. Chadderton, *Hanging a Legend*. For a summary of the debate, see Greenhous, "Billy Bishop"; Greenhous, *The Making of Billy Bishop*; and McCaffery, *Billy Bishop*. On the controversy over command performance at Ypres, see Grodzinski, "The Use and Abuse of Battle"; and Iarocci, *Shoestring Soldiers*, 6–10. Beginning with Archer Duguid, several writers charted the evolution of the CEF from an "amateur colonial contingent" to seasoned and feared "shock troops." Iarocci challenged these claims, arguing that the CEF was a well-trained and capable force from the outset.

49 Robert Fulford, "The First World War," *National Post*, 8 February 2000.

50 David Bercuson, "Crime or Commitment?" *National Post*, 11 February 2000; Jonathan Vance, "Turning Point of a Nation," *National Post*, 11 February 2000; Keshen, "The Great War Soldier," 3 (Keshen's list included Armstrong, *The Crisis of Quebec*; Neatby, *Laurier and a Liberal Quebec*; Brown and Cook, *Canada 1896–1921*; Brown, *Robert Laird Borden*; and Granatstein and Hitsman, *Broken Promises*); Grodzinski, "The Use and Abuse of Battle," 85. For examples of the disdain for Quebec's influence on foreign policy, see Creighton, *The Forked Road*, 56, 69; J.L. Granatstein, "Multiculturalism and Canadian Foreign Policy," in Carment and Bercuson, *The World in Canada*, 87–9.

51 Mead, *The Doughboys*, ix; Cooper, "The Great War and American Memory"; Richard Simon, "Fight over National World War I Memorial continues in 2013," *Los Angeles Times*, 1 January 2013. Mosier's *The Myth of the Great War* advances one of the more controversial components of the affirmative view of US participation: that without it, Germany would have prevailed in the conflict. Veterans Day in the United States vies for attention with the May commemoration of Memorial Day. The US Department of Veterans affairs concedes that "most Americans confuse [Veterans Day] with Memorial Day" and are unclear about what is being commemorated on November 11. In contrast to Memorial Day (and to Remembrance Day in Canada), many stores and schools remain open on Veterans Day. See "The History of Veterans Day," Military.com, http://www.military.com/veterans-day/history-of-veterans-day.html. (18 August 2013). http://articles.latimes.com/2013/jan/01/nation/la-na-nn-national-world-war-1-memorial-20130101 (accessed 18 August 2013).

52 Senator George Norris of Nebraska hit all of these notes in his speech
opposing Woodrow Wilson's War Message. See George W. Norris,
"Wealth's Terrible Mandate," in Polner and Woods, *We Who Dared*, 118–23;
53 Combs, *American Diplomatic History*, 96.
54 Ibid., 118; US War Department casualty estimates cited in Bradley, *No
Strategic Targets Left*, 7; Cooper, "The Great War and American Memory."
On Harding, the title of Philip Payne's review of public opinion of the
president says it all: *Dead Last: The Public Memory of Warren G. Harding's
Scandalous Legacy*.
55 Fay, "New Light"; Fay, *The Origins of the World War*, esp. 547–8 and 556.
56 Barnes, *The Genesis of the World War*, 6–9, 10 (first quote), xi (second quote),
xviii (third quote), xiii (fourth quote).
57 Barnes, *The Genesis of the World War*, 3; Murray Rothband, "Harry Elmer
Barnes RIP," *Left and Right* 4.1 (1968): 4. For a highly readable and
informative summary of the Scopes trial, see Larson, *Summer for the
Gods*. Barnes' introduction of evolution to the debate is somewhat less
provocative when we consider that by the beginning of the twentieth
century, most American scientists, like those in Canada and Britain, had
accepted evolutionary ideas, a fact that was reflected in the full incorporation
of Darwin's model in American high school textbooks of the era (Larson,
Trial and Error, 8–9). On Sanger, see Chesler, *Woman of Valor*. On the influence
of Barnes and other revisionists, see Riggenbach, *Why American History is
Not what they Say*, 77; Combs, *American Diplomatic History*, 136.
58 Engelbrecht and Hanighen, *Merchants of Death*; Nye Committee addressed
in Kleidman, *Organizing for Peace*, 60; and Olmstead, *Real Enemies*, 31–43;
Walter Millis, "Editor's Introduction" and "1939 is not 1914," *Life*, 6
November 1939, 69; Millis, *Road to War*. Some of the more influential
disapproving interwar publications included Beard, *The Devil Theory of
War*, which pointed to the economic impetus for war; Borchard and Lange,
Neutrality for the United States, which condemned Wilson's fumbling of
the principal of neutrality, Grattan, *Why We Fought*, which positioned
propaganda and profit as the leading motivators; and Morrissey, *The
American Defense*, which argued that the supposedly neutral United States
had in fact favoured Britain and treated Germany unfairly.
59 Combs, *American Diplomatic History*, 144–5, 152 (quote); Holsti, *Public
Opinion and American Foreign Policy*, 17–18. For a conservative critique
of US intervention, see Tansill, *America Goes to War*, which regarded US
intervention as a tragic and decidedly avoidable error.
60 Bodnar, *The "Good War*," 237.
61 Trout, *On the Battlefield of Memory*, 9, 43–4 (quote).

62 Combs, *American Diplomatic History*, 258, 279; William Earl Weeks, "New Directions in the Study of Early American Foreign Relations," in Hogan, *Paths to Power*, 20; Siracusa, *New Left Diplomatic Histories and Historians*, 63–72; Mead, *The Doughboys*, xiii.

63 Cooper, "The Great War and American Memory"; Unger, *Fighting Bob La Follette*, xi; David L. Porter, "America's Ten Greatest Senators," in Pederson and McLaurin, *The Rating Game*; Hibben, *The Peerless Leader*; Werner; *Bryan*; Curti, *Bryan and World Peace*; Abrams, *The Nobel Peace Prize*, 122. On the reverence for war opponents, see, for example, DeBenedetti, *Peace Heroes*; Zinn, *A People's History*, 140–6; and Benjamin F. Shearer, ed., *Home Front Heroes: A Biographical Dictionary of Americans During Wartime*, 3 vols. (Westport, Connecticut: Greenwood Press, 2007), which gives equal billing to those who supported and opposed America's wars.

64 Zinn, *A People's History*, 137; Polner and Woods, "Introduction," *We Who Dared*, xii; Ian McKay and Jamie Swift, "Alexandre Boulerice: Another casualty of the Great War," *Toronto Star*, 5 May 2013.

2 Wars Good, Cold, and Forgotten

1 For example, in Ferguson's *The Pity of War*, the author suggested that the United Kingdom should have permitted the German takeover of Europe in 1914 in the name of preserving the British Empire.

2 Brokaw, *The Greatest Generation*. Adams, *The Best War Ever*, provides a critical analysis of these themes.

3 "Is Bush the Churchill of the 21st Century?" *BBC News*, 29 August, 2002, http://news.bbc.co.uk/2/hi/uk_news/2223075.stm (accessed 4 October 2013); J.L. Granatstein, "In Peacetime, Soldiers are Scorned," *Ottawa Citizen*, 5 July 2011. As Margaret MacMillan noted, "the cult of Winston Churchill … is perhaps even more pronounced in North America than in it is in the United Kingdom," where greater familiarity with Churchill's entire career reveals blunders as well as triumphs (*The Uses and Abuses*, 17).

4 Adams, *The Best War Ever*, 2; MacMillan, *The Uses and Abuses*, 17. For a small sampling of the outpouring of analysis on the Enola Gay controversy, see Linenthal and Engelhardt, *History Wars*; Nobile, *Judgment at the Smithsonian*; and Bird and Lifschultz, *Hiroshima's Shadow*. On the Canadian controversies, see Weisbord and Mohr, *The Valour and the Horror*; Bercuson and Wise, *The Valour and the Horror Revisited*; MacMillan, Bothwell and Hansen, "Controversy, Commemoration, and Capitulation"; Hansen, *Fire and Fury*; and MacMillan, *The Uses and Abuses*. For a summary

of the ongoing debates over Allied strategic bombing from an international perspective, see Grayling, *Among the Dead Cities*.

5 Adams, *The Best War Ever*, xiii, 2–4; Fousek, *To Lead the Free World*, 17.

6 Rosenberg, *A Day Which Will Live*, 17–18, 34–43; Lippmann, *U.S. Foreign Policy*, ix; Zuhlsdorff, *Hitler's Exiles*, 43.

7 Bodnar, *The "Good War,"* 3; Roya Nikkhah, "Sir Tim Rice on his New Musical and Working with Andrew Lloyd Webber," *The Telegraph*, 4 September 2013, http://www.telegraph.co.uk/culture/theatre/9164512/Sir-Tim-Rice-on-his-new-musical-and-working-with-Andrew-Lloyd-Webber.html (accessed 13 October 2013). For an excellent and extended analysis of these authors' themes and impact, see Bodnar, *The "Good War,"* 34–43.

8 Williams, *The Tragedy of American Diplomacy*, 150; Kolko, *The Politics of War*.

9 Dower, *War without Mercy*, 4, 9; Hogan, "The Enola Gay Controversy," 225. The beginning of atomic bomb revisionism is often associated with Alperovitz, *Atomic Diplomacy*. For essays that summarize the enormous body of literature on the bombings, see Asada, "The Shock of the Atomic Bomb"; and Walker, "Recent Literature."

10 Pease, *The New American Exceptionalism*, 61–2; Rosenberg, *A Date Which Will Live*, 115–8. The term "the good war" entered popular consciousness after the 1984 publication of Studs Terkel's oral history of the same name.

11 Rosenberg, *A Date Which Will Live*, 117; Bodnar, *The "Good War,"* 213; Niemi, *History in the Media*, 137; Ambrose, *Band of Brothers*. The D-Day Museum was later renamed the National World War II Museum.

12 Farber, "War Stories," 318 (first Fussell quote); second Fussell quote cited in Bodnar, *The "Good War,"* 56.

13 Bailey and Farber, *The First Strange Place*; Adams, *The Best War Ever*, xiii, 90; Fussell cited in Oostdijk, "Debunking the 'Good War' Myth," 274; Niemi, *History in the Media*, 138. For other revisionist accounts, see Jeffries, *Wartime America*; Erenberg and Hirsch, *The War in American Culture*; Baker, *Human Smoke*; Hitchcock, *The Bitter Road*; Hixson, *The Myth of American Diplomacy*; Rose, *Myth and the Greatest Generation*.

14 The suggestion that modern historians introduce controversy where none existed and impose today's moral standards on the past was a recurrent theme in the 1995 debates over the Enola Gay. See Hogan, "The Enola Gay Controversy."

15 Birney cited in Whitaker, *Great Canadian War Stories*, 213 (see also Keith, *Canadian Literature in English*, 51–2; and Keshen, *Saints, Sinners, and Soldiers*, 10); Stacey, "Second World War (WWII)," revised by Richard Foot, *The Canadian Encyclopedia* online ed. (Historica Canada, 2014),

http://www.thecanadianencyclopedia.ca/en/article/second-world-war-wwii/ (accessed 1 November 2013).

16 McInnis, *Canada*, 482; officer cited in Zuehlke, *Tragedy at Dieppe*, 58; Morton, *The Kingdom of Canada*, 482–3.

17 English, *The Canadian Army*; Careless, *Canada*, 380; McInnis, *Canada*, 485; Stacey cited in Copp, *Cinderella Army*, 287.

18 DiJoseph, *Noble Cause*, 4; Granatstein and Morton, *A Nation Forged in Fire*, 114; Schurman, "Writing About War," 242. Some of the early titles on Canada at war include Stacey, *Canada's Battle*; Department of National Defence, *The Canadian Army*; Department of National Defence, *Six Years of War*; Department of National Defence, *Official History of the Canadian Army*.

19 Cook, *Clio's Warriors*, 211, 210; McCullough, "We Are the Blue Berets"; Wittner, *Toward Nuclear Abolition*, 197–201. For a summary of the historiographical trends noted here, see Berger, *The Writing of Canadian History*, 259–320.

20 Stacey, *Arms, Men and Governments*; Granatstein and Hitsman, *Broken Promises*; Read, *The Great War*; for a summary of these trends, see Cook, *Clio's Warriors*, 216–21. Findley, *The Wars*; Vanderhaeghe, 'Introduction,' in ibid., xvi; Mowatt, *And No Birds Sang*.

21 Douglas and Greenhous, *Out of the Shadows*, 193, 235, 241, 248–53, 269; Thompson, Eric. "Of Wars and Men." *Canadian Literature* 78 (Autumn 1978), 100.

22 Douglas and Greenhous, *Out of the Shadows*, 6.

23 Pierson, *They're Still Women After All*; Jeanette Sloniowski, "The Valour and the Horror," *Museum of Broadcasting Communications*, http://www.museum.tv/archives/etv/V/htmlV/valourandth/valourandth.htm (accessed 5 November 2013); Keshen, *Saints, Sinners, and Soldiers*, 3; area bombing is covered in the third volume of the DND series, Greenhous, Harris, Johnston, and Rawling, *The Crucible of War*; Bercuson and Wise, *The Valour and the Horror Revisited*; Granatstein cited in McKay and Swift, *Warrior Nation*, 190–1.

24 MacMillan, Bothwell and Hansen, "Controversy, Commemoration, and Capitulation"; Richler, *What We Talk About*, 65.

25 Keshen, *Saints, Sinners, and Soldiers*, 9. For the latest British offering along these lines, see Heartfield, *An Unpatriotic History*.

26 Jackson, *One of the Boys*. The American precursor was BÃ©rubÃ©, *Coming Out Under Fire*; MacMillan, *The Uses and Abuses*; Hanson, *Fire and Fury*, 287.

27 Granatstein and Neary, *The Good Fight*; Granatstein, *The Last Good War*; Granatstein (quote), *The Last Good War*, viii; Copp, *Fields of Fire*, 267;

Copp, *Cinderella Army*; Bercuson, *Maple Leaf Against the Axis*, 274–5; Engen *Canadians Under Fire*.

28 Adams, *The Best War Ever*, 4. The title of Tim Cook's recent book on the conflict, *The Necessary War*, speaks to the more limited claims prominent among US historians.

29 Braun and McCullough, "Reviewing the History Textbooks," 47–8; Edwards, *To Acknowledge a War*, 16–17; Melady, *Korea*, 13.

30 Teigrob, *Warming Up to the Cold War*, 181–8; 200; Edwards, *To Acknowledge a War*, 30, 32.

31 Ibid., 33–4; Watson, *Far Eastern Tour*, 176.

32 Hastings, *The Korean War*; Edwards, *To Acknowledge a War*, 152–3; Johnson, *A War of Patrols*, xvi-xviii.

33 See, for instance, Hastings, *The Korean War*; Edwards, *To Acknowledge a War*, 152–3; Johnson, *A War of Patrols*, xvi-xviii. Writing in 2003, Erin Carrière, Marc O'Reilly, and Richard Vengroff summed up the particular lessons that Canadian diplomats, cognizant of the limitations of Canadian resources, gleaned from Korea: "Such a setback reminded them that they could not consider the prosecution of wars as a national talent" (Carrière, O'Reilly, and Vengroff, "In the Service of Peace," 12–13).

34 Edwards, *To Acknowledge a War*, 122, 123.

35 Stone, *The Hidden History*, 116, 179; Voorhees, *Korean Tales*, 49.

36 Guttenplan, *American Radical*, 265–6; Edwards, *To Acknowledge a War*, 123; Huebner, *Warrior Image*, 9, 12. For an excellent summary on the vast body of revisionist literature, see Stueck, "Revisionism and the Korean War." For a general survey of Korean War historiography, see Millett, "The Korean War."

37 Rose, *Roots of Tragedy*; Alexander, *Korea: The First War We Lost*. Other critical accounts written by US veterans of the war include Goulden, *Korea: The Untold Story*; and Weintraub, *MacArthur's War*.

38 Cumings, *The Origins of the Korean War*, 48–50; Young, "An Incident at No Gun Ri," 243.

39 Cumings, *The Korean War*, 5.

40 *Tribune* cited in McKay and Swift, *Warrior Nation*, 131; Endicott and Hagerman, *The United States and Biological Warfare*; Cumings, "Occurrence at Nog Ŭn-ri Bridge"; Stueck, "Revisionism and the Korean War," 25. For more on these debates, see Chen, "History of Three Mobilizations."

41 Edwards, *To Acknowledge a War*, 12–13; The *New York Times* reprinted the entire first chapter of Cumings' incendiary *The Korean War* (Bruce Cumings, "Excerpt: The Korean War," *New York Times*, 21 July 2010); see also Doug Bandow, "A Revisionist's Korean War," *The American Spectator*, 1 November 2010, http://spectator.org/articles/38668/revisionists-korean-war

(accessed 11 November 2013). Wood, *Strange Battleground*, 179, 259–60.
Roughly four million Koreans, or 10 per cent of the total population, were
casualties of the conflict, and 70 per cent of those killed in the fighting
were civilians (Malkasian, *The Korean War*, 88; Cho, *Haunting the Korean
Diaspora*, 52).

42 Stairs, *The Diplomacy of Constraint*, 333. For authors who supported the
constraint thesis, see Lee, *Outposts of Empire*; Keating, *Canada and World
Order*, 34–5, 38; and Stueck, *The Korean War*, 4. A more skeptical take on
the ability of Canadians to moderate US foreign policymaking in Korea is
offered in Prince, "The Limits of Constraint."

43 Melady, *Korea*, 31–2, 45, 267, 12; Bercuson, *Blood on the Hills*, xiii, xiv; Johnston,
A War of Patrols; David Bercuson, "Introduction" in Barris, *Deadlock in
Korea*, xvi. Brent Byron Watson's handling of the issue of war origins is
representative: "Within this bipolar context," he wrote without further
qualification, "Western governments largely viewed North Korea's invasion
of South Korea as an act of Soviet-sponsored aggression" (*Far Eastern Tour*, 5).

44 Bjarnason, *Triumph at Kapyong*, 22, 16.

45 Watson, *Far Eastern Tour*, 177, 134.

46 Price, *Orienting Canada*, 265 (quote), 257–68; Watson, *Far Eastern Tour*, 172;
Granatstein, *Canada's Army*, 334.

47 See Edwards, *To Acknowledge a War*, 126, for a discussion of the "reverse
heroic" mode.

48 See, for example, the use of the term in Desmond Morton's excellent
annotated bibliography of Canadian military history in *A Military History
of Canada*, 319–38.

3 Wars for and against Empire

1 Here I adopt Jerry Bentley's periodization, which holds that West-
European expansion ushered in "the modern age, extending from 1500
to the present, a period during which all the world's regions and peoples
ultimately became engaged in sustained encounter with each other, thus
a period that inaugurated a genuinely global epoch of world history"
(Bentley, "Cross-Cultural Interaction," 769). For an early and influential
study of the transformative nature of imperialism, see Crosby, *The
Columbian Exchange*; for a more recent account, see Mann, *1493*.

2 Schurman, "Writing About War," 241. Patrick O'Brien makes a convincing
case for the pre-eminence of American imperialism in "The Pax Britannica
and American Hegemony: Precedent, Antecedent or Just Another
History?" in O'Brien and Clesse, *Two Hegemonies*, 3–65.

3 Cited in Ferguson, "Hegemony or Empire," 154.
4 Heiss, "The Evolution of the Imperial Idea," 521; Kaufman, *Ain't My America*, 3–5, 13.
5 Knowles, *Inventing the Loyalists*, 4; Coates and Morgan, *Heroines and History*.
6 Phillip Buckner, "Introduction: Canada and the British Empire," in Buckner, *Canada and the British Empire*, 4; Coates and Morgan, *Heroines and History*, 140–1; Knowles, *Inventing the Loyalists*, 26–7; Paradis, "Acadia," 36–7; Bannister, "The Loyalist Order Framework," 104.
7 Berger, *The Sense of Power*. For more recent analysis of the relationship between imperialism and Canadian nationalism, see Buckner, *Canada and the End of Empire*; Buckner, *Canada and the British Empire*; Champion, *The Strange Demise of British Canada*; Coleman, *White Civility*; and Igartua, *The Other Quiet Revolution*.
8 John Dobson, "Spanish-Cuban/American War," Beede, *The War of 1898*, 521. For a summary of the historiographical debates surrounding the war, see Fry, "From Open Door," 277–303.
9 McKinley cited in Brewer, *Why America Fights*, 34; Howlett and Harris, *Books, Not Bombs*, 14; Zwick, "The Anti-Imperialist Movement," 174; S.L. Clemens to Edward W. Ordway, 1 May 1901, Edward W. Ordway Papers, Box 1, New York Public Library Rare Books and Manuscripts Division. Of Secretary of Defense Donald Rumsfeld's many intentional and/or accidental obfuscations surrounding the Iraq War, his statement on Saddam Hussein's alleged weapons of mass destruction stands out: "There's another way to phrase that and that is that the absence of evidence is not evidence of absence. It is basically saying the same thing in a different way. Simply because you do not have evidence that something exists does not mean that you have evidence that it doesn't exist" ("News Transcript," US Department of Defense, Office of the Assistant Secretary of Defense [Public Affairs], 6 June 2002, http://www.defense.gov/Transcripts/Transcript. aspx?TranscriptID=3490 [accessed 1 February 2014]).
10 Mayers, *Dissenting Voices*, 199–201. As Mayers noted, presidents and professors at Harvard, Stanford, and Northwestern publically opposed annexation, as did scholars at Yale, Princeton, Columbia, Cornell, Chicago, and Michigan. On Bierce and the war, see Berkove, *A Prescription for Adversity*, 22–6; Davis cited in Walter Benn Michaels, "Anti-Imperial Americanism," in Kaplan and Pease, *Cultures of United States Imperialism*, 387 n1. For a summary of racially charged debates over the propriety of absorbing non-Europeans into US society, see Love, *Race Over Empire*.
11 Michaels, "Anti-Imperial Americanism"; Horace Flack, "Spanish-American Diplomatic Relations," 30, 44, 49, 55, 59, 69 (quote), 95.

Benton, *International Law*, 291. Similar cross-examinations were provided by H. Parker Wills, "The Economic Situation in the Philippines," *Journal of Political Economy*, 1905; Carman F. Randolph, "Constitutional Aspects of Annexation," *Harvard Law Review*, 1898; Edwin Burritt Smith, "The Constitution and Inequality of Rights," *Yale Law Journal*, February 1901. Each of these articles was reprinted as a pamphlet by the Anti-Imperialist League. The League published hundreds of such tracts in the years immediately following the war, many of which consisted of reprinted essays, speeches, sermons, editorials, legal analyses, and judicial findings. A good number of these, including the ones cited here, are held in the New York Public Library's Edward W. Ordway Papers.

12　Mayers, *Dissenting Voices*, 201. The Senate voted 57–27 – just one vote more than the two-thirds majority required – in favour of ratifying the Treaty of Paris, which delivered Puerto Rico, Guam, and the Philippines to the United States; Adams cited in Perez, *The War of 1898*, 44; Trask, *The War with Spain in 1898*, 58. For early works that emphasize longstanding US designs on Cuba, see Millis, *The Martial Spirit*, and Storey and Lichauco, *The Conquest of the Philippines*. This is a foundational argument for Perez, *The War of 1898*, as well as many of the New Left and cultural studies of 1898 discussed below.

13　For variations on the "accidental" theme, see Holbo, "Economics, Emotion, and Expansion," 221; and Offner, *An Unwanted War*; McKinley cited in Brewer, *Why America Fights*, 37; Felix Adler to Edward W. Ordway, 2 January 1900, Edward W. Ordway Papers, box 1; Walter LaFeber, "Comments," in Field, "American Imperialism," 669. On Adler's life and thought, see Radest, *Felix Adler*.

14　Michael Adas, "Improving the Civilizing Mission?: Assumptions of United States Exceptionalism in the Colonization of the Philippines," in Gardner and Young, eds., *The New Empire*, 153–81; Wilson cited in Herring, *From Colony to Superpower*, 305. As Adas argued, "most American observers were not only critical of European approaches to colonization in Asia but convinced that their own colonial project was unprecedented in the nature and extent of the process of civilizing that it had set in motion." For a similar view, see Ninkovich, *The United States and Imperialism*, 249.

15　Hendrickson, *Union, Nation, or Empire*, 294.

16　Buckner, "Introduction," in Buckner, ed., *Canada and the End of Empire*, 3; Doug Owram, "Canada and the Empire," in Buckner, *Canada and the British Empire*, 149; Coates and Morgan, *Heroines and History*, 131–41; Miller, *Painting the Map Red*, 9; *Gazette* cited in Wood, *Militia Myths*, 93; Berger, *The Sense of Power*, 233. On clerical support, see Heath, *A War with a Silver Lining*.

17 Goldwin Smith to Edward W. Ordway, 7 November 1901, Ordway Papers, Box 1; *Reader* cited in Threlfall, "Empire over Nation," 36. The imperial ties Smith railed against do go far in explaining Canadian participation, and his analysis of the role of British mining interests in leading that nation to war is likewise defended by the historical record. Like his British contemporary and fellow anti-imperialist J.A. Hobson, however, Smith also provided accusations of a Jewish conspiracy behind Britain's declaration of war. Smith's anti-Semitic rants are peppered throughout his book, *In The Court of History*. On Hobson, see Alan Jeeves, "Hobson's *The War in South Africa*: A Reassessment" in Cuthbertson, Grundlingh, and Suttie, *Writing a Wider War*, 233–46.

18 Marquis, *Canada's Sons on Kopje and Veldt*, iii, iv; George Munro Grant, "Introduction," in ibid., 1–2, 4, 5–6. For a general discussion of the idea of muscular Christianity, see Watson, Weir, and Friend, "The Development of Muscular Christianity." For the Canadian context, see Coleman, *White Civility*, 128–67.

19 Henry, "W. Sanford Evans and the Canadian Club of Winnipeg"; Evans, *The Canadian Contingents*, 2.

20 Pickles, *Female Imperialism and National Identity*, 3.

21 Miller, *Painting the Map Red*, 441–4; Bourassa cited in Cook, *Watching Quebec*, 118; François-Albert Angers, "La pensée de Henri Bourassa: Le problème de la paix," *L'Action nationale*, Montréal, 1954, 92, cited in Richard, "Henri Bourassa and Conscription," 75; Minto cited in Page, *Imperialism and Canada*, 7. While Minto supported Canada's participation in public, in private he called the war "the most iniquitous we had ever engaged in ... The fact is, if we fight we fight for Rhodes, Beit and Co. and the speculators of the Rand, it makes me sick." On Canada's role, he wrote, "I don't see why they should commit their country to the expenditure of lives and money for a quarrel not threatening imperial safety" (cited in Dyer, *Canada in the Great Power Game*, 10–11).

22 Morton, *A Military History of Canada*, 116–17 (as Morton observed, "English-speaking critics of the war learned to curb their tongues"); Goldwin Smith to Edward W. Ordway, 7 November 1901, Edward W. Ordway Papers, Box 1; Miller, *Painting the Map Red*, 442; Smith, *In The Court of History*, 63.

23 Webb, "The Silent Flag in the New Fallen Snow"; Shipley, *To Mark Our Place*, 41–4. For examples of historians' handling of the matter, see Wrong, *The Canadians*, 391; Lower, *Colony to Nation*, 442; Morton, *The Kingdom of Canada*, 399; Penlington, *Canada and Imperialism*, 240–1; Creighton, *Dominion of the North*, 399; Creighton, *The Story of Canada*, 197–8; Careless, *Canada*, 317; McNaught, *The Pelican History of Canada*, 207; Department of

the Secretary of State, *Our History*, 63; Brown and Cook, *Canada 1896–1921*, 38; Morton, *A Shorty History of Canada*, 125; Hardy, *From Sea unto Sea*, 427.

24 Miller, *Painting the Map Red*, 22–4 (quote). Smith had originally made a case for union in *Canada and the Canadian Question*, 1891. Thomas Phillips Thompson, a leftist journalist who founded Toronto's *Labour Advocate*, was another English-Canadian war dissenter, but these were rather isolated figures; as Thompson's 1933 *Toronto Star* obituary noted, he was perpetually "on the side of lost causes" (cited in Mckay, *Reasoning Otherwise*, 94).

25 Mayers, *Dissenting Voices*, 237–8; Robert La Follette, "The People Do Not Want This War," in Polner and Woods Jr, *We Who Dared*, 127; Brewer, *Why America Fights*, 53.

26 Cited in Beard, *The Rise of American Civilization*, 627; Pestritto, *Woodrow Wilson*, 43.

27 La Follete and Borah cited in Mayers, *Dissenting Voices*, 247; Combs, *American Diplomatic History*, 114–19; Hendrickson, *Union, Nation, or Empire*, 316. On the considerable impact of Wilson's anti-imperial rhetoric among peoples struggling against foreign domination, and the considerable disillusionment that followed the Allied powers' refusal to extend the principle of self-determination beyond European borders, see Manela, *The Wilsonian Moment*.

28 Morton, *When Your Number's Up*, 7, 13.

29 Ewart discussed in Berger, *The Sense of Power*, 122–3; Creighton, *Dominion of the North*, 437; Cook, *At the Sharp End*, 21; Macintyre, *Canada at Vimy*, 4; Casser, *Hell in Flanders Fields*, 21.

30 Borden cited in Zuehlke, *Brave Battalion*, 4; *Gazette* cited in ibid., 3; Skelton, *The Canadian Dominion*, 258–9.

31 Skelton, *The Canadian Dominion*, 258–9; 269; Careless, *Canada*, 327; Granatstein, et al., *Twentieth Century Canada*, 93; Cook, *At the Sharp End*, 10; Iarocci, *Shoestring Soldiers*, 15; Creighton, *Canada's First Century*, 157. For examples of Canadian accounts that focus primarily on immediate causes, see Morton, *When Your Number's Up*, 2; Greenfield, *Baptism of Fire*, 2. For those that depict Britain as standing above the quarrels of the continent, see Swettenham, *To Seize the Victory*, 27; Stacey, *Canada and the Age of Conflict*, 173–4; Morton, *A Military History of Canada*, 130; Zuehlke, *Brave Battalion*, 2–3. For those that begin with the Canadian reaction, see Creighton, *Dominion of the North*, 436; Creighton, *Canada's First Century*, 136; Morton, *The Kingdom of Canada*, 420; Cook, Ricker, and Saywell, *Canada, A Modern Study*; McKee, *Vimy Ridge*, 24; Burton, *Vimy*, 29; Cassar, *Hell in Flanders Fields*, 15; Bercuson, *The Fighting Canadians*, 127.

32 Cohen, *The American Revisionists*, 95–7; Hofstadter, *The Progressive Historians*, xii, 437. Turner's thesis first appeared in print as "The Significance of the Frontier in American History," *Proceedings of the State Historical Society of Wisconsin*, 14 December 1893.

33 Cited in Hofstadter, *The Progressive Historians*, 438.

34 Ian Tyrrel comments on both *The Rise of American Civilization* and the Beard's subsequent collaboration, *America in Midpassage* (1939): "Immensely successful, these volumes served a generation as textbooks in high schools and colleges, winning critical praise from reviewers" (Tyrrell, *Historians in Public*, 61); Beard, *The Rise of American Civilization*, 617 (first quote, 630–1; 484 second quote).

35 Ibid., 531.

36 Beard cited in Hofstadter, *The Progressive Historians*, 171 n3; Hendrickson, *Union, Nation, or Empire*, 356. Examples of disapproving looks at the United States in Latin America include Nearing and Freeman, *Dollar Diplomacy*, and Jenks, *Our Cuban Colony*. For a summary of these interwar historiographical trends, see Combs, *American Diplomatic History*, 114–15.

37 Morton, *A Military History of Canada*, 148, 151; Berger, *The Sense of Power*, 264; Yearwood, *Guarantee of Peace*, 143.

38 White cited in Granatstein, *How Britain's Weakness*, 14; Owram, "Canada and the Empire," 154.

39 First Underhill quote cited in Berger, *The Writing of Canadian History*, 77; second cited in Francis, *Frank H. Underhill*, 106; Massolin, *Canadian Intellectuals*, 81–2; "Toronto Professors Censured in the Legislature; Hepburn Demands Curb," *Globe and Mail*, 14 April 1939; "Professors and Politicians," *Hamilton Review*, 26 January 1940.

40 Underhill, "Goldwin Smith," 292–4; Lower to Underhill, 6 October 1940, and Lower to Underhill, 14 November 1936, "A.R.M Lower" file, Box 5, Frank Underhill Fonds, MG 30 D204, Library and Archives Canada; Berger, *The Writing of Canadian History*, 79–80. On Underhill's correspondence with both the University of Toronto and Carlyle King on this issue, see Frank Underhill Fonds, Box 19. On the cancelled subscription, see ibid., Underhill to Laski, 5 February 1937, "Harold Laski" file. King mentions that he was a former student of Underhill's in ibid., King to Underhill, 4 March 1950, Box 5.

41 Buckner, "Introduction: Canada and the British Empire," in Buckner, *Canada and the British Empire*, 5; see speeches by H.S. Hamilton and Mackenzie King, *Hansard*, Fifth (Special War) Session, 18th Parliament, 7–13 September 1939 (Ottawa: King's Printer, 1939), 9, 22.

42 Hamilton cited ibid., 9; Blackmore cited ibid., 47, 50.

43 Hendrickson, *Union, Nation, or Empire*, 358 (Schlesinger quote), 369; "The President's War," *The Christian Century*, 8 January 1941, 49. For a recent study of this virulent debate, Olson's aptly titled *Those Angry Days*.

44 Herring, *From Colony to Superpower*, 484, 519–26, 537; Hendrickson, *Union, Nation, or Empire*, 369.

45 Young, *Postcolonialism*, 180; Heiss, "The Evolution," 533–4; *Life* cited in ibid; Roosevelt cited in Felix Belair, "Roosevelt Warns Americans to Meet Force with Force," *New York Times*, 16 April 1940.

46 Rotter, *Comrades at Odds*, 161. For two excellent summaries of the postwar projection of US power and the ways in which scholars have interpreted it, see La Feber, "The Tension"; and Cox and Kennedy-Pipe, "The Tragedy of American Diplomacy?"

47 Fousek, *To Lead the Free World*, 81–2 (quote); Fenster, *Conspiracy Theories*, 5–7; Breisach, *Historiography*, 361–3; Morgan, *Into New Territory*, 11–15; Hofstadter, The *American Political Tradition*, xxxvi.

48 Boorstin, *The Genius of American Politics*, 1; Bell, *The End of Ideology*; Gilman, *Mandarins of the Future*, 4.

49 Ibid., 11. For a summary of this line of reasoning and some of its leading advocates, see Nashel, "Modernization Theory in Fact and Fiction," 132–54.

50 Breisach, *Historiography*, 364.

51 William Appleman Williams, "The Frontier Thesis and American Foreign Policy," in Berger, *A William Appleman Williams Reader*, 96; William Appleman Williams, "The Age of Corporation Capitalism, 1882-," in Berger, *A William Appleman Williams Reader*, 262.

52 Williams, "The Tragedy of American Diplomacy," 39.

53 Gaddis cited in Crapol, "Coming to Terms with Empire," 103; Schonberger, "William H. Becker," 249; Perkins, *"The Tragedy of American Diplomacy,"* 15. For post-9/11 works that draw extensively on Williams's ideas, see Berman, *Dark Ages America*; Bacevich, *American Empire*; and Phillips, "The Tragedy of American Diplomacy."

54 Paterson, "United States Intervention in Cuba," 354; Williams, "United States Indian Policy," 810–31. For an early racial analysis of the War of 1898, see Merriam, "Racism," 369–80. For a summary of race-based approaches to explaining US intervention, see Paterson, "United States Intervention in Cuba"; Love, *Race Over Empire*; and Tebbel, *America's Great Patriotic War*. On the myriad interpretations of Wilson's Latin American policy, see Brian McKercher, "Reaching for the Brass Ring: The Recent Historiography of Interwar American Foreign Relations," in Hogan, *Paths to Power*, 176–223. On race and the atomic bombings, see Dower,

War Without Mercy. A seminal work on the influence of race on US foreign policy in general is Hunt, *Ideology and U.S. Foreign Policy.*

55 Bacevich, "Breaking Washington's Rules," 25; Johnson, *Nemesis,* 278; Bacevich, *American Empire,* 218–19.

56 Rosenberg, *Spreading the American Dream,* 7–10; Wagnleitner, *Coca-Colonization;* Ninkovich, *The Diplomacy of Ideas.* For a survey of these approaches to culture and empire, see Gienow-Hecht, "Shame on US?"; and Griffin, "The Cultural Turn." On understandings of hegemony, the field's debt to Antonio Gramsci can hardly be overstated. A summary of this influence is provided in Bennett, "Popular Culture," 217–24.

57 Maier, "Introduction," in Gardner and Young, eds., *The New Empire,* xi; Kagan, "The Benevolent Empire"; Krauthammer cited in Emily Eakin, "All Roads Lead To D.C.," *New York Times,* 31 March 2002; Hitchens, "Imperialism"; Cheney seasonal wishes cited in Lieven, *America Right Or Wrong,* 154.

58 Whitaker and Marcuse, *Cold War Canada,* 140; Massolin, *Canadian Intellectuals,* 11; Owram, "Canada and the Empire," 155. For a discussion of the public debates in Canada surrounding the creation of NATO, see Teigrob, *Warming Up to the Cold War,* 127–67.

59 Teigrob, *Warming Up to the Cold War,* 200–2.

60 Creighton, *Canada's First Century,* 245; Innis cited in Massolin, *Canadian Intellectuals,* 199; Grant, *Lament for a Nation;* Buckner, "Introduction," in Buckner, *Canada and the End of Empire,* 2, 5; Davies, *World of Wonders,* in *The Depford Trilogy,* 773. For a concise examination of Canadian intellectual life from this era, and of the "new nationalist" critique of the perceived Americanization of Canada, see Edwardson, "Kicking Uncle Sam Out."

61 Buckner, "Introduction," in Buckner, *Canada and the End of Empire,* 7–9; Minifie, *Peacemaker or Powder-Monkey,* 5. For other examples, see Hertzman et al., *Alliances and Illusions;* Warnock, *Partner to Behemoth;* Igartua, *The Other Quiet Revolution,* 1.

62 Douglas, "Marching to Different Drums," 248.

63 Cook, *Clio's Warriors,* 210–11; Halladay, "Renegotiating National Boundaries." The works cited in note 61 represent a critical leftist analysis of Canadian military and foreign policy, but aim their venom at the nation's Cold War acquiescence to a continental militarism that began with the 1940 Ogdensburg Agreement, not at Canada's wars per se.

64 Innis cited in Massolin, *Canadian Intellectuals,* 199. While certainly not alone, the leading spokesman for these views remains J.L. Granatstein. See "Peacekeeping: Did Canada Make a Difference? And What Difference did Peacekeeping Make to Canada?" in English and Hillmer, *Making a Difference?,* 222–36; and *Who Killed Canadian History?,* 123, 89, xvii.

Bercuson's *Significant Incident* blamed peacekeeping for the malaise that led frustrated Canadian soldiers to commit atrocities against Somali citizens in the 1990s. And writing in the aftermath of an almost universally panned American invasion of Iraq, Granatstein still maintained that Canada's economic dependence on the United States should have brought his nation into the war. "We are extremely vulnerable if the administration in Washington is unhappy with us, and we are in peril if border crossings are slowed even for a few minutes for each truck or if passports are required to cross the border. The need to keep the economy strong ought to have determined the Iraq question for us" (Granatstein, *Whose War is It?*, 151). As Political Scientist Phil Ryan wondered, "would anyone be willing to risk being killed by an IED in order that Ford Canada's shipments to Ford U.S. might spend two minutes less at the border?" (Ryan, "Beware 'Shared Memory,'" 29). This coordinated peacekeeping-bashing is described in Richler, *What We Talk About*, 64–8.

65 Thomas Hardy, *The Dynasts* (1904) cited in Richler, *What We Talk About*, 15; McKay and Swift, *Warrior Nation*, 287.

66 Vance, *Death So Noble*, 26–9; Cook, *Clio's Warriors*, 93, 130; Greenfield, *Baptism of Fire*, 356.

67 Andrew Smith "Canadian Progress and the British Connection: Why Canadian Historians Seeking the Middle Road Should Give 2½ Cheers for the British Empire," in Dummit and Dawson, *Contesting Clio's Craft*, 75.

68 Cook, "A Reconstruction of the World"; Allan Gotlieb and Thomas Delworth, "The Queen has her Place, But So Do the Pellans," *Globe and Mail*, 27 August 2011; Gloria Galloway, "Navy, Air Force will become 'Royal' Again," *Globe and Mail*, 16 August 2011; Christina Blizzard, "Promises were 'Far Surpassed,'" *The Daily Press* (Timmins), 9 July 2011; Jane Taber, "Harper Spins a New Brand of Patriotism," *Globe and Mail*, 20 August 2011; Granatstein cited in Tristen Hopper, "'Royal' Returns for Canada's Armed Forces," *National Post*, 15 August 2011.

69 Robert Finch cited in Gloria Galloway, "Navy, Air Force will become 'Royal' Again," *Globe and Mail*, 16 August 2011.

4 Political Cultures: The Architecture of Governance

1 I use the term "regime" here in the sense employed by political scientists Patrick Malcolmson and Richard Myers: "the form of government and the underlying political principles that provide the legitimate basis for that form of government. It thus provides the answer to the question: who rules and why?" Malcolmson and Myers, *The Canadian Regime*, 3–4.

2 Wiseman, *In Search*, 13.

3 Cited in Billias, *American Constitutionalism*, 59.

4 Kirk, "A Revolution." Kirk borrowed the phrase from Edmund Burke, who coined it to describe Britain's Glorious Revolution of 1688. Shays's Rebellion, an armed uprising by Massachusetts farmers in 1786–7 against farm foreclosures was the most serious of these post-independence revolts. See Leonard L. Richards' *Shays's Rebellion*. This incident was preceded by the smaller Pennsylvania Mutiny of 1783, a protest of some five hundred veterans demanding payment for their service in the American Revolutionary War. The soldiers besieged Philadelphia's State House (now Independence Hall), an act that led the framers of the Constitution to set aside a separate federal district where Congress would provide for its own security. See Powe, *The Fourth Estate*, 31–2. For an excellent recent study of the Constitutional debates, see Maier, *Ratification*.

5 Schaffner, *Politics, Parties, and Elections*, 119–20. While the president doubles as the military commander-in-chief, the decision to declare war rests with Congress; the latter's power to enact legislation is constrained by the presidential veto, which itself can be overturned by a two-thirds vote in Congress. The executive negotiates treaties with foreign powers, but those treaties must be ratified by Congress.

6 Oleszek, "Party Whips."

7 Tocqueville, *Democracy in America*, 99; Ralph Waldo Emerson, "Self-Reliance," 1841, cited in Benjamin Anastas, "The Foul Reign of 'Self-Reliance,'" *New York Times Magazine*, 4 December 2011, 59.

8 Thayer, *Who Shakes the Money Tree?*, 30; Twain cited in ibid., 41; Cameron cited in ibid., 44, 73. As a recent statistical analysis of congressional financing demonstrated, "the more business PAC contributors pairs of U.S. House members share in common, the more similarly they vote," regardless of party affiliation (Peoples and Gortari, "The Impact of Campaign Contributions," 57). Attempts to place a ceiling on what candidates can spend, meanwhile, have been struck down by the Supreme Court as an infringement on free speech ("An Idea Worth Saving," *New York Times*, 6 May 2012).

9 Szilard cited in DeBenedetti and Chatfield, *An American Ordeal*, 55; Colson cited in Douglas Martin, "Stewart R. Mott, 70, Offbeat Philanthropist, Dies," *New York Times*, 14 June 2008. For an early work on the relationship between the military-industrial-complex and politicians, see Adams, *The Politics of Defense Contracting*. See also Hartung, *Prophets of War*; and Craig and Logevall, *America's Cold War*, 7–8.

10 DeConde, *Ethnicity, Race, and American Foreign Policy*, 6; Brewer, *Why America Fights*, 69; Klein, *A Population History*, 112–13, 147–8; Cravins,

"Scandinavian Regions," 172–4. For an engaging study of the Great Migration, see Wilkerson, *The Warmth of Other Suns*.

11　Siracusa and Coleman, *Depression to Cold War*, 50; Wilson, *American Political Leaders*, 41. On the matter of Senate influence over foreign policy, the Constitution gives that body exclusive powers over treaty ratification and ambassadorships.

12　Denison cited in Berger, *The Sense of Power*, 164; see ibid., 162–5 for a range of similar views; DeConde cited in Ambrosio, "Ethnic Identity Groups," 5; Carlisle, *World War I*, 163.

13　Wison cited in Fried, *The Russians are Coming!*, 6; Small, *Democracy and Diplomacy*, xvi.

14　Truman cited in Preston, *Sword of the Spirit*, 437; Kennan cited in Smith, *Foreign Attachments*, 5. For a recent, and highly critical, assessment of Truman's role in the creation of Israel, see Judis, *Genesis*.

15　Congress became, in other words, more like the Westminster system devised by the United Kingdom. This was the charge leveled against the unprecedented partisanship in Washington by moderate Republican Senator Olympia Snowe of Maine in announcing that she would not run for re-election in 2012. "We are becoming more like a Parliamentary system, where everyone simply votes with their party and those in charge employ every possible tactic to block the other side," lamented the three-term senator noted for her capacity for brokering bipartisan consensus. (Frank Bruni, "Snowe's Sad Retreat," *New York Times*, 3 March 2012). On the evolution of voting patterns in the US south, see Shafer and Johnston, *The End of Southern Exceptionalism*. On the increased polarization between Democrats and Republicans, see Polsby, *How Congress Evolves*.

16　Avella, "The President, Congress, and Decisions," 51; Lordan, *The Case for Combat*, 12.

17　Brewer, *Why America Fights*, 94–5; Alterman, *When Presidents Lie*, 16–17.

18　Fulbright cited in Alterman, *When Presidents Lie*, 17; Bonn and Welch, *Mass Deception*, 96.

19　Logevall, "A Critique of Containment"; Marshall and Truman cited in Freeland, *The Truman Doctrine*, 100–1; Lordan, *The Case for Combat*, 12.

20　Woodward, "The Age of Reinterpretation," 8; Preston, *Sword of the Spirit*, 10; McKinley summarized in Brewer, *Why America Fights*, 9–10; Woodrow Wilson, "Wilson's War Message to Congress," *World War I Document Archive*, http://wwi.lib.byu.edu/index.php/Wilson's_War_Message_to_Congress (accessed 6 June 2013); Wilson's charge to the CPI cited in Brewer, *Why America Fights*, 55.

21　Abraham Lincoln, "The Half-Insane Mumbling of a Fever Dream," in Polner and Woods, *We Who Dared*, 31–2; George Frisbie Hoar, "Against

Imperialism," in Ravitch, *The American Reader*, 339. Hoar was not the only Republican to rebuke his own president. Former President Benjamin Harrison publically condemned McKinley's Philippine policy, and McKinley's own secretary of state, John Sherman, spoke out against the campaign against the Filipinos after resigning his position in April 1898 (Mayers, *Dissenting Voices*, 201).

22 Democratic Party Platforms: "Democratic Party Platform of 1900," 4 July 1900, online by Gerhard Peters and John T. Woolley, *The American Presidency Project*, http://www.presidency.ucsb.edu/ws/?pid=29587 (accessed 7 June 2013).

23 "George Norris Assails the Senate Resolution," in Stellato, *Not in Our Name*, 87–8; George McGovern, "This Chamber Reeks of Blood," in Polner and Woods, *We Who Dared*, 238–9. On the anthologies, see, for example, Stellato, *Not in Our Name*; Polner and Woods, *We Who Dared*; Ravitch, *The American Reader*; and Olson, *Landmark Speeches on the Vietnam War*.

24 Hoffer, *The Caning of Charles Sumner*, 11–13, 105; Wineapple, cited in David S. Reynolds, "Patriotic Roar: 'Ecstatic Nation,'" *New York Time Book Review*, 9 August 2013.

25 Alterman, *When Presidents Lie*, 16; Brewer, *Why America Fights*, 8–10, 28–9, 55; Garrison cited in ibid., 38; Truman's about face summarized in ibid., 145; Norris, "Wealth's Terrible Mandate," 119.

26 "Pentagon Papers: The Secret War," *Time*, 28 June 1971, 16.

27 Arendt, *Crises of the Republic*, 14.

28 Eric Schmidt, "Fast Withdrawal of G.I.'s Is Urged by Key Democrat," *New York Times*, 18 November 2005.

29 H. Scadding (first quote) and J.G. Bourinot (second quote) cited in Berger, *A Sense of Power*, 124; Lipset, *Continental Divide*, 12. As Philip Massolin demonstrated, influential English-speaking elites continued to express "contempt for democracy and [a] respect for the role of privilege," and promote Burkean "organic, evolutionary change" over revolution well into the twentieth century; such inclinations were shared and often eclipsed by French Canadian elites (Massolin, *Canadian Intellectuals*, 241, 5).

30 Joseph Wearing, "Ideological and Historical Perspectives," in Azoulay, *Canadian Political Parties*, 9–10. John Ralston Saul ascribes a portion of Canada's commitment to egalitarianism, the balance between group and individual rights, and the emphasis on negotiation rather than conflict to the Métis influence on national development. See Saul, *A Fair Country*.

31 Ajzenstat and Smith, "Liberal Republicanism," 5, 3. The pre-eminence of this liberal orientation in American development is unarguable; since the 1980s, a multitude of scholars from a range of disciplines have likewise

designated liberalism as Canada's predominant motif, notwithstanding
the odes to the "common good" that pepper Canadian political discourse.
See McKay, "The Liberal Order Framework"; and Michel Ducharme and
Jean-François Constant, "Introduction: A Project of Rule Called Canada –
The Liberal Order Framework and Historical Practice," in Constant
and Ducharme, *Liberalism and Hegemony*, 3–32. For Ajzenstat and Smith,
Canada's (American-influenced, and often American-born) radical
republicans represented the more faithful advocates of the common
good; it was William Lyon Mackenzie King, Louis-Joseph Papineau, and
their ilk who inveighed most sincerely against rampant individualism,
competition, greed, and paternalistic elitism, and who petitioned, and later
fought, for a regime premised on equality and virtue (6–7).

32 As Jerry Bannister argued, liberal ideology may have achieved hegemony
in Canada over the course of the nineteenth century, but it was an ideology
preceded and coloured by "an early modern loyalist order," which "ensured
that the nascent liberal order in British North America remained distinct from
the American one" (Bannister, "The Loyalist Order Framework," 99, 128).
Ajzenstat's study of Locke illustrates the ability of mythologies to evolve
into actualities, writing that although the Lockean accent on Confederation
is undeniable, that accent was underappreciated and thus diminished by
the practice and interpretation of Canadian governance undertaken by later
lawmakers and scholars. In consequence, the Canadian polity became more
centralized and elitist, more Burkean and illiberal, than originally envisioned
(Ajzenstat, *The Canadian Founding*, 3–6, 180–94). Legal scholar Paul Romney
made a similar argument, holding that while the framers of the 1867 accord
did not in fact envision a highly centralized union, this strong-state myth
would come to "set the terms of the discussion" and form a permanent
facet of English Canadian identity (Romney, *Getting it Wrong*, 16).

33 Romney, *Getting it Wrong*, 15; *Methodist* cited in Berger, *The Sense of
Power*, 155; criticisms of politicians, ibid., 199–203. For examples of recent
Canadian odes to the (embellished) US-Canada dichotomy, see Bannister,
"The Loyalist Order Framework," 128.

34 William Cross and John Chrysler, "Financing Party Leadership Campaigns,"
in Young and Jansen, *Money, Politics, and Democracy*, 146; Malcolmson and
Myers, *The Canadian Regime*, 125. As Michael Bliss observed, "a ministry with
the confidence of a legislature can do anything it wants within the limits of
the Constitution. And our Constitution imposes very few limits" (Michael
Bliss, "Sending Government to the Box," *Globe and Mail*, 24 October 2012).

35 Dan Azoulay, "The Evolution of Party Organization in Canada, 1900–1984,"
in Azoulay, *Canadian Political Parties*, 29.

36 J.L. Granatstein, "Multiculturalism and Canadian Foreign Policy," in
Carment and Bercuson, *The World in Canada*, 82; Morton, *A Short History
of Canada*, 185; *La Presse* cited in Keshen, *Propaganda and Censorship*, 4.
On the lasting grudge, see Desbarats and Greer, "The Seven Years' War,"
145–78, esp. 156. On concerns over secularism of France, see Ducharme,
"Interpreting the Past," 136–60.

37 Lapointe cited in MacFarlane, *Earnest Lapointe*, 179; King cited ibid., 194.

38 Ibid., 5–7, 197–9. Even though francophones lost the conscription battle,
Donald Creighton carped that the debate over conscription during the
Second World War verified "the basic doctrinal truth that French Canada
possessed rights superior to those of English Canada," and called the
Liberal Party's "sedulous concern for public opinion in Quebec" a defect
which "[e]veryone of any consequence" readily understood (Creighton,
The Forked Road, 69, 56). While recent scholarship points to the increasing
influence of rapidly expanding percentages of minority groups on
Canadian foreign policymaking over the last three decades, the nation
is only now confronting a set of circumstances that has characterized
American policymaking for over a century. Still, a recent study comparing
voting patterns among Canadian and American legislators determined
that in the United States, federal representatives sharing the same ethnic
background were significantly more likely to vote in similar ways
regardless of party affiliation, a consonance that was not found among their
Canadian counterparts (Peoples and Gortari, "The Impact of Campaign
Contributions," 58–9). As Janet Hiebert observed, "[i]ncreasingly, interest
and minority groups have questioned the ability of the traditional political
parties to represent the wide variety of social, cultural and economic
interests that exist in Canada" (Hiebert, "Interest Groups," 8). For a wide-
ranging discussion on the present impact of ethnic groups on Canadian
foreign policy, see Carment and Bercuson, *The World in Canada*.

39 Palmer, "Politics, Religion, and Antisemitism," 193 n51. On Canadian third
parties, see Wearing, "Ideological and Historical Perspectives"; Éric Bélanger,
"Third Party Success in Canada," in Gagnon and Tanguay, *Canadian Parties
in Transition*, 83–109. In early twentieth century Canada, the Progressive
Party emerged to speak for agrarian interests (and tellingly, called for
greater grassroots accountability in Ottawa through the abolition of party
discipline and the institution of American-style primaries); following the
First World War, the party served as the official opposition in Parliament and
formed governments in three provinces. A handful of Labour candidates
won federal and provincial seats during the same period, and in 1932, the
Canadian Commonwealth Federation arose to unite the Progressive and

Labour agenda. By the mid-1940s the CCF had won a provincial election in Saskatchewan and held 28 federal ridings; in 1961, it evolved into the NDP. The Social Credit Party, established in Depression-era British Columbia, appealed to conservative, rural interests in BC, Alberta, and Quebec, and became a force in those provinces and Ottawa in mid-twentieth century. Quebec-only parties also emerged, from the Union National to the Bloc populaire to the Bloc Quebecois. In the United States, only a handful of third party efforts stand out: the agrarian-based Populists emerged as a force in the 1892 election, then were promptly absorbed into the Democratic Party; Socialist Eugene Debs gathered a loyal following in the tumultuous economic climate following the First World War; and southern Democrats who could not countenance their party's progress on civil rights mounted hopeless campaigns for the presidency in 1948 and 1968.

40 As Massolin observed, Canadian elites "explained that Canada was an advanced political entity – far superior to the republic – because of its British connection. The British nexus implied a set of moral virtues that placed the Anglo-Canadian world above other civilizations" (Massolin, *Canadian Intellectuals*, 6). As works by Keshen (*Propaganda and Citizenship*) and Bourrie (*The Fog of War*) make clear, the Canadian state utilized propaganda and censorship extensively during the world wars; my point here is that gross deception was not utilized to manoeuvre the state into foreign conflicts, but rather to maintain support for decisions undertaken by the federal government – often, although not necessarily, through the mechanism of Parliament.

41 Malcolmson and Myers, *The Canadian Regime*, 125. According to a 2010 poll, "two-thirds (66%) of Canadians agree that Question Period is 'just a forum for politicians to grandstand for the media and try to score cheap, political points'" ("Question Period Not Working for Most Canadians," The PPF – Pollara National Dialogue Poll, September 2010, http://www .ppforum.ca/sites/default/files/PPF-Pollara%20FINAL%20ENG.pdf [accessed 8 June 2013]).

42 Laurier cited in Gordon T. Stewart, "The Poverty of Canadian Politics?," in Ware, *Democracy and North America*, 33; Waite, "Sir Oliver Mowat's Canada," 24–5; Frances Ryan, "Can Question Period Be Reformed?," *Canadian Parliamentary Review*, Autumn 2009, 18. For examples of acrimonious debating, see, English, *The Worldly Years*, ch. 8; Malcolmson and Myer, *The Canadian Regime*, 125.

43 Wearing "Ideological and Historical Perspectives," 9; Miller, *Painting the Map Red*, 38–48, 152–4.

44 Bourassa cited in Richard, "Henri Bourassa and Conscription," 82 n3; Miller, *Painting the Map Red*, 442, 155.

45 Morton, *A Military History of Canada*, 130 (Laurier quote), 155; Veatch, *Canada and the League of Nations*, 31.
46 Granatstein and Morton, *A Nation Forged in Fire*, 8; *Hansard*, Fifth (Special War) Session, 18th Parliament, 7–13 September 1939 (Ottawa: King's Printer, 1939), 18, 50.
47 Raymond cited in Granatstein, *The Good Fight*, 28; Keshen, *Sinners, Saints, and Soldiers*, 14.
48 CCF Manifesto cited in Naylor, "Pacifism or Anti-Imperialism?," 217; Woodsworth cited in Granatstein, *The Good Fight*, 26, 27; McNaught, "J.S. Woodsworth and War," 186 (Underhill cited in ibid).
49 W.E.C. Harrison, cited in Stairs, *The Diplomacy of Constraint*, 55.
50 Stairs, *The Diplomacy of Constraint*, 56–7.
51 Smith cited in ibid., 57.
52 Ibid., 55 (Boisvert quote), 56, 111–12. On Quebec opposition, see Gordon O. Rothney, "Quebec and Korea," *Canadian Forum*, June 1951, 56.

5 Political Cultures: The Citizen and the State

1 Randolph Bourne, "The State," in Polner and Woods Jr, *We Who Dared*, 133; La Follette cited in Young, *Dissent in America*, 123.
2 Bourne, "The State," 137–8.
3 Bourne cited in Thompson, *Reformers and War*, 30.
4 Bourne cited in Naveh, *Crown of Thorns*, 126; Friedman, *Rethinking Anti-Americanism*, 7; Twain cited in ibid., 35. On the US public's willing participation in smothering wartime dissent, see McGerr, *A Fierce Discontent*, 289–92; and Nagler, "Propaganda and Social Violence," 66-91.
5 Hall and Patrick, *The Pursuit of Justice*, 78–80. Some of the more prominent works in this area include Murray, *Red Scare*; Scheiber, *The Wilson Administration*; Johnson, *The Challenge to American Freedoms*; Preston, *Aliens and Dissenters*; Chatfield, *For Peace and Justice*; Luebke, *Bonds of Loyalty*; Murphy, *World War I*; Gibbs, *The Great Silent Majority*; Polenberg, *Fighting Faiths*; Foster, *The Women and the Warriors*; Early, *A World Without War*. This list owes much to Showalter, "The United States in the Great War," 9.
6 First Huntington quote cited in Friedberg, *In the Shadow*, 13; second cited in Nye, Zelikow, and King, *Why People Don't Trust Government*, 89.
7 Norquist cited in Monika Bauerlein and Clara Jeffery, "The Job Killers," *Mother Jones*, November/December 2011. http://www.motherjones.com/politics/2011/10/republicans-job-creation-kill (accessed 2 January 2013); Stone cited in Guttenplan, *American Radical*, 443.

8 Fiala, *Public War, Private Conscience*; Levi cited in Arendt, *Crises of the Republic*, 52.

9 McWilliams cited in ibid., n3; Arendt cited in Perry, *Civil Disobedience*, ix.

10 Friedberg, *In the Shadow*, 6, 23; Avrich, *Anarchist Voices*, xi; Goodway, *Anarchist Seeds*, 98; Fousek, *To Lead the Free World*.

11 Plummer, *Rising Wind*; Wills, *A Necessary Evil*.

12 Novak, "The Myth," 754–5; McWilliams, *The Idea of Fraternity*; Dionne, *Our Divided Political Heart*; Thoreau cited in Fiala, *Public War, Private Conscience*, 147. The "Swedenization" smear appears in a number of recent blogs and publications, including Kesler, *I Am the Change*.

13 Mazella, *The Making of Modern Cynicism*, 1–3; Waldman, *America and the Limits*, 68–72.

14 McKinley cited in Hendrickson, *The Spanish-American War*, 158; Carnegie cited in Cashman, *America in the Gilded Age*, 348; Bourne cited in Piehl, *"The Catholic Worker,"* 77.

15 Holsti, *Public Opinion*, 17–18; Lipstadt, *Beyond Belief*.

16 Borstelmann, *The 1970s*, 46. Days before the US invasion of Iraq, a *USA Today* poll found that "by a 2-to-1 ratio, Americans favor invading Iraq with U.S. ground troops to remove Saddam Hussein from power." But a portion of that support was predicated on the Bush administration obtaining UN approval for the invasion. If Bush sought UN Security Council approval and was rejected, support for the invasion dropped to 54 per cent. If the administration did not ask for Security Council approval, only 47 per cent were in favour. Lacking the votes necessary for approval, the invasion proceeded without a Security Council vote (Richard Benedetto, "Poll: Most Back War, But Want U.N. Support," *USA Today*, 16 March 2003, http://usatoday30.usatoday.com/news/world/iraq/2003-03-16-poll-iraq_x.htm [accessed 14 January 2013]). By September 2003, six months following an invasion that produced bitter Iraqi resistance but no weapons of mass destruction, a majority of Americans polled believed the war was not "worth its costs" (Joel Roberts, "Poll: Fading Support For Iraq War," CBSNews.com, 10 October 2005, http://www.cbsnews.com/2100-500160_162-930772.html [accessed 6 March 2013]).

17 Berger, *The Sense of Power*, 240; Smith, *War and Press Freedom*, 3–4.

18 Madison, *James Madison's 'Advice,'* 106–7.

19 Higginbotham, *Revolution in America*, 124 n31.

20 Wood, *Militia Myths*, 5; Adams cited in Sarkesianalse, *America's Forgotten Wars*, 105.

21 Stevenson, *Warriors and Politicians*, 2–3; Rubenstein, *Reasons to Kill*, 2.

22 Wood, *Militia Myths*, 5; *Globe* cited in ibid., 6. See Stanley, *Canada's Soldiers*, esp. 417–18, for a later reiteration of the myth.

23 Granatstein, *Canada's Army*, 33; militia officer cited in Wood, *Militia Myths*, 20; Morton cited in Moss, *Manliness and Militarism*, 22.

24 Morton, *A Military History of Canada*, 93, 110; Leacock cited in Ware, "English-Canadian Literature," 113–14. For a detailed study of these transformations, see Wood, *Militia Myths*; and Moss, *Manliness and Militarism*.

25 Berger, *The Sense of Power*, 233; Smith cited in Wood, *Militia Myths*, 151; Morton, *A Military History of Canada*, 116–17.

26 Fisher, *The War Power*, 17 (Lincoln quote), 18; Schlesinger Jr, "War and the Constitution," 176.

27 Seymour, *American Insurgents*, 42; Charles Howlet, "Parrington's Opposition," 53.

28 McKay, *Reasoning Otherwise*, 1; Tunnell, "Worker Insurgency and Social Control," 79; Gauvreau, "Beyond the Search," 55–6; Underhill cited in Berger, *The Writing of Canadian History*, 64.

29 Brison, *Rockefeller, Carnegie, and Canada*, 72; Gauvreau, "Beyond the Search," 56; Mackey, *The House of Difference*, 54; Iacovetta, "Making Model Citizens," 154–67.

30 Berger, *The Sense of Power*, 175; "Anarchism," *The Canadian Encyclopedia*, http://www.thecanadianencyclopedia.com/articles/anarchism (accessed 6 March 2013); Tomchuck, "Transnational Radicals"; McKay, *Reasoning Otherwise*, 80–2, 192, 536n67. Estimates for the total number of casualties in wars between white Americans and indigenous peoples from 1775 to 1890 range from 57,500 to 72,500, with roughly 70 per cent of these being indigenous (Pierpaoli, "American Indian Wars," 12). A series of notorious massacres during the nineteenth century saw white assailants – both civilian and military – ritually mutilate their adversaries. During this same era, the Canadian government generally avoided using the military to enforce Indian policy, and the country often served as a safe haven for indigenous peoples fleeing the violence to the south (Utley and Washburn, *Indian Wars*). The most notorious clash, the Northwest Rebellion, resulted in roughly 200 deaths, making it "by far the bloodiest incident in [post-Confederation] Canadian history" (Torrance, *Public Violence in Canada*, 21).

31 Clark, *The Developing Canadian Community*, 232; Presthus, *Elite Accommodation*, 32.

32 Taylor, *Radical Tories*, 168; Underhill cited in ibid.

33 Wise, "Colonial Attitudes," 23; Fierlbeck, *Political Thought in Canada*, 50. I am not entirely clear on whether Feirlbeck is endorsing the idea of peaceful settlement or reporting on the way the issue has been framed by Canadian

analysts. In the sense that the author is presenting evidence that has been *routinely deployed* to "prove" Canadians' lawfulness, her statement is incontestable. For a harrowing look the Canadian government's program of ethnic cleansing, see Daschuk, *Clearing the Plains*; and Louis A. Knafla, "Violence on the Western Canadian Frontier: A Historical Perspective," in Ross, *Violence in Canada*, 10–39.

34 Fierlbeck, *Political Thought in Canada*, 127; Hale, *The Politics of Taxation*, 149; Béland and Lecours, *Nationalism and Social Policy*, 53. Polls revealed that the percentage of Canadians who considered "big government" a greater threat to the nation than labour unions or big business sat at 23 percent in 1969, but jumped to 56 per cent in 1991 (Roberts, *Recent Social Trends*, 435).

35 Creighton, *Canada's First Century*, 138; Doherty cited in Bushnell, *Captive Court*, 201. See also Creighton, *Dominion of the North*, 439.

36 Kealey, "State Repression," 286–7; Cook and Brown, *Canada, 1896–1921*, 226; Keshen, *Propaganda and Censorship*, 67.

37 McCormack, *Reformers, Rebels, and Revolutionaries*, 118; Bannister, "The Loyalist Order Framework," 127. For examples of more recent and less buoyant views on domestic wartime policies see Keshen, *Propaganda and Citizens*; Kealey, "State Repression of Labour"; Greenhous and Douglas, *Out of the Shadows*, 252; Bushnell, *Captive Court*, 201; and Bothwell, *Canada and Quebec*, 93. On Muriel Duckworth, see Marion Kerans, "Muriel Duckworth: the Peace Movement's Best Friend," *Peace Magazine* (October-November 1988): 8, http://peacemagazine.org/archive/v04n5p08.htm (accessed 5 February 2013); and Kerans, *Muriel Duckworth*.

38 Cooke, *Reporting the War*, 1; Collins and Chatlain, *We Must Not Be Afraid*, 65–6; Jefferson cited in Humphrey *The Press of the Young Republic*, 72; Smith, *War and Press Freedom*, 4.

39 For a survey of twentieth-century American muckraking and investigative reporting that includes reprints of some of the more influential examples, see Jensen, *Stories that Changed America*. For the rather tepid press protests against the First World War Espionage and Sedition Acts, see Cooke, *Reporting the War*, 99–101.

40 McGerr, *A Fierce Discontent*, 289; Robert La Follette, "The People Do Not Want This War," in Polner and Woods Jr, *We Who Dared*, 128–9; Overbeck and Belmas, *Major Principles*, 46.

41 Hall and Patrick, *The Pursuit of Justice*, 78; Zinn, *A People's History*, 145; O'Hare cited in Zinn, *Declarations of Independence*, 158; Brewer, *Why America Fights*, 71, 82 (Beard quote); Walker, *In Defense of American Liberties*, 21.

42 Brewer, *Why America Fights*, 88, 103; Smith, *War and Press Freedom*, 63. For a summary of the vast scholarship on Japanese internment, see Pederson, *A Companion to Franklin D. Roosevelt*.

43 May, *The Big Tomorrow*; Brewer, *Why America Fights*, 90.

44 Henry R. Luce, "The American Century," *Life*, 17 February 1941, reprinted in Hogan, *The Ambiguous Legacy*, 11–29; Schlesinger, *The Vital Center*; Hunt, *The Turning*, 4, 92.

45 "Our Mission," Veterans for Peace website, http://www.veteransforpeace. org/who-we-are/our-mission/ (accessed 8 February 2013); Bush impeachment call cited in Laufer, *Mission Rejected*, 125; Obama impeachment call dated 22 August 2011, cited in Veterans for Peace, "Impeachment Of President Barack H. Obama For War Crimes," Global Research, http://www.globalresearch.ca/impeachment-of-president-barack-h-obama-for-war-crimes/5318950 (accessed 14 January 2013). On US veterans' outspokenness, see Paul Koring, "Speaking Truth to Power Part of U.S. Military Tradition," *Globe and Mail*, 8 October 2009.

46 Johnson, *Nemesis*, 278. Johnson's other titles include *Blowback*, *The Sorrows of Empire*, and *Dismantling the Empire*. For a small sampling of similar works, see Bacevich, *Washington Rules*; Bacevich, *The New American Militarism*; Boggs, *Imperial Delusions*; Goodman, *National Insecurity*; Denson, *Costs of War*; Glain, *State vs. Defense*; Rothbard, *The Betrayal*. On Johnson's background and motivations, see Tom Engelhardt, "On Our Military Empire – Part I: Cold Warrior in a Strange Land," *Mother Jones*, 21 March 2006, http://www.motherjones.com/politics/2006/03/our-military-empire (accessed 4 March 2013).

47 Bacevich, "Breaking Washington's Rules," 25.

48 Guttenplan, *American Radical*, xiv; Hersh's original dispatches on My Lai are reprinted in Bates, Lichty, Miles, Spector, and Young, *Reporting Vietnam, Part Two*, 13–27. On Hersh's work and its influence, see Miraldi, *Seymour Hersh*. Hersh's reliance on the Constitution to motivate citizen opposition to war was obvious in a column written on the 10th anniversary of the invasion of Iraq: "What's up with our Constitution?," he asked. "How could a small group of hard-line conservatives around President Bush, including Dick Cheney, Donald Rumsfeld, and a few neoconservatives so quickly throw us over the cliff? This included not only a war fought on false pretenses but also a system of torture and indefinite detention that, in far too many cases, ran against our laws and values (and was only partially checked by the Supreme Court) … What happened to our press corps with its alleged independence and its commitment to the First Amendment and the values of the rest of the Bill of Rights? What

about Congressional oversight [?] … Is our Constitution that fragile?" (Seymour Hersh, "Iraq, Ten Years Later: What about the Constitution?" *New Yorker*, 14 March 2013, http://www.newyorker.com/magazine/bios/ seymour_m_hersh/search?contributorName=seymour%20m%20hersh [accessed 18 March 2013]).

49 Cooke *Reporting the War*, 164; Collins and Chatlain, *We Must Not Be Afraid*, 81; Black cited in ibid.

50 Cited in ibid, 75.

51 Ibid; Nixon cited in Ellsberg, *Secrets*, 457.

52 Diane Foster, "Ellsberg, Daniel (1931-)," in Shearer, *Home Front Heroes*, 272–4; Katovsky, *Patriots Act*, 287–95; Michael Kazin, "Daniel Ellsberg, the Original Big Leaker," *New Republic*, 26 June 2013, http://www. newrepublic.com/article/113625/daniel-ellsberg-edward-snowden-and-bradley-manning-leakers (accessed 21 August 2013); Emily Ekins, "Poll Finds Public Split on Whether Edward Snowden Is a Hero or Traitor," *Reason.com*, 19 September 2013, http://reason.com/poll/2013/09/19/ poll-finds-public-split-on-whether-edwa2 (accessed 9 February 2014); Christopher Mandel, "Americans Expose Their Politics through Debate Over Bradley Manning," *OpEdNews*, 20 August 2013, http://www. opednews.com/articles/Americans-Expose-Their-Pol-by-Christopher-Mandel-130820-177.html (accessed 9 February 2014); Lucy Kinder, "Nobel Peace Prize 2013: The Nominees," *The Telegraph* (London), 9 October 2013; Julie Tate, "Bradley Manning gets a billboard in Washington," *Washington Post*, 11 January 2012, http://www.washingtonpost.com/ blogs/checkpoint-washington/post/bradley-manning-gets-a-billboard-in-washington/2012/01/10/gIQA53ntoP_blog.html (accessed 9 February 2013); "Courage to Resist" website, http://couragetoresist.org/donate/ bradley-manning.html (accessed 9 February 2013).

53 "The Times and Iraq," *New York Times*, 26 May 2004; Garance Franke-Ruta, "The NSA Leaks and the Pentagon Papers: What's the Difference Between Edward Snowden and Daniel Ellsberg?," *The Atlantic*, 15 June 2013, http://www.theatlantic.com/politics/archive/2013/06/the-nsa-leaks-and-the-pentagon-papers-whats-the-difference-between-edward-snowden-and-daniel-ellsberg/276741/ (accessed 9 July 2013).

54 Dominique Clément, *Canada's Rights Revolution*, 19.

55 Parnaby and Kealey, "The Origins of Political Policing in Canada," 238–9; Bannister, "The Loyalist Order Framework," 126.

56 Nevitte, *The Decline of Deference*; Newman, *The Canadian Revolution*; Smith, *The People's House*; Keshen, *Propaganda and Censorship*, x.

57 Ibid., xii, xvii, 67, 112.

58 Kealey, "State Repression of Labour," 306; Wood, *Militia Myths*, 252; judge cited in Bushnell, *Captive Court*, 203.

59 McKay, *Reasoning Otherwise*, 399, 83.

60 Kealey, 282 n3, 282; Shaw, *Crisis of Conscience*, 10–11. Important recent works in this vein include Keshen, *Propaganda and Censorship*; Joan Sangster, "Mobilizing Women for War," in Mackenzie, *Canada and the First World War*, 157–93; Glassford and Shaw, *A Sisterhood*; Cuthbertson, *Labour Goes to War*.

61 Ross Lambertson, "Suppression and Subversion: Libertarian and Egalitarian Rights up to 1960," in Miron, *A History of Human Rights*, 28–30.

62 Petrou, *Renegades*, 16–23; Canadian volunteer Ron Liversedge cited in ibid., 31; American commissar cited in ibid., 25. On the background and makeup of the American volunteers, see Carroll, *The Odyssey*.

63 Petrou, *Renegades*, 18–19; Whitaker and Marcuse, *Cold War Canada*, 10

64 Kaplan, *State and Salvation*; Lambertson, "Suppression and Subversion," 30.

65 Clément, *Canada's Rights Revolution*, 17–21.

66 Ibid., 22–3; Roberts, *Recent Social Trends*, 433; Watson, *Civil Rights*, 35; Wingrove and Geist cited in Elizabeth Renzetti, "As Government Snoops, Canadians … Take a Nap," *Globe and Mail*, 3 February 2014. In terms of new approaches to war writing, studies of Japanese internment, for instance, began to appear in the late 1970s; see Adachi, *The Enemy that Never Was*; Broadfoot, *Years of Sorrow*; Ward, *White Canada Forever*; and Nakano, *Within the Barbed Wire Fence*. Polls suggested that a majority of Canadians supported the UN intervention in Afghanistan following the 9/11 attacks, but public support turned when Canadian soldiers began taking a central role in ground operations. When the Canadian combat mission ended in 2011, just 30 per cent believed the sacrifice had been worthwhile. See Brian Laghi, "Majority Opposed to Afghan Mission," *Globe and Mail*, 24 February 2006; Thane Burnett, "War Wounds: Poll Suggests We Don't Feel Afghan Mission Was Worth It," *Toronto Sun*, 4 August 2011, http://www.torontosun.com/2011/08/03/war-wounds-poll-suggests-we-dont-feel-afghan-mission-was-worth-it (accessed 30 March 2013).

67 Hedican, *Ipperwash*, 7; Gifford, *Canada's Fighting Seniors*, 137–65; Vipond, "Canadian Nationalism," 43–63. Teigrob, *Warming Up to the Cold War*, 168, 184, 204, 208, 219; Dyer, *Canada in the Great Power Game*, 2–4; Stueck, "Revisionism and the Korean War," 25. As Berger notes, Canadians could also find some of this American-based muckraking journalism reprinted in *Queen's Quarterly* and other Canadian serials (*The Sense of Power*, 190).

68 Hofstadter cited in Combs, *American Diplomatic History*, 212; Rosenberg, *A Day Which Will Live*, 50; Goldberg, "Conspiracy Theories," 1; Knight, *Conspiracy Theories in American History*.

69 Olmsted, *Real Enemies*, 13–44; Combs, *American Diplomatic History*, 140.

70 For a summary of the Pearl Harbor conspiracy theorists, see Rosenberg, *A Date Which Will Live*, 40–3; Edwards, *To Acknowledge a War*, 45; Lisa O'Carroll, "Seymour Hersh on Obama, NSA and the 'Pathetic' American media," *The Guardian*, 27 September 2013, http://www.theguardian.com/media/media-blog/2013/sep/27/seymour-hersh-obama-nsa-american-media (accessed 5 February 2014).

71 See, for instance, Loring Villa, *Unauthorized Action*.

6 Matters of Faith

1 Kramer, *Nationalism*, 1.

2 Timothy Garton Ash offered a different though equally helpful framework, designating states like the United States and Canada "state-nations" rather than "nation-states." "A state-nation," he wrote, "is one in which a shared civic national identity is created by the state, rather than a single ethnic national identity being embodied in it." Timothy Garton Ash, "At Stake in Ukraine's Drama is the Future of Putin, Russia and Europe," *The Guardian*, 21 February 2014.

3 Huntington wrote: "A person can be half-French and half-Arab and simultaneously even a citizen of two countries. It is more difficult to be half-Catholic and half Muslim" (Huntington, "The Clash of Civilizations?," 27); Phillips, *American Theocracy*, 121; Tocqueville, *Democracy in America*, vol. I part 2, chap. 9, 275.

4 Noll, *A History of Christianity*, 546; Heath, *A War with a Silver Lining*, xvi.

5 Horn, *A Land as God Made It*, 24–5; Walsh, *The Role of Religion*, 162.

6 Preston, *Sword of the Spirit*, 25, 32–3.

7 Bailyn, *The Barbarous Years*, 448; Bernard Bailyn, Letter to the Editor, *New York Times Book Review*, 20 January 2013, 6; Hudson, *Religion in America*, 95–6; Preston, *Sword of the Spirit*, 34 (Sutton quote), 45; Martin, *With God on Our Side*, 2.

8 Hudson, *Religion in America*, 6.

9 Ibid., 9–14; Grant, *A Profusion of Spires*, 32; Hudson, *Religion in America*, 96; Crawford and Olson, *Christian Clergy*.

10 Preston, *Sword of the Spirit*, 41; Martin, *With God on Our Side*, 3; Phillips, *American Theocracy*, 122; Hudson, *Religion in America*, 95.

11 Hudson, *Religion in America*, 18; Preston, *Sword of the Spirit*, 117.

12 Massachusetts law cited in ibid., 34; Mayers, *Dissenting Voices*, 87; 167–9; Hudson *Religion in America*, 7, 46, 95, 116. Other prominent Americans who were members of the Society of Friends, or who were raised in the church

and derived a measure of their passion for peace and social justice from the sect, include Lucretia Mott, Susan B. Anthony, Jane Addams, Bayard Rustin, and Mary Calderone. The church's imprint on America's most famous Quaker, Richard Nixon, is less discernible. See Hamm, *The Quakers in America*; and Bacon, *The Quiet Rebels*.

13 Schroth, *The American Jesuits*, 29–30; Noll, *A History of Christianity*, 22–3; Fischer, *Champlain's Dream*, 333.

14 Crowley, "The French Regime," 3, 24, 48 (quote); Greer, *The People of New France*, 14–15.

15 Crowley, "The French Regime," 25; Axtell, *Natives and Newcomers*, 162 (Onondaga quote), 163. On the comparative aspects of English and French missionary efforts, see also page 147 of this same volume.

16 Grant, *A Profusion of Spires*, 15, 29; Knowles, *Inventing the Loyalists*, 14–25. As Grant observed of nineteenth-century Ontario, "in comparison with the United States, [religious affiliation] leaned toward the traditional end of the denominational spectrum" (Grant, *A Profusion of Spires*, 231).

17 Fahey, *In His Name*, 114–15 (Strachan quote), 124, 4; Westfall, *Two Worlds*, 86.

18 Benn, *Historic Fort York*, 61; Grant, *A Profusion of Spires*, 68–70; Choquette, *Canada's Religions*, 206, 208.

19 Fahey, *In His Name*, 124; William Westfall, "Constructing Public Religions at Private Sites: The Anglican Church in the Shadow of Disestablishment," in Van Die, *Religion and Public Life*, 26; Westfall, *Two Worlds*, 83, 85, 119 (*Churchman* quote); Choquette, *Canada's Religions*, 223, 212; Grant, *A Profusion of Spires*, 82.

20 Westfall, *Two Worlds*, 88, 95, 77; Choquette, *Canada's Religions*, 230, 167; Grant, *A Profusion of Spires*, 82, 224; Joseph Wearing, "Ideological and Historical Perspectives," in Azoulay, *Canadian Political Parties*, 9.

21 Westfall, *Two Worlds*, 120, 205 (quote), 193; Grant, *A Profusion of Spires*, 223.

22 Ibid., 196, 231, 233 (United Church quote); William Katerberg, "Consumers and Citizens: Religion, Identity, and Politics in Canada and the United States," in Lyon and Van Die, *Rethinking Church, State, and Modernity*, 286.

23 Grant, *A Profusion of Spires*, 112–13; Phillips, *American Theocracy*, 110–12; Martin, *With God on Our Side*, 4–5.

24 Newlands, "Quakers," *Canadian Encyclopedia*, http://www. thecanadianencyclopedia.com/articles/quakers (accessed 3 April 2014); "About the 1861 Census," *Library and Archives Canada*, http://www. bac-lac.gc.ca/eng/census/1861/Pages/about-census.aspx (accessed 4 April 2014) (by contrast, the US Quakers numbered 90,000 in 2002, down from 121,000 in 1972 ["The Present State of Quakerism," Earlham School

of Religion, http://esr.earlham.edu/support/comprehensive-case/the-vine/present-state-of-quakerism (accessed 30 April 2014)]; Shaw, *Crisis of Conscience*, 48, 135, 48 (Brock quote); Epp, *The Mennonites*, 366. By the end of the century, Canadian Mennonite churches counted nearly 200,000 members; as the group practices adult baptism, this number does not include the children who also attend Mennonite churches (Choquette, *Canada's Religions*, 268).

25 Grant, *A Profusion of Spires*, 23–5; Fair, "Model Farmers," 79–106 (Strachan cited 90).

26 Regehr, *Mennonites in Canada*, 400–8; Wright, *A World Mission*, 13; Shaw, *Crisis of Conscience*, 11, 15 (judge quote).

27 Heath, *A War with a Silver Lining*, 10, 22, 42–5.

28 Ibid., 24; McMaster editorial cited in Berger, *The Sense of Power*, 250; Heath, *A War with a Silver Lining*, 124.

29 Ibid., 62, 80, 50, 60 (quote).

30 Friesen, *In Defense of Privilege*, 365; Heath, *A War with a Silver Lining*, xvii-xviii, 14; Bliss, "The Methodist Church," 214; Miller, *Painting the Map Red*, 23; Meisel, Rocher, and Silver, *As I Recall*, 98. As Carman Miller notes, some English Protestant clergy spoke out against the war and "incurred the wrath of their congregations," while other mainline Protestants "tolerated their minister's pronouncements and sometimes endorsed them" (Miller, *Painting the Map Red*, 23).

31 Wetzel, "Onward Christian Soldiers," 407–11 (Abbot quote).

32 Preston, *Sword of the Spirit*, 6. 217, 221; Shankman, "Southern Methodist Newspapers"; Hudson, *Religion in America*, 249; Quinn, "The Mormon Church"; Abrams, "Remembering the Maine."

33 Henry Van Dyke, "The American Birthright and the Philippine Pottage," in Polner and Woods Jr, *We Who Dared*, 110, 113; Preston, *Sword of the Spirit*, 219, 220 (Simmons quote); Hudson, *Religion in America*, 321.

34 Clarke, "English-Speaking Canada," 335; *Record* cited in Morton and Granatstein, *Marching to Armageddon*, 24; Bliss, "The Methodist Church," 214, 216; Clarke, "English-Speaking Canada," 335; Wright, *A World Mission*, 12; Berger, *The Sense of Power*, 251. On the jingoistic response of the Anglican Church, see Crerar, "The Church in the Furnace."

35 Clarke, "English-Speaking Canada," 337; McGowan, *The Waning of the Green*, 250; McGowan, "To Share in the Burdens," 183, 196 n31.

36 McNaught, *A Prophet in Politics*, 82–7; 97; Wright, *A World Mission*, 13; Shaw, *Crisis of Conscience*, 24, 104–5; Wright, "The Canadian Protestant Tradition," 143.

37 Vance, *Death So Noble*, 36.

38 Ibid., 71, 7; Wright, *A World Mission*, 15; Oliver cited in Clark, "English-Speaking Canada," 339; Wright, *A World Mission*, 14.
39 Vance, *Death So Noble*, 56, 69; Vance, "Sacrifice in Stained Glass," 16. American artist Grant Wood, most famous for his painting *American Gothic*, completed in 1929 one of the more notable stained-glass memorials. Featured in the Veterans Memorial Building in Cedar Rapids, Iowa, the window pays tribute to soldiers from all major American wars to that date, not just the Great War. (Dennis, *Renegade Regionalists*, 106).
40 Berger, *The Writing of Canadian History*, 79. The notion that the sheer scale of the sacrifice inhibited charges of meaninglessness forms a key motif in Vance, *Death So Noble*.
41 Preston, *Sword of the Spirit*, 243.
42 Folly and Palmer, *The A to Z of U.S. Diplomacy*, 270; Preston, *Sword of the Spirit*, 236–245.
43 Ibid., 247, 252; Hudson, *Religion in America*, 326; Bullert, "Reinhold Niebuhr," 272; Sunday cited in Nagler, "Propaganda and Social Violence," 76.
44 Folly and Palmer, *The A to Z of U.S. Diplomacy*, 270; Preston, *Sword of the Spirit*, 266, 271, 273; Gibbons cited in Himes and Cahill, *Modern Catholic Social Teaching*, 495; Capozzola, *Uncle Sam Wants You*, 59–62 (quote on 59).
45 Bullert, "Reinhold Niebuhr," 274; Hudson, *Religion in America*, 365; FCC cited in "The Chaplaincy Question," *The Christian Century*, 16 January 1935, 70; other resolutions cited in Sittser, *A Cautious Patriotism*, 19–20; Abrams, *Preachers Present Arms*; Vance, *Death So Noble*, 30; Page cited in Preston, *Sword of the Spirit*, 298. On the considerable impact of Abrams's book, see Nutt, *The Whole Gospel*, 123.
46 Sittser, *A Cautious Patriotism*, 18–19; Methodists cited in Bullert, "Reinhold Niebuhr," 273; Morrison cited in ibid, 282.
47 Reinhold Niebuhr, "Idealists as Cynics," *The Nation*, 29 January 1940, 73; Brinkley, *Voices of Protest*, 266; Martin, *With God on Our Side*, 19, 11–12; Mayers, *Dissenting Voices*, 270, 275; Abella and Troper, "The Line Must Be Drawn," 181.
48 Preston, *Sword of the Spirit*, 374, 376; Sittser, *A Cautious Patriotism*, 92; Harold E. Fey, "Seventy Years of the Century," *Christian Century*, 28 October 1978, 952; Hudson, *Religion in America*, 389; FCC cited in "American Malvern," *Time*, 16 March 1942, 44; Hudson, *Religion in America*, 389.
49 Preston, *Sword of the Spirit*, 376–9; Boyer, *By the Bomb's Early Light*, 199–200 (final quote); *World* cited in ibid., 203; FCC cited in ibid., 200; Mel Piehl, "The Catholic Worker." On the opposition to the bomb, much of it emerging from various religious communities, see Wittner's magisterial trilogy *One World or None*; *Resisting the Bomb*; and *Toward Nuclear Abolition*.

50 Vance, *Death So Noble*, 71; Wright, *A World Mission*, 4; Wright, "The Canadian Protestant Tradition," 154–6.

51 Clarke, "English-Speaking Canada," 354; Wright, *A World Mission*, 225; Clément, *Canada's Rights Revolution*, 17; Fay, *A History of Canadian Catholics*, 236–8. While Wright's statement captures the overall tenor of Christian church leaders' response to the Nazi persecution of the Jews, Christians' concern for, and activism on behalf of, European Jews varied sometimes markedly according to sect. See Davies and Nefsky, *How Silent Were the Churches?*

52 Clarke, "English-Speaking Canada," 354; Fletcher, "Canadian Anglicanism," 146; Wright, "The Canadian Protestant Tradition," 188; Wright, *A World Mission*, 231; Shaw, *Crisis of Conscience*, 152–3.

53 Miller, *Harry Emerson Fosdick*, 540; Smith cited in Socknat, *Witness against War*, 279; Bangarth, *Voices Raised*, 76, 191. The author's final quote summarizes the findings of Hemmings, "The Church and the Japanese," 136–7.

54 FOR cited in Wittner, *One World or None*, 98; Cecil Swanson, Letter to the Editor, *Canadian Churchman*, 6 September 1945, 7; Socknat, "The Dilemma," 415; Paul Sauriol, "La Bombe Atomique: Nouvelle Arme des Alliés Contre Le Japon," *Le Devoir*, 7 August 1945. For a summary of Canadian denunciations of the bombing on moral grounds, see Teigrob, *Warming Up to the Cold War*, 26–9.

55 Martin, *With God on Our Side*, 13–16; Brinkley, "World War II and American Liberalism," 323; Preston, *Sword of the Spirit*, 441.

56 Martin, *With God on Our Side*, 29 (quote)–33.

57 Preston, *Sword of the Spirit*, 556; Dobson cited in ibid., 557; Martin, *With God on Our Side*, 35; McKay and Swift, *Warrior Nation*, 219; Edwards, *To Acknowledge a War*, 6.

58 Preston, *Sword of the Spirit*, 479–85; "Out of Darkness, Hope!," *Christian Century*, 12 July 1950, 838; second *Century* quote cited in Conway-Lanz, *Collateral Damage*, 153; Swartz, *Moral Minority*.

59 Choquette, *Canada's Religions*, 350; Wright, *A World Mission*, 36; "The Peace Council Men," *Saturday Night*, 29 March 1949, 1; McKay and Swift, *Warrior Nation*, 98, 126; Matthews, "The Christian Churches," 162–3.

60 Choquette, *Canada's Religions*, 349, 351; Matthews, "The Christian Churches," 162–3.

61 Choquette, *Canada's Religions*, 375; Roberts, *Recent Social Trends in Canada*, 359–61; Phillips, *American Theocracy*, 107.

62 McKay and Swift, *Warrior Nation*, 126, 131; Whitaker and Marcuse, *Cold War Canada*, 376; Stevens, *God-Fearing and Free*, 73; Matthews, "Reds and Our Churches," 3.

63 Phillips, *American Theocracy*, 105; Young, "Faith and Politics," 4. For a discussion of the complicated relationship between newer Canadians and national commemorations of war, see Randy Boyagoda, "Toward a More Complex Sense of the Past," *Globe and Mail*, 13 May 2011.

64 Utter and True, *Conservative Christians,*15–16; Choquette, *Canada's Religions*, 320, 374, Clarke, "English-Speaking Canada," 344; John Stackhouse Jr, "Bearing Witness: Christian Groups Engage Politics since 1960," in Lyon and Van Die, *Rethinking Church, State, and Modernity*, 117; McDonald, *The Armageddon Factor*.

7 Race

1 National WWII Museum website, http://www.nationalww2museum.org/visit/exhibits/; Defense News Top 100 for 2012 (accessed 4 January 2013)," *Defense News*, http://special.defensenews.com/top-100/charts/rank_2011.php (accessed 4 January 2013).

2 William Katerberg, "Consumers and Citizens: Religion, Identity, and Politics in Canada and the United States," in Lyon and Van Die, *Rethinking Church, State, and Modernity*, 293. Both the 9/11 attacks and the Bush administration's overt deployment of religious idioms in the prosecution of the subsequent "war on terror" helped to inspire a spate of often condemnatory assessments of religion's role in international relations from Americans and non-Americans alike. See Preston, *Sword of the Spirit*; Martin, *With God on Our Side*; Phillips, *American Theocracy*; Almond, Appleby, and Sivan, *Strong Religion*; Rinehart, *Apocalyptic Faith and Political Violence*; Thomas, *The Global Resurgence of Religion and the Transformation of International Relations*; Harris, *The End of Faith*; and Hitchens, *God is Not Great*.

3 See Goldberg, *Racist Culture*; Goldberg, *The Racial State*.

4 Durham cited in Francis, *National Dreams*, 60; Owram, "Canada and Empire," 147.

5 Blad, *Neoliberalism and National Culture*, 95; Dickinson and Young, *A Short History of Quebec*, 250–3; Morris, *Canadian Language Policies*, 30–1; Meisel, Rocher, and Silver, *As I Recall*, 95, 102.

6 Chartrand, *Canadian Forces in World War II*, 5.

7 Cited in Miller, *Painting the Map Red*, 36.

8 First Bourassa quote cited in Kennedy, *Liberal Nationalisms*, 155; second cited in Meisel, Rocher, and Silver, *As I Recall*, 102; Lavergne cited in ibid; sovereingtists cited in ibid., 105.

9 *Evening News* cited in McKay and Swift, *Warrior Nation*, 57; Hopkins, *The Story of the Dominion*, 549, 550; Hardy, *From Sea unto Sea*, 427; Wrong,

The Canadians, 391; Granatstein, Abella, Bercuson, Brown, and Neatby, *Twentieth Century Canada*, 53.

10 Lower, *Colony to Nation*, 444.

11 Creighton, *Canada's First Century*, 142.

12 Cooper cited in Mayers, *Dissenting Voices*, 196.

13 Aguirre, *Racial and Ethnic Diversity in America*, 26; Frank Hobbs and Nicole Stoops, "Demographic Trends in the 20th Century," US Census Bureau, Census 2000 Special Reports, Series CENSR-4 (Washington, DC: US Government Printing Office, 2002), A-21, A25, http://www.census.gov/prod/2002pubs/censr-4.pdf (accessed 5 February 2013).

14 Vickers and Osei-Kwadwo, *The Politics of Race*, 91 (Macdonald quote)-94; Herberg, *Ethnic Groups in Canada*, 40–2; Reva Joshee, Lauri Johnson, *Multicultural Education Policies in Canada and the United States* (Vancouver: University of British Columbia Press, 2007), 168–9.

15 "NAACP: 100 Years of History," NAACP website, http://www.naacp.org/pages/naacp-history (accessed 12 January 2013); Winegard, *Indigenous Peoples of the British Dominions*, 71; Jeffries, *Wartime America*, 115; Winks, *The Blacks in Canada*, 315, 390–2, 402.

16 Ward, *White Canada Forever*; Oliver Moore, "Burning Cross Ignites Racial Tension in Nova Scotia," *Globe and Mail*, 24 February 2010; Winks, *The Blacks in Canada*, 484.

17 Jacqueline Jones Royster, "Introduction," in Royster, *Southern Horrors and Other Writings*, 10, 26; Keith Thor Carlson, "The Lynching of Louie Sam," *BC Studies*, 109 (Spring 1996): 63–78.

18 Galabuzi, *Canada's Economic Apartheid*, 79; Morton, *A Military History of Canada*, 223; "After the Halifax Riots," *Edmonton Journal*, 16 September 1991 (in the words of the *Journal*, the 1991 Halifax riots "shocked locals" and "Canadians outside Nova Scotia, too. On television they seemed like a scene from an American inner city."); Rucker and Upton, *Encyclopedia of American Race Riots*; Collins, *All Hell Broke Loose*, xv-xvi; Patterson cited in Phillips, *War!*, 10.

19 Backhouse, *Colour-Coded*, 14 (quote); Coleman, *White Civility*, 21, 245 n20; James W. St. G. Walker, "The Law's Confirmation of Racial Inferiority: Christie v. York," in Walker, *The African Canadian Legal Odyssey*, 245; Mensah, *Black Canadians*, 43–4; Barrington Walker, "Introduction: From a Property Right to Citizenship Rights – The African Canadian Legal Odyssey," in Walker, ed., *The African Canadian Legal Odyssey*, 23–4.

20 Myrdal, *An American Dilemma*; Aldridge, "Opportunity Lost." For specialized studies of Cold War activism and internationalism among American blacks, and of the federal government's attempts to "manage"

it, see Dudziak, *Cold War Civil Rights*; Plummer, *Rising Wind*; Von Eschen, *Satchmo Blows up the World*; and Von Eschen, *Race Against Empire*.

21 Singh, *Black is a Country*; Miller, *Benevolent Assimilation*, 127; Dubois, *The Correspondence of W.E.B. Du Bois*, 136. On the battle and the photograph, see Andrew Bacevich, "What Happened at Bud Dajo," *Boston Globe*, 12 March 2006.

22 Gentile, *The Great War and America*, 55; Du Bois cited in Waligora-Davis, *Sanctuary: African Americans and Empire*, 111; Schaffer, *America in the Great War*, 78.

23 Ibid, 79.

24 Aldridge, "Black Powerlessness in a Liberal Era," 89–90.

25 White cited in ibid., 92.

26 Ibid., (Roosevelt quote), 90; NAACP cited in ibid, 96.

27 Plummer, *Rising Wind*, 184–9; Fousek, *To Lead the Free World*, 145; Dudziak, *Cold War Civil Rights*, 62.

28 Westheider, *The African American Experience in Vietnam*, 5–8; Du Bois cited in Phillips, *War!*, 9; Casey, *Selling the Korean War*, 320–1.

29 First Du Bois quote in Schaffer, *America in the Great War*, 80; Reef, *A to Z of African Americans in the Military*, xiii-xiv; second Du Bois quote in Hagedorn *Savage Peace*, 191.

30 Takaki, *Double Victory*, 20; Igartua, *The Other Quiet Revolution*, 11; Dan J. Puckett, "Double V Campaign," 745–6; NAACP cited in Folly, *The United States and World War II*, 61; Reef, *A to Z of African Americans in the Military*, xiv; elderly woman cited in Estes, *I Am a Man!*, 31.

31 *Afro-American* cited in Williams, *Torchbearers of Democracy*, 24; Jeffries, *Wartime America*, 110.

32 Westheider, *The African American Experience*, 5; Baldwin cited in Phillips, *War!* 10; Bodnar, *The "Good War,"* 169–70.

33 Allen, *Vietnam*, 97; King cited in ibid., 98; *Washington Post* cited in ibid., 99.

34 Taylor cited in Chong, *The Oriental Obscene*, 64; Phillips, *War!* 14; Kusch, *All American Boys*, 76. For an in-depth discussion of this transformation of black activism, see Hall, *Peace and Freedom*.

35 Mensah, *Black Canadians*, 49–50, 52; Backhouse, "Bitterly Disappointed," 118; Price, *Orienting Canada*, 145.

36 Barrington Walker, "Introduction: From a Property Right to Citizenship Rights – The African Canadian Legal Odyssey," in Walker, ed., *The African Canadian Legal Odyssey*, 32–4; James W. St. G. Walker, "The Law's Confirmation of Racial Inferiority: Christie v. York," in Walker, *The African Canadian Legal Odyssey*, 243; Backhouse, "Bitterly Disappointed," 117–18; Finkel, *Our Lives*, 10–12.

37 David T. McNab, "A Brief History of the Denial of Indigenous Rights in Canada," in Miron, *A History of Human Rights in Canada*, 99–115.

38 Buckner, "Nationalism in Canada," 114; Mar, *Brokering Belonging*, 12, 126–7; Winegard, *For King and Kanata*, 38; Walker, "Race and Recruitment in World War I," 1; Glasrud, "Introduction: Black Citizen-Soldiers," 1–2.

39 Sheffield, "Fighting a White Man's War?," 69, 73–5; Saugeen letter cited in Winegard, *For King and Kanata*, 36–7; Indian council cited in Schmalz, *The Ojibwa of Southern Ontario*, 230; Morton cited in Mathieu, *North of the Color Line*, 102; Whitney cited in Winks, *The Blacks in Canada*, 316.

40 Chamberlain cited in Winegard, *For King and Kanata*, 37; Winks, *The Blacks in Canada*, 314, 486. As Winks wrote of the situation in the First World War, "Hughes's advisors did not favor an all-Negro unit since at least three thousand black volunteers would be needed to keep a regiment in the field for twelve months." At a time when the total African Canadian population stood at roughly 16,000, this target would have been unattainable (Winks, *The Blacks in Canada*, 314).

41 Walker, "Race and Recruitment," 3–4; Winks, *The Blacks in Canada*, 314–17 (commanders cited 315); Walker, "The Law's Confirmation," 254; Walker, "Race and Recruitment," 7.

42 Walker, "The Law's Confirmation," 255–6; Winks, *The Blacks in Canada*, 318.

43 Chan, *The Chinese in Toronto from 1878*, 66; Walker, "Race and Recruitment," 16–19; officer cited in Mathieu, *North of the Color Line*, 107.

44 Walker, "The Law's Confirmation," 291; Sheffield, "Fighting a White Man's War?" 72; English, *Cream of the Crop*, 23–4.

45 Winegard, *Indigenous Peoples of the British Dominions*, 152; Walker, "Race and Recruitment in World War I," 16.

46 Walker, "The Law's Confirmation," 291; Indian agent cited in Sheffield, "Fighting a White Man's War?" 73; Ross cited in ibid., 79.

47 Ibid., 69–71 (quote, 70), 85 n22; *Star* cited in ibid., 87n43.

48 Winegard, *Indigenous Peoples of the British Dominions*, 152; Sheffield, "Fighting a White Man's War?" 77–9 (quote).

49 Marszalek and Nash, "African Americans in the Military," 1. For an introduction to the vast literature on American blacks and war, for example, see Marszalek and Nash, "African Americans in the Military." As these authors wrote, "*Blacks in the American Armed Forces, 1776–1983: A Bibliography* (1985) by Lenwood G. Davis and George Hall, comps., lists 2,386 books, articles, and dissertations, but this book is already out of date," (Marszalek and Nash, "African Americans in the Military," 1).

50 Brokaw, *The Greatest Generation*, 183 (quote); 185–227; Bodnar, *The 'Good War,'* 175.

51 Walker, "The Law's Confirmation," 290.
52 Winks, *The Blacks in Canada*, 313–14.
53 Creighton, *Canada's First Century*, 142; Morton, "Was The Great War Canada's War Of Independence?"; Bercuson, *Maple Leaf Against the Axis*, 275.
54 Sherene Razack, "From the Somalia Affair to Canada's Afghan Detainee Torture Scandal: How Stories of Torture Define the Nation," in Jerome Klassen and Greg Albo, eds., *Empire's Ally: Canada and the War in Afghanistan* (Toronto: University of Toronto Press, 2013), 367–87; Lori Crowe and Chris Hendershot, "Ambivalent Spectators and Enthusiastic Fans? Mapping Civilian-Military Engagement in Canada," in *War, Ethics and Justice: New Perspectives on a Post 9/11 World* (New York: Routledge, 2011), 79 (quote). See also Smith, *The Dogs are Eating Them Now*, 127–53.
55 Adachi, *The Enemy that Never Was*; Broadfoot, *Years of Sorrow, Years of Shame*; Ward, *White Canada Forever*; Nakano, *Within the Barbed Wire Fence*; Gaffen, *Forgotten Soldiers*. For a summary of subsequent work in this area, see Sheffield, "Fighting a White Man's War?" 67–8; Ruck, *The Black Battalion, 1916–1920*.
56 Granatstein, *Canada's Army*, 72.

8 Making and Breaking Nations

1 According to a recent poll, ninety-four per cent of Americans correctly identified 4 July as Independence Day. The fact that six per cent failed this test troubled *New York Times* columnist Frank Bruni, but for a question on a historical topic, this might be as good as it gets. See Frank Bruni, "America the Clueless," *New York Times*, 12 May 2013.
2 Hickey, *The War of 1812*, 15–17; Borneman, *1812: The War That Forged a Nation*; Henderson, *Stonewall Jackson and the American Civil War*, 127; Rosenberg, *A Day Which Will Live*, 14; Kristin Hoganson, "'Honor Comes First': The Imperatives of Manhood in the Congressional Debate over War," in Bouvier, *Whose America?*, 125, 129 (quote); Roosevelt cited in Zinn, *A People's History*, 93.
3 Rosenberg, *A Day Which Will Live*, 17–18; Roosevelt cited in Clark, *Cold Warriors*, 1. For examples of works on the influence of masculinity on foreign policy see Corber, *Homosexuality in Cold War America*; Cuordileone, "Politics in an Age of Anxiety"; Dean, *Imperial Brotherhood*; Gilbert, *Men in the Middle*; Cuordileone, *Manhood and American Political Culture*.
4 Dean, *Imperial Brotherhood*, 170; Weber, *Faking It*, 32; William Deresiewicz, "An Empty Regard," *New York Times*, 21 August 2011; Rosenberg, *A Day Which Will Live*, 13. See also George, *Awaiting Armageddon*, 118–20.

5 Holman and Thacker, "Literary and Popular Culture," 203–4 (as an
  Ontario primary school student during this era, I can confirm the
  esteemed place of the song in the curriculum). For the considerable impact
  of Henry's words on the American psyche, and his significant debt to
  the Roman orator Cato in crafting the speech, see Shalev, *Rome Reborn on
  Western Shores*, 141–6. As Robin Winks noted, scholars dispute the exact
  wording of Hale's statement from the gallows, but agree on its general
  thrust. See Winks, *Cloak & Gown*, 16.

6 Anderson, *Imagined Communities*; Threlfall, "Empire over Nation"; Knight,
  How the Cold War Began, 155; Ryan Research and Communications, "Royal
  Commission on Renewing and Strengthening Our Place in Canada:
  Provincial Opinion Study" (April 2003), 390–3; Berger, *The Sense of Power*,
  4; Ramsay Cook, "Canadian Centennial Celebrations," 663. Years later,
  Cook did feel compelled to add nuance to his thesis, writing in 2000
  that his earlier taxonomy of Canadian identities had been too static and
  assured. "Identities … are neither hermetically sealed nor easily defined,"
  he argued. "Their edges are always fuzzy and shifting … Identities are
  not essential but contingent, constructed and deconstructed by changing
  historical circumstances" (Cook, "Identities are not like Hats," 264).
  Clearly, this updated view gets us no closer to a fixed, single definition of
  "Canadianism"; indeed, it would appear to render the effort even more
  quixotic.

7 Dandeker, "Nationalism, Nation-States, and Violence at the End of the
  Twentieth Century," 24–5; Gordon, *The Hero and the Historians*, 4; Renan
  cited in Vernes, *Ernest Renan*, 101.

8 Renan cited in ibid; Underhill cited in Mckillop, *Pierre Berton*, 491; Conway
  cited in McKay and Swift, *Warrior Nation*, 257. Canada's citizenship guides
  pointed routinely to these achievements as evidence of citizens' nation-
  building efforts – although the 2009 version demonstrated significantly
  less enthusiasm for the Charter of Rights and Freedoms. See Citizenship
  and Immigration Canada, *Discover Canada*, 14–23; and Marwah,
  Triadafilopoulos, and White, "Immigration, Citizenship, and Canada's
  New Conservative Party," 109.

9 Lower, *Canadians in the Making*, 135–6.

10 Kramer, *Nationalism in Europe and America*, 8; Davidson, *The Origins of
   Scottish Nationhood*, 12–13. Here, Davidson is rephrasing British historian
   Edward Thompson's description of class formation to come up with a
   definition of nationhood.

11 Jonathan Vance, "Battle Verse: Poetry and Nationalism after Vimy Ridge,"
   in Hayes, Iarocci, and Bechthold, *Vimy Ridge*, 265–6.

12 Creighton, *Dominion of the North*, 442, 444; Keshen, "The Great War
Soldier," 14–15; Historica Canada website, "Vimy Ridge." https://www.
historicacanada.ca/content/heritage-minutes/vimy-ridge (accessed
5 May 2014); Chartrand, *The Canadian Corps in World War I*, 20; Joe
O'Connor, "How Vimy Ridge made Canada into a Country of Heroes,"
National Post, 8 April 2013.

13 MacMillan, *The Uses and Abuses*, 66 (Harper quote ibid); Fellman, "Let's
Talk about Creeping Canadian Militarism"; Johnston cited in Natalie
Stechyson, "Battle of Vimy Ridge Marked Canada's Birth as a Nation:
Governor General David Johnston," *National Post*, 9 April 2012.

14 Gary Sheffield, "Vimy Ridge and the Battle of Arras: A British Perspective,"
in Hayes, Iarocci, and Bechthold, *Vimy Ridge*, 17; Turner, *Vimy Ridge*, 24;
Paul Dickson, "The End of the Beginning: The Canadian Corps in 1917,"
in Hayes, Iarocci, and Betchford, *Vimy Ridge*, 33; Gustavson, "Competing
Visions," 143; Jean Martin, "Vimy, April 1917: The Birth of Which Nation?"
Canadian Military Journal, 11, 2 (2011), http://www.journal.forces.gc.ca/
vol11/no2/06-martin-eng.asp#_edn3 (accessed 3 February 2013); Burton,
Vimy, 307–8; Desmond Morton, "Yes, think of November 11 – but 1871,
not 1918," *Globe and Mail*, 11 November 2008; Morton *A Military History
of Canada*, 145 (quote). The increasing popularity of the "coming of age"
theme is evident in reports from various newspapers on commemorations
of the 50th anniversary of Vimy. See "The Battle," *Globe and Mail*, 9 April
1967; "Philip among 15,000 at Vimy but not Charles de Gaulle," *Globe and
Mail*, 10 April 1967; "Vimy Vets Given Warm Welcome at Service," *Halifax
Herald*, 10 April 1967; "50/14 Veterans Pay Tribute to Those Who Died at
Vimy," *Calgary Herald*, 10 April 1967.

15 Underhill, "The Canadian Forces in the War"; Schurman, "Writing About
War," 241; Morton and Granatstein, *Marching to Armageddon*, 1; Granatstein,
Who Killed Canadian History?, 140; John Herd Thompson, "Canada in the
'Third British Empire,' 1901–1939," in Buckner, *Canada and the British
Empire*, 97; Buckner, "Nationalism in Canada," 112.

16 Martin, "Vimy, April 1917"; Wood, *Militia Myths*, 242, 252; Cook, *Clio's
Warriors*, 41.

17 Jeffrey Simpson, "Let's Not Exalt Historical Folly," *Globe and Mail*,
7 October 2011; Ryerson cited in Sheppard, *Plunder, Profit, and Paroles*, 4;
Fraser cited in Donald Graves, "Who Won the War of 1812?," *Canada's
History* (December 2012-January 2013): 23.

18 "Prime Minister's Message: The War of 1812 - The Fight for Canada,"
Government of Canada, The War of 1812, http://1812.gc.ca/
eng/1305743548294/1305743621243 (accessed 9 May 2013). On the

conflicting loyalties demonstrated by those on both sides of the border, see Taylor, *The Civil War of 1812*.

19 Jackson, *The Crown and Canadian Federalism*; Chetanwakanmani cited in Graves, "Who Won the War of 1812?," 26; "Prime Minister's Message: The War of 1812."

20 Gloria Galloway, "War of 1812 Extravaganza Failed to Excite Canadians, Poll Shows," *Globe and Mail*, 21 February 2013. For a similar emphasis regarding the making of Canada, see Saul, *Louis-Hippolyte LaFontaine and Robert Baldwin*. Saul argued that through their painstaking efforts to build responsible government and bind the destinies of anglophones and francophones, these mid-nineteenth-century leaders of Upper and Lower Canada laid the foundation for Confederation and a civic, multiethnic Canada.

21 George Munro Grant, "Introduction," in Marquis, *Canada's Sons on Kopje and Veldt*, 4–5; Vronsky, *Ridgeway*; C.P. Stacey and Richard Foot, "Second World War," *The Canadian Encyclopedia*, http://www.thecanadianencyclopedia. com/en/article/second-world-war-wwii/ (accessed 4 January 2013); Granatstein and Morton, *A Nation Forged in Fire*, 8; Granatstein, *How Britain's Weakness Forced Canada into the Arms of the United States*, 61. The slim volume was a transcript of talks delivered as part of the University of Western Ontario's Joanne Goodman Lecture Series in 1988, midst an intensive public debate over the merits of free trade with the United States. On the book's final page, Granatstein suggested that the trade deal may mark the final triumph of the dependency inaugurated by the wars, noting that "it looks as if we are now asking to be taken over," 62. As suggested on page 364n64, Granatstein has since made peace with Canada's dependent status.

22 English, *The Worldly Years*, 29; Champion, *The Strange Demise of British Canada*, 26; Horn, *Forging a Nation*; Boyko, *Blood and Daring*.

23 Peter MacKay to soldiers withdrawing from Afghanistan in 2011, cited in McKay and Swift, *Warrior Nation*, 13; Granatstein, *Canada's Army*, x; Saldin, *War, the American State, and Politics since 1898*.

24 Ernest J. Chambers, cited in Berger, *The Sense of Power*, 234.

25 Joe Friesen, "Ottawa Pumps Up Military Role in Citizenship Ceremonies," *Globe and Mail*, 1 July 2011. For a similar view of Canada's unique record of peace, see MacMillan, *The Uses and Abuses*, ix, and Richler, *What We Talk About*, 33; McKay and Swift make a distinction between actions and attitudes in discussing Canadians of the late Victorian period: "The peaceable kingdom was always something of an illusion because its many Anglo subjects were so often captivated by warlike visions of the White Man's Burden" (*Warrior Nation*, 62).

26 Howard, "What is Military History?"

27 David Bercuson, "The Military Is a Central Actor in Our Country's Story,"
    Globe and Mail, 12 July 2011.
28 Lackenbauer, *The Canadian Rangers*; Claire Hastings, Policy, Projects &
    Communications Officer, British Consulate General, Toronto, Ontario,
    11 July 2012. Email; Claire K. Nicholson, Public Affairs Officer, Office of
    Communications, US Citizenship and Immigration Services, 12 July 2012.
    Email; J.L. Granatstein, "In Peacetime, Soldiers are Scorned," *Ottawa
    Citizen*, 5 July 2011. The British may have removed their military garrisons
    from Canada in 1871 (save for the mother country's troops stationed
    at the Halifax Citadel, who stood on guard until 1906), but prior to the
    British-American rapprochement of the early twentieth century, Canadian
    officials considered Britain the ultimate guarantor of their nation's
    sovereignty in the face of a potentially aggressive United States. See
    Wood, *Militia Myths*, 54.
29 McKay and Swift, *Warrior Nation*, 26.
30 Judge cited in Shaw, *Crisis of Conscience*, 15; First Duguid quote cited in
    Cook, *Clio's Warriors*, 65; second cited in Gustavson, "Competing Visions,"
    142; Martin cited in Owram, "Canada and Empire," 146; Berger, *The
    Writing of Canadian History*, 219.
31 Buckner, *Canada and the End of Empire*, 2; Gordon, *History and the Historians*,
    8. British Historian Michael Howard referred to stirring nation-building
    narratives as "nursery history," arguing that the historian's true task is to
    tackle, complicate, and sometimes destroy national mythologies. To Howard,
    this is the real path to national maturity. "Such disillusion," he wrote, "is a
    necessary part of growing up in and belonging to an adult society" (Howard,
    "The Use and Abuse of Military History," 4–5). And not all contemporary
    Canadian historians "would deny the [nationalist] label." In the work of
    Granatstein, for one, "history" amounts to the search for a national master
    narrative, and the historian's primary duty is not to reflect the varieties of
    lived experience or the complexities inherent in representing the past, but to
    instill civic pride and inspire fealty to the project of nation-building. As he
    instructed in the preface to his book, *Who Killed Canadian History*, "we have a
    country to build" (xvii).
32 MacMillan, *The Uses and Abuses*, 131; Richler, *What We Talk About*, 219. See
    Gustavson, "Competing Visions," 142–4, for candid expressions of this
    approach among Australian and Canadian military historians. See also
    Keshen, "The Great War Soldier," 3–26; Thompson, *Anzac Memories*; and
    Thompson, "The Anzac Legend," 73–82.
33 Doug Owram, "Canada and the Empire," 149; Denison cited in Wood,
    Militia Myths, 53; Bernd Horn, "Accidental Heroes," 213.

34 Hopkins cited in Wood, *Militia Myths*, 224; Vance, *Death So Noble*, 179, Hurd cited 228–9. On Hurd, see "Obituary: William Burton Hurd (1894–1950),"*The Canadian Journal of Economics and Political Science / Revue canadienne d'Economique et de Science politique* 16. 2 (May 1950), 143–5.

35 George cited in Peart and Schaffter, *The Winds of Change*, 136; Greenfield, *Baptism of Fire*, 347; Berton, *Vimy*, 295. A random sampling of nine popular high school history texts published between 1959 and 1994 found some portion of the George quote in six of the volumes: McInnis, *Canada: A Political and Social History*, 407; Cook, Ricker, and Saywell, *Canada: A Modern Study*, 187; Careless, *Canada: A Story of Challenge*, 330; McNaught, *The Pelican History of Canada*, 213; Saywell, *Canada: Pathways to the Present*, 126; Cook et al., *Canada: A Modern Study*, 163.

36 Hillier cited in Richler, *What We Talk About*, 71; Hamilton cited in ibid., 201; Greenhous and Douglas, *Out of the Shadows*, 287; Cornell, Hamelin, Ouellet, and Trudel, *Canada: Unity in Diversity*, 464; McKay and Swift, *Warrior Nation*, 102–3.

37 "Leaving with our Heads Held High," *Globe and Mail*, 23 May 2012.

38 Ibid. Buchan, *Montrose*. On Buchan, see McKay and Swift, *Warrior Nation*, 16–17. For a hardnosed look at the Canadian Afghan mission that explores these dilemmas and contradictions, see Smith, *The Dogs Are Eating Them Now*.

39 Massie, "Canada's War for Prestige," 282; Whitworth, *Men, Militarism, and UN Peacekeeping*, 87–9; Heinbecker, *Getting Back in the Game*, 35–7; Cass, "A Climate of Obstinacy," 19–20; "Canada's Reputation Worsens: Global Poll," *CBC News*, 11 February 2010, http://www.cbc.ca/news/canada/canada-s-reputation-worsens-global-poll-1.892750 (accessed 12 April 2013); Horn, "Accidental Heroes," 213. As foreign affairs minister John Baird stated in explaining the government's decision not to seek a spot on the Security Council in 2014, "Canada's principled foreign policy is not for sale for a Security Council seat" (Stephanie Levitz, "Canada Not in Running for UN Security Council Seat in 2014," *Toronto Star*, 1 May 2013). Jeffrey Simpson observed: "Canada under this government failed to win a seat on the UN Security Council, a stinging rebuke. Canada's once-sterling reputation for caring about Africa is over. Canada's reputation in the Arab world is mud, because although ministers never criticize anything Israel does, they never miss a chance to lecture the Palestinians" ("Canada is 'Back' on the World Stage? Hardly," *Globe and Mail*, 13 June 2012). See also Yves Engler, *The Ugly Canadian: Stephen Harper's Foreign Policy* (Black Point, Nova Scotia: Fernwood Publishing, 2012).

40 Graebner cited in Schoonover, *Uncle Sam's War of 1898*, 4; Krabbendam and Thompson, "Theodore Roosevelt and the 'Discovery' of Europe," 1.

41 Press, *Calculating Credibility*, 2–3 (Dulles cited 2); Logevall, "America Isolated," 175.

42 Ibid.; Press, *Calculating Credibility*, vii, 4–5, 7, 1.

43 For an analysis of the ways war makes states, see Higgs, *Crisis and Leviathan*; Porter, *War and the Rise of the State*; and Tilly, *Coercion, Capital, and European States*; Drakulic, "Academic Nationalism," 28 (Smith quote), 33. On Canadian apologies and reparations, see Radforth, "Ethnic Minorities and Wartime Injustices"; for an example from the United States, see Shimabukuro, *Born in Seattle*.

44 MacFarlane, *Triquet's Cross*, 60, 95, 151–60. For a modern example of this project of lionising francophone military contributions for functionalist, statist ends, note the frequent exaltation of Van Doos past and present in English-language military histories and the mass media, where the regiment is rarely named without the preceding adjective "legendary." See Matt Hartely and Joanna Smith, "Legendary Vandoos 'Do the Job Right,'" *Globe and Mail*, 16 July 2007, and Zuehlke, *Ortona Street Fight*, 36, for just two of the innumerable examples of the well-worn phrase.

45 MacFarlane, *Triquet's Cross*, 128–30.

46 Democratic platform cited in Saldin, *War, the American State, and Politics*, 59; Richler, *What We Talk About*, 31.

47 For an excellent discussion of the ways in which the First World War has been employed to "reconcile" Canada's disparate communities, and the complexities involved in this task, see Vance, *Death So Noble*, 241–56.

Conclusion

1 Rose, *Myth and the Greatest Generation*; Divine, *Perpetual War for Perpetual Peace*; Barnes cited 14. See also Vidal, *Perpetual War for Perpetual Peace*.

2 Divine, *Perpetual War*, 13, 15; Bourne, "The State," in Polner and Woods, 139; Lippmann cited in Foyle, *Counting the Public In*, 4. Of course there are other responses, including the wholesale rejection of established traditions and institutions implied by anarchism, communism, etc. Here I am simply outlining the more common ways that citizens have accommodated themselves to the emergence of the United States as a warfare state.

3 "Bush Unswayed by Anti-War Demonstrations," *National Public Radio* (transcript), 18 February 2003. http://www.npr.org/programs/atc/transcripts/2003/feb/030218.gonyea.html (accessed 6 February 2014).

4 MacMillan, *The Uses and Abuses*, ix.

5 Sheehan, *Where Have All the Soldiers Gone?* xvi, xix; MacMillan, *The Uses and Abuses*, 131. See also Pinker, *The Better Angels of Our Nature*; Mueller, *Retreat from Doomsday*; Welsh, "Beyond War and Peacekeeping." On the inefficacy of warring for peace, see Regehr, *Disarming Conflict*.
6 Judt, *Reappraisals*, 406.
7 Robert Fulford, "The First World War," *National Post*, 8 February 2000.
8 Halladay, "Renegotiating National Boundaries," 5.
9 Ibid., 16.
10 Randy Boyagoda, "Toward a More Complex Sense of the Past," *Globe and Mail*, 13 May 2011.
11 Rosenberg, *A Date Which Will Live*, 131; Englehardt and Linenthal, "Introduction: History under Siege," 5.

Bibliography

Abella, Irving, and Harold Troper. "'The Line Must Be Drawn Somewhere': Jewish Refugees, 1933–9." *Canadian Historical Review* 60.2 (June 1979): 178–209.

Abrams, Irwin. *The Nobel Peace Prize and the Laureates: An Illustrated Biographical History.* Nantucket, Massachusetts: Watson, 2001.

Abrams, Jeanne. "Remembering the Maine: The Jewish Attitude toward the Spanish-American War as Reflected in 'The American Israelite.'" *American Jewish History* 76. 4 (1987): 439–55.

Abrams, Ray H. *Preachers Present Arms: A Study of the War-time Attitudes and Activities of the Churches and the Clergy in the United States, 1914–1918.* Philadelphia: University of Pennsylvania Press, 1933.

Adachi, Ken. *The Enemy that Never Was: A History of the Japanese Canadians.* Toronto: McClelland and Stewart, 1976.

Adams, Gordon. *The Politics of Defense Contracting: The Iron Triangle.* New York: Transaction, 1981.

Adams, Michael C.C. *The Best War Ever.* Baltimore: Johns Hopkins University Press, 1993.

Aguirre, Adalberto. *Racial and Ethnic Diversity in America: A Reference Handbook.* Santa Barbara, California: ABC-CLIO, 2003.

Ajzenstat, Janet. *The Canadian Founding: John Locke and Parliament.* Montreal/Kingston: McGill-Queen's University Press, 2007.

Ajzenstat, Janet, and Peter J. Smith, "Liberal Republicanism: The Revisionist Picture of Canada's Founding." In Janet Ajzenstat and Peter J. Smith, eds., *Canada's Origins: Liberal, Tory, Or Republican?* 1–18. Ottawa: Carleton University Press, 1995.

Aldridge, Daniel W. III, "Opportunity Lost: African American Public Intellectuals, the Roosevelt Administration, and the Creation of the UN Trusteeship Council, 1941–1945." *Perspectives on International and*

Multicultural Affairs 1.1 (2001). 4 April 2013. http://www2.davidson.edu/
    academics/acad_depts/rusk/prima/Vol1Issue1/opportunity_lost.htm.
– "Black Powerlessness in a Liberal Era: The NAACP, Anti-Colonialism,
    and the United Nations Organization, 1942–1945." In R. M. Douglas,
    Michael Dennis Callahan, and Elizabeth Bishop, eds., *Imperialism on Trial:
    International Oversight of Colonial Rule in Historical Perspective*, 85–100.
    Lanham, Maryland: Lexington Books, 2006.
Alexander, Bevin. *Korea: The First War We Lost.* New York: Hippocrene, 1986.
Allen, Joe. *Vietnam: The (Last) War the U.S. Lost.* Chicago: Haymarket Books,
    2007.
Almond, Gabriel A., R. Scott Appleby, and Emmanuel Sivan. *Strong Religion:
    The Rise of Fundamentalisms around the World.* Chicago: University of Chicago
    Press, 2003.
Alperovitz, Gar. *Atomic Diplomacy: Hiroshima and Potsdam.* New York: Simon
    and Schuster, 1965.
Alterman, Eric. *When Presidents Lie: A History of Official Deception and Its
    Consequences.* New York: Penguin, 2005.
Ambrose, Stephen E. *Band of Brothers: E Company, 506th Regiment, 101st
    Airborne from Normandy to Hitler's Eagle's Nest.* New York: Simon and
    Schuster, 1992.
Ambrosio, Thomas. "Ethnic Identity Groups and United States Foreign
    Policy." In Thomas Ambrosio, ed. *Ethnic Identity Groups and United States
    Foreign Policy*, 1–20. Westport, Connecticut: Praeger, 2002.
Anderson, Benedict. *Imagined Communities: Reflections on the Origin and Spread
    of Nationalism.* London: Verso, 1983.
Arendt, Hannah. *Crises of the Republic.* New York: Houghton Mifflin Harcourt,
    1972.
Armstrong, Elizabeth. *The Crisis in Quebec, 1914–1918.* New York: Columbia
    University Press, 1937.
Armstrong-Reid, Susan E., and David Murray. *Armies of Peace: Canada and the
    UNRRA Years.* Toronto: University of Toronto Press, 2008.
Asada, Sadoa. "The Shock of the Atomic Bomb and Japan's Decision to
    Surrender – A Reconsideration." *Pacific Historical Review* 67 (November
    1998): 477–512.
Athan Billias, George. *American Constitutionalism Heard Round the World,
    1776–1989: A Global Perspective.* New York: New York University Press, 2009.
Atwood, Margaret. *Selected Poems, 1965–1975.* Boston: Houghton Mifflin
    Harcourt, 1987.
Auxier, George. "Middle Western Newspapers and the Spanish-American
    War." *Mississippi Valley Historical Review* 26 (March 1940): 523–34.

Avella, Joseph. "The President, Congress, and Decisions to Employ Military Force." In Phillip Henderson, ed. *The Presidency Then and Now*, 47–68. Lanham, Maryland: Rowman & Littlefield, 2000.

Avrich, Paul. *Anarchist Voices: An Oral History of Anarchism in America.* Oakland, California: AK Press, 2005.

Axtell, James. *Natives and Newcomers: The Cultural Origins of North America.* New York: Oxford University Press, 2001.

Azoulay, Dan, ed. *Canadian Political Parties.* Toronto: Irwin, 1999.

Azzi, Stephen. "The Nationalist Moment in English Canada." In Lara Campbell, Dominique Clément, and Gregory Kealey, eds., *Debating Dissent: Canada and the 1960s*, 213–28. Toronto: University of Toronto Press, 2012.

Bacevich, Andrew J. "Breaking Washington's Rules: How an Empire Can Become a Republic Again." *The American Conservative* (January 2011): 23–6.

– *American Empire: The Realities and Consequences of US Diplomacy.* Cambridge, Massachusetts: Harvard University Press, 2002.

– *Washington Rules: America's Path to Permanent War.* New York: Macmillan, USA, 2010.

– *The New American Militarism: How Americans Are Seduced by War.* New York: Oxford University Press, 2005.

Backhouse, Constance. "'Bitterly Disappointed' at the Spread of 'Colour-Bar Tactics': Viola Desmond's Challenge to Racial Segregation, Nova Scotia, 1946. In Barrington Walker, ed. *The African Canadian Legal Odyssey: Historical Essays*, 101–66. Toronto: University of Toronto Press, 2012.

– *Colour-Coded: A Legal History of Racism in Canada, 1900–1950.* Toronto: Osgoode Society for Canadian Legal History/University of Toronto Press, 2001.

Bacon, Margaret Hope. *The Quiet Rebels: The Story of the Quakers in America.* Philadelphia: New Society, 1985.

Bailey, Beth, and David Farber. *The First Strange Place: Race and Sex in World War II Hawaii.* Baltimore: Johns Hopkins University Press, 1994.

Bailyn, Bernard. *The Barbarous Years: The Peopling of British North America – The Conflict of Civilizations, 1600–1675.* New York: Random House, 2012.

Baker, Nicholson. *Human Smoke: The Beginnings of World War II, the End of Civilization.* New York: Simon and Schuster, 2008.

Bangarth, Stephanie. *Voices Raised in Protest: Defending North American Citizens of Japanese Ancestry, 1942–49.* Vancouver: UBC Press, 2008.

Barnes, Harry Elmer. *In Quest of Truth and Justice: De-Bunking the War Guilt Myth.* Chicago: National Historical Society, 1928.

– *The Genesis of the World War: An Introduction to the Problem of War Guilt.* New York: Alfred A. Knopf, 1926.

Barnett, Louise. *Atrocity and American Military Justice in Southeast Asia: Trial by Army*. New York: Routledge, 2010.

Barris, Ted. *Deadlock in Korea: Canadians at War, 1950–1953*. 60th Anniversary ed. Toronto: Thomas Allen, 2010.

Bates, Milton J., Lawrence Lichty, Paul Miles, Ronald H. Spector, and Marilyn Young. *Reporting Vietnam, Part Two: American Journalism 1969–1975*. New York: Library of America, 1998.

Beard, Charles. *The Devil Theory of War: An Inquiry into the Nature of History and the Possibility of Keeping out of War*. New York: Vanguard, 1936.

Beard, Charles, and Mary Beard. *The Rise of American Civilization*. New One Volume Edition. New York: Macmillan, 1937.

Becker, Walter. *The Dynamics of Business-Government Relations: Industry and Exports, 1893–1921*. Chicago: University of Chicago Press, 1982.

Beede, Benjamin R. ed. *The War of 1898 and U.S. Interventions, 1898–1934: An Encyclopedia*. New York: Garland, 1994.

Béland, Daniel, and André Lecours. *Nationalism and Social Policy: The Politics of Territorial Solidarity*. Oxford: Oxford University Press, 2008.

Bélanger, Eric. "Third Party Success in Canada." In Alain Gagnon and A. Brian Tanguay, eds., *Canadian Parties in Transition*, 83–109. Peterborough, Ontario: Broadview, 2007.

Bell, Daniel. *The End of Ideology: On the Exhaustion of Political Ideas in the Fifties*. Cambridge, Massachusetts: Harvard University Press, 1960.

Benn, Carl. *Historic Fort York, 1793–1993*. Toronto: Dundurn, 1993.

– *Mohawks on the Nile: Natives among the Canadian Voyageurs in Egypt, 1884–1885*. Toronto: Dundurn, 2009.

– *The War of 1812*. New York: Taylor and Francis, 2003.

Bennett, Tony. "Popular Culture and the 'Turn to Gramsci.'" In John Storey, ed., *Cultural Theory and Popular Culture: A Reader*, 217–24. 2nd ed. Athens, Georgia: University of Georgia Press, 1998.

Bentley, Jerry. "Cross-Cultural Interaction and Periodization in World History." *American Historical Review* 101 (1996): 749–70.

Benton, Elbert. *International Law and Diplomacy of the Spanish-American War*. Gloucester, Massachusetts: Peter Smith, 1968 [first published in 1908].

Bercuson, David. *Blood on the Hills*. Toronto: University of Toronto Press, 1999.

– *Maple Leaf Against the Axis: Canada's Second World War*. Toronto: Stoddart, 1995.

– *The Fighting Canadians*. Toronto: Harper Collins, 2008.

Bercuson, David, and S.F. Wise. *The Valour and the Horror Revisited*. Montreal/Kingston: McGill-Queens University Press, 1994.

Berger, Carl. *The Sense of Power: Studies in the Ideas of Canadian Imperialism 1867–1914*. Toronto: University of Toronto Press, 1970.

– *The Writing of Canadian History: Aspects of English-Canadian Historical Writing since 1900*. 2nd ed. Toronto: University of Toronto Press, 1986.

Berger, Henry, ed. *A William Appleman Williams Reader*. Chicago: Ivan R. Dee, 1992.

Berger, Mark. *Under Northern Eyes: Latin American Studies and U.S. Hegemony in the Americas 1898–1990*. Indianapolis: Indiana University Press, 1995.

Berkove, Lawrence. *A Prescription for Adversity: The Moral Art of Ambrose Bierce*. Columbus: Ohio State University Press, 2002.

Berman, Morris. *Dark Ages America: The Final Phase of Empire*. New York: W.W. Norton, 2006.

Berton, Pierre. *Vimy*. Toronto: McClelland and Stewart, 1986.

Bérubé, Allan. *Coming Out under Fire: Gay Men and Women in World War II*. New York: Free Press, 1990.

Bird, Kai, and Lawrence Lifschultz, eds. *Hiroshima's Shadow: Writings on the Denial of History and the Smithsonian Controversy*. Story Creek, Connecticut: Pamphleteers, 1998.

Bird, Will R. *And We Go On: A Story of the War by a Private in the Canadian Black Watch; a Story without Filth or Favor*. Toronto: Hunter-Rose, 1930.

Bjarnason, Dan. *Triumph at Kapyong: Canada's Pivotal Battle in Korea*. Toronto: Dundurn, 2011.

Black, Jeremy. *The Great War and the Making of the Modern World*. New York: Continuum, 2009.

Blad, Cory. *Neoliberalism and National Culture: State-Building and Legitimacy in Canada and Quebec*. Lieden, Netherlands: Brill, 2011.

Blanchard, Margaret. *Revolutionary Sparks: Freedom of Expression in Modern America*. New York: Oxford University Press, 1992.

Bliss, Michael. "The Methodist Church and World War I." *Canadian Historical Review* 49 (1968): 213–27.

Bodnar, John. *The "Good War" in American Memory*. Baltimore: Johns Hopkins University Press, 2010.

Boggs, Carl. *Imperial Delusions: American Militarism and the Endless War*. Lanham, Maryland: Rowman & Littlefield, 2004.

Boggs, Carl, and Tom Pollard. *The Hollywood War Machine: U.S. Militarism and Popular Culture*. Boulder, Colorado: Paradigm, 2007.

Bonn, Scott, and Michael Welch. *Mass Deception: Moral Panic and the U.S. War on Iraq*. New Jersey: Rutgers University Press, 2010.

Boorstin, Daniel. *The Genius of American Politics*. Chicago: University of Chicago Press, 1953.

Borchard, Edwin, and William Potter Lange. *Neutrality for the United States*.
New Haven, Connecticut: Yale University Press, 1937.

Borneman, Walter. *1812: The War That Forged a Nation*. New York: Harper
Collins, 2004.

Borstelmann, Thomas. *The 1970s: A New Global History from Civil Rights to
Economic Inequality*. Princeton, New Jersey: Princeton University Press, 2011.

Bothwell, Robert. *Canada and Quebec: One Country, Two Histories*. Vancouver:
UBC Press, 1993.

Bourke, Joanna. *An Intimate History of Killing: Face- to-Face Killing in Twentieth-
Century Warfare*. London: Granta, 1999.

Bourrie, Mark. *The Fog of War: Censorship of Canada's Media in World War Two*.
Vancouver: Douglas & McIntyre, 2011.

Bouvier, Virginia, ed., *Whose America?: The War of 1898 and the Battles to Define
the Nation*. Westport, Connecticut: Praeger, 2001.

Boyden, Joseph. *Three Day Road*. Toronto: Penguin Canada, 2005.

Boyer, Paul S. *By the Bomb's Early Light: American Thought and Culture at the
Dawn of the Atomic Age*. Chapel Hill, North Carolina: University of North
Carolina Press, 1985.

Boyko, John. *Blood and Daring: How Canada Fought the American Civil War and
Forged a Nation*. Toronto: Knopf Canada, 2013.

Bradford, James, ed. *Crucible of Empire: The Spanish–American War and Its
Aftermath*. Annapolis, Maryland: Naval Institute Press, 1993.

Bradley, F.J. *No Strategic Targets Left*. Paducah, Kentucky: Turner, 1999.

Braun, Irwin, and Robert McCullough. "Reviewing the History Textbooks on
the Korean War." *Graybeards* (August 1998): 47–8.

Brebner, J.B. *The North Atlantic Triangle: The Interplay of Canada, the United
States, and Great Britain*, Carleton Library ed. Toronto: McClelland and
Stewart, 1966.

Breisach, Ernst. *Historiography: Ancient, Medieval, and Modern*, 3rd ed. Chicago:
University of Chicago Press, 2007.

Brewer, Susan A. *Why America Fights: Patriotism and War Propaganda from the
Philippines to Iraq*. New York: Oxford University Press, 2009.

Brinkley, Alan. "World War II and American Liberalism." In Lewis
Erenberg and Susan Hirsch, eds., *The War in American Culture: Society and
Consciousness during World War II*, 313–30. Chicago: University of Chicago
Press, 1996.

– *Voices of Protest: Huey Long, Father Coughlin, and the Great Depression*. New
York: Random House, 2011.

Brison, Jeffrey. *Rockefeller, Carnegie, and Canada: American Philanthropy in the Arts
Letters in Canada*. Montreal/Kingston: McGill-Queens University Press, 2005.

Broadfoot, Barry. *Years of Sorrow, Years of Shame: The Story of the Japanese Canadians in World War II*. New York: Doubleday, 1977.

Brokaw, Tom. *The Greatest Generation*. New York: Random House, 1998.

Brown, Robert Craig, and Ramsay Cook. *Canada 1896–1921: A Nation Transformed*. Toronto: McClelland and Stewart, 1974.

Brown, Robert Craig. *Robert Laird Borden: A Biography*. Vol. 2. Toronto: University of Toronto Press, 1980.

Buchan, John. *Montrose: A History*. Boston: Houghton Mifflin, 1928.

Buckner, Phillip ed. *Canada and the British Empire*. Oxford: Oxford University Press, 2008.

Buckner, Phillip. "Nationalism in Canada." In Don Harrison Doyle, Marco Antonio, and Villela Pamplona, eds., *Nationalism in the New World*, 99–117. Athens, Georgia: University of Georgia Press, 2006.

Bullert, Gary B. "Reinhold Niebuhr and The Christian Century: World War II And The Eclipse Of The Social Gospel." *Journal of Church and State* 44.2 (2002): 271–90.

Bushnell, Ian. *Captive Court: A Study of the Supreme Court of Canada*. Montreal/Kingston: McGill-Queen's University Press, 1992.

Callwood, June. *Portrait of Canada*. New York: Doubleday & Company, 1981.

Campbell, Lara, Michael Dawson, and Catherine Gidney, eds. *Worth Fighting For: Canada's Tradition of War Resistance from 1812 to the War on Terror*. Toronto: Between the Lines, 2015.

Capozzola, Christopher. *Uncle Sam Wants You: World War I and the Making of the Modern American Citizen*. New York: Oxford University Press, 2008.

Careless, J.M.S. *Canada: A Story of Challenge*. Cambridge: Cambridge University Press, 1959.

Carlisle, Rodney. *World War I*. New York: Facts on File, 2006.

Carlson, Keith Thor. "The Lynching of Louie Sam." *BC Studies* 109 (Spring 1996): 63–78.

Carment, David, and David Bercuson, eds. *The World in Canada: Diaspora, Demography, and Domestic Politics*. Montreal/Kingston: McGill-Queen's University Press, 2008.

Carrière, Erin, Marc O'Reilly, and Richard Vengroff. "In the Service of Peace: Reflexive Multilateralism and the Canadian Experience in Bosnia." In Richard Sobel and Eric Shiraev, eds., *International Public Opinion and the Bosnia Crisis*, 1–32. Lanham, Maryland: Lexington Books, 2003.

Carroll, Peter N. *The Odyssey of the Abraham Lincoln Brigade: Americans in the Spanish Civil War*. Stanford, California: Stanford University Press, 1994.

Carty, R. Kenneth, William Paul Cross, and Lisa Young. *Rebuilding Canadian Party Politics*. Vancouver: UBC Press, 2000.

Casey, Steven. *Selling the Korean War: Propaganda, Politics, and Public Opinion,*
1950–1953. New York: Oxford University Press, 2008.

Cashman, Sean Dennis. *America in the Gilded Age: From the Death of Lincoln to*
the Rise of Theodore Roosevelt. 3rd ed. New York: New York University Press,
1993.

Cass, Loren R." A Climate of Obstinacy: Symbolic Politics in Australian and
Canadian Policy." In Paul G. Harris, ed., *The Politics of Climate Change:*
Environmental Dynamics in International Affairs, 17–34. New York: Routledge,
2009.

Casser, George H. *Hell in Flanders Fields: Canadians at the Second Battle of Ypres.*
Toronto: Dundurn, 2010.

Chadderton, H. Clifford. *Hanging a Legend: The NFB's Shameful Attempt to*
Discredit Billy Bishop, VC. Ottawa: The War Amputations of Canada,
1986.

Champion, C.P. *The Strange Demise of British Canada: The Liberals and Canadian*
Nationalism, 1964–68. Montreal/Kingston: McGill-Queens University Press,
2010.

Chan, Arlene. *The Chinese in Toronto from 1878: From Outside to Inside the Circle.*
Toronto: Dundurn, 2011.

Chartrand, René. *Canadian Forces in World War II.* Oxford: Osprey, 2001.
– *The Canadian Corps in World War I.* Oxford: Osprey, 2007.

Chatfield, Charles. *For Peace and Justice: Pacifism in America, 1914–1941.*
Knoxville: University of Tennessee Press, 1971.

Chen, Shiwei. "History of Three Mobilizations: A Reexamination of the
Chinese Biological Warfare Allegations against the United States in the
Korean War." *Journal of American-East Asian Relations* 16.3 (2009): 213–47.

Chesler, Ellen *Woman of Valor: Margaret Sanger and the Birth Control Movement*
in America. New York: Simon and Schuster 2007.

Cho, Grace M. *Haunting the Korean Diaspora: Shame, Secrecy, and the Forgotten*
War. Minneapolis: University of Minnesota Press, 2008.

Chong, Sylvia Shin Huey. *The Oriental Obscene: Violence and Racial Fantasies in*
the Vietnam Era. Durham, North Carolina: Duke University Press, 2012.

Choquette, Robert. *Canada's Religions: An Historical Introduction.* Ottawa:
University of Ottawa Press, 2004.

Citizenship and Immigration Canada. *Discover Canada: The Rights and*
Responsibilities of Citizenship. Ottawa: Queen's Printer, 2009.

Clark, S.D. *The Developing Canadian Community.* Toronto: University of Toronto
Press, 1962.

Clark, Suzanne. *Cold Warriors: Manliness on Trial in the Rhetoric of the West.*
Carbondale, Illinois: Southern Illinois University, 2000.

Clarke, Brian. "English-Speaking Canada from 1854." In Terrance Murphy and Roberto Perin, eds., *A Concise History of Christianity in Canada*, 261–359. Toronto: Oxford University Press, 1996.

Clément, Dominique. *Canada's Rights Revolution: Social Movements and Social Change, 1937–82*. Vancouver: UBC Press, 2008.

Coates, Colin, and Cecilia Morgan. *Heroines and History: Representations of Madeleine de Verchères and Laura Secord*. Toronto: University of Toronto Press, 2002.

Cohen, Warren. *The American Revisionists: The Lessons of Intervention in World War I*. Chicago: University of Chicago Press, 1967.

Coleman, Daniel. *White Civility: The Literary Project of English Canada*. Toronto: University of Toronto Press, 2006.

Collins Ronald K.L., and Sam Chatlain. *We Must Not Be Afraid to Be Free: Stories of Free Expression in America*. New York: Oxford University Press, 2011.

Collins, Ann V. *All Hell Broke Loose: American Race Riots from the Progressive Era to World War II*. Santa Barbara, California: ABC-CLIO, 2012.

Combs, Jerald. *American Diplomatic History: Two Centuries of Changing Interpretations*. Berkeley: University of California Press, 1983.

Constant, Jean-François, and Michel Ducharme, *Liberalism and Hegemony: Debating the Canadian Liberal Revolution*. Toronto: University of Toronto Press, 2009.

Conway-Lanz, Sahr. *Collateral Damage: Americans, Noncombatant Immunity, and Atrocity after World War II*. New York: Routledge, 2006.

Cook, Ramsay. "Canadian Centennial Celebrations." *International Journal* 22.4 (Autumn, 1967): 659–63.

– "Identities Are Not Like Hats." *Canadian Historical Review* 81.2 (June 2000): 260–5.

– *Watching Quebec: Selected Essays*. Montreal/Kingston: McGill-Queen's University Press, 2005.

Cook, Ramsay, John C.Ricker, and John T. Saywell. *Canada: A Modern Study*. Toronto: Clarke, Irwin and Company, 1963.

Cook, Ramsay, and Robert Craig Brown. *Canada, 1896–1921: A Nation Transformed*. Toronto: University of Toronto Press, 1974.

Cook, Terry. "A Reconstruction of the World: George R. Parkin's British Empire Map of 1893." *Cartographica* 21.4 (1984): 53–65.

Cook, Tim. *At the Sharp End: Canadians Fighting the Great War 1914–1916*. Toronto: Viking, 2007.

– *Clio's Warriors: Canadian Historians and the Writing of the World Wars*. Vancouver: UBC Press, 2006.

– *The Necessary War: Canadians Fighting the Second World War*. Vol. 1. Toronto: Allen Lane, 2014.

- "The Politics of Surrender: Canadian Soldiers and the Killing of Prisoners in the Great War." *The Journal of Military History* 70.3 (July 2006): 637-65.
- "Quill and Canon: Writing the Great War in Canada." *American Review of Canadian Studies* 35.3 (2005): 503-30.

Cooke, John Byrne. *Reporting the War: Freedom of the Press from the American Revolution to the War on Terrorism.* New York: Palgrave Macmillan, 2007.

Cooper, John Milton. "The Great War and American Memory." *The Virginia Quarterly Review* 79.1 (Winter 2003). 12 February 2013. http://www.vqronline.org/essay/great-war-and-american-memory.

Copp, Terry. *Cinderella Army: The Canadians in Northwest Europe, 1944–1945.* Toronto: University of Toronto Press, 2006.

- *Fields of Fire: The Canadians in Normandy.* Toronto: University of Toronto Press, 2003.

Corber, Robert J. *Homosexuality in Cold War America: Resistance and the Crisis of Masculinity.* Durham, NC: Duke University Press, 1997.

Cornell, Paul, Jean Hamelin, Fernand Ouellet, and Marcel Trudel. *Canada: Unity in Diversity.* English ed. Toronto, Montreal: Holt, Rineheart and Winston of Canada, Ltd, 1967.

Cox, Michael, and Caroline Kennedy-Pipe. "The Tragedy of American Diplomacy? Rethinking the Marshall Plan." *Journal of Cold War Studies* 7.1 (Winter 2005): 97–134.

Craig, Campbell, and Fredrik Logevall, *America's Cold War: The Politics of Insecurity.* Cambridge, Massachusetts: Harvard University Press, 2009.

Cravins, George G. "Scandinavian Regions of the Upper Midwest." In Andrew R. L. Cayton, Richard Sisson, and Chris Zacher, eds., *The American Midwest: An Interpretive Encyclopedia*, 172–4. Bloomington: University of Indiana Press, 2006.

Crawford, Sue E. S., and Laura R. Olson, eds. *Christian Clergy in American Politics.* Baltimore: Johns Hopkins University Press, 2001.

Creighton, Donald. *Canada's First Century.* Toronto: Macmillan, 1970.

- *Dominion of the North: A History of Canada.* Toronto: Macmillan, 1944.

- *The Forked Road: Canada, 1939–1957.* Toronto: McClelland and Stewart, 1976.

- *The Story of Canada.* London: Faber and Faber, 1959.

Crerar, Duff. "The Church in the Furnace: Canadian Anglican Chaplains Respond to the Great War." *Journal of the Canadian Church Historical Society* 35.2 (November 1993): 75–103.

Crosby, Alfred. *The Columbian Exchange: Biological and Cultural Consequences of 1492.* Westport, CT: Greenwood Press, 1972.

Crowe, Lori, and Chris Hendershot, "Ambivalent Spectators and Enthusiastic Fans? Mapping Civilian-Military Engagement in Canada." In Annika

Bergman-Rosamond and Mark Phythian, eds., *War, Ethics and Justice: New Perspectives on a Post 9/11 World*, 76–90. New York: Routledge, 2011.

Crowley, Terry. "The French Regime to 1760." In Terrance Murphy and Roberto Perin, eds., *A Concise History of Christianity in Canada*, 1–55. Toronto: Oxford University Press, 1996.

Cumings, Bruce. "Occurrence at Nog Ŭn-ri Bridge: An Inquiry into the History and Memory of a Civil War." *Critical Asian Studies* 33.4 (2001): 509–26.

Cumings, Bruce. *The Korean War: A History*. New York: Modern Library, 2010.

– *The Origins of the Korean War*. Vol. 1, *Liberation and the Emergence of Separate Regimes, 1945–1947*. Princeton, New Jersey: Princeton University Press, 1981.

– *The Origins of the Korean War*. Vol. 2, *The Roaring of the Cataract, 1947–1950*. Princeton, New Jersey: Princeton University Press, 1990.

Cuordileone, K.A. "'Politics in an Age of Anxiety': Cold War Political Culture and the Crisis of American Masculinity, 1949–1960." *The Journal of American History* 87.2 (2000): 515–45.

– *Manhood and American Political Culture in the Cold War*. New York: Routledge, 2012.

Curti, Merle. *Bryan and World Peace*. Northampton, Massachusetts: Smith College Studies in History, 17, 1931.

Curti, Merle. *Peace or War: The American Struggle*. New York: W.W. Norton and Company, 1936.

Cuthbertson, Greg, Albert Grundlingh, and Mary-Lynn Suttie, *Writing a Wider War: Rethinking Gender, Race, And Identity in the South African War, 1899–1902*. Athens: Ohio University Press, 2002.

Cuthbertson, Wendy. *Labour Goes to War: The CIO and the Construction of a New Social Order, 1939–45*. Vancouver: UBC Press, 2012.

Dandeker, Christopher. "Nationalism, Nation-States, and Violence at the End of the Twentieth Century: A Sociological View." In Christopher Dandeker, ed., *Nationalism and Violence*, 21–47. London: Transaction, 1998.

Davidson, Neil. *The Origins of Scottish Nationhood*. Sterling, Virginia: Pluto Press, 2000.

Davies, Robertson. *The Deptford Trilogy: Fifth Business, The Manticore, World of Wonders*. Toronto: Penguin, 1990.

Davies, Alan T., and Marilyn F. Nefsky. *How Silent Were the Churches? Canadian Protestantism and the Jewish Plight during the Nazi Era*. Waterloo, Ontario: Wilfrid Laurier University Press, 1997.

Dean, Robert. *Imperial Brotherhood: Gender and the Making of Cold War Foreign Policy*. Boston: University of Massachusetts Press, 2001.

DeBenedetti, Charles. *Peace Heroes in Twentieth-Century America.* Indianapolis: Indiana University Press, 1988.

DeBenedetti, Charles, and Charles Chatfield. *An American Ordeal: The Antiwar Movement of the Vietnam Era.* Syracuse, New York: Syracuse University Press, 1990.

DeConde, Alexander. *Ethnicity, Race, and American Foreign Policy: A History.* Boston: Northeastern University Press, 1992.

Dennis, James M. *Renegade Regionalists: The Modern Independence of Grant Wood, Thomas Hart Benton, and John Steuart Curry.* Madison: University of Wisconsin Press, 1998.

Denson, John V. *Costs of War: America's Pyrrhic Victories.* 2nd ed. New Brunswick, New Jersey: Transaction, 1999.

Department of National Defence, General Staff, *Six Years of War: The Army in Canada, Britain and the Pacific.* Ottawa: Queen's Printer, 1955.

Department of National Defence, General Staff. *Official History of the Canadian Army in the Second World War.* 3 vols. Ottawa: Queen's Printer, 1955–60.

Department of National Defence, General Staff. *The Canadian Army, 1939–1945: An Official Historical Summary.* Ottawa: King's Printer, 1948.

Department of the Secretary of State. *Our History.* Ottawa: Queen's Printer, 1970.

Desbarats, Catherine, and Allan Greer, "The Seven Years' War in Canadian History and Memory." In Warren R. Hofstra, ed., *Cultures in Conflict: The Seven Years' War in North America,* 145–78. Lanham, Maryland: Rowman and Littlefield, 2007.

Dickinson, John A., and Brian Young. *A Short History of Quebec.* Montreal/Kingston: McGill-Queen's University Press, 2008.

DiJoseph, John. *Noble Cause Corruption, the Banality of Evil, and the Threat to American Democracy.* Rowan & Littlefield, 2010.

Dionne, E.J., Jr. *Our Divided Political Heart: The Battle for the American Idea in an Age of Discontent.* New York: Bloomsbury, 2012.

Divine, Robert A. *Perpetual War for Perpetual Peace.* College Station, Texas: Texas A&M University Press, 2000.

Donaldson, Allan. *Maclean.* Halifax: Vagrant Press, 2005.

Douglas, W.A.B., "Marching to Different Drums: Canadian Military History." *Journal of Military History* 56.2 (1992): 245–60.

Douglas, W.A.B., and Brereton Greenhous. *Out of the Shadows: Canada in the Second World War.* Toronto: Oxford University Press, 1977.

Dower, John. *War without Mercy: Race and Power in the Pacific War.* New York: Pantheon Books, 1986.

Drakulic, Slobodan. "Academic Nationalism." In Trevor W. Harrison and Slobodan Drakulic, eds., *Against Orthodoxy: Studies in Nationalism*, 17–38. Vancouver: UBC Press, 2011.

Dubois, W.E.B. *The Correspondence of W. E. B. Du Bois: Selections, 1877–1934.* Edited by Herb Aptheker. Boston: University of Massachusetts Press, 1973.

Ducharme, Michel. "Interpreting the Past, Shaping the Present, and Envisioning the Future: Remembering the Conquest in Nineteenth-Century Quebec." In Phillip Buckner and John G. Reid, eds., *Remembering 1759: The Conquest of Canada in Historical Memory*, 136–60. Toronto: University of Toronto Press, 2012.

Dudziak, Mary. *Cold War Civil Rights: Race and the Image of American Democracy.* Princeton: Princeton University Press, 2000.

Duguid, A.F. *Official History of the Canadian Forces in the Great War, 1914–1919.* Ottawa: King's Printer, 1938.

Dyer, Gwynne. *Canada in the Great Power Game 1914–2014.* Toronto: Random House Canada, 2014.

Dyal, Donald. *Historical Dictionary of the Spanish-American War.* Santa Barbara: Greenwood, 1996.

Early, Francis H. *A World Without War: How U.S. Feminists and Pacifists Resisted World War I.* Syracuse, New York: Syracuse University Press, 1997.

Edwards, Paul M. *To Acknowledge a War: The Korean War in American Memory.* Westport, Connecticut: Greenwood Press, 2000.

Edwardson, Ryan. "'Kicking Uncle Sam out of the Peaceable Kingdom': English-Canadian 'New Nationalism' and Americanization." *Journal of Canadian Studies* 37.4 (Winter 2003): 131–50.

Eksteins, Modris. *The Rites of Spring: The Great War and the Birth of the Modern Age.* Boston: Houghton Mifflin Company, 1989.

Ellsberg, Daniel. *Secrets: A Memoir of Vietnam and the Pentagon Papers.* New York: Penguin 2002.

Endicott, Stephen, and Edward Hagerman. *The United States and Biological Warfare.* Bloomington, Indiana: University of Indiana Press, 1998.

Engelbrecht, H.C., and F.C. Hanighen. *Merchants of Death.* New York: Dodd, Mead, and Co., 1934.

Engen, Robert. *Canadians under Fire: Infantry Effectiveness in the Second World War.* Montreal/Kingston: McGill-Queen's University Press, 2009.

Englehardt, Tom, and Edward Linenthal. "Introduction: History Under Siege." In Edward Linenthal and Tom Engelhardt, eds., *History Wars: The Enola Gay and Other Battles for the American Past*, 1–7. New York: Metropolitan Books, 1996.

English, Allan Douglas. *Cream of the Crop: Canadian Aircrew, 1939–1945.* Montreal/Kingston: McGill-Queen's University Press, 1996.

English, John. *The Canadian Army and the Normandy Campaign: A Study of Failure in High Command.* New York, Praeger, 1991.

– *The Worldly Years: Life of Lester Pearson.* Vol. 2, *1949–1972.* Toronto: Alfred A. Knopf, 1992.

Epp, Frank. *The Mennonites in Canada, 1786–1920: The History of a Separate People.* Toronto: Macmillan, 1974.

Erenberg, Lewis A., and Susan E. Hirsch, eds. *The War in American Culture: Society and Consciousness during World War II.* Chicago: University of Chicago Press, 1996.

Estes, Steve. *I Am a Man! Race, Manhood, and the Civil Rights Movement.* Chapel Hill, North Carolina: University of North Carolina Press, 2006.

Evans, W. Sanford. *The Canadian Contingents.* Toronto: The Publisher's Syndicate, 1901.

Fahey, Curtis. *In His Name: The Anglican Experience in Upper Canada, 1791–1854.* Ottawa: Carleton University Press, 1991.

Fair, Ross. "Model Farmers, Dubious Citizens: Reconsidering the Pennsylvania Germans of Upper Canada, 1786–1834." In Alexander Freund, ed. *Beyond the Nation? Immigrants' Local Lives in Transnational Cultures,* 79–106. Toronto: University of Toronto Press, 2012.

Farber, David. "War Stories." *Reviews in American History* 23.2 (1995): 317–22.

Fay, Sidney. "New Light on the Origins of the World War." *American Historical Review* 25–6 (1920–1921).

– *The Origins of the World War,* 2nd ed. rev. New York: Free Press, 1966.

Fay, Terence. *A History of Canadian Catholics: Gallicanism, Romanism, and Canadianism.* Montreal/Kingston: McGill-Queen's University Press, 2003.

Fenster, Mark. *Conspiracy Theories: Secrecy and Power in American Culture.* Minneapolis: University of Minnesota Press, 1999.

Ferguson, Malcolm. "Canada's Response: The Making and Remaking of the National War Memorial." MA Thesis, Carleton University, 2012.

Ferguson, Niall. "Hegemony or Empire." *Foreign Affairs* (September/October 2003): 154–61.

– *The Pity of War.* New York: Basic Books, 2000.

– "Prisoner Taking and Prisoner Killing in the Age of Total War: Towards a Political Economy of Military Defeat." *War in History* 11.2 (2004): 148–92.

Fiala, Andrew. *Public War, Private Conscience: The Ethics of Political Violence.* New York: Continuum International Publishing Group, 2010.

Field, James, Jr. "American Imperialism: The Worst Chapter in Almost Any Book." *American Historical Review* 83 (June 1978): 644–83.

Fierlbeck, Katherine. *Political Thought in Canada: An Intellectual History.* Toronto: University of Toronto Press, 2006.

Findley, Timothy. *The Wars.* Toronto: Clark, Irwin, 1977.

Finkel, Alvin. *Our Lives: Canada after 1945.* Toronto: James Lorimer & Company, 1997.

Fischer, David Hackett. *Champlain's Dream: The Visionary Adventurer Who Made a New World in Canada.* Toronto: Alfred A. Knopf, 2008.

Fisher, Louis. *The War Power: Original and Contemporary.* Bloomington, Indiana: American Historical Association, 2009.

Flack, Horace. "Spanish-American Diplomatic Relations Preceding the War of 1898." *Johns Hopkins Studies in History and Political Science* 24.1–2 (1906): 7–95.

Fletcher, Wendy. "Canadian Anglicanism and Ethnicity." In Paul Bramadat and David Seljak, eds., *Christianity and Ethnicity in Canada,* 138–67. Toronto: University of Toronto Press, 2008.

Folly, Martin. *The United States and World War II: The Awakening Giant.* Edinburgh: Edinburgh University Press, 2002.

Folly, Martin, and Niall Palmer. *The A to Z of U.S. Diplomacy from World War I through World War II.* Lanham, Maryland: Rowan and Littlefield, 2010.

Foster, Carrie. *The Woman and the Warriors: The U.S. Section of the Women's International League for Peace and Freedom, 1915–1946.* Syracuse, New York: Syracuse University Press, 1995.

Fousek, John. *To Lead the Free World: American Nationalism and the Cultural Roots of the Cold War.* Chapel Hill: University of North Carolina Press, 2000.

Foyle, Douglas C. *Counting the Public In: Presidents, Public Opinion, and Foreign Policy.* New York: Columbia University Press, 2013.

Francis, Daniel. *National Dreams: Myth, Memory, and Canadian History.* Vancouver: Arsenal Press, 1997.

Francis, R. Douglas. *Frank H. Underhill: Intellectual Provocateur.* Toronto: University of Toronto Press, 1986.

Freeland, Richard. *The Truman Doctrine and the Origins of McCarthyism: Foreign Policy, Domestic Politics, and Internal Security, 1946–1948.* New York: New York University Press, 1985.

Freidel, Frank. *The Splendid Little War.* Boston: Little, Brown and Co., 1958.

Fried, Richard. *The Russians Are Coming! The Russians Are Coming! Pageantry and Patriotism in Cold-War America.* New York: Oxford University Press, 1998.

Friedberg, Aaron L. *In the Shadow of the Garrison State: America's Anti-Statism and Its Cold War Grand Strategy.* Princeton, New Jersey: Princeton University Press, 2000.

Friedman, Max Paul. *Rethinking Anti-Americanism: The History of an Exceptional Concept in American Foreign Relations.* Cambridge: Cambridge University Press, 2012.

Friesen, Abraham. *In Defense of Privilege: Russian Mennonites and the State before and during World War I.* Winnipeg: Kindred Productions, 2006.

Fry, Joseph. "From Open Door to World Systems: Economic Interpretations of Late Nineteenth Century American Foreign Relations, *Pacific Historical Review* 65.2 (May 1996): 277-303.

– "William McKinley and the Coming of the Spanish-American War: A Study of the Besmirching and Redemption of an Historical Image." *Diplomatic History* 3 (Winter 1979): 77–97.

Fussell, Paul. *Doing Battle: The Making of a Skeptic.* New York: Oxford University Press, 1996.

– *The Great War and Modern Memory.* New York: Oxford University Press, 1975.

– *Wartime: Understanding and Behavior in the Second World War.* New York: Oxford University Press, 1989.

Gaffen, Fred. *Forgotten Soldiers.* Penticton, British Columbia: Theytus, 1985.

Galabuzi, Grace-Edward. *Canada's Economic Apartheid: The Social Exclusion of Racialized Groups in the New Century.* Toronto: Canadian Scholar's Press, 2006.

Gardner, Lloyd, and Marilyn B. Young. *The New Empire: A 21st-Century Teach-In on U.S. Foreign Policy.* New York: The New Press, 2003.

Gates, Henry Louis, Jr. *The Classic Slave Narratives.* New York: Signet Classics, 2002.

Gauvreau, Michael. "Beyond the Search for Intellectuals: On the Paucity of Paradigms in the Writing of Canadian Intellectual History." In Gerald Friesen and Doug Owram, eds., *Thinkers and Dreamers: Historical Essays in Honour of Carl Berger*, 53–92. Toronto: University of Toronto Press, 2011.

Gentile, Nancy. *The Great War and America: Civil-Military Relations during World War I.* Westport, Connecticut: Ford Praeger Security International, 2008.

George, Alice. *Awaiting Armageddon: How Americans Faced the Cuban Missile Crisis.* Chapel Hill: University of North Carolina Press, 2003.

Gibbs, Christopher. *The Great Silent Majority: Missouri's Resistance to World War I.* Columbia: University of Missouri Press, 1980.

Gienow-Hecht, Jessica. "Shame on US? Academics, Cultural Transfer, and the Cold War – A Critical Review." *Diplomatic History* 24.3 (Summer 2000): 465–94.

Gifford, C.G. *Canada's Fighting Seniors.* Toronto: James Lorimer, 1990.

Gilbert, James. *Men in the Middle: Searching for Masculinity in the 1950s.* Chicago: University of Chicago Press, 2005.

Gilman, Daniel Coit, Harry Thurston Peck, and Frank Moore Colby, eds., *New International Encyclopedia.* New York: Dodd, Mead, 1905.

Gilman, Nils. *Mandarins of the Future: Modernization Theory in Cold War America.* Baltimore: Johns Hopkins University Press, 2007.

Glain, Stephen. *State vs. Defense: The Battle to Define America's Empire.* New York: Crown, 2011.

Glasrud, Bruce A. "Introduction: Black Citizen-Soldiers, 1865-1917." In Bruce A. Glasrud, ed. *Brothers to the Buffalo Soldiers: Perspectives on the African American Militia and Volunteers,* 1–18. Columbia, Missouri: University of Missouri Press, 2011.

Glassford, Sarah, and Amy Shaw, eds. *A Sisterhood of Suffering and Service: Women and Girls of Canada and Newfoundland during the First World War.* Vancouver: UBC Press, 2012.

Go, Julian, and Anne L. Foster, *The American Colonial State in the Philippines: Global Perspectives.* Durham, NC: Duke University Press, 2003.

Godby, Michael. "Confronting Horror: Emily Hobhouse and the Concentration Camp Photographs of the South African War." In Maria Pia Di Bella and James Elkins, *Representations of Pain in Art and Visual Culture,* 157–69. New York: Routledge, 2013.

Godefory, Andrew, ed. *Great War Commands: Historical Perspectives on Canadian Army Leadership, 1914–1918.* Kingston: Canadian Defence Academy Press, 2010.

Golay, Michael. *Spanish American War.* Ann Arbor, Michigan: Facts on File, 2003.

Goldberg, David. *The Racial State.* Malden, Massachusetts: Blackwell, 2001.

– *Racist Culture: Philosophy and the Politics of Meaning.* Malden, Massachusetts: Blackwell, 1993.

Goldberg, Robert Alan. "Conspiracy Theories in American History: A Historical Overview." In Peter Knight, ed. *Conspiracy Theories in American History: An Encyclopedia,* 1–13. Santa Barbara, California: ABC-CLIO, 2003.

Goodman, Melvin A. *National Insecurity: The Cost of American Militarism.* San Francisco: City Lights, 2013.

Goodway, David. *Anarchist Seeds beneath the Snow: Left-Libertarian Thought and British Writers from William Morris to Colin Ward.* Liverpool: Liverpool University Press, 2012.

Gordon, Alan. *The Hero and the Historians: Historiography and the Uses of Jacques Cartier.* Vancouver: UBC Press, 2010.

Goulden, Joseph. *Korea: The Untold Story.* New York: Times Books, 1982.

Granatstein, J. L. *Canada's Army: Waging War and Keeping the Peace*. 2nd ed. Toronto: University of Toronto Press, 2011.

– "Peacekeeping: Did Canada Make a Difference? And What Difference did Peacekeeping Make to Canada?" In John English and Norman Hillmer, eds., *Making a Difference? Canada's Foreign Policy in a Changing World Order*, 222–36. Toronto: Lester, 1992.

– *How Britain's Weakness Forced Canada into the Arms of the United States*. Toronto: University of Toronto Press, 1989.

– *The Last Good War: An Illustrated History of Canada in the Second World War*. Toronto: Douglas and McIntyre, 2005.

– *Who Killed Canadian History?* 2nd ed. Toronto: Harper Collins, 2007.

– *Whose War is It?* Toronto: Harper Collins, 2007.

Granatstein, J.L., and Desmond Morton, *A Nation Forged in Fire: Canadians and the Second World War, 1939–1945*. Toronto: Lester and Orpen Dennys, 1989.

Granatstein, J.L. and J.M. Hitsman. *Broken Promises: A History of Conscription in Canada*. Toronto: Oxford University Press, 1977.

Granatstein, J.L., and Peter Neary, eds. *The Good Fight: Canadians and World War II*. Toronto: Copp Clark, 1995.

Granatstein, J.L., Irving M. Abella, David J. Bercuson, R. Craig Brown, and H. Blair Neatby. *Twentieth Century Canada*. Toronto: McGraw-Hill Ryerson, 1983.

Grant, John Webster. *A Profusion of Spires: Religion in Nineteenth-Century Ontario*. Toronto: University of Toronto Press, 1988.

Grant, George. *Lament for a Nation: The Defeat of Canadian Nationalism*. Toronto: McClelland and Stewart, 1965.

Grattan, C. Hartley. *Why We Fought*. New York: Vanguard Press, 1929.

Grayling, A.C. *Among the Dead Cities: The History and Moral Legacy of the WWII Bombing of Civilians in Germany and Japan*. New York: Walker and Company, 2006.

Greenfield, Nathan M. *Baptism of Fire: The Second Battle of Ypres and the Forging of Canada, April 1915*. Toronto: Harper Collins, 2007.

Greenhous, Brereton. "Billy Bishop – Brave Flyer, Bold Liar." *Canadian Military Journal* (Autumn 2002): 61–4.

– *The Making of Billy Bishop*. Toronto: Dundurn Press, 2002.

Greenhous, Brereton, Stephen J. Harris, William C. Johnston, and William G.P. Rawling. *The Crucible of War, 1939–1945: The Official History of the Royal Canadian Air Force*. Vol 3. Ottawa: National Defence Headquarters, 1994.

Greer, Allan. *The People of New France*. Toronto: University of Toronto Press, 1997.

Griffin, Robert. "The Cultural Turn in Cold War Studies." *Reviews in American History* 29 (2001): 150–7.

Grodzinski, John. "The Use and Abuse of Battle: Vimy Ridge and the Great War over the History of the First World War." *Canadian Military History* 10.1 (2009): 83–6.

Grossman, Dave. *On Killing*. Boston: Little, Brown and Co., 1996.

Guéhenno, Jean-Marie. *The End of the Nation-State*. Minneapolis: University of Minnesota Press, 1995.

Gustavson, Wesley C. "Competing Visions: Canada, Britain, and the Writing of the First World War." In Phillip A. Buckner and R. Douglas Francis, eds., *Canada and the British World: Culture, Migration, and Identity*, 142–56. Vancouver: UBC Press, 2006.

Guttenplan, D.D. *American Radical: The Life and Times of I.F. Stone*. Evantson, Illinois: Northwestern University Press, 2012.

Hagedorn, Ann. *Savage Peace: Hope and Fear in America, 1919*. New York: Simon and Schuster, 2007.

Hale, Geoffrey E. *The Politics of Taxation in Canada*. Toronto: University of Toronto Press, 2002.

Hall, Kermit, and John J. Patrick. *The Pursuit of Justice: Supreme Court Decisions that Shaped America*. New York: Oxford University Press, 2006.

Hall, Simon. *Peace and Freedom: The Civil Rights and Antiwar Movements in the 1960s*. Philadelphia: University of Pennsylvania Press, 2005.

Halladay, Laurel. "Renegotiating National Boundaries: Canadian Military Historians and Thematic Analysis." *Journal of Military and Strategic Studies* 8.2 (Winter 2005–2006): 1–16.

Hamm, Thomas D. *The Quakers in America*. New York: Columbia University Press, 2013.

Hansen, Randall. *Fire and Fury: the Allied Bombing of Germany 1942–1945*. Toronto: Doubleday Canada, 2008.

Hardy, W.G. *From Sea unto Sea: Canada – 1850 to 1910, The Road to Nationhood*. New York: Doubleday & Company, 1960.

Harris, Sam. *The End of Faith: Religion, Terror, and the Future of Reason*. New York: W.W. Norton, 2004.

Hartung, William. *Prophets of War: Lockheed Martin and the Making of the Military-Industrial Complex*. New York: Nation Books, 2010.

Hartz, Louis. *The Liberal Tradition in America: An Interpretation of American Political Thought Since the Revolution*. New York: Harcourt, Brace, 1955.

Hayes, Geoffrey, Andrew Iarocci, and Mike Bechthold, eds. *Vimy Ridge: A Canadian Reassessment*. Waterloo, Ontario: Wilfrid Laurier University Press, 2007.

Healy, David. "One War from Two Sides: The Cuban Assessment of U.S.-Cuban Relations." *Cercles* 5 (2002): 31–8.

Heartfield, James. *An Unpatriotic History of the Second World War.* London: Zero Books, 2012.

Heath, Gordon. "Passion for Empire: War Poetry Published in the Canadian English Protestant Press during the South African War, 1899–1902." *Literature & Theology* [Oxford] 16.2 (2002): 127–47.

– *A War with a Silver Lining: Canadian Protestant Churches and the South African War, 1899–1902.* Montreal/Kingston: McGill-Queens University Press, 2009.

Hedican, Edward J. *Ipperwash: The Tragic Failure of Canada's Aboriginal Policy.* Toronto: University of Toronto Press, 2013.

Heinbecker, Paul. *Getting Back in the Game: A Foreign Policy Handbook for Canada.* Toronto: Dundurn Press, 2011.

Heiss, Mary Ann. "The Evolution of the Imperial Idea and US National Identity." *Diplomatic History* 26.4 (2002): 511–41.

Hemmings, Michael. "The Church and the Japanese in Canada, 1941-1946: Ambulance Wagon to Embattled Army?" MTheol., Vancouver School of Theology, 1990.

Henderson, George Francis Robert. *Stonewall Jackson and the American Civil War.* New York, Grossett & Dunlap, 1943.

Hendrickson, David. *Union, Nation, or Empire: The American Debate over International Relations, 1789–1941.* Lawrence: University of Kansas Press, 2009.

Hendrickson, Kenneth E. *The Spanish-American War.* Westport, Connecticut: Greenwood Publishing Group, 2003.

Henry, Wade. "W. Sanford Evans and the Canadian Club of Winnipeg, 1904-1919." *Manitoba History* 27 (Spring1994). 4 April 2013. http://www.mhs.mb.ca/docs/mb_history/27/evanscanadianclub.shtml.

Herberg, Edward N. *Ethnic Groups in Canada: Adaptations and Transitions.* Scarborough: Nelson Canada 1989.

Herring, George. *From Colony to Superpower: U.S. Foreign Relations since 1776.* New York: Oxford University Press, 2008.

Hertzman Lewis, John W. Warnock and Thomas A Hockin. *Alliances and Illusions: Canada and the NATO-NORAD Question.* Edmonton: M.G. Hurtig Ltd., 1969.

Hibben, Paxton. *The Peerless Leader, William Jennings Bryan.* New York: Farrar and Rinehart, 1929.

Hickey, Donald R. *The War of 1812: A Short History.* Champaign, Illinois: University of Illinois Press, 1995.

Hiebert, Janet. "Interest Groups and Canadian Federal Elections." In F. Leslie Seidle, ed. *Interest Groups and Elections in Canada.* Vol. 2, 72–86. Toronto: Dundurn, 1991.

Higginbotham, Don. *Revolution in America: Considerations & Comparisons.* Charlottesville: University of Virginia Press, 2005.

Higgs, Robert. *Crisis and Leviathan: Critical Episodes in the Growth of American Government.* New York: Oxford University Press, 1987.

Himes, Kenneth R., and Lisa Sowle Cahill, eds. *Modern Catholic Social Teaching: Commentaries and Interpretations.* Washington, D.C.: Georgetown University Press, 2005.

Hitchcock, William I. *The Bitter Road to Freedom: The Human Cost of Allied Victory in World War II Europe.* New York: Free Press, 2009.

Hitchens, Christopher. "Imperialism: Superpower Dominance, Malignant and Benign." *Slate* (10 December 2002). 5 April 2013. http://www.slate.com/id/2075261/.

– *God is Not Great: How Religion Poisons Everything.* New York: Twelve, 2007.

Hixson, William, Jr. *Moorfield Storey and the Abolitionist Tradition.* New York: Oxford University Press, 1972.

Hixson, Walter L. *The Myth of American Diplomacy: National Identity and U.S. Foreign Policy.* New Haven, Connecticut: Yale University Press, 2009.

Hobson, J.A. *The Morals of Economic Nationalism.* Boston: Houghton Mifflin, 1920.

Hodgins, Jack. *Broken Ground.* McClelland and Stewart, 1999.

Hoffer, Williamjames. *The Caning of Charles Sumner: Honor, Idealism, and the Origins of the Civil War.* Hopkins Fulfillment Service, 2010.

Hofstadter, Richard. The *American Political Tradition and the Men Who Made It.* New York: Vintage Books, 1989.

– *The Progressive Historians: Turner, Beard, Parrington.* New York: Vintage, 1971.

Hogan, Michael J. "The Enola Gay Controversy: History, Memory, and the Politics of Presentation." In Michael J. Hogan, ed. *Hiroshima in History and Memory.* New York: Cambridge University Press, 1996. 200–32.

Hogan, Michael J., ed., *The Ambiguous Legacy.* Cambridge: Cambridge University Press, 1999.

– *Paths to Power: The Historiography of American Foreign Relations to 1941.* New York: Cambridge University Press, 1993.

Hoganson, Kristin. *Fighting for American Manhood: How Gender Politics Provoked the Spanish-American and Philippine-American Wars.* New Haven: Yale University Press, 1998.

Holbo, Paul. "Economics, Emotion, and Expansion: An Emerging Foreign Policy." In H. Wayne Morgan, ed. *The Gilded Age*, 199–221. Syracuse: Syracuse University Press, 1970.

Holman, Andrew, and Robert Thacker, "Literary and Popular Culture." In Mark J. Kasoff and Patrick James, eds., *Canadian Studies in the New Millennium*, 2nd ed, 185–224. Toronto: University of Toronto Press, 2013.

Holmes, Nancy. "'In Flanders Fields' – Canada's Official Poem: Breaking Faith." *Studies in Canadian Literature* 30.1 (2005): 11–33.

Holsti, Ole Rudolf. *Public Opinion and American Foreign Policy*, rev. ed. Ann Arbor, Michigan: University of Michigan Press, 2009.

Hopkins, J. Castell. *The Story of the Dominion.* Toronto: Winston, 1901.

Horn, Bernd. "Accidental Heroes: The 'Royal Canadians' Redeem British Honour at Paardeberg." In Bernd Horn, ed. *Show No Fear: Daring Actions in Canadian Military History*, 213–34. Toronto: Dundurn, 2008.

– *Doing Canada Proud: The Second Boer War and the Battle of Paardeberg.* Toronto: Dundurn, 2013.

– *The Canadian Way of War: Serving the National Interest.* Toronto: Dundurn, 2006.

Horn, Bernd, ed. *Forging a Nation: Perspectives on the Canadian Military Experience.* St. Catharines: Vanwell, 2003.

Horn, James. *A Land as God Made It: Jamestown and the Birth of America.* New York: Basic Books, 2006.

Howard, Michael. "The Use and Abuse of Military History." *Royal United Service Institute Journal* 107 (February 1962): 4–10.

– "What is Military History?" *History Today* 34.12 (December 1984). 4 May 2014. http://www.historytoday.com/michael-howard/what-military-history.

Howlet, Charles. "Parrington's Opposition to War: An Undercurrent of his Liberal Thought." *Peace & Change* 5.2–3 (Fall 1978): 52–62.

Howlett, Charles, and Ian Harris. *Books, Not Bombs: Teaching Peace Since the Dawn of the Republic.* Charlotte, North Carolina: Information Age, 2010.

Hudson, Winthrop S. *Religion in America.* 3rd ed. New York: Charles Scribner's Sons, 1981.

Huebner, Andrew J. *Warrior Image: Soldiers in American Culture from the Second World War to the Vietnam Era.* Chapel Hill: The University of North Carolina Press, 2008.

Humphrey, Carol Sue. *The Press of the Young Republic, 1783–1833.* Westport, Connecticut: Greenwood Press, 1996.

Hunt, Andrew. *The Turning: A History of Vietnam Veterans against the War.* New York: New York University Press, 1999.

Hunt, Michael. *Ideology and U.S. Foreign Policy.* New Haven, Connecticut: Yale University Press, 1987.

Huntington, Samuel. "The Clash of Civilizations? The Next Pattern of Conflict." *Foreign Affairs* 72.3 (Summer 1993): 22–49.

Iacobelli, Teresa. *Death or Deliverance: Canadian Courts Martial in the Great War.* Vancouver: UBC Press, 2013.

Iacovetta, Franca. "Making Model Citizens: Gender, Corrupted Democracy, and Immigrant and Refugee Reception Work in Cold War Canada." In Kinsman, Gary, Dieter K. Buse, and Mercedes Steedman, eds., *Whose National Security? Canadian State Surveillance and the Creation of Enemies*, 154–67. Toronto: Between the Lines, 2000.

Iarocci, Andrew. *Shoestring Soldiers: The 1st Canadian Division at War, 1914–1915*. Toronto: University of Toronto Press, 2008.

Igartua, José Eduardo. *The Other Quiet Revolution: National Identities in English Canada, 1945–1971*. Vancouver: UBC Press, 2006.

Jackson, D. Michael. *The Crown and Canadian Federalism*. Toronto: Dundurn, 2013.

Jackson, Paul. *One of the Boys: Homosexuality in the Military during World War II*. Montreal/Kingston: McGill-Queen's University Press, 2004.

Jeffries, John W. *Wartime America: The World War II Home Front*. Chicago: Ivan R Dee, 1996.

Jenks, Leland. *Our Cuban Colony: A Study in Sugar*. New York: Vanguard Press, 1928.

Jensen, Carl. *Stories That Changed America: Muckrakers of the 20th Century*. New York: Seven Stories Press, 2002.

Johnson, Chalmers. *Blowback: The Costs and Consequences of American Empire*. New York: Metropolitan Books, 2000.

– *Dismantling the Empire: America's Last Best Hope*. New York: Metropolitan Books, 2010.

– *Nemesis: The Last Days of the American Republic*. New York: Metropolitan Books, 2006.

– *The Sorrows of Empire: Militarism, Secrecy, and the End of the Republic*. New York: Metropolitan Books, 2004.

Johnson, Donald. *The Challenge to American Freedoms: World War I and the Rise of the American Civil Liberties Union*. Lexington: University of Kentucky Press, 1963.

Johnson, William. *A War of Patrols: Canadian Army Operations in Korea*. Vancouver: UBC Press, 2003.

Joshee, Reva, and Lauri Johnson. *Multicultural Education Policies in Canada and the United States*. Vancouver: UBC Press, 2007.

Judis, John B. *Genesis: Truman, American Jews, and the Origins of the Arab/Israeli Conflict*. New York: Farrar, Straus and Giroux, 2014.

Judt, Tony. *Reappraisals: Reflections on the Forgotten Twentieth Century*. New York: Penguin, 2008.

Kagan, Robert. "The Benevolent Empire." *Foreign Policy* 111 (Summer 1998): 24–35.

Kaplan, Amy, and Donald Pease. *Cultures of United States Imperialism*. Durham, North Carolina: Duke University Press, 1993.

Kaplan, William. *State and Salvation: The Jehovah's Witnesses and Their Fight for Civil Rights*. Toronto: University of Toronto Press, 1989.

Katovsky, Bill. *Patriots Act: Voices of Dissent and the Risk of Speaking Out*. Guilford, Connecticut, 2006.

Kaufman, Bill. *Ain't My America: The Long, Noble History of Antiwar Conservatism and Middle-American Anti-Imperialism*. New York: Metropolitan Books, 2008.

Kaye, Harvey. *Thomas Paine and the Promise of America*. New York: Hill and Wang, 2006.

Kealey, Gregory S. "State Repression of Labour and the Left in Canada, 1914-20: The Impact of the First World War." *Canadian Historical Review* 73.3 (1992): 281–314.

Keating, Tom. *Canada and World Order*. Toronto: Oxford University Press, 2002.

Keith, W.J. *Canadian Literature in English*. Vol. 2. Erin, Ontario: The Porcupine's Quill, 2006.

Kennedy, James. *Liberal Nationalisms: Empire, State, and Civil Society in Scotland and Quebec*. Montreal/Kingston: McGill-Queen's University Press, 2013.

Kerans, Marion. *Muriel Duckworth: A Very Activist Pacifist*. Halifax: Fernwood, 1996.

Keshen, Jeffrey A. "The Great War Soldier as Nation Builder in Canada and Australia." In Briton C. Busch, ed. *Canada and the Great War: Western Front Association Papers*, 3–26. Montreal/Kingston: McGill-Queens University Press, 2003.

– *Propaganda and Censorship during Canada's Great War*. Edmonton: University of Alberta Press, 1996.

– *Saints, Sinners, and Soldiers: Canada's Second World War*. Vancouver: UBC Press, 2004.

Kesler, Charles. *I Am the Change: Barack Obama and the Crisis of Liberalism*. New York: Broadside Books, 2012.

Keynes, John Maynard. *The Economic Consequences of the Peace*. London: Macmillan and Co., 1919.

Kirk, Russell. "A Revolution Not Made but Prevented." *Modern Age* 29 (1985): 295–303.

Kleidman, Robert. *Organizing for Peace: Neutrality, the Test Ban, and the Freeze*. Syracuse, New York: Syracuse University Press, 1993.

Klein, Herbert S. *A Population History of the United States*. 2nd ed. New York: Cambridge University Press, 2012.

Knight, Amy. *How the Cold War Began: The Gouzenko Affair and the Hunt for Soviet Spies*. Toronto: McClelland and Stewart, 2005.

Knowles, Norman. *Inventing the Loyalists: The Ontario Loyalist Tradition and the Creation of Usable Pasts.* Toronto: University of Toronto Press, 1997.

Kohn, Edward. *This Kindred People: Canadian-American Relations and the Anglo-Saxon Ideal, 1895–1903.* Montreal/Kingston: McGill-Queen's University Press, 2004.

Kolko, Gabriel. *The Politics of War: The World and United States Foreign Policy, 1943–1945.* New York: Random House, 1968.

Krabbendam, Hans, and John M. Thompson. "Theodore Roosevelt and the 'Discovery' of Europe: An Introduction." In Hans Krabbendam and John M. Thompson, eds., *America's Transatlantic Turn: Theodore Roosevelt and the "Discovery" of Europe*, 1–14. New York: Palgrave Macmillan, 2012.

Kramer, Lloyd. *Nationalism in Europe and America: Politics, Cultures, and Identities since 1775.* Chapel Hill: University of North Carolina Press, 2011.

Krenn, Michael. *The Color of Empire: Race and American Foreign Relations.* Washington, D.C.: Potomac Books, 2006.

Kusch, Frank. *All American Boys: Draft Dodgers in Canada from the Vietnam War.* Westport, Connecticut: Greenwood, 2001.

Lackenbauer, P. Whitney. *The Canadian Rangers: A Living History.* Vancouver: University of British Columbia Press, 2013.

La Feber, Walter. "The Tension between Democracy and Capitalism during the American Century." *Diplomatic History* 23.2 (Spring 1999): 263–84.

– *The American Search for Opportunity 1865–1913.* New York: Cambridge University Press, 1993.

– *The New Empire: An Interpretation of American Expansion.* 35th Anniversary ed. Ithaca: Cornell University Press, 1998.

Lake, Marilyn, and Henry Reynolds. *Drawing the Global Colour Line: White Men's Countries and the International Challenge of Racial Equality.* Cambridge: Cambridge University Press, 2008.

Larson, Edward. *Trial and Error: The American Controversy over Creation and Evolution.* New York: Oxford University Press, 1989.

– *Summer for the Gods: The Scopes Trial and America's Continuing Debate over Science and Religion.* New York: Basic Books, 1997.

Laufer, Peter. *Mission Rejected: U.S. Soldiers Who Say No to Iraq.* White River, Vermont: Chelsea Green, 2006.

Leach, Norman. *Passchendaele: Canada's Triumph and Tragedy on the Fields of Flanders: an Illustrated History.* Regina: Coteau Books, 2008.

Leacock, Stephen. *Canada: The Foundations of Its Future.* Montreal: The House of Seagram, 1941.

Lee, Steven Hugh. *Outposts of Empire: Korea, Vietnam, and the Origins of the Cold War in Asia, 1949–1954.* Montreal/Kingston: McGill-Queen's University Press, 1995.

Lembcke, Jerry. *The Spitting Image: Myth, Memory and the Legacy of Vietnam.*
New York: New York University Press, 1998.

Leuchtenburg, William. "The Needless War with Spain." *American Heritage*
8 (February 1957): 32–41.

Lieven, Anatol. *America Right or Wrong: An Anatomy of American Nationalism.*
New York: Oxford University Press, 2012.

Linenthal, Edward, and Tom Engelhardt, eds. *History Wars: The Enola Gay and
Other Battles for the American Past.* New York: Metropolitan, 1996.

Lippmann, Walter. *U.S. Foreign Policy: Shield of the Republic.* Boston: Little,
Brown, 1943.

Lipset, Seymour Martin. *Continental Divide: The Values and Institutions of the
United States and Canada.* New York: Routledge, 1990.

Lipstadt, Deborah. *Beyond Belief: The American Press and the Coming of the
Holocaust.* New York: Freedom Press, 1986.

Logevall, Fredrik. "A Critique of Containment." *Diplomatic History* 28.4
(September 2004): 473–99.

– "America Isolated: The Western Powers and the Escalation of the War."
In Andreas W. Daum, Lloyd C. Gardner, and Wilfried Mausbach, eds.,
*America, the Vietnam War, and the World: Comparative and International
Perspectives*, 175–96. Cambridge: Cambridge University Press, 2003.

Lordan, Edward J. *The Case for Combat: How Presidents Persuade Americans to Go
to War.* Santa Barbara, California: Greenwood, 2010.

Loring Villa, Brian. *Unauthorized Action: Mountbatten and the Dieppe Raid.*
Toronto: Oxford University Press, 1989.

Love, Eric. *Race over Empire: Racism and U.S. Imperialism, 1865–1900.* Chapel
Hill, North Carolina: University of North Carolina Press, 2004.

Lower, A.R.M. *Colony to Nation: A History of Canada.* Toronto: Longmans,
1946.

– *Canadians in the Making: A Social History of Canada.* Toronto: Longmans,
Green, 1958.

Lowry, Donal, ed., *The South African War Reappraised.* Manchester: Manchester
University Press, 2000.

Luebke, Frederick. *Bonds of Loyalty: German Americans and World War.* DeKalb,
Illinois: Northern Illinois University Press, 1974.

Lutzker, Michael A. "Themes and Contradictions in the American Peace
Movement, 1895-1917." In Harvey Leonard Dyck, ed. *The Pacifist Impulse in
Historical Perspective*, 320–40. Toronto: University of Toronto Press, 1996.

Lyon, David, and Marguerite Van Die, eds. *Rethinking Church, State, and
Modernity: Canada between Europe and America.* Toronto: University of
Toronto Press, 2000.

MacFarlane, John. *Earnest Lapointe and Quebec's Influence on Canadian Foreign Policy*. Toronto: University of Toronto Press, 1999.

– *Triquet's Cross: A Study of Military Heroism*. Montreal/Kingston: McGill-Queen's University Press, 2009.

Macintyre, D.E. *Canada at Vimy*. Toronto: Peter Martin, 1967.

Mackenzie, David, ed. *Canada and the First World War: Essays in Honour of Robert Craig Brown*. Toronto: University of Toronto Press, 2005.

Mackey, Eva. *The House of Difference: Cultural Politics and National Identity in Canada*. 2nd ed. Toronto: University of Toronto Press, 2002.

MacMillan, Margaret. *The Uses and Abuses of History*. Toronto: Penguin, 2008.

MacMillan, Margaret. *Paris 1919: Six Months That Changed the World*. New York: Random House, 2007.

MacMillan, Margaret, Robert Bothwell, and Randall Hansen. "Controversy, Commemoration, and Capitulation: The Canadian War Museum and Bomber Command." *Queen's Quarterly* 115.3 (Fall 2008): 366–87.

Madison, James. *James Madison's "Advice to My Country."* Charlottesville Virginia: University of Virginia Press, 1997.

Madsen, Chris. *Another Kind of Justice: Canadian Military Law from Confederation to Somalia*. Vancouver: UBC Press, 1999.

Maier, Pauline. *Ratification: The People Debate the Constitution, 1787–1788*. New York: Simon and Schuster, 2010.

Malcolmson, Patrick, and Richard Myers. *The Canadian Regime: An Introduction to Parliamentary Government in Canada*. Toronto: University of Toronto Press, 2009.

Malkasian, Carter. *The Korean War*. Oxford: Osprey, 2001.

Mann, Charles C. *1493: Uncovering the New World Columbus Created*. New York: Random House, 2012.

Manzela, Eric. *The Wilsonian Moment: Self-Determination and the International Origins of Anticolonial Nationalism*. New York: Oxford University Press, 2007.

Mar, Lisa Rose. *Brokering Belonging: Chinese in Canada's Exclusion Era, 1885–1945*. New York: Oxford University Press, 2010.

Markus, Gregory. "American Individualism Reconsidered." In James Kuklinski, ed. *Citizens and Politics: Perspectives from Political Psychology*, 401–32. Urbana-Champaign: University of Illinois Press, 2001.

Marlin, Randal. *Propaganda and the Ethics of Persuasion*. 2nd ed. Peterborough, Ontario: Broadview Press, 2013.

Marquis, T.G. *Canada's Sons on Kopje and Veldt*. Toronto: Canada's Sons Publishing Co., 1900.

Marszalek, John F., and Horace D. Nash. "African Americans in the Military of the United States." In Arvarh E. Strickland and Robert E. Weems Jr, eds., *The*

African American Experience: An Historiographical and Bibliographical Guide,
231–54. Westport, Connecticut: Greenwood Press, 2001.

Martin, Jean. "Vimy, April 1917: The Birth of Which Nation?" *Canadian Military Journal* 11.2 (2011). 8 June 2013. http://www.journal.forces.gc.ca/vo11/no2/06-martin-eng.asp#_edn3.

Martin, William. *With God on Our Side: The Rise of the Religious Right in America*. New York: Broadway Books, 2005.

Marwah, Inder, Triadafilos Triadafilopoulos, and Stephen White. "Immigration, Citizenship, and Canada's New Conservative Party." In James Farney and David Rayside, eds., *Conservatism in Canada*, 95–119. Toronto: University of Toronto Press, 2013.

Massie, Justin. "Canada's War for Prestige in Afghanistan: A Realist Paradox?" *International Journal* 68.2 (June 2013): 274–88.

Massolin, Philip. *Canadian Intellectuals, the Tory Tradition, and the Challenge of Modernity, 1939–1970*. Toronto: University of Toronto Press, 2001.

Mathieu, Sarah-Jane. *North of the Color Line: Migration and the Black Resistance in Canada, 1870–1955*. Chapel Hill: University of North Carolina Press, 2010.

Matthews, J.B. "Reds and Our Churches." *The American Mercury* (July 1953): 3–13.

Matthews, Robert. "The Christian Churches and Foreign Policy: An Assessment." In Bonnie Green, ed. *Canadian Churches and Foreign Policy* 160–79. Toronto: James Lorimer, 1990.

May, Lary. *The Big Tomorrow: Hollywood and the Politics of the American Way*. Chicago: University of Chicago Press, 2000.

Mayers, David. *Dissenting Voices in America's Rise to Power*. Cambridge: Cambridge University Press, 2007.

Mazella, David. *The Making of Modern Cynicism*. Charlottesville, Virginia: University of Virginia Press, 2007.

McCaffery, Dan. *Billy Bishop: Canadian Hero*. 3rd ed. Toronto: Lorimer, 2002.

McClung, Nellie. *The Complete Autobiography: Clearing the West and The Stream Runs Fast*. Veronica Strong-Boag and Michelle Lynn Rosa, eds. Toronto: Broadview Press, 2003.

McCormack, Ross. *Reformers, Rebels, and Revolutionaries: The Western Canadian Radical Movement, 1899–1919*. Toronto: University of Toronto Press, 1977.

McCoy, Alfred, and Francisco Scarano, eds. *Colonial Crucible: Empire in the Making of the Modern American State*. Madison, Wisconsin: University of Wisconsin Press, 2009.

McCullough, Colin. "We Are the Blue Berets: Problematizing Peacekeeping in Postwar Canada." Ph.D. Dissertation. York University, 2013.

McDonald, Marci. *The Armageddon Factor: The Rise of Christian Nationalism in Canada.* Toronto: Random House, 2010.

McGerr, Michael. *A Fierce Discontent: The Rise and Fall of the Progressive Movement in America.* New York: Free Press, 2003.

McGowan, Mark G. "'To Share in the Burdens of Empire': Toronto's Catholics and the Great War." In Mark G. McGowan and Brian P. Clarke, eds., *Catholics at the Gathering Place: Historical Essays on the Archdiocese of Toronto, 1841–1991,* 177–207. Toronto: Dundurn, 1993.

– *The Waning of the Green: Catholics, the Irish, and Identity in Toronto, 1887–1922.* Montreal/Kingston: McGill-Queen's University Press, 1999.

McInnis, Edgar. *Canada: A Political and Social History.* Toronto: Clarke, Irwin, and Company, 1959.

McKay, Ian. "The Liberal Order Framework: A Prospectus for a Reconnaissance of Canadian History." *Canadian Historical Review* 81 (2000): 617–45.

– *Reasoning Otherwise: Leftists and the People's Enlightenment in Canada, 1890–1920.* Toronto: Between the Lines, 2008.

McKay, Ian, and Jamie Swift. *Warrior Nation: Rebranding Canada in an Age of Anxiety.* Toronto: Between the Lines, 2012.

McKay, Ian, and Robin Bates. *In the Province of History: The Making of the Public Past in Twentieth-Century Nova Scotia.* Montreal/Kingston: McGill-Queen's University Press, 2010.

McKee, Alexander. *Vimy Ridge.* Toronto: Ryerson Press, 1965.

Mckillop, Brian. *Pierre Berton: A Biography.* Toronto: McClelland and Stewart, 2010.

McNaught, Kenneth. "J.S. Woodsworth and War." In Peter Brock and Thomas Socknat, eds., *Challenge to Mars: Pacifism from 1918 to 1945,* 186–98. Toronto: University of Toronto Press.

– *A Prophet in Politics: A Biography of J. S. Woodsworth.* Toronto: University of Toronto Press, 2001.

McNaught, Kenneth. *The Pelican History of Canada.* Markham, Ontario: Penguin, 1976.

McWilliams, Wilson Carey. *The Idea of Fraternity in America.* Berkeley: University of California Press, 1973.

Mead, Gary. *The Doughboys: America and the First World War.* Woodstock: The Overlook Press, 2000.

Meisel, John, Guy Rocher, and A. I. Silver. *As I Recall / Si je me souviens bien: Historical Perspectives.* Montreal: Institute for Research on Public Policy, 1999.

Melady, John L. *Korea: Canada's Forgotten War.* 2nd ed. Toronto: Dundurn Press, 2011.

Mensah, Joseph. *Black Canadians: History, Experiences, Social Conditions.* Halifax: Fernwood, 2002.

Merriam, Allen H. "Racism in the Expansionist Controversy of 1898-1900." *Phylon* 39.4 (4th Qtr., 1978): 369–80.

Miller, Carman. *Painting the Map Red: Canada and the South African War, 1899–1902.* Montreal/Kingston: McGill-Queens University Press, 1993.

Miller, Charles A. "Endgame for the West in Afghanistan? Explaining the Decline in Support for the War in Afghanistan in the United States, Great Britain, Canada, Australia, France and Germany." *Strategic Studies Institute Letort Papers,* June 2010. 12 May 2013. http://www.strategicstudiesinstitute.army.mil/pdffiles/pub994.pdf.

Miller, Joshua. *The Rise and Fall of Democracy in Early America, 1630–1789: The Legacy for Contemporary Politics.* University Park, Pennsylvania: Penn State University Press, 1994.

Miller, Perry. *The New England Mind: The Seventeenth Century.* Cambridge: Harvard University Press, 1939.

Miller, Stuart Creighton. *Benevolent Assimilation: The American Conquest of the Philippines, 1899–1903.* New Haven: Yale University Press, 1983.

Miller, Robert Moats. *Harry Emerson Fosdick: Preacher, Pastor, Prophet.* New York: Oxford University Press, 1985.

Millett, Allan. "The Korean War: A 50 Year Critical Historiography." *Journal of Strategic Studies* 24 (March 2001): 188–224.

Millis, Walter. *The Martial Spirit: A Study of Our War with Spain.* Boston: Houghton Mifflin, 1931.

– *Road to War: America, 1914–1917.* Boston: Houghton Mifflin, 1935.

Minifie, James M. *Peacemaker or Powder-Monkey: Canada's Role in a Revolutionary World.* Toronto: McClelland and Stewart, 1960.

Miraldi, Robert. *Seymour Hersh: Scoop Artist.* Dulles, Virginia: Potomac Books, 2013.

Miron, Janet, ed. *A History of Human Rights in Canada: Essential Issues.* Toronto: Canadian Scholars Press, 2009.

Mollov, M. Benjamin. *Power and Transcendence: Hans Morgenthau and the Jewish Experience.* Lanham, Maryland: Lexington Books, 2002.

Morgan, James G. *Into New Territory: American Historians and the Concept of US Imperialism.* Madison: University of Wisconsin Press, 2014.

Morgenthau, Hans. *In Defense of the National Interest.* New York: Alfred A. Knopf, 1951.

Morris, Michael A. *Canadian Language Policies in Comparative Perspective.* Montreal/Kingston: McGill-Queen's University Press, 2010.

Morrissey, Alice M. *The American Defense of Neutral Rights, 1914–1917.* Cambridge, Massachusetts: Harvard University Press, 1939.

Morton, Desmond. *Canada and War: A Military and Political History.* Toronto:
   Butterworth & Co., 1981.
– *A Military History of Canada.* 5th ed. Toronto: McClelland and Stewart, 2007.
– *A Short History of Canada.* 6th ed. Toronto: McClelland and Stewart, 2006.
– *A Short History of Canada.* Edmonton: Hurtig, 1983.
– *When Your Number's Up: The Canadian Soldier in the First World War.* Toronto:
   Vintage, 1994.
Morton, Desmond, and J.L. Granatstein. *Marching to Armageddon: Candians and
   the Great War, 1914–1919.* Toronto: Lester and Orpen Dennys, 1989.
Morton, W.L. *The Kingdom of Canada: A General History from Earliest Times.*
   Toronto: McClelland and Stewart, 1963.
Mosier, John. *The Myth of the Great War: A New Military History of World War I.*
   New York: Harper Perennial, 2002.
Moss, Mark Howard. *Manliness and Militarism: Educating Young Boys in Ontario
   for War.* Toronto: University of Toronto Press, 2001.
Mowatt, Farley. *And No Birds Sang.* Toronto: McClelland and Stewart, 1979.
Mueller, John. *Retreat from Doomsday: The Obsolescence of Major War.* New York:
   Basic Books, 1989.
Murphy, Paul. *World War I and the Origin of Civil Liberties in the United States.*
   New York: W.W. Norton, 1979.
Murray, Robert K. *Red Scare: A Study in National Hysteria.* Minneapolis: University
   of Minnesota Press, 1955.
Myrdal, Gunnar. *An American Dilemma: The Negro Problem and Modern Democracy.*
   New York: Harper, 1944.
Nagler, Jörg. "Propaganda and Social Violence on the American Home
   Front during World War I." In Jessica C. E. Gienow-Hecht, ed. *Emotions in
   American History: An International Assessment,* 66–91. New York: Berghahn
   Books, 2010.
Nakano, Takeo. *Within the Barbed Wire Fence.* Toronto: University of Toronto
   Press, 1980.
Nash, David. "The Boer War and its Humanitarian Critics." *History Today* 49
   (June 1999): 42–9.
Nashel, Jonathan. "Modernization Theory in Fact and Fiction." In Christian Appy,
   ed. *Cold War Constructions: The Political Culture of United States Imperialism,
   1945–1966,* 132–54. Amherst: University of Massachusetts Press, 2000.
Naveh, Eyal. *Crown of Thorns: Political Martyrdom in America from Abraham
   Lincoln to Martin Luther King Jr.* New York: New York University Press, 1990.
Naylor, James. "Pacifism or Anti-Imperialism?: The CCF Response to the
   Outbreak of World War II." *Journal of the Canadian Historical Association*
   8 (1997): 213–37.

Nearing, Scott, and Joseph Freeman. *Dollar Diplomacy: A Study in American Imperialism.* New York: Heubsch, 1925.

Neatby, H. Blair. *Laurier and a Liberal Quebec: A Study in Political Management.* Toronto: McClelland and Stewart, 1973.

Nevitte, Neil. *The Decline of Deference: Canadian Value Change in Cross National Perspective.* Toronto: University of Toronto Press, 1996.

Newman, Peter C. *The Canadian Revolution: From Deference to Defiance.* Toronto: Penguin, 1996.

Nicholson, G.W.L. *The Canadian Expeditionary Force, 1914–1919.* Ottawa: Queen's Printer, 1962.

Nicholson, George. *Official History of the Canadian Army in the First World War: Canadian Expeditionary Force 1914–1919.* Ottawa: Queen's Printer, 1962.

Niemi, Robert. *History in the Media: Film and Television.* Santa Barbara, California: ABC-CLIO, 2006.

Ninkovich, Frank A. *The Diplomacy of Ideas: U.S. Foreign Policy and Cultural Relations, 1938–1950.* Cambridge: Cambridge University Press, 1981.

– *The United States and Imperialism.* London: Blackwell, 2001.

Nobile, Philip, ed., *Judgment at the Smithsonian.* New York: Marlowe, 1995.

Noble, Roger. "Raising the White Flag: The Surrender of Australian Soldiers on the Western Front." *Revue Internationale d'Histoire Militaire* 72 (1990): 48–79.

Noll, Mark A. *A History of Christianity in the United States and Canada.* Grand Rapids, Michigan: Eerdmans, 1992.

Novak, William. "The Myth of the 'Weak' American State." *American Historical Review* (June 2008): 752–72.

Nutt, Rick. *The Whole Gospel for the Whole World: Sherwood Eddy and the American Protestant Mission.* Macon, Georgia: Mercer University Press, 1988.

Nye, Joseph S., Philip Zelikow, David C. King, eds. *Why People Don't Trust Government.* Cambridge, Mass: Harvard University Press, 1997.

O'Brien, P.K., and A. Clesse, eds. *Two Hegemonies: Britain 1846–1914 and the United States, 1941–2001.* Aldershot: Ashgate, 2002.

Offner, John. *An Unwanted War: The Diplomacy of the United States and Spain over Cuba, 1895–1898.* Chapel Hill, North Carolina: University of North Carolina Press, 1992.

Oleszek, Walter. "Party Whips in the United States Senate." *Journal of Politics* 33 (November 1971): 955–79.

Olmsted, Kathryn S. *Real enemies: Conspiracy Theories and American Democracy, World War I to 9/11.* New York: Oxford University Press, 2009.

Olson, Gregory Allen, ed., *Landmark Speeches on the Vietnam War.* College Station, TX: Texas A&M University Press, 2010.

Olson, Lynn. *Those Angry Days: Roosevelt, Lindbergh, and America's Fight over World War II, 1939–1941*. New York: Random House, 2013.

Oostdijk, Diederik. "Debunking the 'Good War' Myth: Howard Nemerov's War Poetry." In Wilfried Wilms and William Rasch, eds., *Bombs Away! Representing the Air War over Europe and Japan*, 265–80. New York: Ropodi, 2006.

Osmissi, David, and Andrew Stuart Thompson, eds. *The Impact of the South African War*. New York: Palgrave Macmillan, 2002.

Overbeck, Wayne, and Genelle Belmas. *Major Principles of Media Law*. Boston: Wadsworth, 2011.

Owram, D.R. "Canada and Empire." In Robin W. Winks, ed. *The Oxford History of the British Empire*. Vol. 5, *Historiography*, 146–62. Oxford: Oxford University Press, 1999.

Page, Robert J.D. *The Boer War and Canadian Imperialism*. Canadian Historical Association Historical Booklet No. 44. Ottawa: CHA, 1987.

– "Canada and the Imperial Idea in the Boer War Years." *Journal of Canadian Studies* 5.1 (1970): 33–49.

– *Imperialism and Canada, 1895–1903*. Toronto: Holt, Rinehart and Winston, 1972.

Palmer, Howard. "Politics, Religion, and Antisemitism in Alberta, 1880-1950." In Alan T. Davies, ed. *Antisemitism in Canada: History and Interpretation*, 167–96. Waterloo: Wilfrid Laurier University Press, 1992.

Paradis, Francoise. "Acadia: From 'Le Grand Derangement' to 'The Great Upheaval.'" In Henry Wadswoth Longfellow, *Evangeline: A Tale of Acadie*, 17–42. Buxton, Maine: Hidden Springs, 2004.

Parnaby, Andrew, and Gregory S. Kealey. "The Origins of Political Policing in Canada: Class, Law, and the Burden of Empire." *Osgoode Law Journal* 41.2, 3 (2003): 211–40.

Paterson, "United States Intervention in Cuba, 1898: Interpretations of the Spanish-American-Cuban-Filipino War." *The History Teacher* 29.3 (May 1996): 341–61.

Patten, Steven. "The Evolution of the Canadian Party System." In Alain Gagnon and A. Brian Tanguay, eds., *Canadian Parties in Transition*, 55–81. Peterborough, Ontario: Broadview Press, 2007.

Payne, Philip. *Dead Last: The Public Memory of Warren G. Harding's Scandalous Legacy*. Athens, Ohio: Ohio University Press, 2009.

Peart, Hugh W., and John Schaffter. *The Winds of Change: A History of Canada and Canadians in the Twentieth Century*. Toronto: McGraw-Hill Ryerson, 1961.

Pease, Donald E. *The New American Exceptionalism*. Minneapolis: University of Minnesota Press, 2009.

Pederson, William D., ed. *A Companion to Franklin D. Roosevelt*. West Sussex, UK: Blackwell, 2011.

Pederson, William D., and Ann M. McLaurin, eds. *The Rating Game in American Politics: An Interdisciplinary Approach*. New York: Irvington, 1987.

Penlington, Norman. *Canada and Imperialism, 1896–1899*. Toronto: University of Toronto Press, 1965.

Peoples, Clayton, and Michael Gortari. "The Impact of Campaign Contributions on Policymaking in the U.S. and Canada: Theoretical and Public Policy Implications." In Harland N. Prechel, ed. *Politics and Public Policy*, 43–63. Bingley, UK: JAI Press, 2008.

Perez, Louis, Jr. *Cuba between Empires, 1878–1902*. Pittsburgh: University of Pittsburgh Press, 1983.

– *The War of 1898: The United States and Cuba in History and Historiography*. Chapel Hill: University of North Carolina Press, 1998.

Perkins, Bradford. "The Tragedy of American Diplomacy: Twenty-Five Years After." *Reviews in American History* 12.1 (March 1984): 1–18.

Perry, Lewis. *Civil Disobedience: An American Tradition*. New Haven: Yale University Press, 2012.

Pestritto, Ronald. *Woodrow Wilson and the Roots of Modern Liberalism*. Lanham, Maryland: Rowman & Littlefield, 2005.

Petrou, Michael. *Renegades: Canadians in the Spanish Civil War*. Vancouver: UBC Press, 2008.

Phillips, Dennis. "The Tragedy of American Diplomacy: A Tribute to the Legacy of William Appleman Williams." *Australasian Journal of American Studies* 26.2 (December 2007): 89–98.

Phillips, Kevin. *American Theocracy: The Peril and Politics of Radical Religion, Oil, and Borrowed Money in the 21st Century*. New York: Penguin Books, 2007.

Phillips, Kimberley L. *War! What Is It Good For? Black Freedom Struggles and the U.S. Military from World War II to Iraq*. Chapel Hill: University of North Carolina Press, 2011.

Pierson, Ruth Roach. *They're Still Women after All: The Second World War and Canadian Womanhood*. Toronto: McClelland and Stewart 1986.

Pickles, Katie. *Female Imperialism and National Identity: Imperial Order Daughters of the Empire*. New York: Manchester University Press, 2002.

Piehl, Mel. "The *Catholic Worker* and Peace in the Early Cold War Era." In Anne Klejment and Nancy L. Roberts, eds., *American Catholic Pacifism: The Influence of Dorothy Day and the Catholic Worker Movement*, 77–90. Westport, Connecticut: Greenwood, 1996.

Pierpaoli, Paul G., Jr. "American Indian Wars, Massacres during the."
    In Alexander Mikaberidze, *Atrocities, Massacres and War Crimes: An
    Encyclopedia*. Vol. 1. Santa Barbara, California: ABC-CLIO, 2013. 12.

Pinker, Steven. *The Better Angels of Our Nature: Why Violence Has Declined*. New
    York: Penguin, 2011.

Plummer, Brenda Gayle. *Rising Wind: Black Americans and US Foreign Affairs,
    1935–1960*. Chapel Hill: University of North Carolina Press, 1996.

Polenberg, Richard. *Fighting Faiths: The Abrams Case, the Supreme Court, and
    Free Speech*. New York: Viking, 1987.

Polner, Murray, and Thomas Woods Jr. *We Who Dared to Say No to War:
    American Antiwar Writing from 1812 to Now*. New York: Basic Books, 2008.

Polsby, Nelson. *How Congress Evolves: Social Bases of Institutional Change*. New
    York: Oxford University Press, 2004.

Porter, Bruce. *War and the Rise of the State: The Military Foundations of Modern
    Politics*. New York: Free Press, 1994.

Postel, Charles. *The Populist Vision*. New York: Oxford University Press, 2007.

Powe, Lucas. *The Fourth Estate and the Constitution: Freedom of the Press in
    America*. Berkeley: University of California Press, 1991.

Pratt, Julius. *The Expansionists of 1898: The Acquisition of Hawaii and the Spanish
    Islands*. Baltimore: Johns Hopkins University Press, 1936.

Press, Daryl G. *Calculating Credibility: How Leaders Assess Military Threats*.
    Ithaca, New York: Cornell University Press, 2005.

Presthus, Robert Vance. *Elite Accommodation in Canadian Politics*. Cambridge:
    Cambridge University Press, 1973.

Preston, Andrew. *Sword of the Spirit, Shield of Faith: Religion in American War
    and Diplomacy*. New York: Alfred A Knopf, 2012.

Preston, William, Jr. *Aliens and Dissenters: Federal Suppression of Radicals,
    1903–1933*. Cambridge, Massachusetts: Harvard University Press, 1963.

Price, John. *Orienting Canada: Race, Empire, and the Transpacific*. Vancouver:
    UBC Press, 2011.

Prince, Robert S. "The Limits of Constraint: Canadian-American Relations and
    the Korean War, 1950–51." *Journal of Canadian Studies* 27.4 (1992–3): 129–52.

Puckett, Dan J. "Double V Campaign." In Leslie Alexander, ed. *Encyclopedia of
    African American History*, 745–6. Santa Barbara, California: ABC-CLIO, 2010.

Queen, Edward L. II, Stephen R. Prothero, and Gardiner H. Shattuck Jr, eds.
    Encyclopedia of American Religious History. Vol. 1. New York: Facts on File,
    2009.

Quinn, Michael D. "The Mormon Church and the Spanish-American War:
    An End to Selective Pacifism." *Pacific Historical Review* 43.3 (August 1974):
    342–66.

Radforth, Ian. "Ethnic Minorities and Wartime Injustices: Redress Campaigns and Historical Narratives in Late Twentieth-Century Canada." In Nicole Neatby and Peter Hodgins, eds., *Settling and Unsettling Memories: Essays in Canadian Public History*, 369–418. Toronto: University of Toronto Press, 2012.

Ravitch, Diane, ed. *The American Reader: Words That Moved a Nation.* New York: Harper Collins, 2010.

Razack, Sherene. "From the Somalia Affair to Canada's Afghan Detainee Torture Scandal: How Stories of Torture Define the Nation." In Jerome Klassen and Greg Albo, eds., *Empire's Ally: Canada and the War in Afghanistan*, 367–87. Toronto: University of Toronto Press, 2013.

Read, Daphne. *The Great War and Canadian Society: An Oral History.* Toronto: New Hogtown Press, 1978.

Reef, Catherine. *A to Z of African Americans in the Military.* Rev. ed. New York: Facts on File, 2010.

Regehr, Ernie. *Disarming Conflict: Why Peace Cannot Be Won on the Battlefield.* Toronto: Between the Lines, 2015.

Regehr, T. D. *Mennonites in Canada, 1939–1970: A People Transformed.* Toronto: University of Toronto Press, 1996.

Richard, Béatrice. "Henri Bourassa and Conscription: Traitor or Saviour?" *Canadian Military Journal* (Winter 2006–2007): 75–83.

Richards, Leonard L. *Shays's Rebellion: The American Revolution's Final Battle.* Philadelphia: University of Pennsylvania Press, 2002.

Richler, Noah. *What We Talk about When We Talk about War.* Fredericton: Goose Lane Editions, 2012.

Riggenbach, Jeff. *Why American History Is Not What They Say: An Introduction to Revisionism.* Auburn, Alabama: Ludwig von Mises Institute, 2009.

Rinehart, James F. *Apocalyptic Faith and Political Violence: Prophets of Terror.* New York: Palgrave Macmillan, 2006.

Roberts, Lance, ed. *Recent Social Trends in Canada, 1960–2000.* Montreal/Kingston: McGill-Queen's University Press, 2005.

Robertson, Ian. *Sir Andrew Macphail: The Life and Legacy of a Canadian Man of Letters.* Montreal/Kingston: McGill-Queen's University Press, 2008.

Romney, Paul. *Getting It Wrong: How Canadians Forgot Their Past and Imperilled Confederation.* Toronto: University of Toronto Press, 1999.

Rose, Kenneth. *Myth and the Greatest Generation: A Social History of Americans in World War II.* New York: Routledge, 2013.

Rose, Lisle. *Roots of Tragedy: The United States and the Struggle for Asia, 1945–1953.* Westport, Connecticut: Greenwood Press, 1976.

Rosenberg, Emily S. *A Day Which Will Live in Infamy: Pearl Harbor in American Memory.* Chapel Hill, North Carolina: Duke University Press, 2003.

– *Spreading the American Dream: American Economic and Cultural Expansion, 1890–1945*. New York: Hill and Wang, 1982.

Ross, Jeffrey Ian. *Violence in Canada: Sociopolitical Perspectives*. 2nd ed. Piscataway, New Jersey: Transaction, 2004.

Rothbard, Murray N. *The Betrayal of the American Right*. Auburn, Alabama: Ludwig von Mises Institute, 2007.

Rotter, Andrew. *Comrades at Odds: The United States and India, 1947–1964*. Ithaca: Cornell University Press, 2000.

Royster, Jacqueline Jones, ed. *Southern Horrors and Other Writings: The Anti-Lynching Campaign of Ida B. Wells, 1892–1900*. Boston: Bedford Books, 1997.

Rubenstein, Richard E. *Reasons to Kill: Why Americans Choose War*. New York: Bloomsbury Press, 2010.

Ruck, Calvin W. *The Black Battalion, 1916–1920: Canada's Best Kept Military Secret*. Halifax: Nimbus, 1987.

Rucker, Walter, and James Nathaniel Upton, eds. *Encyclopedia of American Race Riots*. Westport, Connecticut: Greenwood Press, 2006.

Ryan, Frances. "Can Question Period Be Reformed?" *Canadian Parliamentary Review*, (Autumn 2009):18–22.

Ryan, Phil. "Beware 'Shared Memory.'" *Canadian Issues/Thèmes Canadiens* (Winter 2010): 28–31.

Saldin, Robert. *War, the American State, and Politics since 1898*. New York: Cambridge University Press, 2011.

Sarkesianalse, Sam Charles. *America's Forgotten Wars: The Counterrevolutionary Past and Lessons for the Future*. Westport, Connecticut: Praeger, 1984.

Saul, John Ralston. *A Fair Country: Telling Truths about Canada*. Toronto: Penguin, 2008.

– *Louis-Hippolyte LaFontaine and Robert Baldwin: A Penguin Lives Biography*. Toronto: Penguin, 2010.

Saywell, John. *Canada: Pathways to the Present*. Toronto: Stoddart, 1994.

Schaffer, Ronald. *America in the Great War: The Rise of the War Welfare State*. New York: Oxford University Press, 1991.

Schaffner, Brian. *Politics, Parties, and Elections in America*. Boston: Wadsworth, 2012.

Scheiber, Harry N. *The Wilson Administration and Civil Liberties, 1917–1921*. Ithaca, New York: Cornell University Press, 1960.

Schlesinger, Arthur, Jr. *The Vital Center: The Politics of Freedom*. Boston: Houghton Mifflin, 1949.

– "War and the Constitution: Abraham Lincoln and Franklin D. Roosevelt." In Gabor S. Boritt, ed. *Lincoln, the War President: The Gettysburg Lectures*, 145–78. New York: Oxford University Press, 1992.

– *The Cycles of American History*. Boston: Houghton Mifflin, 1986.

Schmalz, Peter S. *The Ojibwa of Southern Ontario*. Toronto: University of Toronto Press, 1991.

Schonberger, Howard. "William H. Becker and the New Left Revisionists: A Rebuttal." *Pacific Historical Review* 44.2 (May 1975), 249–55.

Schoonover, Thomas D. *Uncle Sam's War of 1898 and the Origins of Globalization*. Louisville: University of Kentucky Press, 2013.

Schroth, Raymond A. *The American Jesuits: A History*. New York: New York University Press, 2007.

Schurman, Donald. "Writing about War." In John Schultz, ed. *Writing about Canada: A Handbook for Modern Canadian History*, 231–50. Scarborough: Prentice-Hall, 1990.

Schwarzmantel, John. "Introduction: Gramsci in His Time and Ours." In Mark McNally and John Schwarzmantel, eds., *Gramsci and Global Politics: Hegemony and Resistance*, 1–16. New York: Routledge, 2009.

Scowen, Peter. *Rogue Nation: The America the Rest of the World Knows*. Toronto: McClelland and Stewart, 2003.

Seymour, Richard. *American Insurgents: A Brief History of American Anti-imperialism*. Chicago: Haymarket Books, 2012.

Shafer, Byron, and Richard Johnston. *The End of Southern Exceptionalism: Class, Race, and Partisan Change in the Postwar South*. Cambridge, Massachusetts: Harvard University Press, 2006.

Shalev, Eran. *Rome Reborn on Western Shores: Historical Imagination and the Creation of the American Republic*. Charlottesville, Virginia: University of Virginia Press, 2009.

Shankman, Arnold M. "Southern Methodist Newspapers and the Coming of the Spanish-American War: A Research Note." *Journal of Southern History* 39 (1973): 93–6.

Sharpe, Robert. *The Last Day, the Last Hour: The Currie Libel Trial*. Toronto: University of Toronto Press, 2009.

Shaw, Amy J. *Crisis of Conscience: Conscientious Objection in Canada during the First World War*. Vancouver: UBC Press, 2009.

Shearer, Benjamin F. ed. *Home Front Heroes: A Biographical Dictionary of Americans during Wartime*. Westport, Connecticut: Greenwood Press, 2007.

Sheehan, James J. *Where Have All the Soldiers Gone? The Transformation of Modern Europe*. New York: Houghton and Mifflin, 2008.

Sheffield, Scott. "Fighting a White Man's War? First Nations' Participation in the Canadian War Effort, 1939-1945." In Geoffrey Hayes, Mike Bechtold, and Matt Stymes, eds., *Canada and the Second World War: Essays in Honour of Terry Copp*, 67–92. Waterloo, Ontario: Wilfrid Laurier Press, 2012

Sheppard, George. *Plunder, Profit, and Paroles: A Social History of the War of 1812 in Upper Canada*. Montreal/Kingston: McGill-Queen's University Press, 1994.

Shimabukuro, Robert Sadamu. *Born in Seattle: The Campaign for Japanese American Redress*. Seattle: University of Washington Press, 2001.

Shipley, Robert. *To Mark Our Place: A History of Canadian War Memorials*. Toronto: N.C. Press, 1987.

Showalter, Dennis. "The United States in the Great War: A Historiography." *OAH Magazine of History* 17.1 (October 2002): 5–12.

Sillars, Stuart. *Fields of Agony: British Poetry of the First World War*. Humanities Ebooks, 2010.

Singh, Nikhil Pal. *Black Is a Country: Race and the Unfinished Struggle for Democracy*. Cambridge, Massachusetts: Harvard University Press, 2004.

Siracusa, Joseph. *New Left Diplomatic Histories and Historians: The American Revisionists*. Port Washington, New York: Kennikat Press, 1973.

Siracusa, Joseph, and David Coleman. *Depression to Cold War: A History of America from Herbert Hoover to Ronald Reagan*. Westport, Connecticut: Greenwood, 2002.

Sittser, Gerald Lawson. *A Cautious Patriotism: The American Churches and the Second World War*. Chapel Hill: University of North Carolina Press, 1997.

Skelton, O.D. *The Canadian Dominion: A Chronicle of Our Northern Neighbor*. New Haven: Yale University Press, 1921.

Small, Melvin. *Democracy and Diplomacy: The Impact of Domestic Policy on U.S. Foreign Policy, 1789–1994*. Baltimore: Johns Hopkins University Press, 1996.

Smith, Andrew. "Canadian Progress and the British Connection: Why Canadian Historians Seeking the Middle Road Should Give 2½ Cheers for the British Empire." In Christopher Dummit and Michael Dawson, eds., *Contesting Clio's Craft: New Directions and Debates in Canadian History*, 75–97. Vancouver: UBC Press, 2008.

Smith, David E. *The People's House of Commons: Theories of Democracy in Contention*. Toronto: University of Toronto Press, 2007.

Smith, Goldwin. *In The Court of History: An Apology of Canadians Opposed to the Boer War*. Toronto: William Tyrrell and Company, 1902.

Smith, Graeme. *The Dogs Are Eating Them Now: Our War in Afghanistan*. Toronto: Knopf Canada, 2013.

Smith, Jeffrey A. *War and Press Freedom: The Problem of Prerogative Power*. New York: Oxford University Press, 1999.

Smith, Tony. *Foreign Attachments: The Power of Ethnic Groups in the Making of American Foreign Policy*. Cambridge, Massachusetts: Harvard University Press, 2000.

Socknat, Thomas P. "The Dilemma of Canadian Pacifists during the Early Cold War Years." In Harvey L. Dyck, ed., *The Pacifist Impulse in Historical Perspective*, 413–24. Toronto: University of Toronto Press, 1996.

– *Witness against War: Pacifism in Canada 1900–1945*. Toronto: University of Toronto Press, 1987.

Stacey, C.P. *Arms, Men and Governments: The War Policies of Canada, 1939–1945*. Ottawa: Queen's Printer, 1970.

– *Canada's Battle in Normandy*. Ottawa: Minister of National Defence, 1946.

– *Canada and the Age of Conflict*. Vol. 1, *1867–1921*. Toronto: Macmillan, 1977.

– "Nationality: The Experience of Canada." *Canadian Historical Association Historical Papers* (1967): 10–19.

Stairs, Denis. *The Diplomacy of Constraint: Canada, the Korean War, and the United States*. Toronto: University of Toronto Press, 1974.

Stanley, George. *Canada's Soldiers: The Military History of an Unmilitary People*. Rev. ed. Toronto: Macmillan, 1954.

Stellato, Jesse, ed. *Not in Our Name: American Antiwar Speeches, 1846 to the Present*. University Park, Pennsylvania: Pennsylvania State University Press, 2012.

Stevens, Jason W. *God-Fearing and Free: A Spiritual History of America's Cold War*. Cambridge, Massachusetts: Harvard University Press, 2011.

Stevenson, Charles A. *Warriors and Politicians: US Civil-Military Relations under Stress*. New York: Routledge, 2006.

Stewart, Gordon T. "The Poverty of Canadian Politics?" In Alan Ware, ed., *Democracy and North America*, 28–45. New York: Routledge, 1996.

Stone, I.F. *The Hidden History of the Korean War*. New York: Monthly Review Press, 1952.

Storey, Moorfield, and Marcial Lichauco. *The Conquest of the Philippines by the United States*. Reprint. Freeport, New York: Books for Libraries Press, 1971.

Stueck, William. *The Korean War: An International History*. Princeton: Princeton University Press, 1995.

– "Revisionism and the Korean War." *Journal of Conflict Studies* 22.1 (2002): 17–27.

Swartz, David. *Moral Minority: The Evangelical Left in an Age of Conservatism*. Philadelphia: University of Pennsylvania Press, 2012.

Swettenham, John. *To Seize the Victory: The Canadian Corps in World War I*. Toronto: Ryerson Press, 1965.

Takaki, Ronald. *Double Victory: A Multicultural History of America in World War II*. New York: Little, Brown and Co., 2000.

Tansill, Charles. *America Goes to War*. Boston: Little Brown, 1938.

Taylor, Alan. *The Civil War of 1812: American Citizens, British Subjects, Irish Rebels, and Indian Allies*. New York: Alfred A. Knopf, 2010.

Taylor, Charles. *Radical Tories*. Toronto: Anansi, 1982.

Tebbel, John William. *America's Great Patriotic War with Spain: Mixed Motives, Lies, and Racism in Cuba and the Philippines, 1898–1915*. Manchester Center, Vermont: Marshall Jones, 1996.

Teigrob, Robert. "Glad Adventures, Tragedies, Silences: Remembering and Forgetting Wars for Empire in Canada and the United States." *International Journal of Canadian Studies / Revue international d'études canadiennes* 45–46 (2012): 441–65.

– *Warming Up to the Cold War: Canada and the United States Coalition of the Willing, from Hiroshima to Korea*. Toronto: University of Toronto Press, 2009.

Terkel, Studs. *"The Good War": An Oral History of World War Two*. New York: Pantheon, 1984.

Thayer, George. *Who Shakes the Money Tree? American Campaign Financing Practices from 1789 to the Present*. New York: Simon and Schuster, 1973.

Theobald, Andrew. "Divided Once More: Social Memory and the Canadian Conscription Crisis of the First World War." *Past Imperfect* 12 (2006): 1–19.

Thomas, Scott. *The Global Resurgence of Religion and the Transformation of International Relations: The Struggle for the Soul of the Twenty-First Century*. New York: Palgrave Macmillan, 2005.

Thompson, Alistair. "The Anzac Legend: Exploring National Myth and Memory in Australia." In Ralph Samuel, ed., *The Myths We Live By*, 73–82. London: Routledge, 1990.

– *Anzac Memories: Living with the Legend*. New York: Oxford University Press, 1994.

Thompson, J.A. "William Appleman Williams and the 'American Empire,'" *Journal of American Studies* 7 (1973): 91–104.

– *Reformers and War: American Progressive Publicists and the First World War*. Cambridge: Cambridge University Press, 1987.

Thornton, A.P. *The Imperial Idea and Its Enemies*. London: Macmillan, 1959.

Threlfall, John. "Empire over Nation: Victoria Newspapers and the Boer War" *B.C. Historical News* 30.1 (Winter 1996–1997).

Tilly, Charles. *Coercion, Capital, and European States, AD 990–1990*. Oxford, UK: Blackwell, 1990.

Tocqueville, Alex de. *Democracy in America*. Vol. 2. Trans. by Harry Reeve. New York: Langley, 1840.

Tomchuck, Travis. "Transnational Radicals: Italian Anarchist Networks in Southern Ontario and the Northeastern United States, 1915–1940." PhD Thesis. Queen's University, 2010.

Trask, David. *The War with Spain in 1898*. New York: The Free Press, 1981.

Tremblay, Yves. "Du suicide, militaire et bibliographique." *Bulletin d'histoire politique* (Fall, 2010): 115–27.

Trout, Steven. *On the Battlefield of Memory: The First World War and American Remembrance, 1919–1941*. Tuscaloosa, Alabama: University of Alabama Press, 2012.

Turner, Alexander. *Vimy Ridge 1917: Byng's Canadians Triumph at Arras*. London: Osprey, 2005.

Turner, Frederick Jackson. "The Significance of the Frontier in American History." *Proceedings of the State Historical Society of Wisconsin*. 14 December 1893.

Tyrrell, Ian. *Historians in Public: The Practice of American History, 1890–1970*. Chicago: University of Chicago Press, 2005.

Underhill, Frank H. "The Canadian Forces in the War." In Sir Charles Lucas, ed. *The Empire at War*. Vol. 2. Toronto: Oxford University Press, 1923.

Underhill, Frank. "Goldwin Smith." *University of Toronto Quarterly* 2.3 (April 1933): 285–309.

Unger, Nancy C. *Fighting Bob La Follette: The Righteous Reformer*. Madison, Wisconsin: Wisconsin Historical Society, 2008.

Utley, Robert Marshall, and Wilcomb E. Washburn. *Indian Wars*. Boston: Mariner Books, 2002.

Utter, Glenn H., and James L. True. *Conservative Christians and Political Participation: A Reference Handbook*. Santa Barbara, California: ABC-CLIO, 2004.

Vance, Jonathan. "Sacrifice in Stained Glass: Memorial Windows of the Great War." *Canadian Military History* 5.2 (Autumn 1996): 16–24.

Vance, Jonathon. *Death So Noble: Memory, Meaning, and the First World War*. Vancouver: UBC Press, 1996.

Veatch, Richard. *Canada and the League of Nations*. Toronto: University of Toronto Press, 1975.

Vernes, Maurice. *Ernest Renan*. New York: Twayne, 1968.

Vickers, Jill, and Edward Osei-Kwadwo. *The Politics of Race: Canada, Australia, the United States*. Toronto: Dundurn Press, 2002.

Vidal, Gore. *Perpetual War for Perpetual Peace: How We Got to Be So Hated – Causes of Conflict in the Last Empire.* New York: Thunders' Mouth Press, 2002.

Vipond, Mary. "Canadian Nationalism and the Plight of Canadian Magazines in the 1920s." *Canadian Historical Review* 58 (March 1977): 43–63.

Von Eschen, Penny. *Race against Empire: Black Americans and Anticolonialism, 1937–1957*. Ithaca: Cornell University Press, 1997.

– *Satchmo Blows up the World: Jazz Ambassadors Play the Cold War*. Cambridge, Massachusetts: Harvard University Press, 2006.

Voorhees, Melvin B. *Korean Tales*. New York: Simon and Schuster, 1952.

Vronsky, Peter. *Ridgeway: The American Fenian Invasion and the 1866 Battle That Made Canada*. Toronto: Penguin-Allen Lane, 2011.

Wagnleitner, Richard. *Coca-Colonization: The Cultural Mission of the United States in Austria after the Second World War*. Chapel Hill, North Carolina: University of North Carolina Press, 1994.

Waite, P.B. "Sir Oliver Mowat's Canada: Reflections on an Un-Victorian Society." In Donald Swainson, ed. *Oliver Mowat's Ontario*, 12–32. Toronto: Macmillan 1972.

Waldman, Sidney. *America and the Limits of the Politics of Selfishness*. Plymouth, UK: Lexington Books, 2007.

Waligora-Davis, Nicole. *Sanctuary: African Americans and Empire*. New York: Oxford University Press, 2011.

Walker, Barrington, ed. *The African Canadian Legal Odyssey*. Toronto: University of Toronto Press, 2012.

Walker, James W. St.G. "Race and Recruitment in World War I: Enlistment of Visible Minorities in the Canadian Expedition Force." *Canadian Historical Review* 70.1 (1989):1–26.

Walker, Samuel J. "Recent Literature on Truman's Atomic Bomb Decision: A Search for Middle Ground." *Diplomatic History* 29.2 (April 2005): 311–34.

– *In Defense of American Liberties: A History of the ACLU*. New York: Oxford University Press, 1990.

Walsh, George. *The Role of Religion in History*. New Brunswick, New Jersey: Transaction, 1998.

Ward, Peter W. *White Canada Forever*. Montreal/Kingston: McGill-Queens University Press, 1978.

Ware, Tracey. "English-Canadian Literature, 1867–1918: The Making of a Nation." In Reingard M. Nischik, ed. *History of Literature in Canada: English-Canadian and French Canadian*, 113–14. Rochester, New York: Camden House, 2008.

Warnock, John W. *Partner to Behemoth: The Military Policy of a Satellite Canada*. Toronto: New Press, 1970.

Watson, Bradley C. S. *Civil Rights and the Paradox of Liberal Democracy*. Lanham, Maryland: Lexington Books, 1999.

Watson, Brent Byron. *Far Eastern Tour: The Canadian Infantry in Korea, 1950–1953*. Montreal/Kingston: McGill-Queen's University Press, 2002.

Watson, Nick, Stuart Weir, and Stephen Friend. "The Development of Muscular Christianity in Victorian Britain and Beyond." *Journal of Religion and Society* 7 (2005): 1–21.

Webb, Peter. "'A Righteous Cause': War Propaganda and Canadian Fiction, 1915–1921." *British Journal of Canadian Studies* 24.1 (2011): 31–48.

- "'The Silent Flag in the New Fallen Snow': Sara Jeannette Duncan and the Legacy of the South African War." *Journal of Canadian Studies/Revue d'etudes canadiennes* 44.1 (Winter 2010): 75–89.

Weber, Cynthia. *Faking It: U.S. Hegemony in a "Post-Phallic" Era.* Minneapolis: University of Minnesota Press, 1999.

Weigley, Russell. "Walter Millis and the Conscience of the Military Historian." *Reviews in American History* 16.3 (September 1988): 500–5.

Weintraub, Stanley. *MacArthur's War: Korea and the Undoing of an American Hero.* New York: The Free Press, 2000.

Weisbord, Merrily, and Merilyn Simonds Mohr. *The Valour and the Horror: The Untold Story of Canadians in the Second World War.* Toronto: Harper Collins, 1991.

Welch, Richard E., Jr. "American Atrocities in the Philippines: The Indictment and the Response." *Pacific Historical Review* 43.2 (May 1974): 233–53.

Welsh, Jennifer. "Beyond War and Peacekeeping: With Armed Conflict in Steady Decline, the Usual Debates over Canada's Military Seem Increasingly Dated." *Literary Review of Canada* (June 2012). 6 March 2013. http://reviewcanada.ca/magazine/2012/06/beyond-war-and-peacekeeping/.

Werner, M.R. *Bryan.* New York: Harcourt Brace, 1929.

Westfall, William. "Constructing Public Religions at Private Sites: The Anglican Church in the Shadow of Disestablishment." In Marguerite Van Die, ed., *Religion and Public Life in Canada: Historical and Comparative Perspectives*, 23–49. Toronto: University of Toronto Press, 2001.

- *Two Worlds: The Protestant Culture of Nineteenth Century Ontario.* Montreal/ Kingston: McGill-Queen's University Press, 1990.

Westheider, James E. *The African American Experience in Vietnam: Brothers in Arms.* Lanham, Maryland: Rowan and Littlefield, 2008.

Wetzel, Benjamin J. "Onward Christian Soldiers: Lyman Abbott's Justification of the Spanish-American War." *Journal of Church and State* 54.3 (September 2012): 406–25.

Whitaker, Reginald, and Gary Marcuse. *Cold War Canada: The Making of a National Insecurity State.* Toronto: University of Toronto Press, 1994.

Whitaker, Muriel, ed. *Great Canadian War Stories.* Edmonton: University of Alberta Press, 2001.

Whitworth, Sandra. *Men, Militarism, and UN Peacekeeping: A Gendered Analysis.* Boulder, Colorado: Lynne Rienner, 2004.

Wilkerson, Isabel. *The Warmth of Other Suns: The Epic Story of America's Great Migration.* New York: Random House, 2010.

Wilkinson, Marcus. *Public Opinion and the Spanish-American War: A Study in Propaganda.* Baton Rouge: University of Louisiana Press, 1932.

Williams, Chad Louis. *Torchbearers of Democracy: African American Soldiers in the World War I Era*. Chapel Hill: University of North Carolina Press, 2010.

Williams, Walter. "United States Indian Policy and the Debate over Philippine Annexation: Implications for the Origins of American Imperialism." *Journal of American History* 56 (1980): 810–31.

Williams, William Appleman. *The Tragedy of American Diplomacy*. Cleveland: World, 1959.

Wills, Gary. *A Necessary Evil: A History of American Distrust of Government*. New York: Simon and Schuster, 2002.

Wilson, Richard. *American Political Leaders*. New York: Facts on File, 2002.

Wilton, Shauna. "Immigration Policy and Literature: Contradictions of a 'Post-National' State?" In Gunilla Florby, Mark Shackleton, and Katri Suhonen, eds., *Canada: Images of a Post/national Society/ Canada: Images D'une Société Post/nationale*, 25–38. New York: P.I.E.-Peter Lang, 2009.

Wineapple, Brenda. *Ecstatic Nation: Confidence, Crisis, and Compromise, 1848–1877*. New York: Harper, 2013.

Winegard, Timothy C. *Indigenous Peoples of the British Dominions and the First World War*. Cambridge, Massachusetts: Cambridge University Press 2011.

– *For King and Kanata: Canadian Indians and the First World War*. Winnipeg: University of Manitoba Press, 2012.

Winks, Robin W. *Cloak & Gown: Scholars in the Secret War, 1939–1961*. 2nd ed. New Haven, Connecticut: Yale University Press, 1996.

– *The Blacks in Canada: A History*. 2nd ed. Montreal/Kingston: McGill-Queen's University Press, 1997.

Winter, Jay, and Antoine Prost. *The Great War in History: Debates and Controversies, 1914 to the Present*. Cambridge: Cambridge University Press, 2005.

Wisan, Joseph. *The Cuban Crisis as Reflected in the New York Press, 1895–1898*. New York: Octagon, 1934.

Wise, S.F. "Colonial Attitudes from the Era of the War of 1812 to the Rebellions of 1837." In S.F Wise and Robert Craig Brown, eds., *Canada Views the United States: Nineteenth-Century Political Attitudes*. Toronto: Macmillan, 1967.

Wiseman, Nelson. *In Search of Canadian Political Culture*. Vancouver: UBC Press, 2007.

Wittner, Lawrence. *One World or None: A History of the World Nuclear Disarmament Movement through 1953*. Stanford, California: Stanford University Press, 1993.

– *Resisting the Bomb: A History of the World Nuclear Disarmament Movement, 1954–1970*. Stanford, California: Stanford University Press, 1997.

– *Toward Nuclear Abolition: A History of the World Nuclear Disarmament Movement, 1971 to the Present*. Stanford, California: Stanford University Press, 2003.

Wolin, Sheldon. *Politics and Vision: Continuity and Innovation in Western Political Thought.* Expanded ed. Princeton: Princeton University Press, 2004.

Wood, Herbert Fairlie. *Strange Battleground: Official History of the Canadian Army in Korea.* Ottawa: Queen's Printer, 1966.

Wood, James. *Militia Myths: Ideas of the Citizen Soldier.* Vancouver: UBC Press, 2010.

Woodward, C. Vann. "The Age of Reinterpretation." *American Historical Review* 66 (October 1960): 2–8.

Wright, Robert. "The Canadian Protestant Tradition, 1914-1945." In George A. Rawlyk, ed. *The Canadian Protestant Experience, 1760 to 1990*, 139–97. Montreal/Kingston: McGill-Queen's University Press, 1994.

– *A World Mission: Canadian Protestantism and the Quest for a New International Order, 1919–1939.* Montreal/Kingston: McGill-Queen's University Press, 1991.

Wrong, George. *The Canadians: The Story of a People.* New York: Macmillan, 1938.

Yearwood, Peter J. *Guarantee of Peace: The League of Nations in British Policy 1914–1925.* Oxford: Oxford University Press, 2009.

Young, John. "Faith and Politics in Canada." In John Young and Boris Dewiel, eds., *Faith in Democracy? Religion and Politics in Canada*, 1–12. Newcastle: Cambridge Scholars, 2009.

Young, Lisa, and Harold J. Jansen, eds. *Money, Politics, and Democracy: Canada's Party Finance Reforms.* Vancouver: UBC Press, 2011.

Young, Marilyn B. "An Incident at No Gun Ri." In Omer Bartov, Atina Grossman, and Mary Nolan, eds., *Crimes of War: Guilt and Denial in the Twentieth Century*, 242–58. New York: The New Press, 2002.

– *The Vietnam Wars, 1945–1990.* New York: Harper Collins, 1990.

Young, Ralph F. *Dissent in America.* Vol. 2, *Since 1865.* New York: Longman, 2004.

Young, Robert. *Postcolonialism: An Historical Introduction.* Oxford: Blackwell, 2001.

Zinn, Howard. *A People's History of the United States.* Vol. 2, *The Civil War to the Present.* Rev. and Abridged Teaching Ed. New York: New Press, 2003.

– *Declarations of Independence: Cross-Examining American Ideology.* New York: Harper Perennial, 1990.

Zuehlke, Mark. *Brave Battalion: The Remarkable Saga of the 16th Battalion (Canadian Scottish) in the First World War.* Mississauga: John Wiley and Sons, 2008.

– *Ortona Street Fight.* Victoria: Orca Book, 2011.

– *Tragedy at Dieppe: Operation Jubilee, August 19, 1942.* Toronto: Douglas & McIntyre, 2012.

Zuhlsdorff, Volkmar. *Hitler's Exiles: The German Cultural Resistance in America and Europe.* New York: Continuum, 2004.

Index